MW00781661

genesis

the first book of moses, called

genesis

authorized king james version

grove press
new york

with an introduction by | e. l. doctorow

The Pocket Canons were originally published in the U.K. in 1998 by Canongate Books, Ltd.
Published simultaneously in Canada
Printed in the United States of America

FIRST AMERICAN EDITION

Copyright information is on file with the Library of Congress
ISBN 0-8021-3610-9

Design by Paddy Cramsie

Grove Press
841 Broadway
New York, NY 10003

99 00 01 02 10 9 8 7 6 5 4 3 2 1

a note about pocket canons

The Authorized King James Version of the Bible, translated between 1603 and 1611, coincided with an extraordinary flowering of English literature. This version, more than any other, and possibly more than any other work in history, has had an influence in shaping the language we speak and write today. Presenting individual books from the Bible as separate volumes, as they were originally conceived, encourages the reader to approach them as literary works in their own right.

The first twelve books in this series encompass categories as diverse as history, fiction, philosophy, love poetry, and law. Each Pocket Canon also has its own introduction, specially commissioned from an impressive range of writers, which provides a personal interpretation of the text and explores its contemporary relevance.

E. L. Doctorow's books include the novels Ragtime, Billy Bathgate, Loon Lake, *and* The Book of Daniel. *His work has won two National Book Critics Circle Awards, the National Book Award, the PEN/Faulkner Award, the Edith Wharton citation for fiction, and the William Dean Howells medal from the American Academy of Arts and Letters. He lives and works in New York City.*

introduction by e. l. doctorow

The King James Version of The Bible, an early-seventeenth-century translation, seems, by its now venerable diction, to have added a degree of poetic luster to the ancient tales, genealogies, and covenantal events of the original. It is the version preachers quote from who believe in the divinity of the text.

Certainly in the case of Genesis 1–4, in which the world is formed and populated and Adam and Eve are sent from the Garden, there could be no more appropriate language than the English of Shakespeare's time. The King James does not suffer at all from what is inconsistent or self-contradictory in the text any more than do the cryptic ancient Hebrew and erring Greek from which it is derived. Once you assume poetically divine authorship, only your understanding is imperfect.

But when you read of these same matters in the contemporary diction of the English Revised Bible, the Jamesian voice of Holy Scripture is not quite what you hear. In plain-spoken modern English, Genesis—especially as it moves on from the Flood and the Tower of Babel, and comes up in time through the lives of Abraham, Sarah, Isaac, Rebecca, and then to the more detailed adventures of Jacob and Rachel and Joseph and his brothers—seems manifestly of the oral tradition of preliterate storytelling out of which the biblical documents emerged, when history and moral instruction, genealogy, law, science, and momentous confrontations with God were not recorded on papyrus or clay tablets but held in the mind for transmittal by generations of narrators. And so Genesis in the English Revised Version is homier—something like a collection of stories about people trying to work things out.

The contemporary reader would do well to read the King James herein side by side with the English Revised. Some lovely stereophonic truths come of the fact that a devotion to God did not preclude the use of narrative strategies.

If not in all stories, certainly in all mystery stories, the writer works backward. The ending is known and the story is designed to arrive at the ending. If you know the people of the world speak many languages, that is the ending: The story of the Tower of Babel gets you there. The known ending of life is death: The story of Adam and Eve, and the forbidden fruit of the Tree of the Knowledge of Good and Evil, arrives at that ending. Why do we suffer, why must we die? Well, you see, there was this Garden. . . . The story has turned the human condition into a sequential narrative of how it came to be; it has used conflict and suspense to create a moral framework for *being*. And in suggesting that things might have worked out another way for humanity if the fruit had not been eaten, it has, not incidentally, left itself open to revision by some subsequent fantasist who will read into it the idea of original sin.

Artistry is at work also in the blessings the dying Jacob bestows on his twelve eponymous sons. Each blessing, an astute judgment of character, will explain the fate of the twelve tribes led by the sons. A beginning is invented for each of the historical tribal endings the writer knows. Never mind that we understand from the documentary thesis of Bible sources—for it is, after all, the work of various storytellers and their editors—that different sons are accorded hands-on leadership by their father according to which writer is telling the story. Character is fate. And life under God is always an allegory.

Another venerable storytelling practice is the appropriation of an already existing story. Otherwise known as adaptation, it is the principle of literary communalism that allows us to use other people's myths, legends, and histories in the way that serves ourselves—Shakespeare's reliance on Hollinshed's Chronicles, for example, which should have, in honor, disposed him to share his royalites. Here in Genesis, the ancient scribes have retooled the story of the Flood recounted earlier in Mesopotamia and Sumer, including the vivid rendition in the Epic of Gilgamesh. Yet though the plot is the same, the resounding meanings are different, as befits an adaptation. Noah is unprecedented as the last godfearing, righteous man on earth . . . who may nevertheless drink a bit more wine than is good for him. And the God of Genesis is a Presence beyond the conception of the Sumerian epic.

The cosmology of Genesis is beautiful and, for all we know, may even turn out to be as metaphorically prescient as some believers think it is. One imagines the ancient storytellers convening to consider what they had to work with: day and night, land and sea, earth and sky, trees that bore fruit, plants that bore seed, wild animals, domesticated animals, birds, fish, and everything that crept. In their brilliant imaginations, inflamed by the fear and love of God, it seemed more than possible that these elements and forms of life, this organization of the animate and inanimate, would have been produced from a chaos of indeterminate dark matter by spiritual intent—here was the story to get to the ending—and that it was done by a process of discretion, the separation of day from night, air from water, earth from sky, one thing from another in, presumably, a six-day sequence culminating in the human race.

Every writer has to be awed by the staying power of the Genesis stories that have passed through the embellishing realms of oral transmission and the literate multilingual cultures of thousands of years. They are a group effort but not at all afflicted with the bureaucratic monotone that would be expected to characterize written collaborations. One reason for this may be the wisdom of the later scribes in leaving intact on the page those chronicles they felt obligated to improve upon. As a result we get more than one point of view, which has the effect, in the depiction of human character, of a given roundness or ambiguity that we recognize as realistic. Consider Jacob for example, who will wrestle with God or His representative and be named Israel, after all, but is impelled twice in his life to acts of gross deception—of his brother, Esau, and of his father, Isaac. Or the lovely gentle Rebecca, who as a maid displays the innocent generosity that the servant of Abraham seeks, offering him the water from her water jar, and then seeing to his camels . . . but years later, as the mother of Jacob, shrewishly assists her son in depriving Esau of his rightful patrimony.

In general, family life does not go all that smoothly for the founding generations. Beginning with Cain and Abel and persisting to the time of Joseph, brothers seem—like the brothers in fairy tales—to be seriously lacking in the fraternal spirit. Wives who are not themselves sufficiently fertile foist slave women on their husbands for purposes of impregnation, and then become jealous of those women and have them sent away. There seem to be two stations of wife, high and low—Hagar and Leah being examples of the low—and the anger and resentment this creates is palpable. Overall, the women of Genesis may be subject to an exclusively biological destiny as childbearers—theirs is a nomadic society that to survive must be fruitful—and the movable tent kingdoms in which they live may be unquestioningly paternalistic, but the modern reader cannot help but notice with relief how much grumbling they do.

It is in the pages of Genesis that the first two of the three major covenants between God and humanity are described. After the Flood, God assures Noah that He will not again lay waste to all creation in a flood. The sign of this covenant will be a rainbow in the clouds. Later, Abraham is commanded by God to resettle in Canaan, where he will be assured that he will eventually prevail as the father of many nations. Circumcision is the way Abraham and his descendants are to give sign of keeping this covenant. It is only in the next book, Exodus, that the final element of the covenantal religion, the Ten Commandments, will be given through Moses to his people. It is here that God will be identified as Yahweh and a ritualized sabbath—a simulation of God's day of rest after the Creation—is to be identified as the sign.

Apart from their religious profundity, this graduated series of exchanges between God and man have to remind us of the struggle for human distinction or identity in a precarious, brute life. This was the Bronze Age, after all. The Abrahamic generations were desert nomads, outlanders, who lived in tents while people such as the Egyptians lived in cities that were the heart of civilization. The territory that Abraham and his descendants were called to was abuzz with Amorites and other tribes of ethnically diverse Canaanites. Under such difficult circumstances it is understandable that the Abrahamic nomads' desire to be a designated people living in a state of moral consequence would direct them to bond with one God rather than many gods, and to find their solace and their courage in His singularity, His totality. But that they did so was tantamount to genius—and a considerable advance in the moral career of the human race.

For finally, as to literary strategies, it is the invention of character that is most telling, and in the Genesis narratives it is God Himself who is the most complex and riveting character. He seems at times to be as troubled and conflicted, as moved by the range of human feelings, as the human beings He has created. The personality of God cannot be an entirely unwitting set of traits in a theological text that declares that we are made in His image, after His likeness. There is an unmistakable implication of codependence. And it is no doubt some of the incentive for the idea expressed by the late Rabbi Abraham Joshua Heschel that the immanence of God, His existence in us, is manifest in the goodness of human works, the *mitzvot* or good deeds that reflect His nature. "Reverence," says the rabbi, "is the discovery of the world as an allusion to God." And so in reverence and ethical action do our troubled, conflicted minds find holiness, or bring it into being. Recognizing the glory of God is presumably our redemption, and our redemption is, presumably, His.

the first book of moses, called genesis

In the beginning God created the heaven and the earth. [2]And
the earth was without form, and void; and darkness was
upon the face of the deep. And the Spirit of God moved upon
the face of the waters. [3]And God said, 'Let there be light':
and there was light. [4]And God saw the light, that it was good;
and God divided the light from the darkness. [5]And God
called the light Day, and the darkness he called Night. And
the evening and the morning were the first day.

[6]And God said, 'Let there be a firmament in the midst of
the waters, and let it divide the waters from the waters.' [7]And
God made the firmament, and divided the waters which
were under the firmament from the waters which were above
the firmament; and it was so. [8]And God called the firmament Heaven. And the evening and the morning were the
second day.

[9]And God said, 'Let the waters under the heaven be gathered together unto one place, and let the dry land appear,'
and it was so. [10]And God called the dry land Earth; and the
gathering together of the waters called he Seas; and God saw
that it was good. [11]And God said, 'Let the earth bring forth
grass, the herb yielding seed, and the fruit tree yielding fruit
after his kind, whose seed is in itself, upon the earth,' and it

was so. 12And the earth brought forth grass, and herb yielding
seed after his kind, and the tree yielding fruit, whose seed
was in itself, after his kind; and God saw that it was good.
13And the evening and the morning were the third day.

14And God said, 'Let there be lights in the firmament of
the heaven to divide the day from the night; and let them be
for signs, and for seasons, and for days, and years; 15and let
them be for lights in the firmament of the heaven to give
light upon the earth,' and it was so. 16And God made two great
lights: the greater light to rule the day, and the lesser light to
rule the night; he made the stars also. 17And God set them in
the firmament of the heaven to give light upon the earth, 18and
to rule over the day and over the night, and to divide the light
from the darkness; and God saw that it was good. 19And the
evening and the morning were the fourth day. 20And God said,
'Let the waters bring forth abundantly the moving creature
that hath life, and fowl that may fly above the earth in the
open firmament of heaven.' 21And God created great whales,
and every living creature that moveth, which the waters
brought forth abundantly, after their kind, and every winged
fowl after his kind; and God saw that it was good. 22And
God blessed them, saying, 'Be fruitful, and multiply, and fill
the waters in the seas, and let fowl multiply in the earth.'
23And the evening and the morning were the fifth day.

24And God said, 'Let the earth bring forth the living creature after his kind, cattle, and creeping thing, and beast of
the earth after his kind,' and it was so. 25And God made the
beast of the earth after his kind, and cattle after their kind,

and every thing that creepeth upon the earth after his kind: and God saw that it was good.

[26]And God said, 'Let us make man in our image, after our likeness: and let them have dominion over the fish of the sea, and over the fowl of the air, and over the cattle, and over all the earth, and over every creeping thing that creepeth upon the earth.' [27]So God created man in his own image, in the image of God created he him; male and female created he them. [28]And God blessed them, and God said unto them, 'Be fruitful, and multiply, and replenish the earth, and subdue it: and have dominion over the fish of the sea, and over the fowl of the air, and over every living thing that moveth upon the earth.'

[29]And God said, 'Behold, I have given you every herb bearing seed, which is upon the face of all the earth, and every tree, in the which is the fruit of a tree yielding seed; to you it shall be for meat. [30]And to every beast of the earth, and to every fowl of the air, and to every thing that creepeth upon the earth, wherein there is life, I have given every green herb for meat,' and it was so. [31]And God saw every thing that he had made, and, behold, it was very good. And the evening and the morning were the sixth day.

2 Thus the heavens and the earth were finished, and all the host of them. [2]And on the seventh day God ended his work which he had made; and he rested on the seventh day from all his work which he had made. [3]And God blessed the seventh day, and sanctified it; because that in it he had

rested from all his work which God created and made.
4 These are the generations of the heavens and of the earth
when they were created, in the day that the Lord God made
the earth and the heavens, 5 and every plant of the field before
it was in the earth, and every herb of the field before it grew;
for the Lord God had not caused it to rain upon the earth,
and there was not a man to till the ground. 6 But there went
up a mist from the earth, and watered the whole face of the
ground. 7 And the Lord God formed man of the dust of the
ground, and breathed into his nostrils the breath of life; and
man became a living soul.
8 And the Lord God planted a garden eastward in Eden;
and there he put the man whom he had formed. 9 And out of
the ground made the Lord God to grow every tree that is
pleasant to the sight, and good for food; the tree of life also
in the midst of the garden, and the tree of knowledge of
good and evil. 10 And a river went out of Eden to water the
garden; and from thence it was parted, and became into four
heads. 11 The name of the first is Pison: that is it which compasseth the whole land of Havilah, where there is gold;
12 and the gold of that land is good; there is bdellium and the
onyx stone. 13 And the name of the second river is Gihon: the
same is it that compasseth the whole land of Ethiopia. 14 And
the name of the third river is Hiddekel: that is it which goeth
toward the east of Assyria. And the fourth river is Euphrates. 15 And the Lord God took the man, and put him into the
garden of Eden to dress it and to keep it. 16 And the Lord God
commanded the man, saying, 'Of every tree of the garden

thou mayest freely eat; 17 but of the tree of the knowledge of
good and evil, thou shalt not eat of it; for in the day that
thou eatest thereof thou shalt surely die.'
18 And the Lord God said, 'It is not good that the man
should be alone; I will make him an help meet for him.'
19 And out of the ground the Lord God formed every beast of
the field, and every fowl of the air; and brought them unto
Adam to see what he would call them; and whatsoever
Adam called every living creature, that was the name thereof. 20 And Adam gave names to all cattle, and to the fowl of
the air, and to every beast of the field; but for Adam there
was not found an help meet for him. 21 And the Lord God
caused a deep sleep to fall upon Adam, and he slept: and he
took one of his ribs, and closed up the flesh instead thereof;
22 and the rib, which the Lord God had taken from man,
made he a woman, and brought her unto the man. 23 And
Adam said, 'This is now bone of my bones, and flesh of my
flesh; she shall be called Woman, because she was taken out
of Man.' 24 Therefore shall a man leave his father and his
mother, and shall cleave unto his wife; and they shall be one
flesh. 25 And they were both naked, the man and his wife,
and were not ashamed.

3 Now the serpent was more subtil than any beast of the
field which the Lord God had made. And he said unto
the woman, 'Yea, hath God said, "Ye shall not eat of every
tree of the garden"?' 2 And the woman said unto the serpent,
'We may eat of the fruit of the trees of the garden; 3 but of the

fruit of the tree which is in the midst of the garden, God hath
said, "Ye shall not eat of it, neither shall ye touch it, lest ye
die."' 4And the serpent said unto the woman, 'Ye shall not
surely die; 5for God doth know that in the day ye eat thereof,
then your eyes shall be opened, and ye shall be as gods,
knowing good and evil.' 6And when the woman saw that the
tree was good for food, and that it was pleasant to the eyes,
and a tree to be desired to make one wise, she took of the
fruit thereof, and did eat, and gave also unto her husband
with her; and he did eat. 7And the eyes of them both were
opened, and they knew that they were naked; and they sewed
fig leaves together, and made themselves aprons.

8And they heard the voice of the Lord God walking in
the garden in the cool of the day; and Adam and his wife hid
themselves from the presence of the Lord God amongst the
trees of the garden. 9And the Lord God called unto Adam,
and said unto him, 'Where art thou?' 10And he said, 'I heard
thy voice in the garden, and I was afraid, because I was naked;
and I hid myself.' 11And he said, 'Who told thee that thou
wast naked? Hast thou eaten of the tree, whereof I commanded thee that thou shouldest not eat?' 12And the man
said, 'The woman whom thou gavest to be with me, she
gave me of the tree, and I did eat.' 13And the Lord God said
unto the woman, 'What is this that thou hast done?' And the
woman said, 'The serpent beguiled me, and I did eat.' 14And
the Lord God said unto the serpent, 'Because thou hast done
this, thou art cursed above all cattle, and above every beast
of the field; upon thy belly shalt thou go, and dust shalt thou

eat all the days of thy life. 15And I will put enmity between
thee and the woman, and between thy seed and her seed; it
shall bruise thy head, and thou shalt bruise his heel.' 16 Unto
the woman he said, 'I will greatly multiply thy sorrow and
thy conception; in sorrow thou shalt bring forth children;
and thy desire shall be to thy husband, and he shall rule over
thee.' 17And unto Adam he said, 'Because thou hast hearkened unto the voice of thy wife, and hast eaten of the tree, of
which I commanded thee, saying, "Thou shalt not eat of it":
cursed is the ground for thy sake; in sorrow shalt thou eat of
it all the days of thy life; 18 thorns also and thistles shall it
bring forth to thee; and thou shalt eat the herb of the field;
19 in the sweat of thy face shalt thou eat bread, till thou return
unto the ground; for out of it wast thou taken; for dust thou
art, and unto dust shalt thou return.' 20And Adam called his
wife's name Eve; because she was the mother of all living.
21 Unto Adam also and to his wife did the Lord God make
coats of skins, and clothed them.

22And the Lord God said, 'Behold, the man is become as
one of us, to know good and evil; and now, lest he put forth
his hand, and take also of the tree of life, and eat, and live for
ever.' 23 Therefore the Lord God sent him forth from the garden of Eden, to till the ground from whence he was taken.
24 So he drove out the man; and he placed at the east of the
garden of Eden Cherubims, and a flaming sword which
turned every way, to keep the way of the tree of life.

4 And Adam knew Eve his wife; and she conceived, and
bare Cain, and said, 'I have gotten a man from the Lord.'
[2]And she again bare his brother Abel. And Abel was a keeper
of sheep, but Cain was a tiller of the ground. [3]And in process
of time it came to pass that Cain brought of the fruit of the
ground an offering unto the Lord. [4]And Abel, he also brought
of the firstlings of his flock and of the fat thereof. And the
Lord had respect unto Abel and to his offering; [5]but unto
Cain and to his offering he had not respect. And Cain was
very wroth, and his countenance fell. [6]And the Lord said
unto Cain, 'Why art thou wroth? And why is thy countenance fallen? [7]If thou doest well, shalt thou not be accepted?
And if thou doest not well, sin lieth at the door. And unto
thee shall be his desire, and thou shalt rule over him.' [8]And
Cain talked with Abel his brother; and it came to pass, when
they were in the field, that Cain rose up against Abel his
brother, and slew him.

[9]And the Lord said unto Cain, 'Where is Abel thy brother?'
And he said, 'I know not. Am I my brother's keeper?' [10]And
he said, 'What hast thou done? The voice of thy brother's
blood crieth unto me from the ground. [11]And now art thou
cursed from the earth, which hath opened her mouth to
receive thy brother's blood from thy hand; [12]when thou till-
est the ground, it shall not henceforth yield unto thee her
strength; a fugitive and a vagabond shalt thou be in the earth.'
[13]And Cain said unto the Lord, 'My punishment is greater
than I can bear. [14]Behold, thou hast driven me out this day
from the face of the earth; and from thy face shall I be hid;

and I shall be a fugitive and a vagabond in the earth; and it
shall come to pass, that every one that findeth me shall slay
me.' [15]And the Lord said unto him, 'Therefore whosoever
slayeth Cain, vengeance shall be taken on him sevenfold.'
And the Lord set a mark upon Cain, lest any finding him
should kill him.

[16]And Cain went out from the presence of the Lord, and
dwelt in the land of Nod, on the east of Eden. [17]And Cain
knew his wife; and she conceived, and bare Enoch; and he
builded a city, and called the name of the city, after the name
of his son, Enoch. [18]And unto Enoch was born Irad; and
Irad begat Mehujael; and Mehujael begat Methusael; and
Methusael begat Lamech.

[19]And Lamech took unto him two wives: the name of the
one was Adah, and the name of the other Zillah. [20]And Adah
bare Jabal; he was the father of such as dwell in tents, and of
such as have cattle. [21]And his brother's name was Jubal: he
was the father of all such as handle the harp and organ.
[22]And Zillah, she also bare Tubalcain, an instructer of every
artificer in brass and iron; and the sister of Tubalcain was
Naamah. [23]And Lamech said unto his wives, Adah and Zillah, 'Hear my voice; ye wives of Lamech, hearken unto my
speech; for I have slain a man to my wounding, and a young
man to my hurt. [24]If Cain shall be avenged sevenfold, truly
Lamech seventy and sevenfold.'

[25]And Adam knew his wife again; and she bare a son, and
called his name Seth; 'For God,' said she, 'hath appointed me
another seed instead of Abel, whom Cain slew.' [26]And to Seth,

to him also there was born a son; and he called his name
Enos; then began men to call upon the name of the Lord.

5 This is the book of the generations of Adam. In the day
that God created man, in the likeness of God made he
him; 2 male and female created he them; and blessed them, and
called their name Adam, in the day when they were created.
3 And Adam lived an hundred and thirty years, and begat
a son in his own likeness, after his image; and called his name
Seth; 4 and the days of Adam after he had begotten Seth were
eight hundred years; and he begat sons and daughters; 5 and
all the days that Adam lived were nine hundred and thirty
years; and he died. 6 And Seth lived an hundred and five
years, and begat Enos; 7 and Seth lived after he begat Enos
eight hundred and seven years, and begat sons and daughters; 8 and all the days of Seth were nine hundred and twelve
years; and he died.
9 And Enos lived ninety years, and begat Cainan; 10 and
Enos lived after he begat Cainan eight hundred and fifteen
years, and begat sons and daughters; 11 and all the days of
Enos were nine hundred and five years; and he died.
12 And Cainan lived seventy years, and begat Mahalaleel;
13 and Cainan lived after he begat Mahalaleel eight hundred
and forty years, and begat sons and daughters; 14 and all the
days of Cainan were nine hundred and ten years; and he died.
15 And Mahalaleel lived sixty and five years, and begat
Jared; 16 and Mahalaleel lived after he begat Jared eight hundred and thirty years, and begat sons and daughters; 17 and

all the days of Mahalaleel were eight hundred ninety and
five years; and he died.

18 And Jared lived an hundred sixty and two years, and he
begat Enoch; 19 and Jared lived after he begat Enoch eight hundred years, and begat sons and daughters; 20 and all the days
of Jared were nine hundred sixty and two years; and he died.

21 And Enoch lived sixty and five years, and begat Methuselah; 22 and Enoch walked with God after he begat Methuselah three hundred years, and begat sons and daughters;
23 and all the days of Enoch were three hundred sixty and
five years; 24 and Enoch walked with God; and he was not;
for God took him. 25 And Methuselah lived an hundred eighty
and seven years, and begat Lamech; 26 and Methuselah lived
after he begat Lamech seven hundred eighty and two years,
and begat sons and daughters; 27 and all the days of Methuselah were nine hundred sixty and nine years; and he died.

28 And Lamech lived an hundred eighty and two years,
and begat a son; 29 and he called his name Noah, saying, 'This
same shall comfort us concerning our work and toil of our
hands, because of the ground which the Lord hath cursed.'
30 And Lamech lived after he begat Noah five hundred ninety
and five years, and begat sons and daughters; 31 and all the
days of Lamech were seven hundred seventy and seven
years; and he died. 32 And Noah was five hundred years old;
and Noah begat Shem, Ham, and Japheth.

6 And it came to pass, when men began to multiply on
the face of the earth, and daughters were born unto

them, [2] that the sons of God saw the daughters of men that
they were fair; and they took them wives of all which they
chose. [3]And the Lord said, 'My spirit shall not always strive
with man, for that he also is flesh; yet his days shall be an
hundred and twenty years.' [4]There were giants in the earth
in those days; and also after that, when the sons of God
came in unto the daughters of men, and they bare children
to them, the same became mighty men which were of old,
men of renown.

[5]And God saw that the wickedness of man was great in
the earth, and that every imagination of the thoughts of his
heart was only evil continually. [6]And it repented the Lord
that he had made man on the earth, and it grieved him at his
heart. [7]And the Lord said, 'I will destroy man whom I have
created from the face of the earth; both man, and beast, and
the creeping thing, and the fowls of the air; for it repenteth
me that I have made them.' [8]But Noah found grace in the
eyes of the Lord.

[9]There are the generations of Noah: Noah was a just man
and perfect in his generations, and Noah walked with God.
[10]And Noah begat three sons, Shem, Ham, and Japheth. [11]The
earth also was corrupt before God, and the earth was filled
with violence. [12]And God looked upon the earth, and, behold, it was corrupt; for all flesh had corrupted his way upon
the earth. [13]And God said unto Noah, 'The end of all flesh is
come before me; for the earth is filled with violence through
them; and, behold, I will destroy them with the earth.

[14]'Make thee an ark of gopher wood; rooms shalt thou

make in the ark, and shalt pitch it within and without with
pitch. [15]And this is the fashion which thou shalt make it of:
the length of the ark shall be three hundred cubits, the
breadth of it fifty cubits, and the height of it thirty cubits. [16]A
window shalt thou make to the ark, and in a cubit shalt thou
finish it above; and the door of the ark shalt thou set in the
side thereof; with lower, second, and third stories shalt thou
make it. [17]And, behold, I, even I, do bring a flood of waters
upon the earth, to destroy all flesh, wherein is the breath of
life, from under heaven; and every thing that is in the earth
shall die. [18]But with thee will I establish my covenant; and
thou shalt come into the ark, thou, and thy sons, and thy
wife, and thy sons' wives with thee. [19]And of every living
thing of all flesh, two of every sort shalt thou bring into the
ark, to keep them alive with thee; they shall be male and
female. [20]Of fowls after their kind, and of cattle after their
kind, of every creeping thing of the earth after his kind, two
of every sort shall come unto thee, to keep them alive. [21]And
take thou unto thee of all food that is eaten, and thou shalt
gather it to thee; and it shall be for food for thee, and for
them.' [22]Thus did Noah; according to all that God commanded him, so did he.

7 And the Lord said unto Noah, 'Come thou and all thy
house into the ark; for thee have I seen righteous before
me in this generation. [2]Of every clean beast thou shalt take
to thee by sevens, the male and his female; and of beasts that
are not clean by two, the male and his female. [3]Of fowls also

of the air by sevens, the male and the female; to keep seed
alive upon the face of all the earth. 4 For yet seven days, and I
will cause it to rain upon the earth forty days and forty nights;
and every living substance that I have made will I destroy
from off the face of the earth.' 5And Noah did according unto
all that the Lord commanded him. 6And Noah was six hundred years old when the flood of waters was upon the earth.

7And Noah went in, and his sons, and his wife, and his
sons' wives with him, into the ark, because of the waters of
the flood. 8 Of clean beasts, and of beasts that are not clean,
and of fowls, and of every thing that creepeth upon the earth,
9 there went in two and two unto Noah into the ark, the male
and the female, as God had commanded Noah. 10And it came
to pass after seven days, that the waters of the flood were
upon the earth.

11 In the six hundredth year of Noah's life, in the second
month, the seventeenth day of the month, the same day were
all the fountains of the great deep broken up, and the windows of heaven were opened. 12And the rain was upon the
earth forty days and forty nights. 13 In the selfsame day entered
Noah, and Shem, and Ham, and Japheth, the sons of Noah,
and Noah's wife, and the three wives of his sons with them,
into the ark; 14 they, and every beast after his kind, and all the
cattle after their kind, and every creeping thing that creepeth
upon the earth after his kind, and every fowl after his kind,
every bird of every sort. 15And they went in unto Noah into
the ark, two and two of all flesh, wherein is the breath of life.
16And they that went in, went in male and female of all flesh,

as God had commanded him: and the Lord shut him in. 17And
the flood was forty days upon the earth; and the waters
increased, and bare up the ark, and it was lift up above the
earth. 18And the waters prevailed, and were increased greatly
upon the earth; and the ark went upon the face of the waters.
19And the waters prevailed exceedingly upon the earth; and
all the high hills, that were under the whole heaven, were covered. 20 Fifteen cubits upward did the waters prevail; and the
mountains were covered. 21And all flesh died that moved
upon the earth, both of fowl, and of cattle, and of beast, and of
every creeping thing that creepeth upon the earth, and every
man; 22 all in whose nostrils was the breath of life, of all that
was in the dry land, died. 23And every living substance was
destroyed which was upon the face of the ground, both man,
and cattle, and the creeping things, and the fowl of the heaven;
and they were destroyed from the earth: and Noah only
remained alive, and they that were with him in the ark. 24And
the waters prevailed upon the earth an hundred and fifty days.

8 And God remembered Noah, and every living thing, and
all the cattle that was with him in the ark: and God made
a wind to pass over the earth, and the waters asswaged; 2 the
fountains also of the deep and the windows of heaven were
stopped, and the rain from heaven was restrained; 3 and the
waters returned from off the earth continually: and after the
end of the hundred and fifty days the waters were abated.
4And the ark rested in the seventh month, on the seventeenth
day of the month, upon the mountains of Ararat. 5And the

waters decreased continually until the tenth month; in the
tenth month, on the first day of the month, were the tops of
the mountains seen.

6And it came to pass at the end of forty days that Noah
opened the window of the ark which he had made; 7and he
sent forth a raven, which went forth to and fro, until the
waters were dried up from off the earth. 8Also he sent forth a
dove from him, to see if the waters were abated from off the
face of the ground; 9 but the dove found no rest for the sole
of her foot, and she returned unto him into the ark, for the
waters were on the face of the whole earth; then he put forth
his hand, and took her, and pulled her in unto him into the
ark. 10And he stayed yet other seven days; and again he sent
forth the dove out of the ark; 11 and the dove came in to him
in the evening; and, lo, in her mouth was an olive leaf pluckt
off; so Noah knew that the waters were abated from off the
earth. 12And he stayed yet other seven days; and sent forth
the dove; which returned not again unto him any more.

13And it came to pass in the six hundredth and first year,
in the first month, the first day of the month, the waters were
dried up from off the earth; and Noah removed the covering
of the ark, and looked, and, behold, the face of the ground
was dry. 14And in the second month, on the seven and twentieth day of the month, was the earth dried.

15And God spake unto Noah, saying, 16'Go forth of the
ark, thou, and thy wife, and thy sons, and thy sons' wives
with thee. 17 Bring forth with thee every living thing that is
with thee, of all flesh, both of fowl, and of cattle, and of every

creeping thing that creepeth upon the earth; that they may
breed abundantly in the earth, and be fruitful, and multiply
upon the earth.' 18 And Noah went forth, and his sons, and
his wife, and his sons' wives with him; 19 every beast, every
creeping thing, and every fowl, and whatsoever creepeth
upon the earth, after their kinds, went forth out of the ark.

20 And Noah builded an altar unto the Lord; and took of
every clean beast, and of every clean fowl, and offered burnt
offerings on the altar. 21 And the Lord smelled a sweet savour;
and the Lord said in his heart, 'I will not again curse the
ground any more for man's sake; for the imagination of man's
heart is evil from his youth; neither will I again smite any
more every thing living, as I have done. 22 While the earth
remaineth, seed-time and harvest, and cold and heat, and
summer and winter, and day and night shall not cease.'

9 And God blessed Noah and his sons, and said unto
them, 'Be fruitful, and multiply, and replenish the earth.
2 And the fear of you and the dread of you shall be upon every
beast of the earth, and upon every fowl of the air, upon all
that moveth upon the earth, and upon all the fishes of the
sea; into your hand are they delivered. 3 Every moving thing
that liveth shall be meat for you; even as the green herb have
I given you all things. 4 But flesh with the life thereof, which
is the blood thereof, shall ye not eat. 5 And surely your blood
of your lives will I require; at the hand of every beast will I
require it, and at the hand of man; at the hand of every man's
brother will I require the life of man. 6 Whoso sheddeth man's

blood, by man shall his blood be shed: for in the image of
God made he man. [7]And you, be ye fruitful, and multiply;
bring forth abundantly in the earth, and multiply therein.'

[8]And God spake unto Noah, and to his sons with him,
saying, [9]'And I, behold, I establish my covenant with you, and
with your seed after you; [10]and with every living creature that
is with you, of the fowl, of the cattle, and of every beast of the
earth with you; from all that go out of the ark, to every beast of
the earth. [11]And I will establish my covenant with you; neither
shall all flesh be cut off any more by the waters of a flood;
neither shall there any more be a flood to destroy the earth.'

[12]And God said, 'This is the token of the covenant which I
make between me and you and every living creature that is
with you, for perpetual generations: [13]I do set my bow in the
cloud, and it shall be for a token of a covenant between me
and the earth. [14]And it shall come to pass, when I bring a
cloud over the earth, that the bow shall be seen in the cloud:
[15]and I will remember my covenant, which is between me and
you and every living creature of all flesh; and the waters shall
no more become a flood to destroy all flesh. [16]And the bow
shall be in the cloud; and I will look upon it, that I may remember the everlasting covenant between God and every living
creature of all flesh that is upon the earth.' [17]And God said
unto Noah, 'This is the token of the covenant, which I have
established between me and all flesh that is upon the earth.'

[18]And the sons of Noah, that went forth of the ark, were
Shem, and Ham, and Japheth; and Ham is the father of Canaan. [19]These are the three sons of Noah; and of them was the

whole earth overspread. 20And Noah began to be an husbandman, and he planted a vineyard; 21and he drank of the wine,
and was drunken; and he was uncovered within his tent.
22And Ham, the father of Canaan, saw the nakedness of his
father, and told his two brethren without. 23And Shem and
Japheth took a garment, and laid it upon both their shoulders, and went backward, and covered the nakedness of their
father; and their faces were backward, and they saw not
their father's nakedness. 24And Noah awoke from his wine,
and knew what his younger son had done unto him. 25And
he said, 'Cursed be Canaan; a servant of servants shall he be
unto his brethren.' 26And he said, 'Blessed be the Lord God
of Shem; and Canaan shall be his servant. 27God shall enlarge
Japheth, and he shall dwell in the tents of Shem; and Canaan
shall be his servant.'

28And Noah lived after the flood three hundred and fifty
years. 29And all the days of Noah were nine hundred and
fifty years: and he died.

10 Now these are the generations of the sons of Noah,
Shem, Ham, and Japheth: and unto them were sons
born after the flood. 2The sons of Japheth: Gomer, and Magog,
and Madai, and Javan, and Tubal, and Meshech, and Tiras.
3And the sons of Gomer: Ashkenaz, and Riphath, and Toga-
rmah. 4And the sons of Javan: Elishah, and Tarshish, Kittim,
and Dodanim. 5By these were the isles of the Gentiles divided in their lands; every one after his tongue, after their
families, in their nations.

6 And the sons of Ham: Cush, and Mizraim, and Phut,
and Canaan. 7 And the sons of Cush: Seba, and Havilah, and
Sabtah, and Raamah, and Sabtecha; and the sons of Raamah:
Sheba, and Dedan. 8 And Cush begat Nimrod; he began to be
a mighty one in the earth. 9 He was a mighty hunter before
the Lord: wherefore it is said, 'Even as Nimrod the mighty
hunter before the Lord.' 10 And the beginning of his kingdom
was Babel, and Erech, and Accad, and Calneh, in the land of
Shinar. 11 Out of that land went forth Asshur, and builded
Nineveh, and the city Rehoboth, and Calah, 12 and Resen
between Nineveh and Calah: the same is a great city. 13 And
Mizraim begat Ludim, and Anamim, and Lehabim, and Naph-
tuhim, 14 and Pathrusim, and Casluhim (out of whom came
Philistim) and Caphtorim.

15 And Canaan begat Sidon his firstborn, and Heth, 16 and
the Jebusite, and the Amorite, and the Girgasite, 17 and the
Hivite, and the Arkite, and the Sinite, 18 and the Arvadite, and
the Zemarite, and the Hamathite: and afterward were the
families of the Canaanites spread abroad. 19 And the border
of the Canaanites was from Sidon, as thou comest to Gerar,
unto Gaza; as thou goest, unto Sodom, and Gomorrah, and
Admah, and Zeboim, even unto Lasha. 20 These are the sons
of Ham, after their families, after their tongues, in their countries, and in their nations.

21 Unto Shem also, the father of all the children of Eber,
the brother of Japheth the elder, even to him were children
born. 22 The children of Shem: Elam, and Asshur, and Arphaxad, and Lud, and Aram. 23 And the children of Aram: Uz,

and Hul, and Gether, and Mash. 24And Arphaxad begat Salah;
and Salah begat Eber. 25And unto Eber were born two sons:
the name of one was Peleg; for in his days was the earth
divided; and his brother's name was Joktan. 26And Joktan
begat Almodad, and Sheleph, and Hazarmaveth, and Jerah,
27and Hadoram, and Uzal, and Diklah, 28and Obal, and Abi-
mael, and Sheba, 29and Ophir, and Havilah, and Jobab: all
these were the sons of Joktan.30And their dwelling was from
Mesha, as thou goest unto Sephar a mount of the east.
31These are the sons of Shem, after their families, after their
tongues, in their lands, after their nations. 32These are the
families of the sons of Noah, after their generations, in their
nations: and by these were the nations divided in the earth
after the flood.

11 And the whole earth was of one language, and of one
speech. 2And it came to pass, as they journeyed from
the east, that they found a plain in the land of Shinar; and
they dwelt there. 3And they said one to another, 'Go to, let us
make brick, and burn them throughly.' And they had brick
for stone, and slime had they for morter. 4And they said, 'Go
to, let us build us a city and a tower, whose top may reach
unto heaven; and let us make us a name, lest we be scattered
abroad upon the face of the whole earth.' 5And the Lord
came down to see the city and the tower, which the children
of men builded. 6And the Lord said, 'Behold, the people is
one, and they have all one language; and this they begin to
do; and now nothing will be restrained from them, which

they have imagined to do. 7 Go to, let us go down, and there
confound their language, that they may not understand one
another's speech.' 8 So the Lord scattered them abroad from
thence upon the face of all the earth; and they left off to build
the city. 9 Therefore is the name of it called Babel; because
the Lord did there confound the language of all the earth:
and from thence did the Lord scatter them abroad upon the
face of all the earth.

10 These are the generations of Shem: Shem was an hundred years old, and begat Arphaxad two years after the flood;
11 and Shem lived after he begat Arphaxad five hundred years,
and begat sons and daughters. 12 And Arphaxad lived five and
thirty years, and begat Salah; 13 and Arphaxad lived after he
begat Salah four hundred and three years, and begat sons
and daughters.

14 And Salah lived thirty years, and begat Eber; 15 and Salah
lived after he begat Eber four hundred and three years, and
begat sons and daughters.

16 And Eber lived four and thirty years, and begat Peleg;
17 and Eber lived after he begat Peleg four hundred and thirty
years, and begat sons and daughters.

18 And Peleg lived thirty years, and begat Reu; 19 and Peleg
lived after he begat Reu two hundred and nine years, and
begat sons and daughters.

20 And Reu lived two and thirty years, and begat Serug:
21 and Reu lived after he begat Serug two hundred and seven
years, and begat sons and daughters.

22 And Serug lived thirty years, and begat Nahor; 23 and

Serug lived after he begat Nahor two hundred years, and
begat sons and daughters.

24 And Nahor lived nine and twenty years, and begat
Terah; 25 and Nahor lived after he begat Terah an hundred
and nineteen years, and begat sons and daughters.

26 And Terah lived seventy years, and begat Abram, Nahor,
and Haran.

27 Now these are the generations of Terah: Terah begat
Abram, Nahor, and Haran; and Haran begat Lot. 28 And Haran
died before his father Terah in the land of his nativity, in Ur
of the Chaldees. 29 And Abram and Nahor took them wives:
the name of Abram's wife was Sarai; and the name of Nahor's
wife, Milcah, the daughter of Haran, the father of Milcah,
and the father of Iscah. 30 But Sarai was barren; she had no
child. 31 And Terah took Abram his son, and Lot the son of
Haran his son's son, and Sarai his daughter in law, his son
Abram's wife; and they went forth with them from Ur of the
Chaldees, to go into the land of Canaan; and they came unto
Haran, and dwelt there. 32 And the days of Terah were two
hundred and five years; and Terah died in Haran.

12 Now the Lord had said unto Abram, 'Get thee out of
thy country, and from thy kindred, and from thy
father's house, unto a land that I will shew thee; 2 and I will
make of thee a great nation, and I will bless thee, and make
thy name great; and thou shalt be a blessing; 3 and I will
bless them that bless thee, and curse him that curseth thee;
and in thee shall all families of the earth be blessed.' 4 So

Abram departed, as the Lord had spoken unto him; and Lot
went with him: and Abram was seventy and five years old
when he departed out of Haran. 5And Abram took Sarai his
wife, and Lot his brother's son, and all their substance that
they had gathered, and the souls that they had gotten in
Haran; and they went forth to go into the land of Canaan;
and into the land of Canaan they came.

6And Abram passed through the land unto the place of
Sichem, unto the plain of Moreh. And the Canaanite was then
in the land. 7And the Lord appeared unto Abram, and said,
'Unto thy seed will I give this land,' and there builded he an
altar unto the Lord, who appeared unto him. 8And he removed
from thence unto a mountain on the east of Beth-el, and
pitched his tent, having Beth-el on the west, and Hai on the
east; and there he builded an altar unto the Lord, and called
upon the name of the Lord. 9And Abram journeyed, going
on still toward the south.

10And there was a famine in the land; and Abram went
down into Egypt to sojourn there; for the famine was grievous in the land. 11And it came to pass, when he was come
near to enter into Egypt, that he said unto Sarai his wife,
'Behold now, I know that thou art a fair woman to look upon.
12Therefore it shall come to pass, when the Egyptians shall
see thee, that they shall say, "This is his wife," and they will
kill me, but they will save thee alive. 13Say, I pray thee, thou
art my sister: that it may be well with me for thy sake; and
my soul shall live because of thee.'

14And it came to pass, that, when Abram was come into

Egypt, the Egyptians beheld the woman that she was very
fair. 15 The princes also of Pharaoh saw her, and commended
her before Pharaoh: and the woman was taken into Pharaoh's
house. 16 And he entreated Abram well for her sake; and he had
sheep, and oxen, and he asses, and menservants, and maidservants, and she asses, and camels. 17 And the Lord plagued
Pharaoh and his house with great plagues because of Sarai
Abram's wife. 18 And Pharaoh called Abram, and said, 'What
is this that thou hast done unto me? Why didst thou not tell
me that she was thy wife? 19 Why saidst thou, "She is my sister" so I might have taken her to me to wife? Now therefore
behold thy wife, take her, and go thy way.' 20 And Pharaoh
commanded his men concerning him: and they sent him
away, and his wife, and all that he had.

13 And Abram went up out of Egypt, he, and his wife,
and all that he had, and Lot with him, into the south.
2 And Abram was very rich in cattle, in silver, and in gold.
3 And he went on his journeys from the south even to Beth-el,
unto the place where his tent had been at the beginning,
between Beth-el and Hai; 4 unto the place of the altar, which
he had made there at the first: and there Abram called on the
name of the Lord.

5 And Lot also, which went with Abram, had flocks, and
herds, and tents. 6 And the land was not able to bear them, that
they might dwell together: for their substance was great, so
that they could not dwell together. 7 And there was a strife
between the herdmen of Abram's cattle and the herdmen of

Lot's cattle; and the Canaanite and the Perizzite dwelled then in the land. [8]And Abram said unto Lot, 'Let there be no strife, I pray thee, between me and thee, and between my herdmen and thy herdmen; for we be brethren. [9]Is not the whole land before thee? Separate thyself, I pray thee, from me: if thou wilt take the left hand, then I will go to the right; or if thou depart to the right hand, then I will go to the left.' [10]And Lot lifted up his eyes, and beheld all the plain of Jordan, that it was well watered every where, before the Lord destroyed Sodom and Gomorrah, even as the garden of the Lord, like the land of Egypt, as thcu comest unto Zoar. [11]Then Lot chose him all the plain of Jordan; and Lot journeyed east: and they separated themselves the one from the other. [12]Abram dwelled in the land of Canaan, and Lot dwelled in the cities of the plain, and pitched his tent toward Sodom. [13]But the men of Sodom were wicked and sinners before the Lord exceedingly.

[14]And the Lord said unto Abram, after that Lot was separated from him, 'Lift up now thine eyes, and look from the place where thou art northward, and southward, and eastward, and westward: [15]for all the land which thou seest, to thee will I give it, and to thy seed for ever. [16]And I will make thy seed as the dust of the earth; so that if a man can number the dust of the earth, then shall thy seed also be numbered. [17]Arise, walk through the land in the length of it and in the breadth of it; for I will give it unto thee.' [18]Then Abram removed his tent, and came and dwelt in the plain of Mamre, which is in Hebron, and built there an altar unto the Lord.

14 And it came to pass in the days of Amraphel king of
Shinar, Arioch king of Ellasar, Chedorlaomer king of
Elam, and Tidal king of nations; 2 that these made war with
Bera king of Sodom, and with Birsha king of Gomorrah,
Shinab king of Admah, and Shemeber king of Zeboiim, and
the king of Bela, which is Zoar. 3 All these were joined
together in the vale of Siddim, which is the salt sea. 4 Twelve
years they served Chedorlaomer, and in the thirteenth year
they rebelled. 5 And in the fourteenth year came Chedorlaomer, and the kings that were with him, and smote the
Rephaims in Ashteroth Karnaim, and the Zuzims in Ham,
and the Emims in Shaveh Kiriathaim, 6 and the Horites in
their mount Seir, unto El-paran, which is by the wilderness.
7 And they returned, and came to Enmishpat, which is Kadesh, and smote all the country of the Amalekites, and also
the Amorites, that dwelt in Hazezontamar. 8 And there went
out the king of Sodom, and the king of Gomorrah, and the
king of Admah, and the king of Zeboiim, and the king of
Bela (the same is Zoar); and they joined battle with them in
the vale of Siddim; 9 with Chedorlaomer the king of Elam,
and with Tidal king of nations, and Amraphel king of Shinar, and Arioch king of Ellasar; four kings with five. 10 And
the vale of Siddim was full of slimepits; and the kings of
Sodom and Gomorrah fled, and fell there; and they that
remained fled to the mountain. 11 And they took all the goods
of Sodom and Gomorrah, and all their victuals, and went
their way. 12 And they took Lot, Abram's brother's son, who
dwelt in Sodom, and his goods, and departed.

[13]And there came one that had escaped, and told Abram
the Hebrew; for he dwelt in the plain of Mamre the Amorite,
brother of Eshcol, and brother of Aner: and these were con-
federate with Abram. [14]And when Abram heard that his brother was taken captive, he armed his trained servants, born
in his own house, three hundred and eighteen, and pursued
them unto Dan. [15]And he divided himself against them, he
and his servants, by night, and smote them, and pursued them
unto Hobah, which is on the left hand of Damascus. [16]And he
brought back all the goods, and also brought again his brother Lot, and his goods, and the women also, and the people.

[17]And the king of Sodom went out to meet him after his
return from the slaughter of Chedorlaomer, and of the kings
that were with him, at the valley of Shaveh, which is the
king's dale.

[18]And Melchizedek king of Salem brought forth bread
and wine; and he was the priest of the most high God. [19]And
he blessed him, and said, 'Blessed be Abram of the most
high God, possessor of heaven and earth; [20]and blessed be
the most high God, which hath delivered thine enemies into
thy hand.' And he gave him tithes of all. [21]And the king of
Sodom said unto Abram, 'Give me the persons, and take the
goods to thyself.' [22]And Abram said to the king of Sodom, 'I
have lift up mine hand unto the Lord, the most high God,
the possessor of heaven and earth, [23]that I will not take from
a thread even to a shoelatchet, and that I will not take any
thing that is thine, lest thou shouldest say, "I have made
Abram rich," [24]save only that which the young men have

eaten, and the portion of the men which went with me, Aner, Eshcol, and Mamre; let them take their portion.'

15 After these things the word of the Lord came unto Abram in a vision, saying, 'Fear not, Abram: I am thy shield, and thy exceeding great reward.' 2And Abram said, 'Lord God, what wilt thou give me, seeing I go childless, and the steward of my house is this Eliezer of Damascus?' 3And Abram said, 'Behold, to me thou hast given no seed; and, lo, one born in my house is mine heir.' 4And, behold, the word of the Lord came unto him, saying, 'This shall not be thine heir; but he that shall come forth out of thine own bowels shall be thine heir.' 5And he brought Abram forth abroad, and said, 'Look now toward heaven, and tell the stars, if thou be able to number them,' and he said unto him, 'So shall thy seed be.'

6And he believed in the Lord; and he counted it to him for righteousness. 7And he said unto him, 'I am the Lord that brought thee out of Ur of the Chaldees, to give thee this land to inherit it.' 8And he said, 'Lord God, whereby shall I know that I shall inherit it?' 9And the Lord said unto him, 'Take me an heifer of three years old, and a she goat of three years old, and a ram of three years old, and a turtledove, and a young pigeon.' 10And he took unto him all these, and divided them in the midst, and laid each piece one against another; but the birds divided he not. 11And when the fowls came down upon the carcases, Abram drove them away. 12And when the sun was going down, a deep sleep fell upon Abram; and, lo, an

horror of great darkness fell upon him. 13And he said unto
Abram, 'Know of a surety that thy seed shall be a stranger in
a land that is not theirs, and shall serve them; and they shall
afflict them four hundred years; 14and also that nation, whom
they shall serve, will I judge: and afterward shall they come
out with great substance. 15And thou shalt go to thy fathers
in peace; thou shalt be buried in a good old age. 16But in the
fourth generation they shall come hither again: for the iniquity of the Amorites is not yet full.' 17And it came to pass, that,
when the sun went down, and it was dark, behold a smoking
furnace, and a burning lamp that passed between those pieces.
18In the same day the Lord made a covenant with Abram,
saying, 'Unto thy seed have I given this land, from the river
of Egypt unto the great river, the river Euphrates: 19the Ken-
ites, and the Kenizzites, and the Kadmonites, 20and the Hittites, and the Perizzites, and the Rephaims, 21and the Amorites,
and the Canaanites, and the Girgashites, and the Jebusites.'

16 Now Sarai Abram's wife bare him no children; and
she had an handmaid, an Egyptian, whose name was
Hagar. 2And Sarai said unto Abram, 'Behold now, the Lord
hath restrained me from bearing; I pray thee, go in unto my
maid; it may be that I may obtain children by her.' And Abram
hearkened to the voice of Sarai. 3And Sarai Abram's wife
took Hagar her maid the Egyptian, after Abram had dwelt
ten years in the land of Canaan, and gave her to her husband
Abram to be his wife.

4And he went in unto Hagar, and she conceived; and when

she saw that she had conceived, her mistress was despised
in her eyes. 5And Sarai said unto Abram, 'My wrong be upon
thee: I have given my maid into thy bosom; and when she
saw that she had conceived, I was despised in her eyes; the
Lord judge between me and thee.' 6But Abram said unto Sarai,
'Behold, thy maid is in thy hand; do to her as it pleaseth thee.'
And when Sarai dealt hardly with her, she fled from her face.

7And the angel of the Lord found her by a fountain of
water in the wilderness, by the fountain in the way to Shur.
8And he said, 'Hagar, Sarai's maid, whence camest thou?
And whither wilt thou go?' And she said, 'I flee from the face
of my mistress Sarai.' 9And the angel of the Lord said unto
her, 'Return to thy mistress, and submit thyself under her
hands.' 10And the angel of the Lord said unto her, 'I will multiply thy seed exceedingly, that it shall not be numbered for
multitude.' 11And the angel of the Lord said unto her, 'Behold,
thou art with child, and shalt bear a son, and shalt call his
name Ishmael; because the Lord hath heard thy affliction.
12And he will be a wild man; his hand will be against every
man, and every man's hand against him; and he shall dwell
in the presence of all his brethren.' 13And she called the name
of the Lord that spake unto her, 'Thou God seest me,' for she
said, 'Have I also here looked after him that seeth me?'
14Wherefore the well was called Beerlahai-roi; behold, it is
between Kadesh and Bered.

15And Hagar bare Abram a son; and Abram called his son's
name, which Hagar bare, Ishmael. 16And Abram was fourscore and six years old, when Hagar bare Ishmael to Abram.

17 And when Abram was ninety years old and nine, the
Lord appeared to Abram, and said unto him, 'I am the
Almighty God; walk before me, and be thou perfect. 2 And I
will make my covenant between me and thee, and will multiply thee exceedingly.' 3 And Abram fell on his face: and
God talked with him, saying, 4 'As for me, behold, my covenant is with thee, and thou shalt be a father of many nations.
5 Neither shall thy name any more be called Abram, but thy
name shall be Abraham; for a father of many nations have I
made thee. 6 And I will make thee exceeding fruitful, and I
will make nations of thee, and kings shall come out of thee.
7 And I will establish my covenant between me and thee and
thy seed after thee in their generations for an everlasting
covenant, to be a God unto thee, and to thy seed after thee.
8 And I will give unto thee, and to thy seed after thee, the
land wherein thou art a stranger, all the land of Canaan, for
an everlasting possession; and I will be their God.'

9 And God said unto Abraham, 'Thou shalt keep my covenant therefore, thou, and thy seed after thee in their generations. 10 This is my covenant, which ye shall keep, between me
and you and thy seed after thee; every man child among you
shall be circumcised. 11 And ye shall circumcise the flesh of your
foreskin; and it shall be a token of the covenant betwixt me
and you. 12 And he that is eight days old shall be circumcised
among you, every man child in your generations, he that is
born in the house, or bought with money of any stranger,
which is not of thy seed. 13 He that is born in thy house, and he
that is bought with thy money, must needs be circumcised;

and my covenant shall be in your flesh for an everlasting
covenant. 14And the uncircumcised man child whose flesh of
his foreskin is not circumcised, that soul shall be cut off from
his people; he hath broken my covenant.'

15And God said unto Abraham, 'As for Sarai thy wife, thou
shalt not call her name Sarai, but Sarah shall her name be.
16And I will bless her, and give thee a son also of her; yea, I
will bless her, and she shall be a mother of nations; kings of
people shall be of her.' 17Then Abraham fell upon his face, and
laughed, and said in his heart, 'Shall a child be born unto him
that is an hundred years old? And shall Sarah, that is ninety
years old, bear?' 18And Abraham said unto God, 'O that Ishmael might live before thee!' 19And God said, 'Sarah thy wife
shall bear thee a son indeed; and thou shalt call his name Isaac;
and I will establish my covenant with him for an everlasting
covenant, and with his seed after him. 20And as for Ishmael, I
have heard thee. Behold, I have blessed him, and will make
him fruitful, and will multiply him exceedingly; twelve princes
shall he beget, and I will make him a great nation. 21But my
covenant will I establish with Isaac, which Sarah shall bear
unto thee at this set time in the next year.' 22And he left off
talking with him, and God went up from Abraham.

23And Abraham took Ishmael his son, and all that were born
in his house, and all that were bought with his money, every
male among the men of Abraham's house; and circumcised
the flesh of their foreskin in the selfsame day, as God had
said unto him. 24And Abraham was ninety years old and nine,
when he was circumcised in the flesh of his foreskin. 25And

Ishmael his son was thirteen years old, when he was circumcised in the flesh of his foreskin. 26 In the selfsame day was
Abraham circumcised, and Ishmael his son. 27 And all the men
of his house, born in the house, and bought with money of
the stranger, were circumcised with him.

18 And the Lord appeared unto him in the plains of
Mamre; and he sat in the tent door in the heat of the
day; 2 and he lift up his eyes and looked, and, lo, three men
stood by him: and when he saw them, he ran to meet them
from the tent door, and bowed himself toward the ground,
3 and said, 'My Lord, if now I have found favour in thy sight,
pass not away, I pray thee, from thy servant; 4 let a little water,
I pray you, be fetched, and wash your feet, and rest yourselves under the tree; 5 and I will fetch a morsel of bread, and
comfort ye your hearts; after that ye shall pass on; for therefore are ye come to your servant.' And they said, 'So do, as
thou hast said.' 6 And Abraham hastened into the tent unto
Sarah, and said, 'Make ready quickly three measures of fine
meal, knead it, and make cakes upon the hearth.' 7 And Abraham ran unto the herd, and fetcht a calf tender and good,
and gave it unto a young man; and he hasted to dress it.
8 And he took butter, and milk, and the calf which he had
dressed, and set it before them; and he stood by them under
the tree, and they did eat.

9 And they said unto him, 'Where is Sarah thy wife?' And
he said, 'Behold, in the tent.' 10 And he said, 'I will certainly
return unto thee according to the time of life; and, lo, Sarah

thy wife shall have a son.' And Sarah heard it in the tent door, which was behind him. 11 Now Abraham and Sarah were old and well stricken in age; and it ceased to be with Sarah after the manner of women. 12 Therefore Sarah laughed within herself, saying, 'After I am waxed old shall I have pleasure, my lord being old also?' 13 And the Lord said unto Abraham, 'Wherefore did Sarah laugh, saying, "Shall I of a surety bear a child, which am old?" 14 Is any thing too hard for the Lord? At the time appointed I will return unto thee, according to the time of life, and Sarah shall have a son.' 15 Then Sarah denied, saying, 'I laughed not', for she was afraid. And he said, 'Nay; but thou didst laugh.'

16 And the men rose up from thence, and looked toward Sodom; and Abraham went with them to bring them on the way. 17 And the Lord said, 'Shall I hide from Abraham that thing which I do; 18 seeing that Abraham shall surely become a great and mighty nation, and all the nations of the earth shall be blessed in him? 19 For I know him, that he will command his children and his household after him, and they shall keep the way of the Lord, to do justice and judgment; that the Lord may bring upon Abraham that which he hath spoken of him.' 20 And the Lord said, 'Because the cry of Sodom and Gomorrah is great, and because their sin is very grievous; 21 I will go down now, and see whether they have done altogether according to the cry of it, which is come unto me; and if not, I will know.' 22 And the men turned their faces from thence, and went toward Sodom; but Abraham stood yet before the Lord.

23And Abraham drew near, and said, 'Wilt thou also destroy the righteous with the wicked? 24 Peradventure there be
fifty righteous within the city; wilt thou also destroy and not
spare the place for the fifty righteous that are therein? 25 That
be far from thee to do after this manner, to slay the righteous
with the wicked: and that the righteous should be as the
wicked, that be far from thee; shall not the Judge of all the
earth do right?' 26And the Lord said, 'If I find in Sodom fifty
righteous within the city, then I will spare all the place for
their sakes.' 27And Abraham answered and said, 'Behold
now, I have taken upon me to speak unto the Lord, which am
but dust and ashes: 28 peradventure there shall lack five of the
fifty righteous; wilt thou destroy all the city for lack of five?'
And he said, 'If I find there forty and five, I will not destroy it.'
29And he spake unto him yet again, and said, 'Peradventure
there shall be forty found there.' And he said, 'I will not do it
for forty's sake.' 30And he said unto him, 'Oh let not the Lord
be angry, and I will speak: peradventure there shall thirty be
found there.' And he said, 'I will not do it, if I find thirty there.'
31And he said, 'Behold now, I have taken upon me to speak
unto the Lord: peradventure there shall be twenty found
there.' And he said, 'I will not destroy it for twenty's sake.'
32And he said, 'Oh let not the Lord be angry, and I will speak
yet but this once: peradventure ten shall be found there.'
And he said, 'I will not destroy it for ten's sake.' 33And the
Lord went his way, as soon as he had left communing with
Abraham; and Abraham returned unto his place.

19 And there came two angels to Sodom at even; and Lot sat in the gate of Sodom; and Lot seeing them rose up to meet them; and he bowed himself with his face toward the ground; 2 and he said, 'Behold now, my lords, turn in, I pray you, into your servant's house, and tarry all night, and wash your feet, and ye shall rise up early, and go on your ways.' And they said, 'Nay; but we will abide in the street all night.' 3 And he pressed upon them greatly; and they turned in unto him, and entered into his house; and he made them a feast, and did bake unleavened bread, and they did eat.

4 But before they lay down, the men of the city, even the men of Sodom, compassed the house round, both old and young, all the people from every quarter; 5 and they called unto Lot, and said unto him, 'Where are the men which came in to thee this night? Bring them out unto us, that we may know them.' 6 And Lot went out at the door unto them, and shut the door after him, 7 and said, 'I pray you, brethren, do not so wickedly. 8 Behold now, I have two daughters which have not known man; let me, I pray you, bring them out unto you, and do ye to them as is good in your eyes: only unto these men do nothing; for therefore came they under the shadow of my roof.' 9 And they said, 'Stand back.' And they said again, 'This one fellow came in to sojourn, and he will needs be a judge; now will we deal worse with thee, than with them.' And they pressed sore upon the man, even Lot, and came near to break the door. 10 But the men put forth their hand, and pulled Lot into the house to them, and shut to the door. 11 And they smote the men that were at the door

of the house with blindness, both small and great; so that
they wearied themselves to find the door.
12 And the men said unto Lot, 'Hast thou here any besides?
Son in law, and thy sons, and thy daughters, and whatsoever thou hast in the city, bring them out of this place, 13 for
we will destroy this place, because the cry of them is waxen
great before the face of the Lord; and the Lord hath sent us
to destroy it.' 14 And Lot went out, and spake unto his sons in
law, which married his daughters, and said, 'Up, get you out
of this place; for the Lord will destroy this city.' But he
seemed as one that mocked unto his sons in law.
15 And when the morning arose, then the angels hastened
Lot, saying, 'Arise, take thy wife, and thy two daughters,
which are here; lest thou be consumed in the iniquity of the
city.' 16 And while he lingered, the men laid hold upon his
hand, and upon the hand of his wife, and upon the hand of
his two daughters; the Lord being merciful unto him; and
they brought him forth, and set him without the city.
17 And it came to pass, when they had brought them forth
abroad, that he said, 'Escape for thy life; look not behind
thee, neither stay thou in all the plain; escape to the mountain, lest thou be consumed.' 18 And Lot said unto them, 'Oh,
not so, my Lord: 19 behold now, thy servant hath found grace
in thy sight, and thou hast magnified thy mercy, which thou
hast shewed unto me in saving my life; and I cannot escape
to the mountain, lest some evil take me, and I die; 20 behold
now, this city is near to flee unto, and it is a little one; oh, let
me escape thither (is it not a little one?) and my soul shall

live.' 21 And he said unto him, 'See, I have accepted thee concerning this thing also, that I will not overthrow this city, for
the which thou hast spoken. 22 Haste thee, escape thither; for
I cannot do any thing till thou be come thither.' Therefore
the name of the city was called Zoar.

23 The sun was risen upon the earth when Lot entered
into Zoar. 24 Then the Lord rained upon Sodom and upon
Gomorrah brimstone and fire from the Lord out of heaven;
25 and he overthrew those cities, and all the plain, and all the
inhabitants of the cities, and that which grew upon the ground.

26 But his wife looked back from behind him, and she
became a pillar of salt.

27 And Abraham gat up early in the morning to the place
where he stood before the Lord; 28 and he looked toward
Sodom and Gomorrah, and toward all the land of the plain,
and beheld, and, lo, the smoke of the country went up as the
smoke of a furnace.

29 And it came to pass, when God destroyed the cities of
the plain, that God remembered Abraham, and sent Lot out
of the midst of the overthrow, when he overthrew the cities
in the which Lot dwelt.

30 And Lot went up out of Zoar, and dwelt in the mountain, and his two daughters with him; for he feared to dwell
in Zoar; and he dwelt in a cave, he and his two daughters.
31 And the firstborn said unto the younger, 'Our father is old,
and there is not a man in the earth to come in unto us after
the manner of all the earth; 32 come, let us make our father
drink wine, and we will lie with him, that we may preserve

seed of our father.' 33And they made their father drink wine
that night: and the firstborn went in, and lay with her father;
and he perceived not when she lay down, nor when she arose.
34And it came to pass on the morrow, that the firstborn said
unto the younger, 'Behold, I lay yesternight with my father;
let us make him drink wine this night also; and go thou in,
and lie with him, that we may preserve seed of our father.'
35And they made their father drink wine that night also; and
the younger arose, and lay with him; and he perceived not
when she lay down, nor when she arose. 36Thus were both
the daughters of Lot with child by their father. 37And the
firstborn bare a son, and called his name Moab; the same is
the father of the Moabites unto this day. 38And the younger,
she also bare a son, and called his name Ben-ammi: the same
is the father of the children of Ammon unto this day.

20 And Abraham journeyed from thence toward the
south country, and dwelled between Kadesh and
Shur, and sojourned in Gerar. 2And Abraham said of Sarah
his wife, 'She is my sister,' and Abimelech king of Gerar sent,
and took Sarah. 3But God came to Abimelech in a dream by
night, and said to him, 'Behold, thou art but a dead man, for
the woman which thou hast taken; for she is a man's wife.'
4But Abimelech had not come near her; and he said, 'Lord,
wilt thou slay also a righteous nation? 5Said he not unto me,
"She is my sister"? And she, even she herself said, "He is my
brother"; in the integrity of my heart and innocency of my
hands have I done this.' 6And God said unto him in a dream,

'Yea, I know that thou didst this in the integrity of thy heart;
for I also withheld thee from sinning against me; therefore
suffered I thee not to touch her. [7] Now therefore restore the
man his wife; for he is a prophet, and he shall pray for thee,
and thou shalt live; and if thou restore her not, know thou
that thou shalt surely die, thou, and all that are thine.' [8] Therefore Abimelech rose early in the morning, and called all his
servants, and told all these things in their ears; and the men
were sore afraid. [9] Then Abimelech called Abraham, and said
unto him, 'What hast thou done unto us? And what have I
offended thee, that thou hast brought on me and on my kingdom a great sin? Thou hast done deeds unto me that ought
not to be done.' [10] And Abimelech said unto Abraham, 'What
sawest thou, that thou hast done this thing?' [11] And Abraham
said, 'Because I thought, surely the fear of God is not in this
place; and they will slay me for my wife's sake. [12] And yet
indeed she is my sister; she is the daughter of my father, but
not the daughter of my mother; and she became my wife.
[13] And it came to pass, when God caused me to wander from
my father's house, that I said unto her, "This is thy kindness
which thou shalt shew unto me; at every place whither we
shall come, say of me, 'He is my brother.'"' [14] And Abimelech
took sheep, and oxen, and menservants, and womenservants, and gave them unto Abraham, and restored him Sarah
his wife. [15] And Abimelech said, 'Behold, my land is before
thee; dwell where it pleaseth thee.' [16] And unto Sarah he said,
'Behold, I have given thy brother a thousand pieces of silver;
behold, he is to thee a covering of the eyes, unto all that are

with thee, and with all other'; thus she was reproved.

17 So Abraham prayed unto God: and God healed Abimelech, and his wife, and his maidservants; and they bare children. 18 For the Lord had fast closed up all the wombs of the house of Abimelech, because of Sarah Abraham's wife.

21 And the Lord visited Sarah as he had said, and the Lord did unto Sarah as he had spoken. 2 For Sarah conceived, and bare Abraham a son in his old age, at the set time of which God had spoken to him. 3 And Abraham called the name of his son that was born unto him, whom Sarah bare to him, Isaac. 4 And Abraham circumcised his son Isaac being eight days old, as God had commanded him. 5 And Abraham was an hundred years old, when his son Isaac was born unto him.

6 And Sarah said, 'God hath made me to laugh, so that all that hear will laugh with me.' 7 And she said, 'Who would have said unto Abraham, that Sarah should have given children suck? For I have born him a son in his old age.' 8 And the child grew, and was weaned; and Abraham made a great feast the same day that Isaac was weaned.

9 And Sarah saw the son of Hagar the Egyptian, which she had born unto Abraham, mocking. 10 Wherefore she said unto Abraham, 'Cast out this bondwoman and her son: for the son of this bondwoman shall not be heir with my son, even with Isaac.' 11 And the thing was very grievous in Abraham's sight because of his son.

12 And God said unto Abraham, 'Let it not be grievous in

thy sight because of the lad, and because of thy bondwoman;
in all that Sarah hath said unto thee, hearken unto her voice;
for in Isaac shall thy seed be called. [13]And also of the son of
the bondwoman will I make a nation, because he is thy seed.'
[14]And Abraham rose up early in the morning, and took bread,
and a bottle of water, and gave it unto Hagar, putting it on her
shoulder, and the child, and sent her away; and she departed,
and wandered in the wilderness of Beer-sheba. [15]And the
water was spent in the bottle, and she cast the child under
one of the shrubs. [16]And she went, and sat her down over
against him a good way off, as it were a bowshot; for she
said, 'Let me not see the death of the child.' And she sat over
against him, and lift up her voice, and wept. [17]And God heard
the voice of the lad; and the angel of God called to Hagar out
of heaven, and said unto her, 'What aileth thee, Hagar? Fear
not; for God hath heard the voice of the lad where he is.
[18]Arise, lift up the lad, and hold him in thine hand; for I will
make him a great nation.' [19]And God opened her eyes, and
she saw a well of water; and she went, and filled the bottle
with water, and gave the lad drink. [20]And God was with the
lad; and he grew, and dwelt in the wilderness, and became
an archer. [21]And he dwelt in the wilderness of Paran; and his
mother took him a wife out of the land of Egypt.

[22]And it came to pass at that time, that Abimelech and
Phichol the chief captain of his host spake unto Abraham,
saying, 'God is with thee in all that thou doest; [23]now therefore swear unto me here by God that thou wilt not deal
falsely with me, nor with my son, nor with my son's son; but

according to the kindness that I have done unto thee, thou shalt do unto me, and to the land wherein thou hast sojourned.' [24]And Abraham said, 'I will swear.' [25]And Abraham reproved Abimelech because of a well of water, which Abimelech's servants had violently taken away. [26]And Abimelech said, 'I wot not who hath done this thing; neither didst thou tell me, neither yet heard I of it, but to day.' [27]And Abraham took sheep and oxen, and gave them unto Abimelech; and both of them made a covenant. [28]And Abraham set seven ewe lambs of the flock by themselves. [29]And Abimelech said unto Abraham, 'What mean these seven ewe lambs which thou hast set by themselves?' [30]And he said, 'For these seven ewe lambs shalt thou take of my hand, that they may be a witness unto me, that I have digged this well.' [31]Wherefore he called that place Beer-sheba; because there they sware both of them. [32]Thus they made a covenant at Beer-sheba; then Abimelech rose up, and Phichol the chief captain of his host, and they returned into the land of the Philistines.

[33]And Abraham planted a grove in Beer-sheba, and called there on the name of the Lord, the everlasting God. [34]And Abraham sojourned in the Philistines' land many days.

22 And it came to pass after these things, that God did tempt Abraham, and said unto him, 'Abraham,' and he said, 'Behold, here I am.' [2]And he said, 'Take now thy son, thine only son Isaac, whom thou lovest, and get thee into the land of Moriah; and offer him there for a burnt offering upon one of the mountains which I will tell thee of.'

3And Abraham rose up early in the morning, and saddled his ass, and took two of his young men with him, and
Isaac his son, and clave the wood for the burnt offering, and
rose up, and went unto the place of which God had told him.
4Then on the third day Abraham lifted up his eyes, and saw
the place afar off. 5And Abraham said unto his young men,
'Abide ye here with the ass; and I and the lad will go yonder
and worship, and come again to you.' 6And Abraham took
the wood of the burnt offering, and laid it upon Isaac his
son; and he took the fire in his hand, and a knife; and they
went both of them together. 7And Isaac spake unto Abraham
his father, and said, 'My father,' and he said, 'Here am I, my
son.' And Isaac said, 'Behold the fire and the wood; but where
is the lamb for a burnt offering?' 8And Abraham said, 'My
son, God will provide himself a lamb for a burnt offering'; so
they went both of them together. 9And they came to the
place which God had told him of; and Abraham built an
altar there, and laid the wood in order, and bound Isaac his
son, and laid him on the altar upon the wood. 10And Abraham stretched forth his hand, and took the knife to slay his
son. 11And the angel of the Lord called unto him out of heaven,
and said, 'Abraham, Abraham,' and he said, 'Here am I.' 12And
he said, 'Lay not thine hand upon the lad, neither do thou
any thing unto him; for now I know that thou fearest God,
seeing thou hast not withheld thy son, thine only son from
me.' 13And Abraham lifted up his eyes, and looked, and
behold behind him a ram caught in a thicket by his horns;
and Abraham went and took the ram, and offered him up

for a burnt offering in the stead of his son. [14]And Abraham
called the name of that place Jehovah-jireh: as it is said to
this day, in the mount of the Lord it shall be seen.

[15]And the angel of the Lord called unto Abraham out of
heaven the second time, [16]and said, 'By myself have I sworn,
saith the Lord, for because thou hast done this thing, and
hast not withheld thy son, thine only son: [17]that in blessing I
will bless thee, and in multiplying I will multiply thy seed as
the stars of the heaven, and as the sand which is upon the
sea shore; and thy seed shall possess the gate of his enemies;
[18]and in thy seed shall all the nations of the earth be blessed;
because thou hast obeyed my voice.' [19]So Abraham returned
unto his young men, and they rose up and went together to
Beer-sheba; and Abraham dwelt at Beer-sheba.

[20]And it came to pass after these things, that it was told
Abraham, saying, 'Behold, Milcah, she hath also born children unto thy brother Nahor; [21]Huz his firstborn, and Buz his
brother, and Kemuel the father of Aram, [22]and Chesed, and
Hazo, and Pildash, and Jidlaph, and Bethuel. [23]And Bethuel
begat Rebekah: these eight Milcah did bear to Nahor, Abraham's brother. [24]And his concubine, whose name was Reumah,
she bare also Tebah, and Gaham, and Thahash, and Maachah.'

23 And Sarah was an hundred and seven and twenty
years old: these were the years of the life of Sarah.
[2]And Sarah died in Kirjath-arba; the same is Hebron in the
land of Canaan; and Abraham came to mourn for Sarah, and
to weep for her.

3And Abraham stood up from before his dead, and spake
unto the sons of Heth, saying, 4 'I am a stranger and a sojour-
ner with you; give me a possession of a buryingplace with
you, that I may bury my dead out of my sight.' 5And the children of Heth answered Abraham, saying unto him, 6 'Hear
us, my lord: thou art a mighty prince among us; in the choice
of our sepulchres bury thy dead; none of us shall withhold
from thee his sepulchre, but that thou mayest bury thy dead.'
7And Abraham stood up, and bowed himself to the people
of the land, even to the children of Heth. 8And he communed with them, saying, 'If it be your mind that I should
bury my dead out of my sight; hear me, and intreat for me to
Ephron the son of Zohar, 9 that he may give me the cave of
Machpelah, which he hath, which is in the end of his field;
for as much money as it is worth he shall give it me for a
possession of a buryingplace amongst you.' 10And Ephron
dwelt among the children of Heth: and Ephron the Hittite
answered Abraham in the audience of the children of Heth,
even of all that went in at the gate of his city, saying, 11 'Nay,
my lord, hear me: the field give I thee, and the cave that is
therein, I give it thee; in the presence of the sons of my people give I it thee; bury thy dead.' 12And Abraham bowed down
himself before the people of the land. 13And he spake unto
Ephron in the audience of the people of the land, saying,
'But if thou wilt give it, I pray thee, hear me: I will give thee
money for the field; take it of me, and I will bury my dead
there.' 14And Ephron answered Abraham, saying unto him,
15 'My lord, hearken unto me: the land is worth four hundred

shekels of silver; what is that betwixt me and thee? Bury
therefore thy dead.' 16And Abraham hearkened unto Ephron;
and Abraham weighed to Ephron the silver, which he had
named in the audience of the sons of Heth, four hundred
shekels of silver, current money with the merchant.

17And the field of Ephron, which was in Machpelah, which
was before Mamre, the field, and the cave which was therein,
and all the trees that were in the field, that were in all the
borders round about, were made sure 18 unto Abraham for a
possession in the presence of the children of Heth, before all
that went in at the gate of his city. 19And after this, Abraham
buried Sarah his wife in the cave of the field of Machpelah
before Mamre: the same is Hebron in the land of Canaan.
20And the field, and the cave that is therein, were made sure
unto Abraham for a possession of a buryingplace by the
sons of Heth.

24 And Abraham was old, and well stricken in age: and
the Lord had blessed Abraham in all things. 2And
Abraham said unto his eldest servant of his house, that ruled
over all that he had, 'Put, I pray thee, thy hand under my
thigh; 3and I will make thee swear by the Lord, the God of
heaven, and the God of the earth, that thou shalt not take a
wife unto my son of the daughters of the Canaanites, among
whom I dwell; 4but thou shalt go unto my country, and to
my kindred, and take a wife unto my son Isaac.' 5And the
servant said unto him, 'Peradventure the woman will not be
willing to follow me unto this land; must I needs bring thy

son again unto the land from whence thou camest?' [6]And
Abraham said unto him, 'Beware thou that thou bring not
my son thither again.

[7]"The Lord God of heaven, which took me from my father's
house, and from the land of my kindred, and which spake
unto me, and that sware unto me, saying, "Unto thy seed
will I give this land"; he shall send his angel before thee, and
thou shalt take a wife unto my son from thence. [8]And if the
woman will not be willing to follow thee, then thou shalt be
clear from this my oath: only bring not my son thither again.'
[9]And the servant put his hand under the thigh of Abraham his
master, and sware to him concerning that matter.

[10]And the servant took ten camels of the camels of his
master, and departed; for all the goods of his master were in
his hand; and he arose, and went to Mesopotamia, unto the
city of Nahor. [11]And he made his camels to kneel down without the city by a well of water at the time of the evening,
even the time that women go out to draw water. [12]And he
said, 'O Lord God of my master Abraham, I pray thee, send
me good speed this day, and shew kindness unto my master
Abraham. [13]Behold, I stand here by the well of water; and
the daughters of the men of the city come out to draw water;
[14]and let it come to pass that the damsel to whom I shall say,
"Let down thy pitcher, I pray thee, that I may drink"; and
she shall say, "Drink, and I will give thy camels drink also";
let the same be she that thou hast appointed for thy servant
Isaac; and thereby shall I know that thou hast shewed kindness unto my master.'

15And it came to pass, before he had done speaking, that,
behold, Rebekah came out, who was born to Bethuel, son of
Milcah, the wife of Nahor, Abraham's brother, with her pitcher upon her shoulder. 16And the damsel was very fair to
look upon, a virgin, neither had any man known her; and
she went down to the well, and filled her pitcher, and came
up. 17And the servant ran to meet her, and said, 'Let me, I
pray thee, drink a little water of thy pitcher.' 18And she said,
'Drink, my lord'; and she hasted, and let down her pitcher
upon her hand, and gave him drink. 19And when she had
done giving him drink, she said, 'I will draw water for thy
camels also, until they have done drinking.' 20And she hasted,
and emptied her pitcher into the trough, and ran again unto
the well to draw water, and drew for all his camels. 21And
the man wondering at her held his peace, to wit whether the
Lord had made his journey prosperous or not. 22And it came
to pass, as the camels had done drinking, that the man took
a golden earring of half a shekel weight, and two bracelets for
her hands of ten shekels weight of gold; 23and said, 'Whose
daughter art thou? Tell me, I pray thee; is there room in thy
father's house for us to lodge in?' 24And she said unto him, 'I
am the daughter of Bethuel the son of Milcah, which she bare
unto Nahor.' 25She said moreover unto him, 'We have both
straw and provender enough, and room to lodge in.' 26And
the man bowed down his head, and worshipped the Lord.
27And he said, 'Blessed be the Lord God of my master Abraham, who hath not left destitute my master of his mercy and
his truth; I being in the way, the Lord led me to the house of

my master's brethren.' 28 And the damsel ran, and told them
of her mother's house these things.

29 And Rebekah had a brother, and his name was Laban;
and Laban ran out unto the man, unto the well. 30 And it came
to pass, when he saw the earring and bracelets upon his sister's hands, and when he heard the words of Rebekah his
sister, saying, 'Thus spake the man unto me'; that he came
unto the man; and, behold, he stood by the camels at the well.
31 And he said, 'Come in, thou blessed of the Lord; wherefore
standest thou without? For I have prepared the house, and
room for the camels.'

32 And the man came into the house; and he ungirded his
camels, and gave straw and provender for the camels, and
water to wash his feet, and the men's feet that were with
him. 33 And there was set meat before him to eat; but he said,
'I will not eat, until I have told mine errand.' And he said,
'Speak on.' 34 And he said, 'I am Abraham's servant. 35 And the
Lord hath blessed my master greatly; and he is become great;
and he hath given him flocks, and herds, and silver, and gold,
and menservants, and maidservants, and camels, and asses.
36 And Sarah my master's wife bare a son to my master when
she was old; and unto him hath he given all that he hath.
37 And my master made me swear, saying, "Thou shalt not
take a wife to my son of the daughters of the Canaanites, in
whose land I dwell; 38 but thou shalt go unto my father's house,
and to my kindred, and take a wife unto my son." 39 And I
said unto my master, "Peradventure the woman will not follow me." 40 And he said unto me, "The Lord, before whom I

walk, will send his angel with thee, and prosper thy way;
and thou shalt take a wife for my son of my kindred, and of
my father's house; 41 then shalt thou be clear from this my
oath, when thou comest to my kindred; and if they give not
thee one, thou shalt be clear from my oath." 42And I came
this day unto the well, and said, "O Lord God of my master
z I stand by the well of water; and it shall come to pass, that
when the virgin cometh forth to draw water, and I say to her,
'Give me, I pray thee, a little water of thy pitcher to drink';
44And she say to me, 'Both drink thou, and I will also draw
for thy camels': let the same be the woman whom the Lord
hath appointed out for my master's son." 45And before I had
done speaking in mine heart, behold, Rebekah came forth
with her pitcher on her shoulder; and she went down unto
the well, and drew water; and I said unto her, "Let me drink,
I pray thee." 46And she made haste, and let down her pitcher
from her shoulder, and said, "Drink, and I will give thy
camels drink also"; so I drank, and she made the camels
drink also. 47And I asked her, and said, "Whose daughter art
thou?" And she said, "The daughter of Bethuel, Nahor's son,
whom Milcah bare unto him"; and I put the earring upon
her face, and the bracelets upon her hands. 48And I bowed
down my head, and worshipped the Lord, and blessed the
Lord God of my master Abraham, which had led me in the
right way to take my master's brother's daughter unto his
son. 49And now if ye will deal kindly and truly with my master, tell me; and if not, tell me; that I may turn to the right
hand, or to the left.'

50 Then Laban and Bethuel answered and said, 'The thing
proceedeth from the Lord; we cannot speak unto thee bad or
good. 51 Behold, Rebekah is before thee, take her, and go, and
let her be thy master's son's wife, as the Lord hath spoken.'
52 And it came to pass, that, when Abraham's servant heard
their words, he worshipped the Lord, bowing himself to the
earth. 53 And the servant brought forth jewels of silver, and
jewels of gold, and raiment, and gave them to Rebekah; he
gave also to her brother and to her mother precious things.
54 And they did eat and drink, he and the men that were with
him, and tarried all night; and they rose up in the morning,
and he said, 'Send me away unto my master.' 55 And her
brother and her mother said, 'Let the damsel abide with us a
few days, at the least ten; after that she shall go.' 56 And he
said unto them, 'Hinder me not, seeing the Lord hath prospered my way; send me away that I may go to my master.'
57 And they said, 'We will call the damsel, and enquire at her
mouth.' 58 And they called Rebekah, and said unto her, 'Wilt
thou go with this man?' And she said, 'I will go.' 59 And they
sent away Rebekah their sister, and her nurse, and Abraham's servant, and his men. 60 And they blessed Rebekah,
and said unto her, 'Thou art our sister, be thou the mother of
thousands of millions, and let thy seed possess the gate of
those which hate them.'

61 And Rebekah arose, and her damsels, and they rode
upon the camels, and followed the man; and the servant
took Rebekah, and went his way. 62 And Isaac came from the
way of the well Lahai-roi; for he dwelt in the south country.

63And Isaac went out to meditate in the field at the eventide:
and he lifted up his eyes, and saw, and, behold, the camels
were coming. 64And Rebekah lifted up her eyes, and when
she saw Isaac, she lighted off the camel. 65For she had said
unto the servant, 'What man is this that walketh in the field
to meet us?' And the servant had said, 'It is my master'; therefore she took a vail, and covered herself. 66And the servant
told Isaac all things that he had done. 67And Isaac brought
her into his mother Sarah's tent, and took Rebekah, and she
became his wife; and he loved her; and Isaac was comforted
after his mother's death.

25 Then again Abraham took a wife, and her name was
Keturah. 2And she bare him Zimran, and Jokshan,
and Medan, and Midian, and Ishbak, and Shuah. 3And Jok-
shan begat Sheba, and Dedan. And the sons of Dedan were
Asshurim, and Letushim, and Leummim. 4And the sons of
Midian: Ephah, and Epher, and Hanoch, and Abida, and
Eldaah. All these were the children of Keturah.

5And Abraham gave all that he had unto Isaac. 6But unto
the sons of the concubines, which Abraham had, Abraham
gave gifts, and sent them away from Isaac his son, while he
yet lived, eastward, unto the east country. 7And these are the
days of the years of Abraham's life which he lived, an hundred threescore and fifteen years. 8Then Abraham gave up
the ghost, and died in a good old age, an old man, and full of
years; and was gathered to his people. 9And his sons Isaac
and Ishmael buried him in the cave of Machpelah, in the

field of Ephron the son of Zohar the Hittite, which is before
Mamre; 10 the field which Abraham purchased of the sons of
Heth; there was Abraham buried, and Sarah his wife.

11 And it came to pass after the death of Abraham, that God
blessed his son Isaac; and Isaac dwelt by the well Lahai-roi.

12 Now these are the generations of Ishmael, Abraham's
son, whom Hagar the Egyptian, Sarah's handmaid, bare unto
Abraham; 13 and these are the names of the sons of Ishmael,
by their names, according to their generations: the firstborn
of Ishmael, Nebajoth; and Kedar, and Adbeel, and Mibsam,
14 and Mishma, and Dumah, and Massa, 15 Hadar, and Tema,
Jetur, Naphish, and Kedemah. 16 These are the sons of Ishmael, and these are their names, by their towns, and by their
castles; twelve princes according to their nations. 17 And these
are the years of the life of Ishmael, an hundred and thirty
and seven years; and he gave up the ghost and died; and
was gathered unto his people. 18 And they dwelt from Havilah unto Shur, that is before Egypt, as thou goest toward
Assyria; and he died in the presence of all his brethren.

19 And these are the generations of Isaac, Abraham's son:
Abraham begat Isaac; 20 and Isaac was forty years old when
he took Rebekah to wife, the daughter of Bethuel the Syrian
of Padan-aram, the sister to Laban the Syrian. 21 And Isaac
intreated the Lord for his wife, because she was barren; and
the Lord was intreated of him, and Rebekah his wife conceived. 22 And the children struggled together within her; and
she said, 'If it be so, why am I thus?' And she went to enquire
of the Lord. 23 And the Lord said unto her, 'Two nations are

in thy womb, and two manner of people shall be separated
from thy bowels; and the one people shall be stronger than
the other people; and the elder shall serve the younger.'

24 And when her days to be delivered were fulfilled, behold,
there were twins in her womb. 25 And the first came out red,
all over like an hairy garment; and they called his name Esau.
26 And after that came his brother out, and his hand took hold
on Esau's heel; and his name was called Jacob; and Isaac was
threescore years old when she bare them. 27 And the boys
grew; and Esau was a cunning hunter, a man of the field;
and Jacob was a plain man, dwelling in tents. 28 And Isaac
loved Esau, because he did eat of his venison; but Rebekah
loved Jacob.

29 And Jacob sod pottage; and Esau came from the field,
and he was faint; 30 and Esau said to Jacob, 'Feed me, I pray
thee, with that same red pottage; for I am faint'; therefore was
his name called Edom. 31 And Jacob said, 'Sell me this day thy
birthright.' 32 And Esau said, 'Behold, I am at the point to die;
and what profit shall this birthright do to me?' 33 And Jacob
said, 'Swear to me this day'; and Esau sware unto him; and
he sold his birthright unto Jacob. 34 Then Jacob gave Esau
bread and pottage of lentiles; and he did eat and drink, and
rose up, and went his way; thus Esau despised his birthright.

26 And there was a famine in the land, beside the first
famine that was in the days of Abraham. And Isaac
went unto Abimelech king of the Philistines unto Gerar. 2 And
the Lord appeared unto him, and said, 'Go not down into

Egypt; dwell in the land which I shall tell thee of; [3] sojourn in
this land, and I will be with thee, and will bless thee; for unto
thee, and unto thy seed, I will give all these countries, and I
will perform the oath which I sware unto Abraham thy father;
[4] and I will make thy seed to multiply as the stars of heaven,
and will give unto thy seed all these countries; and in thy
seed shall all the nations of the earth be blessed; [5] because
that Abraham obeyed my voice, and kept my charge, my
commandments, my statues, and my laws.'

[6]And Isaac dwelt in Gerar. [7]And the men of the place
asked him of his wife; and he said, 'She is my sister', for he
feared to say, 'She is my wife', lest, said he, 'the men of the
place should kill me for Rebekah;' because she was fair to
look upon. [8]And it came to pass, when he had been there a
long time, that Abimelech king of the Philistines looked out
at a window, and saw, and, behold, Isaac was sporting with
Rebekah his wife. [9]And Abimelech called Isaac, and said,
'Behold, of a surety she is thy wife: and how saidst thou, "She
is my sister"?' And Isaac said unto him, 'Because I said, Lest
I die for her.' [10]And Abimelech said, 'What is this thou hast
done unto us? One of the people might lightly have lien
with thy wife, and thou shouldest have brought guiltiness
upon us.' [11]And Abimelech charged all his people, saying,
'He that toucheth this man or his wife shall surely be put to
death.' [12] Then Isaac sowed in that land, and received in the
same year an hundred-fold: and the Lord blessed him. [13]And
the man waxed great, and went forward, and grew until he
became very great; [14] for he had possession of flocks, and

possession of herds, and great store of servants: and the
Philistines envied him. 15 For all the wells which his father's
servants had digged in the days of Abraham his father, the
Philistines had stopped them, and filled them with earth.
16 And Abimelech said unto Isaac, 'Go from us; for thou art
much mightier than we.'

17 And Isaac departed thence, and pitched his tent in the
valley of Gerar, and dwelt there. 18 And Isaac digged again
the wells of water, which they had digged in the days of
Abraham his father; for the Philistines had stopped them
after the death of Abraham; and he called their names after
the names by which his father had called them. 19 And Isaac's
servants digged in the valley, and found there a well of
springing water. 20 And the herdmen of Gerar did strive with
Isaac's herdmen, saying, 'The water is ours,' and he called
the name of the well Esek; because they strove with him.
21 And they digged another well, and strove for that also; and
he called the name of it Sitnah. 22 And he removed from thence,
and digged another well; and for that they strove not; and
he called the name of it Rehoboth; and he said, 'For now the
Lord hath made room for us, and we shall be fruitful in the
land.' 23 And he went up from thence to Beer-sheba. 24 And
the Lord appeared unto him the same night, and said, 'I am
the God of Abraham thy father: fear not, for I am with thee,
and will bless thee, and multiply thy seed for my servant
Abraham's sake.' 25 And he builded an altar there, and called
upon the name of the Lord, and pitched his tent there; and
there Isaac's servants digged a well.

26 Then Abimelech went to him from Gerar, and Ahuz-
zath one of his friends, and Phichol the chief captain of his
army. 27 And Isaac said unto them, 'Wherefore come ye to
me, seeing ye hate me, and have sent me away from you?'
28 And they said, 'We saw certainly that the Lord was with
thee; and we said, "Let there be now an oath betwixt us,
even betwixt us and thee, and let us make a covenant with
thee"; 29 that thou wilt do us no hurt, as we have not touched
thee, and as we have done unto thee nothing but good, and
have sent thee away in peace: thou art now the blessed of
the Lord.' 30 And he made them a feast, and they did eat and
drink. 31 And they rose up betimes in the morning, and sware
one to another; and Isaac sent them away, and they departed
from him in peace. 32 And it came to pass the same day, that
Isaac's servants came, and told him concerning the well which
they had digged, and said unto him, 'We have found water.'
33 And he called it Shebah: therefore the name of the city is
Beer-sheba unto this day.

34 And Esau was forty years old when he took to wife
Judith the daughter of Beeri the Hittite, and Bashemath the
daughter of Elon the Hittite: 35 which were a grief of mind
unto Isaac and to Rebekah.

27 And it came to pass that, when Isaac was old, and
his eyes were dim, so that he could not see, he called
Esau his eldest son, and said unto him, 'My son,' and he said
unto him, 'Behold, here am I.' 2 And Isaac said, 'Behold now,
I am old, I know not the day of my death; 3 now therefore

take, I pray thee, thy weapons, thy quiver and thy bow, and
go out to the field, and take me some venison; 4 and make me
savoury meat, such as I love, and bring it to me, that I may
eat; that my soul may bless thee before I die.' 5 And Rebekah
heard when Isaac spake to Esau his son. And Esau went to
the field to hunt for venison, and to bring it.

6 And Rebekah spake unto Jacob her son, saying, 'Behold, I
heard thy father speak unto Esau thy brother, saying, 7 "Bring
me venison, and make me savoury meat, that I may eat, and
bless thee before the Lord before my death." 8 Now therefore, my son, obey my voice according to that which I command thee. 9 Go now to the flock, and fetch me from thence
two good kids of the goats; and I will make them savoury
meat for thy father, such as he loveth; 10 and thou shalt bring
it to thy father, that he may eat, and that he may bless thee
before his death.' 11 And Jacob said to Rebekah his mother,
'Behold, Esau my brother is a hairy man, and I am a smooth
man: 12 my father peradventure will feel me, and I shall seem
to him as a deceiver; and I shall bring a curse upon me, and
not a blessing.' 13 And his mother said unto him, 'Upon me be
thy curse, my son; only obey my voice, and go fetch me them.'
14 And he went, and fetched, and brought them to his mother;
and his mother made savoury meat, such as his father loved.
15 And Rebekah took goodly raiment of her eldest son Esau,
which were with her in the house, and put them upon Jacob
her younger son; 16 and she put the skins of the kids of the
goats upon his hands, and upon the smooth of his neck;
17 and she gave the savoury meat and the bread, which she

had prepared, into the hand of her son Jacob.
18And he came unto his father, and said, 'My father,' and
he said, 'Here am I; who art thou, my son?' 19And Jacob said
unto his father, 'I am Esau thy firstborn; I have done according as thou badest me; arise, I pray thee, sit and eat of my
venison, that thy soul may bless me.' 20And Isaac said unto
his son, 'How is it that thou hast found it so quickly, my
son?' And he said, 'Because the Lord thy God brought it to
me.' 21And Isaac said unto Jacob, 'Come near, I pray thee,
that I may feel thee, my son, whether thou be my very son
Esau or not.' 22And Jacob went near unto Isaac his father;
and he felt him, and said, 'The voice is Jacob's voice, but the
hands are the hands of Esau.' 23And he discerned him not,
because his hands were hairy, as his brother Esau's hands; so
he blessed him. 24And he said, 'Art thou my very son Esau?'
And he said, 'I am.' 25And Isaac said, 'Bring it near to me, and
I will eat of my son's venison, that my soul may bless thee.'
And he brought it near to him, and he did eat; and he brought
him wine, and he drank. 26And his father Isaac said unto
him, 'Come near now, and kiss me, my son.' 27And he came
near, and kissed him: and he smelled the smell of his raiment, and blessed him, and said, 'See, the smell of my son is
as the smell of a field which the Lord hath blessed; 28there-
fore God give thee of the dew of heaven, and the fatness of
the earth, and plenty of corn and wine; 29let people serve
thee, and nations bow down to thee; be lord over thy brethren,
and let thy mother's sons bow down to thee; cursed be every
one that curseth thee, and blessed be he that blesseth thee.'

30 And it came to pass, as soon as Isaac had made an end
of blessing Jacob, and Jacob was yet scarce gone out from the
presence of Isaac his father, that Esau his brother came in
from his hunting. 31 And he also had made savoury meat, and
brought it unto his father, and said unto his father, 'Let my
father arise, and eat of his son's venison, that thy soul may
bless me.' 32 And Isaac his father said unto him, 'Who art thou?'
And he said, 'I am thy son, thy firstborn Esau.' 33 And Isaac
trembled very exceedingly, and said, 'Who? Where is he that
hath taken venison, and brought it me, and I have eaten of
all before thou camest, and have blessed him? Yea, and he
shall be blessed.' 34 And when Esau heard the words of his
father, he cried with a great and exceeding bitter cry, and
said unto his father, 'Bless me, even me also, O my father.'
35 And he said, 'Thy brother came with subtilty, and hath
taken away thy blessing.' 36 And Esau said, 'Is not he rightly
named Jacob? For he hath supplanted me these two times:
he took away my birthright; and, behold, now he hath taken
away my blessing.' And he said, 'Hast thou not reserved a
blessing for me?' 37 And Isaac answered and said unto Esau,
'Behold, I have made him thy lord, and all his brethren have
I given to him for servants; and with corn and wine have I
sustained him: and what shall I do now unto thee, my son?'
38 And Esau said unto his father, 'Hast thou but one blessing,
my father? Bless me, even me also, O my father.' And Esau
lifted up his voice, and wept. 39 And Isaac his father answered
and said unto him, 'Behold, thy dwelling shall be the fatness
of the earth, and of the dew of heaven from above; 40 and by

thy sword shalt thou live, and shalt serve thy brother; and it
shall come to pass when thou shalt have the dominion, that
thou shalt break his yoke from off thy neck.'
41And Esau hated Jacob because of the blessing wherewith his father blessed him; and Esau said in his heart, 'The
days of mourning for my father are at hand; then will I slay
my brother Jacob.' 42And these words of Esau her elder son
were told to Rebekah; and she sent and called Jacob her
younger son, and said unto him, 'Behold, thy brother Esau,
as touching thee, doth comfort himself, purposing to kill thee.
43Now therefore, my son, obey my voice; and arise, flee thou
to Laban my brother to Haran; 44and tarry with him a few
days, until thy brother's fury turn away; 45until thy brother's
anger turn away from thee, and he forget that which thou
hast done to him; then I will send, and fetch thee from thence;
why should I be deprived also of you both in one day?' 46And
Rebekah said to Isaac, 'I am weary of my life because of the
daughters of Heth; if Jacob take a wife of the daughters of
Heth, such as these which are of the daughters of the land,
what good shall my life do me?'

28 And Isaac called Jacob, and blessed him, and charged
him, and said unto him, 'Thou shalt not take a wife
of the daughters of Canaan. 2Arise, go to Padan-aram, to the
house of Bethuel thy mother's father; and take thee a wife
from thence of the daughters of Laban thy mother's brother.
3And God Almighty bless thee, and make thee fruitful, and
multiply thee, that thou mayest be a multitude of people;

[4]and give thee the blessing of Abraham, to thee, and to thy
seed with thee; that thou mayest inherit the land wherein
thou art a stranger, which God gave unto Abraham.' [5]And
Isaac sent away Jacob; and he went to Padan-aram unto
Laban, son of Bethuel the Syrian, the brother of Rebekah,
Jacob's and Esau's mother.

[6]When Esau saw that Isaac had blessed Jacob, and sent
him away to Padan-aram, to take him a wife from thence; and
that as he blessed him he gave him a charge, saying, 'Thou
shalt not take a wife of the daughters of Canaan,' [7]and that
Jacob obeyed his father and his mother, and was gone to
Padan-aram; [8]and Esau seeing that the daughters of Canaan
pleased not Isaac his father; [9]then went Esau unto Ishmael,
and took unto the wives which he had Mahalath the daughter of Ishmael Abraham's son, the sister of Nebajoth, to be
his wife.

[10]And Jacob went out from Beer-sheba, and went toward
Haran. [11]And he lighted upon a certain place, and tarried there
all night, because the sun was set; and he took of the stones
of that place, and put them for his pillows, and lay down in
that place to sleep. [12]And he dreamed, and behold a ladder
set up on the earth, and the top of it reached to heaven: and
behold the angels of God ascending and descending on it.
[13]And, behold, the Lord stood above it, and said, 'I am the
Lord God of Abraham thy father, and the God of Isaac: the
land whereon thou liest, to thee will I give it, and to thy seed;
[14]and thy seed shall be as the dust of the earth, and thou
shalt spread abroad to the west, and to the east, and to the

north, and to the south; and in thee and in thy seed shall all
the families of the earth be blessed. 15And, behold, I am with
thee, and will keep thee in all places whither thou goest, and
will bring thee again into this land; for I will not leave thee,
until I have done that which I have spoken to thee of.'

16And Jacob awaked out of his sleep, and he said, 'Surely
the Lord is in this place; and I knew it not.' 17And he was
afraid, and said, 'How dreadful is this place! This is none
other but the house of God, and this is the gate of heaven.'
18And Jacob rose up early in the morning, and took the stone
that he had put for his pillows, and set it up for a pillar, and
poured oil upon the top of it. 19And he called the name of
that place Beth-el: but the name of that city was called Luz at
the first. 20And Jacob vowed a vow, saying, 'If God will be
with me, and will keep me in this way that I go, and will
give me bread to eat, and raiment to put on, 21so that I come
again to my father's house in peace; then shall the Lord be
my God; 22and this stone, which I have set for a pillar, shall
be God's house; and of all that thou shalt give me I will
surely give the tenth unto thee.'

29 Then Jacob went on his journey, and came into the
land of the people of the east. 2And he looked, and
behold a well in the field, and, lo, there were three flocks of
sheep lying by it; for out of that well they watered the flocks;
and a great stone was upon the well's mouth. 3And thither
were all the flocks gathered; and they rolled the stone from
the well's mouth, and watered the sheep, and put the stone

again upon the well's mouth in his place. [4]And Jacob said
unto them, 'My brethren, whence be ye?' And they said, 'Of
Haran are we.' [5]And he said unto them, 'Know ye Laban the
son of Nahor?' And they said, 'We know him.' [6]And he said
unto them, 'Is he well?' And they said, 'He is well; and,
behold, Rachel his daughter cometh with the sheep.' [7]And he
said, 'Lo, it is yet high day, neither is it time that the cattle
should be gathered together; water ye the sheep, and go and
feed them.' [8]And they said, 'We cannot, until all the flocks be
gathered together, and till they roll the stone from the well's
mouth; then we water the sheep.'

[9]And while he yet spake with them, Rachel came with her
father's sheep; for she kept them. [10]And it came to pass, when
Jacob saw Rachel the daughter of Laban his mother's brother,
and the sheep of Laban his mother's brother, that Jacob went
near, and rolled the stone from the well's mouth, and
watered the flock of Laban his mother's brother. [11]And Jacob
kissed Rachel, and lifted up his voice, and wept. [12]And Jacob
told Rachel that he was her father's brother, and that he was
Rebekah's son; and she ran and told her father. [13]And it came
to pass, when Laban heard the tidings of Jacob his sister's son,
that he ran to meet him, and embraced him, and kissed him,
and brought him to his house. And he told Laban all these
things. [14]And Laban said to him, 'Surely thou art my bone
and my flesh.' And he abode with him the space of a month.

[15]And Laban said unto Jacob, 'Because thou art my brother,
shouldest thou therefore serve me for nought? Tell me, what
shall thy wages be?' [16]And Laban had two daughters: the

name of the elder was Leah, and the name of the younger
was Rachel. 17 Leah was tender eyed; but Rachel was beautiful and well favoured. 18 And Jacob loved Rachel; and said, 'I
will serve thee seven years for Rachel thy younger daughter.' 19 And Laban said, 'It is better that I give her to thee, than
that I should give her to another man: abide with me.' 20 And
Jacob served seven years for Rachel; and they seemed unto
him but a few days, for the love he had to her.

21 And Jacob said unto Laban, 'Give me my wife, for my
days are fulfilled, that I may go in unto her.' 22 And Laban
gathered together all the men of the place, and made a feast.
23 And it came to pass in the evening, that he took Leah his
daughter, and brought her to him; and he went in unto her.
24 And Laban gave unto his daughter Leah Zilpah his maid
for an handmaid. 25 And it came to pass that in the morning,
behold, it was Leah: and he said to Laban, 'What is this thou
hast done unto me? Did not I serve with thee for Rachel?
Wherefore then hast thou beguiled me?' 26 And Laban said,
'It must not be so done in our country, to give the younger
before the firstborn. 27 Fulfil her week, and we will give thee
this also for the service which thou shalt serve with me yet
seven other years.' 28 And Jacob did so, and fulfilled her week;
and he gave him Rachel his daughter to wife also. 29 And
Laban gave to Rachel his daughter Bilhah his handmaid to
be her maid. 30 And he went in also unto Rachel, and he
loved also Rachel more than Leah, and served with him yet
seven other years.

31 And when the Lord saw that Leah was hated, he opened

her womb: but Rachel was barren. 32And Leah conceived,
and bare a son, and she called his name Reuben; for she said,
'Surely the Lord hath looked upon my affliction; now therefore my husband will love me.' 33And she conceived again,
and bare a son; and said, 'Because the Lord hath heard that I
was hated, he hath therefore given me this son also', and she
called his name Simeon. 34And she conceived again, and bare
a son; and said, 'Now this time will my husband be joined
unto me, because I have born him three sons'; therefore was
his name called Levi. 35And she conceived again, and bare a
son; and she said, 'Now will I praise the Lord'; therefore she
called his name Judah; and left bearing.

30 And when Rachel saw that she bare Jacob no children, Rachel envied her sister; and said unto Jacob,
'Give me children, or else I die.' 2And Jacob's anger was kindled against Rachel; and he said, 'Am I in God's stead, who
hath withheld from thee the fruit of the womb?' 3And she
said, 'Behold my maid Bilhah, go in unto her; and she shall
bear upon my knees, that I may also have children by her.'
4And she gave him Bilhah her handmaid to wife; and Jacob
went in unto her. 5And Bilhah conceived, and bare Jacob a
son. 6And Rachel said, 'God hath judged me, and hath also
heard my voice, and hath given me a son'; therefore called
she his name Dan. 7And Bilhah Rachel's maid conceived
again, and bare Jacob a second son. 8And Rachel said, 'With
great wrestlings have I wrestled with my sister, and I have
prevailed'; and she called his name Naphtali. 9When Leah

saw that she had left bearing, she took Zilpah her maid, and
gave her Jacob to wife. [10]And Zilpah Leah's maid bare Jacob
a son. [11]And Leah said, 'A troop cometh', and she called his
name Gad. [12]And Zilpah Leah's maid bare Jacob a second
son. [13]And Leah said, 'Happy am I, for the daughters will call
me blessed,' and she called his name Asher.

[14]And Reuben went in the days of wheat harvest, and
found mandrakes in the field, and brought them unto his
mother Leah. Then Rachel said to Leah, 'Give me, I pray thee,
of thy son's mandrakes.' [15]And she said unto her, 'Is it a small
matter that thou hast taken my husband? And wouldest
thou take away my son's mandrakes also?' And Rachel said,
'Therefore he shall lie with thee to night for thy son's mandrakes.' [16]And Jacob came out of the field in the evening, and
Leah went out to meet him, and said, 'Thou must come in
unto me; for surely I have hired thee with my son's mandrakes.' And he lay with her that night. [17]And God hearkened
unto Leah, and she conceived, and bare Jacob the fifth son.
[18]And Leah said, 'God hath given me my hire, because I have
given my maiden to my husband,' and she called his name
Issachar. [19]And Leah conceived again, and bare Jacob the sixth
son. [20]And Leah said, 'God hath endued me with a good
dowry; now will my husband dwell with me, because I have
born him six sons,' and she called his name Zebulun. [21]And
afterwards she bare a daughter, and called her name Dinah.

[22]And God remembered Rachel, and God hearkened to
her, and opened her womb. [23]And she conceived, and bare a
son; and said, 'God hath taken away my reproach,' [24]and she

called his name Joseph; and said, 'The Lord shall add to me
another son.'

25 And it came to pass, when Rachel had born Joseph, that
Jacob said unto Laban, 'Send me away, that I may go unto
mine own place, and to my country. 26 Give me my wives and
my children, for whom I have served thee, and let me go; for
thou knowest my service which I have done thee.' 27 And
Laban said unto him, 'I pray thee, if I have found favour in
thine eyes, tarry: for I have learned by experience that the
Lord hath blessed me for thy sake.' 28 And he said, 'Appoint
me thy wages, and I will give it.' 29 And Jacob said unto him,
'Thou knowest how I have served thee, and how thy cattle
was with me. 30 For it was little which thou hadst before I
came, and it is now increased unto a multitude; and the Lord
hath blessed thee since my coming; and now when shall I
provide for mine own house also?' 31 And Laban said, 'What
shall I give thee?' And Jacob said, 'Thou shalt not give me
any thing; if thou wilt do this thing for me, I will again feed
and keep thy flock. 32 I will pass through all thy flock to day,
removing from thence all the speckled and spotted cattle,
and all the brown cattle among the sheep, and the spotted
and speckled among the goats; and of such shall be my hire.
33 So shall my righteousness answer for me in time to come,
when it shall come for my hire before thy face; every one
that is not speckled and spotted among the goats, and
brown among the sheep, that shall be counted stolen with
me.' 34 And Laban said, 'Behold, I would it might be according to thy word.' 35 And he removed that day the he goats

that were ringstraked and spotted, and all the she goats that were speckled and spotted, and every one that had some white in it, and all the brown among the sheep, and gave them into the hand of his sons. 36 And he set three days' journey betwixt himself and Jacob: and Jacob fed the rest of Laban's flocks.

37 And Jacob took him rods of green poplar, and of the hazel and chesnut tree; and pilled white strakes in them, and made the white appear which was in the rods. 38 And he set the rods which he had pilled before the flocks in the gutters in the watering troughs when the flocks came to drink, that they should conceive when they came to drink. 39 And the flocks conceived before the rods, and brought forth cattle ringstraked, speckled, and spotted. 40 And Jacob did separate the lambs, and set the faces of the flocks toward the ringstraked, and all the brown in the flock of Laban; and he put his own flocks by themselves, and put them not unto Laban's cattle. 41 And it came to pass, whensoever the stronger cattle did conceive, that Jacob laid the rods before the eyes of the cattle in the gutters, that they might conceive among the rods. 42 But when the cattle were feeble, he put them not in: so the feebler were Laban's, and the stronger Jacob's. 43 And the man increased exceedingly, and had much cattle, and maidservants, and menservants, and camels, and asses.

31 And Jacob heard the words of Laban's sons, saying, 'Jacob hath taken away all that was our father's; and of that which was our father's hath he gotten all this glory.'

2And Jacob beheld the countenance of Laban, and, behold, it
was not toward him as before. 3And the Lord said unto Jacob,
'Return unto the land of thy fathers, and to thy kindred; and
I will be with thee.' 4And Jacob sent and called Rachel and
Leah to the field unto his flock, 5and said unto them, 'I see
your father's countenance, that it is not toward me as before;
but the God of my father hath been with me. 6And ye know
that with all my power I have served your father. 7And your
father hath deceived me, and changed my wages ten times;
but God suffered him not to hurt me. 8If he said thus, "The
speckled shall be thy wages," then all the cattle bare speckled: and if he said thus, "The ringstraked shall be thy hire,"
then bare all the cattle ringstraked. 9Thus God hath taken
away the cattle of your father, and given them to me. 10And it
came to pass at the time that the cattle conceived, that I lifted
up mine eyes, and saw in a dream, and, behold, the rams
which leaped upon the cattle were ringstraked, speckled,
and grisled. 11And the angel of God spake unto me in a dream,
saying, "Jacob," and I said, "Here am I." 12And he said, "Lift
up now thine eyes, and see, all the rams which leap upon the
cattle are ringstraked, speckled, and grisled; for I have seen
all that Laban doeth unto thee. 13I am the God of Beth-el,
where thou anointedst the pillar, and where thou vowedst a
vow unto me; now arise, get thee out from this land, and
return unto the land of thy kindred."' 14And Rachel and Leah
answered and said unto him, 'Is there yet any portion or
inheritance for us in our father's house? 15Are we not counted of him strangers? For he hath sold us, and hath quite

devoured also our money. 16 For all the riches which God
hath taken from our father, that is ours, and our children's;
now then, whatsoever God hath said unto thee, do.'

17 Then Jacob rose up, and set his sons and his wives upon
camels; 18 and he carried away all his cattle, and all his goods
which he had gotten, the cattle of his getting, which he had
gotten in Padan-aram, for to go to Isaac his father in the land
of Canaan. 19 And Laban went to shear his sheep: and Rachel
had stolen the images that were her father's. 20 And Jacob
stole away unawares to Laban the Syrian, in that he told him
not that he fled. 21 So he fled with all that he had; and he rose
up, and passed over the river, and set his face toward the
mount Gilead. 22 And it was told Laban on the third day that
Jacob was fled. 23 And he took his brethren with him, and
pursued after him seven days' journey; and they overtook
him in the mount Gilead. 24 And God came to Laban the Syrian in a dream by night, and said unto him, 'Take heed that
thou speak not to Jacob either good or bad.'

25 Then Laban overtook Jacob. Now Jacob had pitched
his tent in the mount; and Laban with his brethren pitched
in the mount of Gilead. 26 And Laban said to Jacob, 'What
hast thou done, that thou hast stolen away unawares to me,
and carried away my daughters, as captives taken with the
sword? 27 Wherefore didst thou flee away secretly, and steal
away from me; and didst not tell me, that I might have sent
thee away with mirth, and with songs, with tabret, and with
harp? 28 And hast not suffered me to kiss my sons and my
daughters? Thou hast now done foolishly in so doing. 29 It is

in the power of my hand to do you hurt; but the God of your
father spake unto me yesternight, saying, "Take thou heed
that thou speak not to Jacob either good or bad." 30 And now,
though thou wouldest needs be gone, because thou sore long-
edst after thy father's house, yet wherefore hast thou stolen
my gods?' 31 And Jacob answered and said to Laban, 'Because
I was afraid: for I said, peradventure thou wouldest take by
force thy daughters from me. 32 With whomsoever thou find-
est thy gods, let him not live; before our brethren discern
thou what is thine with me, and take it to thee.' For Jacob
knew not that Rachel had stolen them. 33 And Laban went
into Jacob's tent, and into Leah's tent, and into the two maidservants' tents; but he found them not. Then went he out of
Leah's tent, and entered into Rachel's tent. 34 Now Rachel
had taken the images, and put them in the camel's furniture,
and sat upon them. And Laban searched all the tent, but
found them not. 35 And she said to her father, 'Let it not displease my lord that I cannot rise up before thee; for the custom of women is upon me.' And he searched, but found not
the images.

36 And Jacob was wroth, and chode with Laban; and Jacob
answered and said to Laban, 'What is my trespass? What is
my sin, that thou hast so hotly pursued after me? 37 Whereas
thou hast searched all my stuff, what hast thou found of all
thy household stuff? Set it here before my brethren and thy
brethren, that they may judge betwixt us both. 38 This twenty
years have I been with thee; thy ewes and thy she goats have
not cast their young, and the rams of thy flock have I not

eaten. [39] That which was torn of beasts I brought not unto
thee; I bare the loss of it; of my hand didst thou require it,
whether stolen by day, or stolen by night. [40] Thus I was; in
the day the drought consumed me, and the frost by night;
and my sleep departed from mine eyes. [41] Thus have I been
twenty years in thy house; I served thee fourteen years for
thy two daughters, and six years for thy cattle; and thou hast
changed my wages ten times. [42] Except the God of my father,
the God of Abraham, and the fear of Isaac, had been with me,
surely thou hadst sent me away now empty. God hath seen
mine affliction and the labour of my hands, and rebuked
thee yesternight.'

[43] And Laban answered and said unto Jacob, 'These daughters are my daughters, and these children are my children,
and these cattle are my cattle, and all that thou seest is mine;
and what can I do this day unto these my daughters, or unto
their children which they have born? [44] Now therefore come
thou, let us make a covenant, I and thou; and let it be for a
witness between me and thee.' [45] And Jacob took a stone, and
set it up for a pillar. [46] And Jacob said unto his brethren, 'Gather
stones'; and they took stones, and made an heap; and they
did eat there upon the heap. [47] And Laban called it Jegar-saha-
dutha; but Jacob called it Galeed. [48] And Laban said, 'This
heap is a witness between me and thee this day.' Therefore
was the name of it called Galeed; [49] and Mizpah; for he said,
'The Lord watch between me and thee, when we are absent
one from another. [50] If thou shalt afflict my daughters, or if
thou shalt take other wives beside my daughters, no man is

with us; see, God is witness betwixt me and thee.' 51And
Laban said to Jacob, 'Behold this heap, and behold this pillar, which I have cast betwixt me and thee; 52 this heap be
witness, and this pillar be witness, that I will not pass over
this heap to thee, and that thou shalt not pass over this heap
and this pillar unto me, for harm. 53 The God of Abraham,
and the God of Nahor, the God of their father, judge betwixt
us.' And Jacob sware by the fear of his father Isaac. 54 Then
Jacob offered sacrifice upon the mount, and called his brethren
to eat bread; and they did eat bread, and tarried all night in
the mount. 55And early in the morning Laban rose up, and
kissed his sons and his daughters, and blessed them; and
Laban departed, and returned unto his place.

32 And Jacob went on his way, and the angels of God
met him. 2And when Jacob saw them, he said, 'This
is God's host,' and he called the name of that place Maha-
naim. 3And Jacob sent messengers before him to Esau his
brother unto the land of Seir, the country of Edom. 4And he
commanded them, saying, 'Thus shall ye speak unto my lord
Esau: thy servant Jacob saith thus, I have sojourned with
Laban, and stayed there until now; 5 and I have oxen, and
asses, flocks, and menservants, and womenservants: and I
have sent to tell my lord, that I may find grace in thy sight.'

6And the messengers returned to Jacob, saying, 'We
came to thy brother Esau, and also he cometh to meet thee,
and four hundred men with him.' 7 Then Jacob was greatly
afraid and distressed; and he divided the people that was

with him, and the flocks, and herds, and the camels, into two
bands; [8]and said, 'If Esau come to the one company, and
smite it, then the other company which is left shall escape.'

[9]And Jacob said, 'O God of my father Abraham, and God
of my father Isaac, the Lord which saidst unto me, "Return
unto thy country, and to thy kindred, and I will deal well
with thee"; [10]I am not worthy of the least of all the mercies,
and of all the truth, which thou hast shewed unto thy servant; for with my staff I passed over this Jordan; and now I
am become two bands. [11]Deliver me, I pray thee, from the
hand of my brother, from the hand of Esau; for I fear him,
lest he will come and smite me, and the mother with the
children. [12]And thou saidst, "I will surely do thee good, and
make thy seed as the sand of the sea, which cannot be numbered for multitude."'

[13]And he lodged there that same night; and took of that
which came to his hand a present for Esau his brother: [14]two
hundred she goats, and twenty he goats, two hundred ewes,
and twenty rams, [15]thirty milch camels with their colts, forty
kine, and ten bulls, twenty she asses, and ten foals. [16]And he
delivered them into the hand of his servants, every drove by
themselves; and said unto his servants, 'Pass over before me,
and put a space betwixt drove and drove.' [17]And he commanded the foremost, saying, 'When Esau my brother meeteth
thee, and asketh thee, saying, "Whose art thou? And whither
goest thou? And whose are these before thee?" [18]Then thou
shalt say, "They be thy servant Jacob's; it is a present sent
unto my lord Esau; and, behold, also he is behind us."' [19]And

so commanded he the second, and the third, and all that followed the droves, saying, 'On this manner shall ye speak unto
Esau, when ye find him. 20 And say ye moreover, "Behold,
thy servant Jacob is behind us."' For he said, 'I will appease
him with the present that goeth before me, and afterward I
will see his face; peradventure he will accept of me.' 21 So
went the present over before him; and himself lodged that
night in the company. 22 And he rose up that night, and took
his two wives, and his two womenservants, and his eleven
sons, and passed over the ford Jabbok. 23 And he took them,
and sent them over the brook, and sent over that he had.

24 And Jacob was left alone; and there wrestled a man
with him until the breaking of the day. 25 And when he saw
that he prevailed not against him, he touched the hollow of
his thigh; and the hollow of Jacob's thigh was out of joint, as
he wrestled with him. 26 And the man said, 'Let me go, for the
day breaketh.' And Jacob said, 'I will not let thee go, except
thou bless me.' 27 And the man said unto him, 'What is thy
name?' And he said, 'Jacob.' 28 And the man said, 'Thy name
shall be called no more Jacob, but Israel; for as a prince hast
thou power with God and with men, and hast prevailed.'
29 And Jacob asked him, and said, 'Tell me, I pray thee, thy
name.' And he said, 'Wherefore is it that thou dost ask after
my name?' And he blessed him there. 30 And Jacob called the
name of the place Peniel; 'for I have seen God face to face,
and my life is preserved'. 31 And as he passed over Penuel the
sun rose upon him, and he halted upon his thigh. 32 Therefore the children of Israel eat not of the sinew which shrank,

which is upon the hollow of the thigh, unto this day: because he touched the hollow of Jacob's thigh in the sinew that shrank.

33 And Jacob lifted up his eyes, and looked, and, behold,
Esau came, and with him four hundred men. And he
divided the children unto Leah, and unto Rachel, and unto
the two handmaids. 2And he put the handmaids and their
children foremost, and Leah and her children after, and
Rachel and Joseph hindermost. 3And he passed over before
them, and bowed himself to the ground seven times, until he
came near to his brother. 4And Esau ran to meet him, and
embraced him, and fell on his neck, and kissed him; and
they wept. 5And he lifted up his eyes, and saw the women
and the children; and said, 'Who are those with thee?' And
Jacob said, 'The children which God hath graciously given
thy servant.' 6Then the handmaidens came near, they and
their children, and they bowed themselves. 7And Leah also
with her children came near, and bowed themselves; and
after came Joseph near and Rachel, and they bowed themselves. 8And Esau said, 'What meanest thou by all this drove
which I met?' And Jacob said, 'These are to find grace in the
sight of my lord.' 9And Esau said, 'I have enough, my brother;
keep that thou hast unto thyself.' 10And Jacob said, 'Nay, I pray
thee, if now I have found grace in thy sight, then receive my
present at my hand; for therefore I have seen thy face, as
though I had seen the face of God, and thou wast pleased
with me. 11Take, I pray thee, my blessing that is brought to

thee; because God hath dealt graciously with me, and because
I have enough.' And he urged him, and he took it. 12And
Esau said, 'Let us take our journey, and let us go, and I will
go before thee.' 13And Jacob said unto him, 'My lord knoweth
that the children are tender, and the flocks and herds with
young are with me; and if men should overdrive them one
day, all the flock will die. 14Let my lord, I pray thee, pass
over before his servant: and I will lead on softly, according
as the cattle that goeth before me and the children be able to
endure, until I come unto my lord unto Seir.' 15And Esau
said, 'Let me now leave with thee some of the folk that are
with me.' And he said, 'What needeth it? Let me find grace
in the sight of my lord.'

16So Esau returned that day on his way unto Seir. 17And
Jacob journeyed to Succoth, and built him an house, and
made booths for his cattle; therefore the name of the place is
called Succoth.

18And Jacob came to Shalem, a city of Shechem, which is
in the land of Canaan, when he came from Padan-aram; and
pitched his tent before the city. 19And he bought a parcel of a
field, where he had spread his tent, at the hand of the children
of Hamor, Shechem's father, for an hundred pieces of money.
20And he erected there an altar, and called it El-elohe-Israel.

34 And Dinah the daughter of Leah, which she bare unto
Jacob, went out to see the daughters of the land.
2And when Shechem the son of Hamor the Hivite, prince of
the country, saw her, he took her, and lay with her, and

defiled her. 3And his soul clave unto Dinah the daughter of
Jacob, and he loved the damsel, and spake kindly unto the
damsel. 4And Shechem spake unto his father Hamor, saying,
'Get me this damsel to wife.' 5And Jacob heard that he had
defiled Dinah his daughter; now his sons were with his cattle in the field: and Jacob held his peace until they were come.

6And Hamor the father of Shechem went out unto Jacob
to commune with him. 7And the sons of Jacob came out of
the field when they heard it: and the men were grieved, and
they were very wroth, because he had wrought folly in
Israel in lying with Jacob's daughter; which thing ought not
to be done. 8And Hamor communed with them, saying, 'The
soul of my son Shechem longeth for your daughter; I pray
you give her him to wife. 9And make ye marriages with us,
and give your daughters unto us, and take our daughters
unto you. 10And ye shall dwell with us; and the land shall be
before you; dwell and trade ye therein, and get you possessions therein.' 11And Shechem said unto her father and unto
her brethren, 'Let me find grace in your eyes, and what ye
shall say unto me I will give. 12Ask me never so much dowry
and gift, and I will give according as ye shall say unto me;
but give me the damsel to wife.' 13And the sons of Jacob
answered Shechem and Hamor his father deceitfully, and
said, because he had defiled Dinah their sister: 14and they
said unto them, 'We cannot do this thing, to give our sister to
one that is uncircumcised; for that were a reproach unto us;
15but in this will we consent unto you: if ye will be as we be,
that every male of you be circumcised; 16then will we give

our daughters unto you, and we will take your daughters to
us, and we will dwell with you, and we will become one
people. 17 But if ye will not hearken unto us, to be circumcised; then will we take our daughter, and we will be gone.'
18 And their words pleased Hamor, and Shechem Hamor's son.
19 And the young man deferred not to do the thing, because
he had delight in Jacob's daughter; and he was more
honourable than all the house of his father.

20 And Hamor and Shechem his son came unto the gate of
their city, and communed with the men of their city, saying,
21 'These men are peaceable with us; therefore let them dwell
in the land, and trade therein; for the land, behold, it is large
enough for them; let us take their daughters to us for wives,
and let us give them our daughters. 22 Only herein will the
men consent unto us for to dwell with us, to be one people, if
every male among us be circumcised, as they are circumcised. 23 Shall not their cattle and their substance and every
beast of theirs be ours? Only let us consent unto them, and
they will dwell with us.' 24 And unto Hamor and unto Shechem his son hearkened all that went out of the gate of his
city; and every male was circumcised, all that went out of
the gate of his city.

25 And it came to pass on the third day, when they were
sore, that two of the sons of Jacob, Simeon and Levi, Dinah's
brethren, took each man his sword, and came upon the city
boldly, and slew all the males. 26 And they slew Hamor and
Shechem his son with the edge of the sword, and took Dinah
out of Shechem's house, and went out. 27 The sons of Jacob

came upon the slain, and spoiled the city, because they had
defiled their sister. 28 They took their sheep, and their oxen,
and their asses, and that which was in the city, and that which
was in the field, 29 and all their wealth, and all their little ones,
and their wives took they captive, and spoiled even all that
was in the house. 30 And Jacob said to Simeon and Levi, 'Ye
have troubled me to make me to stink among the inhabitants
of the land, among the Canaanites and the Perizzites; and I
being few in number, they shall gather themselves together
against me, and slay me; and I shall be destroyed, I and my
house.' 31 And they said, 'Should he deal with our sister as
with an harlot?'

35 And God said unto Jacob, 'Arise, go up to Beth-el, and
dwell there; and make there an altar unto God, that
appeared unto thee when thou fleddest from the face of
Esau thy brother.' 2 Then Jacob said unto his household, and
to all that were with him, 'Put away the strange gods that are
among you, and be clean, and change your garments; 3 and
let us arise, and go up to Beth-el; and I will make there an
altar unto God, who answered me in the day of my distress,
and was with me in the way which I went.' 4 And they gave
unto Jacob all the strange gods which were in their hand, and
all their earrings which were in their ears; and Jacob hid them
under the oak which was by Shechem. 5 And they journeyed;
and the terror of God was upon the cities that were round
about them, and they did not pursue after the sons of Jacob.
6 So Jacob came to Luz, which is in the land of Canaan,

that is, Beth-el, he and all the people that were with him.
[7]And he built there an altar, and called the place El-beth-el;
because there God appeared unto him, when he fled from
the face of his brother. [8] But Deborah Rebekah's nurse died,
and she was buried beneath Beth-el under an oak; and the
name of it was called Allon-bachuth.

[9]And God appeared unto Jacob again, when he came out
of Padan-aram, and blessed him. [10]And God said unto him,
'Thy name is Jacob: thy name shall not be called any more
Jacob, but Israel shall be thy name,' and he called his name
Israel. [11]And God said unto him, 'I am God Almighty: be fruitful and multiply; a nation and a company of nations shall be
of thee, and kings shall come out of thy loins; [12] and the land
which I gave Abraham and Isaac, to thee I will give it, and to
thy seed after thee will I give the land.' [13]And God went up
from him in the place where he talked with him. [14]And Jacob
set up a pillar in the place where he talked with him, even a
pillar of stone; and he poured a drink offering thereon, and
he poured oil thereon. [15]And Jacob called the name of the
place where God spake with him, Beth-el.

[16]And they journeyed from Beth-el; and there was but a
little way to come to Ephrath; and Rachel travailed, and she
had hard labour. [17]And it came to pass, when she was in hard
labour, that the midwife said unto her, 'Fear not; thou shalt
have this son also.' [18]And it came to pass, as her soul was in
departing (for she died) that she called his name Ben-oni;
but his father called him Benjamin. [19]And Rachel died, and
was buried in the way to Ephrath, which is Bethlehem. [20]And

Jacob set a pillar upon her grave; that is the pillar of Rachel's
grave unto this day.

21And Israel journeyed, and spread his tent beyond the
tower of Edar. 22And it came to pass, when Israel dwelt in
that land, that Reuben went and lay with Bilhah his father's
concubine; and Israel heard it. Now the sons of Jacob were
twelve. 23The sons of Leah: Reuben, Jacob's firstborn, and Simeon, and Levi, and Judah, and Issachar, and Zebulun; 24the
sons of Rachel: Joseph, and Benjamin; 25and the sons of Bilhah, Rachel's handmaid: Dan, and Naphtali; 26and the sons of
Zilpah, Leah's handmaid: Gad, and Asher: these are the sons
of Jacob, which were born to him in Padan-aram.

27And Jacob came unto Isaac his father unto Mamre, unto
the city of Arbah, which is Hebron, where Abraham and
Isaac sojourned. 28And the days of Isaac were an hundred
and fourscore years. 29And Isaac gave up the ghost, and
died, and was gathered unto his people, being old and full
of days; and his sons Esau and Jacob buried him.

36 Now these are the generations of Esau, who is Edom.
2Esau took his wives of the daughters of Canaan;
Adah the daughter of Elon the Hittite, and Aholibamah the
daughter of Anah the daughter of Zibeon the Hivite; 3and
Bashemath Ishmael's daughter, sister of Nebajoth. 4And Adah
bare to Esau Eliphaz; and Bashemath bare Reuel; 5and
Aholibamah bare Jeush, and Jaalam, and Korah. These are
the sons of Esau, which were born unto him in the land of
Canaan. 6And Esau took his wives, and his sons, and his

daughters, and all the persons of his house, and his cattle, and all his beasts, and all his substance, which he had got in the land of Canaan; and went into the country from the face of his brother Jacob. 7 For their riches were more than that they might dwell together; and the land wherein they were strangers could not bear them because of their cattle. 8 Thus dwelt Esau in mount Seir: Esau is Edom.

9 And these are the generations of Esau the father of the Edomites in mount Seir. 10 These are the names of Esau's sons: Eliphaz the son of Adah the wife of Esau, Reuel the son of Bashemath the wife of Esau. 11 And the sons of Eliphaz were Teman, Omar, Zepho, and Gatam, and Kenaz. 12 And Timna was concubine to Eliphaz Esau's son; and she bare to Eliphaz Amalek. These were the sons of Adah Esau's wife. 13 And these are the sons of Reuel: Nahath, and Zerah, Shammah, and Mizzah. These were the sons of Bashemath Esau's wife.

14 And these were the sons of Aholibamah, the daughter of Anah the daughter of Zibeon, Esau's wife: and she bare to Esau Jeush, and Jaalam, and Korah.

15 These were dukes of the sons of Esau; the sons of Eliphaz the firstborn son of Esau; duke Teman, duke Omar, duke Zepho, duke Kenaz, 16 duke Korah, duke Gatam, and duke Amalek: these are the dukes that came of Eliphaz in the land of Edom. These were the sons of Adah.

17 And these are the sons of Reuel Esau's son: duke Nahath, duke Zerah, duke Shammah, duke Mizzah. These are the dukes that came of Reuel in the land of Edom; these are the sons of Bashemath Esau's wife.

18 And these are the sons of Aholibamah Esau's wife: duke
Jeush, duke Jaalam, duke Korah. These were the dukes that
came of Aholibamah the daughter of Anah, Esau's wife. 19 These
are the sons of Esau, who is Edom, and these are their dukes.

20 These are the sons of Seir the Horite, who inhabited the
land: Lotan, and Shobal, and Zibeon, and Anah, 21 and Dishon,
and Ezer, and Dishan. These are the dukes of the Horites,
the children of Seir in the land of Edom. 22 And the children
of Lotan were Hori and Hemam; and Lotan's sister was
Timna. 23 And the children of Shobal were these: Alvan, and
Manahath, and Ebal, Shepho, and Onam. 24 And these are the
children of Zibeon: both Ajah, and Anah. This was that Anah
that found the mules in the wilderness, as he fed the asses of
Zibeon his father. 25 And the children of Anah were these:
Dishon, and Aholibamah the daughter of Anah. 26 And these
are the children of Dishon: Hemdan, and Eshban, and Ithran,
and Cheran. 27 The children of Ezer are these: Bilhan, and
Zaavan, and Akan. 28 The children of Dishan are these: Uz,
and Aran. 29 These are the dukes that came of the Horites:
duke Lotan, duke Shobal, duke Zibeon, duke Anah, 30 duke
Dishon, duke Ezer, duke Dishan. These are the dukes that
came of Hori, among their dukes in the land of Seir.

31 And these are the kings that reigned in the land of Edom,
before there reigned any king over the children of Israel.
32 And Bela the son of Beor reigned in Edom; and the name of
his city was Dinhabah. 33 And Bela died, and Jobab the son of
Zerah of Bozrah reigned in his stead. 34 And Jobab died, and
Husham of the land of Temani reigned in his stead. 35 And

Husham died, and Hadad the son of Bedad, who smote
Midian in the field of Moab, reigned in his stead; and the
name of his city was Avith. 36 And Hadad died, and Samlah
of Masrekah reigned in his stead. 37 And Samlah died, and
Saul of Rehoboth by the river reigned in his stead. 38 And Saul
died, and Baal-hanan the son of Achbor reigned in his stead.
39 And Baal-hanan the son of Achbor died, and Hadar reigned
in his stead: and the name of his city was Pau; and his wife's
name was Mehetabel, the daughter of Matred, the daughter
of Mezahab. 40 And these are the names of the dukes that came
of Esau, according to their families, after their places, by
their names: duke Timnah, duke Alvah, duke Jetheth, 41 duke
Aholibamah, duke Elah, duke Pinon, 42 duke Kenaz, duke
Teman, duke Mibzar, 43 duke Magdiel, duke Iram. These be
the dukes of Edom, according to their habitations in the land
of their possession; he is Esau the father of the Edomites.

37 And Jacob dwelt in the land wherein his father was a
stranger, in the land of Canaan. 2 These are the generations of Jacob. Joseph, being seventeen years old, was feeding the flock with his brethren; and the lad was with the sons
of Bilhah, and with the sons of Zilpah, his father's wives;
and Joseph brought unto his father their evil report. 3 Now
Israel loved Joseph more than all his children, because he
was the son of his old age; and he made him a coat of many
colours. 4 And when his brethren saw that their father loved
him more than all his brethren, they hated him, and could
not speak peaceably unto him.

[5]And Joseph dreamed a dream, and he told it his brethren; and they hated him yet the more. [6]And he said unto
them, 'Hear, I pray you, this dream which I have dreamed:
[7]for, behold, we were binding sheaves in the field, and, lo,
my sheaf arose, and also stood upright; and, behold, your
sheaves stood round about, and made obeisance to my sheaf.'
[8]And his brethren said to him, 'Shalt thou indeed reign over
us? Or shalt thou indeed have dominion over us?' And they
hated him yet the more for his dreams, and for his words.

[9]And he dreamed yet another dream, and told it his brethren, and said, 'Behold, I have dreamed a dream more; and,
behold, the sun and the moon and the eleven stars made
obeisance to me.' [10]And he told it to his father, and to his
brethren; and his father rebuked him, and said unto him,
'What is this dream that thou hast dreamed? Shall I and thy
mother and thy brethren indeed come to bow down ourselves to thee to the earth?' [11]And his brethren envied him;
but his father observed the saying.

[12]And his brethren went to feed their father's flock in Shechem. [13]And Israel said unto Joseph, 'Do not thy brethren
feed the flock in Shechem? Come, and I will send thee unto
them.' And he said to him, 'Here am I.' [14]And he said to him,
'Go, I pray thee, see whether it be well with thy brethren, and
well with the flocks; and bring me word again.' So he sent
him out of the vale of Hebron, and he came to Shechem.

[15]And a certain man found him, and, behold, he was wandering in the field; and the man asked him, saying, 'What
seekest thou?' [16]And he said, 'I seek my brethren; tell me, I

pray thee, where they feed their flocks.' [17]And the man said,
'They are departed hence; for I heard them say, "Let us go to
Dothan."' And Joseph went after his brethren, and found them
in Dothan. [18]And when they saw him afar off, even before he
came near unto them, they conspired against him to slay him.
[19]And they said one to another, 'Behold, this dreamer cometh.
[20]Come now therefore, and let us slay him, and cast him into
some pit, and we will say, "Some evil beast hath devoured
him;" and we shall see what will become of his dreams.'
[21]And Reuben heard it, and he delivered him out of their
hands; and said, 'Let us not kill him.' [22]And Reuben said unto
them, 'Shed no blood, but cast him into this pit that is in the
wilderness, and lay no hand upon him,' that he might rid
him out of their hands, to deliver him to his father again.

[23]And it came to pass, when Joseph was come unto his
brethren, that they stript Joseph out of his coat, his coat of
many colours that was on him; [24]and they took him, and cast
him into a pit; and the pit was empty, there was no water in
it. [25]And they sat down to eat bread; and they lifted up their
eyes and looked, and, behold, a company of Ishmeelites came
from Gilead with their camels bearing spicery and balm and
myrrh, going to carry it down to Egypt. [26]And Judah said
unto his brethren, 'What profit is it if we slay our brother,
and conceal his blood? [27]Come, and let us sell him to the Ishmeelites, and let not our hand be upon him; for he is our
brother and our flesh.' And his brethren were content. [28]Then
there passed by Midianite merchantmen; and they drew
and lifted up Joseph out of the pit, and sold Joseph to the

Ishmeelites for twenty pieces of silver; and they brought
Joseph into Egypt.

29 And Reuben returned unto the pit; and, behold, Joseph
was not in the pit; and he rent his clothes. 30 And he returned
unto his brethren, and said, 'The child is not; and I, whither
shall I go?' 31 And they took Joseph's coat, and killed a kid of
the goats, and dipped the coat in the blood; 32 and they sent
the coat of many colours, and they brought it to their father;
and said, 'This have we found: know now whether it be thy
son's coat or no.' 33 And he knew it, and said, 'It is my son's
coat; an evil beast hath devoured him; Joseph is without
doubt rent in pieces.' 34 And Jacob rent his clothes, and put
sackcloth upon his loins, and mourned for his son many
days. 35 And all his sons and all his daughters rose up to comfort him; but he refused to be comforted; and he said, 'For I
will go down into the grave unto my son mourning.' Thus
his father wept for him. 36 And the Midianites sold him into
Egypt unto Potiphar, an officer of Pharaoh's, and captain of
the guard.

38 And it came to pass at that time that Judah went
down from his brethren, and turned in to a certain
Adullamite, whose name was Hirah. 2 And Judah saw there a
daughter of a certain Canaanite, whose name was Shuah;
and he took her, and went in unto her. 3 And she conceived,
and bare a son; and he called his name Er. 4 And she conceived again, and bare a son; and she called his name Onan.
5 And she yet again conceived, and bare a son; and called his

name Shelah; and he was at Chezib, when she bare him. 6And Judah took a wife for Er his firstborn, whose name was Tamar. 7And Er, Judah's firstborn, was wicked in the sight of the Lord; and the Lord slew him. 8And Judah said unto Onan, 'Go in unto thy brother's wife, and marry her, and raise up seed to thy brother.' 9And Onan knew that the seed should not be his; and it came to pass, when he went in unto his brother's wife, that he spilled it on the ground, lest that he should give seed to his brother. 10And the thing which he did displeased the Lord; wherefore he slew him also. 11Then said Judah to Tamar his daughter in law, 'Remain a widow at thy father's house, till Shelah my son be grown,' for he said, 'lest peradventure he die also, as his brethren did.' And Tamar went and dwelt in her father's house.

12And in process of time the daughter of Shuah Judah's wife died; and Judah was comforted, and went up unto his sheepshearers to Timnath, he and his friend Hirah the Adullamite. 13And it was told Tamar, saying, 'Behold thy father in law goeth up to Timnath to shear his sheep.' 14And she put her widow's garments off from her, and covered her with a vail, and wrapped herself, and sat in an open place, which is by the way to Timnath; for she saw that Shelah was grown, and she was not given unto him to wife. 15When Judah saw her, he thought her to be an harlot; because she had covered her face. 16And he turned unto her by the way, and said, 'Go to, I pray thee, let me come in unto thee' (for he knew not that she was his daughter in law). And she said, 'What wilt thou give me, that thou mayest come in unto me?' 17And he

said, 'I will send thee a kid from the flock.' And she said, 'Wilt
thou give me a pledge, till thou send it?' 18And he said, 'What
pledge shall I give thee?' And she said, 'Thy signet, and thy
bracelets, and thy staff that is in thine hand.' And he gave it
her, and came in unto her, and she conceived by him. 19And
she arose, and went away, and laid by her vail from her, and
put on the garments of her widowhood. 20And Judah sent the
kid by the hand of his friend the Adullamite, to receive his
pledge from the woman's hand: but he found her not. 21Then
he asked the men of that place, saying, 'Where is the harlot,
that was openly by the way side?' And they said, 'There was
no harlot in this place.' 22And he returned to Judah, and said,
'I cannot find her; and also the men of the place said, that
there was no harlot in this place.' 23And Judah said, 'Let her
take it to her, lest we be shamed; behold, I sent this kid, and
thou hast not found her.'

24And it came to pass about three months after, that it was
told Judah, saying, 'Tamar thy daughter in law hath played
the harlot; and also, behold, she is with child by whoredom.'
And Judah said, 'Bring her forth, and let her be burnt.' 25When
she was brought forth, she sent to her father in law, saying,
'By the man, whose these are, am I with child,' and she said,
'Discern, I pray thee, whose are these, the signet, and bracelets, and staff.' 26And Judah acknowledged them, and said,
'She hath been more righteous than I; because that I gave her
not to Shelah my son.' And he knew her again no more.

27And it came to pass in the time of her travail, that, behold,
twins were in her womb. 28And it came to pass, when she

travailed, that the one put out his hand: and the midwife
took and bound upon his hand a scarlet thread, saying, 'This
came out first.' [29]And it came to pass, as he drew back his
hand, that, behold, his brother came out; and she said, 'How
hast thou broken forth? This breach be upon thee'; therefore
his name was called Pharez. [30]And afterward came out his
brother, that had the scarlet thread upon his hand; and his
name was called Zarah.

39 And Joseph was brought down to Egypt; and Potiphar, an officer of Pharaoh, captain of the guard, an
Egyptian, bought him of the hands of the Ishmeelites, which
had brought him down thither. [2]And the Lord was with
Joseph, and he was a prosperous man; and he was in the
house of his master the Egyptian. [3]And his master saw that
the Lord was with him, and that the Lord made all that he
did to prosper in his hand. [4]And Joseph found grace in his
sight, and he served him; and he made him overseer over
his house, and all that he had he put into his hand. [5]And it
came to pass from the time that he had made him overseer
in his house, and over all that he had, that the Lord blessed
the Egyptian's house for Joseph's sake; and the blessing of
the Lord was upon all that he had in the house, and in the
field. [6]And he left all that he had in Joseph's hand; and he
knew not ought he had, save the bread which he did eat.
And Joseph was a goodly person, and well favoured.

[7]And it came to pass after these things that his master's
wife cast her eyes upon Joseph; and she said, 'Lie with me.'

8 But he refused, and said unto his master's wife, 'Behold, my
master wotteth not what is with me in the house, and he
hath committed all that he hath to my hand; 9 there is none
greater in this house than I; neither hath he kept back any
thing from me but thee, because thou art his wife; how then
can I do this great wickedness, and sin against God?' 10 And it
came to pass, as she spake to Joseph day by day, that he hearkened not unto her, to lie by her, or to be with her. 11 And it
came to pass about this time, that Joseph went into the house
to do his business; and there was none of the men of the
house there within. 12 And she caught him by his garment,
saying, 'Lie with me'; and he left his garment in her hand,
and fled, and got him out. 13 And it came to pass, when she
saw that he had left his garment in her hand, and was fled
forth, 14 that she called unto the men of her house, and spake
unto them, saying, 'See, he hath brought in an Hebrew unto
us to mock us; he came in unto me to lie with me, and I cried
with a loud voice; 15 and it came to pass, when he heard that I
lifted up my voice and cried, that he left his garment with
me, and fled, and got him out.' 16 And she laid up his garment
by her, until his lord came home. 17 And she spake unto him
according to these words, saying, 'The Hebrew servant, which
thou hast brought unto us, came in unto me to mock me;
18 and it came to pass, as I lifted up my voice and cried, that
he left his garment with me, and fled out.' 19 And it came to
pass, when his master heard the words of his wife, which
she spake unto him, saying, 'After this manner did thy servant
to me,' that his wrath was kindled. 20 And Joseph's master

took him, and put him into the prison, a place where the
king's prisoners were bound; and he was there in the prison.
21 But the Lord was with Joseph, and shewed him mercy,
and gave him favour in the sight of the keeper of the prison.
22 And the keeper of the prison committed to Joseph's hand
all the prisoners that were in the prison; and whatsoever they
did there, he was the doer of it. 23 The keeper of the prison
looked not to any thing that was under his hand; because
the Lord was with him, and that which he did, the Lord made
it to prosper.

40 And it came to pass after these things, that the butler of the king of Egypt and his baker had offended
their lord the king of Egypt. 2 And Pharaoh was wroth against
two of his officers, against the chief of the butlers, and
against the chief of the bakers. 3 And he put them in ward in
the house of the captain of the guard, into the prison, the
place where Joseph was bound. 4 And the captain of the guard
charged Joseph with them, and he served them; and they
continued a season in ward.
5 And they dreamed a dream both of them, each man his
dream in one night, each man according to the interpretation
of his dream, the butler and the baker of the king of Egypt,
which were bound in the prison. 6 And Joseph came in unto
them in the morning, and looked upon them, and, behold,
they were sad. 7 And he asked Pharaoh's officers that were
with him in the ward of his lord's house, saying, 'Wherefore
look ye so sadly to day?' 8 And they said unto him, 'We have

dreamed a dream, and there is no interpreter of it.' And Joseph
said unto them, 'Do not interpretations belong to God? Tell
me them, I pray you.' 9 And the chief butler told his dream to
Joseph, and said to him, 'In my dream, behold, a vine was
before me; 10 and in the vine were three branches: and it was
as though it budded, and her blossoms shot forth; and the
clusters thereof brought forth ripe grapes; 11 and Pharaoh's
cup was in my hand; and I took the grapes, and pressed
them into Pharaoh's cup, and I gave the cup into Pharaoh's
hand.' 12 And Joseph said unto him, 'This is the interpretation
of it. The three branches are three days; 13 yet within three
days shall Pharaoh lift up thine head, and restore thee unto
thy place; and thou shalt deliver Pharaoh's cup into his hand,
after the former manner when thou wast his butler. 14 But
think on me when it shall be well with thee, and shew kindness, I pray thee, unto me, and make mention of me unto Pharaoh, and bring me out of this house; 15 for indeed I was stolen
away out of the land of the Hebrews; and here also have I
done nothing that they should put me into the dungeon.'

16 When the chief baker saw that the interpretation was
good, he said unto Joseph, 'I also was in my dream, and, behold,
I had three white baskets on my head; 17 and in the uppermost basket there was of all manner of bakemeats for Pharaoh;
and the birds did eat them out of the basket upon my head.'
18 And Joseph answered and said, 'This is the interpretation
thereof. The three baskets are three days; 19 yet within three days
shall Pharaoh lift up thy head from off thee, and shall hang
thee on a tree; and the birds shall eat thy flesh from off thee.'

[20]And it came to pass the third day, which was Pharaoh's
birthday, that he made a feast unto all his servants; and he lifted
up the head of the chief butler and of the chief baker among
his servants. [21]And he restored the chief butler unto his butler-
ship again; and he gave the cup into Pharaoh's hand; [22] but he
hanged the chief baker, as Joseph had interpreted to them. [23] Yet
did not the chief butler remember Joseph, but forgat him.

41 And it came to pass at the end of two full years, that
Pharaoh dreamed; and, behold, he stood by the river.
[2]And, behold, there came up out of the river seven well favoured kine and fatfleshed; and they fed in a meadow. [3]And,
behold, seven other kine came up after them out of the river,
ill favoured and leanfleshed; and stood by the other kine
upon the brink of the river. [4]And the ill favoured and leanfleshed kine did eat up the seven well favoured and fat kine.
So Pharaoh awoke. [5]And he slept and dreamed the second
time; and, behold, seven ears of corn came up upon one stalk,
rank and good. [6]And, behold, seven thin ears and blasted
with the east wind sprung up after them. [7]And the seven
thin ears devoured the seven rank and full ears. And Pharoah awoke, and, behold, it was a dream. [8]And it came to pass
in the morning that his spirit was troubled; and he sent and
called for all the magicians of Egypt, and all the wise men
thereof; and Pharaoh told them his dream; but there was
none that could interpret them unto Pharaoh.

[9]Then spake the chief butler unto Pharaoh, saying, 'I do
remember my faults this day: [10]Pharaoh was wroth with his

servants, and put me in ward in the captain of the guard's
house, both me and the chief baker; 11 and we dreamed a
dream in one night, I and he; we dreamed each man according to the interpretation of his dream. 12 And there was there
with us a young man, an Hebrew, servant to the captain of
the guard; and we told him, and he interpreted to us our
dreams; to each man according to his dream he did interpret. 13 And it came to pass, as he interpreted to us, so it was;
me he restored unto mine office, and him he hanged.'

14 Then Pharaoh sent and called Joseph, and they brought
him hastily out of the dungeon; and he shaved himself, and
changed his raiment, and came in unto Pharoah. 15 And Pharaoh said unto Joseph, 'I have dreamed a dream, and there is
none that can interpret it; and I have heard say of thee, that
thou canst understand a dream to interpret it.' 16 And Joseph
answered Pharaoh, saying, 'It is not in me: God shall give
Pharaoh an answer of peace.' 17 And Pharaoh said unto Joseph,
'In my dream, behold, I stood upon the bank of the river;
18 and, behold, there came up out of the river seven kine, fatfleshed and well favoured; and they fed in a meadow; 19 and,
behold, seven other kine came up after them, poor and very
ill favoured and leanfleshed, such as I never saw in all the
land of Egypt for badness; 20 and the lean and the ill favoured
kine did eat up the first seven fat kine; 21 and when they had
eaten them up, it could not be known that they had eaten
them; but they were still ill favoured, as at the beginning. So
I awoke. 22 And I saw in my dream, and, behold, seven ears
came up in one stalk, full and good; 23 and, behold, seven

ears, withered, thin, and blasted with the east wind, sprung
up after them; 24 and the thin ears devoured the seven good
ears; and I told this unto the magicians; but there was none
that could declare it to me.'

25 And Joseph said unto Pharaoh, 'The dream of Pharaoh
is one: God hath shewed Pharaoh what he is about to do.
26 The seven good kine are seven years; and the seven good
ears are seven years: the dream is one. 27 And the seven thin
and ill favoured kine that came up after them are seven years;
and the seven empty ears blasted with the east wind shall be
seven years of famine. 28 This is the thing which I have spoken unto Pharaoh: what God is about to do he sheweth unto
Pharaoh. 29 Behold, there come seven years of great plenty
throughout all the land of Egypt; 30 and there shall arise after
them seven years of famine; and all the plenty shall be forgotten in the land of Egypt; and the famine shall consume
the land; 31 and the plenty shall not be known in the land by
reason of that famine following; for it shall be very grievous.
32 And for that the dream was doubled unto Pharaoh twice; it
is because the thing is established by God, and God will
shortly bring it to pass. 33 Now therefore let Pharaoh look out
a man discreet and wise, and set him over the land of Egypt.
34 Let Pharaoh do this, and let him appoint officers over the
land, and take up the fifth part of the land of Egypt in the
seven plenteous years. 35 And let them gather all the food of
those good years that come, and lay up corn under the hand
of Pharaoh, and let them keep food in the cities. 36 And that
food shall be for store to the land against the seven years of

famine, which shall be in the land of Egypt; that the land perish not through the famine.'

37 And the thing was good in the eyes of Pharaoh, and in
the eyes of all his servants. 38 And Pharaoh said unto his servants, 'Can we find such a one as this is, a man in whom the
Spirit of God is?' 39 And Pharaoh said unto Joseph, 'Forasmuch as God hath shewed thee all this, there is none so discreet and wise as thou art. 40 Thou shalt be over my house,
and according unto thy word shall all my people be ruled;
only in the throne will I be greater than thou.' 41 And Pharaoh
said unto Joseph, 'See, I have set thee over all the land of
Egypt.' 42 And Pharaoh took off his ring from his hand, and
put it upon Joseph's hand, and arrayed him in vestures of
fine linen, and put a gold chain about his neck; 43 and he made
him to ride in the second chariot which he had; and they
cried before him, 'Bow the knee,' and he made him ruler over
all the land of Egypt. 44 And Pharaoh said unto Joseph, 'I am
Pharaoh, and without thee shall no man lift up his hand or
foot in all the land of Egypt.' 45 And Pharaoh called Joseph's
name Zaphnath-paaneah; and he gave him to wife Asenath
the daughter of Potipherah priest of On. And Joseph went
out over all the land of Egypt.

46 And Joseph was thirty years old when he stood before
Pharaoh king of Egypt. And Joseph went out from the presence of Pharaoh, and went throughout all the land of Egypt.
47 And in the seven plenteous years the earth brought forth
by handfuls. 48 And he gathered up all the food of the seven
years, which were in the land of Egypt, and laid up the food

in the cities; the food of the field, which was round about
every city, laid he up in the same. 49And Joseph gathered corn
as the sand of the sea, very much, until he left numbering;
for it was without number. 50And unto Joseph were born two
sons before the years of famine came, which Asenath the
daughter of Potipherah priest of On bare unto him. 51And
Joseph called the name of the firstborn Manasseh: 'For God,'
said he, 'hath made me forget all my toil, and all my father's
house.' 52And the name of the second called he Ephraim: 'For
God hath caused me to be fruitful in the land of my affliction.'

53And the seven years of plenteousness, that was in the
land of Egypt, were ended. 54And the seven years of dearth
began to come, according as Joseph had said; and the dearth
was in all lands; but in all the land of Egypt there was bread.
55And when all the land of Egypt was famished, the people
cried to Pharaoh for bread; and Pharaoh said unto all the
Egyptians, 'Go unto Joseph; what he saith to you, do.' 56And
the famine was over all the face of the earth. And Joseph
opened all the storehouses, and sold unto the Egyptians;
and the famine waxed sore in the land of Egypt. 57And all
countries came into Egypt to Joseph for to buy corn; because
that the famine was so sore in all lands.

42 Now when Jacob saw that there was corn in Egypt,
Jacob said unto his sons, 'Why do ye look one upon
another?' 2And he said, 'Behold, I have heard that there is
corn in Egypt; get you down thither, and buy for us from
thence; that we may live, and not die.'

3And Joseph's ten brethren went down to buy corn in
Egypt. 4But Benjamin, Joseph's brother, Jacob sent not with
his brethren; for he said, 'Lest peradventure mischief befall
him.' 5And the sons of Israel came to buy corn among those
that came; for the famine was in the land of Canaan. 6And
Joseph was the governor over the land, and he it was that
sold to all the people of the land; and Joseph's brethren came,
and bowed down themselves before him with their faces to
the earth. 7And Joseph saw his brethren, and he knew them,
but made himself strange unto them, and spake roughly unto
them; and he said unto them, 'Whence come ye?' And they
said, 'From the land of Canaan to buy food.' 8And Joseph knew
his brethren, but they knew not him. 9And Joseph remembered the dreams which he dreamed of them, and said unto
them, 'Ye are spies; to see the nakedness of the land ye are
come.' 10And they said unto him, 'Nay, my lord, but to buy
food are thy servants come. 11We are all one man's sons; we
are true men, thy servants are no spies.' 12And he said unto
them, 'Nay, but to see the nakedness of the land ye are come.'
13And they said, 'Thy servants are twelve brethren, the sons
of one man in the land of Canaan; and, behold, the youngest
is this day with our father, and one is not.' 14And Joseph said
unto them, 'That is it that I spake unto you, saying, "Ye are
spies"; 15hereby ye shall be proved: by the life of Pharaoh ye
shall not go forth hence, except your youngest brother come
hither. 16Send one of you, and let him fetch your brother, and
ye shall be kept in prison, that your words may be proved,
whether there be any truth in you; or else by the life of Pharaoh

surely ye are spies.' 17 And he put them all together into ward
three days.

18 And Joseph said unto them the third day, 'This do, and
live; for I fear God: 19 if ye be true men, let one of your brethren
be bound in the house of your prison; go ye, carry corn for
the famine of your houses; 20 but bring your youngest brother
unto me; so shall your words be verified, and ye shall not
die.' And they did so.

21 And they said one to another, 'We are verily guilty concerning our brother, in that we saw the anguish of his soul,
when he besought us, and we would not hear; therefore is
this distress come upon us.' 22 And Reuben answered them,
saying, 'Spake I not unto you, saying, "Do not sin against the
child," and ye would not hear? Therefore, behold, also his
blood is required.' 23 And they knew not that Joseph understood them; for he spake unto them by an interpreter. 24 And
he turned himself about from them, and wept; and returned
to them again, and communed with them, and took from
them Simeon, and bound him before their eyes.

25 Then Joseph commanded to fill their sacks with corn,
and to restore every man's money into his sack, and to give
them provision for the way: and thus did he unto them.
26 And they laded their asses with the corn, and departed
thence. 27 And as one of them opened his sack to give his ass
provender in the inn, he espied his money; for, behold, it
was in his sack's mouth. 28 And he said unto his brethren, 'My
money is restored; and, lo, it is even in my sack,' and their
heart failed them, and they were afraid, saying one to another,

'What is this that God hath done unto us?'
29 And they came unto Jacob their father unto the land of
Canaan, and told him all that befell unto them; saying, 30 'The
man, who is the lord of the land, spake roughly to us, and
took us for spies of the country. 31 And we said unto him,
"We are true men; we are no spies: 32 we be twelve brethren,
sons of our father; one is not, and the youngest is this day
with our father in the land of Canaan." 33 And the man, the
lord of the country, said unto us, "Hereby shall I know that
ye are true men; leave one of your brethren here with me,
and take food for the famine of your households, and be
gone; 34 and bring your youngest brother unto me: then shall
I know that ye are no spies, but that ye are true men: so will
I deliver you your brother, and ye shall traffick in the land."'
35 And it came to pass as they emptied their sacks, that,
behold, every man's bundle of money was in his sack: and
when both they and their father saw the bundles of money,
they were afraid. 36 And Jacob their father said unto them, 'Me
have ye bereaved of my children: Joseph is not, and Simeon
is not, and ye will take Benjamin away; all these things are
against me.' 37 And Reuben spake unto his father, saying, 'Slay
my two sons, if I bring him not to thee; deliver him into my
hand, and I will bring him to thee again.' 38 And Jacob said,
'My son shall not go down with you; for his brother is dead,
and he is left alone; if mischief befall him by the way in the
which ye go, then shall ye bring down my gray hairs with
sorrow to the grave.'

43 And the famine was sore in the land. [2]And it came
to pass, when they had eaten up the corn which they
had brought out of Egypt, their father said unto them, 'Go
again, buy us a little food.' [3]And Judah spake unto him, saying, 'The man did solemnly protest unto us, saying, "Ye shall
not see my face, except your brother be with you." [4]If thou
wilt send our brother with us, we will go down and buy thee
food; [5]but if thou wilt not send him, we will not go down;
for the man said unto us, "Ye shall not see my face, except
your brother be with you."' [6]And Israel said, 'Wherefore dealt
ye so ill with me, as to tell the man whether ye had yet a
brother?' [7]And they said, 'The man asked us straitly of our
state, and of our kindred, saying, "Is your father yet alive?
Have ye another brother?" And we told him according to
the tenor of these words: could we certainly know that he
would say, "Bring your brother down"?' [8]And Judah said
unto Israel his father, 'Send the lad with me, and we will
arise and go; that we may live, and not die, both we, and thou,
and also our little ones. [9]I will be surety for him; of my hand
shalt thou require him; if I bring him not unto thee, and set
him before thee, then let me bear the blame for ever; [10]for
except we had lingered, surely now we had returned this
second time.' [11]And their father Israel said unto them, 'If it
must be so now, do this; take of the best fruits in the land in
your vessels, and carry down the man a present, a little balm,
and a little honey, spices, and myrrh, nuts, and almonds;
[12]and take double money in your hand; and the money that
was brought again in the mouth of your sacks, carry it again

in your hand; peradventure it was an oversight; 13 take also
your brother, and arise, go again unto the man; 14 and God
Almighty give you mercy before the man, that he may send
away your other brother, and Benjamin. If I be bereaved of
my children, I am bereaved.'

15 And the men took that present, and they took double
money in their hand, and Benjamin; and rose up, and went
down to Egypt, and stood before Joseph. 16 And when Joseph
saw Benjamin with them, he said to the ruler of his house,
'Bring these men home, and slay, and make ready; for these
men shall dine with me at noon.' 17 And the man did as Joseph
bade; and the man brought the men into Joseph's house.
18 And the men were afraid, because they were brought into
Joseph's house; and they said, 'Because of the money that
was returned in our sacks at the first time are we brought in;
that he may seek occasion against us, and fall upon us, and
take us for bondmen, and our asses.' 19 And they came near to
the steward of Joseph's house, and they communed with
him at the door of the house, 20 And said, 'O sir, we came
indeed down at the first time to buy food; 21 and it came to
pass, when we came to the inn, that we opened our sacks,
and, behold, every man's money was in the mouth of his
sack, our money in full weight; and we have brought it again
in our hand. 22 And other money have we brought down in
our hands to buy food; we cannot tell who put our money in
our sacks.' 23 And he said, 'Peace be to you, fear not: your God,
and the God of your father, hath given you treasure in your
sacks; I had your money.' And he brought Simeon out unto

them. 24 And the man brought the men into Joseph's house, and gave them water, and they washed their feet; and he gave their asses provender. 25 And they made ready the present against Joseph came at noon; for they heard that they should eat bread there.

26 And when Joseph came home, they brought him the present which was in their hand into the house, and bowed themselves to him to the earth. 27 And he asked them of their welfare, and said, 'Is your father well, the old man of whom ye spake? Is he yet alive?' 28 And they answered, 'Thy servant our father is in good health, he is yet alive.' And they bowed down their heads, and made obeisance. 29 And he lifted up his eyes, and saw his brother Benjamin, his mother's son, and said, 'Is this your younger brother, of whom ye spake unto me?' And he said, 'God be gracious unto thee, my son.' 30 And Joseph made haste; for his bowels did yearn upon his brother: and he sought where to weep; and he entered into his chamber, and wept there. 31 And he washed his face, and went out, and refrained himself, and said, 'Set on bread.' 32 And they set on for him by himself, and for them by themselves, and for the Egyptians, which did eat with him, by themselves; because the Egyptians might not eat bread with the Hebrews; for that is an abomination unto the Egyptians. 33 And they sat before him, the firstborn according to his birthright, and the youngest according to his youth; and the men marvelled one at another. 34 And he took and sent messes unto them from before him; but Benjamin's mess was five times so much as any of theirs. And they drank, and were merry with him.

44 And he commanded the steward of his house, saying, 'Fill the men's sacks with food, as much as they
can carry, and put every man's money in his sack's mouth.
2And put my cup, the silver cup, in the sack's mouth of the
youngest, and his corn money.' And he did according to the
word that Joseph had spoken. 3As soon as the morning was
light, the men were sent away, they and their asses. 4And
when they were gone out of the city, and not yet far off,
Joseph said unto his steward, 'Up, follow after the men; and
when thou dost overtake them, say unto them, "Wherefore
have ye rewarded evil for good? 5Is not this it in which my
lord drinketh, and whereby indeed he divineth? Ye have
done evil in so doing."'

6And he overtook them, and he spake unto them these same
words. 7And they said unto him, 'Wherefore saith my lord
these words? God forbid that thy servants should do according to this thing; 8behold, the money, which we found in our
sacks' mouths, we brought again unto thee out of the land of
Canaan; how then should we steal out of thy lord's house
silver or gold? 9With whomsoever of thy servants it be found,
both let him die, and we also will be my lord's bondmen.'
10And he said, 'Now also let it be according unto your words:
he with whom it is found shall be my servant; and ye shall
be blameless.' 11Then they speedily took down every man his
sack to the ground, and opened every man his sack. 12And he
searched, and began at the eldest, and left at the youngest; and
the cup was found in Benjamin's sack. 13Then they rent their
clothes, and laded every man his ass, and returned to the city.

14 And Judah and his brethren came to Joseph's house; for
he was yet there; and they fell before him on the ground.
15 And Joseph said unto them, 'What deed is this that ye have
done? Wot ye not that such a man as I can certainly divine?'
16 And Judah said, 'What shall we say unto my lord? What
shall we speak? Or how shall we clear ourselves? God hath
found out the iniquity of thy servants: behold, we are my
lord's servants, both we, and he also with whom the cup is
found.' 17 And Joseph said, 'God forbid that I should do so;
but the man in whose hand the cup is found, he shall be my
servant; and as for you, get you up in peace unto your father.'

18 Then Judah came near unto him, and said, 'Oh my lord,
let thy servant, I pray thee, speak a word in my lord's ears,
and let not thine anger burn against thy servant; for thou art
even as Pharaoh. 19 My lord asked his servants, saying, "Have
ye a father, or a brother?" 20 And we said unto my lord, "We
have a father, an old man, and a child of his old age, a little
one; and his brother is dead, and he alone is left of his mother,
and his father loveth him." 21 And thou saidst unto thy servants, "Bring him down unto me, that I may set mine eyes
upon him." 22 And we said unto my lord, "The lad cannot
leave his father; for if he should leave his father, his father
would die." 23 And thou saidst unto thy servants, "Except your
youngest brother come down with you, ye shall see my face
no more." 24 And it came to pass when we came up unto thy
servant my father, we told him the words of my lord. 25 And
our father said, "Go again, and buy us a little food." 26 And
we said, "We cannot go down: if our youngest brother be with

us, then will we go down; for we may not see the man's face,
except our youngest brother be with us." 27And thy servant
my father said unto us, "Ye know that my wife bare me two
sons; 28and the one went out from me, and I said, 'Surely he
is torn in pieces; and I saw him not since,' 29and if ye take
this also from me, and mischief befall him, ye shall bring
down my gray hairs with sorrow to the grave." 30Now therefore when I come to thy servant my father, and the lad be
not with us; seeing that his life is bound up in the lad's life;
31it shall come to pass, when he seeth that the lad is not with
us, that he will die; and thy servants shall bring down the
gray hairs of thy servant our father with sorrow to the grave.
32For thy servant became surety for the lad unto my father,
saying, "If I bring him not unto thee, then I shall bear the
blame to my father for ever." 33Now therefore, I pray thee,
let thy servant abide instead of the lad a bondman to my
lord; and let the lad go up with his brethren. 34For how shall
I go up to my father, and the lad be not with me? Lest peradventure I see the evil that shall come on my father.'

45 Then Joseph could not refrain himself before all them
that stood by him; and he cried, 'Cause every man
to go out from me.' And there stood no man with him, while
Joseph made himself known unto his brethren. 2And he wept
aloud; and the Egyptians and the house of Pharaoh heard.
3And Joseph said unto his brethren, 'I am Joseph; doth my
father yet live?' And his brethren could not answer him; for
they were troubled at his presence. 4And Joseph said unto

his brethren, 'Come near to me, I pray you.' And they came
near. And he said, 'I am Joseph your brother, whom ye sold
into Egypt. [5] Now therefore be not grieved, nor angry with
yourselves, that ye sold me hither; for God did send me before
you to preserve life. [6] For these two years hath the famine
been in the land; and yet there are five years, in the which
there shall neither be earing nor harvest. [7] And God sent me
before you to preserve you a posterity in the earth, and to
save your lives by a great deliverance. [8] So now it was not
you that sent me hither, but God; and he hath made me a
father to Pharaoh, and lord of all his house, and a ruler
throughout all the land of Egypt. [9] Haste ye, and go up to my
father, and say unto him, "Thus saith thy son Joseph, God
hath made me lord of all Egypt: come down unto me, tarry
not; [10] and thou shalt dwell in the land of Goshen, and thou
shalt be near unto me, thou, and thy children, and thy children's children, and thy flocks, and thy herds, and all that
thou hast; [11] and there will I nourish thee; for yet there are
five years of famine; lest thou, and thy household, and all
that thou hast, come to poverty." [12] And, behold, your eyes
see, and the eyes of my brother Benjamin, that it is my mouth
that speaketh unto you. [13] And ye shall tell my father of all
my glory in Egypt, and of all that ye have seen; and ye shall
haste and bring down my father hither.' [14] And he fell upon
his brother Benjamin's neck, and wept; and Benjamin wept
upon his neck. [15] Moreover he kissed all his brethren, and
wept upon them; and after that his brethren talked with him.

[16] And the fame thereof was heard in Pharaoh's house,

saying, 'Joseph's brethren are come'; and it pleased Pharaoh
well, and his servants. [17]And Pharaoh said unto Joseph, 'Say
unto thy brethren, "This do ye; lade your beasts, and go, get
you unto the land of Canaan; [18]And take your father and your
households, and come unto me; and I will give you the good
of the land of Egypt, and ye shall eat the fat of the land." [19]Now
thou art commanded, this do ye: "Take you wagons out of the
land of Egypt for your little ones, and for your wives, and bring
your father, and come. [20]Also regard not your stuff; for the
good of all the land of Egypt is yours."' [21]And the children of
Israel did so; and Joseph gave them wagons, according to the
commandment of Pharaoh, and gave them provision for the
way. [22]To all of them he gave each man changes of raiment; but
to Benjamin he gave three hundred pieces of silver, and five
changes of raiment. [23]And to his father he sent after this manner: ten asses laden with the good things of Egypt, and ten
she asses laden with corn and bread and meat for his father
by the way. [24]So he sent his brethren away, and they departed:
and he said unto them, 'See that ye fall not out by the way.'

[25]And they went up out of Egypt, and came into the land
of Canaan unto Jacob their father, [26]and told him, saying,
'Joseph is yet alive, and he is governor over all the land of
Egypt.' And Jacob's heart fainted, for he believed them not.
[27]And they told him all the words of Joseph, which he had
said unto them; and when he saw the wagons which Joseph
had sent to carry him, the spirit of Jacob their father revived;
[28]and Israel said, 'It is enough. Joseph my son is yet alive; I
will go and see him before I die.'

46 And Israel took his journey with all that he had, and
came to Beer-sheba, and offered sacrifices unto the
God of his father Isaac. 2 And God spake unto Israel in the
visions of the night, and said, 'Jacob, Jacob.' And he said,
'Here am I.' 3 And God said, 'I am God, the God of thy father:
fear not to go down into Egypt; for I will there make of thee
a great nation; 4 I will go down with thee into Egypt; and I
will also surely bring thee up again; and Joseph shall put his
hand upon thine eyes.' 5 And Jacob rose up from Beer-sheba:
and the sons of Israel carried Jacob their father, and their little ones, and their wives, in the wagons which Pharaoh had
sent to carry him. 6 And they took their cattle, and their goods,
which they had gotten in the land of Canaan, and came into
Egypt, Jacob, and all his seed with him: 7 his sons, and his
sons' sons with him, his daughters, and his sons' daughters,
and all his seed brought he with him into Egypt.

8 And these are the names of the children of Israel, which
came into Egypt, Jacob and his sons: Reuben, Jacob's firstborn.
9 And the sons of Reuben: Hanoch, and Phallu, and Hezron,
and Carmi.

10 And the sons of Simeon: Jemuel, and Jamin, and Ohad, and
Jachin, and Zohar, and Shaul the son of a Canaanitish woman.

11 And the sons of Levi: Gershon, Kohath, and Merari.

12 And the sons of Judah: Er, and Onan, and Shelah, and
Pharez, and Zerah; but Er and Onan died in the land of
Canaan. And the sons of Pharez were Hezron and Hamul.

13 And the sons of Issachar: Tola, and Phuvah, and Job,
and Shimron.

14 And the sons of Zebulun: Sered, and Elon, and Jahleel.
15 These be the sons of Leah, which she bare unto Jacob in
Padan-aram, with his daughter Dinah: all the souls of his
sons and his daughters were thirty and three.

16 And the sons of Gad: Ziphion, and Haggi, Shuni, and
Ezbon, Eri, and Arodi, and Areli.

17 And the sons of Asher: Jimnah, and Ishuah, and Isui, and
Beriah, and Serah their sister: and the sons of Beriah: Heber, and
Malchiel. 18 These are the sons of Zilpah, whom Laban gave to
Leah his daughter, and these she bare unto Jacob, even sixteen
souls. 19 The sons of Rachel Jacob's wife: Joseph, and Benjamin.

20 And unto Joseph in the land of Egypt were born Manasseh and Ephraim, which Asenath the daughter of Potipherah priest of On bare unto him.

21 And the sons of Benjamin were Belah, and Becher, and
Ashbel, Gera, and Naaman, Ehi, and Rosh, Muppim, and
Huppim, and Ard. 22 These are the sons of Rachel, which were
born to Jacob: all the souls were fourteen.

23 And the sons of Dan: Hushim.

24 And the sons of Naphtali: Jahzeel, and Guni, and Jezer,
and Shillem. 25 These are the sons of Bilhah, which Laban
gave unto Rachel his daughter, and she bare these unto Jacob:
all the souls were seven. 26 All the souls that came with Jacob
into Egypt, which came out of his loins, besides Jacob's sons'
wives, all the souls were threescore and six; 27 and the sons of
Joseph, which were born him in Egypt, were two souls: all
the souls of the house of Jacob, which came into Egypt, were
threescore and ten.

28 And he sent Judah before him unto Joseph, to direct his
face unto Goshen; and they came into the land of Goshen.
29 And Joseph made ready his chariot, and went up to meet
Israel his father, to Goshen, and presented himself unto him;
and he fell on his neck, and wept on his neck a good while.
30 And Israel said unto Joseph, 'Now let me die, since I have
seen thy face, because thou art yet alive.' 31 And Joseph said
unto his brethren, and unto his father's house, 'I will go up,
and shew Pharaoh, and say unto him, "My brethren, and my
father's house, which were in the land of Canaan, are come
unto me; 32 and the men are shepherds, for their trade hath
been to feed cattle; and they have brought their flocks, and
their herds, and all that they have." 33 And it shall come to
pass, when Pharaoh shall call you, and shall say, "What is your
occupation?" 34 That ye shall say, "Thy servants' trade hath
been about cattle from our youth even until now, both we,
and also our fathers," that ye may dwell in the land of Goshen;
for every shepherd is an abomination unto the Egyptians.'

47 Then Joseph came and told Pharaoh, and said, 'My
father and my brethren, and their flocks, and their
herds, and all that they have, are come out of the land of
Canaan; and, behold, they are in the land of Goshen.' 2 And
he took some of his brethren, even five men, and presented
them unto Pharaoh. 3 And Pharaoh said unto his brethren,
'What is your occupation?' And they said unto Pharaoh,
'Thy servants are shepherds, both we, and also our fathers.'
4 They said moreover unto Pharaoh, 'For to sojourn in the

land are we come; for thy servants have no pasture for their flocks; for the famine is sore in the land of Canaan; now therefore, we pray thee, let thy servants dwell in the land of Goshen.' [5]And Pharaoh spake unto Joseph, saying, 'Thy father and thy brethren are come unto thee; [6]the land of Egypt is before thee; in the best of the land make thy father and brethren to dwell; in the land of Goshen let them dwell; and if thou knowest any men of activity among them, then make them rulers over my cattle.' [7]And Joseph brought in Jacob his father, and set him before Pharaoh; and Jacob blessed Pharaoh. [8]And Pharaoh said unto Jacob, 'How old art thou?' [9]And Jacob said unto Pharaoh, 'The days of the years of my pilgrimage are an hundred and thirty years; few and evil have the days of the years of my life been, and have not attained unto the days of the years of the life of my fathers in the days of their pilgrimage.' [10]And Jacob blessed Pharaoh, and went out from before Pharaoh.

[11]And Joseph placed his father and his brethren, and gave them a possession in the land of Egypt, in the best of the land, in the land of Rameses, as Pharaoh had commanded. [12]And Joseph nourished his father, and his brethren, and all his father's household, with bread, according to their families.

[13]And there was no bread in all the land; for the famine was very sore, so that the land of Egypt and all the land of Canaan fainted by reason of the famine. [14]And Joseph gathered up all the money that was found in the land of Egypt, and in the land of Canaan, for the corn which they bought; and Joseph brought the money into Pharaoh's house. [15]And

when money failed in the land of Egypt, and in the land of
Canaan, all the Egyptians came unto Joseph, and said, 'Give
us bread; for why should we die in thy presence? For the
money faileth.' 16 And Joseph said, 'Give your cattle; and I will
give you for your cattle, if money fail.' 17 And they brought
their cattle unto Joseph: and Joseph gave them bread in
exchange for horses, and for the flocks, and for the cattle of
the herds, and for the asses; and he fed them with bread for
all their cattle for that year. 18 When that year was ended,
they came unto him the second year, and said unto him, 'We
will not hide it from my lord, how that our money is spent;
my lord also hath our herds of cattle; there is not ought left
in the sight of my lord, but our bodies, and our lands.
19 Wherefore shall we die before thine eyes, both we and our
land? Buy us and our land for bread, and we and our land
will be servants unto Pharaoh; and give us seed, that we may
live, and not die, that the land be not desolate.' 20 And Joseph
bought all the land of Egypt for Pharaoh; for the Egyptians
sold every man his field, because the famine prevailed over
them; so the land became Pharaoh's. 21 And as for the people,
he removed them to cities from one end of the borders of
Egypt even to the other end thereof. 22 Only the land of the
priests bought he not; for the priests had a portion assigned
them of Pharaoh, and did eat their portion which Pharaoh
gave them; wherefore they sold not their lands.

23 Then Joseph said unto the people, 'Behold, I have bought
you this day and your land for Pharaoh; lo, here is seed for
you, and ye shall sow the land. 24 And it shall come to pass in

the increase, that ye shall give the fifth part unto Pharaoh,
and four parts shall be your own, for seed of the field, and
for your food, and for them of your households, and for food
for your little ones.' 25And they said, 'Thou hast saved our
lives: let us find grace in the sight of my lord, and we will be
Pharaoh's servants.' 26And Joseph made it a law over the
land of Egypt unto this day, that Pharaoh should have the
fifth part; except the land of the priests only, which became
not Pharaoh's.

27And Israel dwelt in the land of Egypt, in the country of
Goshen; and they had possessions therein, and grew, and
multiplied exceedingly. 28And Jacob lived in the land of Egypt
seventeen years; so the whole age of Jacob was an hundred
forty and seven years. 29And the time drew nigh that Israel
must die; and he called his son Joseph, and said unto him, 'If
now I have found grace in thy sight, put, I pray thee, thy
hand under my thigh, and deal kindly and truly with me;
bury me not, I pray thee, in Egypt: 30 but I will lie with my
fathers, and thou shalt carry me out of Egypt, and bury me
in their buryingplace.' And Joseph said, 'I will do as thou
hast said.' 31And he said, 'Swear unto me.' And he sware unto
him. And Israel bowed himself upon the bed's head.

48 And it came to pass after these things, that one told
Joseph, 'Behold, thy father is sick,' and he took with
him his two sons, Manasseh and Ephraim. 2And one told
Jacob, and said, 'Behold, thy son Joseph cometh unto thee,'
and Israel strengthened himself, and sat upon the bed. 3And

Jacob said unto Joseph, 'God Almighty appeared unto me at
Luz in the land of Canaan, and blessed me, [4]and said unto
me, "Behold, I will make thee fruitful, and multiply thee, and
I will make of thee a multitude of people; and will give this
land to thy seed after thee for an everlasting possession."
[5]'And now thy two sons, Ephraim and Manasseh, which
were born unto thee in the land of Egypt before I came unto
thee into Egypt, are mine; as Reuben and Simeon, they shall
be mine. [6]And thy issue, which thou begettest after them,
shall be thine, and shall be called after the name of their
brethren in their inheritance. [7]And as for me, when I came
from Padan, Rachel died by me in the land of Canaan in the
way, when yet there was but a little way to come unto
Ephrath: and I buried her there in the way of Ephrath; the
same is Beth-lehem.' [8]And Israel beheld Joseph's sons, and
said, 'Who are these?' [9]And Joseph said unto his father,
'They are my sons, whom God hath given me in this place.'
And he said, 'Bring them, I pray thee, unto me, and I will
bless them.' [10]Now the eyes of Israel were dim for age, so
that he could not see. And he brought them near unto him;
and he kissed them, and embraced them. [11]And Israel said
unto Joseph, 'I had not thought to see thy face; and, lo, God
hath shewed me also thy seed.' [12]And Joseph brought them
out from between his knees, and he bowed himself with his
face to the earth. [13]And Joseph took them both, Ephraim in
his right hand toward Israel's left hand, and Manasseh in his
left hand toward Israel's right hand, and brought them near
unto him. [14]And Israel stretched out his right hand, and laid

it upon Ephraim's head, who was the younger, and his left hand upon Manasseh's head, guiding his hands wittingly; for Manasseh was the first-born.

15 And he blessed Joseph, and said, 'God, before whom my fathers Abraham and Isaac did walk, the God which fed me all my life long unto this day, 16 the Angel which redeemed me from all evil, bless the lads; and let my name be named on them, and the name of my fathers Abraham and Isaac; and let them grow into a multitude in the midst of the earth.' 17 And when Joseph saw that his father laid his right hand upon the head of Ephraim, it displeased him; and he held up his father's hand, to remove it from Ephraim's head unto Manasseh's head. 18 And Joseph said unto his father, 'Not so, my father, for this is the firstborn; put thy right hand upon his head.' 19 And his father refused, and said, 'I know it, my son, I know it. He also shall become a people, and he also shall be great; but truly his younger brother shall be greater than he, and his seed shall become a multitude of nations.' 20 And he blessed them that day, saying, 'In thee shall Israel bless, saying, "God make thee as Ephraim and as Manasseh,"' and he set Ephraim before Manasseh. 21 And Israel said unto Joseph, 'Behold, I die; but God shall be with you, and bring you again unto the land of your fathers. 22 Moreover I have given to thee one portion above thy brethren, which I took out of the hand of the Amorite with my sword and with my bow.'

49 And Jacob called unto his sons, and said, 'Gather yourselves together, that I may tell you that which

shall befall you in the last days. 2 Gather yourselves together,
and hear, ye sons of Jacob; and hearken unto Israel your
father. 3 'Reuben, thou art my firstborn, my might, and the
beginning of my strength, the excellency of dignity, and the
excellency of power: 4 unstable as water, thou shalt not excel;
because thou wentest up to thy father's bed; then defiledst
thou it: he went up to my couch.

5 'Simeon and Levi are brethren; instruments of cruelty
are in their habitations. 6 O my soul, come not thou into their
secret; unto their assembly, mine honour, be not thou united;
for in their anger they slew a man, and in their self-will they
digged down a wall. 7 Cursed be their anger, for it was fierce;
and their wrath, for it was cruel. I will divide them in Jacob,
and scatter them in Israel.

8 'Judah, thou art he whom thy brethren shall praise: thy
hand shall be in the neck of thine enemies; thy father's children shall bow down before thee. 9 Judah is a lion's whelp:
from the prey, my son, thou art gone up; he stooped down,
he couched as a lion, and as an old lion; who shall rouse him
up? 10 The sceptre shall not depart from Judah, nor a law-
giver from between his feet, until Shiloh come; and unto him
shall the gathering of the people be. 11 Binding his foal unto the
vine, and his ass's colt unto the choice vine; he washed his garments in wine, and his clothes in the blood of grapes; 12 his
eyes shall be red with wine, and his teeth white with milk.

13 'Zebulun shall dwell at the haven of the sea; and he shall
be for an haven of ships; and his border shall be unto Zidon.

14 'Issachar is a strong ass couching down between two

burdens; 15 and he saw that rest was good, and the land that
it was pleasant; and bowed his shoulder to bear, and became
a servant unto tribute.

16 'Dan shall judge his people, as one of the tribes of Israel.
17 Dan shall be a serpent by the way, an adder in the path,
that biteth the horse heels, so that his rider shall fall backward. 18 I have waited for thy salvation, O Lord.

19 'Gad, a troop shall overcome him; but he shall overcome at the last.

20 'Out of Asher his bread shall be fat, and he shall yield
royal dainties.

21 'Naphtali is a hind let loose: he giveth goodly words.

22 'Joseph is a fruitful bough, even a fruitful bough by a
well; whose branches run over the wall. 23 The archers have
sorely grieved him, and shot at him, and hated him; 24 but
his bow abode in strength, and the arms of his hands were
made strong by the hands of the mighty God of Jacob (from
thence is the shepherd, the stone of Israel); 25 even by the
God of thy father, who shall help thee; and by the Almighty,
who shall bless thee with blessings of heaven above, blessings of the deep that lieth under, blessings of the breasts,
and of the womb. 26 The blessings of thy father have prevailed above the blessings of my progenitors unto the utmost
bound of the everlasting hills; they shall be on the head of
Joseph, and on the crown of the head of him that was separate from his brethren.

27 'Benjamin shall ravin as a wolf; in the morning he shall
devour the prey, and at night he shall divide the spoil.'

28 All these are the twelve tribes of Israel; and this is it that
their father spake unto them, and blessed them; every one
according to his blessing he blessed them. 29 And he charged
them, and said unto them, 'I am to be gathered unto my people; bury me with my fathers in the cave that is in the field of
Ephron the Hittite, 30 in the cave that is in the field of Machpelah, which is before Mamre, in the land of Canaan, which
Abraham bought with the field of Ephron the Hittite for a
possession of a buryingplace. 31 There they buried Abraham
and Sarah his wife; there they buried Isaac and Rebekah his
wife; and there I buried Leah. 32 The purchase of the field
and of the cave that is therein was from the children of Heth.'
33 And when Jacob had made an end of commanding his
sons, he gathered up his feet into the bed, and yielded up the
ghost, and was gathered unto his people.

50 And Joseph fell upon his father's face, and wept upon
him, and kissed him. 2 And Joseph commanded his
servants the physicians to embalm his father; and the physicians embalmed Israel. 3 And forty days were fulfilled for
him; for so are fulfilled the days of those which are embalmed;
and the Egyptians mourned for him threescore and ten days.
4 And when the days of his mourning were past, Joseph spake
unto the house of Pharaoh, saying, 'If now I have found grace
in your eyes, speak, I pray you, in the ears of Pharaoh, saying, 5 My father made me swear, saying, "Lo, I die; in my
grave which I have digged for me in the land of Canaan,
there shalt thou bury me." Now therefore let me go up, I

pray thee, and bury my father, and I will come again.' [6]And
Pharaoh said, 'Go up, and bury thy father, according as he
made thee swear.'

[7]And Joseph went up to bury his father; and with him
went up all the servants of Pharaoh, the elders of his house,
and all the elders of the land of Egypt, [8]and all the house of
Joseph, and his brethren, and his father's house; only their
little ones, and their flocks, and their herds, they left in the
land of Goshen. [9]And there went up with him both chariots
and horsemen; and it was a very great company. [10]And they
came to the threshingfloor of Atad, which is beyond Jordan,
and there they mourned with a great and very sore lamentation: and he made a mourning for his father seven days.
[11]And when the inhabitants of the land, the Canaanites, saw
the mourning in the floor of Atad, they said, 'This is a grievous mourning to the Egyptians,' wherefore the name of it
was called Abel-mizraim, which is beyond Jordan. [12]And his
sons did unto him according as he commanded them; [13]for
his sons carried him into the land of Canaan, and buried him
in the cave of the field of Machpelah, which Abraham bought
with the field for a possession of a buryingplace of Ephron
the Hittite, before Mamre.

[14]And Joseph returned into Egypt, he, and his brethren,
and all that went up with him to bury his father, after he had
buried his father.

[15]And when Joseph's brethren saw that their father was
dead, they said, 'Joseph will peradventure hate us, and will
certainly requite us all the evil which we did unto him.' [16]And

they sent a messenger unto Joseph, saying, 'Thy father did
command before he died, saying, 17 "So shall ye say unto
Joseph: Forgive, I pray thee now, the trespass of thy brethren, and their sin; for they did unto thee evil"; and now, we
pray thee, forgive the trespass of the servants of the God of
thy father.' And Joseph wept when they spake unto him.
18 And his brethren also went and fell down before his face;
and they said, 'Behold, we be thy servants.' 19 And Joseph
said unto them, 'Fear not; for am I in the place of God? 20 But
as for you, ye thought evil against me; but God meant it unto
good, to bring to pass, as it is this day, to save much people
alive. 21 Now therefore fear ye not: I will nourish you, and
your little ones.' And he comforted them, and spake kindly
unto them.

22 And Joseph dwelt in Egypt, he, and his father's house;
and Joseph lived an hundred and ten years. 23 And Joseph
saw Ephraim's children of the third generation: the children
also of Machir the son of Manasseh were brought up upon
Joseph's knees. 24 And Joseph said unto his brethren, 'I die:
and God will surely visit you, and bring you out of this land
unto the land which he sware to Abraham, to Isaac, and to
Jacob.' 25 And Joseph took an oath of the children of Israel,
saying, 'God will surely visit you, and ye shall carry up my
bones from hence.' 26 So Joseph died, being an hundred and
ten years old; and they embalmed him, and he was put in a
coffin in Egypt.

titles in the series

genesis – *introduced by e. l. doctorow*
exodus – *introduced by david grossman*
job – *introduced by charles frazier*
selections from the book of psalms – *introduced by bono*
proverbs – *introduced by charles johnson*
ecclesiastes – *introduced by doris lessing*
matthew – *introduced by francisco goldman*
mark – *introduced by barry hannah*
luke – *introduced by thomas cahill*
john – *introduced by darcey steinke*
corinthians – *introduced by fay weldon*
revelation – *introduced by kathleen norris*

exodus

the second book of moses, called

exodus

authorized king james version

grove press
new york

with an introduction by | david grossman

The Pocket Canons were originally published in the U.K. in 1998 by Canongate Books, Ltd.
Published simultaneously in Canada
Printed in the United States of America

FIRST AMERICAN EDITION

Copyright information is on file with the Library of Congress
ISBN 0-8021-3611-7

Design by Paddy Cramsie

Grove Press
841 Broadway
New York, NY 10003

99 00 01 02 10 9 8 7 6 5 4 3 2 1

a note about pocket canons

The Authorized King James Version of the Bible, translated between 1603 and 1611, coincided with an extraordinary flowering of English literature. This version, more than any other, and possibly more than any other work in history, has had an influence in shaping the language we speak and write today. Presenting individual books from the Bible as separate volumes, as they were originally conceived, encourages the reader to approach them as literary works in their own right.

The first twelve books in this series encompass categories as diverse as history, fiction, philosophy, love poetry, and law. Each Pocket Canon also has its own introduction, specially commissioned from an impressive range of writers, which provides a personal interpretation of the text and explores its contemporary relevance.

David Grossman is one of Israel's leading writers. He is author of four award-winning and internationally acclaimed novels including See Under: Love, The Smile of the Lamb, The Book of Intimate Grammar *and* The Zigzag Kid. *He has also writtten two powerful journalistic accounts about his encounters with Palestinians,* The Yellow Wind *and* Sleeping on a Wire, *as well as a number of children's books and a play. He was born in Jerusalem, where he now lives with his wife and three children.*

introduction by david grossman

Into the swirl of events at the beginning *The Book of Exodus* – the tale of the bondage and oppression of the children of Israel and the growing enmity between the Israelites and Egyptians – seeps another, more personal and poignant story: a Hebrew child is born and his mother, who would save him from the death decreed for all sons by Pharaoh, lays him in a basket of bulrushes and sets the basket in the Nile. There, among the reeds, the daughter of the King of Egypt finds him. Pharaoh's daughter knows instantly that he is 'one of the Hebrews' children', but nevertheless decides to raise him as her son; she is the one who gives him his name, Moses.

How enchanting the entwining of this winsome tale with the tempestuous, epic myth of the birth of a nation. In a sense, this is the fabric of the entire book, an almost illusive weaving of fairy tale with strict legal and religious code: the warp – rods that turn into serpents, a vicious, cruel king, a land blighted by a plague of frogs; the woof – the giving of the law on Mount Sinai, the moment at which a people becomes welded to its destiny.

Reading *The Book of Exodus* is charged with tension: between the miserable, 'childlike' state of the children of

Israel, a people physically and spiritually enslaved, and the exalted role God has chosen for them, heedless of the pace of their spiritual and moral development. Perhaps this is the truly demanding journey made by the children of Israel in *The Book of Exodus*: from clan to nation, from slavery to freedom.

II

Here in my study in Jerusalem, in Israel, in 'the promised land' to which the Jews have returned time and again from exile, I think about my forefathers, the children of Israel, during those first days after the maelstrom that uprooted them from Egypt. They are in the desert, and the desert is empty. They are being led, like an immense herd, to an unknown destination. What can they cling to? They escaped bondage in Egypt, but also abandoned their daily routine, their habits and customs, a familiar place and the social interactions and hierarchies that had become fixed over the course of generations. Suddenly everything is new and strange. Nothing can be taken for granted. What had appeared to be the end of the road, now appears to be its beginning. Somewhere in the heavens hovers the spirit of a God who seems to be benevolent; yet they, who have seen how He dealt with the Egyptians, know how unpredictable, brutal and fierce He can be.

Stunned, they stride onward, as if in a void. They follow their leader, a man who never lived among them, who from the time he was weaned lived in the king's palace and then in Midian. He tells them they are at long last free men, but perhaps free is the last thing they feel or want to be. Every day brings new experiences, new religious regulations and laws, and strange food – enough for one day – that falls from the skies.

If they have any spirit left they will realize that a miracle has befallen them, that they are privileged to have been given the chance to reinvent themselves, to be redeemed. If they dare, they can fashion a new identity for themselves. But to do so they must fight the ponderous gravity of habit, of anxiety and doubt, of inner bondage.

Maybe their hearts swelled at times – the expansive, dramatic landscapes of Sinai could have awakened unfamiliar feelings in the hearts of those who had for generations lived the choked lives of slaves in the confines of huts. Suddenly the body could try broader, more daring movements. Perhaps an ancient memory, thousands of years old, flickered, of their forefathers' wending their way toward Egypt across this very desert on a journey of which only shards of legend remain. Perhaps their carrying the body of Joseph, son of Jacob, to burial in the land of Israel made tangible for them the abstract promise of return to their country; return to the place where Joseph was a child, and Jacob before him lived; return home.

In addition, a new factor entered their lives: calendar time. God determined the cycle of their days, sealing the week with the Sabbath (*Exodus* 16:23). Since the six days of creation this concept of the 'week' had hovered over the

Torah, yet only now does it become clear to the reader that this concept was apparently known to God alone. Now He imparts it to His people. Can we, who were born within calendar time, fathom the impact this conceptual change must have had on human beings? Did it strengthen their sense of the circular, the cyclical, the monotonous? Or did time suddenly seem to be just another dimension of the desert in which they were trapped?

Not only did God create the 'circle of the week', but He designated holidays and festivals, setting the new year at Passover to emphasize its historic, religious and national significance. What did the children of Israel feel about God's having inscribed them in the historical consciousness of generations to come, while they themselves were but the dust of men, bewildered and frightened? Did they know they were only one step on the road to another, more exalted existence? At the end of a long day's wandering, as they sat by a dying fire, did a bitter, tragic silence fall as they realized, vaguely, that they were but putty in God's hands, their tortured existence destined to become a 'history' and a religion, an 'epic' tale, and their ability to comprehend this tale no more than that of letters to comprehend a book?

III

In *The Book of Numbers* (14:18 ff), God decrees that the entire generation of those who fled Egypt – a defiant generation that consistently refused to believe in God wholeheartedly and with complete faith – will be destroyed in the desert and not brought into the promised land. Yet the *Zohar*[1] calls this generation the 'generation of knowledge'; some envy its having witnessed God's wondrous acts during the exodus from Egypt, and its presence at the giving of the law on Mount Sinai. Nevertheless, throughout their history the Jewish people have conceived of the 'desert generation' as a lost, transitional generation, rootless and lacking identity and faith, a generation tossed in the 'chasm' between past and future, consumed by anxiety regarding its destiny. According to ancient Jewish legend, on the eve of *Tisha B'Av*[2] during the sojourn in the desert, the children of Israel would dig themselves graves and lie in them, rising in the morning to see who had remained alive.

Even today, the Jewish people read in the Passover *Haggadah* that 'in every generation, each individual is bound to regard himself as if he personally had gone forth from Egypt'. This is a direct summons to the people of Israel to examine the essential components of their identity.

It is difficult to grasp just how crucial those forty years in the desert were to the formation of the Jewish people as a people. During those years, the lines of its 'national character' were drawn through the crucible of slavery and 'victimhood'

---

[1] A commentary on the *Five Books of Moses*, the *Zohar* is a fundamental work of Judaism's mystic teachings (trans.).

[2] The ninth day of the Hebrew month of *Av* is observed by fasting, prayer and mourning in commemoration of the destruction of the first and second Temples, and other calamities that have befallen the Jewish people on that date (trans.).

and the ensuing phenomenal propensity for redemption and rejuvenation. Moreover, a complex pattern of contradictory emotions was formed: pride, indeed arrogance, over being 'the chosen people', tempered by a sense of having been banished, even cursed – the price of such mysterious chosenness; comfort and security in the knowledge of being the people of Yahweh, tempered by a fear of that same invisible and fickle God, Himself seemingly buffeted by internal storms rife with contradiction; and a taste for wandering, branded on the consciousness during the wandering in the desert, tempered by an intense longing for a 'promised land' where – and only where – existence could at last be merged with identity, and a zest for living could be freed.

Wandering is also searching, and longing always gives rise to new ideas and abstract thought. Gradually, searching and longing affect the dormant consciousness of this people that for generations had been subjugated, tethered to physical distress and hardship, become ossified. Searching and longing leave a unique mark on this people, reflected in its ideological motivation, its penchant for the abstract and talent at keeping an entire reality alive in its imagination, its aspirations and yearnings and, above all, its ability to be revitalized by the power of a dream, to use a dream to rise above real affliction.

IV

The people of Israel was formed as a result of a commandment to wander to a new place. God said to our forefather

Abraham, 'Get thee out of thy country, and from thy kindred, and from thy father's house, unto a land that I will show thee' (*Genesis* 12:1). While at that time many tribes and peoples wandered constantly in search of sustenance, such wandering was never an end in itself – a national end in itself – as it was for the Jewish people, and as it is presented in the Books of *Genesis* and *Exodus*.

In retrospect, it seems that during those years in the desert these two contradictory elements – the urge to wander and the longing for a 'place' – became forces so integral to the soul of the Jewish people that it is difficult to know which is stronger. Perhaps this is one reason why for centuries the people of Israel have been mired in the same dilemma, lacking a sense of inner conviction: are they a people of place, or a people of time? That is, can the people of Israel live in a country with traceable, permanent borders and a distinctly national (or any other) 'character', or are they doomed, inherently, to seek out a 'borderless' existence of perpetual movement, of alternate exile and return, assimilation and individuation, restoration and change generation after generation, forever eluding definition and vulnerable to surrounding forces that would fortify or destroy them by turn?

Perhaps this also explains why for centuries other peoples have been so eager to determine just what a 'Jew' is, hemming him in to some 'definition' or other based on distinct characteristics, confining his fields of commerce or even penning him into a ghetto, as if to make him comprehensible, easy to monitor.

After all, this is also a description of the utter, onerous foreignness of one people among many. Indeed, from the harsh and violent exodus from Egypt to God's insistence on the separateness of this people and His exclusive 'possession' of it, *The Book of Exodus* brings into sharp relief the unique status of the Jewish people: its ability to quickly uproot itself, as if cutting itself out along an ever-present dotted line, coupled with a trenchant need to mingle with others, to become lost in them and thereby, paradoxically, to distill its identity, to define itself for itself.

This may further explain the necessity to the Jewish people of spending those forty years in the desert, almost completely cut off from other peoples and identities. Those years served as a lengthy cocoon stage, the final one before the Jewish people was hatched into its history, giving it time to formulate its identity solely through internal dialogue and an acceptance of its essential components, through countless occurrences, crises and climaxes.

V

More than any other of the *Five Books of Moses, The Book of Exodus* lays the foundation for the sense of 'epic', of myth, that has dogged the Jewish people since the exodus from Egypt, until the present. This is a most complex, disturbing feeling; perhaps it has contributed to Jewish existence having become, in the eyes of other peoples, an immense 'drama' – too immense – that cannot be confronted without being turned into a symbol or metaphor for something else.

In other words, that existence is never just an existence, the Jews never just a people among peoples. This attitude is so entrenched, so ancient that it is difficult to know whether it resulted from the historic fate of the Jews or was 'projected' onto them and determined their fate. It burdens the 'Jew' by ascribing him either a heavy load of sentimental ideals or a refutably demonic character. The Jew is stretched between these two extremes, suffering from them, of course, but also surely finding solace in the equally ancient sense that his suffering and wandering has 'meaning', that a hidden author's intent will at some point lend the whole story significance.

It is no less interesting to ponder the extent to which the Israelis of today, citizens of a sovereign, free, strong Israel, are impaired by a perception of themselves as a 'symbol' of something else – one they may not really, truly want to give up. To what extent does this warped self-perception cause them to fall short of their aspiration to be at long last a people living in its country, a people that has fully internalized its sovereignty and might, and that is capable of conducting a life of minutiae, of concessions, of practical compromises with its neighbours, a normal people, a people like any other?

As one who was born in Israel and has lived there all his life, I read *The Book of Exodus* and wonder how it is that even today, and even by its inhabitants, Israel is still called 'the promised land'. That is, not 'the land that was promised' or 'a land of promise', but the land that is still promised, and that, even after the return to Zion, has not yet been fulfilled, and whose people have not yet fully realized their potential. It would seem that the disenfranchisement of the 'desert generation' still casts its spell within Israel, fifty years after the State's establishment.

This 'eternal promise' carries with it the hope of growth and a potential for almost limitless freedom of thought, and flexibility of perspective, regarding things that have become fossilized in their definitions. However, it is inevitably tainted by the 'curse of the eternal', a latent, deep-seated sense of inability to ever achieve fulfilment, and a concomitant inability to address fundamental questions of identity, of belonging to a place or of that place's permanent borders, vis à vis its neighbours.

This may be the principal anomaly of the Jewish people's identity, in Israel as in the diaspora. It may be the secret of that people's endurance and vitality, but it doubtless also makes it constantly vulnerable to tragedy in a world that is all definitions and borders. *The Book of Exodus*, the grand story of the childhood of the Jewish people, sketches the primordial face of that people as it is being formed and, as we now know, describes what will be its fate throughout thousands of years of history.

Translated from the Hebrew by Marsha Weinstein

the second book of moses, called exodus

Now these are the names of the children of Israel, which
came into Egypt; every man and his household came with
Jacob: 2 Reuben, Simeon, Levi, and Judah, 3 Issachar, Zebulun, and Benjamin, 4 Dan, and Naphtali, Gad, and Asher. 5 And
all the souls that came out of the loins of Jacob were seventy
souls, for Joseph was in Egypt already. 6 And Joseph died,
and all his brethren, and all that generation.

7 And the children of Israel were fruitful, and increased
abundantly, and multiplied, and waxed exceeding mighty,
and the land was filled with them. 8 Now there arose up a
new king over Egypt, which knew not Joseph. 9 And he said
unto his people, 'Behold, the people of the children of Israel
are more and mightier than we. 10 Come on, let us deal wisely
with them, lest they multiply, and it come to pass, that, when
there falleth out any war, they join also unto our enemies,
and fight against us, and so get them up out of the land.'
11 Therefore they did set over them taskmasters to afflict them
with their burdens. And they built for Pharaoh treasure
cities, Pithom and Raamses. 12 But the more they afflicted
them, the more they multiplied and grew. And they were
grieved because of the children of Israel. 13 And the Egyptians
made the children of Israel to serve with rigour, 14 and they

made their lives bitter with hard bondage, in morter, and in brick, and in all manner of service in the field. All their service, wherein they made them serve, was with rigour.

15 And the king of Egypt spake to the Hebrew midwives, of which the name of the one was Shiphrah, and the name of the other Puah, 16 and he said, 'When ye do the office of a midwife to the Hebrew women, and see them upon the stools; if it be a son, then ye shall kill him: but if it be a daughter, then she shall live.' 17 But the midwives feared God, and did not as the king of Egypt commanded them, but saved the men children alive. 18 And the king of Egypt called for the midwives, and said unto them, 'Why have ye done this thing, and have saved the men children alive?' 19 And the midwives said unto Pharaoh, 'Because the Hebrew women are not as the Egyptian women; for they are lively, and are delivered ere the midwives come in unto them.' 20 Therefore God dealt well with the midwives: and the people multiplied, and waxed very mighty. 21 And it came to pass, because the midwives feared God, that he made them houses. 22 And Pharaoh charged all his people, saying, 'Every son that is born ye shall cast into the river, and every daughter ye shall save alive.'

2 And there went a man of the house of Levi, and took to wife a daughter of Levi. 2 And the woman conceived, and bare a son: and when she saw him that he was a goodly child, she hid him three months. 3 And when she could not longer hide him, she took for him an ark of bulrushes, and daubed it with slime and with pitch, and put the child

therein; and she laid it in the flags by the river's brink. 4And
his sister stood afar off, to wit what would be done to him.
5And the daughter of Pharaoh came down to wash herself at the river; and her maidens walked along by the river's
side; and when she saw the ark among the flags, she sent her
maid to fetch it. 6And when she had opened it, she saw the
child; and, behold, the babe wept. And she had compassion
on him, and said, 'This is one of the Hebrews' children.'
7Then said his sister to Pharaoh's daughter, 'Shall I go and
call to thee a nurse of the Hebrew women, that she may
nurse the child for thee?' 8And Pharaoh's daughter said to
her, 'Go.' And the maid went and called the child's mother.
9And Pharaoh's daughter said unto her, 'Take this child away,
and nurse it for me, and I will give thee thy wages.' And the
woman took the child, and nursed it. 10And the child grew,
and she brought him unto Pharaoh's daughter, and he became
her son. And she called his name Moses: and she said, 'Because
I drew him out of the water.'

11And it came to pass in those days, when Moses was
grown, that he went out unto his brethren, and looked on their
burdens, and he spied an Egyptian smiting an Hebrew, one
of his brethren. 12And he looked this way and that way, and
when he saw that there was no man, he slew the Egyptian,
and hid him in the sand. 13And when he went out the second
day, behold, two men of the Hebrews strove together, and
he said to him that did the wrong, 'Wherefore smitest thou
thy fellow?' 14And he said, 'Who made thee a prince and a
judge over us? Intendest thou to kill me, as thou killedst the

Egyptian?' And Moses feared, and said, 'Surely this thing is
known.' 15 Now when Pharaoh heard this thing, he sought to
slay Moses. But Moses fled from the face of Pharaoh, and
dwelt in the land of Midian; and he sat down by a well. 16 Now
the priest of Midian had seven daughters, and they came
and drew water, and filled the troughs to water their father's
flock. 17 And the shepherds came and drove them away, but
Moses stood up and helped them, and watered their flock.
18 And when they came to Reuel their father, he said, 'How is
it that ye are come so soon today?' 19 And they said, 'An
Egyptian delivered us out of the hand of the shepherds, and
also drew water enough for us, and watered the flock.' 20 And
he said unto his daughters, 'And where is he? Why is it that
ye have left the man? Call him, that he may eat bread.' 21 And
Moses was content to dwell with the man, and he gave
Moses Zipporah his daughter. 22 And she bare him a son, and
he called his name Gershom, for he said, 'I have been a
stranger in a strange land.'

23 And it came to pass in process of time, that the king of
Egypt died, and the children of Israel sighed by reason of the
bondage, and they cried, and their cry came up unto God by
reason of the bondage. 24 And God heard their groaning, and
God remembered his covenant with Abraham, with Isaac,
and with Jacob. 25 And God looked upon the children of Israel,
and God had respect unto them.

3 Now Moses kept the flock of Jethro his father-in-law,
the priest of Midian; and he led the flock to the backside

of the desert, and came to the mountain of God, even to
Horeb. [2]And the angel of the Lord appeared unto him in a
flame of fire out of the midst of a bush, and he looked, and,
behold, the bush burned with fire, and the bush was not
consumed. [3]And Moses said, 'I will now turn aside, and see
this great sight, why the bush is not burnt.' [4]And when the
Lord saw that he turned aside to see, God called unto him
out of the midst of the bush, and said, 'Moses, Moses.' And
he said, 'Here am I.' [5]And he said, 'Draw not nigh hither: put
off thy shoes from off thy feet, for the place whereon thou
standest is holy ground.' [6]Moreover he said, 'I am the God of
thy father, the God of Abraham, the God of Isaac, and the
God of Jacob.' And Moses hid his face, for he was afraid to
look upon God.

[7]And the Lord said, 'I have surely seen the affliction of
my people which are in Egypt, and have heard their cry by
reason of their taskmasters, for I know their sorrows; [8]and I
am come down to deliver them out of the hand of the Egyptians, and to bring them up out of that land unto a good land
and a large, unto a land flowing with milk and honey; unto
the place of the Canaanites, and the Hittites, and the Amorites, and the Perizzites, and the Hivites, and the Jebusites.
[9]Now therefore, behold, the cry of the children of Israel is
come unto me, and I have also seen the oppression wherewith the Egyptians oppress them. [10]Come now therefore,
and I will send thee unto Pharaoh, that thou mayest bring
forth my people the children of Israel out of Egypt.'

[11]And Moses said unto God, 'Who am I, that I should go

unto Pharaoh, and that I should bring forth the children of
Israel out of Egypt?' 12And he said, 'Certainly I will be with
thee; and this shall be a token unto thee, that I have sent
thee: when thou hast brought forth the people out of Egypt,
ye shall serve God upon this mountain. 13And Moses said
unto God, 'Behold, when I come unto the children of Israel,
and shall say unto them, "The God of your fathers hath sent
me unto you," and they shall say to me, "What is his name?",
what shall I say unto them?' 14And God said unto Moses, 'I
am that I am,' and he said, 'Thus shalt thou say unto the children of Israel, "'I am' hath sent me unto you."' 15And God said
moreover unto Moses, 'Thus shalt thou say unto the children
of Israel, "The Lord God of your fathers, the God of Abraham, the God of Isaac, and the God of Jacob, hath sent me
unto you." This is my name for ever, and this is my memorial unto all generations. 16Go, and gather the elders of Israel
together, and say unto them, "The Lord God of your fathers,
the God of Abraham, of Isaac, and of Jacob, appeared unto
me, saying, 'I have surely visited you, and seen that which is
done to you in Egypt. 17And I have said I will bring you up
out of the affliction of Egypt unto the land of the Canaanites,
and the Hittites, and the Amorites, and the Perizzites, and
the Hivites, and the Jebusites, unto a land flowing with milk
and honey.'" 18And they shall hearken to thy voice; and thou
shalt come, thou and the elders of Israel, unto the king of
Egypt, and ye shall say unto him, "The Lord God of the
Hebrews hath met with us; and now let us go, we beseech
thee, three days' journey into the wilderness, that we may

sacrifice to the Lord our God."

19 'And I am sure that the king of Egypt will not let you go, no, not by a mighty hand. 20 And I will stretch out my hand, and smite Egypt with all my wonders which I will do in the midst thereof, and after that he will let you go. 21 And I will give this people favour in the sight of the Egyptians; and it shall come to pass, that, when ye go, ye shall not go empty. 22 But every woman shall borrow of her neighbour, and of her that sojourneth in her house, jewels of silver, and jewels of gold, and raiment; and ye shall put them upon your sons, and upon your daughters; and ye shall spoil the Egyptians.'

4 And Moses answered and said, 'But, behold, they will not believe me, nor hearken unto my voice, for they will say, "The Lord hath not appeared unto thee."' 2 And the Lord said unto him, 'What is that in thine hand?' And he said, 'A rod.' 3 And he said, 'Cast it on the ground.' And he cast it on the ground, and it became a serpent; and Moses fled from before it. 4 And the Lord said unto Moses, 'Put forth thine hand, and take it by the tail,' and he put forth his hand, and caught it, and it became a rod in his hand: 5 'that they may believe that the Lord God of their fathers, the God of Abraham, the God of Isaac, and the God of Jacob, hath appeared unto thee.'

6 And the Lord said furthermore unto him, 'Put now thine hand into thy bosom.' And he put his hand into his bosom, and when he took it out, behold, his hand was leprous as snow. 7 And he said, 'Put thine hand into thy bosom again.' And he put his hand into his bosom again, and plucked it

out of his bosom, and, behold, it was turned again as his
other flesh. 8 'And it shall come to pass, if they will not
believe thee, neither hearken to the voice of the first sign,
that they will believe the voice of the latter sign. 9 And it shall
come to pass, if they will not believe also these two signs,
neither hearken unto thy voice, that thou shalt take of the
water of the river, and pour it upon the dry land; and the
water which thou takest out of the river shall become blood
upon the dry land.'

10 And Moses said unto the Lord, 'O my Lord, I am not
eloquent, neither heretofore, nor since thou hast spoken unto
thy servant: but I am slow of speech, and of a slow tongue.'
11 And the Lord said unto him, 'Who hath made man's mouth?
Or who maketh the dumb, or deaf, or the seeing, or the
blind? Have not I the Lord? 12 Now therefore go, and I will
be with thy mouth, and teach thee what thou shalt say.' 13 And
he said, 'O my Lord, send, I pray thee, by the hand of him
whom thou wilt send.' 14 And the anger of the Lord was kindled against Moses, and he said, 'Is not Aaron the Levite thy
brother? I know that he can speak well. And also, behold, he
cometh forth to meet thee: and when he seeth thee, he will be
glad in his heart. 15 And thou shalt speak unto him, and put
words in his mouth; and I will be with thy mouth, and with
his mouth, and will teach you what ye shall do. 16 And he
shall be thy spokesman unto the people; and he shall be,
even he shall be to thee instead of a mouth, and thou shalt be
to him instead of God. 17 And thou shalt take this rod in thine
hand, wherewith thou shalt do signs.'

[18]And Moses went and returned to Jethro his father-in-law,
and said unto him, 'Let me go, I pray thee, and return unto
my brethren which are in Egypt, and see whether they be yet
alive.' And Jethro said to Moses, 'Go in peace.' [19]And the Lord
said unto Moses in Midian, 'Go, return into Egypt: for all the
men are dead which sought thy life.' [20]And Moses took his
wife and his sons, and set them upon an ass, and he returned
to the land of Egypt, and Moses took the rod of God in his
hand. [21]And the Lord said unto Moses, 'When thou goest to
return into Egypt, see that thou do all those wonders before
Pharaoh, which I have put in thine hand: but I will harden
his heart, that he shall not let the people go. [22]And thou shalt
say unto Pharaoh, "Thus saith the Lord, 'Israel is my son,
even my firstborn. [23]And I say unto thee, let my son go, that
he may serve me, and if thou refuse to let him go, behold, I
will slay thy son, even thy firstborn.'"'

[24]And it came to pass by the way in the inn, that the Lord
met him, and sought to kill him. [25]Then Zipporah took a
sharp stone, and cut off the foreskin of her son, and cast it at
his feet, and said, 'Surely a bloody husband art thou to me.'
[26]So he let him go: then she said, 'A bloody husband thou
art, because of the circumcision.'

[27]And the Lord said to Aaron, 'Go into the wilderness to
meet Moses.' And he went, and met him in the mount of God,
and kissed him. [28]And Moses told Aaron all the words of the
Lord who had sent him, and all the signs which he had commanded him.

[29]And Moses and Aaron went and gathered together all

the elders of the children of Israel, 30 and Aaron spake all the
words which the Lord had spoken unto Moses, and did the
signs in the sight of the people. 31 And the people believed;
and when they heard that the Lord had visited the children
of Israel, and that he had looked upon their affliction, then
they bowed their heads and worshipped.

5 And afterward Moses and Aaron went in, and told Pharaoh, 'Thus saith the Lord God of Israel, "Let my people
go, that they may hold a feast unto me in the wilderness."'
2 And Pharaoh said, 'Who is the Lord, that I should obey his
voice to let Israel go? I know not the Lord, neither will I let
Israel go.' 3 And they said, 'The God of the Hebrews hath met
with us: let us go, we pray thee, three days' journey into the
desert, and sacrifice unto the Lord our God; lest he fall upon
us with pestilence, or with the sword.' 4 And the king of
Egypt said unto them, 'Wherefore do ye, Moses and Aaron,
let the people from their works? Get you unto your burdens.' 5 And Pharaoh said, 'Behold, the people of the land
now are many, and ye make them rest from their burdens.'
6 And Pharaoh commanded the same day the taskmasters of
the people, and their officers, saying, 7 'Ye shall no more give
the people straw to make brick, as heretofore; let them go
and gather straw for themselves. 8 And the tale of the bricks,
which they did make heretofore, ye shall lay upon them; ye
shall not diminish ought thereof, for they be idle; therefore
they cry, saying, "Let us go and sacrifice to our God." 9 Let
there more work be laid upon the men, that they may labour

therein; and let them not regard vain words.'
[10]And the taskmasters of the people went out, and their
officers, and they spake to the people, saying, 'Thus saith
Pharaoh, "I will not give you straw. [11] Go ye, get you straw
where ye can find it; yet not ought of your work shall be
diminished."' [12] So the people were scattered abroad throughout all the land of Egypt to gather stubble instead of straw.
[13]And the taskmasters hasted them, saying, 'Fulfil your works,
your daily tasks, as when there was straw.' [14]And the officers
of the children of Israel, which Pharaoh's taskmasters had
set over them, were beaten, and demanded, 'Wherefore have
ye not fulfilled your task in making brick both yesterday and
to day, as heretofore?'
[15] Then the officers of the children of Israel came and cried
unto Pharaoh, saying, 'Wherefore dealest thou thus with thy
servants? [16] There is no straw given unto thy servants, and
they say to us, "Make brick," and, behold, thy servants are
beaten; but the fault is in thine own people.' [17] But he said,
'Ye are idle, ye are idle; therefore ye say, "Let us go and do
sacrifice to the Lord." [18] Go therefore now, and work; for there
shall no straw be given you, yet shall ye deliver the tale of
bricks.' [19]And the officers of the children of Israel did see that
they were in evil case, after it was said, 'Ye shall not minish
ought from your bricks of your daily task.'
[20]And they met Moses and Aaron, who stood in the way,
as they came forth from Pharaoh, [21]and they said unto them,
'The Lord look upon you, and judge; because ye have made
our savour to be abhorred in the eyes of Pharaoh, and in the

eyes of his servants, to put a sword in their hand to slay us.' 22 And Moses returned unto the Lord, and said, 'Lord, wherefore hast thou so evil entreated this people? Why is it that thou hast sent me? 23 For since I came to Pharaoh to speak in thy name, he hath done evil to this people; neither hast thou delivered thy people at all.'

6 Then the Lord said unto Moses, 'Now shalt thou see what I will do to Pharaoh, for with a strong hand shall he let them go, and with a strong hand shall he drive them out of his land.' 2 And God spake unto Moses, and said unto him, 'I am the Lord, 3 and I appeared unto Abraham, unto Isaac, and unto Jacob, by the name of God Almighty, but by my name "Jehovah" was I not known to them. 4 And I have also established my covenant with them, to give them the land of Canaan, the land of their pilgrimage, wherein they were strangers. 5 And I have also heard the groaning of the children of Israel, whom the Egyptians keep in bondage; and I have remembered my covenant. 6 Wherefore say unto the children of Israel, "I am the Lord, and I will bring you out from under the burdens of the Egyptians, and I will rid you out of their bondage, and I will redeem you with a stretched out arm, and with great judgments. 7 And I will take you to me for a people, and I will be to you a God, and ye shall know that I am the Lord your God, which bringeth you out from under the burdens of the Egyptians. 8 And I will bring you in unto the land, concerning the which I did swear to give it to Abraham, to Isaac, and to Jacob; and I will give it

you for an heritage. I am the Lord.'"

9 And Moses spake so unto the children of Israel, but they
hearkened not unto Moses for anguish of spirit, and for cruel
bondage. 10 And the Lord spake unto Moses, saying, 11 'Go in,
speak unto Pharaoh king of Egypt, that he let the children of
Israel go out of his land.' 12 And Moses spake before the Lord,
saying, 'Behold, the children of Israel have not hearkened
unto me; how then shall Pharaoh hear me, who am of uncircumcised lips?' 13 And the Lord spake unto Moses and unto
Aaron, and gave them a charge unto the children of Israel,
and unto Pharaoh king of Egypt, to bring the children of
Israel out of the land of Egypt. 14 These be the heads of their
fathers' houses: the sons of Reuben the firstborn of Israel;
Hanoch, and Pallu, Hezron, and Carmi; these be the families
of Reuben. 15 And the sons of Simeon: Jemuel, and Jamin, and
Ohad, and Jachin, and Zohar, and Shaul the son of a Canaan-
itish woman; these are the families of Simeon. 16 And these are
the names of the sons of Levi according to their generations:
Gershon, and Kohath, and Merari; and the years of the life of
Levi were an hundred thirty and seven years. 17 The sons of
Gershon: Libni, and Shimi, according to their families. 18 And
the sons of Kohath: Amram, and Izhar, and Hebron, and
Uzziel; and the years of the life of Kohath were an hundred
thirty and three years. 19 And the sons of Merari: Mahali and
Mushi; these are the families of Levi according to their generations. 20 And Amram took him Jochebed his father's sister
to wife; and she bare him Aaron and Moses; and the years of
the life of Amram were an hundred and thirty and seven

years. 21 And the sons of Izhar: Korah, and Nepheg, and Zichri. 22 And the sons of Uzziel: Mishael, and Elzaphan, and Zithri. 23 And Aaron took him Elisheba, daughter of Amminadab, sister of Naashon, to wife; and she bare him Nadab, and Abihu, Eleazar, and Ithamar. 24 And the sons of Korah: Assir, and Elkanah, and Abiasaph; these are the families of the Korhites. 25 And Eleazar Aaron's son took him one of the daughters of Putiel to wife; and she bare him Phinehas. These are the heads of the fathers of the Levites according to their families. 26 These are that Aaron and Moses, to whom the Lord said, 'Bring out the children of Israel from the land of Egypt according to their armies.' 27 These are they which spake to Pharaoh king of Egypt, to bring out the children of Israel from Egypt; these are that Moses and Aaron.

28 And it came to pass on the day when the Lord spake unto Moses in the land of Egypt, 29 that the Lord spake unto Moses, saying, 'I am the Lord. Speak thou unto Pharaoh king of Egypt all that I say unto thee.' 30 And Moses said before the Lord, 'Behold, I am of uncircumcised lips, and how shall Pharaoh hearken unto me?'

7 And the Lord said unto Moses, 'See, I have made thee a god to Pharaoh, and Aaron thy brother shall be thy prophet. 2 Thou shalt speak all that I command thee: and Aaron thy brother shall speak unto Pharaoh, that he send the children of Israel out of his land. 3 And I will harden Pharaoh's heart, and multiply my signs and my wonders in the land of Egypt. 4 But Pharaoh shall not hearken unto you, that I may

lay my hand upon Egypt, and bring forth mine armies, and
my people the children of Israel, out of the land of Egypt by
great judgments. 5And the Egyptians shall know that I am
the Lord, when I stretch forth mine hand upon Egypt, and
bring out the children of Israel from among them.' 6And
Moses and Aaron did as the Lord commanded them, so did
they. 7And Moses was fourscore years old, and Aaron fourscore and three years old, when they spake unto Pharaoh.

8And the Lord spake unto Moses and unto Aaron, saying,
9'When Pharaoh shall speak unto you, saying, "Shew a miracle for you," then thou shalt say unto Aaron, "Take thy rod,
and cast it before Pharaoh, and it shall become a serpent."'

10And Moses and Aaron went in unto Pharaoh, and they
did so as the Lord had commanded; and Aaron cast down
his rod before Pharaoh, and before his servants, and it became
a serpent. 11Then Pharaoh also called the wise men and the
sorcerers; now the magicians of Egypt, they also did in like
manner with their enchantments. 12For they cast down every
man his rod, and they became serpents, but Aaron's rod
swallowed up their rods. 13And he hardened Pharaoh's heart,
that he hearkened not unto them, as the Lord had said.

14And the Lord said unto Moses, 'Pharaoh's heart is hardened, he refuseth to let the people go. 15Get thee unto Pharaoh in the morning; lo, he goeth out unto the water; and
thou shalt stand by the river's brink against he come; and
the rod which was turned to a serpent shalt thou take in
thine hand. 16And thou shalt say unto him, "The Lord God of
the Hebrews hath sent me unto thee, saying, 'Let my people

go, that they may serve me in the wilderness,' and, behold,
hitherto thou wouldest not hear. 17 Thus saith the Lord, 'In
this thou shalt know that I am the Lord: Behold, I will smite
with the rod that is in mine hand upon the waters which are
in the river, and they shall be turned to blood. 18 And the fish
that is in the river shall die, and the river shall stink; and the
Egyptians shall lothe to drink of the water of the river.'"'

19 And the Lord spake unto Moses, 'Say unto Aaron, "Take
thy rod, and stretch out thine hand upon the waters of Egypt,
upon their streams, upon their rivers, and upon their ponds,
and upon all their pools of water, that they may become
blood; and that there may be blood throughout all the land
of Egypt, both in vessels of wood, and in vessels of stone."'
20 And Moses and Aaron did so, as the Lord commanded;
and he lifted up the rod, and smote the waters that were in
the river, in the sight of Pharaoh, and in the sight of his servants; and all the waters that were in the river were turned
to blood. 21 And the fish that was in the river died; and the
river stank, and the Egyptians could not drink of the water
of the river; and there was blood throughout all the land of
Egypt. 22 And the magicians of Egypt did so with their enchantments; and Pharaoh's heart was hardened, neither did he
hearken unto them, as the Lord had said. 23 And Pharaoh
turned and went into his house, neither did he set his heart
to this also. 24 And all the Egyptians digged round about the
river for water to drink; for they could not drink of the water
of the river. 25 And seven days were fulfilled, after that the
Lord had smitten the river.

8 And the Lord spake unto Moses, 'Go unto Pharaoh, and
say unto him, "Thus saith the Lord, 'Let my people go,
that they may serve me. 2And if thou refuse to let them go,
behold, I will smite all thy borders with frogs. 3And the river
shall bring forth frogs abundantly, which shall go up and
come into thine house, and into thy bed-chamber, and upon
thy bed, and into the house of thy servants, and upon thy
people, and into thine ovens, and into thy kneadingtroughs.
4And the frogs shall come up both on thee, and upon thy
people, and upon all thy servants.'"'

5And the Lord spake unto Moses, 'Say unto Aaron, "Stretch
forth thine hand with thy rod over the streams, over the
rivers, and over the ponds, and cause frogs to come up upon
the land of Egypt."' 6And Aaron stretched out his hand over
the waters of Egypt; and the frogs came up, and covered the
land of Egypt. 7And the magicians did so with their enchantments, and brought up frogs upon the land of Egypt.

8Then Pharaoh called for Moses and Aaron, and said,
'Intreat the Lord, that he may take away the frogs from me,
and from my people; and I will let the people go, that they
may do sacrifice unto the Lord.' 9And Moses said unto Pharaoh, 'Glory over me: when shall I intreat for thee, and for thy
servants, and for thy people, to destroy the frogs from thee
and thy houses, that they may remain in the river only?'
10And he said, 'Tomorrow.' And he said, 'Be it according to
thy word, that thou mayest know that there is none like unto
the Lord our God. 11And the frogs shall depart from thee,
and from thy houses, and from thy servants, and from thy

people; they shall remain in the river only.' [12]And Moses and
Aaron went out from Pharaoh, and Moses cried unto the
Lord because of the frogs which he had brought against
Pharaoh. [13]And the Lord did according to the word of Moses;
and the frogs died out of the houses, out of the villages, and
out of the fields. [14]And they gathered them together upon
heaps, and the land stank. [15]But when Pharaoh saw that there
was respite, he hardened his heart, and hearkened not unto
them, as the Lord had said.

[16]And the Lord said unto Moses, 'Say unto Aaron, "Stretch
out thy rod, and smite the dust of the land, that it may become
lice throughout all the land of Egypt."' [17]And they did so; for
Aaron stretched out his hand with his rod, and smote the
dust of the earth, and it became lice in man, and in beast; all
the dust of the land became lice throughout all the land of
Egypt. [18]And the magicians did so with their enchantments
to bring forth lice, but they could not, so there were lice upon
man, and upon beast. [19]Then the magicians said unto Pharaoh,
'This is the finger of God' and Pharaoh's heart was hardened, and he hearkened not unto them, as the Lord had said.

[20]And the Lord said unto Moses, 'Rise up early in the morning, and stand before Pharaoh; lo, he cometh forth to the
water; and say unto him, "Thus saith the Lord, 'Let my people go, that they may serve me. [21]Else, if thou wilt not let my
people go, behold, I will send swarms of flies upon thee, and
upon thy servants, and upon thy people, and into thy houses:
and the houses of the Egyptians shall be full of swarms of
flies, and also the ground whereon they are. [22]And I will sever

in that day the land of Goshen, in which my people dwell,
that no swarms of flies shall be there; to the end thou mayest
know that I am the Lord in the midst of the earth. 23And I will
put a division between my people and thy people: tomorrow shall this sign be.'"' 24And the Lord did so; and there
came a grievous swarm of flies into the house of Pharaoh,
and into his servants' houses, and into all the land of Egypt:
the land was corrupted by reason of the swarm of flies.

25And Pharaoh called for Moses and for Aaron, and said,
'Go ye, sacrifice to your God in the land.' 26And Moses said,
'It is not meet so to do; for we shall sacrifice the abomination
of the Egyptians to the Lord our God. Lo, shall we sacrifice
the abomination of the Egyptians before their eyes, and will
they not stone us? 27We will go three days' journey into the
wilderness, and sacrifice to the Lord our God, as he shall
command us.' 28And Pharaoh said, 'I will let you go, that ye
may sacrifice to the Lord your God in the wilderness; only ye
shall not go very far away. Intreat for me.' 29And Moses said,
'Behold, I go out from thee, and I will intreat the Lord that the
swarms of flies may depart from Pharaoh, from his servants,
and from his people, tomorrow: but let not Pharaoh deal deceitfully any more in not letting the people go to sacrifice to the
Lord.' 30And Moses went out from Pharaoh, and intreated the
Lord. 31And the Lord did according to the word of Moses; and
he removed the swarms of flies from Pharaoh, from his servants, and from his people; there remained not one. 32And
Pharaoh hardened his heart at this time also, neither would
he let the people go.

9 Then the Lord said unto Moses, 'Go in unto Pharaoh, and tell him, "Thus saith the Lord God of the Hebrews, 'Let my people go, that they may serve me.' 2For if thou refuse to let them go, and wilt hold them still, 3behold, the hand of the Lord is upon thy cattle which is in the field, upon the horses, upon the asses, upon the camels, upon the oxen, and upon the sheep; there shall be a very grievous murrain. 4And the Lord shall sever between the cattle of Israel and the cattle of Egypt, and there shall nothing die of all that is the children's of Israel."' 5And the Lord appointed a set time, saying, 'Tomorrow the Lord shall do this thing in the land.' 6And the Lord did that thing on the morrow, and all the cattle of Egypt died, but of the cattle of the children of Israel died not one. 7And Pharaoh sent, and, behold, there was not one of the cattle of the Israelites dead. And the heart of Pharaoh was hardened, and he did not let the people go.

8And the Lord said unto Moses and unto Aaron, 'Take to you handfuls of ashes of the furnace, and let Moses sprinkle it toward the heaven in the sight of Pharaoh. 9And it shall become small dust in all the land of Egypt, and shall be a boil breaking forth with blains upon man, and upon beast, throughout all the land of Egypt.' 10And they took ashes of the furnace, and stood before Pharaoh; and Moses sprinkled it up toward heaven; and it became a boil breaking forth with blains upon man, and upon beast. 11And the magicians could not stand before Moses because of the boils; for the boil was upon the magicians, and upon all the Egyptians. 12And the Lord hardened the heart of Pharaoh, and he hearkened not

unto them, as the Lord had spoken unto Moses.
[13]And the Lord said unto Moses, 'Rise up early in the morning, and stand before Pharaoh, and say unto him, "Thus saith
the Lord God of the Hebrews, 'Let my people go, that they
may serve me. [14]For I will at this time send all my plagues
upon thine heart, and upon thy servants, and upon thy people; that thou mayest know that there is none like me in all
the earth. [15]For now I will stretch out my hand, that I may
smite thee and thy people with pestilence; and thou shalt be
cut off from the earth. [16]And in very deed for this cause have
I raised thee up, for to shew in thee my power; and that my
name may be declared throughout all the earth. [17]As yet exal-
test thou thyself against my people, that thou wilt not let
them go? [18]Behold, tomorrow about this time I will cause it
to rain a very grievous hail, such as hath not been in Egypt
since the foundation thereof even until now. [19]Send therefore now, and gather thy cattle, and all that thou hast in the
field; for upon every man and beast which shall be found in
the field, and shall not be brought home, the hail shall come
down upon them, and they shall die.'"' [20]He that feared the
word of the Lord among the servants of Pharaoh made his
servants and his cattle flee into the houses: [21]and he that
regarded not the word of the Lord left his servants and his
cattle in the field.
[22]And the Lord said unto Moses, 'Stretch forth thine hand
toward heaven, that there may be hail in all the land of Egypt,
upon man, and upon beast, and upon every herb of the field,
throughout the land of Egypt. [23]And Moses stretched forth

his rod toward heaven: and the Lord sent thunder and hail,
and the fire ran along upon the ground; and the Lord rained
hail upon the land of Egypt.' 24 So there was hail, and fire
mingled with the hail, very grievous, such as there was none
like it in all the land of Egypt since it became a nation. 25 And
the hail smote throughout all the land of Egypt all that was in
the field, both man and beast; and the hail smote every herb
of the field, and brake every tree of the field. 26 Only in the
land of Goshen, where the children of Israel were, was there
no hail.

27 And Pharaoh sent, and called for Moses and Aaron, and
said unto them, 'I have sinned this time. The Lord is righteous, and I and my people are wicked. 28 Intreat the Lord (for
it is enough) that there be no more mighty thunderings and
hail; and I will let you go, and ye shall stay no longer.' 29 And
Moses said unto him, 'As soon as I am gone out of the city, I
will spread abroad my hands unto the Lord; and the thunder shall cease, neither shall there be any more hail; that
thou mayest know how that the earth is the Lord's. 30 But as
for thee and thy servants, I know that ye will not yet fear the
Lord God.' 31 And the flax and the barley was smitten: for the
barley was in the ear, and the flax was bolled. 32 But the wheat
and the rie were not smitten, for they were not grown up.
33 And Moses went out of the city from Pharaoh, and spread
abroad his hands unto the Lord: and the thunders and hail
ceased, and the rain was not poured upon the earth. 34 And
when Pharaoh saw that the rain and the hail and the thunders were ceased, he sinned yet more, and hardened his

heart, he and his servants. 35And the heart of Pharaoh was
hardened, neither would he let the children of Israel go; as
the Lord had spoken by Moses.

10 And the Lord said unto Moses, 'Go in unto Pharaoh,
for I have hardened his heart, and the heart of his servants, that I might shew these my signs before him; 2and
that thou mayest tell in the ears of thy son, and of thy son's
son, what things I have wrought in Egypt, and my signs
which I have done among them; that ye may know how that
I am the Lord.' 3And Moses and Aaron came in unto Pharaoh,
and said unto him, 'Thus saith the Lord God of the Hebrews,
"How long wilt thou refuse to humble thyself before me?
Let my people go, that they may serve me. 4Else, if thou
refuse to let my people go, behold, tomorrow will I bring the
locusts into thy coast. 5And they shall cover the face of the
earth, that one cannot be able to see the earth; and they shall
eat the residue of that which is escaped, which remaineth
unto you from the hail, and shall eat every tree which groweth for you out of the field. 6And they shall fill thy houses,
and the houses of all thy servants, and the houses of all the
Egyptians; which neither thy fathers, nor thy fathers' fathers
have seen, since the day that they were upon the earth unto
this day."' And he turned himself, and went out from Pharaoh. 7And Pharaoh's servants said unto him, 'How long shall
this man be a snare unto us? Let the men go, that they may
serve the Lord their God. Knowest thou not yet that Egypt is
destroyed?' 8And Moses and Aaron were brought again unto

Pharaoh, and he said unto them, 'Go, serve the Lord your
God, but who are they that shall go?' [9]And Moses said, 'We
will go with our young and with our old, with our sons and
with our daughters, with our flocks and with our herds will
we go; for we must hold a feast unto the Lord.' [10]And he said
unto them, 'Let the Lord be so with you, as I will let you go,
and your little ones. Look to it; for evil is before you. [11]Not so;
go now ye that are men, and serve the Lord; for that ye did
desire.' And they were driven out from Pharaoh's presence.

[12]And the Lord said unto Moses, 'Stretch out thine hand
over the land of Egypt for the locusts, that they may come
up upon the land of Egypt, and eat every herb of the land,
even all that the hail hath left.' [13]And Moses stretched forth
his rod over the land of Egypt, and the Lord brought an east
wind upon the land all that day, and all that night; and when
it was morning, the east wind brought the locusts. [14]And the
locusts went up over all the land of Egypt, and rested in all
the coasts of Egypt: very grievous were they; before them
there were no such locusts as they, neither after them shall
be such. [15]For they covered the face of the whole earth, so
that the land was darkened; and they did eat every herb of
the land, and all the fruit of the trees which the hail had left;
and there remained not any green thing in the trees, or in the
herbs of the field, through all the land of Egypt.

[16]Then Pharaoh called for Moses and Aaron in haste; and
he said, 'I have sinned against the Lord your God, and against
you. [17]Now therefore forgive, I pray thee, my sin only this
once, and intreat the Lord your God, that he may take away

from me this death only.' [18]And he went out from Pharaoh,
and intreated the Lord. [19]And the Lord turned a mighty strong
west wind, which took away the locusts, and cast them into
the Red sea; there remained not one locust in all the coasts of
Egypt. [20]But the Lord hardened Pharaoh's heart, so that he
would not let the children of Israel go.

[21]And the Lord said unto Moses, 'Stretch out thine hand
toward heaven, that there may be darkness over the land of
Egypt, even darkness which may be felt.' [22]And Moses stretched forth his hand toward heaven; and there was a thick
darkness in all the land of Egypt three days. [23]They saw not
one another, neither rose any from his place for three days,
but all the children of Israel had light in their dwellings.

[24]And Pharaoh called unto Moses, and said, 'Go ye, serve
the Lord; only let your flocks and your herds be stayed: let
your little ones also go with you.' [25]And Moses said, 'Thou
must give us also sacrifices and burnt offerings, that we may
sacrifice unto the Lord our God. [26]Our cattle also shall go
with us; there shall not an hoof be left behind; for thereof
must we take to serve the Lord our God; and we know not
with what we must serve the Lord, until we come thither.'

[27]But the Lord hardened Pharaoh's heart, and he would
not let them go. [28]And Pharaoh said unto him, 'Get thee from
me, take heed to thyself, see my face no more; for in that day
thou seest my face thou shalt die.' [29]And Moses said, 'Thou
hast spoken well, I will see thy face again no more.'

11 And the Lord said unto Moses, 'Yet will I bring one
plague more upon Pharaoh, and upon Egypt; afterwards he will let you go hence: when he shall let you go, he
shall surely thrust you out hence altogether. 2 Speak now in
the ears of the people, and let every man borrow of his
neighbour, and every woman of her neighbour, jewels of silver, and jewels of gold.' 3 And the Lord gave the people favour in the sight of the Egyptians. Moreover the man Moses
was very great in the land of Egypt, in the sight of Pharaoh's
servants, and in the sight of the people. 4 And Moses said,
'Thus saith the Lord, "About midnight will I go out into the
midst of Egypt; 5 and all the firstborn in the land of Egypt
shall die, from the firstborn of Pharaoh that sitteth upon his
throne, even unto the firstborn of the maidservant that is
behind the mill; and all the firstborn of beasts. 6 And there
shall be a great cry throughout all the land of Egypt, such as
there was none like it, nor shall be like it any more. 7 But
against any of the children of Israel shall not a dog move his
tongue, against man or beast, that ye may know how that
the Lord doth put a difference between the Egyptians and
Israel." 8 And all these thy servants shall come down unto
me, and bow down themselves unto me, saying, "Get thee
out, and all the people that follow thee," and after that I will
go out.' And he went out from Pharaoh in a great anger.
9 And the Lord said unto Moses, 'Pharaoh shall not hearken
unto you; that my wonders may be multiplied in the land of
Egypt.' 10 And Moses and Aaron did all these wonders before
Pharaoh, and the Lord hardened Pharaoh's heart, so that he

would not let the children of Israel go out of his land.

12 And the Lord spake unto Moses and Aaron in the land of Egypt, saying, [2]"This month shall be unto you the beginning of months; it shall be the first month of the year to you.

[3]'Speak ye unto all the congregation of Israel, saying, "In the tenth day of this month they shall take to them every man a lamb, according to the house of their fathers, a lamb for an house. [4]And if the household be too little for the lamb, let him and his neighbour next unto his house take it according to the number of the souls; every man according to his eating shall make your count for the lamb. [5]Your lamb shall be without blemish, a male of the first year; ye shall take it out from the sheep, or from the goats. [6]And ye shall keep it up until the fourteenth day of the same month; and the whole assembly of the congregation of Israel shall kill it in the evening. [7]And they shall take of the blood, and strike it on the two side posts and on the upper door post of the houses, wherein they shall eat it. [8]And they shall eat the flesh in that night, roast with fire, and unleavened bread; and with bitter herbs they shall eat it. [9]Eat not of it raw, nor sodden at all with water, but roast with fire; his head with his legs, and with the purtenance thereof. [10]And ye shall let nothing of it remain until the morning; and that which remaineth of it until the morning ye shall burn with fire.

[11]'"And thus shall ye eat it; with your loins girded, your shoes on your feet, and your staff in your hand; and ye shall eat it in haste; it is the Lord's passover. [12]For I will pass

through the land of Egypt this night, and will smite all the
firstborn in the land of Egypt, both man and beast; and
against all the gods of Egypt I will execute judgment: I am
the Lord. 13 And the blood shall be to you for a token upon
the houses where ye are: and when I see the blood, I will pass
over you, and the plague shall not be upon you to destroy
you, when I smite the land of Egypt. 14 And this day shall be
unto you for a memorial; and ye shall keep it a feast to the
Lord throughout your generations; ye shall keep it a feast by
an ordinance for ever. 15 Seven days shall ye eat unleavened
bread; even the first day ye shall put away leaven out of your
houses; for whosoever eateth leavened bread from the first
day until the seventh day, that soul shall be cut off from Israel.
16 And in the first day there shall be an holy convocation, and
in the seventh day there shall be an holy convocation to you;
no manner of work shall be done in them, save that which
every man must eat, that only may be done of you. 17 And ye
shall observe the feast of unleavened bread; for in this selfsame day have I brought your armies out of the land of
Egypt; therefore shall ye observe this day in your generations by an ordinance for ever.

18 '"In the first month, on the fourteenth day of the month
at even, ye shall eat unleavened bread, until the one and
twentieth day of the month at even. 19 Seven days shall
there be no leaven found in your houses: for whosoever
eateth that which is leavened, even that soul shall be cut off
from the congregation of Israel, whether he be a stranger,
or born in the land. 20 Ye shall eat nothing leavened; in all

your habitations shall ye eat unleavened bread.'"

21 Then Moses called for all the elders of Israel, and said unto them, 'Draw out and take you a lamb according to your families, and kill the passover. 22 And ye shall take a bunch of hyssop, and dip it in the blood that is in the bason, and strike the lintel and the two side posts with the blood that is in the bason; and none of you shall go out at the door of his house until the morning. 23 For the Lord will pass through to smite the Egyptians; and when he seeth the blood upon the lintel, and on the two side posts, the Lord will pass over the door, and will not suffer the destroyer to come in unto your houses to smite you. 24 And ye shall observe this thing for an ordinance to thee and to thy sons for ever. 25 And it shall come to pass, when ye be come to the land which the Lord will give you, according as he hath promised, that ye shall keep this service. 26 And it shall come to pass, when your children shall say unto you, "What mean ye by this service?" 27 That ye shall say, "It is the sacrifice of the Lord's passover, who passed over the houses of the children of Israel in Egypt, when he smote the Egyptians, and delivered our houses."' And the people bowed the head and worshipped. 28 And the children of Israel went away, and did as the Lord had commanded Moses and Aaron, so did they.

29 And it came to pass, that at midnight the Lord smote all the firstborn in the land of Egypt, from the firstborn of Pharaoh that sat on his throne unto the firstborn of the captive that was in the dungeon; and all the firstborn of cattle. 30 And Pharaoh rose up in the night, he, and all his servants, and all

the Egyptians; and there was a great cry in Egypt; for there
was not a house where there was not one dead.
31 And he called for Moses and Aaron by night, and said,
'Rise up, and get you forth from among my people, both ye
and the children of Israel; and go, serve the Lord, as ye have
said. 32 Also take your flocks and your herds, as ye have said,
and be gone; and bless me also.' 33 And the Egyptians were
urgent upon the people, that they might send them out of
the land in haste; for they said, 'We be all dead men.' 34 And
the people took their dough before it was leavened, their
kneading-troughs being bound up in their clothes upon their
shoulders. 35 And the children of Israel did according to the
word of Moses; and they borrowed of the Egyptians jewels
of silver, and jewels of gold, and raiment. 36 And the Lord gave
the people favour in the sight of the Egyptians, so that they
lent unto them such things as they required. And they spoiled
the Egyptians.
37 And the children of Israel journeyed from Rameses to
Succoth, about six hundred thousand on foot that were men,
beside children. 38 And a mixed multitude went up also with
them; and flocks, and herds, even very much cattle. 39 And they
baked unleavened cakes of the dough which they brought
forth out of Egypt, for it was not leavened; because they
were thrust out of Egypt, and could not tarry, neither had
they prepared for themselves any victual.
40 Now the sojourning of the children of Israel, who dwelt
in Egypt, was four hundred and thirty years. 41 And it came
to pass at the end of the four hundred and thirty years, even

the selfsame day it came to pass, that all the hosts of the Lord
went out from the land of Egypt. [42]It is a night to be much
observed unto the Lord for bringing them out from the land
of Egypt. This is that night of the Lord to be observed of all
the children of Israel in their generations.

[43]And the Lord said unto Moses and Aaron, 'This is the
ordinance of the passover. There shall no stranger eat thereof; [44] but every man's servant that is bought for money, when
thou hast circumcised him, then shall he eat thereof. [45]A for-
eigner and an hired servant shall not eat thereof. [46]In one
house shall it be eaten; thou shalt not carry forth ought of
the flesh abroad out of the house; neither shall ye break a
bone thereof. [47]All the congregation of Israel shall keep it.
[48]And when a stranger shall sojourn with thee, and will keep
the passover to the Lord, let all his males be circumcised, and
then let him come near and keep it; and he shall be as one
that is born in the land, for no uncircumcised person shall
eat thereof. [49]One law shall be to him that is homeborn, and
unto the stranger that sojourneth among you.' [50]Thus did all
the children of Israel; as the Lord commanded Moses and
Aaron, so did they. [51]And it came to pass the selfsame day,
that the Lord did bring the children of Israel out of the land
of Egypt by their armies.

13 And the Lord spake unto Moses, saying, [2]'Sanctify unto
me all the firstborn, whatsoever openeth the womb among
the children of Israel, both of man and of beast: it is mine.'

[3]And Moses said unto the people, 'Remember this day, in

which ye came out from Egypt, out of the house of bondage;
for by strength of hand the Lord brought you out from this
place; there shall no leavened bread be eaten. [4] This day came
ye out in the month Abib.

[5] 'And it shall be when the Lord shall bring thee into the
land of the Canaanites, and the Hittites, and the Amorites, and
the Hivites, and the Jebusites, which he sware unto thy fathers
to give thee, a land flowing with milk and honey, that thou
shalt keep this service in this month. [6] Seven days thou shalt
eat unleavened bread, and in the seventh day shall be a feast
to the Lord. [7] Unleavened bread shall be eaten seven days;
and there shall no leavened bread be seen with thee, neither
shall there be leaven seen with thee in all thy quarters.

[8] 'And thou shalt shew thy son in that day, saying, "This
is done because of that which the Lord did unto me when I
came forth out of Egypt." [9] And it shall be for a sign unto thee
upon thine hand, and for a memorial between thine eyes,
that the Lord's law may be in thy mouth; for with a strong
hand hath the Lord brought thee out of Egypt. [10] Thou shalt
therefore keep this ordinance in his season from year to year.

[11] 'And it shall be when the Lord shall bring thee into
the land of the Canaanites, as he sware unto thee and to thy
fathers, and shall give it thee, [12] that thou shalt set apart unto
the Lord all that openeth the matrix, and every firstling that
cometh of a beast which thou hast; the males shall be the
Lord's. [13] And every firstling of an ass thou shalt redeem with
a lamb; and if thou wilt not redeem it, then thou shalt break
his neck; and all the firstborn of man among thy children

shalt thou redeem.

[14]'And it shall be when thy son asketh thee in time to come, saying, "What is this?" that thou shalt say unto him, "By strength of hand the Lord brought us out from Egypt, from the house of bondage: [15]And it came to pass, when Pharaoh would hardly let us go, that the Lord slew all the firstborn in the land of Egypt, both the firstborn of man, and the firstborn of beast; therefore I sacrifice to the Lord all that openeth the matrix, being males; but all the firstborn of my children I redeem." [16]And it shall be for a token upon thine hand, and for frontlets between thine eyes, for by strength of hand the Lord brought us forth out of Egypt.'

[17]And it came to pass, when Pharaoh had let the people go, that God led them not through the way of the land of the Philistines, although that was near; for God said, 'Lest peradventure the people repent when they see war, and they return to Egypt.' [18]But God led the people about, through the way of the wilderness of the Red sea, and the children of Israel went up harnessed out of the land of Egypt. [19]And Moses took the bones of Joseph with him, for he had straitly sworn the children of Israel, saying, 'God will surely visit you; and ye shall carry up my bones away hence with you.'

[20]And they took their journey from Succoth, and encamped in Etham, in the edge of the wilderness. [21]And the Lord went before them by day in a pillar of a cloud, to lead them the way; and by night in a pillar of fire, to give them light; to go by day and night. [22]He took not away the pillar of the cloud by day, nor the pillar of fire by night, from before the people.

14 And the Lord spake unto Moses, saying, 2'Speak unto the children of Israel, that they turn and encamp before Pi-hahiroth, between Migdol and the sea, over against Baal-zephon; before it shall ye encamp by the sea. 3For Pharaoh will say of the children of Israel, "They are entangled in the land, the wilderness hath shut them in." 4And I will harden Pharaoh's heart, that he shall follow after them; and I will be honoured upon Pharaoh, and upon all his host; that the Egyptians may know that I am the Lord.' And they did so.

5And it was told the king of Egypt that the people fled; and the heart of Pharaoh and of his servants was turned against the people, and they said, 'Why have we done this, that we have let Israel go from serving us?' 6And he made ready his chariot, and took his people with him. 7And he took six hundred chosen chariots, and all the chariots of Egypt, and captains over every one of them. 8And the Lord hardened the heart of Pharaoh king of Egypt, and he pursued after the children of Israel: and the children of Israel went out with an high hand. 9But the Egyptians pursued after them, all the horses and chariots of Pharaoh, and his horsemen, and his army, and overtook them encamping by the sea, beside Pi-hahiroth, before Baal-zephon.

10And when Pharaoh drew nigh, the children of Israel lifted up their eyes, and, behold, the Egyptians marched after them; and they were sore afraid; and the children of Israel cried out unto the Lord. 11And they said unto Moses, 'Because there were no graves in Egypt, hast thou taken us away to

die in the wilderness? Wherefore hast thou dealt thus with
us, to carry us forth out of Egypt? 12 Is not this the word that
we did tell thee in Egypt, saying, "Let us alone, that we may
serve the Egyptians"? For it had been better for us to serve
the Egyptians, than that we should die in the wilderness.'

13 And Moses said unto the people, 'Fear ye not, stand
still, and see the salvation of the Lord, which he will shew to
you today, for the Egyptians whom ye have seen to day, ye
shall see them again no more for ever. 14 The Lord shall fight
for you, and ye shall hold your peace.'

15 And the Lord said unto Moses, 'Wherefore criest thou
unto me? Speak unto the children of Israel, that they go forward; 16 but lift thou up thy rod, and stretch out thine hand
over the sea, and divide it, and the children of Israel shall go
on dry ground through the midst of the sea. 17 And I, behold,
I will harden the hearts of the Egyptians, and they shall follow them; and I will get me honour upon Pharaoh, and upon
all his host, upon his chariots, and upon his horsemen. 18 And
the Egyptians shall know that I am the Lord, when I have
gotten me honour upon Pharaoh, upon his chariots, and
upon his horsemen.'

19 And the angel of God, which went before the camp of
Israel, removed and went behind them; and the pillar of the
cloud went from before their face, and stood behind them.
20 And it came between the camp of the Egyptians and the
camp of Israel; and it was a cloud and darkness to them, but
it gave light by night to these; so that the one came not near
the other all the night. 21 And Moses stretched out his hand

over the sea; and the Lord caused the sea to go back by a
strong east wind all that night, and made the sea dry land, and
the waters were divided. [22]And the children of Israel went
into the midst of the sea upon the dry ground, and the waters
were a wall unto them on their right hand, and on their left.
[23]And the Egyptians pursued, and went in after them to
the midst of the sea, even all Pharaoh's horses, his chariots,
and his horsemen. [24]And it came to pass, that in the morning
watch the Lord looked unto the host of the Egyptians
through the pillar of fire and of the cloud, and troubled the
host of the Egyptians, [25]and took off their chariot wheels, that
they drave them heavily, so that the Egyptians said, 'Let us
flee from the face of Israel; for the Lord fighteth for them
against the Egyptians.'
[26]And the Lord said unto Moses, 'Stretch out thine hand
over the sea, that the waters may come again upon the Egyptians, upon their chariots, and upon their horsemen.' [27]And
Moses stretched forth his hand over the sea, and the sea
returned to his strength when the morning appeared; and
the Egyptians fled against it; and the Lord overthrew the
Egyptians in the midst of the sea. [28]And the waters returned,
and covered the chariots, and the horsemen, and all the host
of Pharaoh that came into the sea after them; there remained
not so much as one of them. [29]But the children of Israel
walked upon dry land in the midst of the sea; and the waters
were a wall unto them on their right hand, and on their left.
[30]Thus the Lord saved Israel that day out of the hand of the
Egyptians; and Israel saw the Egyptians dead upon the sea

shore. [31]And Israel saw that great work which the Lord did upon the Egyptians; and the people feared the Lord, and believed the Lord, and his servant Moses.

15 Then sang Moses and the children of Israel this song unto the Lord, and spake, saying,

'I will sing unto the Lord,
for he hath triumphed gloriously.
The horse and his rider
hath he thrown into the sea.
2 The Lord is my strength and song,
and he is become my salvation;
he is my God,
and I will prepare him an habitation;
my father's God, and I will exalt him.
3 The Lord is a man of war; the Lord is his name.
4 Pharaoh's chariots and his host
hath he cast into the sea;
his chosen captains also are drowned
in the Red sea.
5 The depths have covered them;
they sank into the bottom as a stone.
6 Thy right hand, O Lord,
is become glorious in power;
thy right hand, O Lord,
hath dashed in pieces the enemy.
7 And in the greatness of thine excellency thou hast
overthrown them that rose up against thee;

thou sentest forth thy wrath,
which consumed them as stubble.
8 And with the blast of thy nostrils
the waters were gathered together,
the floods stood upright as an heap,
and the depths were congealed
in the heart of the sea.
9 The enemy said, "I will pursue, I will overtake,
I will divide the spoil;
my lust shall be satisfied upon them;
I will draw my sword,
my hand shall destroy them."
10 Thou didst blow with thy wind,
the sea covered them;
they sank as lead in the mighty waters.
11 Who is like unto thee, O Lord, among the gods?
Who is like thee, glorious in holiness,
fearful in praises, doing wonders?
12 Thou stretchedst out thy right hand,
the earth swallowed them.
13 Thou in thy mercy hast led forth the people
which thou hast redeemed;
thou hast guided them in thy strength
unto thy holy habitation.
14 The people shall hear, and be afraid;
sorrow shall take hold
on the inhabitants of Palestina.
15 Then the dukes of Edom shall be amazed;

the mighty men of Moab,
trembling shall take hold upon them;
all the inhabitants of Canaan shall melt away.
16 Fear and dread shall fall upon them;
by the greatness of thine arm
they shall be as still as a stone;
till thy people pass over, O Lord,
till the people pass over,
which thou hast purchased.
17 Thou shalt bring them in, and plant them
in the mountain of thine inheritance,
in the place, O Lord, which thou hast made
for thee to dwell in, in the Sanctuary, O Lord,
which thy hands have established.
18 The Lord shall reign for ever and ever.'

19 For the horse of Pharaoh went in with his chariots and with
his horsemen into the sea, and the Lord brought again the
waters of the sea upon them; but the children of Israel went
on dry land in the midst of the sea.

20 And Miriam the prophetess, the sister of Aaron, took a
timbrel in her hand; and all the women went out after her
with timbrels and with dances. 21 And Miriam answered them,
'Sing ye to the Lord, for he hath triumphed gloriously; the
horse and his rider hath he thrown into the sea.' 22 So Moses
brought Israel from the Red sea, and they went out into the
wilderness of Shur; and they went three days in the wilderness, and found no water.

23 And when they came to Marah, they could not drink of

the waters of Marah, for they were bitter; therefore the name of it was called Marah. 24 And the people murmured against Moses, saying, 'What shall we drink?' 25 And he cried unto the Lord; and the Lord shewed him a tree, which when he had cast into the waters, the waters were made sweet. There he made for them a statute and an ordinance, and there he proved them, 26 and said, 'If thou wilt diligently hearken to the voice of the Lord thy God, and wilt do that which is right in his sight, and wilt give ear to his commandments, and keep all his statutes, I will put none of these diseases upon thee, which I have brought upon the Egyptians, for I am the Lord that healeth thee.'

27 And they came to Elim, where were twelve wells of water, and three-score and ten palm trees, and they encamped there by the waters.

16 And they took their journey from Elim, and all the congregation of the children of Israel came unto the wilderness of Sin, which is between Elim and Sinai, on the fifteenth day of the second month after their departing out of the land of Egypt. 2 And the whole congregation of the children of Israel murmured against Moses and Aaron in the wilderness: 3 And the children of Israel said unto them, 'Would to God we had died by the hand of the Lord in the land of Egypt, when we sat by the flesh pots, and when we did eat bread to the full; for ye have brought us forth into this wilderness, to kill this whole assembly with hunger.'

4 Then said the Lord unto Moses, 'Behold, I will rain bread

from heaven for you; and the people shall go out and gather
a certain rate every day, that I may prove them, whether
they will walk in my law, or no. 5And it shall come to pass,
that on the sixth day they shall prepare that which they
bring in; and it shall be twice as much as they gather daily.'
6And Moses and Aaron said unto all the children of Israel,
'At even, then ye shall know that the Lord hath brought you
out from the land of Egypt, 7and in the morning, then ye
shall see the glory of the Lord; for that he heareth your murmurings against the Lord: and what are we, that ye murmur
against us?' 8And Moses said, 'This shall be, when the Lord
shall give you in the evening flesh to eat, and in the morning
bread to the full; for that the Lord heareth your murmurings
which ye murmur against him; and what are we? Your murmurings are not against us, but against the Lord.'

9And Moses spake unto Aaron, 'Say unto all the congregation of the children of Israel, "Come near before the Lord:
for he hath heard your murmurings."' 10And it came to pass,
as Aaron spake unto the whole congregation of the children
of Israel, that they looked toward the wilderness, and,
behold, the glory of the Lord appeared in the cloud.

11And the Lord spake unto Moses, saying, 12'I have heard
the murmurings of the children of Israel; speak unto them,
saying, "At even ye shall eat flesh, and in the morning ye
shall be filled with bread; and ye shall know that I am the
Lord your God."' 13And it came to pass, that at even the quails
came up, and covered the camp; and in the morning the dew
lay round about the host. 14And when the dew that lay was

gone up, behold, upon the face of the wilderness there lay a
small round thing, as small as the hoar frost on the ground.
[15]And when the children of Israel saw it, they said one to
another, 'It is manna,' for they wist not what it was. And
Moses said unto them, 'This is the bread which the Lord hath
given you to eat.

[16]'This is the thing which the Lord hath commanded:
"Gather of it every man according to his eating, an omer for
every man, according to the number of your persons; take
ye every man for them which are in his tents."' [17]And the
children of Israel did so, and gathered, some more, some less.
[18]And when they did mete it with an omer, he that gathered
much had nothing over, and he that gathered little had no
lack; they gathered every man according to his eating. [19]And
Moses said, 'Let no man leave of it till the morning.' [20]Not-
withstanding they hearkened not unto Moses; but some of
them left of it until the morning, and it bred worms, and
stank; and Moses was wroth with them. [21]And they gathered
it every morning, every man according to his eating; and
when the sun waxed hot, it melted.

[22]And it came to pass, that on the sixth day they gathered
twice as much bread, two omers for one man; and all the
rulers of the congregation came and told Moses. [23]And he said
unto them, 'This is that which the Lord hath said, "Tomorrow is the rest of the holy sabbath unto the Lord. Bake that
which ye will bake to day, and seethe that ye will seethe; and
that which remaineth over lay up for you to be kept until the
morning."' [24]And they laid it up till the morning, as Moses

bade; and it did not stink, neither was there any worm therein.
25 And Moses said, 'Eat that to day; for today is a sabbath unto
the Lord; today ye shall not find it in the field. 26 Six days ye
shall gather it; but on the seventh day, which is the sabbath,
in it there shall be none.'

27 And it came to pass, that there went out some of the
people on the seventh day for to gather, and they found none.
28 And the Lord said unto Moses, 'How long refuse ye to keep
my commandments and my laws? 29 See, for that the Lord
hath given you the sabbath, therefore he giveth you on the
sixth day the bread of two days; abide ye every man in his
place, let no man go out of his place on the seventh day.' 30 So
the people rested on the seventh day. 31 And the house of Israel
called the name thereof Manna; and it was like coriander seed,
white; and the taste of it was like wafers made with honey.

32 And Moses said, 'This is the thing which the Lord commandeth: "Fill an omer of it to be kept for your generations;
that they may see the bread wherewith I have fed you in the
wilderness, when I brought you forth from the land of Egypt."'
33 And Moses said unto Aaron, 'Take a pot, and put an omer
full of manna therein, and lay it up before the Lord, to be
kept for your generations.' 34 As the Lord commanded Moses,
so Aaron laid it up before the Testimony, to be kept. 35 And
the children of Israel did eat manna forty years, until they
came to a land inhabited; they did eat manna, until they came
unto the borders of the land of Canaan. 36 Now an omer is
the tenth part of an ephah.

17 And all the congregation of the children of Israel journeyed from the wilderness of Sin, after their journeys,
according to the commandment of the Lord, and pitched in
Rephidim; and there was no water for the people to drink.
2 Wherefore the people did chide with Moses, and said, 'Give
us water that we may drink.' And Moses said unto them,
'Why chide ye with me? Wherefore do ye tempt the Lord?'
3 And the people thirsted there for water; and the people
murmured against Moses, and said, 'Wherefore is this that
thou hast brought us up out of Egypt, to kill us and our children and our cattle with thirst?' 4 And Moses cried unto the
Lord, saying, 'What shall I do unto this people? They be
almost ready to stone me.' 5 And the Lord said unto Moses,
'Go on before the people, and take with thee of the elders of
Israel; and thy rod, wherewith thou smotest the river, take
in thine hand, and go. 6 Behold, I will stand before thee there
upon the rock in Horeb; and thou shalt smite the rock, and
there shall come water out of it, that the people may drink.'
And Moses did so in the sight of the elders of Israel. 7 And he
called the name of the place Massah, and Meribah, because
of the chiding of the children of Israel, and because they
tempted the Lord, saying, 'Is the Lord among us, or not?'

8 Then came Amalek, and fought with Israel in Rephidim.
9 And Moses said unto Joshua, 'Choose us out men, and go
out, fight with Amalek; tomorrow I will stand on the top of
the hill with the rod of God in mine hand.' 10 So Joshua did as
Moses had said to him, and fought with Amalek; and Moses,
Aaron, and Hur went up to the top of the hill. 11 And it came

to pass, when Moses held up his hand, that Israel prevailed,
and when he let down his hand, Amalek prevailed. 12But
Moses' hands were heavy; and they took a stone, and put it
under him, and he sat thereon; and Aaron and Hur stayed
up his hands, the one on the one side, and the other on the
other side; and his hands were steady until the going down
of the sun. 13And Joshua discomfited Amalek and his people
with the edge of the sword. 14And the Lord said unto Moses,
'Write this for a memorial in a book, and rehearse it in the
ears of Joshua: for I will utterly put out the remembrance of
Amalek from under heaven.' 15And Moses built an altar, and
called the name of it Jehovah-nissi: 16for he said, 'Because the
Lord hath sworn that the Lord will have war with Amalek
from generation to generation.'

18 When Jethro, the priest of Midian, Moses' father in law,
heard of all that God had done for Moses, and for
Israel his people, and that the Lord had brought Israel out of
Egypt, 2then Jethro, Moses' father in law, took Zipporah,
Moses' wife, after he had sent her back, 3and her two sons,
of which the name of the one was Gershom; for he said, 'I
have been an alien in a strange land,' 4and the name of the
other was Eliezer; for 'The God of my father,' said he, 'was
mine help, and delivered me from the sword of Pharaoh.'
5And Jethro, Moses' father in law, came with his sons and
his wife unto Moses into the wilderness, where he
encamped at the mount of God. 6And he said unto Moses, 'I
thy father in law Jethro am come unto thee, and thy wife,

and her two sons with her.'

7 And Moses went out to meet his father in law, and did obeisance, and kissed him; and they asked each other of their welfare; and they came into the tent. 8 And Moses told his father in law all that the Lord had done unto Pharaoh and to the Egyptians for Israel's sake, and all the travail that had come upon them by the way, and how the Lord delivered them. 9 And Jethro rejoiced for all the goodness which the Lord had done to Israel, whom he had delivered out of the hand of the Egyptians. 10 And Jethro said, 'Blessed be the Lord, who hath delivered you out of the hand of the Egyptians, and out of the hand of Pharaoh, who hath delivered the people from under the hand of the Egyptians. 11 Now I know that the Lord is greater than all gods, for in the thing wherein they dealt proudly he was above them.' 12 And Jethro, Moses' father in law, took a burnt offering and sacrifices for God; and Aaron came, and all the elders of Israel, to eat bread with Moses' father in law before God.

13 And it came to pass on the morrow, that Moses sat to judge the people: and the people stood by Moses from the morning unto the evening. 14 And when Moses' father in law saw all that he did to the people, he said, 'What is this thing that thou doest to the people? Why sittest thou thyself alone, and all the people stand by thee from morning unto even?' 15 And Moses said unto his father in law, 'Because the people come unto me to enquire of God. 16 When they have a matter, they come unto me; and I judge between one and another, and I do make them know the statutes of God, and his laws.'

17 And Moses' father in law said unto him, 'The thing that thou
doest is not good. 18 Thou wilt surely wear away, both thou,
and this people that is with thee, for this thing is too heavy
for thee; thou art not able to perform it thyself alone. 19 Hearken now unto my voice, I will give thee counsel, and God
shall be with thee. Be thou for the people to Godward, that
thou mayest bring the causes unto God. 20 And thou shalt
teach them ordinances and laws, and shalt shew them the
way wherein they must walk, and the work that they must
do. 21 Moreover thou shalt provide out of all the people able
men, such as fear God, men of truth, hating covetousness;
and place such over them, to be rulers of thousands, and
rulers of hundreds, rulers of fifties, and rulers of tens. 22 And
let them judge the people at all seasons; and it shall be, that
every great matter they shall bring unto thee, but every
small matter they shall judge; so shall it be easier for thyself,
and they shall bear the burden with thee. 23 If thou shalt do
this thing, and God command thee so, then thou shalt be
able to endure, and all this people shall also go to their place
in peace.' 24 So Moses hearkened to the voice of his father in
law, and did all that he had said. 25 And Moses chose able men
out of all Israel, and made them heads over the people, rulers
of thousands, rulers of hundreds, rulers of fifties, and rulers
of tens. 26 And they judged the people at all seasons; the hard
causes they brought unto Moses, but every small matter they
judged themselves.

27 And Moses let his father in law depart; and he went his
way into his own land.

19 In the third month, when the children of Israel were
gone forth out of the land of Egypt, the same day came
they into the wilderness of Sinai. 2 For they were departed
from Rephidim, and were come to the desert of Sinai, and
had pitched in the wilderness; and there Israel camped before
the mount. 3 And Moses went up unto God, and the Lord
called unto him out of the mountain, saying, 'Thus shalt thou
say to the house of Jacob, and tell the children of Israel, 4 "Ye
have seen what I did unto the Egyptians, and how I bare you
on eagles' wings, and brought you unto myself. 5 Now therefore, if ye will obey my voice indeed, and keep my covenant,
then ye shall be a peculiar treasure unto me above all
people, for all the earth is mine. 6 And ye shall be unto me
a kingdom of priests, and an holy nation." These are the
words which thou shalt speak unto the children of Israel.'

7 And Moses came and called for the elders of the people,
and laid before their faces all these words which the Lord
commanded him. 8 And all the people answered together,
and said, 'All that the Lord hath spoken we will do.' And Moses
returned the words of the people unto the Lord. 9 And the
Lord said unto Moses, 'Lo, I come unto thee in a thick cloud,
that the people may hear when I speak with thee, and believe
thee for ever.' And Moses told the words of the people unto
the Lord.

10 And the Lord said unto Moses, 'Go unto the people, and
sanctify them today and tomorrow, and let them wash their
clothes, 11 and be ready against the third day; for the third day
the Lord will come down in the sight of all the people upon

mount Sinai. 12And thou shalt set bounds unto the people round about, saying, "Take heed to yourselves, that ye go not up into the mount, or touch the border of it." Whosoever toucheth the mount shall be surely put to death. 13There shall not an hand touch it, but he shall surely be stoned, or shot through; whether it be beast or man, it shall not live. When the trumpet soundeth long, they shall come up to the mount.'

14And Moses went down from the mount unto the people, and sanctified the people; and they washed their clothes. 15And he said unto the people, 'Be ready against the third day: come not at your wives.'

16And it came to pass on the third day in the morning, that there were thunders and lightnings, and a thick cloud upon the mount, and the voice of the trumpet exceeding loud; so that all the people that was in the camp trembled. 17And Moses brought forth the people out of the camp to meet with God; and they stood at the nether part of the mount. 18And mount Sinai was altogether on a smoke, because the Lord descended upon it in fire: and the smoke thereof ascended as the smoke of a furnace, and the whole mount quaked greatly. 19And when the voice of the trumpet sounded long, and waxed louder and louder, Moses spake, and God answered him by a voice. 20And the Lord came down upon mount Sinai, on the top of the mount; and the Lord called Moses up to the top of the mount; and Moses went up. 21And the Lord said unto Moses, 'Go down, charge the people, lest they break through unto the Lord to gaze, and many of them perish. 22And let the priests also, which come near to the

Lord, sanctify themselves, lest the Lord break forth upon
them.' 23And Moses said unto the Lord, 'The people cannot
come up to mount Sinai; for thou chargedst us, saying, "Set
bounds about the mount, and sanctify it."' 24And the Lord
said unto him, 'Away, get thee down, and thou shalt come
up, thou, and Aaron with thee, but let not the priests and the
people break through to come up unto the Lord, lest he
break forth upon them.' 25So Moses went down unto the
people, and spake unto them.

20 And God spake all these words, saying, 2'I am the
Lord thy God, which have brought thee out of the
land of Egypt, out of the house of bondage.

3Thou shalt have no other gods before me.
4Thou shalt not make unto thee any graven image,
  or any likeness of any thing
    that is in heaven above,
  or that is in the earth beneath,
    or that is in the water under the earth.
5Thou shalt not bow down thyself to them,
    nor serve them;
  for I the Lord thy God am a jealous God,
    visiting the iniquity of the fathers
  upon the children unto the third and
    fourth generation of them that hate me;
6and shewing mercy unto thousands of them
  that love me, and keep my commandments.

7 Thou shalt not take the name
of the Lord thy God in vain;
for the Lord will not hold him guiltless
that taketh his name in vain.
8 Remember the sabbath day, to keep it holy.
9 Six days shalt thou labour, and do all thy work,
10 But the seventh day is the sabbath
of the Lord thy God;
in it thou shalt not do any work, thou,
nor thy son, nor thy daughter, thy manservant,
nor thy maidservant, nor thy cattle,
nor thy stranger that is within thy gates.
11 For in six days the Lord made heaven and earth,
the sea, and all that in them is,
and rested the seventh day;
wherefore the Lord blessed the sabbath day,
and hallowed it.
12 Honour thy father and thy mother:
that thy days may be long upon the land
which the Lord thy God giveth thee.
13 Thou shalt not kill.
14 Thou shalt not commit adultery.
15 Thou shalt not steal.
16 Thou shalt not bear false witness
against thy neighbour.
17 Thou shalt not covet thy neighbour's house,
thou shalt not covet thy neighbour's wife,
nor his manservant, nor his maidservant,

nor his ox, nor his ass,
nor any thing that is thy neighbour's.'

18And all the people saw the thunderings, and the lightnings,
and the noise of the trumpet, and the mountain smoking;
and when the people saw it, they removed, and stood afar off.
19And they said unto Moses, 'Speak thou with us, and we will
hear, but let not God speak with us, lest we die.' 20And Moses
said unto the people, 'Fear not, for God is come to prove
you, and that his fear may be before your faces, that ye sin
not.' 21And the people stood afar off, and Moses drew near
unto the thick darkness where God was.

22And the Lord said unto Moses, 'Thus thou shalt say unto
the children of Israel, "Ye have seen that I have talked with
you from heaven. 23Ye shall not make with me gods of silver, neither shall ye make unto you gods of gold.

24'"An altar of earth thou shalt make unto me, and shalt
sacrifice thereon thy burnt offerings, and thy peace offerings,
thy sheep, and thine oxen. In all places where I record my
name I will come unto thee, and I will bless thee. 25And if
thou wilt make me an altar of stone, thou shalt not build it of
hewn stone, for if thou lift up thy tool upon it, thou hast polluted it. 26Neither shalt thou go up by steps unto mine altar,
that thy nakedness be not discovered thereon."

21 'Now these are the judgments which thou shalt set
before them. 2"If thou buy an Hebrew servant, six
years he shall serve, and in the seventh he shall go out free

for nothing. 3 If he came in by himself, he shall go out by
himself; if he were married, then his wife shall go out with
him. 4 If his master have given him a wife, and she have born
him sons or daughters, the wife and her children shall be her
master's, and he shall go out by himself. 5 And if the servant
shall plainly say, 'I love my master, my wife, and my children, I will not go out free': 6 then his master shall bring him
unto the judges; he shall also bring him to the door, or unto
the door post; and his master shall bore his ear through with
an aul; and he shall serve him for ever.

7 '"And if a man sell his daughter to be a maidservant,
she shall not go out as the menservants do. 8 If she please not
her master, who hath betrothed her to himself, then shall he
let her be redeemed; to sell her unto a strange nation he shall
have no power, seeing he hath dealt deceitfully with her.
9 And if he have betrothed her unto his son, he shall deal with
her after the manner of daughters. 10 If he take him another
wife; her food, her raiment, and her duty of marriage, shall
he not diminish. 11 And if he do not these three unto her, then
shall she go out free without money.

12 '"He that smiteth a man, so that he die, shall be surely
put to death. 13 And if a man lie not in wait, but God deliver
him into his hand, then I will appoint thee a place whither
he shall flee. 14 But if a man come presumptuously upon his
neighbour, to slay him with guile, thou shalt take him from
mine altar, that he may die.

15 '"And he that smiteth his father, or his mother, shall be
surely put to death.

16 '"And he that stealeth a man, and selleth him, or if he
be found in his hand, he shall surely be put to death.
17 '"And he that curseth his father, or his mother, shall
surely be put to death.
18 '"And if men strive together, and one smite another with
a stone, or with his fist, and he die not, but keepeth his bed,
19 if he rise again, and walk abroad upon his staff, then shall
he that smote him be quit; only he shall pay for the loss of
his time, and shall cause him to be thoroughly healed.
20 '"And if a man smite his servant, or his maid, with a
rod, and he die under his hand, he shall be surely punished.
21 Notwithstanding, if he continue a day or two, he shall not
be punished, for he is his money.
22 '"If men strive, and hurt a woman with child, so that her
fruit depart from her, and yet no mischief follow, he shall be
surely punished, according as the woman's husband will lay
upon him; and he shall pay as the judges determine. 23 And if
any mischief follow, then thou shalt give life for life, 24 eye
for eye, tooth for tooth, hand for hand, foot for foot, 25 burning for burning, wound for wound, stripe for stripe.
26 '"And if a man smite the eye of his servant, or the eye
of his maid, that it perish, he shall let him go free for his eye's
sake. 27 And if he smite out his manservant's tooth, or his maidservant's tooth; he shall let him go free for his tooth's sake.
28 '"If an ox gore a man or a woman, that they die, then the
ox shall be surely stoned, and his flesh shall not be eaten; but
the owner of the ox shall be quit. 29 But if the ox were wont to
push with his horn in time past, and it hath been testified to

his owner, and he hath not kept him in, but that he hath
killed a man or a woman; the ox shall be stoned, and his
owner also shall be put to death. [30] If there be laid on him a
sum of money, then he shall give for the ransom of his life
whatsoever is laid upon him. [31] Whether he have gored a
son, or have gored a daughter, according to this judgment
shall it be done unto him. [32] If the ox shall push a manservant
or a maidservant, he shall give unto their master thirty shekels of silver, and the ox shall be stoned.

[33] '"And if a man shall open a pit, or if a man shall dig a
pit, and not cover it, and an ox or an ass fall therein, [34] the
owner of the pit shall make it good, and give money unto
the owner of them; and the dead beast shall be his.

[35] '"And if one man's ox hurt another's, that he die, then they
shall sell the live ox, and divide the money of it; and the dead
ox also they shall divide. [36] Or if it be known that the ox hath
used to push in time past, and his owner hath not kept him
in, he shall surely pay ox for ox; and the dead shall be his own.

22 '"If a man shall steal an ox, or a sheep, and kill it, or
sell it, he shall restore five oxen for an ox, and four
sheep for a sheep.

[2] '"If a thief be found breaking up, and be smitten that he
die, there shall no blood be shed for him. [3] If the sun be risen
upon him, there shall be blood shed for him; for he should
make full restitution. If he have nothing, then he shall be sold
for his theft. [4] If the theft be certainly found in his hand alive,
whether it be ox, or ass, or sheep, he shall restore double.

5 '"If a man shall cause a field or vineyard to be eaten, and
shall put in his beast, and shall feed in another man's field,
of the best of his own field, and of the best of his own vineyard, shall he make restitution.

6 '"If fire break out, and catch in thorns, so that the stacks
of corn, or the standing corn, or the field, be consumed therewith, he that kindled the fire shall surely make restitution.

7 '"If a man shall deliver unto his neighbour money or
stuff to keep, and it be stolen out of the man's house, if the
thief be found, let him pay double. 8 If the thief be not found,
then the master of the house shall be brought unto the
judges, to see whether he have put his hand unto his neighbour's goods. 9 For all manner of trespass, whether it be for
ox, for ass, for sheep, for raiment, or for any manner of lost
thing, which another challengeth to be his, the cause of both
parties shall come before the judges; and whom the judges
shall condemn, he shall pay double unto his neighbour. 10 If a
man deliver unto his neighbour an ass, or an ox, or a sheep,
or any beast, to keep, and it die, or be hurt, or driven away,
no man seeing it, 11 then shall an oath of the Lord be between
them both, that he hath not put his hand unto his neighbour's goods, and the owner of it shall accept thereof, and he
shall not make it good. 12 And if it be stolen from him, he shall
make restitution unto the owner thereof. 13 If it be torn in
pieces, then let him bring it for witness, and he shall not make
good that which was torn.

14 '"And if a man borrow ought of his neighbour, and it be
hurt, or die, the owner thereof being not with it, he shall surely

make it good. 15 But if the owner thereof be with it, he shall
not make it good: if it be an hired thing, it came for his hire.

16 '"And if a man entice a maid that is not betrothed, and
lie with her, he shall surely endow her to be his wife. 17 If her
father utterly refuse to give her unto him, he shall pay money
according to the dowry of virgins.

18 '"Thou shalt not suffer a witch to live. 19 Whosoever lieth
with a beast shall surely be put to death.

20 '"He that sacrificeth unto any god, save unto the Lord
only, he shall be utterly destroyed.

21 '"Thou shalt neither vex a stranger, nor oppress him,
for ye were strangers in the land of Egypt.

22 '"Ye shall not afflict any widow, or fatherless child. 23 If
thou afflict them in any wise, and they cry at all unto me, I
will surely hear their cry, 24 and my wrath shall wax hot, and
I will kill you with the sword; and your wives shall be widows, and your children fatherless.

25 '"If thou lend money to any of my people that is poor by
thee, thou shalt not be to him as an usurer, neither shalt thou
lay upon him usury. 26 If thou at all take thy neighbour's raiment
to pledge, thou shalt deliver it unto him by that the sun goeth
down, 27 For that is his covering only, it is his raiment for his
skin. Wherein shall he sleep? And it shall come to pass, when
he crieth unto me, that I will hear, for I am gracious.

28 '"Thou shalt not revile the gods, nor curse the ruler of
thy people.

29 '"Thou shalt not delay to offer the first of thy ripe fruits,
and of thy liquors; the firstborn of thy sons shalt thou give

unto me. 30 Likewise shalt thou do with thine oxen, and with
thy sheep. Seven days it shall be with his dam; on the eighth
day thou shalt give it me.

31 '"And ye shall be holy men unto me. Neither shall ye
eat any flesh that is torn of beasts in the field; ye shall cast it
to the dogs.

23 '"Thou shalt not raise a false report; put not thine
hand with the wicked to be an unrighteous witness.
2 Thou shalt not follow a multitude to do evil; neither shalt thou
speak in a cause to decline after many to wrest judgment.
3 Neither shalt thou countenance a poor man in his cause.

4 '"If thou meet thine enemy's ox or his ass going astray,
thou shalt surely bring it back to him again. 5 If thou see the
ass of him that hateth thee lying under his burden, and
wouldest forbear to help him, thou shalt surely help with
him. 6 Thou shalt not wrest the judgment of thy poor in his
cause. 7 Keep thee far from a false matter; and the innocent
and righteous slay thou not, for I will not justify the wicked.

8 '"And thou shalt take no gift, for the gift blindeth the
wise, and perverteth the words of the righteous.

9 '"Also thou shalt not oppress a stranger, for ye know
the heart of a stranger, seeing ye were strangers in the land
of Egypt. 10 And six years thou shalt sow thy land, and shalt
gather in the fruits thereof, 11 but the seventh year thou shalt
let it rest and lie still, that the poor of thy people may eat,
and what they leave the beasts of the field shall eat. In like
manner thou shalt deal with thy vineyard, and with thy olive-

yard. 12 Six days thou shalt do thy work, and on the seventh day thou shalt rest, that thine ox and thine ass may rest, and the son of thy handmaid, and the stranger, may be refreshed. 13 And in all things that I have said unto you be circumspect, and make no mention of the name of other gods, neither let it be heard out of thy mouth.

14 '"Three times thou shalt keep a feast unto me in the year. 15 Thou shalt keep the feast of unleavened bread (thou shalt eat unleavened bread seven days, as I commanded thee, in the time appointed of the month Abib, for in it thou camest out from Egypt, and none shall appear before me empty); 16 and the feast of harvest, the firstfruits of thy labours, which thou hast sown in the field; and the feast of ingathering, which is in the end of the year, when thou hast gathered in thy labours out of the field. 17 Three times in the year all thy males shall appear before the Lord God. 18 Thou shalt not offer the blood of my sacrifice with leavened bread; neither shall the fat of my sacrifice remain until the morning. 19 The first of the first-fruits of thy land thou shalt bring into the house of the Lord thy God. Thou shalt not seethe a kid in his mother's milk.

20 '"Behold, I send an Angel before thee, to keep thee in the way, and to bring thee into the place which I have prepared. 21 Beware of him, and obey his voice; provoke him not, for he will not pardon your transgressions, for my name is in him. 22 But if thou shalt indeed obey his voice, and do all that I speak, then I will be an enemy unto thine enemies, and an adversary unto thine adversaries. 23 For mine Angel shall go before thee, and bring thee in unto the Amorites, and the

Hittites, and the Perizzites, and the Canaanites, the Hivites,
and the Jebusites; and I will cut them off. 24 Thou shalt not
bow down to their gods, nor serve them, nor do after their
works; but thou shalt utterly overthrow them, and quite break
down their images. 25 And ye shall serve the Lord your God,
and he shall bless thy bread, and thy water; and I will take
sickness away from the midst of thee.

26 '"There shall nothing cast their young, nor be barren, in
thy land; the number of thy days I will fulfil. 27 I will send
my fear before thee, and will destroy all the people to whom
thou shalt come, and I will make all thine enemies turn their
backs unto thee. 28 And I will send hornets before thee, which
shall drive out the Hivite, the Canaanite, and the Hittite,
from before thee. 29 I will not drive them out from before thee
in one year, lest the land become desolate, and the beast of
the field multiply against thee. 30 By little and little I will drive
them out from before thee, until thou be increased, and
inherit the land. 31 And I will set thy bounds from the Red sea
even unto the sea of the Philistines, and from the desert unto
the river, for I will deliver the inhabitants of the land into
your hand; and thou shalt drive them out before thee. 32 Thou
shalt make no covenant with them, nor with their gods.
33 They shall not dwell in thy land, lest they make thee sin
against me, for if thou serve their gods, it will surely be a
snare unto thee."'

24 And he said unto Moses, 'Come up unto the Lord,
thou, and Aaron, Nadab, and Abihu, and seventy of

the elders of Israel; and worship ye afar off. [2]And Moses alone shall come near the Lord, but they shall not come nigh; neither shall the people go up with him.'

[3]And Moses came and told the people all the words of the Lord, and all the judgments; and all the people answered with one voice, and said, 'All the words which the Lord hath said will we do.' [4]And Moses wrote all the words of the Lord, and rose up early in the morning, and builded an altar under the hill, and twelve pillars, according to the twelve tribes of Israel. [5]And he sent young men of the children of Israel, which offered burnt offerings, and sacrificed peace offerings of oxen unto the Lord. [6]And Moses took half of the blood, and put it in basons; and half of the blood he sprinkled on the altar. [7]And he took the book of the covenant, and read in the audience of the people; and they said, 'All that the Lord hath said will we do, and be obedient.' [8]And Moses took the blood, and sprinkled it on the people, and said, 'Behold the blood of the covenant, which the Lord hath made with you concerning all these words.'

[9]Then went up Moses, and Aaron, Nadab, and Abihu, and seventy of the elders of Israel. [10]And they saw the God of Israel. And there was under his feet as it were a paved work of a sapphire stone, and as it were the body of heaven in his clearness. [11]And upon the nobles of the children of Israel he laid not his hand; also they saw God, and did eat and drink.

[12]And the Lord said unto Moses, 'Come up to me into the mount, and be there, and I will give thee tables of stone, and a law, and commandments which I have written, that thou

mayest teach them.' [13]And Moses rose up, and his minister Joshua, and Moses went up into the mount of God. [14]And he said unto the elders, 'Tarry ye here for us, until we come again unto you, and, behold, Aaron and Hur are with you. If any man have any matters to do, let him come unto them.' [15]And Moses went up into the mount, and a cloud covered the mount. [16]And the glory of the Lord abode upon mount Sinai, and the cloud covered it six days; and the seventh day he called unto Moses out of the midst of the cloud. [17]And the sight of the glory of the Lord was like devouring fire on the top of the mount in the eyes of the children of Israel. [18]And Moses went into the midst of the cloud, and gat him up into the mount; and Moses was in the mount forty days and forty nights.

25 And the Lord spake unto Moses, saying, [2]'Speak unto the children of Israel, that they bring me an offering; of every man that giveth it willingly with his heart ye shall take my offering. [3]And this is the offering which ye shall take of them: gold, and silver, and brass, [4]and blue, and purple, and scarlet, and fine linen, and goats' hair, [5]and rams' skins dyed red, and badgers' skins, and shittim wood, [6]oil for the light, spices for anointing oil, and for sweet incense, [7]onyx stones, and stones to be set in the ephod, and in the breastplate. [8]And let them make me a sanctuary, that I may dwell among them. [9]According to all that I shew thee, after the pattern of the tabernacle, and the pattern of all the instruments thereof, even so shall ye make it.

[10]'And they shall make an ark of shittim wood: two cubits

and a half shall be the length thereof, and a cubit and a half
the breadth thereof, and a cubit and a half the height thereof.
11 And thou shalt overlay it with pure gold, within and without shalt thou overlay it, and shalt make upon it a crown of
gold round about. 12 And thou shalt cast four rings of gold for
it, and put them in the four corners thereof; and two rings
shall be in the one side of it, and two rings in the other side
of it. 13 And thou shalt make staves of shittim wood, and overlay them with gold. 14 And thou shalt put the staves into the
rings by the sides of the ark, that the ark may be borne with
them. 15 The staves shall be in the rings of the ark; they shall
not be taken from it. 16 And thou shalt put into the ark the testimony which I shall give thee. 17 And thou shalt make a mercy
seat of pure gold; two cubits and a half shall be the length
thereof, and a cubit and a half the breadth thereof. 18 And thou
shalt make two cherubims of gold, of beaten work shalt thou
make them, in the two ends of the mercy seat. 19 And make
one cherub on the one end, and the other cherub on the other
end; even of the mercy seat shall ye make the cherubims on
the two ends thereof. 20 And the cherubims shall stretch forth
their wings on high, covering the mercy seat with their
wings, and their faces shall look one to another; toward the
mercy seat shall the faces of the cherubims be. 21 And thou
shalt put the mercy seat above upon the ark; and in the ark
thou shalt put the testimony that I shall give thee. 22 And
there I will meet with thee, and I will commune with thee
from above the mercy seat, from between the two cherubims
which are upon the ark of the testimony, of all things which I

will give thee in commandment unto the children of Israel.
[23] 'Thou shalt also make a table of shittim wood; two cubits
shall be the length thereof, and a cubit the breadth thereof,
and a cubit and a half the height thereof. [24]And thou shalt
overlay it with pure gold, and make thereto a crown of gold
round about. [25]And thou shalt make unto it a border of an
hand breadth round about, and thou shalt make a golden
crown to the border thereof round about. [26]And thou shalt
make for it four rings of gold, and put the rings in the four
corners that are on the four feet thereof. [27]Over against the
border shall the rings be for places of the staves to bear the
table. [28]And thou shalt make the staves of shittim wood, and
overlay them with gold, that the table may be borne with
them. [29]And thou shalt make the dishes thereof, and spoons
thereof, and covers thereof, and bowls thereof, to cover withal;
of pure gold shalt thou make them. [30]And thou shalt set upon
the table shewbread before me alway.
[31] 'And thou shalt make a candlestick of pure gold; of
beaten work shall the candlestick be made. His shaft, and his
branches, his bowls, his knops, and his flowers, shall be of
the same. [32]And six branches shall come out of the sides of it;
three branches of the candlestick out of the one side, and
three branches of the candlestick out of the other side; [33] three
bowls made like unto almonds, with a knop and a flower in
one branch; and three bowls made like almonds in the other
branch, with a knop and a flower; so in the six branches that
come out of the candlestick. [34]And in the candlestick shall be
four bowls made like unto almonds, with their knops and

their flowers. 35 And there shall be a knop under two branches of the same, and a knop under two branches of the same, and a knop under two branches of the same, according to the six branches that proceed out of the candlestick. 36 Their knops and their branches shall be of the same; all it shall be one beaten work of pure gold. 37 And thou shalt make the seven lamps thereof, and they shall light the lamps thereof, that they may give light over against it. 38 And the tongs thereof, and the snuffdishes thereof, shall be of pure gold. 39 Of a talent of pure gold shall he make it, with all these vessels. 40 And look that thou make them after their pattern, which was shewed thee in the mount.

26 'Moreover thou shalt make the tabernacle with ten curtains of fine twined linen, and blue, and purple, and scarlet; with cherubims of cunning work shalt thou make them. 2 The length of one curtain shall be eight and twenty cubits, and the breadth of one curtain four cubits, and every one of the curtains shall have one measure. 3 The five curtains shall be coupled together one to another; and other five curtains shall be coupled one to another. 4 And thou shalt make loops of blue upon the edge of the one curtain from the selvedge in the coupling; and likewise shalt thou make in the uttermost edge of another curtain, in the coupling of the second. 5 Fifty loops shalt thou make in the one curtain, and fifty loops shalt thou make in the edge of the curtain that is in the coupling of the second; that the loops may take hold one of another. 6 And thou shalt make fifty taches of

gold, and couple the curtains together with the taches, and it
shall be one tabernacle.
7 'And thou shalt make curtains of goats' hair to be a
covering upon the tabernacle; eleven curtains shalt thou
make. 8 The length of one curtain shall be thirty cubits, and
the breadth of one curtain four cubits; and the eleven curtains shall be all of one measure. 9 And thou shalt couple five
curtains by themselves, and six curtains by themselves, and
shalt double the sixth curtain in the forefront of the tabernacle. 10 And thou shalt make fifty loops on the edge of the one
curtain that is outmost in the coupling, and fifty loops in the
edge of the curtain which coupleth the second. 11 And thou
shalt make fifty taches of brass, and put the taches into the
loops, and couple the tent together, that it may be one. 12 And
the remnant that remaineth of the curtains of the tent, the
half curtain that remaineth, shall hang over the backside of
the tabernacle. 13 And a cubit on the one side, and a cubit on
the other side of that which remaineth in the length of the
curtains of the tent, it shall hang over the sides of the tabernacle on this side and on that side, to cover it. 14 And thou
shalt make a covering for the tent of rams' skins dyed red,
and a covering above of badgers' skins.
15 'And thou shalt make boards for the tabernacle of shittim wood standing up. 16 Ten cubits shall be the length of a
board, and a cubit and a half shall be the breadth of one board.
17 Two tenons shall there be in one board, set in order one
against another: thus shalt thou make for all the boards of
the tabernacle. 18 And thou shalt make the boards for the

tabernacle, twenty boards on the south side southward.
19And thou shalt make forty sockets of silver under the
twenty boards; two sockets under one board for his two
tenons, and two sockets under another board for his two
tenons. 20And for the second side of the tabernacle on the
north side there shall be twenty boards; 21and their forty
sockets of silver; two sockets under one board, and two
sockets under another board. 22And for the sides of the tabernacle westward thou shalt make six boards. 23And two
boards shalt thou make for the corners of the tabernacle in
the two sides. 24And they shall be coupled together beneath,
and they shall be coupled together above the head of it unto
one ring; thus shall it be for them both; they shall be for the
two corners. 25And they shall be eight boards, and their sockets of silver, sixteen sockets; two sockets under one board,
and two sockets under another board.

26'And thou shalt make bars of shittim wood; five for the
boards of the one side of the tabernacle, 27and five bars for
the boards of the other side of the tabernacle, and five bars
for the boards of the side of the tabernacle, for the two sides
westward. 28And the middle bar in the midst of the boards
shall reach from end to end. 29And thou shalt overlay the
boards with gold, and make their rings of gold for places for
the bars, and thou shalt overlay the bars with gold. 30And
thou shalt rear up the tabernacle according to the fashion
thereof which was shewed thee in the mount.

31'And thou shalt make a vail of blue, and purple, and scarlet, and fine twined linen of cunning work; with cherubims

shall it be made; 32 and thou shalt hang it upon four pillars of
shittim wood overlaid with gold. Their hooks shall be of gold,
upon the four sockets of silver.

33 'And thou shalt hang up the vail under the taches, that
thou mayest bring in thither within the vail the ark of the
testimony; and the vail shall divide unto you between the
holy place and the most holy. 34 And thou shalt put the mercy
seat upon the ark of the testimony in the most holy place.
35 And thou shalt set the table without the vail, and the candlestick over against the table on the side of the tabernacle
toward the south; and thou shalt put the table on the north
side. 36 And thou shalt make an hanging for the door of the
tent, of blue, and purple, and scarlet, and fine twined linen,
wrought with needlework. 37 And thou shalt make for the
hanging five pillars of shittim wood, and overlay them with
gold, and their hooks shall be of gold, and thou shalt cast
five sockets of brass for them.

27 'And thou shalt make an altar of shittim wood, five
cubits long, and five cubits broad; the altar shall be
foursquare, and the height thereof shall be three cubits. 2 And
thou shalt make the horns of it upon the four corners thereof;
his horns shall be of the same; and thou shalt overlay it with
brass. 3 And thou shalt make his pans to receive his ashes,
and his shovels, and his basons, and his fleshhooks, and his
firepans; all the vessels thereof thou shalt make of brass.
4 And thou shalt make for it a grate of network of brass; and
upon the net shalt thou make four brasen rings in the four

corners thereof. 5And thou shalt put it under the compass
of the altar beneath, that the net may be even to the midst of
the altar. 6And thou shalt make staves for the altar, staves of
shittim wood, and overlay them with brass. 7And the staves
shall be put into the rings, and the staves shall be upon the
two sides of the altar, to bear it. 8Hollow with boards shalt
thou make it; as it was shewed thee in the mount, so shall
they make it.

9'And thou shalt make the court of the tabernacle; for the
south side southward there shall be hangings for the court of
fine twined linen of an hundred cubits long for one side.
10And the twenty pillars thereof and their twenty sockets
shall be of brass; the hooks of the pillars and their fillets shall
be of silver. 11And likewise for the north side in length there
shall be hangings of an hundred cubits long, and his twenty
pillars and their twenty sockets of brass; the hooks of the pillars and their fillets of silver.

12'And for the breadth of the court on the west side shall
be hangings of fifty cubits; their pillars ten, and their sockets
ten. 13And the breadth of the court on the east side eastward
shall be fifty cubits. 14The hangings of one side of the gate
shall be fifteen cubits; their pillars three, and their sockets
three. 15And on the other side shall be hangings fifteen cubits:
their pillars three, and their sockets three.

16'And for the gate of the court shall be an hanging of
twenty cubits, of blue, and purple, and scarlet, and fine twined
linen, wrought with needlework; and their pillars shall be
four, and their sockets four. 17All the pillars round about the

court shall be filleted with silver; their hooks shall be of silver, and their sockets of brass.

[18] 'The length of the court shall be an hundred cubits, and the breadth fifty every where, and the height five cubits of fine twined linen, and their sockets of brass. [19] All the vessels of the tabernacle in all the service thereof, and all the pins thereof, and all the pins of the court, shall be of brass.

[20] 'And thou shalt command the children of Israel, that they bring thee pure oil olive beaten for the light, to cause the lamp to burn always. [21] In the tabernacle of the congregation without the vail, which is before the testimony, Aaron and his sons shall order it from evening to morning before the Lord; it shall be a statute for ever unto their generations on the behalf of the children of Israel.

28 'And take thou unto thee Aaron thy brother, and his sons with him, from among the children of Israel, that he may minister unto me in the priest's office, even Aaron, Nadab and Abihu, Eleazar and Ithamar, Aaron's sons. [2] And thou shalt make holy garments for Aaron thy brother for glory and for beauty. [3] And thou shalt speak unto all that are wise hearted, whom I have filled with the spirit of wisdom, that they may make Aaron's garments to consecrate him, that he may minister unto me in the priest's office. [4] And these are the garments which they shall make: a breastplate, and an ephod, and a robe, and a broidered coat, a mitre, and a girdle; and they shall make holy garments for Aaron thy brother, and his sons, that he may minister unto me in the priest's

office. 5And they shall take gold, and blue, and purple, and scarlet, and fine linen.

6'And they shall make the ephod of gold, of blue, and of purple, of scarlet, and fine twined linen, with cunning work. 7It shall have the two shoulderpieces thereof joined at the two edges thereof; and so it shall be joined together. 8And the curious girdle of the ephod, which is upon it, shall be of the same, according to the work thereof; even of gold, of blue, and purple, and scarlet, and fine twined linen. 9And thou shalt take two onyx stones, and grave on them the names of the children of Israel; 10six of their names on one stone, and the other six names of the rest on the other stone, according to their birth. 11With the work of an engraver in stone, like the engravings of a signet, shalt thou engrave the two stones with the names of the children of Israel; thou shalt make them to be set in ouches of gold. 12And thou shalt put the two stones upon the shoulders of the ephod for stones of memorial unto the children of Israel: and Aaron shall bear their names before the Lord upon his two shoulders for a memorial.

13'And thou shalt make ouches of gold, 14and two chains of pure gold at the ends; of wreathen work shalt thou make them, and fasten the wreathen chains to the ouches.

15'And thou shalt make the breastplate of judgment with cunning work; after the work of the ephod thou shalt make it; of gold, of blue, and of purple, and of scarlet, and of fine twined linen, shalt thou make it. 16Foursquare it shall be being doubled; a span shall be the length thereof, and a span shall be the breadth thereof. [17]And thou shalt set in it settings of stones, even four rows of stones. The first row shall be a sardius, a topaz, and a carbuncle; this shall be the first row. [18]And the second row shall be an emerald, a sapphire, and a diamond. [19]And the third row a ligure, an agate, and an amethyst. [20]And the fourth row a beryl, and an onyx, and a jasper; they shall be set in gold in their inclosings. [21]And the stones shall be with the names of the children of Israel, twelve, according to their names, like the engravings of a signet; every one with his name shall they be according to the twelve tribes.

[22]'And thou shalt make upon the breastplate chains at the ends of wreathen work of pure gold. [23]And thou shalt make upon the breastplate two rings of gold, and shalt put the two rings on the two ends of the breastplate. [24]And thou shalt put the two wreathen chains of gold in the two rings which are on the ends of the breastplate. [25]And the other two ends of the two wreathen chains thou shalt fasten in the two ouches, and put them on the shoulderpieces of the ephod before it.

[26]'And thou shalt make two rings of gold, and thou shalt put them upon the two ends of the breastplate in the border thereof, which is in the side of the ephod inward. [27]And two other rings of gold thou shalt make, and shalt put them on the two sides of the ephod underneath, toward the forepart thereof, over against the other coupling thereof, above the curious girdle of the ephod. [28]And they shall bind the breastplate by the rings thereof unto the rings of the ephod with a lace of blue, that it may be above the curious girdle of the

ephod, and that the breastplate be not loosed from the ephod.
29 And Aaron shall bear the names of the children of Israel in
the breastplate of judgment upon his heart, when he goeth in
unto the holy place, for a memorial before the Lord continually.

30 'And thou shalt put in the breast-plate of judgment the
Urim and the Thummim; and they shall be upon Aaron's
heart, when he goeth in before the Lord; and Aaron shall bear
the judgment of the children of Israel upon his heart before
the Lord continually.

31 'And thou shalt make the robe of the ephod all of blue.
32 And there shall be an hole in the top of it, in the midst thereof;
it shall have a binding of woven work round about the hole
of it, as it were the hole of an habergeon, that it be not rent.

33 'And beneath upon the hem of it thou shalt make pomegranates of blue, and of purple, and of scarlet, round about the
hem thereof; and bells of gold between them round about:
34 a golden bell and a pomegranate, a golden bell and a pomegranate, upon the hem of the robe round about. 35 And it shall
be upon Aaron to minister; and his sound shall be heard
when he goeth in unto the holy place before the Lord, and
when he cometh out, that he die not.

36 'And thou shalt make a plate of pure gold, and grave
upon it, like the engravings of a signet, "Holiness to the Lord"
37 and thou shalt put it on a blue lace, that it may be upon the
mitre; upon the forefront of the mitre it shall be. 38 And it
shall be upon Aaron's forehead, that Aaron may bear the iniquity of the holy things, which the children of Israel shall hallow in all their holy gifts; and it shall be always upon his

forehead, that they may be accepted before the Lord.
39 'And thou shalt embroider the coat of fine linen, and
thou shalt make the mitre of fine linen, and thou shalt make
the girdle of needlework.
40 'And for Aaron's sons thou shalt make coats, and thou
shalt make for them girdles, and bonnets shalt thou make
for them, for glory and for beauty. 41 And thou shalt put them
upon Aaron thy brother, and his sons with him; and shalt
anoint them, and consecrate them, and sanctify them, that
they may minister unto me in the priest's office. 42 And thou
shalt make them linen breeches to cover their nakedness;
from the loins even unto the thighs they shall reach. 43 And
they shall be upon Aaron, and upon his sons, when they come
in unto the tabernacle of the congregation, or when they come
near unto the altar to minister in the holy place; that they
bear not iniquity, and die; it shall be a statute for ever unto
him and his seed after him.

29 'And this is the thing that thou shalt do unto them to
hallow them, to minister unto me in the priest's
office: take one young bullock, and two rams without blemish, 2 and unleavened bread, and cakes unleavened tempered
with oil, and wafers unleavened anointed with oil; of
wheaten flour shalt thou make them. 3 And thou shalt put
them into one basket, and bring them in the basket, with the
bullock and the two rams. 4 And Aaron and his sons thou
shalt bring unto the door of the tabernacle of the congregation, and shalt wash them with water. 5 And thou shalt take

the garments, and put upon Aaron the coat, and the robe of
the ephod, and the ephod, and the breastplate, and gird him
with the curious girdle of the ephod. [6]And thou shalt put the
mitre upon his head, and put the holy crown upon the mitre.
[7]Then shalt thou take the anointing oil, and pour it upon his
head, and anoint him. [8]And thou shalt bring his sons, and
put coats upon them. [9]And thou shalt gird them with girdles, Aaron and his sons, and put the bonnets on them; and
the priest's office shall be theirs for a perpetual statute; and
thou shalt consecrate Aaron and his sons. [10]And thou shalt
cause a bullock to be brought before the tabernacle of the
congregation; and Aaron and his sons shall put their hands
upon the head of the bullock. [11]And thou shalt kill the bullock before the Lord, by the door of the tabernacle of the
congregation. [12]And thou shalt take of the blood of the bullock, and put it upon the horns of the altar with thy finger,
and pour all the blood beside the bottom of the altar. [13]And
thou shalt take all the fat that covereth the inwards, and the
caul that is above the liver, and the two kidneys, and the fat
that is upon them, and burn them upon the altar. [14]But the
flesh of the bullock, and his skin, and his dung, shalt thou
burn with fire without the camp; it is a sin offering.

[15]'Thou shalt also take one ram; and Aaron and his sons
shall put their hands upon the head of the ram. [16]And thou
shalt slay the ram, and thou shalt take his blood, and sprinkle it round about upon the altar. [17]And thou shalt cut the
ram in pieces, and wash the inwards of him, and his legs,
and put them unto his pieces, and unto his head. [18]And thou

shalt burn the whole ram upon the altar; it is a burnt offering unto the Lord; it is a sweet savour, an offering made by
fire unto the Lord.
19 'And thou shalt take the other ram; and Aaron and his
sons shall put their hands upon the head of the ram. 20 Then
shalt thou kill the ram, and take of his blood, and put it upon
the tip of the right ear of Aaron, and upon the tip of the right
ear of his sons, and upon the thumb of their right hand, and
upon the great toe of their right foot, and sprinkle the blood
upon the altar round about. 21 And thou shalt take of the
blood that is upon the altar, and of the anointing oil, and
sprinkle it upon Aaron, and upon his garments, and upon
his sons, and upon the garments of his sons with him; and
he shall be hallowed, and his garments, and his sons, and his
sons' garments with him. 22 Also thou shalt take of the ram
the fat and the rump, and the fat that covereth the inwards,
and the caul above the liver, and the two kidneys, and the
fat that is upon them, and the right shoulder; for it is a ram
of consecration. 23 And one loaf of bread, and one cake of oiled
bread, and one wafer out of the basket of the unleavened
bread that is before the Lord. 24 And thou shalt put all in the
hands of Aaron, and in the hands of his sons; and shalt wave
them for a wave offering before the Lord. 25 And thou shalt
receive them of their hands, and burn them upon the altar
for a burnt offering, for a sweet savour before the Lord; it is
an offering made by fire unto the Lord. 26 And thou shalt take
the breast of the ram of Aaron's consecration, and wave it for
a wave offering before the Lord, and it shall be thy part.

27 And thou shalt sanctify the breast of the wave offering, and
the shoulder of the heave offering, which is waved, and
which is heaved up, of the ram of the consecration, even of
that which is for Aaron, and of that which is for his sons.
28 And it shall be Aaron's and his sons' by a statute for ever
from the children of Israel, for it is an heave offering: and it
shall be an heave offering from the children of Israel of the
sacrifice of their peace offerings, even their heave offering
unto the Lord.

29 'And the holy garments of Aaron shall be his sons' after
him, to be anointed therein, and to be consecrated in them.
30 And that son that is priest in his stead shall put them on
seven days, when he cometh into the tabernacle of the congregation to minister in the holy place.

31 'And thou shalt take the ram of the consecration, and
seethe his flesh in the holy place. 32 And Aaron and his sons
shall eat the flesh of the ram, and the bread that is in the basket, by the door of the tabernacle of the congregation. 33 And
they shall eat those things wherewith the atonement was
made, to consecrate and to sanctify them; but a stranger shall
not eat thereof, because they are holy. 34 And if ought of the
flesh of the consecrations, or of the bread, remain unto the
morning, then thou shalt burn the remainder with fire; it
shall not be eaten, because it is holy. 35 And thus shalt thou
do unto Aaron, and to his sons, according to all things which
I have commanded thee; seven days shalt thou consecrate
them. 36 And thou shalt offer every day a bullock for a sin
offering for atonement; and thou shalt cleanse the altar, when

thou hast made an atonement for it, and thou shalt anoint it,
to sanctify it. [37] Seven days thou shalt make an atonement for
the altar, and sanctify it; and it shall be an altar most holy;
whatsoever toucheth the altar shall be holy.

[38] 'Now this is that which thou shalt offer upon the altar:
two lambs of the first year day by day continually. [39] The one
lamb thou shalt offer in the morning; and the other lamb
thou shalt offer at even. [40] And with the one lamb a tenth deal
of flour mingled with the fourth part of an hin of beaten oil;
and the fourth part of an hin of wine for a drink offering.
[41] And the other lamb thou shalt offer at even, and shalt do
thereto according to the meat offering of the morning, and
according to the drink offering thereof, for a sweet savour,
an offering made by fire unto the Lord. [42] This shall be a continual burnt offering throughout your generations at the door
of the tabernacle of the congregation before the Lord, where
I will meet you, to speak there unto thee. [43] And there I will
meet with the children of Israel, and the tabernacle shall be
sanctified by my glory. [44] And I will sanctify the tabernacle of
the congregation, and the altar. I will sanctify also both Aaron
and his sons, to minister to me in the priest's office.

[45] 'And I will dwell among the children of Israel, and will
be their God. [46] And they shall know that I am the Lord their
God, that brought them forth out of the land of Egypt, that I
may dwell among them. I am the Lord their God.

30 'And thou shalt make an altar to burn incense upon;
of shittim wood shalt thou make it. [2] A cubit shall be

the length thereof, and a cubit the breadth thereof; foursquare shall it be. And two cubits shall be the height thereof;
the horns thereof shall be of the same. 3And thou shalt overlay it with pure gold, the top thereof, and the sides thereof
round about, and the horns thereof; and thou shalt make
unto it a crown of gold round about. 4And two golden rings
shalt thou make to it under the crown of it, by the two corners thereof, upon the two sides of it shalt thou make it; and
they shall be for places for the staves to bear it withal. 5And
thou shalt make the staves of shittim wood, and overlay
them with gold. 6And thou shalt put it before the vail that is
by the ark of the testimony, before the mercy seat that is over
the testimony, where I will meet with thee. 7And Aaron shall
burn thereon sweet incense every morning. When he dres-
seth the lamps, he shall burn incense upon it. 8And when
Aaron lighteth the lamps at even, he shall burn incense upon
it, a perpetual incense before the Lord throughout your generations. 9Ye shall offer no strange incense thereon, nor
burnt sacrifice, nor meat offering; neither shall ye pour drink
offering thereon. 10And Aaron shall make an atonement upon
the horns of it once in a year with the blood of the sin offering of atonements. Once in the year shall he make atonement upon it throughout your generations. It is most holy
unto the Lord.'

11And the Lord spake unto Moses, saying, 12'When thou
takest the sum of the children of Israel after their number,
then shall they give every man a ransom for his soul unto
the Lord, when thou numberest them; that there be no

plague among them, when thou numberest them. [13] This they
shall give, every one that passeth among them that are numbered, half a shekel after the shekel of the sanctuary (a shekel is twenty gerahs); an half shekel shall be the offering
of the Lord. [14] Every one that passeth among them that are
numbered, from twenty years old and above, shall give an
offering unto the Lord. [15] The rich shall not give more, and
the poor shall not give less than half a shekel, when they give an offering unto the Lord, to make an atonement for
your souls. [16] And thou shalt take the atonement money of
the children of Israel, and shalt appoint it for the service of the tabernacle of the congregation; that it may be a memorial unto the children of Israel before the Lord, to make an atonement for your souls.'

[17] And the Lord spake unto Moses, saying, [18] 'Thou shalt
also make a laver of brass, and his foot also of brass, to wash withal; and thou shalt put it between the tabernacle of the congregation and the altar, and thou shalt put water therein.
[19] For Aaron and his sons shall wash their hands and their
feet thereat. [20] When they go into the tabernacle of the congregation, they shall wash with water, that they die not; or when they come near to the altar to minister, to burn offering made by fire unto the Lord; [21] so they shall wash their
hands and their feet, that they die not; and it shall be a statute for ever to them, even to him and to his seed throughout their generations.'

[22] Moreover the Lord spake unto Moses, saying, [23] 'Take thou
also unto thee principal spices, of pure myrrh five hundred

shekels, and of sweet cinnamon half so much, even two hundred and fifty shekels, and of sweet calamus two hundred and fifty shekels, 24 and of cassia five hundred shekels, after the shekel of the sanctuary, and of oil olive an hin; 25 and thou shalt make it an oil of holy ointment, an ointment compound after the art of the apothecary; it shall be an holy anointing oil. 26 And thou shalt anoint the tabernacle of the congregation therewith, and the ark of the testimony, 27 and the table and all his vessels, and the candlestick and his vessels, and the altar of incense, 28 and the altar of burnt offering with all his vessels, and the laver and his foot. 29 And thou shalt sanctify them, that they may be most holy; whatsoever toucheth them shall be holy. 30 And thou shalt anoint Aaron and his sons, and consecrate them, that they may minister unto me in the priest's office. 31 And thou shalt speak unto the children of Israel, saying, "This shall be an holy anointing oil unto me throughout your generations. 32 Upon man's flesh shall it not be poured, neither shall ye make any other like it, after the composition of it; it is holy, and it shall be holy unto you. 33 Whosoever compoundeth any like it, or whosoever putteth any of it upon a stranger, shall even be cut off from his people."'

34 And the Lord said unto Moses, 'Take unto thee sweet spices, stacte, and onycha, and galbanum. These sweet spices with pure frankincense; of each shall there be a like weight, 35 and thou shalt make it a perfume, a confection after the art of the apothecary, tempered together, pure and holy. 36 And thou shalt beat some of it very small, and put of it before the

testimony in the tabernacle of the congregation, where I will meet with thee; it shall be unto you most holy. 37 And as for the perfume which thou shalt make, ye shall not make to yourselves according to the composition thereof; it shall be unto thee holy for the Lord. 38 Whosoever shall make like unto that, to smell thereto, shall even be cut off from his people.'

31 And the Lord spake unto Moses, saying, 2 'See, I have called by name Bezaleel the son of Uri, the son of Hur, of the tribe of Judah: 3 And I have filled him with the spirit of God, in wisdom, and in understanding, and in knowledge, and in all manner of workmanship, 4 to devise cunning works, to work in gold, and in silver, and in brass, 5 and in cutting of stones, to set them, and in carving of timber, to work in all manner of workmanship. 6 And I, behold, I have given with him Aholiab, the son of Ahisamach, of the tribe of Dan; and in the hearts of all that are wise hearted I have put wisdom, that they may make all that I have commanded thee: 7 the tabernacle of the congregation, and the ark of the testimony, and the mercy seat that is thereupon, and all the furniture of the tabernacle, 8 and the table and his furniture, and the pure candlestick with all his furniture, and the altar of incense, 9 and the altar of burnt offering with all his furniture, and the laver and his foot, 10 and the cloths of service, and the holy garments for Aaron the priest, and the garments of his sons, to minister in the priest's office, 11 and the anointing oil, and sweet incense for the holy place; according to all that I have commanded thee shall they do.'

[12]And the Lord spake unto Moses, saying, [13]'Speak thou also unto the children of Israel, saying, "Verily my sabbaths ye shall keep, for it is a sign between me and you throughout your generations; that ye may know that I am the Lord that doth sanctify you. [14]Ye shall keep the sabbath therefore; for it is holy unto you; every one that defileth it shall surely be put to death, for whosoever doeth any work therein, that soul shall be cut off from among his people. [15]Six days may work be done; but in the seventh is the sabbath of rest, holy to the Lord; whosoever doeth any work in the sabbath day, he shall surely be put to death. [16]Wherefore the children of Israel shall keep the sabbath, to observe the sabbath throughout their generations, for a perpetual covenant. [17]It is a sign between me and the children of Israel for ever, for in six days the Lord made heaven and earth, and on the seventh day he rested, and was refreshed."'

[18]And he gave unto Moses, when he had made an end of communing with him upon mount Sinai, two tables of testimony, tables of stone, written with the finger of God.

32 And when the people saw that Moses delayed to come down out of the mount, the people gathered themselves together unto Aaron, and said unto him, 'Up, make us gods, which shall go before us; for as for this Moses, the man that brought us up out of the land of Egypt, we wot not what is become of him.' [2]And Aaron said unto them, 'Break off the golden earrings, which are in the ears of your wives, of your sons, and of your daughters, and bring them unto me.' [3]And

all the people brake off the golden earrings which were in
their ears, and brought them unto Aaron. 4 And he received
them at their hand, and fashioned it with a graving tool, after
he had made it a molten calf, and they said, 'These be thy
gods, O Israel, which brought thee up out of the land of
Egypt.' 5 And when Aaron saw it, he built an altar before it;
and Aaron made proclamation, and said, 'To morrow is a feast
to the Lord.' 6 And they rose up early on the morrow, and
offered burnt offerings, and brought peace offerings; and
the people sat down to eat and to drink, and rose up to play.

7 And the Lord said unto Moses, 'Go, get thee down; for
thy people, which thou broughtest out of the land of Egypt,
have corrupted themselves. 8 They have turned aside quickly
out of the way which I commanded them: they have made
them a molten calf, and have worshipped it, and have sacrificed thereunto, and said, "These be thy gods, O Israel, which
have brought thee up out of the land of Egypt."' 9 And the
Lord said unto Moses, 'I have seen this people, and, behold,
it is a stiffnecked people. 10 Now therefore let me alone, that
my wrath may wax hot against them, and that I may consume
them, and I will make of thee a great nation.' 11 And Moses
besought the Lord his God, and said, 'Lord, why doth thy
wrath wax hot against thy people, which thou hast brought
forth out of the land of Egypt with great power, and with a
mighty hand? 12 Wherefore should the Egyptians speak, and
say, "For mischief did he bring them out, to slay them in the
mountains, and to consume them from the face of the earth?"
Turn from thy fierce wrath, and repent of this evil against

thy people. 13 Remember Abraham, Isaac, and Israel, thy servants, to whom thou swarest by thine own self, and saidst unto them, "I will multiply your seed as the stars of heaven, and all this land that I have spoken of will I give unto your seed, and they shall inherit it for ever."' 14 And the Lord repented of the evil which he thought to do unto his people.

15 And Moses turned, and went down from the mount, and the two tables of the testimony were in his hand. The tables were written on both their sides; on the one side and on the other were they written. 16 And the tables were the work of God, and the writing was the writing of God, graven upon the tables. 17 And when Joshua heard the noise of the people as they shouted, he said unto Moses, 'There is a noise of war in the camp.' 18 And he said, 'It is not the voice of them that shout for mastery, neither is it the voice of them that cry for being overcome, but the noise of them that sing do I hear.'

19 And it came to pass, as soon as he came nigh unto the camp, that he saw the calf, and the dancing; and Moses' anger waxed hot, and he cast the tables out of his hands, and brake them beneath the mount. 20 And he took the calf which they had made, and burnt it in the fire, and ground it to powder, and strawed it upon the water, and made the children of Israel drink of it. 21 And Moses said unto Aaron, 'What did this people unto thee, that thou hast brought so great a sin upon them?' 22 And Aaron said, 'Let not the anger of my lord wax hot; thou knowest the people, that they are set on mischief. 23 For they said unto me, "Make us gods, which shall go before us, for as for this Moses, the man that brought us

up out of the land of Egypt, we wot not what is become of him." 24And I said unto them, "Whosoever hath any gold, let them break it off." So they gave it me; then I cast it into the fire, and there came out this calf.'

25And when Moses saw that the people were naked (for Aaron had made them naked unto their shame among their enemies), 26then Moses stood in the gate of the camp, and said, 'Who is on the Lord's side? Let him come unto me.' And all the sons of Levi gathered themselves together unto him. 27And he said unto them, 'Thus saith the Lord God of Israel, "Put every man his sword by his side, and go in and out from gate to gate throughout the camp, and slay every man his brother, and every man his companion, and every man his neighbour."' 28And the children of Levi did according to the word of Moses, and there fell of the people that day about three thousand men. 29For Moses had said, 'Consecrate yourselves today to the Lord, even every man upon his son, and upon his brother, that he may bestow upon you a blessing this day.'

30And it came to pass on the morrow, that Moses said unto the people, 'Ye have sinned a great sin, and now I will go up unto the Lord; peradventure I shall make an atonement for your sin.' 31And Moses returned unto the Lord, and said, 'Oh, this people have sinned a great sin, and have made them gods of gold. 32Yet now, if thou wilt forgive their sin—; and if not, blot me, I pray thee, out of thy book which thou hast written.' 33And the Lord said unto Moses, 'Whosoever hath sinned against me, him will I blot out of my book.

34 Therefore now go, lead the people unto the place of which
I have spoken unto thee. Behold, mine Angel shall go before
thee; nevertheless in the day when I visit I will visit their sin
upon them.' 35 And the Lord plagued the people, because
they made the calf, which Aaron made.

33 And the Lord said unto Moses, 'Depart, and go up
hence, thou and the people which thou hast brought
up out of the land of Egypt, unto the land which I sware unto
Abraham, to Isaac, and to Jacob, saying, "Unto thy seed will I
give it." 2 And I will send an angel before thee; and I will drive
out the Canaanite, the Amorite, and the Hittite, and the Perizzite, the Hivite, and the Jebusite, 3 unto a land flowing with
milk and honey, for I will not go up in the midst of thee; for
thou art a stiffnecked people, lest I consume thee in the way.'

4 And when the people heard these evil tidings, they mourned, and no man did put on him his ornaments. 5 For the
Lord had said unto Moses, 'Say unto the children of Israel,
"Ye are a stiffnecked people. I will come up into the midst of
thee in a moment, and consume thee; therefore now put off
thy ornaments from thee, that I may know what to do unto
thee."' 6 And the children of Israel stripped themselves of their
ornaments by the mount Horeb. 7 And Moses took the tabernacle, and pitched it without the camp, afar off from the
camp, and called it the Tabernacle of the congregation. And
it came to pass, that every one which sought the Lord went
out unto the tabernacle of the congregation, which was without the camp. 8 And it came to pass, when Moses went out

unto the tabernacle, that all the people rose up, and stood
every man at his tent door, and looked after Moses, until he
was gone into the tabernacle. 9And it came to pass, as Moses
entered into the tabernacle, the cloudy pillar descended, and
stood at the door of the tabernacle, and the Lord talked with
Moses. 10And all the people saw the cloudy pillar stand at the
tabernacle door, and all the people rose up and worshipped,
every man in his tent door. 11And the Lord spake unto Moses
face to face, as a man speaketh unto his friend. And he turned
again into the camp, but his servant Joshua, the son of Nun,
a young man, departed not out of the tabernacle.

12And Moses said unto the Lord, 'See, thou sayest unto
me, "Bring up this people,' and thou hast not let me know
whom thou wilt send with me. Yet thou hast said, "I know
thee by name, and thou hast also found grace in my sight."
13Now therefore, I pray thee, if I have found grace in thy
sight, shew me now thy way, that I may know thee, that I may
find grace in thy sight; and consider that this nation is thy
people.' 14And he said, 'My presence shall go with thee, and I
will give thee rest.' 15And he said unto him, 'If thy presence
go not with me, carry us not up hence. 16For wherein shall it
be known here that I and thy people have found grace in thy
sight? Is it not in that thou goest with us? So shall we be separated, I and thy people, from all the people that are upon
the face of the earth.' 17And the Lord said unto Moses, 'I will
do this thing also that thou hast spoken, for thou hast found
grace in my sight, and I know thee by name.' 18And he said, 'I
beseech thee, shew me thy glory.' 19And he said, 'I will make

all my goodness pass before thee, and I will proclaim the
name of the Lord before thee; and will be gracious to whom
I will be gracious, and will shew mercy on whom I will shew
mercy.’ 20And he said, ‘Thou canst not see my face, for there
shall no man see me, and live.’ 21And the Lord said, ‘Behold,
there is a place by me, and thou shalt stand upon a rock. 22And
it shall come to pass, while my glory passeth by, that I will
put thee in a clift of the rock, and will cover thee with my
hand while I pass by. 23And I will take away mine hand, and
thou shalt see my back parts, but my face shall not be seen.’

34 And the Lord said unto Moses, ‘Hew thee two tables
of stone like unto the first, and I will write upon
these tables the words that were in the first tables, which
thou brakest. 2And be ready in the morning, and come up in
the morning unto mount Sinai, and present thyself there to
me in the top of the mount. 3And no man shall come up with
thee, neither let any man be seen throughout all the mount;
neither let the flocks nor herds feed before that mount.’

4And he hewed two tables of stone like unto the first; and
Moses rose up early in the morning, and went up unto mount
Sinai, as the Lord had commanded him, and took in his hand
the two tables of stone. 5And the Lord descended in the cloud,
and stood with him there, and proclaimed the name of the
Lord. 6And the Lord passed by before him, and proclaimed,
‘The Lord, The Lord God, merciful and gracious, long-suf-
fering, and abundant in goodness and truth, 7keeping mercy
for thousands, forgiving iniquity and transgression and sin,

and that will by no means clear the guilty, visiting the iniquity of the fathers upon the children, and upon the children's
children, unto the third and to the fourth generation.' 8And
Moses made haste, and bowed his head toward the earth, and
worshipped. 9And he said, 'If now I have found grace in thy
sight, O Lord, let my Lord, I pray thee, go among us; for it is
a stiffnecked people; and pardon our iniquity and our sin,
and take us for thine inheritance.'

10And he said, 'Behold, I make a covenant; before all thy
people I will do marvels, such as have not been done in all
the earth, nor in any nation; and all the people among which
thou art shall see the work of the Lord, for it is a terrible thing
that I will do with thee. 11Observe thou that which I command
thee this day; behold, I drive out before thee the Amorite,
and the Canaanite, and the Hittite, and the Perizzite, and the
Hivite, and the Jebusite. 12Take heed to thyself, lest thou make
a covenant with the inhabitants of the land whither thou
goest, lest it be for a snare in the midst of thee. 13But ye shall
destroy their altars, break their images, and cut down their
groves, 14for thou shalt worship no other god, for the Lord,
whose name is Jealous, is a jealous God, 15lest thou make a
covenant with the inhabitants of the land, and they go a whoring after their gods, and do sacrifice unto their gods, and one
call thee, and thou eat of his sacrifice; 16and thou take of their
daughters unto thy sons, and their daughters go a whoring
after their gods, and make thy sons go a whoring after their
gods. 17Thou shalt make thee no molten gods.

18'The feast of unleavened bread shalt thou keep. Seven

days thou shalt eat unleavened bread, as I commanded thee,
in the time of the month Abib, for in the month Abib thou
camest out from Egypt. 19 All that openeth the matrix is mine;
and every firstling among thy cattle, whether ox or sheep,
that is male. 20 But the firstling of an ass thou shalt redeem with
a lamb, and if thou redeem him not, then shalt thou break
his neck. All the firstborn of thy sons thou shalt redeem. And
none shall appear before me empty.

21 'Six days thou shalt work, but on the seventh day thou
shalt rest; in earing time and in harvest thou shalt rest.

22 'And thou shalt observe the feast of weeks, of the firstfruits of wheat harvest, and the feast of ingathering at the
year's end.

23 'Thrice in the year shall all your men children appear
before the Lord God, the God of Israel. 24 For I will cast out
the nations before thee, and enlarge thy borders; neither shall
any man desire thy land, when thou shalt go up to appear
before the Lord thy God thrice in the year. 25 Thou shalt not
offer the blood of my sacrifice with leaven; neither shall the
sacrifice of the feast of the passover be left unto the morning.
26 The first of the firstfruits of thy land thou shalt bring unto
the house of the Lord thy God. Thou shalt not seethe a kid in
his mother's milk.' 27 And the Lord said unto Moses, 'Write
thou these words, for after the tenor of these words I have
made a covenant with thee and with Israel.' 28 And he was
there with the Lord forty days and forty nights; he did neither eat bread, nor drink water. And he wrote upon the tables
the words of the covenant, the ten commandments.

[29]And it came to pass, when Moses came down from
mount Sinai with the two tables of testimony in Moses' hand,
when he came down from the mount, that Moses wist not
that the skin of his face shone while he talked with him. [30]And
when Aaron and all the children of Israel saw Moses, behold,
the skin of his face shone; and they were afraid to come nigh
him. [31]And Moses called unto them; and Aaron and all the
rulers of the congregation returned unto him; and Moses
talked with them. [32]And afterward all the children of Israel
came nigh; and he gave them in commandment all that the
Lord had spoken with him in mount Sinai. [33]And till Moses
had done speaking with them, he put a vail on his face. [34] But
when Moses went in before the Lord to speak with him, he
took the vail off, until he came out. And he came out, and
spake unto the children of Israel that which he was commanded. [35]And the children of Israel saw the face of Moses,
that the skin of Moses' face shone, and Moses put the vail
upon his face again, until he went in to speak with him.

35 And Moses gathered all the congregation of the children of Israel together, and said unto them, 'These
are the words which the Lord hath commanded, that ye
should do them. [2]"Six days shall work be done, but on the
seventh day there shall be to you an holy day, a sabbath of
rest to the Lord; whosoever doeth work therein shall be put
to death. [3] Ye shall kindle no fire throughout your habitations
upon the sabbath day."'

[4]And Moses spake unto all the congregation of the children

of Israel, saying, 'This is the thing which the Lord commanded, saying, [5] "Take ye from among you an offering unto
the Lord; whosoever is of a willing heart, let him bring it, an
offering of the Lord; gold, and silver, and brass, [6] and blue,
and purple, and scarlet, and fine linen, and goats' hair, [7] and
rams' skins dyed red, and badgers' skins, and shittim wood,
[8] and oil for the light, and spices for anointing oil, and for the
sweet incense, [9] and onyx stones, and stones to be set for the
ephod, and for the breastplate. [10] And every wise hearted among
you shall come, and make all that the Lord hath commanded:
[11] the tabernacle, his tent, and his covering, his taches, and his
boards, his bars, his pillars, and his sockets, [12] the ark, and the
staves thereof, with the mercy seat, and the vail of the covering, [13] the table, and his staves, and all his vessels, and the
shewbread, [14] the candlestick also for the light, and his furniture, and his lamps, with the oil for the light, [15] and the incense
altar, and his staves, and the anointing oil, and the sweet
incense, and the hanging for the door at the entering in of
the tabernacle, [16] the altar of burnt offering, with his brasen
grate, his staves, and all his vessels, the laver and his foot,
[17] the hangings of the court, his pillars, and their sockets, and
the hanging for the door of the court, [18] the pins of the tabernacle, and the pins of the court, and their cords, [19] the cloths
of service, to do service in the holy place, the holy garments
for Aaron the priest, and the garments of his sons, to minister in the priest's office."'

[20] And all the congregation of the children of Israel departed
from the presence of Moses. [21] And they came, every one

whose heart stirred him up, and every one whom his spirit
made willing, and they brought the Lord's offering to the
work of the tabernacle of the congregation, and for all his
service, and for the holy garments. 22 And they came, both men
and women, as many as were willing hearted, and brought
bracelets, and earrings, and rings, and tablets, all jewels of
gold; and every man that offered an offering of gold unto
the Lord. 23 And every man, with whom was found blue, and
purple, and scarlet, and fine linen, and goats' hair, and red
skins of rams, and badgers' skins, brought them. 24 Every one
that did offer an offering of silver and brass brought the
Lord's offering; and every man, with whom was found shittim wood for any work of the service, brought it. 25 And all
the women that were wise hearted did spin with their hands,
and brought that which they had spun, both of blue, and of
purple, and of scarlet, and of fine linen. 26 And all the women
whose heart stirred them up in wisdom spun goats' hair.
27 And the rulers brought onyx stones, and stones to be set,
for the ephod, and for the breastplate; 28 and spice, and oil for
the light, and for the anointing oil, and for the sweet incense.
29 The children of Israel brought a willing offering unto the
Lord, every man and woman, whose heart made them willing to bring for all manner of work, which the Lord had
commanded to be made by the hand of Moses.

30 And Moses said unto the children of Israel, 'See, the Lord
hath called by name Bezaleel the son of Uri, the son of Hur,
of the tribe of Judah; 31 and he hath filled him with the spirit
of God, in wisdom, in understanding, and in knowledge,

and in all manner of workmanship; 32 and to devise curious
works, to work in gold, and in silver, and in brass, 33 and in
the cutting of stones, to set them, and in carving of wood, to
make any manner of cunning work. 34 And he hath put in his
heart that he may teach, both he, and Aholiab, the son of
Ahisamach, of the tribe of Dan. 35 Them hath he filled with
wisdom of heart, to work all manner of work, of the engraver,
and of the cunning workman, and of the embroiderer, in
blue, and in purple, in scarlet, and in fine linen, and of the
weaver, even of them that do any work, and of those that
devise cunning work.'

36 Then wrought Bezaleel and Aholiab, and every wise
hearted man, in whom the Lord put wisdom and
understanding to know how to work all manner of work for
the service of the sanctuary, according to all that the Lord
had commanded. 2 And Moses called Bezaleel and Aholiab,
and every wise hearted man, in whose heart the Lord had
put wisdom, even every one whose heart stirred him up to
come unto the work to do it; 3 and they received of Moses all
the offering, which the children of Israel had brought for
the work of the service of the sanctuary, to make it withal.
And they brought yet unto him free offerings every morning. 4 And all the wise men, that wrought all the work of the
sanctuary, came every man from his work which they made;
5 and they spake unto Moses, saying, 'The people bring much
more than enough for the service of the work, which the
Lord commanded to make.' 6 And Moses gave commandment,

and they caused it to be proclaimed throughout the camp,
saying, 'Let neither man nor woman make any more work
for the offering of the sanctuary.' So the people were restrained from bringing. 7 For the stuff they had was sufficient
for all the work to make it, and too much.

8 And every wise hearted man among them that wrought
the work of the tabernacle made ten curtains of fine twined
linen, and blue, and purple, and scarlet; with cherubims of
cunning work made he them. 9 The length of one curtain was
twenty and eight cubits, and the breadth of one curtain four
cubits; the curtains were all of one size. 10 And he coupled the
five curtains one unto another, and the other five curtains he
coupled one unto another. 11 And he made loops of blue on
the edge of one curtain from the selvedge in the coupling;
likewise he made in the uttermost side of another curtain, in
the coupling of the second. 12 Fifty loops made he in one curtain, and fifty loops made he in the edge of the curtain which
was in the coupling of the second; the loops held one curtain
to another. 13 And he made fifty taches of gold, and coupled
the curtains one unto another with the taches; so it became
one tabernacle.

14 And he made curtains of goats' hair for the tent over the
tabernacle; eleven curtains he made them. 15 The length of one
curtain was thirty cubits, and four cubits was the breadth of
one curtain; the eleven curtains were of one size. 16 And he
coupled five curtains by themselves, and six curtains by themselves. 17 And he made fifty loops upon the uttermost edge of
the curtain in the coupling, and fifty loops made he upon the

edge of the curtain which coupleth the second. 18And he made
fifty taches of brass to couple the tent together, that it might
be one. 19And he made a covering for the tent of rams' skins
dyed red, and a covering of badgers' skins above that.

20And he made boards for the tabernacle of shittim wood,
standing up. 21The length of a board was ten cubits, and the
breadth of a board one cubit and a half. 22One board had two
tenons, equally distant one from another; thus did he make
for all the boards of the tabernacle. 23And he made boards for
the tabernacle; twenty boards for the south side southward.
24And forty sockets of silver he made under the twenty
boards; two sockets under one board for his two tenons, and
two sockets under another board for his two tenons. 25And
for the other side of the tabernacle, which is toward the north
corner, he made twenty boards, 26and their forty sockets of
silver; two sockets under one board, and two sockets under
another board. 27And for the sides of the tabernacle westward he made six boards. 28And two boards made he for the
corners of the tabernacle in the two sides. 29And they were
coupled beneath, and coupled together at the head thereof,
to one ring; thus he did to both of them in both the corners.
30And there were eight boards; and their sockets were sixteen sockets of silver, under every board two sockets.

31And he made bars of shittim wood; five for the boards
of the one side of the tabernacle, 32and five bars for the
boards of the other side of the tabernacle, and five bars for
the boards of the tabernacle for the sides westward. 33And he
made the middle bar to shoot through the boards from the

one end to the other. 34 And he overlaid the boards with gold,
and made their rings of gold to be places for the bars, and
overlaid the bars with gold.

35 And he made a vail of blue, and purple, and scarlet, and
fine twined linen; with cherubims made he it of cunning
work. 36 And he made thereunto four pillars of shittim wood,
and overlaid them with gold; their hooks were of gold; and
he cast for them four sockets of silver.

37 And he made an hanging for the tabernacle door of blue,
and purple, and scarlet, and fine twined linen, of needlework; 38 and the five pillars of it with their hooks; and he
overlaid their chapiters and their fillets with gold; but their
five sockets were of brass.

37 And Bezaleel made the ark of shittim wood; two
cubits and a half was the length of it, and a cubit and
a half the breadth of it, and a cubit and a half the height of it;
2 and he overlaid it with pure gold within and without, and
made a crown of gold to it round about. 3 And he cast for it
four rings of gold, to be set by the four corners of it; even
two rings upon the one side of it, and two rings upon the
other side of it. 4 And he made staves of shittim wood, and
overlaid them with gold. 5 And he put the staves into the
rings by the sides of the ark, to bear the ark.

6 And he made the mercy seat of pure gold; two cubits
and a half was the length thereof, and one cubit and a half
the breadth thereof. 7 And he made two cherubims of gold,
beaten out of one piece made he them, on the two ends of

the mercy seat; [8]one cherub on the end on this side, and
another cherub on the other end on that side; out of the
mercy seat made he the cherubims on the two ends thereof.
[9]And the cherubims spread out their wings on high, and
covered with their wings over the mercy seat, with their
faces one to another; even to the mercy seatward were the
faces of the cherubims.

[10]And he made the table of shittim wood; two cubits was
the length thereof, and a cubit the breadth thereof, and a
cubit and a half the height thereof. [11]And he overlaid it with
pure gold, and made thereunto a crown of gold round about.
[12]Also he made thereunto a border of an handbreadth round
about; and made a crown of gold for the border thereof
round about. [13]And he cast for it four rings of gold, and put
the rings upon the four corners that were in the four feet
thereof. [14]Over against the border were the rings, the places
for the staves to bear the table. [15]And he made the staves of
shittim wood, and overlaid them with gold, to bear the table.
[16]And he made the vessels which were upon the table, his
dishes, and his spoons, and his bowls, and his covers to
cover withal, of pure gold.

[17]And he made the candlestick of pure gold; of beaten
work made he the candlestick; his shaft, and his branch, his
bowls, his knops, and his flowers, were of the same; [18]and
six branches going out of the sides thereof; three branches of
the candlestick out of the one side thereof, and three branches
of the candlestick out of the other side thereof; [19]three bowls
made after the fashion of almonds in one branch, a knop and

a flower; and three bowls made like almonds in another
branch, a knop and a flower; so throughout the six branches
going out of the candlestick. 20And in the candlestick were
four bowls made like almonds, his knops, and his flowers;
21and a knop under two branches of the same, and a knop
under two branches of the same, and a knop under two branches of the same, according to the six branches going out of
it. 22Their knops and their branches were of the same; all of it
was one beaten work of pure gold. 23And he made his seven
lamps, and his snuffers, and his snuffdishes, of pure gold. 24Of
a talent of pure gold made he it, and all the vessels thereof.

25And he made the incense altar of shittim wood; the
length of it was a cubit, and the breadth of it a cubit; it was
foursquare; and two cubits was the height of it; the horns
thereof were of the same. 26And he overlaid it with pure gold,
both the top of it, and the sides thereof round about, and the
horns of it; also he made unto it a crown of gold round about.
27And he made two rings of gold for it under the crown
thereof, by the two corners of it, upon the two sides thereof,
to be places for the staves to bear it withal. 28And he made
the staves of shittim wood, and overlaid them with gold.

29And he made the holy anointing oil, and the pure incense
of sweet spices, according to the work of the apothecary.

38

And he made the altar of burnt offering of shittim
wood; five cubits was the length thereof, and five
cubits the breadth thereof; it was foursquare; and three cubits
the height thereof. 2And he made the horns thereof on the

four corners of it; the horns thereof were of the same; and he
overlaid it with brass. [3]And he made all the vessels of the
altar, the pots, and the shovels, and the basons, and the fleshhooks, and the firepans; all the vessels thereof made he of
brass. [4]And he made for the altar a brasen grate of network
under the compass thereof beneath unto the midst of it.
[5]And he cast four rings for the four ends of the grate of brass,
to be places for the staves. [6]And he made the staves of shittim wood, and overlaid them with brass. [7]And he put the
staves into the rings on the sides of the altar, to bear it withal;
he made the altar hollow with boards.

[8]And he made the laver of brass, and the foot of it of brass,
of the looking-glasses of the women assembling, which assembled at the door of the tabernacle of the congregation.

[9]And he made the court; on the south side southward the
hangings of the court were of fine twined linen, an hundred
cubits; [10]their pillars were twenty, and their brasen sockets
twenty; the hooks of the pillars and their fillets were of silver. [11]And for the north side the hangings were an hundred
cubits, their pillars were twenty, and their sockets of brass
twenty; the hooks of the pillars and their fillets of silver.
[12]And for the west side were hangings of fifty cubits, their
pillars ten, and their sockets ten; the hooks of the pillars and
their fillets of silver. [13]And for the east side eastward fifty
cubits. [14]The hangings of the one side of the gate were fifteen
cubits; their pillars three, and their sockets three. [15]And for
the other side of the court gate, on this hand and that hand,
were hangings of fifteen cubits; their pillars three, and their

sockets three. [16]All the hangings of the court round about
were of fine twined linen. [17]And the sockets for the pillars
were of brass; the hooks of the pillars and their fillets of silver; and the overlaying of their chapiters of silver; and all
the pillars of the court were filleted with silver. [18]And the
hanging for the gate of the court was needlework, of blue,
and purple, and scarlet, and fine twined linen; and twenty
cubits was the length, and the height in the breadth was five
cubits, answerable to the hangings of the court. [19]And their
pillars were four, and their sockets of brass four; their hooks
of silver, and the overlaying of their chapiters and their fillets of silver. [20]And all the pins of the tabernacle, and of the
court round about, were of brass.

[21]This is the sum of the tabernacle, even of the tabernacle
of testimony, as it was counted, according to the commandment of Moses, for the service of the Levites, by the hand of
Ithamar, son to Aaron the priest. [22]And Bezaleel the son of
Uri, the son of Hur, of the tribe of Judah, made all that the
Lord commanded Moses. [23]And with him was Aholiab, son
of Ahisamach, of the tribe of Dan, an engraver, and a cunning workman, and an embroiderer in blue, and in purple,
and in scarlet, and fine linen. [24]All the gold that was occupied for the work in all the work of the holy place, even the
gold of the offering, was twenty and nine talents, and seven
hundred and thirty shekels, after the shekel of the sanctuary.
[25]And the silver of them that were numbered of the congregation was an hundred talents, and a thousand seven hundred and threescore and fifteen shekels, after the shekel of

the sanctuary: 26 a bekah for every man, that is, half a shekel,
after the shekel of the sanctuary, for every one that went to
be numbered, from twenty years old and upward, for six
hundred thousand and three thousand and five hundred
and fifty men. 27 And of the hundred talents of silver were
cast the sockets of the sanctuary, and the sockets of the vail;
an hundred sockets of the hundred talents, a talent for a
socket. 28 And of the thousand seven hundred seventy and
five shekels he made hooks for the pillars, and overlaid their
chapiters, and filleted them. 29 And the brass of the offering
was seventy talents, and two thousand and four hundred
shekels. 30 And therewith he made the sockets to the door
of the tabernacle of the congregation, and the brasen altar,
and the brasen grate for it, and all the vessels of the altar,
31 and the sockets of the court round about, and the sockets of
the court gate, and all the pins of the tabernacle, and all the
pins of the court round about.

39 And of the blue, and purple, and scarlet, they made
cloths of service, to do service in the holy place, and
made the holy garments for Aaron; as the Lord commanded
Moses. 2 And he made the ephod of gold, blue, and purple,
and scarlet, and fine twined linen. 3 And they did beat the
gold into thin plates, and cut it into wires, to work it in the
blue, and in the purple, and in the scarlet, and in the fine linen,
with cunning work. 4 They made shoulderpieces for it, to
couple it together; by the two edges was it coupled together.
5 And the curious girdle of his ephod, that was upon it, was

of the same, according to the work thereof; of gold, blue, and purple, and scarlet, and fine twined linen; as the Lord commanded Moses.

[6]And they wrought onyx stones inclosed in ouches of gold, graven, as signets are graven, with the names of the children of Israel. [7]And he put them on the shoulders of the ephod, that they should be stones for a memorial to the children of Israel, as the Lord commanded Moses.

[8]And he made the breastplate of cunning work, like the work of the ephod; of gold, blue, and purple, and scarlet, and fine twined linen. [9]It was foursquare; they made the breastplate double; a span was the length thereof, and a span the breadth thereof, being doubled. [10]And they set in it four rows of stones; the first row was a sardius, a topaz, and a carbuncle; this was the first row. [11]And the second row, an emerald, a sapphire, and a diamond. [12]And the third row, a ligure, an agate, and an amethyst. [13]And the fourth row, a beryl, an onyx, and a jasper; they were inclosed in ouches of gold in their inclosings. [14]And the stones were according to the names of the children of Israel, twelve, according to their names, like the engravings of a signet, every one with his name, according to the twelve tribes. [15]And they made upon the breastplate chains at the ends, of wreathen work of pure gold. [16]And they made two ouches of gold, and two gold rings; and put the two rings in the two ends of the breastplate. [17]And they put the two wreathen chains of gold in the two rings on the ends of the breastplate. [18]And the two ends of the two wreathen chains they fastened in the two ouches, and put them

on the shoulderpieces of the ephod, before it. 19And they
made two rings of gold, and put them on the two ends of the
breastplate, upon the border of it, which was on the side of
the ephod inward. 20And they made two other golden rings,
and put them on the two sides of the ephod underneath,
toward the forepart of it, over against the other coupling
thereof, above the curious girdle of the ephod. 21And they
did bind the breastplate by his rings unto the rings of the
ephod with a lace of blue, that it might be above the curious
girdle of the ephod, and that the breastplate might not be
loosed from the ephod; as the Lord commanded Moses.

22And he made the robe of the ephod of woven work, all
of blue. 23And there was an hole in the midst of the robe, as
the hole of an habergeon, with a band round about the hole,
that it should not rend. 24And they made upon the hems of
the robe pomegranates of blue, and purple, and scarlet, and
twined linen. 25And they made bells of pure gold, and put
the bells between the pomegranates upon the hem of the
robe, round about between the pomegranates: 26a bell and a
pomegranate, a bell and a pomegranate, round about the hem
of the robe to minister in; as the Lord commanded Moses.

27And they made coats of fine linen of woven work for
Aaron, and for his sons, 28and a mitre of fine linen, and goodly
bonnets of fine linen, and linen breeches of fine twined linen,
29and a girdle of fine twined linen, and blue, and purple, and
scarlet, of needlework, as the Lord commanded Moses.

30And they made the plate of the holy crown of pure
gold, and wrote upon it a writing, like to the engravings of a

signet, 'Holiness to the Lord.' 31 And they tied unto it a lace of blue, to fasten it on high upon the mitre; as the Lord commanded Moses.

32 Thus was all the work of the tabernacle of the tent of the congregation finished; and the children of Israel did according to all that the Lord commanded Moses, so did they.

33 And they brought the tabernacle unto Moses, the tent, and all his furniture, his taches, his boards, his bars, and his pillars, and his sockets, 34 and the covering of rams' skins dyed red, and the covering of badgers' skins, and the vail of the covering, 35 the ark of the testimony, and the staves thereof, and the mercy seat, 36 the table, and all the vessels thereof, and the shewbread, 37 the pure candlestick, with the lamps thereof, even with the lamps to be set in order, and all the vessels thereof, and the oil for light, 38 and the golden altar, and the anointing oil, and the sweet incense, and the hanging for the tabernacle door, 39 the brasen altar, and his grate of brass, his staves, and all his vessels, the laver and his foot, 40 the hangings of the court, his pillars, and his sockets, and the hanging for the court gate, his cords, and his pins, and all the vessels of the service of the tabernacle, for the tent of the congregation, 41 the cloths of service to do service in the holy place, and the holy garments for Aaron the priest, and his sons' garments, to minister in the priest's office. 42 According to all that the Lord commanded Moses, so the children of Israel made all the work. 43 And Moses did look upon all the work, and, behold, they had done it as the Lord had commanded, even so had they done it; and Moses blessed them.

40 And the Lord spake unto Moses, saying, 2'On the
first day of the first month shalt thou set up the tabernacle of the tent of the congregation. 3And thou shalt put
therein the ark of the testimony, and cover the ark with the
vail. 4And thou shalt bring in the table, and set in order the
things that are to be set in order upon it; and thou shalt
bring in the candlestick, and light the lamps thereof. 5And
thou shalt set the altar of gold for the incense before the ark
of the testimony, and put the hanging of the door to the tabernacle. 6And thou shalt set the altar of the burnt offering
before the door of the tabernacle of the tent of the congregation. 7And thou shalt set the laver between the tent of the
congregation and the altar, and shalt put water therein. 8And
thou shalt set up the court round about, and hang up the
hanging at the court gate. 9And thou shalt take the anointing
oil, and anoint the tabernacle, and all that is therein, and
shalt hallow it, and all the vessels thereof; and it shall be
holy. 10And thou shalt anoint the altar of the burnt offering,
and all his vessels, and sanctify the altar; and it shall be an
altar most holy. 11And thou shalt anoint the laver and his
foot, and sanctify it. 12And thou shalt bring Aaron and his
sons unto the door of the tabernacle of the congregation, and
wash them with water. 13And thou shalt put upon Aaron the
holy garments, and anoint him, and sanctify him, that he
may minister unto me in the priest's office. 14And thou shalt
bring his sons, and clothe them with coats; 15and thou shalt
anoint them, as thou didst anoint their father, that they may
minister unto me in the priest's office: for their anointing

shall surely be an everlasting priesthood throughout their generations.' 16 Thus did Moses; according to all that the Lord commanded him, so did he.

17 And it came to pass in the first month in the second year, on the first day of the month, that the tabernacle was reared up. 18 And Moses reared up the tabernacle, and fastened his sockets, and set up the boards thereof, and put in the bars thereof, and reared up his pillars. 19 And he spread abroad the tent over the tabernacle, and put the covering of the tent above upon it, as the Lord commanded Moses.

20 And he took and put the testimony into the ark, and set the staves on the ark, and put the mercy seat above upon the ark. 21 And he brought the ark into the tabernacle, and set up the vail of the covering, and covered the ark of the testimony, as the Lord commanded Moses.

22 And he put the table in the tent of the congregation, upon the side of the tabernacle northward, without the vail. 23 And he set the bread in order upon it before the Lord, as the Lord had commanded Moses.

24 And he put the candlestick in the tent of the congregation, over against the table, on the side of the tabernacle southward. 25 And he lighted the lamps before the Lord, as the Lord commanded Moses.

26 And he put the golden altar in the tent of the congregation before the vail; 27 and he burnt sweet incense thereon, as the Lord commanded Moses.

28 And he set up the hanging at the door of the tabernacle. 29 And he put the altar of burnt offering by the door of the

tabernacle of the tent of the congregation, and offered upon it the burnt offering and the meat offering, as the Lord commanded Moses.

30 And he set the laver between the tent of the congregation and the altar, and put water there, to wash withal. 31 And Moses and Aaron and his sons washed their hands and their feet thereat. 32 When they went into the tent of the congregation, and when they came near unto the altar, they washed, as the Lord commanded Moses. 33 And he reared up the court round about the tabernacle and the altar, and set up the hanging of the court gate. So Moses finished the work.

34 Then a cloud covered the tent of the congregation, and the glory of the Lord filled the tabernacle. 35 And Moses was not able to enter into the tent of the congregation, because the cloud abode thereon, and the glory of the Lord filled the tabernacle. 36 And when the cloud was taken up from over the tabernacle, the children of Israel went onward in all their journeys; 37 but if the cloud were not taken up, then they journeyed not till the day that it was taken up. 38 For the cloud of the Lord was upon the tabernacle by day, and fire was on it by night, in the sight of all the house of Israel, throughout all their journeys.

titles in the series

genesis – *introduced by e. l. doctorow*
exodus – *introduced by david grossman*
job – *introduced by charles frazier*
selections from the book of psalms – *introduced by bono*
proverbs – *introduced by charles johnson*
ecclesiastes – *introduced by doris lessing*
matthew – *introduced by francisco goldman*
mark – *introduced by barry hannah*
luke – *introduced by thomas cahill*
john – *introduced by darcey steinke*
corinthians – *introduced by fay weldon*
revelation – *introduced by kathleen norris*

the book of

job

authorized king james version

grove press
new york

with an introduction by | charles frazier

The Pocket Canons were originally published in the U.K. in 1998 by Canongate Books, Ltd.
Published simultaneously in Canada
Printed in the United States of America

FIRST AMERICAN EDITION

Copyright information is on file with the Library of Congress
ISBN 0-8021-3612-5

Design by Paddy Cramsie

Grove Press
841 Broadway
New York, NY 10003

99 00 01 02 10 9 8 7 6 5 4 3 2 1

a note about pocket canons

The Authorized King James Version of the Bible, translated between 1603 and 1611, coincided with an extraordinary flowering of English literature. This version, more than any other, and possibly more than any other work in history, has had an influence in shaping the language we speak and write today. Presenting individual books from the Bible as separate volumes, as they were originally conceived, encourages the reader to approach them as literary works in their own right.

The first twelve books in this series encompass categories as diverse as history, fiction, philosophy, love poetry, and law. Each Pocket Canon also has its own introduction, specially commissioned from an impressive range of writers, which provides a personal interpretation of the text and explores its contemporary relevance.

Charles Frazier is the author of the novel Cold Mountain, *which won the National Book Award. He, his wife, and their daughter have a farm in Raleigh, North Carolina, where they raise horses.*

introduction by charles frazier

Have pity upon me, have pity upon me,
O ye my friends;
for the hand of God hath touched me. (19:21)

As a piece of writing, the great Book of Job strikes me as somewhat similar to watching people thresh grain with a herd of horses: it is all kinds of things trying to go in many different directions at once. Among these are a desperate plea for ultimate justice, an examination of how the individual relates to force and authority, an eloquent and affecting cry of despair, a great and healing song of the power of Creation, and a turgid philosophical drama patched together with a framing device that apparently includes leftover bits of a considerably more ancient Mesopotamian happy-ever-after folktale. Most strikingly, it tells what a fearful and sorrowful thing it is to fall into the hands of a torn and discordant God.

Mark Twain, in his late bitter years, wrote frequently about the Bible. He called the Old Testament's account of God's doings "perhaps the most damnatory biography that exists in print anywhere." Twain catalogs the offenses: "He was an unfair God; he was a God of unsound judgment; he was a God of failures and miscalculations; he was given to odd ideas and fantastic devices."

To be sure, the Book of Job is filled with such behavior. The plot, frail as it is, hinges on a troubling bet between God and Satan—depicted not as real enemies but as affable adversaries. Satan is rather less the Prince of Darkness here than a folkloric trickster figure, slyly but pointedly challenging power and authority. The wager, a test of Job's faith, requires the murder of all Job's ten children and countless servants, the theft and arson of all his vast holdings. This is a measure of destructiveness that even God—at the very least an accessory to these crimes—later calls "without cause."

God initiates the action, dangling Job in Satan's face, saying, "Hast thou considered my servant Job." He calls Job "perfect," holds him out as an example of "an upright man, one that feareth God." Satan very reasonably takes the implied challenge, arguing that the prosperous Job has little reason for fear, since he has always been protected by God: "But put forth thine hand now, and touch all that he hath, and he will curse thee to thy face," Satan says.

God—apparently forgetting his own omniscience in the heat of the moment—falls for this trap and gives Satan almost free rein to test his theory, restraining him in but one regard: "Only upon himself [Job] put not forth thine hand." So Satan pours down tornadic winds, marauding Sabeans and Chaldeans, and the fire of God from Heaven. Job responds much as God expects: he tears his clothes, shaves his head, and falls on the ground to pray, saying, among other things:

> the Lord gave, and the Lord hath taken away;
> blessed be the name of the Lord. (1:21)

Kierkegaard, in his Discourse on Job, makes much of that pair of lines, and he appears to have lost interest at this point, choosing to see Job as a story of unquestioning faith in the face of adversity. Satan, on the other hand, is not yet ready to call the game. He suggests that one's property is one thing, "But put forth thine hand now, and touch his bone and his flesh, and he will curse thee to thy face." With God's blessing Satan then smites Job with boils from crown to sole, leaving him sitting in an ash heap scraping his sores with a potsherd. Job's wife's best advice at this most recent downturn in fortune is that he should "curse God, and die." Job, though, insists on some accounting. What did he do to call down such weight of calamity? Not a thing that he can figure. As stand-in for mankind under constant attack—both physical and spiritual—until woe overbrims our frail vessels, Job demands an explanation for his fate, some justice, an assurance of cosmic fairness. Lacking that, he demands at the very least a chance to yowl his fear and despair at a God that by all the evidence of his actions holds man in contempt and the strictures of justice that bind civilized cultures in weak regard.

> For the arrows of the Almighty are within me,
> the poison whereof drinketh up my spirit:
> the terrors of God do set themselves
> in array against me. (6:4)

At Enfield, Connecticut, in 1741, Jonathan Edwards delivered the most famous of American sermons, "Sinners in the Hands of an Angry God." Edwards's violent, unknowable God, like the one in the Book of Job, expresses much of His power through boundless and easily provoked rage. This is the way Edwards recommends we consider such a Deity:

> How awful are those words, Isaiah 63:3, which are the words of the great God: "I will tread them in mine anger, and trample them in my fury; and their blood shall be sprinkled upon my garments, and I will stain all my raiment." It is perhaps impossible to conceive of words that carry in them greater manifestations of these three things, viz., contempt, and hatred, and fierceness of indignation. If you cry to God to pity you, He will be so far from pitying you in your doleful case, or showing you the least regard or favor, that instead of that He will only tread you under foot; and though He will know that you cannot bear the weight of omnipotence treading upon you, He will not regard that, but He will crush you under His feet without mercy; He will crush out your blood and make it fly, and it shall be sprinkled on His garments, so as to stain all His raiment. He will not only hate you, but He will have you in the utmost contempt; no place shall be thought fit for you but under his feet, to be trodden down as mire in the streets.

In the city and suburban churches of the current version of America, God is really not much that way at all anymore. On the rare occasions I attend such churches, I am struck with the overriding conviction of pastor and congregation that to the extent God is angry at anyone, it is certainly not with people remotely like you and me. God's dark moods have lifted. He is love, and our flaws are really quite understandable and totally forgivable. So minor indeed that, honestly, personal change—at least of any radical or inconvenient kind—is not in order, not the least bit called for.

It is only when I am driving in the rural bits of the country—the regions—that I find any remnant of the old mad God of Edwards and Job, and that confined to the extremes of the AM band where vestigial spittle-spewing preachers rant the breathless and urgent message that God might very well despise us all, and with good cause. It is easy to ridicule such men, to find them humorous or, worse, quaint. But it may be a dangerous proposition to dismiss their views out of hand. Look about you; go to and fro in the world, walk up and down in it like Satan in the Book of Job; make a fair report and then try to present a convincing argument against them.

> When I say, My bed shall comfort me,
> my couch shall ease my complaint;
> Then thou scarest me with dreams,
> and terrifiest me through visions;
> So that my soul chooseth strangling,
> and death rather than my life. (7:13-15)

In my line of work it is often incumbent upon me to read the great spiritual texts of our many people. I am fondest of the Buddhist writings, and also those of various shamans and visionaries and anchorites and desert fathers. All useful in their own ways. I have not, however, read the Book of Job since I was perhaps twelve, when I was, for a brief time, Methodist. Each month I took from a stand in the church foyer a copy of *The Upper Room,* a booklet of suggested daily Bible readings with suggested interpretations. The cover of it was always an artistic rendering of a biblical event, done in rich saturated colors like Caravaggio or Dell Comics. My Bible had a black leather zippered cover with my name stamped in gold letters, and for a bookmark I used a cross twisted from a palm frond. It was the height of the Cold War, and I read the Bible with a certain superstitious consistency every night before turning out the light and tuning in to WLAC's fifty thousand clear watts through the earphone of a gray plastic Zenith transistor radio.

I had trouble sleeping. We lived in a cup of Appalachian valley that lay as the crow flies only a short way from Oak Ridge, a place all my teachers assured me was a first target for Soviet nuclear attack. Some of my friends had bomb shelters buried underneath their houses. You reached them through twisting tunnels, as if visiting the tombs of pharaohs. Inside were canned goods, jugs of water, reading matter. All the things you'd need when you got to the other side. We did not have a shelter.

Sometimes as I lay awake listening to Stax and Chess R&B—John R and Daddy Gene emphatically naming the tunes and reading mail-order offers for Ernie's Record Mart and a thousand baby chicks—I was convinced that this night was the night it all would fall. The siren down at the town fire station would sound, and then before I even had time to get out of bed, the whole broad sky out the window would flash up bright as the flame at the tip of a welder's torch toward which one dare not look.

My bedroom window opened out onto our neighbor's house. It was a log cabin with pale plaster chinking between the dark logs. It sat under a big black walnut tree, and the man that lived alone in it was a sweet old drunk who woke every morning at four no matter what shape he was in or what hour the sun rose. If we locked our keys in our house he would come over with a hammer and a screwdriver and make a single delicate tap and the door would spring open. When, long before dawn, he turned on his lights, it seemed to me that the night watch had changed and I could go to sleep. Old Doug was awake behind his yellow windows, and not much bad could happen.

> Therefore I will not refrain my mouth;
> I will speak in the anguish of my spirit;
> I will complain in the bitterness of my soul. (7:11)

So there sits Job, on the wrong side of God, scraping his boils with a sherd, wondering what he did wrong. And saddled with such a wife. Then three old friends—Bildad the Shuhite, Zophar the Naamathite, and Eliphaz the Temanite—show up to sit with him. They do not, however, commiserate with him; they argue at great length that despite the severity and apparent injustice of his afflictions, he must have had it coming. They're not sure why, but there has to be a reason. Undeserved suffering cannot be. William Blake, in plate X of his *Illustrations of the Book of Job,* shows these men kneeling, their staring faces close together in expressions of self-righteous condemnation, all bearing a great family resemblance to demons. They all point at weeping Job with the fingers of their hands held in creepy, incantatory gestures.

In Blake's reading of Job, despair seems to come—if not wholly, at least significantly—from isolation, a devastating inturning that finds visual expression in several ways. One is a lonely set-apartness in the relation of Job to other human figures in the plates; they turn from him, space themselves away from him, hide their faces from him. They draw away; he pulls into himself. Or the other way around. When they do look at him, they mock and scorn and condemn. Most affectingly, Job's isolation is evident in the odd and troubling resemblances of God, Satan, and Job—as if Blake were suggesting that Job has fallen so far in upon himself that he has created a God and a Devil in his own image.

It is at this point in the narrative that Job—utterly ruined, all his vast holdings and the people he presumably loved yanked from him—begins speaking powerful poems cursing his personal existence. "Why me, Lord" is a good question, and one we've all cast out at one time or another to an unresponsive universe. But Job fashions the simple query into some of the greatest and most terse expressions of despair and soul weariness we have. Job's laments are as blunt and stripped in their pain as Delta blues. I'd like to think there's influence there, to imagine Charlie Patton sitting down with a huge limp Bible flapped open on his lap to chapter 3 of Job and then switching to his guitar and making up "When Your Way Gets Dark" or "Down the Dirt Road." I'll just point out, rather at random, some personal high points of Job's blues: "My face is foul with weeping, and on my eyelids is the shadow of death" (16:16); "My days are swifter than a weaver's shuttle, and are spent without hope" (7:6); "My soul is weary of my life" (10:1); "My days are past, my purposes are broken off, even the thoughts of my heart" (17:11); "For now shall I sleep in the dust; and thou shalt seek me in the morning, but I shall not be" (7:21).

It is some reimbursement, at least, with everything you have taken from you, everything you desire denied you, everything you fear come to pass, to have language of such force and simplicity at your command as both weapon and balm.

> Hast thou perceived the breadth of the earth?
> Declare if thou knowest it all. (38:18)

One of the central questions the Book of Job asks is: How might man and Deity communicate in order to settle the issues Job raises? Job offers logic as a path. "Surely I would speak to the Almighty, and I would desire to reason with God," he says (13:3). It is tempting to view God's entrance in a whirlwind and his subsequent boastful listing of his creative accomplishments, his power and authority as dodging the question, a victory of force over reason, of fear over all else. The Almighty supports such a reading when He asks, "Hast thou an arm like God? Or canst thou thunder with a voice like him?" (40:9).

But his long speech also offers hope for an alternative reading, one that proposes quite a different channel of communication than the one Job recommends. What God holds out for consideration is Creation, all that is the world, its bigness and smallness, its infinite detail, its differing statements of motif and theme, their complex variations and repetitions, beauty and terror intermixed. It is a construct so finely made that even its wild and violent and enormous elements—Leviathan is an example God offers with particular pleasure—contain in their details the smallest and most delicate elements, for the eyes of the monster are "like the eyelids of the morning" (41:18). God is also rightfully pleased with the concept and execution of water in its various forms, rain and dew and ice and frost. His pride is the understandable pride of the artist who has succeeded in creating a whole world. The details of horse anatomy, he feels, worked out particularly well: "The glory of his nostrils is terrible" (39:20).

Blake seems to have liked this line too, for in plate XIV—his illustration of this bit of the text—one of the details of Creation he chooses to include are four horses, nostrils flaring. Blake's God stares out from this frame, just missing eye contact with the viewer, an oddly stricken expression on His face, but His arms are stretched out to encompass ranks of jubilant angels, stars, beasts and humans, mountains and rivers, birds and plants and creeping things. Look at it all, God seems to be saying. Don't trouble me with reason; what you need to know is there in the art and the mystery and ultimate unknowableness of my elegant design. Love it and fear it. Submit to it.

> For the thing which I greatly feared
> is come upon me, and that
> which I was afraid of is come unto me. (3:25)

A number of years ago I read the account of Black Elk, an old Sioux visionary and a friend of Crazy Horse. He lived to see catastrophes to his people at least the like of Job's. They lost as close to everything as you can and not just be extinct. He lived on past his particular apocalypse, to be another exile in the twentieth century. In telling his story, he dwells in great detail on a time in his earlier life when he had become consumed with fear, "afraid of being afraid." He then had a powerful vision that featured the four quarters of the earth, the weathers of the sky, animals and man. In other words, all of Creation. The great lesson of this all-encompassing vision was the conviction that we should not fear the universe. I remember writing the line down in a lost notebook along with a poem by Stephen Dunn and some lines from a Thomas McGuane novel expressing what struck me as somewhat the same ideas.

Not fearing the universe is a useful and comforting attitude if you can sustain it. And with varying degrees of success, I've tried to do it many times. Once I was lost in the Bolivian cloud forest, the damp brow of mountain between the Andes and the Amazon. I had walked down from a barren eighteen-thousand-foot pass, and gradually my map and the land came more and more to disresemble one another. And then fairly suddenly the trail was gone. My one companion waited by a river for me to scout a route.

I walked a mile or so, contouring around a heavily treed hillside and over a ridge, and then I came to a high cliff. Stretched out far beneath my feet was the Amazon basin. I could see for what must have been a hundred miles before the jungle faded into haze. There was not a road or clearing or feather of smoke, just unmarked green treetops. It was a sensation similar to lying on your back in a Cherry County,

Nebraska, field and looking up into the moonless night sky. So to say, the legendary indifference of nature to man's individual existence was much in evidence. I sat on a rock for a long time looking out, and one of the word-strings I remember crossing my mind was, Do not fear the universe. I remember that it helped. And that is about all that you can ask of words.

I thought them again after two days of bushwhacking, when in the dark I stumbled through a banana grove and cutters came out from their camp and stood with machetes in their hands, the thick blades backlit in the glare of pressurized gas lanterns. As it turned out, the men were as scared of me and my thrashing as I was of them. They had warm beer in liter bottles, and they showed me where to camp. I slept by a black river and the night was so quiet I could hear the rocks in the riverbed moving against each other in the current.

It is easy enough when the universe behaves in such a benign way not to fear it. But the Book of Job and its God of the whirlwind are of a different turn of mind. They say—also usefully—"Yes, sometimes do."

the book of job

There was a man in the land of Uz, whose name was Job; and that man was perfect and upright, and one that feared God, and eschewed evil. 2And there were born unto him seven sons and three daughters. 3His substance also was seven thousand sheep, and three thousand camels, and five hundred yoke of oxen, and five hundred she asses, and a very great household; so that this man was the greatest of all the men of the east. 4And his sons went and feasted in their houses, every one his day; and sent and called for their three sisters to eat and to drink with them. 5And it was so, when the days of their feasting were gone about, that Job sent and sanctified them, and rose up early in the morning, and offered burnt offerings according to the number of them all: for Job said, 'It may be that my sons have sinned, and cursed God in their hearts.' Thus did Job continually.

6Now there was a day when the sons of God came to present themselves before the Lord, and Satan came also among them. 7And the Lord said unto Satan, 'Whence comest thou?' Then Satan answered the Lord, and said, 'From going to and fro in the earth, and from walking up and down in it.' 8And the Lord said unto Satan, 'Hast thou considered my servant Job, that there is none like him in the earth, a perfect

and an upright man, one that feareth God, and escheweth
evil?' 9 Then Satan answered the Lord, and said, 'Doth Job
fear God for nought? 10 Hast not thou made an hedge about
him, and about his house, and about all that he hath on every
side? Thou hast blessed the work of his hands, and his substance is increased in the land. 11 But put forth thine hand now,
and touch all that he hath, and he will curse thee to thy face.'
12 And the Lord said unto Satan, 'Behold, all that he hath is in
thy power; only upon himself put not forth thine hand.' So
Satan went forth from the presence of the Lord.

13 And there was a day when his sons and his daughters
were eating and drinking wine in their eldest brother's house,
14 and there came a messenger unto Job, and said, 'The oxen
were plowing, and the asses feeding beside them; 15 and the
Sabeans fell upon them, and took them away; yea, they have
slain the servants with the edge of the sword; and I only am
escaped alone to tell thee.' 16 While he was yet speaking, there
came also another, and said, 'The fire of God is fallen from
heaven, and hath burned up the sheep, and the servants, and
consumed them; and I only am escaped alone to tell thee.'
17 While he was yet speaking, there came also another, and
said, 'The Chaldeans made out three bands, and fell upon
the camels, and have carried them away, yea, and slain the
servants with the edge of the sword; and I only am escaped
alone to tell thee.' 18 While he was yet speaking, there came
also another, and said, 'Thy sons and thy daughters were eating and drinking wine in their eldest brother's house; 19 and,
behold, there came a great wind from the wilderness, and

smote the four corners of the house, and it fell upon the young
men, and they are dead; and I only am escaped alone to tell
thee.' 20 Then Job arose, and rent his mantle, and shaved his
head, and fell down upon the ground, and worshipped,
21 and said,

'Naked came I out of my mother's womb,
and naked shall I return thither:
the Lord gave, and the Lord hath taken away;
blessed be the name of the Lord.'

22 In all this Job sinned not, nor charged God foolishly.

2 Again there was a day when the sons of God came to
present themselves before the Lord, and Satan came
also among them to present himself before the Lord. 2 And
the Lord said unto Satan, 'From whence comest thou?' And
Satan answered the Lord, and said, 'From going to and fro in
the earth, and from walking up and down in it.' 3 And the
Lord said unto Satan, 'Hast thou considered my servant Job,
that there is none like him in the earth, a perfect and an
upright man, one that feareth God, and escheweth evil? And
still he holdeth fast his integrity, although thou movedst me
against him, to destroy him without cause.' 4 And Satan
answered the Lord, and said, 'Skin for skin, yea, all that a
man hath will he give for his life. 5 But put forth thine hand
now, and touch his bone and his flesh, and he will curse thee
to thy face.' 6 And the Lord said unto Satan, 'Behold, he is in
thine hand; but save his life.'

7 So went Satan forth from the presence of the Lord, and
smote Job with sore boils from the sole of his foot unto his
crown. 8 And he took him a potsherd to scrape himself withal;
and he sat down among the ashes.

9 Then said his wife unto him, 'Dost thou still retain thine
integrity? Curse God, and die.' 10 But he said unto her, 'Thou
speakest as one of the foolish women speaketh. What? Shall
we receive good at the hand of God, and shall we not receive
evil?' In all this did not Job sin with his lips.

11 Now when Job's three friends heard of all this evil that
was come upon him, they came every one from his own place:
Eliphaz the Temanite, and Bildad the Shuhite, and Zophar
the Naamathite; for they had made an appointment together
to come to mourn with him and to comfort him. 12 And when
they lifted up their eyes afar off, and knew him not, they
lifted up their voice, and wept; and they rent every one his
mantle, and sprinkled dust upon their heads toward heaven.
13 So they sat down with him upon the ground seven days
and seven nights, and none spake a word unto him: for they
saw that his grief was very great.

3 After this opened Job his mouth, and cursed his day.
2 And Job spake, and said,

3 'Let the day perish wherein I was born,
and the night in which it was said,
"There is a man child conceived."
4 Let that day be darkness;

let not God regard it from above,
neither let the light shine upon it.
5 Let darkness and the shadow of death stain it;
let a cloud dwell upon it;
let the blackness of the day terrify it.
6 As for that night, let darkness seize upon it;
let it not be joined unto the days of the year;
let it not come into the number of the months.
7 Lo, let that night be solitary,
let no joyful voice come therein.
8 Let them curse it that curse the day,
who are ready to raise up their mourning.
9 Let the stars of the twilight thereof be dark;
let it look for light, but have none;
neither let it see the dawning of the day:
10 because it shut not up the doors of my mother's
womb, nor hid sorrow from mine eyes.
11 Why died I not from the womb?
why did I not give up the ghost
when I came out of the belly?
12 Why did the knees prevent me?
Or why the breasts that I should suck?
13 For now should I have lain still and been quiet,
I should have slept: then had I been at rest,
14 with kings and counsellors of the earth,
which built desolate places for themselves;
15 or with princes that had gold,
who filled their houses with silver:

16 or as an hidden untimely birth I had not been;
as infants which never saw light.
17 There the wicked cease from troubling;
and there the weary be at rest.
18 There the prisoners rest together;
they hear not the voice of the oppressor.
19 The small and great are there;
and the servant is free from his master.
20 Wherefore is light given to him that is in misery,
and life unto the bitter in soul;
21 which long for death, but it cometh not,
and dig for it more than for hid treasures;
22 which rejoice exceedingly, and are glad,
when they can find the grave?
23 Why is light given to a man whose way is hid,
and whom God hath hedged in?
24 For my sighing cometh before I eat,
and my roarings are poured out like the waters.
25 For the thing which I greatly feared
is come upon me, and that
which I was afraid of is come unto me.
26 I was not in safety, neither had I rest,
neither was I quiet; yet trouble came.'

4 Then Eliphaz the Temanite answered and said, 2 'If we
assay to commune with thee, wilt thou be grieved? But
who can withhold himself from speaking? 3 Behold, thou hast
instructed many, and thou hast strengthened the weak hands.

4 Thy words have upholden him that was falling, and thou
hast strengthened the feeble knees. 5 But now it is come upon
thee, and thou faintest; it toucheth thee, and thou art troubled. 6 Is not this thy fear, thy confidence, thy hope, and the
uprightness of thy ways? 7 Remember, I pray thee, who ever
perished, being innocent? Or where were the righteous cut
off? 8 Even as I have seen, they that plow iniquity, and sow
wickedness, reap the same. 9 By the blast of God they perish,
and by the breath of his nostrils are they consumed. 10 The
roaring of the lion, and the voice of the fierce lion, and the
teeth of the young lions, are broken. 11 The old lion perisheth
for lack of prey, and the stout lion's whelps are scattered
abroad. 12 Now a thing was secretly brought to me, and mine
ear received a little thereof. 13 In thoughts from the visions of
the night, when deep sleep falleth on men, 14 fear came upon
me, and trembling, which made all my bones to shake. 15 Then
a spirit passed before my face; the hair of my flesh stood up.
16 It stood still, but I could not discern the form thereof: an
image was before mine eyes, there was silence, and I heard a
voice, saying, 17 "Shall mortal man be more just than God?
Shall a man be more pure than his maker? 18 Behold, he put
no trust in his servants; and his angels he charged with folly;
19 how much less in them that dwell in houses of clay, whose
foundation is in the dust, which are crushed before the
moth? 20 They are destroyed from morning to evening; they
perish for ever without any regarding it. 21 Doth not their
excellency which is in them go away? They die, even without wisdom."'

5 1 Call now, if there be any that will answer thee; and to
which of the saints wilt thou turn? 2 For wrath killeth
the foolish man, and envy slayeth the silly one. 3 I have seen
the foolish taking root; but suddenly I cursed his habitation.
4 His children are far from safety, and they are crushed in the
gate, neither is there any to deliver them. 5 Whose harvest the
hungry eateth up, and taketh it even out of the thorns, and
the robber swalloweth up their substance. 6 Although affliction
cometh not forth of the dust, neither doth trouble spring out
of the ground; 7 yet man is born unto trouble, as the sparks
fly upward. 8 I would seek unto God, and unto God would I
commit my cause: 9 which doeth great things and unsearchable, marvellous things without number; 10 who giveth rain
upon the earth, and sendeth waters upon the fields; 11 to set
up on high those that be low, that those which mourn may
be exalted to safety. 12 He disappointeth the devices of the
crafty, so that their hands cannot perform their enterprise.
13 He taketh the wise in their own craftiness; and the counsel
of the forward is carried headlong. 14 They meet with darkness in the daytime, and grope in the noonday as in the
night. 15 But he saveth the poor from the sword, from their
mouth, and from the hand of the mighty. 16 So the poor hath
hope, and iniquity stoppeth her mouth. 17 Behold, happy is
the man whom God correcteth; therefore despise not thou
the chastening of the Almighty: 18 for he maketh sore, and
bindeth up; he woundeth, and his hands make whole. 19 He
shall deliver thee in six troubles; yea, in seven there shall no
evil touch thee. 20 In famine he shall redeem thee from death;

and in war from the power of the sword. 21 Thou shalt be hid
from the scourge of the tongue; neither shalt thou be afraid
of destruction when it cometh. 22 At destruction and famine
thou shalt laugh; neither shalt thou be afraid of the beasts
of the earth. 23 For thou shalt be in league with the stones of
the field; and the beasts of the field shall be at peace with
thee. 24 And thou shalt know that thy tabernacle shall be in
peace; and thou shalt visit thy habitation, and shalt not sin.
25 Thou shalt know also that thy seed shall be great, and thine
offspring as the grass of the earth. 26 Thou shalt come to thy
grave in a full age, like as a shock of corn cometh in his season. 27 Lo this, we have searched it, so it is; hear it, and know
thou it for thy good.'

6 But Job answered and said,

2 'Oh that my grief were throughly weighed,
and my calamity laid in the balances together!
3 For now it would be heavier
than the sand of the sea;
therefore my words are swallowed up.
4 For the arrows of the Almighty are within me,
the poison whereof drinketh up my spirit:
the terrors of God do set themselves
in array against me.
5 Doth the wild ass bray when he hath grass?
Or loweth the ox over his fodder?
6 Can that which is unsavoury be eaten without salt?

Or is there any taste in the white of an egg?
7 The things that my soul refused to touch
are as my sorrowful meat.
8 Oh that I might have my request; and that
God would grant me the thing that I long for!
9 Even that it would please God to destroy me;
that he would let loose his hand, and cut me off!
10 Then should I yet have comfort;
yea, I would harden myself in sorrow:
let him not spare; for I have not concealed
the words of the Holy One.
11 What is my strength, that I should hope?
And what is mine end,
that I should prolong my life?
12 Is my strength the strength of stones?
Or is my flesh of brass?
13 Is not my help in me?
And is wisdom driven quite from me?
14 To him that is afflicted pity
should be shewed from his friend;
but he forsaketh the fear of the Almighty.
15 My brethren have dealt deceitfully as a brook,
and as the stream of brooks they pass away;
16 which are blackish by reason of the ice,
and wherein the snow is hid.
17 What time they wax warm, they vanish;
when it is hot,
they are consumed out of their place.

18 The paths of their way are turned aside;
they go to nothing, and perish.
19 The troops of Tema looked,
the companies of Sheba waited for them.
20 They were confounded because they had hoped;
they came thither, and were ashamed.
21 For now ye are nothing;
ye see my casting down, and are afraid.
22 Did I say, "Bring unto me?"
or, "Give a reward for me of your substance?"
23 or, "Deliver me from the enemy's hand?"
or, "Redeem me from the hand of the mighty?"
24 Teach me, and I will hold my tongue;
and cause me to understand
wherein I have erred.
25 How forcible are right words!
But what doth your arguing reprove?
26 Do ye imagine to reprove words,
and the speeches of one that is desperate,
which are as wind?
27 Yea, ye overwhelm the fatherless,
and ye dig a pit for your friend.
28 Now therefore be content, look upon me;
for it is evident unto you if I lie.
29 Return, I pray you, let it not be iniquity;
yea, return again, my righteousness is in it.
30 Is there iniquity in my tongue?
Cannot my taste discern perverse things?'

7

[1]Is there not an appointed time to man upon earth?
Are not his days also like the days of an hireling?
[2]As a servant earnestly desireth the shadow, and as
an hireling looketh for the reward of his work,
[3]so am I made to possess months of vanity,
and wearisome nights are appointed to me.
[4]When I lie down, I say,
"When shall I arise, and the night be gone?"
and I am full of tossings to and fro
unto the dawning of the day.
[5]My flesh is clothed with worms and clods of dust;
my skin is broken, and become loathsome.
[6]My days are swifter than a weaver's shuttle,
and are spent without hope.
[7]O remember that my life is wind:
mine eye shall no more see good.
[8]The eye of him that hath seen me
shall see me no more:
thine eyes are upon me, and I am not.
[9]As the cloud is consumed and vanisheth away,
so he that goeth down to the grave
shall come up no more.
[10]He shall return no more to his house,
neither shall his place know him any more.
[11]Therefore I will not refrain my mouth;
I will speak in the anguish of my spirit;
I will complain in the bitterness of my soul.

12 Am I a sea, or a whale,
that thou settest a watch over me?
13 When I say, "My bed shall comfort me,
my couch shall ease my complaint";
14 then thou scarest me with dreams,
and terrifiest me through visions;
15 so that my soul chooseth strangling,
and death rather than my life.
16 I loathe it; I would not live alway.
Let me alone; for my days are vanity.
17 What is man, that thou shouldest magnify him?
And that thou shouldest
set thine heart upon him?
18 And that thou shouldest visit him every morning,
and try him every moment?
19 How long wilt thou not depart from me,
nor let me alone till I swallow down my spittle?
20 I have sinned; what shall I do unto thee,
O thou preserver of men?
Why hast thou set me as a mark against thee,
so that I am a burden to myself?
21 And why dost thou not pardon my transgression,
and take away mine iniquity?
For now shall I sleep in the dust;
and thou shalt seek me in the morning,
but I shall not be.'

8 Then answered Bildad the Shuhite, and said, 2 'How long
wilt thou speak these things? And how long shall the
words of thy mouth be like a strong wind? 3 Doth God pervert judgement? Or doth the Almighty pervert justice? 4 If
thy children have sinned against him, and he have cast them
away for their transgression; 5 if thou wouldest seek unto God
betimes, and make thy supplication to the Almighty; 6 if thou
wert pure and upright; surely now he would awake for thee,
and make the habitation of thy righteousness prosperous.
7 Though thy beginning was small, yet thy latter end should
greatly increase. 8 For enquire, I pray thee, of the former age,
and prepare thyself to the search of their fathers 9 (for we are
but of yesterday, and know nothing, because our days upon
earth are a shadow). 10 Shall not they teach thee, and tell thee,
and utter words out of their heart? 11 Can the rush grow up
without mire? Can the flag grow without water? 12 Whilst it
is yet in his greenness, and not cut down, it withereth before
any other herb. 13 So are the paths of all that forget God, and
the hypocrite's hope shall perish; 14 whose hope shall be cut
off, and whose trust shall be a spider's web. 15 He shall lean
upon his house, but it shall not stand; he shall hold it fast,
but it shall not endure. 16 He is green before the sun, and his
branch shooteth forth in his garden. 17 His roots are wrapped
about the heap, and seeth the place of stones. 18 If he destroy
him from his place, then it shall deny him, saying, I have not
seen thee. 19 Behold, this is the joy of his way, and out of the
earth shall others grow. 20 Behold, God will not cast away a
perfect man, neither will he help the evil doers; 21 till he fill

thy mouth with laughing, and thy lips with rejoicing. 22 They
that hate thee shall be clothed with shame; and the dwelling
place of the wicked shall come to nought.'

9 Then Job answered and said,

2 'I know it is so of a truth;
but how should man be just with God?
3 If he will contend with him,
he cannot answer him one of a thousand.
4 He is wise in heart, and mighty in strength:
who hath hardened himself against him,
and hath prospered?
5 Which removeth the mountains, and they know not;
which overturneth them in his anger.
6 Which shaketh the earth out of her place,
and the pillars thereof tremble.
7 Which commandeth the sun, and it riseth not;
and sealeth up the stars.
8 Which alone spreadeth out the heavens,
and treadeth upon the waves of the sea.
9 Which maketh Arcturus, Orion, and Pleiades,
and the chambers of the south.
10 Which doeth great things past finding out;
yea, and wonders without number.
11 Lo, he goeth by me, and I see him not;
he passeth on also, but I perceive him not.
12 Behold, he taketh away, who can hinder him?

Who will say unto him, "What doest thou?"
13 If God will not withdraw his anger,
the proud helpers do stoop under him.
14 How much less shall I answer him,
and choose out my words to reason with him?
15 Whom, though I were righteous,
yet would I not answer,
but I would make supplication to my judge.
16 If I had called, and he had answered me;
yet would I not believe that he had
hearkened unto my voice.
17 For he breaketh me with a tempest,
and multiplieth my wounds without cause.
18 He will not suffer me to take my breath,
but filleth me with bitterness.
19 If I speak of strength, lo, he is strong; and,
if of judgment, who shall set me a time to plead?
20 If I justify myself, mine own mouth shall
condemn me; if I say I am perfect,
it shall also prove me perverse.
21 Though I were perfect,
yet would I not know my soul:
I would despise my life.
22 This is one thing, therefore I said it,
He destroyeth the perfect and the wicked.
23 If the scourge slay suddenly,
he will laugh at the trial of the innocent.

24 The earth is given into the hand of the wicked;
he covereth the faces of the judges thereof;
if not, where and who is he?
25 Now my days are swifter than a post:
they flee away, they see no good.
26 They are passed away as the swift ships;
as the eagle that hasteth to the prey.
27 If I say, "I will forget my complaint,
I will leave off my heaviness,
and comfort myself,"
28 I am afraid of all my sorrows,
I know that thou wilt not hold me innocent.
29 If I be wicked, why then labour I in vain?
30 If I wash myself with snow water,
and make my hands never so clean;
31 yet shalt thou plunge me in the ditch,
and mine own clothes shall abhor me.
32 For he is not a man, as I am,
that I should answer him,
and we should come together in judgment.
33 Neither is there any daysman betwixt us,
that might lay his hand upon us both.
34 Let him take his rod away from me,
and let not his fear terrify me;
35 then would I speak, and not fear him;
but it is not so with me.'

10 'My soul is weary of my life;
I will leave my complaint upon myself;
I will speak in the bitterness of my soul.
2 I will say unto God, "Do not condemn me;
shew me wherefore thou contendest with me.
3 Is it good unto thee that thou shouldest oppress,
that thou shouldest despise the work of thine hands,
and shine upon the counsel of the wicked?
4 Hast thou eyes of flesh? Or seest thou as man seeth?
5 Are thy days as the days of man?
Are thy years as man's days,
6 that thou enquirest after mine iniquity,
and searchest after my sin?
7 Thou knowest that I am not wicked; and
there is none that can deliver out of thine hand.
8 Thine hands have made me
and fashioned me together round about;
yet thou dost destroy me.
9 Remember, I beseech thee,
that thou hast made me as the clay;
and wilt thou bring me into dust again?
10 Hast thou not poured me out as milk,
and curdled me like cheese?
11 Thou hast clothed me with skin and flesh,
and hast fenced me with bones and sinews.
12 Thou hast granted me life and favour,
and thy visitation hath preserved my spirit.
13 And these things hast thou hid in thine heart;

I know that this is with thee.
14 If I sin, then thou markest me,
and thou wilt not acquit me from mine iniquity.
15 If I be wicked, woe unto me;
and if I be righteous, yet will I not lift up my head.
I am full of confusion;
therefore see thou mine affliction,
16 for it increaseth.
Thou huntest me as a fierce lion;
and again thou shewest thyself
marvellous upon me.
17 Thou renewest thy witnesses against me,
and increasest thine indignation upon me;
changes and war are against me.
18 "Wherefore then hast thou brought me forth
out of the womb?
Oh that I had given up the ghost,
and no eye had seen me!
19 I should have been as though I had not been;
I should have been carried
from the womb to the grave.
20 Are not my days few?
Cease then, and let me alone,
that I may take comfort a little,
21 before I go whence I shall not return,
even to the land of darkness
and the shadow of death;
22 a land of darkness, as darkness itself;

and of the shadow of death, without any order,
and where the light is as darkness."'

11 Then answered Zophar the Naamathite, and said, 2 'Should not the multitude of words be answered? And should a man full of talk be justified? 3 Should thy lies make men hold their peace? And when thou mockest, shall no man make thee ashamed? 4 For thou hast said, "My doctrine is pure, and I am clean in thine eyes." 5 But oh that God would speak, and open his lips against thee; 6 and that he would shew thee the secrets of wisdom, that they are double to that which is! Know therefore that God exacteth of thee less than thine iniquity deserveth. 7 Canst thou by searching find out God? Canst thou find out the Almighty unto perfection? 8 It is as high as heaven; what canst thou do? Deeper than hell; what canst thou know? 9 The measure thereof is longer than the earth, and broader than the sea. 10 If he cut off, and shut up, or gather together, then who can hinder him? 11 For he knoweth vain men. He seeth wickedness also; will he not then consider it? 12 For vain man would be wise, though man be born like a wild ass's colt. 13 If thou prepare thine heart, and stretch out thine hands toward him; 14 if iniquity be in thine hand, put it far away, and let not wickedness dwell in thy tabernacles. 15 For then shalt thou lift up thy face without spot; yea, thou shalt be stedfast, and shalt not fear, 16 because thou shalt forget thy misery, and remember it as waters that pass away. 17 And thine age shall be clearer than the noonday; thou shalt shine forth, thou shalt be as the morning.

18 And thou shalt be secure, because there is hope; yea, thou
shalt dig about thee, and thou shalt take thy rest in safety. 19 Also
thou shalt lie down, and none shall make thee afraid; yea,
many shall make suit unto thee. 20 But the eyes of the wicked
shall fail, and they shall not escape, and their hope shall be as
the giving up of the ghost.'

12

And Job answered and said,

2 'No doubt but ye are the people,
and wisdom shall die with you.
3 But I have understanding as well as you;
I am not inferior to you:
yea, who knoweth not such things as these?
4 I am as one mocked of his neighbour,
I who calleth upon God, and he answereth him:
the just upright man is laughed to scorn.
5 He that is ready to slip with his feet
is as a lamp despised in the thought of him
that is at ease.
6 The tabernacles of robbers prosper,
and they that provoke God are secure;
into whose hand God bringeth abundantly.
7 But ask now the beasts, and they shall teach thee;
and the fowls of the air, and they shall tell thee.
8 Or speak to the earth, and it shall teach thee;
and the fishes of the sea shall declare unto thee.
9 Who knoweth not in all these that the hand of

the Lord hath wrought this?
10 In whose hand is the soul of every living thing,
and the breath of all mankind.
11 Doth not the ear try words?
And the mouth taste his meat?
12 With the ancient is wisdom;
and in length of days understanding.
13 With him is wisdom and strength,
he hath counsel and understanding.
14 Behold, he breaketh down,
and it cannot be built again;
he shutteth up a man,
and there can be no opening.
15 Behold, he withholdeth the waters, and they dry up;
also he sendeth them out,
and they overturn the earth.
16 With him is strength and wisdom;
the deceived and the deceiver are his.
17 He leadeth counsellors away spoiled,
and maketh the judges fools.
18 He looseth the bond of kings,
and girdeth their loins with a girdle.
19 He leadeth princes away spoiled,
and overthroweth the mighty.
20 He removeth away the speech of the trusty,
and taketh away the understanding of the aged.
21 He poureth contempt upon princes,
and weakeneth the strength of the mighty.

22 He discovereth deep things out of darkness,
and bringeth out to light the shadow of death.
23 He increaseth the nations, and destroyeth them;
he enlargeth the nations,
and straiteneth them again.
24 He taketh away the heart of the chief of
the people of the earth,
and causeth them to wander
in a wilderness where there is no way.
25 They grope in the dark without light, and
he maketh them to stagger like a drunken man.'

13 'Lo, mine eye hath seen all this,
mine ear hath heard and understood it.
2 What ye know, the same do I know also:
I am not inferior unto you.
3 Surely I would speak to the Almighty,
and I desire to reason with God.
4 But ye are forgers of lies,
ye are all physicians of no value.
5 O that ye would altogether hold your peace!
And it should be your wisdom.
6 Hear now my reasoning,
and hearken to the pleadings of my lips.
7 Will ye speak wickedly for God?
And talk deceitfully for him?
8 Will ye accept his person? Will ye contend for God?
9 Is it good that he should search you out?

Or as one man mocketh another,
do ye so mock him?
10 He will surely reprove you,
if ye do secretly accept persons.
11 Shall not his excellency make you afraid?
And his dread fall upon you?
12 Your remembrances are like unto ashes,
your bodies to bodies of clay.
13 Hold your peace, let me alone, that I may speak,
and let come on me what will.
14 Wherefore do I take my flesh in my teeth,
and put my life in mine hand?
15 Though he slay me, yet will I trust in him;
but I will maintain mine own ways before him.
16 He also shall be my salvation;
for an hypocrite shall not come before him.
17 Hear diligently my speech,
and my declaration with your ears.
18 Behold now I have ordered my cause;
I know that I shall be justified.
19 Who is he that will plead with me?
For now, if I hold my tongue,
I shall give up the ghost.
20 Only do not two things unto me;
then will I not hide myself from thee.
21 Withdraw thine hand far from me;
and let not thy dread make me afraid.
22 Then call thou, and I will answer;

or let me speak, and answer thou me.
23 How many are mine iniquities and sins?
Make me to know my transgression and my sin.
24 Wherefore hidest thou thy face,
and holdest me for thine enemy?
25 Wilt thou break a leaf driven to and fro?
And wilt thou pursue the dry stubble?
26 For thou writest bitter things against me, and
makest me to possess the iniquities of my youth.
27 Thou puttest my feet also in the stocks,
and lookest narrowly unto all my paths;
thou settest a print upon the heels of my feet.
28 And he, as a rotten thing, consumeth,
as a garment that is moth eaten.'

14 'Man that is born of a woman is of few days,
and full of trouble.
2 He cometh forth like a flower, and is cut down;
he fleeth also as a shadow, and continueth not.
3 And dost thou open thine eyes upon such an one,
and bringest me into judgment with thee?
4 Who can bring a clean thing out of an unclean?
Not one.
5 Seeing his days are determined,
the number of his months are with thee,
and thou hast appointed his bounds
that he cannot pass,
6 turn from him, that he may rest,

till he shall accomplish, as an hireling, his day.
7 For there is hope of a tree, if it be cut down,
that it will sprout again, and
that the tender branch thereof will not cease.
8 Though the root thereof wax old in the earth,
and the stock thereof die in the ground,
9 yet through the scent of water it will bud,
and bring forth boughs like a plant.
10 But man dieth, and wasteth away;
yea, man giveth up the ghost, and where is he?
11 As the waters fail from the sea,
and the flood decayeth and drieth up,
12 so man lieth down, and riseth not;
till the heavens be no more, they shall not awake,
nor be raised out of their sleep.
13 O that thou wouldest hide me in the grave,
that thou wouldest keep me secret,
until thy wrath be past, that thou wouldest
appoint me a set time, and remember me!
14 If a man die, shall he live again?
all the days of my appointed time will I wait,
till my change come.
15 Thou shalt call, and I will answer thee:
thou wilt have a desire to the work of thine hands.
16 For now thou numberest my steps;
dost thou not watch over my sin?
17 My transgression is sealed up in a bag,
and thou sewest up mine iniquity.

18 And surely the mountain falling cometh to nought,
and the rock is removed out of his place.
19 The waters wear the stones;
thou washest away the things
which grow out of the dust of the earth;
and thou destroyest the hope of man.
20 Thou prevailest for ever against him,
and he passeth; thou changest his countenance,
and sendest him away.
21 His sons come to honour, and he knoweth it not;
and they are brought low,
but he perceiveth it not of them.
22 But his flesh upon him shall have pain,
and his soul within him shall mourn.'

15 Then answered Eliphaz the Temanite, and said, 2 'Should
a wise man utter vain knowledge, and fill his belly with
the east wind? 3 Should he reason with unprofitable talk? Or
with speeches wherewith he can do no good? 4 Yea, thou cast-
est off fear, and restrainest prayer before God. 5 For thy mouth
uttereth thine iniquity, and thou choosest the tongue of the
crafty. 6 Thine own mouth condemneth thee, and not I; yea,
thine own lips testify against thee. 7 Art thou the first man that
was born? Or wast thou made before the hills? 8 Hast thou
heard the secret of God? And dost thou restrain wisdom to
thyself? 9 What knowest thou, that we know not? What understandest thou, which is not in us? 10 With us are both the gray-
headed and very aged men, much elder than thy father. 11 Are

the consolations of God small with thee? Is there any secret
thing with thee? 12 Why doth thine heart carry thee away?
And what do thy eyes wink at, 13 that thou turnest thy spirit
against God, and lettest such words go out of thy mouth?
14 What is man, that he should be clean? And he which is born
of a woman, that he should be righteous? 15 Behold, he putteth no trust in his saints; yea, the heavens are not clean in
his sight. 16 How much more abominable and filthy is man,
which drinketh iniquity like water? 17 I will shew thee, hear
me; and that which I have seen I will declare; 18 which wise
men have told from their fathers, and have not hid it: 19 unto
whom alone the earth was given, and no stranger passed
among them. 20 The wicked man travaileth with pain all his
days, and the number of years is hidden to the oppressor.
21 A dreadful sound is in his ears; in prosperity the destroyer
shall come upon him. 22 He believeth not that he shall return
out of darkness, and he is waited for of the sword. 23 He wandereth abroad for bread, saying, "Where is it?" He knoweth
that the day of darkness is ready at his hand. 24 Trouble and
anguish shall make him afraid; they shall prevail against him,
as a king ready to the battle. 25 For he stretcheth out his hand
against God, and strengtheneth himself against the Almighty.
26 He runneth upon him, even on his neck, upon the thick bos-
ses of his bucklers; 27 because he covereth his face with his
fatness, and maketh collops of fat on his flanks. 28 And he
dwelleth in desolate cities, and in houses which no man inhab-
iteth, which are ready to become heaps. 29 He shall not be rich,
neither shall his substance continue, neither shall he prolong

the perfection thereof upon the earth. [30] He shall not depart
out of darkness; the flame shall dry up his branches, and by
the breath of his mouth shall he go away. [31] Let not him that
is deceived trust in vanity; for vanity shall be his recompence.
[32] It shall be accomplished before his time, and his branch
shall not be green. [33] He shall shake off his unripe grape as
the vine, and shall cast off his flower as the olive. [34] For the
congregation of hypocrites shall be desolate, and fire shall
consume the tabernacles of bribery. [35] They conceive mischief,
and bring forth vanity, and their belly prepareth deceit.'

16 Then Job answered and said,

[2] 'I have heard many such things:
miserable comforters are ye all.
[3] Shall vain words have an end?
Or what emboldeneth thee that thou answerest?
[4] I also could speak as ye do;
if your soul were in my soul's stead,
I could heap up words against you,
and shake mine head at you.
[5] But I would strengthen you with my mouth, and
the moving of my lips should asswage your grief.
[6] Though I speak, my grief is not asswaged;
and though I forbear, what am I eased?
[7] But now he hath made me weary;
thou hast made desolate all my company.
[8] And thou hast filled me with wrinkles,

which is a witness against me; and my leanness
rising up in me beareth witness to my face.
9 He teareth me in his wrath, who hateth me;
he gnasheth upon me with his teeth;
mine enemy sharpeneth his eyes upon me.
10 They have gaped upon me with their mouth;
they have smitten me upon
the cheek reproachfully; they have gathered
themselves together against me.
11 God hath delivered me to the ungodly,
and turned me over into the hands of the wicked.
12 I was at ease, but he hath broken me asunder;
he hath also taken me by my neck, and shaken
me to pieces, and set me up for his mark.
13 His archers compass me round about,
he cleaveth my reins asunder, and doth not spare;
he poureth out my gall upon the ground.
14 He breaketh me with breach upon breach,
he runneth upon me like a giant.
15 I have sewed sackcloth upon my skin,
and defiled my horn in the dust.
16 My face is foul with weeping,
and on my eyelids is the shadow of death;
17 not for any injustice in mine hands,
also my prayer is pure.
18 O earth, cover not thou my blood,
and let my cry have no place.
19 Also now, behold, my witness is in heaven,

and my record is on high.
20 My friends scorn me;
but mine eye poureth out tears unto God.
21 O that one might plead for a man with God,
as a man pleadeth for his neighbour!
22 When a few years are come,
then I shall go the way whence I shall not return.'

17 'My breath is corrupt, my days are extinct,
the graves are ready for me.
2 Are there not mockers with me? And doth not
mine eye continue in their provocation?
3 Lay down now, put me in a surety with thee;
who is he that will strike hands with me?
4 For thou hast hid their heart from understanding;
therefore shalt thou not exalt them.
5 He that speaketh flattery to his friends,
even the eyes of his children shall fail.
6 He hath made me also a byword of the people;
and aforetime I was as a tabret.
7 Mine eye also is dim by reason of sorrow,
and all my members are as a shadow.
8 Upright men shall be astonied at this,
and the innocent shall stir up himself
against the hypocrite.
9 The righteous also shall hold on his way,
and he that hath clean hands
shall be stronger and stronger.

[10] But as for you all, do ye return, and come now;
for I cannot find one wise man among you.
[11] My days are past, my purposes are broken off,
even the thoughts of my heart.
[12] They change the night into day;
the light is short because of darkness.
[13] If I wait, the grave is mine house;
I have made my bed in the darkness.
[14] I have said to corruption, "Thou art my father;"
to the worm, "Thou art my mother, and my sister."
[15] And where is now my hope?
As for my hope, who shall see it?
[16] They shall go down to the bars of the pit,
when our rest together is in the dust.'

18 Then answered Bildad the Shuhite, and said, [2] 'How
long will it be ere ye make an end of words? Mark,
and afterwards we will speak. [3] Wherefore are we counted as
beasts, and reputed vile in your sight? [4] He teareth himself in
his anger; shall the earth be forsaken for thee? And shall the
rock be removed out of his place? [5] Yea, the light of the wicked
shall be put out, and the spark of his fire shall not shine.
[6] The light shall be dark in his tabernacle, and his candle shall
be put out with him. [7] The steps of his strength shall be straitened, and his own counsel shall cast him down. [8] For he is
cast into a net by his own feet, and he walketh upon a snare.
[9] The gin shall take him by the heel, and the robber shall prevail against him. [10] The snare is laid for him in the ground,

and a trap for him in the way. 11 Terrors shall make him afraid
on every side, and shall drive him to his feet. 12 His strength
shall be hungerbitten, and destruction shall be ready at his
side. 13 It shall devour the strength of his skin; even the firstborn of death shall devour his strength. 14 His confidence shall
be rooted out of his tabernacle, and it shall bring him to the
king of terrors. 15 It shall dwell in his tabernacle, because it is
none of his; brimstone shall be scattered upon his habitation.
16 His roots shall be dried up beneath, and above shall his
branch be cut off. 17 His remembrance shall perish from the
earth, and he shall have no name in the street. 18 He shall be
driven from light into darkness, and chased out of the world.
19 He shall neither have son nor nephew among his people,
nor any remaining in his dwellings. 20 They that come after
him shall be astonied at his day, as they that went before
were affrighted. 21 Surely such are the dwellings of the wicked,
and this is the place of him that knoweth not God.'

19 Then Job answered and said,

2 'How long will ye vex my soul,
and break me in pieces with words?
3 These ten times have ye reproached me;
ye are not ashamed that ye make
yourselves strange to me.
4 And be it indeed that I have erred,
mine error remaineth with myself.
5 If indeed ye will magnify yourselves against me,

and plead against me my reproach,
6 know now that God hath overthrown me,
and hath compassed me with his net.
7 Behold, I cry out of wrong, but I am not heard;
I cry aloud, but there is no judgment.
8 He hath fenced up my way that I cannot pass,
and he hath set darkness in my paths.
9 He hath stripped me of my glory,
and taken the crown from my head.
10 He hath destroyed me on every side,
and I am gone;
and mine hope hath he removed like a tree.
11 He hath also kindled his wrath against me, and
he counteth me unto him as one of his enemies.
12 His troops come together,
and raise up their way against me,
and encamp round about my tabernacle.
13 He hath put my brethren far from me, and
mine acquaintance are verily estranged from me.
14 My kinsfolk have failed,
and my familiar friends have forgotten me.
15 They that dwell in mine house,
and my maids, count me for a stranger:
I am an alien in their sight.
16 I called my servant, and he gave me no answer;
I intreated him with my mouth.
17 My breath is strange to my wife, though I intreated
for the children's sake of mine own body.

18 Yea, young children despised me;
I arose, and they spake against me.
19 All my inward friends abhorred me:
and they whom I loved are turned against me.
20 My bone cleaveth to my skin and to my flesh,
and I am escaped with the skin of my teeth.
21 Have pity upon me, have pity upon me,
O ye my friends;
for the hand of God hath touched me.
22 Why do ye persecute me as God,
and are not satisfied with my flesh?
23 'Oh that my words were now written!
Oh that they were printed in a book!
24 That they were graven with an iron pen
and lead in the rock for ever!
25 For I know that my redeemer liveth, and that
he shall stand at the latter day upon the earth;
26 and though after my skin worms destroy this body,
yet in my flesh shall I see God,
27 whom I shall see for myself,
and mine eyes shall behold, and not another,
though my reins be consumed within me.
28 But ye should say, "Why persecute we him,
seeing the root of the matter is found in me?"
29 Be ye afraid of the sword;
for wrath bringeth the punishments of the sword,
that ye may know there is a judgment.'

20 Then answered Zophar the Naamathite, and said,
2 "Therefore do my thoughts cause me to answer, and
for this I make haste. 3 I have heard the check of my reproach,
and the spirit of my understanding causeth me to answer.
4 Knowest thou not this of old, since man was placed upon
earth, 5 that the triumphing of the wicked is short, and the joy
of the hypocrite but for a moment? 6 Though his excellency
mount up to the heavens, and his head reach unto the clouds,
7 yet he shall perish for ever like his own dung; they which
have seen him shall say, "Where is he?" 8 He shall fly away
as a dream, and shall not be found; yea, he shall be chased
away as a vision of the night. 9 The eye also which saw him
shall see him no more; neither shall his place any more behold
him. 10 His children shall seek to please the poor, and his
hands shall restore their goods. 11 His bones are full of the sin
of his youth, which shall lie down with him in the dust.
12 Though wickedness be sweet in his mouth, though he hide
it under his tongue; 13 though he spare it, and forsake it not,
but keep it still within his mouth; 14 yet his meat in his bowels is turned; it is the gall of asps within him. 15 He hath swallowed down riches, and he shall vomit them up again: God
shall cast them out of his belly. 16 He shall suck the poison of
asps: the viper's tongue shall slay him. 17 He shall not see the
rivers, the floods, the brooks of honey and butter. 18 That which
he laboured for shall he restore, and shall not swallow it down;
according to his substance shall the restitution be, and he shall
not rejoice therein. 19 Because he hath oppressed and hath forsaken the poor, because he hath violently taken away an house

which he builded not, [20] surely he shall not feel quietness in
his belly; he shall not save of that which he desired. [21] There
shall none of his meat be left; therefore shall no man look for
his goods. [22] In the fulness of his sufficiency he shall be in straits;
every hand of the wicked shall come upon him. [23] When he is
about to fill his belly, God shall cast the fury of his wrath
upon him, and shall rain it upon him while he is eating. [24] He
shall flee from the iron weapon, and the bow of steel shall
strike him through. [25] It is drawn, and cometh out of the body;
yea, the glittering sword cometh out of his gall: terrors are
upon him. [26] All darkness shall be hid in his secret places; a
fire not blown shall consume him; it shall go ill with him that
is left in his tabernacle. [27] The heaven shall reveal his iniquity;
and the earth shall rise up against him. [28] The increase of his
house shall depart, and his goods shall flow away in the day
of his wrath. [29] This is the portion of a wicked man from God,
and the heritage appointed unto him by God.'

21

But Job answered and said,

[2] 'Hear diligently my speech,
  and let this be your consolations.
[3] Suffer me that I may speak;
  and after that I have spoken, mock on.
[4] As for me, is my complaint to man?
  And if it were so,
    why should not my spirit be troubled?
[5] Mark me, and be astonished,

and lay your hand upon your mouth.
6 Even when I remember I am afraid,
and trembling taketh hold on my flesh.
7 Wherefore do the wicked live, become old,
yea, are mighty in power?
8 Their seed is established in their sight with them,
and their offspring before their eyes.
9 Their houses are safe from fear;
neither is the rod of God upon them.
10 Their bull gendereth, and faileth not;
their cow calveth, and casteth not her calf.
11 They send forth their little ones like a flock,
and their children dance.
12 They take the timbrel and harp,
and rejoice at the sound of the organ.
13 They spend their days in wealth,
and in a moment go down to the grave.
14 Therefore they say unto God,
"Depart from us; for we desire not
the knowledge of thy ways.
15 What is the Almighty, that we should serve him?
And what profit should we have,
if we pray unto him?"
16 Lo, their good is not in their hand:
the counsel of the wicked is far from me.
17 How oft is the candle of the wicked put out!
And how oft cometh their destruction upon them!
God distributeth sorrows in his anger.

18 They are as stubble before the wind,
and as chaff that the storm carrieth away.
19 God layeth up his iniquity for his children;
he rewardeth him, and he shall know it.
20 His eyes shall see his destruction,
and he shall drink of the wrath of the Almighty.
21 For what pleasure hath he in his house after him,
when the number of his months
is cut off in the midst?
22 Shall any teach God knowledge,
seeing he judgeth those that are high?
23 One dieth in his full strength,
being wholly at ease and quiet.
24 His breasts are full of milk,
and his bones are moistened with marrow.
25 And another dieth in the bitterness of his soul,
and never eateth with pleasure.
26 They shall lie down alike in the dust,
and the worms shall cover them.
27 Behold, I know your thoughts,
and the devices which ye wrongfully
imagine against me.
28 For ye say, "Where is the house of the prince?
And where are the dwelling places of the wicked?"
29 Have ye not asked them that go by the way?
And do ye not know their tokens,
30 that the wicked is reserved to the day of destruction?
They shall be brought forth to the day of wrath.

[31] Who shall declare his way to his face?
And who shall repay him what he hath done?
[32] Yet shall he be brought to the grave,
and shall remain in the tomb.
[33] The clods of the valley shall be sweet unto him,
and every man shall draw after him,
as there are innumerable before him.
[34] How then comfort ye me in vain,
seeing in your answers
there remaineth falsehood?'

22 Then Eliphaz the Temanite answered and said, [2] 'Can
a man be profitable unto God, as he that is wise may
be profitable unto himself? [3] Is it any pleasure to the Almighty,
that thou art righteous? Or is it gain to him, that thou makest
thy ways perfect? [4] Will he reprove thee for fear of thee? Will
he enter with thee into judgment? [5] Is not thy wickedness
great? And thine iniquities infinite? [6] For thou hast taken a
pledge from thy brother for nought, and stripped the naked
of their clothing. [7] Thou hast not given water to the weary to
drink, and thou hast withholden bread from the hungry. [8] But
as for the mighty man, he had the earth; and the honourable
man dwelt in it. [9] Thou hast sent widows away empty, and
the arms of the fatherless have been broken. [10] Therefore
snares are round about thee, and sudden fear troubleth thee,
[11] Or darkness, that thou canst not see; and abundance of
waters cover thee. [12] Is not God in the height of heaven? And
behold the height of the stars, how high they are! [13] And thou

sayest, "How doth God know? Can he judge through the
dark cloud?" [14] Thick clouds are a covering to him, that he
seeth not; and he walketh in the circuit of heaven. [15] Hast
thou marked the old way which wicked men have trodden?
[16] Which were cut down out of time, whose foundation was
overflown with a flood; [17] which said unto God, "Depart from
us" and "What can the Almighty do for them?" [18] Yet he filled
their houses with good things; but the counsel of the wicked
is far from me. [19] The righteous see it, and are glad; and the
innocent laugh them to scorn. [20] Whereas our substance is
not cut down, but the remnant of them the fire consumeth.
[21] Acquaint now thyself with him, and be at peace; thereby
good shall come unto thee. [22] Receive, I pray thee, the law
from his mouth, and lay up his words in thine heart. [23] If
thou return to the Almighty, thou shalt be built up; thou shalt
put away iniquity far from thy tabernacles. [24] Then shalt thou
lay up gold as dust, and the gold of Ophir as the stones of
the brooks. [25] Yea, the Almighty shall be thy defence, and
thou shalt have plenty of silver. [26] For then shalt thou have
thy delight in the Almighty, and shalt lift up thy face unto
God. [27] Thou shalt make thy prayer unto him, and he shall
hear thee, and thou shalt pay thy vows. [28] Thou shalt also
decree a thing, and it shall be established unto thee; and the
light shall shine upon thy ways. [29] When men are cast down,
then thou shalt say, "There is lifting up"; and he shall save
the humble person. [30] He shall deliver the island of the innocent; and it is delivered by the pureness of thine hands.'

23 Then Job answered and said,

[2] 'Even to day is my complaint bitter;
my stroke is heavier than my groaning.
[3] Oh that I knew where I might find him!
That I might come even to his seat!
[4] I would order my cause before him,
and fill my mouth with arguments.
[5] I would know the words which he would answer me,
and understand what he would say unto me.
[6] Will he plead against me with his great power?
No, but he would put strength in me.
[7] There the righteous might dispute with him;
so should I be delivered for ever from my judge.
[8] Behold, I go forward, but he is not there;
and backward, but I cannot perceive him;
[9] on the left hand, where he doth work,
but I cannot behold him;
he hideth himself on the right hand,
that I cannot see him.
[10] But he knoweth the way that I take;
when he hath tried me, I shall come forth as gold.
[11] My foot hath held his steps;
his way have I kept, and not declined.
[12] Neither have I gone back from
the commandment of his lips;
I have esteemed the words of his mouth
more than my necessary food.

13 But he is in one mind, and who can turn him?
And what his soul desireth, even that he doeth.
14 For he performeth the thing that is appointed for me;
and many such things are with him.
15 Therefore am I troubled at his presence;
when I consider, I am afraid of him.
16 For God maketh my heart soft,
and the Almighty troubleth me,
17 Because I was not cut off before the darkness,
neither hath he covered the darkness from my face.'

24 'Why, seeing times are not hidden from the Almighty,
do they that know him not see his days?
2 Some remove the landmarks;
they violently take away flocks, and feed thereof.
3 They drive away the ass of the fatherless,
they take the widow's ox for a pledge.
4 They turn the needy out of the way;
the poor of the earth hide themselves together.
5 Behold, as wild asses in the desert,
go they forth to their work,
rising betimes for a prey;
the wilderness yieldeth food for them
and for their children.
6 They reap every one his corn in the field;
and they gather the vintage of the wicked.
7 They cause the naked to lodge without clothing,
that they have no covering in the cold.

8 They are wet with the showers of the mountains,
and embrace the rock for want of a shelter.
9 They pluck the fatherless from the breast,
and take a pledge of the poor.
10 They cause him to go naked without clothing,
and they take away the sheaf from the hungry;
11 which make oil within their walls,
and tread their winepresses, and suffer thirst.
12 Men groan from out of the city,
and the soul of the wounded crieth out;
yet God layeth not folly to them.
13 They are of those that rebel against the light;
they know not the ways thereof,
nor abide in the paths thereof.
14 The murderer rising with the light killeth the poor
and needy, and in the night is as a thief.
15 The eye also of the adulterer waiteth for
the twilight, saying, "No eye shall see me;"
and disguiseth his face.
16 In the dark they dig through houses,
which they had marked for themselves
in the daytime;
they know not the light.
17 For the morning is to them
even as the shadow of death;
if one know them,
they are in the terrors of the shadow of death.
18 He is swift as the waters;

their portion is cursed in the earth;
he beholdeth not the way of the vineyards.
19 Drought and heat consume the snow waters;
so doth the grave those which have sinned.
20 The womb shall forget him;
the worm shall feed sweetly on him;
he shall be no more remembered;
and wickedness shall be broken as a tree.
21 He evil entreateth the barren that beareth not;
and doeth not good to the widow.
22 He draweth also the mighty with his power;
he riseth up, and no man is sure of life.
23 Though it be given him to be in safety,
whereon he resteth;
yet his eyes are upon their ways.
24 They are exalted for a little while,
but are gone and brought low;
they are taken out of the way as all other,
and cut off as the tops of the ears of corn.
25 And if it be not so now, who will make me a liar,
and make my speech nothing worth?'

25 Then answered Bildad the Shuhite, and said, 2 'Dominion and fear are with him, he maketh peace in his
high places. 3 Is there any number of his armies? And upon
whom doth not his light arise? 4 How then can man be justified with God? Or how can he be clean that is born of a
woman? 5 Behold even to the moon, and it shineth not; yea,

the stars are not pure in his sight. [6] How much less man, that
is a worm? And the son of man, which is a worm?'

26 But Job answered and said,

[2] 'How hast thou helped him that is without power?
How savest thou the arm that hath no strength?
[3] How hast thou counselled him that hath no wisdom?
And how hast thou plentifully declared
the thing as it is?
[4] To whom hast thou uttered words?
And whose spirit came from thee?
[5] Dead things are formed from under the waters,
and the inhabitants thereof.
[6] Hell is naked before him,
and destruction hath no covering.
[7] He stretcheth out the north over the empty place,
and hangeth the earth upon nothing.
[8] He bindeth up the waters in his thick clouds;
and the cloud is not rent under them.
[9] He holdeth back the face of his throne,
and spreadeth his cloud upon it.
[10] He hath compassed the waters with bounds,
until the day and night come to an end.
[11] The pillars of heaven tremble
and are astonished at his reproof.
[12] He divideth the sea with his power, and by his
understanding he smiteth through the proud.

13 By his spirit he hath garnished the heavens;
his hand hath formed the crooked serpent.
14 Lo, these are parts of his ways;
but how little a portion is heard of him?
But the thunder of his power
who can understand?'

27 Moreover Job continued his parable, and said,

2 'As God liveth, who hath taken away my judgment,
and the Almighty, who hath vexed my soul,
3 all the while my breath is in me,
and the spirit of God is in my nostrils,
4 my lips shall not speak wickedness,
nor my tongue utter deceit.
5 God forbid that I should justify you;
till I die I will not remove mine integrity from me.
6 My righteousness I hold fast, and will not let it go;
my heart shall not reproach me so long as I live.
7 Let mine enemy be as the wicked, and
he that riseth up against me as the unrighteous.
8 For what is the hope of the hypocrite,
though he hath gained,
when God taketh away his soul?
9 Will God hear his cry when trouble
cometh upon him?
10 Will he delight himself in the Almighty?
Will he always call upon God?

11 I will teach you by the hand of God;
that which is with the Almighty will I not conceal.
12 Behold, all ye yourselves have seen it;
why then are ye thus altogether vain?
13 This is the portion of a wicked man with God,
and the heritage of oppressors,
which they shall receive of the Almighty.
14 If his children be multiplied, it is for the sword;
and his offspring shall not be satisfied with bread.
15 Those that remain of him shall be buried in death;
and his widows shall not weep.
16 Though he heap up silver as the dust,
and prepare raiment as the clay,
17 he may prepare it, but the just shall put it on,
and the innocent shall divide the silver.
18 He buildeth his house as a moth,
and as a booth that the keeper maketh.
19 The rich man shall lie down,
but he shall not be gathered;
he openeth his eyes, and he is not.
20 Terrors take hold on him as waters,
a tempest stealeth him away in the night.
21 The east wind carrieth him away, and he departeth;
and as a storm hurleth him out of his place.
22 For God shall cast upon him, and not spare;
he would fain flee out of his hand.
23 Men shall clap their hands at him,
and shall hiss him out of his place.'

28 'Surely there is a vein for the silver,
and a place for gold where they fine it.
2 Iron is taken out of the earth,
and brass is molten out of the stone.
3 He setteth an end to darkness,
and searcheth out all perfection;
the stones of darkness, and the shadow of death.
4 The flood breaketh out from the inhabitant,
even the waters forgotten of the foot;
they are dried up,
they are gone away from men.
5 As for the earth, out of it cometh bread;
and under it is turned up as it were fire.
6 The stones of it are the place of sapphires;
and it hath dust of gold.
7 There is a path which no fowl knoweth,
and which the vulture's eye hath not seen;
8 the lion's whelps have not trodden it,
nor the fierce lion passed by it.
9 He putteth forth his hand upon the rock;
he overturneth the mountains by the roots.
10 He cutteth out rivers among the rocks;
and his eye seeth every precious thing.
11 He bindeth the floods from overflowing;
and the thing that is hid bringeth he forth to light.
12 But where shall wisdom be found?
And where is the place of understanding?
13 Man knoweth not the price thereof;

neither is it found in the land of the living.
14 The depth saith, "It is not in me;"
and the sea saith, "It is not with me."
15 It cannot be gotten for gold, neither shall silver
be weighed for the price thereof.
16 It cannot be valued with the gold of Ophir,
with the precious onyx, or the sapphire.
17 The gold and the crystal cannot equal it;
and the exchange of it
shall not be for jewels of fine gold.
18 No mention shall be made of coral, or of pearls,
for the price of wisdom is above rubies.
19 The topaz of Ethiopia shall not equal it,
neither shall it be valued with pure gold.
20 Whence then cometh wisdom?
And where is the place of understanding,
21 seeing it is hid from the eyes of all living,
and kept close from the fowls of the air?
22 Destruction and death say,
"We have heard the fame thereof with our ears."
23 God understandeth the way thereof,
and he knoweth the place thereof.
24 For he looketh to the ends of the earth,
and seeth under the whole heaven,
25 to make the weight for the winds;
and he weigheth the waters by measure.
26 When he made a decree for the rain,
and a way for the lightning of the thunder,

27 then did he see it, and declare it;
he prepared it, yea, and searched it out.
28 And unto man he said,
"Behold, the fear of the Lord, that is wisdom;
and to depart from evil is understanding."'

29

Moreover Job continued his parable, and said,

2 'Oh that I were as in months past,
as in the days when God preserved me;
3 when his candle shined upon my head,
and when by his light I walked through darkness,
4 as I was in the days of my youth,
when the secret of God was upon my tabernacle;
5 when the Almighty was yet with me,
when my children were about me;
6 when I washed my steps with butter,
and the rock poured me out rivers of oil;
7 when I went out to the gate through the city,
when I prepared my seat in the street,
8 the young men saw me, and hid themselves;
and the aged arose, and stood up.
9 The princes refrained talking,
and laid their hand on their mouth.
10 The nobles held their peace, and their tongue
cleaved to the roof of their mouth.
11 When the ear heard me, then it blessed me;
and when the eye saw me, it gave witness to me;

12 because I delivered the poor that cried, and
the fatherless, and him that had none to help him.
13 The blessing of him that was ready to perish
came upon me;
and I caused the widow's heart to sing for joy.
14 I put on righteousness, and it clothed me;
my judgment was as a robe and a diadem.
15 I was eyes to the blind, and feet was I to the lame.
16 I was a father to the poor;
and the cause which I knew not I searched out.
17 And I brake the jaws of the wicked,
and plucked the spoil out of his teeth.
18 Then I said, "I shall die in my nest,
and I shall multiply my days as the sand."
19 My root was spread out by the waters,
and the dew lay all night upon my branch.
20 My glory was fresh in me,
and my bow was renewed in my hand.
21 Unto me men gave ear, and waited,
and kept silence at my counsel.
22 After my words they spake not again;
and my speech dropped upon them.
23 And they waited for me as for the rain;
and they opened their mouth wide
as for the latter rain.
24 If I laughed on them, they believed it not;
and the light of my countenance
they cast not down.

25 I chose out their way, and sat chief,
and dwelt as a king in the army,
as one that comforteth the mourners.'

30 'But now they that are younger than I
have me in derision,
whose fathers I would have disdained
to have set with the dogs of my flock.
2 Yea, whereto might the strength of their hands
profit me, in whom old age was perished?
3 For want and famine they were solitary;
fleeing into the wilderness in former time
desolate and waste;
4 who cut up mallows by the bushes,
and juniper roots for their meat.
5 They were driven forth from among men
(they cried after them as after a thief)
6 to dwell in the clifts of the valleys,
in caves of the earth, and in the rocks.
7 Among the bushes they brayed;
under the nettles they were gathered together.
8 They were children of fools,
yea, children of base men;
they were viler than the earth.
9 And now am I their song, yea, I am their byword.
10 They abhor me, they flee far from me,
and spare not to spit in my face.
11 Because he hath loosed my cord, and afflicted me,

they have also let loose the bridle before me.
12 Upon my right hand rise the youth;
they push away my feet,
and they raise up against me
the ways of their destruction.
13 They mar my path, they set forward my calamity,
they have no helper.
14 They came upon me as a wide breaking in of waters;
in the desolation they rolled themselves upon me.
15 Terrors are turned upon me;
they pursue my soul as the wind;
and my welfare passeth away as a cloud.
16 And now my soul is poured out upon me;
the days of affliction have taken hold upon me.
17 My bones are pierced in me in the night season;
and my sinews take no rest.
18 By the great force of my disease
is my garment changed;
it bindeth me about as the collar of my coat.
19 He hath cast me into the mire,
and I am become like dust and ashes.
20 I cry unto thee, and thou dost not hear me:
I stand up, and thou regardest me not.
21 Thou art become cruel to me;
with thy strong hand
thou opposest thyself against me.
22 Thou liftest me up to the wind;
thou causest me to ride upon it,

and dissolvest my substance.
23 For I know that thou wilt bring me to death,
and to the house appointed for all living.
24 Howbeit he will not stretch out
his hand to the grave,
though they cry in his destruction.
25 Did not I weep for him that was in trouble?
Was not my soul grieved for the poor?
26 When I looked for good, then evil came unto me;
and when I waited for light, there came darkness.
27 My bowels boiled, and rested not;
the days of affliction prevented me.
28 I went mourning without the sun;
I stood up, and I cried in the congregation.
29 I am a brother to dragons,
and a companion to owls.
30 My skin is black upon me,
and my bones are burned with heat.
31 My harp also is turned to mourning,
and my organ into the voice of them that weep.'

31 'I made a covenant with mine eyes;
why then should I think upon a maid?
2 For what portion of God is there from above?
And what inheritance
of the Almighty from on high?
3 Is not destruction to the wicked?
And a strange punishment

to the workers of iniquity?
4 Doth not he see my ways, and count all my steps?
5 If I have walked with vanity,
or if my foot hath hasted to deceit,
6 let me be weighed in an even balance,
that God may know mine integrity.
7 If my step hath turned out of the way,
and mine heart walked after mine eyes,
and if any blot hath cleaved to mine hands,
8 then let me sow, and let another eat;
yea, let my offspring be rooted out.
9 If mine heart have been deceived by a woman,
or if I have laid wait at my neighbour's door,
10 then let my wife grind unto another,
and let others bow down upon her.
11 For this is an heinous crime;
yea, it is an iniquity to be punished by the judges.
12 For it is a fire that consumeth to destruction,
and would root out all mine increase.
13 If I did despise the cause of my manservant
or of my maidservant,
when they contended with me,
14 what then shall I do when God riseth up?
And when he visiteth, what shall I answer him?
15 Did not he that made me in the womb make him?
And did not one fashion us in the womb?
16 If I have withheld the poor from their desire,
or have caused the eyes of the widow to fail;

17 or have eaten my morsel myself alone,
and the fatherless hath not eaten thereof
18 (for from my youth he was brought up with me,
as with a father,
and I have guided her
from my mother's womb);
19 if I have seen any perish for want of clothing,
or any poor without covering;
20 if his loins have not blessed me,
and if he were not warmed
with the fleece of my sheep;
21 if I have lifted up my hand against the fatherless,
when I saw my help in the gate:
22 then let mine arm fall from my shoulder blade,
and mine arm be broken from the bone.
23 For destruction from God was a terror to me,
and by reason of his highness I could not endure.
24 If I have made gold my hope,
or have said to the fine gold,
"Thou art my confidence;"
25 if I rejoiced because my wealth was great,
and because mine hand had gotten much;
26 if I beheld the sun when it shined,
or the moon walking in brightness;
27 and my heart hath been secretly enticed,
or my mouth hath kissed my hand:
28 this also were an iniquity
to be punished by the judge;

for I should have denied the God that is above.
29 If I rejoiced at the destruction of him that hated me,
or lifted up myself when evil found him,
30 neither have I suffered my mouth to sin
by wishing a curse to his soul.
31 If the men of my tabernacle said not,
"Oh that we had of his flesh!"
we cannot be satisfied.
32 The stranger did not lodge in the street;
but I opened my doors to the traveller.
33 If I covered my transgressions as Adam,
by hiding mine iniquity in my bosom,
34 did I fear a great multitude,
or did the contempt of families terrify me,
that I kept silence,
and went not out of the door?
35 Oh that one would hear me!
Behold, my desire is that the Almighty
would answer me,
and that mine adversary had written a book.
36 Surely I would take it upon my shoulder,
and bind it as a crown to me.
37 I would declare unto him the number of my steps;
as a prince would I go near unto him.
38 If my land cry against me,
or that the furrows likewise thereof complain;
39 if I have eaten the fruits thereof without money,
or have caused the owners thereof to lose their life,

40 let thistles grow instead of wheat,
and cockle instead of barley.'

The words of Job are ended.

32 So these three men ceased to answer Job, because he
was righteous in his own eyes. 2 Then was kindled
the wrath of Elihu the son of Barachel the Buzite, of the kindred of Ram; against Job was his wrath kindled, because he
justified himself rather than God. 3 Also against his three
friends was his wrath kindled, because they had found no
answer, and yet had condemned Job. 4 Now Elihu had waited
till Job had spoken, because they were elder than he. 5 When
Elihu saw that there was no answer in the mouth of these
three men, then his wrath was kindled. 6 And Elihu the son
of Barachel the Buzite answered and said,

'I am young, and ye are very old; wherefore I was afraid,
and durst not shew you mine opinion. 7 I said, "Days should
speak, and multitude of years should teach wisdom." 8 But
there is a spirit in man; and the inspiration of the Almighty
giveth them understanding. 9 Great men are not always wise;
neither do the aged understand judgment. 10 Therefore I said,
"Hearken to me; I also will shew mine opinion."

11 'Behold, I waited for your words; I gave ear to your reasons, whilst ye searched out what to say. 12 Yea, I attended
unto you, and, behold, there was none of you that convinced
Job, or that answered his words: 13 lest ye should say, "We
have found out wisdom: God thrusteth him down, not man."

14 Now he hath not directed his words against me; neither
will I answer him with your speeches.

15 'They were amazed, they answered no more; they left
off speaking. 16 When I had waited (for they spake not, but
stood still, and answered no more), 17 I said, "I will answer
also my part, I also will shew mine opinion." 18 For I am full
of matter; the spirit within me constraineth me. 19 Behold, my
belly is as wine which hath no vent; it is ready to burst like
new bottles. 20 I will speak, that I may be refreshed; I will
open my lips and answer. 21 Let me not, I pray you, accept any
man's person, neither let me give flattering titles unto man.
22 For I know not to give flattering titles; in so doing my
maker would soon take me away.

33 'Wherefore, Job, I pray thee, hear my speeches, and
hearken to all my words. 2 Behold, now I have opened
my mouth, my tongue hath spoken in my mouth. 3 My words
shall be of the uprightness of my heart; and my lips shall
utter knowledge clearly. 4 The Spirit of God hath made me,
and the breath of the Almighty hath given me life. 5 If thou
canst answer me, set thy words in order before me, stand up.
6 Behold, I am according to thy wish in God's stead; I also am
formed out of the clay. 7 Behold, my terror shall not make
thee afraid, neither shall my hand be heavy upon thee.

8 'Surely thou hast spoken in mine hearing, and I have
heard the voice of thy words, saying, 9 "I am clean without
transgression, I am innocent; neither is there iniquity in me."
10 Behold, he findeth occasions against me, he counteth me

for his enemy, [11]he putteth my feet in the stocks, he marketh
all my paths.
[12]'Behold, in this thou art not just; I will answer thee, that
God is greater than man. [13]Why dost thou strive against
him? For he giveth not account of any of his matters. [14]For
God speaketh once, yea twice, yet man perceiveth it not. [15]In
a dream, in a vision of the night, when deep sleep falleth
upon men, in slumberings upon the bed; [16]then he openeth
the ears of men, and sealeth their instruction, [17]that he may
withdraw man from his purpose, and hide pride from man.
[18]He keepeth back his soul from the pit, and his life from
perishing by the sword. [19]He is chastened also with pain
upon his bed, and the multitude of his bones with strong
pain; [20]so that his life abhorreth bread, and his soul dainty
meat. [21]His flesh is consumed away, that it cannot be seen;
and his bones that were not seen stick out. [22]Yea, his soul
draweth near unto the grave, and his life to the destroyers.
[23]If there be a messenger with him, an interpreter, one among
a thousand, to shew unto man his uprightness; [24]then he is
gracious unto him, and saith, "Deliver him from going down
to the pit; I have found a ransom. [25]His flesh shall be fresher
than a child's: he shall return to the days of his youth." [26]He
shall pray unto God, and he will be favour-able unto him,
and he shall see his face with joy; for he will render unto
man his righteousness. [27]He looketh upon men, and if any
say, "I have sinned, and perverted that which was right, and
it profited me not;" [28]he will deliver his soul from going into
the pit, and his life shall see the light.

29 'Lo, all these things worketh God oftentimes with man,
30 to bring back his soul from the pit, to be enlightened with
the light of the living. 31 Mark well, O Job, hearken unto me:
hold thy peace, and I will speak. 32 If thou hast any thing to say,
answer me; speak, for I desire to justify thee. 33 If not, heark-
en unto me: hold thy peace, and I shall teach thee wisdom.'

34 Furthermore Elihu answered and said, 2 'Hear my
words, O ye wise men; and give ear unto me, ye that
have knowledge. 3 For the ear trieth words, as the mouth tast-
eth meat. 4 Let us choose to us judgment; let us know among
ourselves what is good. 5 For Job hath said, I am righteous;
and God hath taken away my judgment. 6 Should I lie against
my right? My wound is incurable without transgression.
7 What man is like Job, who drinketh up scorning like water,
8 which goeth in company with the workers of iniquity, and
walketh with wicked men? 9 For he hath said, "It profiteth a
man nothing that he should delight himself with God."
10 'Therefore hearken unto me, ye men of understanding: far
be it from God, that he should do wickedness; and from the
Almighty, that he should commit iniquity. 11 For the work of a
man shall he render unto him, and cause every man to find
according to his ways. 12 Yea, surely God will not do wickedly,
neither will the Almighty pervert judgment. 13 Who hath
given him a charge over the earth? Or who hath disposed
the whole world? 14 If he set his heart upon man, if he gather
unto himself his spirit and his breath, 15 all flesh shall perish
together, and man shall turn again unto dust.

16 'If now thou hast understanding, hear this: hearken to
the voice of my words. 17 Shall even he that hateth right govern? And wilt thou condemn him that is most just? 18 Is it fit
to say to a king, "Thou art wicked?" and to princes, "Ye are
ungodly"? 19 How much less to him that accepteth not the
persons of princes, nor regardeth the rich more than the poor?
For they all are the work of his hands. 20 In a moment shall
they die, and the people shall be troubled at midnight, and
pass away; and the mighty shall be taken away without hand.

21 'For his eyes are upon the ways of man, and he seeth all
his goings. 22 There is no darkness, nor shadow of death,
where the workers of iniquity may hide themselves. 23 For he
will not lay upon man more than right; that he should enter
into judgment with God. 24 He shall break in pieces mighty
men without number, and set others in their stead. 25 Therefore he knoweth their works, and he overturneth them in the
night, so that they are destroyed. 26 He striketh them as
wicked men in the open sight of others, 27 because they turned
back from him, and would not consider any of his ways, 28 so
that they cause the cry of the poor to come unto him, and he
heareth the cry of the afflicted. 29 When he giveth quietness,
who then can make trouble? And when he hideth his face,
who then can behold him? Whether it be done against a
nation, or against a man only: 30 that the hypocrite reign not,
lest the people be ensnared.

31 'Surely it is meet to be said unto God, "I have borne
chastisement, I will not offend any more; 32 that which I see
not teach thou me. If I have done iniquity, I will do no more."

33 Should it be according to thy mind? He will recompense it,
whether thou refuse, or whether thou choose; and not I.
Therefore speak what thou knowest. 34 Let men of understanding tell me, and let a wise man hearken unto me. 35 Job
hath spoken without knowledge, and his words were without wisdom. 36 My desire is that Job may be tried unto the
end because of his answers for wicked men. 37 For he addeth
rebellion unto his sin, he clappeth his hands among us, and
multiplieth his words against God.'

35 Elihu spake moreover, and said, 2 'Thinkest thou this
to be right, that thou saidst, "My righteousness is
more than God's"? 3 For thou saidst, "What advantage will it
be unto thee?" and "What profit shall I have, if I be cleansed
from my sin?" 4 I will answer thee, and thy companions with
thee. 5 Look unto the heavens, and see; and behold the clouds
which are higher than thou. 6 If thou sinnest, what doest thou
against him? Or if thy transgressions be multiplied, what doest
thou unto him? 7 If thou be righteous, what givest thou him?
Or what receiveth he of thine hand? 8 Thy wickedness may
hurt a man as thou art; and thy righteousness may profit the
son of man.

9 'By reason of the multitude of oppressions they make
the oppressed to cry; they cry out by reason of the arm of the
mighty. 10 But none saith, "Where is God my maker, who
giveth songs in the night; 11 who teacheth us more than the
beasts of the earth, and maketh us wiser than the fowls of
heaven?" 12 There they cry, but none giveth answer, because

of the pride of evil men. 13 Surely God will not hear vanity, neither will the Almighty regard it. 14 Although thou sayest thou shalt not see him, yet judgment is before him; therefore trust thou in him. 15 But now, because it is not so, he hath visited in his anger; yet he knoweth it not in great extremity. 16 Therefore doth Job open his mouth in vain; he multiplieth words without knowledge.'

36 Elihu also proceeded, and said, 2 'Suffer me a little, and I will shew thee that I have yet to speak on God's behalf. 3 I will fetch my knowledge from afar, and will ascribe righteousness to my Maker. 4 For truly my words shall not be false; he that is perfect in knowledge is with thee.

5 'Behold, God is mighty, and despiseth not any; he is mighty in strength and wisdom. 6 He preserveth not the life of the wicked, but giveth right to the poor. 7 He withdraweth not his eyes from the righteous; but with kings are they on the throne; yea, he doth establish them for ever, and they are exalted. 8 And if they be bound in fetters, and be holden in cords of affliction; 9 then he sheweth them their work, and their transgressions that they have exceeded. 10 He openeth also their ear to discipline, and commandeth that they return from iniquity. 11 If they obey and serve him, they shall spend their days in prosperity, and their years in pleasures. 12 But if they obey not, they shall perish by the sword, and they shall die without knowledge. 13 'But the hypocrites in heart heap up wrath: they cry not when he bindeth them. 14 They die in youth, and their life is among the unclean. 15 He delivereth

the poor in his affliction, and openeth their ears in oppression. 16 Even so would he have removed thee out of the strait
into a broad place, where there is no straitness; and that which
should be set on thy table should be full of fatness.

17 'But thou hast fulfilled the judgment of the wicked; judgment and justice take hold on thee. 18 Because there is wrath,
beware lest he take thee away with his stroke; then a great
ransom cannot deliver thee. 19 Will he esteem thy riches? No,
not gold, nor all the forces of strength. 20 Desire not the night,
when people are cut off in their place. 21 Take heed, regard
not iniquity; for this hast thou chosen rather than affliction.
22 Behold, God exalteth by his power; who teacheth like him?
23 Who hath enjoined him his way? Or who can say, "Thou
hast wrought iniquity"?

24 'Remember that thou magnify his work, which men
behold. 25 Every man may see it; man may behold it afar off.
26 Behold, God is great, and we know him not, neither can the
number of his years be searched out. 27 For he maketh small
the drops of water; they pour down rain according to the
vapour thereof, 28 which the clouds do drop and distil upon
man abundantly. 29 Also can any understand the spreadings
of the clouds, or the noise of his tabernacle? 30 Behold, he
spreadeth his light upon it, and covereth the bottom of the
sea. 31 For by them judgeth he the people; he giveth meat in
abundance. 32 With clouds he covereth the light; and commandeth it not to shine by the cloud that cometh betwixt.
33 The noise thereof sheweth concerning it, the cattle also
concerning the vapour.

37 'At this also my heart trembleth, and is moved out of
his place. 2 Hear attentively the noise of his voice, and
the sound that goeth out of his mouth. 3 He directeth it under
the whole heaven, and his lightning unto the ends of the
earth. 4 After it a voice roareth; he thundereth with the voice
of his excellency; and he will not stay them when his voice is
heard. 5 God thundereth marvellously with his voice; great
things doeth he, which we cannot comprehend. 6 For he saith
to the snow, "Be thou on the earth;" likewise to the small
rain, and to the great rain of his strength. 7 He sealeth up the
hand of every man; that all men may know his work. 8 Then
the beasts go into dens, and remain in their places. 9 Out of
the south cometh the whirlwind; and cold out of the north.
10 By the breath of God frost is given; and the breadth of the
waters is straitened. 11 Also by watering he wearieth the thick
cloud, he scattereth his bright cloud; 12 and it is turned round
about by his counsels, that they may do whatsoever he commandeth them upon the face of the world in the earth. 13 He
causeth it to come, whether for correction, or for his land, or
for mercy.

14 'Hearken unto this, O Job: stand still, and consider the
wondrous works of God. 15 Dost thou know when God disposed them, and caused the light of his cloud to shine? 16 Dost
thou know the balancings of the clouds, the wondrous works
of him which is perfect in knowledge? 17 How thy garments
are warm, when he quieteth the earth by the south wind?
18 Hast thou with him spread out the sky, which is strong,
and as a molten looking glass? 19 Teach us what we shall say

unto him; for we cannot order our speech by reason of darkness. 20 Shall it be told him that I speak? If a man speak,
surely he shall be swallowed up. 21 And now men see not the
bright light which is in the clouds; but the wind passeth, and
cleanseth them. 22 Fair weather cometh out of the north; with
God is terrible majesty. 23 Touching the Almighty, we cannot
find him out; he is excellent in power, and in judg-ment, and
in plenty of justice; he will not afflict. 24 Men do therefore fear
him; he respecteth not any that are wise of heart.'

38 Then the Lord answered Job out of the whirlwind, and said,

2 'Who is this that darkeneth counsel by words
without knowledge?
3 Gird up now thy loins like a man;
for I will demand of thee, and answer thou me.
4 Where wast thou when I laid
the foundations of the earth?
Declare, if thou hast understanding.
5 Who hath laid the measures thereof,
if thou knowest?
Or who hath stretched the line upon it?
6 Whereupon are the foundations thereof fastened?
Or who laid the corner stone thereof,
7 when the morning stars sang together,
and all the sons of God shouted for joy?
8 Or who shut up the sea with doors,

when it brake forth,
as if it had issued out of the womb,
9 when I made the cloud the garment thereof,
and thick darkness a swaddling-band for it,
10 and brake up for it my decreed place,
and set bars and doors,
11 and said, "Hitherto shalt thou come, but no further:
and here shall thy proud waves be stayed"?
12 Hast thou commanded the morning since thy days,
and caused the dayspring to know his place;
13 that it might take hold of the ends of the earth,
that the wicked might be shaken out of it?
14 It is turned as clay to the seal;
and they stand as a garment.
15 And from the wicked their light is withholden,
and the high arm shall be broken.
16 Hast thou entered into the springs of the sea?
Or hast thou walked in the search of the depth?
17 Have the gates of death been opened unto thee?
Or hast thou seen the doors of
the shadow of death?
18 Hast thou perceived the breadth of the earth?
Declare if thou knowest it all.
19 Where is the way where light dwelleth?
And as for darkness, where is the place thereof,
20 that thou shouldest take it to the bound thereof,
and that thou shouldest know the paths
to the house thereof?

21 Knowest thou it, because thou wast then born?
Or because the number of thy days is great?
22 Hast thou entered into the treasures of the snow?
Or hast thou seen the treasures of the hail,
23 which I have reserved against the time of trouble,
against the day of battle and war?
24 By what way is the light parted,
which scattereth the east wind upon the earth?
25 Who hath divided a watercourse
for the overflowing of waters,
or a way for the lightning of thunder;
26 to cause it to rain on the earth, where no man is;
on the wilderness, wherein there is no man;
27 to satisfy the desolate and waste ground;
and to cause the bud of the tender herb
to spring forth?
28 Hath the rain a father?
Or who hath begotten the drops of dew?
29 Out of whose womb came the ice?
And the hoary frost of heaven,
who hath gendered it?
30 The waters are hid as with a stone,
and the face of the deep is frozen.
31 Canst thou bind the sweet influences of Pleiades,
or loose the bands of Orion?
32 Canst thou bring forth Mazzaroth in his season?
Or canst thou guide Arcturus with his sons?
33 Knowest thou the ordinances of heaven?

Canst thou set the dominion thereof in the earth?
34 Canst thou lift up thy voice to the clouds,
that abundance of waters may cover thee?
35 Canst thou send lightnings, that they may go,
and say unto thee, "Here we are"?
36 Who hath put wisdom in the inward parts?
Or who hath given understanding to the heart?
37 Who can number the clouds in wisdom?
Or who can stay the bottles of heaven,
38 when the dust groweth into hardness,
and the clods cleave fast together?
39 Wilt thou hunt the prey for the lion,
or fill the appetite of the young lions,
40 when they couch in their dens,
and abide in the covert to lie in wait?
41 Who provideth for the raven his food
when his young ones cry unto God,
they wander for lack of meat.'

39 'Knowest thou the time when the wild goats of
the rock bring forth?
Or canst thou mark when the hinds do calve?
2 Canst thou number the months that they fulfil?
Or knowest thou the time when they bring forth?
3 They bow themselves,
they bring forth their young ones,
they cast out their sorrows.
4 Their young ones are in good liking,

they grow up with corn;
they go forth, and return not unto them.
5 Who hath sent out the wild ass free?
Or who hath loosed the bands of the wild ass
6 whose house I have made the wilderness,
and the barren land his dwellings?
7 He scorneth the multitude of the city,
neither regardeth he the crying of the driver.
8 The range of the mountains is his pasture,
and he searcheth after every green thing.
9 Will the unicorn be willing to serve thee,
or abide by the crib?
10 Canst thou bind the unicorn
with his band in the furrow?
Or will he harrow the valleys after thee?
11 Wilt thou trust him, because his strength is great?
Or wilt thou leave thy labour to him?
12 Wilt thou believe him,
that he will bring home thy seed,
and gather it into thy barn?
13 Gavest thou the goodly wings unto the peacocks
or wings and feathers unto the ostrich
14 which leaveth her eggs in the earth,
and warmeth them in dust,
15 and forgetteth that the foot may crush them,
or that the wild beast may break them?
16 She is hardened against her young ones,
as though they were not hers;

her labour is in vain without fear,
17 because God hath deprived her of wisdom,
neither hath he imparted to her understanding.
18 What time she lifteth up herself on high,
she scorneth the horse and his rider.
19 Hast thou given the horse strength?
Hast thou clothed his neck with thunder?
20 Canst thou make him afraid as a grasshopper?
The glory of his nostrils is terrible.
21 He paweth in the valley,
and rejoiceth in his strength;
he goeth on to meet the armed men.
22 He mocketh at fear, and is not affrighted;
neither turneth he back from the sword.
23 The quiver rattleth against him,
the glittering spear and the shield.
24 He swalloweth the ground with fierceness and rage;
neither believeth he
that it is the sound of the trumpet.
25 He saith among the trumpets, "Ha, ha;"
and he smelleth the battle afar off,
the thunder of the captains, and the shouting.
26 Doth the hawk fly by thy wisdom,
and stretch her wings toward the south?
27 Doth the eagle mount up at thy command,
and make her nest on high?
28 She dwelleth and abideth on the rock,
upon the crag of the rock, and the strong place.

29 From thence she seeketh the prey,
and her eyes behold afar off.
30 Her young ones also suck up blood;
and where the slain are, there is she.'

40 Moreover the Lord answered Job, and said,
2 'Shall he that contendeth with the Almighty instruct him?
He that reproveth God, let him answer it.'

3 Then Job answered the Lord, and said,

4 'Behold, I am vile; what shall I answer thee?
I will lay mine hand upon my mouth.
5 Once have I spoken, but I will not answer;
yea, twice, but I will proceed no further.'

6 Then answered the Lord unto Job out of the whirlwind,
and said,

7 'Gird up thy loins now like a man;
I will demand of thee, and declare thou unto me.
8 Wilt thou also disannul my judgment?
Wilt thou condemn me,
that thou mayest be righteous?
9 Hast thou an arm like God?
Or canst thou thunder with a voice like him?
10 Deck thyself now with majesty and excellency;
and array thyself with glory and beauty.

11 Cast abroad the rage of thy wrath:
and behold every one that is proud,
and abase him.
12 Look on every one that is proud,
and bring him low;
and tread down the wicked in their place.
13 Hide them in the dust together;
and bind their faces in secret.
14 Then will I also confess unto thee
that thine own right hand can save thee.
15 Behold now behemoth, which I made with thee;
he eateth grass as an ox.
16 Lo now, his strength is in his loins,
and his force is in the navel of his belly.
17 He moveth his tail like a cedar:
the sinews of his stones are wrapped together.
18 His bones are as strong pieces of brass;
his bones are like bars of iron.
19 He is the chief of the ways of God;
he that made him can make his sword
to approach unto him.
20 Surely the mountains bring him forth food,
where all the beasts of the field play.
21 He lieth under the shady trees,
in the covert of the reed, and fens.
22 The shady trees cover him with their shadow;
the willows of the brook compass him about.
23 Behold, he drinketh up a river, and hasteth not;

he trusteth that he can draw up Jordan
into his mouth.
24 He taketh it with his eyes;
his nose pierceth through snares.'

41 'Canst thou draw out leviathan with an hook?
Or his tongue with a cord which thou lettest down?
2 Canst thou put an hook into his nose?
Or bore his jaw through with a thorn?
3 Will he make many supplications unto thee?
Will he speak soft words unto thee?
4 Will he make a covenant with thee?
Wilt thou take him for a servant for ever?
5 Wilt thou play with him as with a bird?
Or wilt thou bind him for thy maidens?
6 Shall the companions make a banquet of him?
Shall they part him among the merchants?
7 Canst thou fill his skin with barbed irons
or his head with fish spears?
8 Lay thine hand upon him,
remember the battle, do no more.
9 Behold, the hope of him is in vain; shall not one
be cast down even at the sight of him?
10 None is so fierce that dare stir him up;
who then is able to stand before me?
11 Who hath prevented me, that I should repay him?
Whatsoever is under the whole heaven is mine.
12 I will not conceal his parts, nor his power,

nor his comely proportion.
13 Who can discover the face of his garment?
Or who can come to him with his double bridle?
14 Who can open the doors of his face?
His teeth are terrible round about.
15 His scales are his pride, shut up together
as with a close seal.
16 One is so near to another,
that no air can come between them.
17 They are joined one to another, they stick together,
that they cannot be sundered.
18 By his neesings a light doth shine,
and his eyes are like the eyelids of the morning.
19 Out of his mouth go burning lamps,
and sparks of fire leap out.
20 Out of his nostrils goeth smoke,
as out of a seething pot or caldron.
21 His breath kindleth coals,
and a flame goeth out of his mouth.
22 In his neck remaineth strength,
and sorrow is turned into joy before him.
23 The flakes of his flesh are joined together;
they are firm in themselves;
they cannot be moved.
24 His heart is as firm as a stone;
yea, as hard as a piece of the nether millstone.
25 When he raiseth up himself, the mighty are afraid;
by reason of breakings they purify themselves.

26 The sword of him that layeth at him cannot hold
the spear, the dart, nor the habergeon.
27 He esteemeth iron as straw,
and brass as rotten wood.
28 The arrow cannot make him flee;
slingstones are turned with him into stubble.
29 Darts are counted as stubble;
he laugheth at the shaking of a spear.
30 Sharp stones are under him;
he spreadeth sharp pointed things upon the mire.
31 He maketh the deep to boil like a pot;
he maketh the sea like a pot of ointment.
32 He maketh a path to shine after him;
one would think the deep to be hoary.
33 Upon earth there is not his like,
who is made without fear.
34 He beholdeth all high things;
he is a king over all the children of pride.'

42 Then Job answered the Lord, and said,

2 'I know that thou canst do every thing,
and that no thought can be withholden from thee.
3 Who is he that hideth counsel without knowledge?
Therefore have I uttered that I understood not;
things too wonderful for me,
which I knew not.
4 Hear, I beseech thee, and I will speak;

I will demand of thee, and declare thou unto me.
5 I have heard of thee by the hearing of the ear;
but now mine eye seeth thee.
6 Wherefore I abhor myself,
and repent in dust and ashes.'

7 And it was so, that after the Lord had spoken these words
unto Job, the Lord said to Eliphaz the Temanite, 'My wrath
is kindled against thee, and against thy two friends; for ye
have not spoken of me the thing that is right, as my servant
Job hath. 8 Therefore take unto you now seven bullocks and
seven rams, and go to my servant Job, and offer up for yourselves a burnt offering; and my servant Job shall pray for you,
for him will I accept lest I deal with you after your folly, in
that ye have not spoken of me the thing which is right, like
my servant Job.' 9 So Eliphaz the Temanite and Bildad the
Shuhite and Zophar the Naamathite went, and did according as the Lord commanded them; the Lord also accepted Job.
10 And the Lord turned the captivity of Job, when he prayed
for his friends; also the Lord gave Job twice as much as he
had before. 11 Then came there unto him all his brethren, and
all his sisters, and all they that had been of his acquaintance
before, and did eat bread with him in his house; and they
bemoaned him, and comforted him over all the evil that the
Lord had brought upon him; every man also gave him a piece
of money, and every one an earring of gold. 12 So the Lord
blessed the latter end of Job more than his beginning; for he
had fourteen thousand sheep, and six thousand camels, and a

thousand yoke of oxen, and a thousand she asses. 13 He had
also seven sons and three daughters. 14 And he called the
name of the first Jemima; and the name of the second Kezia;
and the name of the third Kerenhappuch. 15 And in all the
land were no women found so fair as the daughters of Job;
and their father gave them inheritance among their brethren.
16 After this lived Job an hundred and forty years, and saw
his sons, and his sons' sons, even four generations. 17 So Job
died, being old and full of days.

selections from the book of

psalms

authorized king james version

grove press
new york

with an introduction by | bono

The Pocket Canons were originally published in the U.K. in 1998 by Canongate Books, Ltd.
Published simultaneously in Canada
Printed in the United States of America

FIRST AMERICAN EDITION

Copyright information is on file with the Library of Congress
ISBN 0-8021-3675-3

Design by Paddy Cramsie

Grove Press
841 Broadway
New York, NY 10003

99 00 01 02 10 9 8 7 6 5 4 3 2 1

a note about pocket canons

The Authorized King James Version of the Bible, translated between 1603 and 1611, coincided with an extraordinary flowering of English literature. This version, more than any other, and possibly more than any other work in history, has had an influence in shaping the language we speak and write today. Presenting individual books from the Bible as separate volumes, as they were originally conceived, encourages the reader to approach them as literary works in their own right.

The first twelve books in this series encompass categories as diverse as history, fiction, philosophy, love poetry, and law. Each Pocket Canon also has its own introduction, specially commissioned from an impressive range of writers, which provides a personal interpretation of the text and explores its contemporary relevance.

Bono was born (Paul David Hewson) in Dublin in 1960. At seventeen he joined the embryonic U2 with three school friends. U2 released their first record with Island Records in April 1980 and have gone on to sell 87 million albums worldwide, gathering seven Grammies in the U.S. and five Brit Awards in the U.K. along the way. In 1992 their ground-breaking Zoo TV *tour was hailed as the most innovative spectacle ever staged. The follow-up, 1997's* PopMart *tour, built on that inventiveness, and played to a record-breaking four million people worldwide. In 1994 Bono was invited to present the Lifetime Achievement Award to Frank Sinatra at the Grammies. He was the guest speaker at the U.K. International Year of Literature in 1995.* The Million Dollar Hotel, *a film based on a story, written by Bono, is currently in production starring Mel Gibson and directed by Wim Wenders. Bono lives in Dublin with his wife and three children.*

introduction by bono

Explaining belief has always been difficult. How do you explain a love and logic at the heart of the universe when the world is so out of whack? How about the poetic versus the actual truth found in the scriptures? Has free will got *us* crucified? And what about the dodgy characters who inhabit the tome, known as the bible, who claim to hear the voice of God?

You have to be interested, but is God?

Explaining faith is impossible ... Vision over visibility ... Instinct over intellect ... A songwriter plays a chord with the faith that he will hear the next one in his head.

One of the writers of the psalms was a musician, a harp-player whose talents were required at 'the palace' as the only medicine that would still the demons of the moody and insecure King Saul of Israel; a thought that still inspires, if not quite explaining Marilyn singing for Kennedy, or the Spice Girls in the court of Prince Charles ...

At age 12, I was a fan of David, he felt familiar ... like a pop star could feel familiar. The words of the psalms were as poetic as they were religious and he was a star. A dramatic character, because before David could fulfil the prophecy and become the king of Israel, he had to take quite a beating. He was forced into exile and ended up in a cave in some no-name border town facing the collapse of his ego and abandonment by God. But this is where the soap opera got interesting, this is where David was said to have composed his first psalm – a blues. That's what a lot of the psalms feel like to me, the blues. Man shouting at God – 'My God, my God why hast thou forsaken me? Why art thou so far from helping me?' (Psalm 22).

I hear echoes of this holy row when un-holy bluesman Robert Johnson howls 'There's a hellhound on my trail' or Van Morrison sings 'Sometimes I feel like a motherless child'. Texas Alexander mimics the psalms in 'Justice Blues': 'I cried Lord my father, Lord eh Kingdom come. Send me back my woman, then thy will be done'. Humorous, sometimes blasphemous, the blues was backslidin' music; but by its very opposition, flattered the subject of its perfect cousin Gospel.

Abandonment, displacement, is the stuff of my favourite psalms. The Psalter may be a font of gospel music, but for me it's in his despair that the psalmist really reveals the nature of his special relationship with God. Honesty, even to the point of anger. 'How long, Lord? Wilt thou hide thyself forever?' (Psalm 89) or 'Answer me when I call' (Psalm 5).

Psalms and hymns were my first taste of inspirational music. I liked the words but I wasn't sure about the tunes – with the exception of Psalm 23, 'The Lord is my Shepherd'. I remember them as droned and chanted rather than sung. Still, in an odd way, they prepared me for the honesty of John Lennon, the baroque language of Bob Dylan and Leonard Cohen, the open throat of Al Green and Stevie Wonder – when I hear these singers, I am reconnected to a part of me I have no explanation for … my 'soul' I guess.

Words and music did for me what solid, even rigorous, religious argument could never do, they introduced me to God, not belief in God, more an experiential sense of GOD. Over art, literature, reason, the way in to my spirit was a combination of words and music. As a result the Book of *Psalms* always felt open to me and led me to the poetry of *Ecclesiastes*, the *Song of Solomon*, the book of *John* … My religion could not be fiction but it had to transcend facts. It could be mystical, but not mythical and definitely not ritual …

My mother was Protestant, my father Catholic; anywhere other than Ireland that would be unremarkable. The 'Prods' at that time had the better tunes and the Catholics had the better stage-gear. My mate Gavin Friday used to say: 'Roman Catholicism is the Glamrock of religion' with its candles and psychedelic colours … Cardinal blues, scarlets and purples, smoke bombs of incense and the ring of the little bell. The Prods were better at the bigger bells, they could afford them. In Ireland wealth and Protestantism went together; to have either, was to have collaborated with the enemy, i.e. Britain. This did not fly in our house.

After going to Mass at the top of the hill, in Finglas on the north side of Dublin, my father waited outside the little Church of Ireland chapel at the bottom of the hill, where my mother had brought her two sons …

I kept myself awake thinking of the clergyman's daughter and let my eyes dive into the cinema of the stained glass. These Christian artisans had invented the movies … light projected through colour to tell their story. In the '70s the story was 'the Troubles' and the Troubles came through the stained glass; with rocks thrown more in mischief than in anger, but the message was the same; the country was to be divided along sectarian lines. I had a foot in both camps, so my Goliath became religion itself; I began to see religion as the perversion of faith. As to the five smooth stones for the sling ... I began to see God everywhere else. In girls, fun, music, justice but still – despite the lofty King James translation – the scriptures ...

I loved these stories for the basest reasons, not just the New Testament with its mind-altering concept that God might reveal himself as a baby born in straw poverty – but even the Old Testament. These were action movies, with some hardcore men and women ... the car chases, the casualties, the blood and guts; there was very little kissing ...

David was a star, the Elvis of the bible, if we can believe the chiselling of Michelangelo (check the face – but I still can't figure out this most famous Jew's foreskin). And unusually for such a 'rock star', with his lust for power, lust for women, lust for life, he had the humility of one who knew his gift worked harder than he ever would. He even danced naked in front of his troops ... the biblical equivalent of the royal walkabout. David was definitely more performance artist than politician.

Anyway, I stopped going to churches and got myself into a different kind of religion. Don't laugh, that's what being in a rock 'n' roll band is, not pseudo-religion either ... Showbusiness is Shamanism: Music is Worship; whether it's worship of women or their designer, the world or its destroyer, whether it comes from that ancient place we call soul or simply the spinal cortex, whether the prayers are on fire with a dumb rage or dove-like desire ... the smoke goes upwards ... to God or something you replace God with ... usually yourself.

Years ago, lost for words and forty minutes of recording time left before the end of our studio time, we were still looking for a song to close our third album, *War*. We wanted to put something explicitly spiritual on the record to balance the politics and the romance of it; like Bob Marley or Marvin Gaye would. We thought about the psalms ... 'Psalm 40' ... There was some squirming. We were a very 'white' rock group, and such plundering of the scriptures was taboo for a white rock group unless it was in the 'service of Satan'. Or worse, Goth.

'Psalm 40' is interesting in that it suggests a time in which grace will replace karma, and love replace the very strict laws of Moses (i.e. fulfil them). I love that thought. David, who committed some of the most selfish as well as selfless acts, was depending on it. That the scriptures are brim full of hustlers, murderers, cowards, adulterers and mercenaries used to shock me; now it is a source of great comfort.

'40' became the closing song at U2 shows and on hundreds of occasions, literally hundreds of thousands of people of every size and shape t-shirt have shouted back the refrain, pinched from 'Psalm 6': "'How long' (to sing this song)". I had thought of it as a nagging question – pulling at the hem of an invisible deity whose presence we glimpse only when we act in love. How long ... hunger? How long ... hatred?

How long until creation grows up and the chaos of its precocious, hell-bent adolescence has been discarded? I thought it odd that the vocalising of such questions could bring such comfort; to me too.

But to get back to David, it is not clear how many, if any, of these psalms David or his son Solomon really wrote. Some scholars suggest the royals never dampened their nibs and that there was a host of Holy Ghost writers ... Who cares? I didn't buy Leiber and Stoller ... they were just his songwriters ... I bought Elvis.

the book of psalms

1

Blessed is the man that walketh not
in the counsel of the ungodly,
nor standeth in the way of sinners,
nor sitteth in the seat of the scornful.
2 But his delight is in the law of the Lord;
and in his law doth he meditate day and night.
3 And he shall be like a tree planted
by the rivers of water,
that bringeth forth his fruit in his season;
his leaf also shall not wither;
and whatsoever he doeth shall prosper.
4 The ungodly are not so, but are like the chaff
which the wind driveth away.
5 Therefore the ungodly shall not stand
in the judgment,
nor sinners in the congregation
of the righteous.
6 For the Lord knoweth the way of the righteous;
but the way of the ungodly shall perish.

2 Why do the heathen rage,
and the people imagine a vain thing?
2 The kings of the earth set themselves, and the rulers
take counsel together, against the Lord,
and against his anointed, saying,
3 'Let us break their bands asunder,
and cast away their cords from us.'
4 He that sitteth in the heavens shall laugh:
the Lord shall have them in derision.
5 Then shall he speak unto them in his wrath,
and vex them in his sore displeasure.
6 Yet have I set my king
upon my holy hill of Zion.
7 I will declare the decree:
the Lord hath said unto me,
'Thou art my Son;
this day have I begotten thee.
8 Ask of me, and I shall give thee the heathen
for thine inheritance,
and the uttermost parts of the earth
for thy possession.
9 Thou shalt break them with a rod of iron;
thou shalt dash them in pieces
like a potter's vessel.'
10 Be wise now therefore, O ye kings:
be instructed, ye judges of the earth.
11 Serve the Lord with fear,
and rejoice with trembling.

[12] Kiss the Son, lest he be angry,
and ye perish from the way,
when his wrath is kindled but a little.
Blessed are all they
that put their trust in him.

4

To the chief musician on Neginoth,
a psalm of David.

Hear me when I call, O God of my righteousness:
thou hast enlarged me when I was in distress;
have mercy upon me, and hear my prayer.
[2] O ye sons of men, how long will ye turn
my glory into shame?
How long will ye love vanity,
and seek after leasing? Selah.
[3] But know that the Lord hath set apart him
that is godly for himself:
the Lord will hear when I call unto him.
[4] Stand in awe, and sin not:
commune with your own heart upon your bed,
and be still. Selah.
[5] Offer the sacrifices of righteousness,
and put your trust in the Lord.
[6] There be many that say,
'Who will shew us any good?
Lord, lift thou up the light
of thy countenance upon us.'

7 Thou hast put gladness in my heart,
more than in the time that their corn
and their wine increased.
8 I will both lay me down in peace, and sleep,
for thou, Lord, only makest me dwell
in safety.

5

To the chief musician upon Nehiloth,
a psalm of David.

Give ear to my words, O Lord,
consider my meditation.
2 Hearken unto the voice of my cry, my King,
and my God, for unto thee will I pray.
3 My voice shalt thou hear in the morning, O Lord;
in the morning will I direct my prayer unto thee,
and will look up.
4 For thou art not a God
that hath pleasure in wickedness;
neither shall evil dwell with thee.
5 The foolish shall not stand in thy sight:
thou hatest all workers of iniquity.
6 Thou shalt destroy them that speak leasing:
the Lord will abhor the bloody and deceitful man.
7 But as for me, I will come into thy house
in the multitude of thy mercy:
and in thy fear will I worship
toward thy holy temple.

8 Lead me, O Lord, in thy righteousness
because of mine enemies;
make thy way straight before my face.
9 For there is no faithfulness in their mouth;
their inward part is very wickedness;
their throat is an open sepulchre;
they flatter with their tongue.
10 Destroy thou them, O God;
let them fall by their own counsels;
cast them out in the multitude
of their transgressions;
for they have rebelled against thee.
11 But let all those that put their trust in thee rejoice:
let them ever shout for joy,
because thou defendest them:
let them also that love thy name
be joyful in thee.
12 For thou, Lord, wilt bless the righteous;
with favour wilt thou compass him
as with a shield.

6

To the chief musician on Neginoth upon Sheminith,
a psalm of David.

O Lord, rebuke me not in thine anger,
neither chasten me in thy hot displeasure.
2 Have mercy upon me,
O Lord; for I am weak:

O Lord, heal me; for my bones are vexed.
3 My soul is also sore vexed;
but thou, O Lord, how long?
4 Return, O Lord, deliver my soul:
oh save me for thy mercies' sake.
5 For in death there is no remembrance of thee:
in the grave who shall give thee thanks?
6 I am weary with my groaning;
all the night make I my bed to swim;
I water my couch with my tears.
7 Mine eye is consumed because of grief;
it waxeth old because of all mine enemies.
8 Depart from me, all ye workers of iniquity;
for the Lord hath heard the voice of my weeping.
9 The Lord hath heard my supplication;
the Lord will receive my prayer.
10 Let all mine enemies be ashamed and sore vexed:
let them return and be ashamed suddenly.

8

To the chief musician upon Gittith,
a psalm of David.

O Lord our Lord, how excellent is thy name
in all the earth,
who hast set thy glory above the heavens!
2 Out of the mouth of babes and sucklings hast thou
ordained strength because of thine enemies,
that thou mightest still the enemy

and the avenger.
3 When I consider thy heavens,
the work of thy fingers, the moon and the stars,
which thou hast ordained;
4 what is man, that thou art mindful of him?
And the son of man, that thou visitest him?
5 For thou hast made him a little lower
than the angels,
and hast crowned him with glory and honour.
6 Thou madest him to have dominion over
the works of thy hands;
thou hast put all things under his feet:
7 all sheep and oxen, yea,
and the beasts of the field;
8 the fowl of the air, and the fish of the sea,
and whatsoever passeth through
the paths of the seas.
9 O Lord our Lord, how excellent is thy name
in all the earth!

15

A psalm of David.

Lord, who shall abide in thy tabernacle?
Who shall dwell in thy holy hill?
2 He that walketh uprightly,
and worketh righteousness,
and speaketh the truth in his heart.
3 He that backbiteth not with his tongue,

nor doeth evil to his neighbour, nor taketh up
a reproach against his neighbour.
4 In whose eyes a vile person is contemned;
but he honoureth them that fear the Lord.
He that sweareth to his own hurt,
and changeth not.
5 He that putteth not out his money to usury,
nor taketh reward against the innocent.
He that doeth these things
shall never be moved.

16

Michtam of David.

Preserve me, O God, for in thee
do I put my trust.
2 O my soul, thou hast said unto the Lord
Thou art my Lord: my goodness extendeth
not to thee,
3 but to the saints that are in the earth,
and to the excellent,
in whom is all my delight.'
4 Their sorrows shall be multiplied
that hasten after another god:
their drink offerings of blood will I not offer,
nor take up their names into my lips.
5 The Lord is the portion of mine inheritance
and of my cup: thou maintainest my lot.
6 The lines are fallen unto me in pleasant places;

yea, I have a goodly heritage.
7 I will bless the Lord, who hath given me counsel:
my reins also instruct me in the night seasons.
8 I have set the Lord always before me:
because he is at my right hand,
I shall not be moved.
9 Therefore my heart is glad, and my glory rejoiceth:
my flesh also shall rest in hope.
10 For thou wilt not leave my soul in hell;
neither wilt thou suffer thine Holy One
to see corruption.
11 Thou wilt shew me the path of life:
in thy presence is fulness of joy;
at thy right hand there are pleasures
for evermore.

19

To the chief musician, a psalm of David.

The heavens declare the glory of God;
and the firmament sheweth his handywork.
2 Day unto day uttereth speech,
and night unto night sheweth knowledge.
3 There is no speech nor language,
where their voice is not heard.
4 Their line is gone out through all the earth,
and their words to the end of the world.
In them hath he set a tabernacle for the sun,
5 which is as a bridegroom

coming out of his chamber,
and rejoiceth as a strong man to run a race.
6 His going forth is from the end of the heaven,
and his circuit unto the ends of it;
and there is nothing hid
from the heat thereof.
7 The law of the Lord is perfect, converting the soul:
the testimony of the Lord is sure,
making wise the simple.
8 The statutes of the Lord are right,
rejoicing the heart:
the commandment of the Lord is pure,
enlightening the eyes.
9 The fear of the Lord is clean, enduring for ever:
the judgments of the Lord are true
and righteous altogether.
10 More to be desired are they than gold,
yea, than much fine gold:
sweeter also than honey and the honeycomb.
11 Moreover by them is thy servant warned;
and in keeping of them there is great reward.
12 Who can understand his errors?
Cleanse thou me from secret faults.
13 Keep back thy servant also
from presumptuous sins;
let them not have dominion over me:
then shall I be upright, and I shall be innocent
from the great transgression.

14 Let the words of my mouth,
and the meditation of my heart,
be acceptable in thy sight, O Lord,
my strength, and my redeemer.

20

To the chief musician, a psalm of David.

The Lord hear thee in the day of trouble;
the name of the God of Jacob defend thee;
2 send thee help from the sanctuary,
and strengthen thee out of Zion;
3 remember all thy offerings,
and accept thy burnt sacrifice; Selah.
4 Grant thee according to thine own heart,
and fulfil all thy counsel.
5 We will rejoice in thy salvation,
and in the name of our God
we will set up our banners:
the Lord fulfil all thy petitions.
6 Now know I that the Lord saveth his anointed;
he will hear him from his holy heaven with the
saving strength of his right hand.
7 Some trust in chariots, and some in horses;
but we will remember the name
of the Lord our God.
8 They are brought down and fallen;
but we are risen, and stand upright.
9 Save, Lord: let the king hear us when we call.

22

To the chief musician upon Aijeleth Shahar,
a psalm of David.

My God, my God, why hast thou forsaken me?
Why art thou so far from helping me,
and from the words of my roaring?
2 O my God, I cry in the daytime,
but thou hearest not;
and in the night season, and am not silent.
3 But thou art holy,
O thou that inhabitest the praises of Israel.
4 Our fathers trusted in thee:
they trusted, and thou didst deliver them.
5 They cried unto thee, and were delivered:
they trusted in thee, and were not confounded.
6 But I am a worm, and no man;
a reproach of men, and despised of the people.
7 All they that see me laugh me to scorn:
they shoot out the lip, they shake the head,
saying,
8 'He trusted on the Lord that he would deliver him:
let him deliver him,
seeing he delighted in him.'
9 But thou art he that took me out of the womb:
thou didst make me hope when I was upon
my mother's breasts.
10 I was cast upon thee from the womb:
thou art my God from my mother's belly.

11 Be not far from me;
for trouble is near; for there is none to help.
12 Many bulls have compassed me:
strong bulls of Bashan have beset me round.
13 They gaped upon me with their mouths,
as a ravening and a roaring lion.
14 I am poured out like water,
and all my bones are out of joint:
my heart is like wax; it is melted
in the midst of my bowels.
15 My strength is dried up like a potsherd;
and my tongue cleaveth to my jaws;
and thou hast brought me
into the dust of death.
16 For dogs have compassed me:
the assembly of the wicked have inclosed me:
they pierced my hands and my feet.
17 I may tell all my bones:
they look and stare upon me.
18 They part my garments among them,
and cast lots upon my vesture.
19 But be not thou far from me, O Lord:
O my strength, haste thee to help me.
20 Deliver my soul from the sword;
my darling from the power of the dog.
21 Save me from the lion's mouth,
for thou hast heard me from the horns
of the unicorns.

22 I will declare thy name unto my brethren:
in the midst of the congregation
will I praise thee.
23 Ye that fear the Lord, praise him;
all ye the seed of Jacob, glorify him;
and fear him, all ye the seed of Israel.
24 For he hath not despised nor abhorred
the affliction of the afflicted;
neither hath he hid his face from him;
but when he cried unto him, he heard.
25 My praise shall be of thee
in the great congregation:
I will pay my vows before them
that fear him.
26 The meek shall eat and be satisfied:
they shall praise the Lord that seek him:
your heart shall live for ever.
27 All the ends of the world shall remember
and turn unto the Lord:
and all the kindreds of the nations
shall worship before thee.
28 For the kingdom is the Lord's:
and he is the governor among the nations.
29 All they that be fat upon earth shall eat
and worship: all they that go down to the dust
shall bow before him:
and none can keep alive his own soul.
30 A seed shall serve him; it shall be accounted

to the Lord for a generation.
31 They shall come, and shall declare
his righteousness unto a people
that shall be born, that he hath done this.

23

A psalm of David.

The Lord is my shepherd; I shall not want.
2 He maketh me to lie down in green pastures:
he leadeth me beside the still waters.
3 He restoreth my soul:
he leadeth me in the paths of righteousness
for his name's sake.
4 Yea, though I walk
through the valley of
the shadow of death,
I will fear no evil;
for thou art with me;
thy rod and thy staff they comfort me.
5 Thou preparest a table before me
in the presence of mine enemies;
thou anointest my head with oil;
my cup runneth over.
6 Surely goodness and mercy shall follow me
all the days of my life;
and I will dwell
in the house of the Lord for ever.

24

A psalm of David.

The earth is the Lord's, and the fulness thereof;
the world, and they that dwell therein.
2 For he hath founded it upon the seas,
and established it upon the floods.
3 Who shall ascend into the hill of the Lord?
Or who shall stand in his holy place?
4 He that hath clean hands, and a pure heart;
who hath not lifted up his soul unto vanity,
nor sworn deceitfully.
5 He shall receive the blessing from the Lord,
and righteousness from the God
of his salvation.
6 This is the generation of them that seek him,
that seek thy face, O Jacob. Selah.
7 Lift up your heads, O ye gates;
and be ye lift up, ye everlasting doors;
and the King of glory shall come in.
8 Who is this King of glory?
The Lord strong and mighty,
the Lord mighty in battle.
9 Lift up your heads, O ye gates;
even lift them up, ye everlasting doors;
and the King of glory shall come in.
10 Who is this King of glory?
The Lord of hosts, he is the King of glory. Selah.

25

A psalm of David.

Unto thee, O Lord, do I lift up my soul.
2 O my God, I trust in thee: let me not be ashamed,
let not mine enemies triumph over me.
3 Yea, let none that wait on thee be ashamed:
let them be ashamed
which transgress without cause.
4 Shew me thy ways, O Lord;
teach me thy paths.
5 Lead me in thy truth, and teach me:
for thou art the God of my salvation;
on thee do I wait all the day.
6 Remember, O Lord,
thy tender mercies and thy lovingkindnesses;
for they have been ever of old.
7 Remember not the sins of my youth,
nor my transgressions:
according to thy mercy, remember thou me
for thy goodness' sake, O Lord.
8 Good and upright is the Lord;
therefore will he teach sinners in the way.
9 The meek will he guide in judgment;
and the meek will he teach his way.
10 All the paths of the Lord are mercy and truth
unto such as keep his covenant
and his testimonies.
11 For thy name's sake, O Lord,

pardon mine iniquity; for it is great.
12 What man is he that feareth the Lord?
Him shall he teach in the way
that he shall choose.
13 His soul shall dwell at ease;
and his seed shall inherit the earth.
14 The secret of the Lord is with them that fear him;
and he will shew them his covenant.
15 Mine eyes are ever toward the Lord;
for he shall pluck my feet out of the net.
16 Turn thee unto me, and have mercy upon me;
for I am desolate and afflicted.
17 The troubles of my heart are enlarged:
O bring thou me out of my distresses.
18 Look upon mine affliction and my pain;
and forgive all my sins.
19 Consider mine enemies; for they are many;
and they hate me with cruel hatred.
20 O keep my soul, and deliver me:
let me not be ashamed;
for I put my trust in thee.
21 Let integrity and uprightness preserve me;
for I wait on thee.
22 Redeem Israel, O God, out of all his troubles.

27

A psalm of David.

The Lord is my light and my salvation;

whom shall I fear?
The Lord is the strength of my life;
of whom shall I be afraid?
2 When the wicked, even mine enemies and my foes,
came upon me to eat up my flesh,
they stumbled and fell.
3 Though an host should encamp against me,
my heart shall not fear:
though war should rise against me,
in this will I be confident.
4 One thing have I desired of the Lord,
that will I seek after;
that I may dwell in the house of the Lord
all the days of my life,
to behold the beauty of the Lord,
and to enquire in his temple.
5 For in the time of trouble he shall hide me
in his pavilion:
in the secret of his tabernacle
shall he hide me;
he shall set me up upon a rock.
6 And now shall mine head be lifted up
above mine enemies round about me:
therefore will I offer in his tabernacle
sacrifices of joy; I will sing,
yea, I will sing praises unto the Lord.
7 Hear, O Lord, when I cry with my voice:
have mercy also upon me, and answer me.

8 When thou saidst, 'Seek ye my face',
my heart said unto thee,
'Thy face, Lord, will I seek.'
9 Hide not thy face far from me;
put not thy servant away in anger:
thou hast been my help;
leave me not, neither forsake me,
O God of my salvation.
10 When my father and my mother forsake me,
then the Lord will take me up.
11 Teach me thy way, O Lord,
and lead me in a plain path,
because of mine enemies.
12 Deliver me not over unto the will of mine enemies:
for false witnesses are risen up against me,
and such as breathe out cruelty.
13 I had fainted, unless I had believed
to see the goodness of the Lord
in the land of the living.
14 Wait on the Lord: be of good courage,
and he shall strengthen thine heart:
wait, I say, on the Lord.

29

A psalm of David.

Give unto the Lord, O ye mighty,
give unto the Lord glory and strength.
2 Give unto the Lord the glory due unto his name;

worship the Lord in the beauty of holiness.
3 The voice of the Lord is upon the waters:
the God of glory thundereth:
the Lord is upon many waters.
4 The voice of the Lord is powerful;
the voice of the Lord is full of majesty.
5 The voice of the Lord breaketh the cedars;
yea, the Lord breaketh the cedars of Lebanon.
6 He maketh them also to skip like a calf;
Lebanon and Sirion like a young unicorn.
7 The voice of the Lord divideth the flames of fire.
8 The voice of the Lord shaketh the wilderness;
the Lord shaketh the wilderness of Kadesh.
9 The voice of the Lord maketh the hinds to calve,
and discovereth the forests:
and in his temple doth every one speak
of his glory.
10 The Lord sitteth upon the flood;
yea, the Lord sitteth King for ever.
11 The Lord will give strength unto his people;
the Lord will bless his people with peace.

30

A psalm and song at the dedication of the house of David.

I will extol thee, O Lord;
for thou hast lifted me up,
and hast not made my foes to rejoice over me.

2 O Lord my God, I cried unto thee,
and thou hast healed me.
3 O Lord, thou hast brought up my soul
from the grave: thou hast kept me alive,
that I should not go down to the pit.
4 Sing unto the Lord, O ye saints of his,
and give thanks at the remembrance
of his holiness.
5 For his anger endureth but a moment;
in his favour is life:
weeping may endure for a night,
but joy cometh in the morning.
6 And in my prosperity I said,
'I shall never be moved.'
7 Lord, by thy favour thou hast made my mountain
to stand strong: thou didst hide thy face,
and I was troubled.
8 I cried to thee, O Lord;
and unto the Lord I made supplication.
9 What profit is there in my blood,
when I go down to the pit?
Shall the dust praise thee?
Shall it declare thy truth?
10 Hear, O Lord, and have mercy upon me:
Lord, be thou my helper.
11 Thou hast turned for me my mourning
into dancing:
thou hast put off my sackcloth,

and girded me with gladness;
12 to the end that my glory may sing praise to thee,
and not be silent.
O Lord my God,
I will give thanks unto thee for ever.

31

To the chief musician, a psalm of David.

In thee, O Lord, do I put my trust;
let me never be ashamed;
deliver me in thy righteousness.
2 Bow down thine ear to me;
deliver me speedily:
be thou my strong rock,
for an house of defence to save me.
3 For thou art my rock and my fortress;
therefore for thy name's sake lead me,
and guide me.
4 Pull me out of the net that they have laid
privily for me; for thou art my strength.
5 Into thine hand I commit my spirit:
thou hast redeemed me, O Lord God of truth.
6 I have hated them that regard lying vanities;
but I trust in the Lord.
7 I will be glad and rejoice in thy mercy;
for thou hast considered my trouble;
thou hast known my soul in adversities,
8 and hast not shut me up into the hand of the enemy:

thou hast set my feet in a large room.
9 Have mercy upon me, O Lord,
for I am in trouble:
mine eye is consumed with grief,
yea, my soul and my belly.
10 For my life is spent with grief,
and my years with sighing:
my strength faileth because of mine iniquity,
and my bones are consumed.
11 I was a reproach among all mine enemies,
but especially among my neighbours,
and a fear to mine acquaintance:
they that did see me without fled from me.
12 I am forgotten as a dead man out of mind:
I am like a broken vessel.
13 For I have heard the slander of many:
fear was on every side:
while they took counsel together against me,
they devised to take away my life.
14 But I trusted in thee, O Lord:
I said, 'Thou art my God.'
15 My times are in thy hand:
deliver me from the hand of mine enemies,
and from them that persecute me.
16 Make thy face to shine upon thy servant:
save me for thy mercies' sake.
17 Let me not be ashamed, O Lord;
for I have called upon thee:

let the wicked be ashamed,
and let them be silent in the grave.
18 Let the lying lips be put to silence,
which speak grievous things proudly
and contemptuously against the righteous.
19 Oh how great is thy goodness,
which thou hast laid up for them that fear thee;
which thou hast wrought for them
that trust in thee before the sons of men!
20 Thou shalt hide them in the secret of thy presence
from the pride of man:
thou shalt keep them secretly in a pavilion
from the strife of tongues.
21 Blessed be the Lord;
for he hath shewed me his marvellous kindness
in a strong city.
22 For I said in my haste,
'I am cut off from before thine eyes':
nevertheless thou heardest the voice
of my supplications when I cried unto thee.
23 O love the Lord, all ye his saints;
for the Lord preserveth the faithful,
and plentifully rewardeth the proud doer.
24 Be of good courage, and he shall strengthen
your heart, all ye that hope in the Lord.

32

A psalm of David, Maschil.

Blessed is he whose transgression is forgiven,
whose sin is covered.
[2] Blessed is the man unto whom
the Lord imputeth not iniquity,
and in whose spirit there is no guile.
[3] When I kept silence, my bones waxed old
through my roaring all the day long.
[4] For day and night thy hand was heavy upon me:
my moisture is turned
into the drought of summer. Selah.
[5] I acknowledged my sin unto thee,
and mine iniquity have I not hid.
I said, 'I will confess my transgressions
unto the Lord'; and thou forgavest the iniquity
of my sin. Selah.
[6] For this shall every one that is godly pray
unto thee in a time when thou mayest be found:
surely in the floods of great waters
they shall not come nigh unto him.
[7] Thou art my hiding place;
thou shalt preserve me from trouble;
thou shalt compass me about
with songs of deliverance. Selah.
[8] I will instruct thee and teach thee in the way
which thou shalt go:
I will guide thee with mine eye.

9 Be ye not as the horse, or as the mule,
which have no understanding:
whose mouth must be held in with bit
and bridle, lest they come near unto thee.
10 Many sorrows shall be to the wicked:
but he that trusteth in the Lord,
mercy shall compass him about.
11 Be glad in the Lord, and rejoice, ye righteous:
and shout for joy, all ye that are upright in heart.

33

Rejoice in the Lord, O ye righteous;
for praise is comely for the upright.
2 Praise the Lord with harp:
sing unto him with the psaltery
and an instrument of ten strings.
3 Sing unto him a new song;
play skilfully with a loud noise.
4 For the word of the Lord is right;
and all his works are done in truth.
5 He loveth righteousness and judgment:
the earth is full of the goodness of the Lord.
6 By the word of the Lord were the heavens made;
and all the host of them
by the breath of his mouth.
7 He gathereth the waters of the sea together
as an heap:
he layeth up the depth in storehouses.

8 Let all the earth fear the Lord:
let all the inhabitants of the world
stand in awe of him.
9 For he spake, and it was done;
he commanded, and it stood fast.
10 The Lord bringeth the counsel of the heathen
to nought:
he maketh the devices of the people
of none effect.
11 The counsel of the Lord standeth for ever,
the thoughts of his heart to all generations.
12 Blessed is the nation whose God is the Lord;
and the people whom he hath chosen
for his own inheritance.
13 The Lord looketh from heaven;
he beholdeth all the sons of men.
14 From the place of his habitation
he looketh upon all the inhabitants of the earth.
15 He fashioneth their hearts alike;
he considereth all their works.
16 There is no king saved by the multitude of an host:
a mighty man is not delivered by much strength.
17 An horse is a vain thing for safety:
neither shall he deliver any by his great strength.
18 Behold, the eye of the Lord is upon them that
fear him, upon them that hope in his mercy;
19 to deliver their soul from death,
and to keep them alive in famine.

20 Our soul waiteth for the Lord:
he is our help and our shield.
21 For our heart shall rejoice in him,
because we have trusted in his holy name.
22 Let thy mercy, O Lord,
be upon us, according as we hope in thee.

34

A psalm of David, when he changed his behaviour before Abimelech, who drove him away, and he departed.

I will bless the Lord at all times:
his praise shall continually be in my mouth.
2 My soul shall make her boast in the Lord:
the humble shall hear thereof, and be glad.
3 O magnify the Lord with me,
and let us exalt his name together.
4 I sought the Lord, and he heard me,
and delivered me from all my fears.
5 They looked unto him, and were lightened:
and their faces were not ashamed.
6 This poor man cried, and the Lord heard him,
and saved him out of all his troubles.
7 The angel of the Lord encampeth round about
them that fear him, and delivereth them.
8 O taste and see that the Lord is good:
blessed is the man that trusteth in him.
9 O fear the Lord, ye his saints;

for there is no want to them that fear him.
10 The young lions do lack, and suffer hunger;
but they that seek the Lord shall not want
any good thing.
11 Come, ye children, hearken unto me:
I will teach you the fear of the Lord.
12 What man is he that desireth life,
and loveth many days, that he may see good?
13 Keep thy tongue from evil,
and thy lips from speaking guile.
14 Depart from evil, and do good;
seek peace, and pursue it.
15 The eyes of the Lord are upon the righteous,
and his ears are open unto their cry.
16 The face of the Lord is against them that do evil,
to cut off the remembrance of them
from the earth.
17 The righteous cry, and the Lord heareth,
and delivereth them out of all their troubles.
18 The Lord is nigh unto them
that are of a broken heart;
and saveth such as be of a contrite spirit.
19 Many are the afflictions of the righteous;
but the Lord delivereth him out of them all.
20 He keepeth all his bones:
not one of them is broken.
21 Evil shall slay the wicked:
and they that hate the righteous shall be desolate.

22 The Lord redeemeth the soul of his servants:
and none of them that trust in him
shall be desolate.

36

To the chief musician, a psalm of David the servant of the Lord.

The transgression of the wicked
saith within my heart, that there is
no fear of God before his eyes.
2 For he flattereth himself in his own eyes,
until his iniquity be found to be hateful.
3 The words of his mouth are iniquity and deceit:
he hath left off to be wise, and to do good.
4 He deviseth mischief upon his bed;
he setteth himself in a way that is not good;
he abhorreth not evil.
5 Thy mercy, O Lord, is in the heavens;
and thy faithfulness reacheth
unto the clouds.
6 Thy righteousness is like the great mountains;
thy judgments are a great deep:
O Lord, thou preservest man and beast.
7 How excellent is thy lovingkindness, O God!
Therefore the children of men put their trust
under the shadow of thy wings.
8 They shall be abundantly satisfied with the fatness
of thy house; and thou shalt make them drink

of the river of thy pleasures.
9 For with thee is the fountain of life:
in thy light shall we see light.
10 O continue thy lovingkindness
unto them that know thee;
and thy righteousness
to the upright in heart.
11 Let not the foot of pride come against me,
and let not the hand of the wicked remove me.
12 There are the workers of iniquity fallen:
they are cast down,
and shall not be able to rise.

37

A psalm of David.

Fret not thyself because of evildoers,
neither be thou envious
against the workers of iniquity.
2 For they shall soon be cut down like the grass,
and wither as the green herb.
3 Trust in the Lord, and do good;
so shalt thou dwell in the land,
and verily thou shalt be fed.
4 Delight thyself also in the Lord;
and he shall give thee the desires of thine heart.
5 Commit thy way unto the Lord;
trust also in him; and he shall bring it to pass.
6 And he shall bring forth thy righteousness

as the light, and thy judgment as the noonday.
7 Rest in the Lord, and wait patiently for him:
fret not thyself because of him who prospereth
in his way, because of the man who bringeth
wicked devices to pass.
8 Cease from anger, and forsake wrath:
fret not thyself in any wise to do evil.
9 For evildoers shall be cut off:
but those that wait upon the Lord,
they shall inherit the earth.
10 For yet a little while, and the wicked shall not be:
yea, thou shalt diligently consider his place,
and it shall not be.
11 But the meek shall inherit the earth;
and shall delight themselves
in the abundance of peace.
12 The wicked plotteth against the just,
and gnasheth upon him with his teeth.
13 The Lord shall laugh at him:
for he seeth that his day is coming.
14 The wicked have drawn out the sword,
and have bent their bow,
to cast down the poor and needy,
and to slay such as be of upright conversation.
15 Their sword shall enter into their own heart,
and their bows shall be broken.
16 A little that a righteous man hath
is better than the riches of many wicked.

17 For the arms of the wicked shall be broken;
but the Lord upholdeth the righteous.
18 The Lord knoweth the days of the upright:
and their inheritance shall be for ever.
19 They shall not be ashamed in the evil time:
and in the days of famine they shall be satisfied.
20 But the wicked shall perish, and the enemies
of the Lord shall be as the fat of lambs;
they shall consume;
into smoke shall they consume away.
21 The wicked borroweth, and payeth not again;
but the righteous sheweth mercy, and giveth.
22 For such as be blessed of him shall inherit
the earth;
and they that be cursed of him
shall be cut off.
23 The steps of a good man are ordered by the Lord,
and he delighteth in his way.
24 Though he fall, he shall not be utterly cast down;
for the Lord upholdeth him with his hand.
25 I have been young, and now am old;
yet have I not seen the righteous forsaken,
nor his seed begging bread.
26 He is ever merciful, and lendeth;
and his seed is blessed.
27 Depart from evil, and do good;
and dwell for evermore.
28 For the Lord loveth judgment,

and forsaketh not his saints;
they are preserved for ever;
but the seed of the wicked shall be cut off.
29 The righteous shall inherit the land,
and dwell therein for ever.
30 The mouth of the righteous speaketh wisdom,
and his tongue talketh of judgment.
31 The law of his God is in his heart;
none of his steps shall slide.
32 The wicked watcheth the righteous,
and seeketh to slay him.
33 The Lord will not leave him in his hand,
nor condemn him when he is judged.
34 Wait on the Lord, and keep his way,
and he shall exalt thee to inherit the land:
when the wicked are cut off,
thou shalt see it.
35 I have seen the wicked in great power,
and spreading himself like a green bay tree.
36 Yet he passed away, and, lo, he was not:
yea, I sought him, but he could not be found.
37 Mark the perfect man, and behold the upright;
for the end of that man is peace.
38 But the transgressors shall be destroyed together:
the end of the wicked shall be cut off.
39 But the salvation of the righteous is of the Lord:
he is their strength in the time of trouble.
40 And the Lord shall help them, and deliver them:

he shall deliver them from the wicked, and save
them, because they trust in him.

40 To the chief musician, a psalm of David.

I waited patiently for the Lord;
and he inclined unto me, and heard my cry.
2 He brought me up also out of an horrible pit,
out of the miry clay,
and set my feet upon a rock,
and established my goings.
3 And he hath put a new song in my mouth,
even praise unto our God:
many shall see it, and fear,
and shall trust in the Lord.
4 Blessed is that man that maketh the Lord his trust,
and respecteth not the proud,
nor such as turn aside to lies.
5 Many, O Lord my God, are thy wonderful works
which thou hast done,
and thy thoughts which are to us-ward:
they cannot be reckoned up in order unto thee:
if I would declare and speak of them,
they are more than can be numbered.
6 Sacrifice and offering thou didst not desire;
mine ears hast thou opened:
burnt offering and sin offering
hast thou not required.

7 Then said I, 'Lo, I come:
in the volume of the book it is written of me,
8 I delight to do thy will, O my God:
yea, thy law is within my heart.'
9 I have preached righteousness in the great
congregation: lo, I have not refrained my lips,
O Lord, thou knowest.
10 I have not hid thy righteousness within my heart;
I have declared thy faithfulness
and thy salvation;
I have not concealed thy lovingkindness
and thy truth from the great congregation.
11 Withhold not thou thy tender mercies from me,
O Lord: let thy lovingkindness
and thy truth continually preserve me.
12 For innumerable evils have compassed me about:
mine iniquities have taken hold upon me,
so that I am not able to look up;
they are more than the hairs of mine head;
therefore my heart faileth me.
13 Be pleased, O Lord, to deliver me:
O Lord, make haste to help me.
14 Let them be ashamed and confounded together
that seek after my soul to destroy it;
let them be driven backward
and put to shame that wish me evil.
15 Let them be desolate for a reward of their shame
that say unto me, 'Aha, aha.'

[16] Let all those that seek thee rejoice
and be glad in thee:
let such as love thy salvation say continually,
'The Lord be magnified.'
[17] But I am poor and needy;
yet the Lord thinketh upon me:
thou art my help and my deliverer;
make no tarrying, O my God.

42

To the chief musician, Maschil, for the sons of Korah.

As the hart panteth after the water brooks,
so panteth my soul after thee, O God.
[2] My soul thirsteth for God, for the living God:
when shall I come and appear before God?
[3] My tears have been my meat day and night,
while they continually say unto me,
'Where is thy God?'
[4] When I remember these things,
I pour out my soul in me;
for I had gone with the multitude,
I went with them to the house of God,
with the voice of joy and praise,
with a multitude that kept holyday.
[5] Why art thou cast down, O my soul?
And why art thou disquieted in me?
Hope thou in God;

for I shall yet praise him for the help of his
countenance.
6 O my God, my soul is cast down within me;
therefore will I remember thee
from the land of Jordan,
and of the Hermonites, from the hill Mizar.
7 Deep calleth unto deep at the noise
of thy waterspouts: all thy waves and thy billows
are gone over me.
8 Yet the Lord will command his lovingkindness
in the daytime,
and in the night his song shall be with me,
and my prayer unto the God of my life.
9 I will say unto God my rock,
'Why hast thou forgotten me?
Why go I mourning because of
the oppression of the enemy?'
10 As with a sword in my bones,
mine enemies reproach me;
while they say daily unto me,
'Where is thy God?'
11 Why art thou cast down, O my soul?
And why art thou disquieted within me?
Hope thou in God;
for I shall yet praise him, who is the health
of my countenance, and my God.

46 To the chief musician for the sons of Korah, a song upon Alamoth.

God is our refuge and strength,
a very present help in trouble.
2 Therefore will not we fear,
though the earth be removed,
and though the mountains be carried
into the midst of the sea;
3 though the waters thereof roar and be troubled,
though the mountains shake
with the swelling thereof. Selah.
4 There is a river, the streams whereof
shall make glad the city of God, the holy place
of the tabernacles of the most High.
5 God is in the midst of her;
she shall not be moved:
God shall help her, and that right early.
6 The heathen raged, the kingdoms were moved:
he uttered his voice, the earth melted.
7 The Lord of hosts is with us;
the God of Jacob is our refuge. Selah.
8 Come, behold the works of the Lord,
what desolations he hath made in the earth.
9 He maketh wars to cease unto the end of the earth;
he breaketh the bow,
and cutteth the spear in sunder;
he burneth the chariot in the fire.

10 Be still, and know that I am God:
I will be exalted among the heathen,
I will be exalted in the earth.
11 The Lord of hosts is with us;
the God of Jacob is our refuge. Selah.

47

To the chief Musician, a psalm for the sons of Korah.

O clap your hands, all ye people;
shout unto God with the voice of triumph.
2 For the Lord most high is terrible;
he is a great King over all the earth.
3 He shall subdue the people under us,
and the nations under our feet.
4 He shall choose our inheritance for us,
the excellency of Jacob whom he loved. Selah.
5 God is gone up with a shout,
the Lord with the sound of a trumpet.
6 Sing praises to God, sing praises:
sing praises unto our King, sing praises.
7 For God is the King of all the earth:
sing ye praises with understanding.
8 God reigneth over the heathen:
God sitteth upon the throne of his holiness.
9 The princes of the people are gathered together,
even the people of the God of Abraham:
for the shields of the earth belong unto God:

he is greatly exalted.

51 To the chief musician, a psalm of David,
when Nathan the prophet came unto him,
after he had gone in to Bath-sheba.

Have mercy upon me, O God,
according to thy lovingkindness:
according unto the multitude
of thy tender mercies blot out my transgressions.
2 Wash me throughly from mine iniquity,
and cleanse me from my sin.
3 For I acknowledge my transgressions:
and my sin is ever before me.
4 Against thee, thee only, have I sinned,
and done this evil in thy sight:
that thou mightest be justified
when thou speakest,
and be clear when thou judgest.
5 Behold, I was shapen in iniquity;
and in sin did my mother conceive me.
6 Behold, thou desirest truth in the inward parts;
and in the hidden part thou shalt make me
to know wisdom.
7 Purge me with hyssop, and I shall be clean:
wash me, and I shall be whiter than snow.
8 Make me to hear joy and gladness;
that the bones which thou hast broken

may rejoice.
9 Hide thy face from my sins,
and blot out all mine iniquities.
10 Create in me a clean heart, O God;
and renew a right spirit within me.
11 Cast me not away from thy presence;
and take not thy holy spirit from me.
12 Restore unto me the joy of thy salvation;
and uphold me with thy free spirit.
13 Then will I teach transgressors thy ways;
and sinners shall be converted unto thee.
14 Deliver me from bloodguiltiness, O God,
thou God of my salvation;
and my tongue shall sing aloud
of thy righteousness.
15 O Lord, open thou my lips;
and my mouth shall shew forth thy praise.
16 For thou desirest not sacrifice;
else would I give it:
thou delightest not in burnt offering.
17 The sacrifices of God are a broken spirit:
a broken and a contrite heart, O God,
thou wilt not despise.
18 Do good in thy good pleasure unto Zion:
build thou the walls of Jerusalem.
19 Then shalt thou be pleased with the sacrifices
of righteousness,
with burnt offering and whole burnt offering:

then shall they offer bullocks upon thine altar.

55 To the chief musician on Neginoth, Maschil, a psalm of David.

Give ear to my prayer, O God;
and hide not thyself from my supplication.
2 Attend unto me, and hear me:
I mourn in my complaint, and make a noise;
3 because of the voice of the enemy,
because of the oppression of the wicked;
for they cast iniquity upon me,
and in wrath they hate me.
4 My heart is sore pained within me;
and the terrors of death are fallen upon me.
5 Fearfulness and trembling are come upon me,
and horror hath overwhelmed me.
6 And I said, 'Oh that I had wings like a dove!
For then would I fly away, and be at rest.
7 Lo, then would I wander far off,
and remain in the wilderness. Selah.
8 I would hasten my escape from the windy storm
and tempest.'
9 Destroy, O Lord, and divide their tongues;
for I have seen violence and strife in the city.
10 Day and night they go about it
upon the walls thereof: mischief also and sorrow
are in the midst of it.

[11] Wickedness is in the midst thereof:
deceit and guile depart not from her streets.
[12] For it was not an enemy that reproached me;
then I could have borne it:
neither was it he that hated me that did
magnify himself against me;
then I would have hid myself from him.
[13] But it was thou, a man mine equal,
my guide, and mine acquaintance.
[14] We took sweet counsel together, and walked
unto the house of God in company.
[15] Let death seize upon them,
and let them go down quick into hell;
for wickedness is in their dwellings,
and among them.
[16] As for me, I will call upon God;
and the Lord shall save me.
[17] Evening, and morning, and at noon,
will I pray, and cry aloud;
and he shall hear my voice.
[18] He hath delivered my soul in peace
from the battle that was against me;
for there were many with me.
[19] God shall hear, and afflict them,
even he that abideth of old. Selah.
Because they have no changes,
therefore they fear not God.
[20] He hath put forth his hands against such as

be at peace with him:
he hath broken his covenant.
21 The words of his mouth were smoother than butter,
but war was in his heart:
his words were softer than oil,
yet were they drawn swords.
22 Cast thy burden upon the Lord,
and he shall sustain thee: he shall
never suffer the righteous to be moved.
23 But thou, O God, shalt bring them down
into the pit of destruction:
bloody and deceitful men shall not live out
half their days; but I will trust in thee.

56

To the chief musician upon Jonath-elem-rechokim,
Michtam of David, when the Philistines
took him in Gath.

Be merciful unto me, O God;
for man would swallow me up;
he fighting daily oppresseth me.
2 Mine enemies would daily swallow me up;
for they be many that fight against me,
O thou most High.
3 What time I am afraid, I will trust in thee.
4 In God I will praise his word,
in God I have put my trust;
I will not fear what flesh can do unto me.

5 Every day they wrest my words:
all their thoughts are against me for evil.
6 They gather themselves together,
they hide themselves, they mark my steps,
when they wait for my soul.
7 Shall they escape by iniquity?
In thine anger cast down the people, O God.
8 Thou tellest my wanderings:
put thou my tears into thy bottle:
are they not in thy book?
9 When I cry unto thee,
then shall mine enemies turn back:
this I know; for God is for me.
10 In God will I praise his word:
in the Lord will I praise his word.
11 In God have I put my trust:
I will not be afraid what man can do unto me.
12 Thy vows are upon me, O God:
I will render praises unto thee.
13 For thou hast delivered my soul from death:
wilt not thou deliver my feet from falling,
that I may walk before God
in the light of the living?

62

To the chief musician, to Jeduthun,
a psalm of David.

Truly my soul waiteth upon God:

from him cometh my salvation.
2 He only is my rock and my salvation;
he is my defence; I shall not be greatly moved.
3 How long will ye imagine mischief against a man?
Ye shall be slain all of you:
as a bowing wall shall ye be,
and as a tottering fence.
4 They only consult to cast him down
from his excellency: they delight in lies:
they bless with their mouth,
but they curse inwardly. Selah.
5 My soul, wait thou only upon God;
for my expectation is from him.
6 He only is my rock and my salvation;
he is my defence; I shall not be moved.
7 In God is my salvation and my glory:
the rock of my strength,
and my refuge, is in God.
8 Trust in him at all times;
ye people, pour out your heart before him:
God is a refuge for us. Selah.
9 Surely men of low degree are vanity,
and men of high degree are a lie:
to be laid in the balance,
they are altogether lighter than vanity.
10 Trust not in oppression,
and become not vain in robbery:
if riches increase, set not your heart upon them.

11 God hath spoken once; twice have I heard this;
that power belongeth unto God.
12 Also unto thee, O Lord, belongeth mercy:
for thou renderest to every man
according to his work.

63

A psalm of David, when he was in the wilderness of Judah.

O God, thou art my God; early will I seek thee:
my soul thirsteth for thee,
my flesh longeth for thee in a dry and thirsty land,
where no water is,
2 to see thy power and thy glory,
so as I have seen thee in the sanctuary.
3 Because thy lovingkindness is better than life,
my lips shall praise thee.
4 Thus will I bless thee while I live:
I will lift up my hands in thy name.
5 My soul shall be satisfied as with marrow
and fatness; and my mouth shall praise thee
with joyful lips:
6 when I remember thee upon my bed,
and meditate on thee in the night watches.
7 Because thou hast been my help,
therefore in the shadow of thy wings
will I rejoice.

8 My soul followeth hard after thee:
thy right hand upholdeth me.
9 But those that seek my soul, to destroy it,
shall go into the lower parts of the earth.
10 They shall fall by the sword:
they shall be a portion for foxes.
11 But the king shall rejoice in God;
every one that sweareth by him shall glory:
but the mouth of them that speak lies
shall be stopped.

65

To the chief musician, a psalm and song of David.

Praise waiteth for thee, O God, in Sion:
and unto thee shall the vow be performed.
2 O thou that hearest prayer,
unto thee shall all flesh come.
3 Iniquities prevail against me:
as for our transgressions,
thou shalt purge them away.
4 Blessed is the man whom thou choosest,
and causest to approach unto thee,
that he may dwell in thy courts:
we shall be satisfied with the goodness
of thy house, even of thy holy temple.
5 By terrible things in righteousness
wilt thou answer us,
O God of our salvation;

who art the confidence of all the ends
of the earth,
and of them that are afar off upon the sea;
6 Which by his strength setteth fast the mountains;
being girded with power;
7 Which stilleth the noise of the seas,
the noise of their waves,
and the tumult of the people.
8 They also that dwell in the uttermost parts
are afraid at thy tokens:
thou makest the outgoings of the morning
and evening to rejoice.
9 Thou visitest the earth, and waterest it:
thou greatly enrichest it with the river of God,
which is full of water:
thou preparest them corn,
when thou hast so provided for it.
10 Thou waterest the ridges thereof abundantly:
thou settlest the furrows thereof:
thou makest it soft with showers:
thou blessest the springing thereof.
11 Thou crownest the year with thy goodness;
and thy paths drop fatness.
12 They drop upon the pastures of the wilderness:
and the little hills rejoice on every side.
13 The pastures are clothed with flocks;
the valleys also are covered over with corn;
they shout for joy, they also sing.

66

To the chief musician, a song or psalm.

Make a joyful noise unto God, all ye lands:
2 sing forth the honour of his name:
make his praise glorious.
3 Say unto God,
'How terrible art thou in thy works!
Through the greatness of thy power
shall thine enemies submit themselves unto thee.
4 All the earth shall worship thee,
and shall sing unto thee;
they shall sing to thy name.' Selah.
5 Come and see the works of God:
he is terrible in his doing toward
the children of men.
6 He turned the sea into dry land:
they went through the flood on foot:
there did we rejoice in him.
7 He ruleth by his power for ever;
his eyes behold the nations: let not
the rebellious exalt themselves. Selah.
8 O bless our God, ye people,
and make the voice of his praise to be heard,
9 Which holdeth our soul in life,
and suffereth not our feet to be moved.
10 For thou, O God, hast proved us:
thou hast tried us, as silver is tried.
11 Thou broughtest us into the net;

thou laidst affliction upon our loins.
12 Thou hast caused men to ride over our heads;
we went through fire and through water:
but thou broughtest us out
into a wealthy place.
13 I will go into thy house with burnt offerings:
I will pay thee my vows,
14 which my lips have uttered, and my mouth hath
spoken, when I was in trouble.
15 I will offer unto thee burnt sacrifices of fatlings,
with the incense of rams;
I will offer bullocks with goats. Selah.
16 Come and hear, all ye that fear God,
and I will declare what he hath done
for my soul.
17 I cried unto him with my mouth,
and he was extolled with my tongue.
18 If I regard iniquity in my heart,
the Lord will not hear me:
19 but verily God hath heard me;
he hath attended to the voice of my prayer.
20 Blessed be God, which hath not turned away
my prayer, nor his mercy from me.

67

To the chief musician on Neginoth, a psalm or song.

God be merciful unto us, and bless us;
and cause his face to shine upon us; Selah.

[2] That thy way may be known upon earth,
thy saving health among all nations.
[3] Let the people praise thee, O God;
let all the people praise thee.
[4] O let the nations be glad and sing for joy:
for thou shalt judge the people righteously,
and govern the nations upon earth. Selah.
[5] Let the people praise thee, O God;
let all the people praise thee.
[6] Then shall the earth yield her increase;
and God, even our own God, shall bless us.
[7] God shall bless us; and all the ends of the earth
shall fear him.

72

A psalm for Solomon.

Give the king thy judgments, O God,
and thy righteousness unto the king's son.
[2] He shall judge thy people with righteousness,
and thy poor with judgment.
[3] The mountains shall bring peace to the people,
and the little hills, by righteousness.
[4] He shall judge the poor of the people,
he shall save the children of the needy,
and shall break in pieces the oppressor.
[5] They shall fear thee as long as the sun
and moon endure, throughout all generations.
[6] He shall come down like rain upon the mown grass,

as showers that water the earth.
7 In his days shall the righteous flourish;
and abundance of peace
so long as the moon endureth.
8 He shall have dominion also from sea to sea,
and from the river unto the ends of the earth.
9 They that dwell in the wilderness shall bow before him;
and his enemies shall lick the dust.
10 The kings of Tarshish and of the isles shall bring presents:
the kings of Sheba and Seba shall offer gifts.
11 Yea, all kings shall fall down before him:
all nations shall serve him.
12 For he shall deliver the needy when he crieth;
the poor also, and him that hath no helper.
13 He shall spare the poor and needy,
and shall save the souls of the needy.
14 He shall redeem their soul from deceit
and violence: and precious
shall their blood be in his sight.
15 And he shall live, and to him shall be given of the gold of Sheba:
prayer also shall be made for him continually;
and daily shall he be praised.
16 There shall be an handful of corn in the earth
upon the top of the mountains;

the fruit thereof shall shake like Lebanon:
and they of the city shall flourish
like grass of the earth.
17 His name shall endure for ever:
his name shall be continued as long as the sun:
and men shall be blessed in him:
all nations shall call him blessed.
18 Blessed be the Lord God, the God of Israel,
who only doeth wondrous things.
19 And blessed be his glorious name for ever:
and let the whole earth be filled with his glory;
Amen, and Amen.
20 The prayers of David the son of Jesse are ended.

80

To the chief musician upon Shoshannim-Eduth,
a psalm of Asaph.

Give ear, O Shepherd of Israel,
thou that leadest Joseph like a flock;
thou that dwellest between the cherubims,
shine forth.
2 Before Ephraim and Benjamin and Manasseh
stir up thy strength, and come and save us.
3 Turn us again, O God, and cause thy face to shine;
and we shall be saved.
4 O Lord God of hosts, how long wilt thou be angry
against the prayer of thy people.
5 Thou feedest them with the bread of tears;

and givest them tears to drink in great measure.
6 Thou makest us a strife unto our neighbours;
and our enemies laugh among themselves.
7 Turn us again, O God of hosts,
and cause thy face to shine; and we shall be saved.
8 Thou hast brought a vine out of Egypt:
thou hast cast out the heathen, and planted it.
9 Thou preparedst room before it,
and didst cause it to take deep root,
and it filled the land.
10 The hills were covered with the shadow of it,
and the boughs thereof were
like the goodly cedars.
11 She sent out her boughs unto the sea,
and her branches unto the river.
12 Why hast thou then broken down her hedges,
so that all they which pass by the way
do pluck her?
13 The boar out of the wood doth waste it,
and the wild beast of the field doth devour it.
14 Return, we beseech thee, O God of hosts:
look down from heaven, and behold,
and visit this vine;
15 and the vineyard which thy right hand
hath planted, and the branch
that thou madest strong for thyself.
16 It is burned with fire, it is cut down:
they perish at the rebuke of thy countenance.
17 Let thy hand be upon the man of thy right hand,

upon the son of man
whom thou madest strong for thyself.
18 So will not we go back from thee:
quicken us, and we will call upon thy name.
19 Turn us again, O Lord God of hosts,
cause thy face to shine;
and we shall be saved.

84

To the chief musician upon Gittith, a psalm for the sons of Korah.

How amiable are thy tabernacles, O Lord of hosts!
2 My soul longeth, yea, even fainteth
for the courts of the Lord:
my heart and my flesh crieth out
for the living God.
3 Yea, the sparrow hath found an house,
and the swallow a nest for herself,
where she may lay her young,
even thine altars, O Lord of hosts,
my King, and my God.
4 Blessed are they that dwell in thy house:
they will be still praising thee. Selah.
5 Blessed is the man whose strength is in thee:
in whose heart are the ways of them.
6 Who passing through the valley of Baca
make it a well;
the rain also filleth the pools.

7 They go from strength to strength,
every one of them in Zion appeareth before God.
8 O Lord God of hosts, hear my prayer:
give ear, O God of Jacob. Selah.
9 Behold, O God our shield,
and look upon the face of thine anointed.
10 For a day in thy courts is better than a thousand.
I had rather be a doorkeeper
in the house of my God,
than to dwell in the tents of wickedness.
11 For the Lord God is a sun and shield:
the Lord will give grace and glory:
no good thing will he withhold
from them that walk uprightly.
12 O Lord of hosts,
blessed is the man that trusteth in thee.

87

A psalm or song for the sons of Korah.

His foundation is in the holy mountains.
2 The Lord loveth the gates of Zion
more than all the dwellings of Jacob.
3 Glorious things are spoken of thee,
O city of God. Selah.
4 I will make mention of Rahab and Babylon
to them that know me: behold Philistia,
and Tyre, with Ethiopia; this man was born
there.

[5] And of Zion it shall be said,
'This and that man was born in her':
and the highest himself shall establish her.
[6] The Lord shall count,
when he writeth up the people,
that this man was born there. Selah.
[7] As well the singers as the players on instruments
shall be there: all my springs are in thee.

89

Maschil of Ethan the Ezrahite.

I will sing of the mercies of the Lord for ever:
with my mouth will I make known
thy faithfulness to all generations.
[2] For I have said, 'Mercy shall be built up for ever:
thy faithfulness shalt thou establish
in the very heavens.'
[3] I have made a covenant with my chosen,
I have sworn unto David my servant,
[4] 'Thy seed will I establish for ever,
and build up thy throne to all generations.' Selah.
[5] And the heavens shall praise thy wonders, O Lord:
thy faithfulness also in the congregation
of the saints.
[6] For who in the heaven can be compared
unto the Lord?
Who among the sons of the mighty
can be likened unto the Lord?

7 God is greatly to be feared in the assembly
of the saints, and to be had in reverence
of all them that are about him.
8 O Lord God of hosts, who is a strong Lord
like unto thee?
Or to thy faithfulness round about thee?
9 Thou rulest the raging of the sea:
when the waves thereof arise, thou stillest them.
10 Thou hast broken Rahab in pieces,
as one that is slain;
thou hast scattered thine enemies
with thy strong arm.
11 The heavens are thine, the earth also is thine:
as for the world and the fulness thereof,
thou hast founded them.
12 The north and the south thou hast created them:
Tabor and Hermon shall rejoice in thy name.
13 Thou hast a mighty arm:
strong is thy hand, and high is thy right hand.
14 Justice and judgment are the habitation
of thy throne:
mercy and truth shall go before thy face.
15 Blessed is the people that know the joyful sound:
they shall walk, O Lord,
in the light of thy countenance.
16 In thy name shall they rejoice all the day;
and in thy righteousness shall they be exalted.
17 For thou art the glory of their strength;

and in thy favour our horn shall be exalted.
18 For the Lord is our defence;
and the Holy One of Israel is our king.
19 Then thou spakest in vision to thy holy one,
and saidst,
'I have laid help upon one that is mighty;
I have exalted one chosen out of the people.
20 I have found David my servant;
with my holy oil have I anointed him,
21 with whom my hand shall be established:
mine arm also shall strengthen him.
22 The enemy shall not exact upon him;
nor the son of wickedness afflict him.
23 And I will beat down his foes before his face,
and plague them that hate him.
24 But my faithfulness and my mercy
shall be with him;
and in my name shall his horn be exalted.
25 I will set his hand also in the sea,
and his right hand in the rivers.
26 He shall cry unto me,
"Thou art my father, my God,
and the rock of my salvation."
27 Also I will make him my firstborn,
higher than the kings of the earth.
28 My mercy will I keep for him for evermore,
and my covenant shall stand fast with him.
29 His seed also will I make to endure for ever,

and his throne as the days of heaven.
30 If his children forsake my law,
and walk not in my judgments;
31 if they break my statutes,
and keep not my commandments;
32 then will I visit their transgression with the rod,
and their iniquity with stripes.
33 Nevertheless my lovingkindness will I not
utterly take from him,
nor suffer my faithfulness to fail.
34 My covenant will I not break,
nor alter the thing that is gone out of my lips.
35 Once have I sworn by my holiness
that I will not lie unto David.
36 His seed shall endure for ever,
and his throne as the sun before me.
37 It shall be established for ever as the moon,
and as a faithful witness in heaven.' Selah.
38 But thou hast cast off and abhorred,
thou hast been wroth with thine anointed.
39 Thou hast made void the covenant of thy servant:
thou hast profaned his crown
by casting it to the ground.
40 Thou hast broken down all his hedges;
thou hast brought his strong holds to ruin.
41 All that pass by the way spoil him:
he is a reproach to his neighbours.
42 Thou hast set up the right hand of his adversaries;

thou hast made all his enemies to rejoice.
43 Thou hast also turned the edge of his sword,
and hast not made him to stand in the battle.
44 Thou hast made his glory to cease,
and cast his throne down to the ground.
45 The days of his youth hast thou shortened:
thou hast covered him with shame. Selah.
46 How long, Lord?
Wilt thou hide thyself for ever?
Shall thy wrath burn like fire?
47 Remember how short my time is:
wherefore hast thou made all men in vain?
48 What man is he that liveth, and shall not see death?
Shall he deliver his soul from the hand
of the grave? Selah.
49 Lord, where are thy former lovingkindnesses,
which thou swarest unto David in thy truth?
50 Remember, Lord, the reproach of thy servants;
how I do bear in my bosom the reproach
of all the mighty people;
51 wherewith thine enemies have reproached, O Lord;
wherewith they have reproached the footsteps
of thine anointed.
52 Blessed be the Lord for evermore.
Amen, and Amen.

90 A prayer of Moses the man of God.

Lord, thou hast been our dwelling place
in all generations.
2 Before the mountains were brought forth,
or ever thou hadst formed the earth
and the world,
even from everlasting
to everlasting, thou art God.
3 Thou turnest man to destruction; and sayest,
'Return, ye children of men.'
4 For a thousand years in thy sight
are but as yesterday when it is past,
and as a watch in the night.
5 Thou carriest them away as with a flood;
they are as a sleep: in the morning they are like grass
which groweth up.
6 In the morning it flourisheth, and groweth up;
in the evening it is cut down, and withereth.
7 For we are consumed by thine anger,
and by thy wrath are we troubled.
8 Thou hast set our iniquities before thee,
our secret sins in the light of thy countenance.
9 For all our days are passed away in thy wrath:
we spend our years as a tale that is told.
10 The days of our years are three-score years and ten;
and if by reason of strength
they be fourscore years,

yet is their strength labour and sorrow;
for it is soon cut off, and we fly away.
11 Who knoweth the power of thine anger?
Even according to thy fear, so is thy wrath.
12 So teach us to number our days,
that we may apply our hearts unto wisdom.
13 Return, O Lord, how long?
And let it repent thee concerning thy servants.
14 O satisfy us early with thy mercy;
that we may rejoice and be glad all our days.
15 Make us glad according to the days
wherein thou hast afflicted us,
and the years wherein we have seen evil.
16 Let thy work appear unto thy servants,
and thy glory unto their children.
17 And let the beauty of the Lord our God be upon us;
and establish thou the work of our hands upon us;
yea, the work of our hands establish thou it.

91 He that dwelleth in the secret place of the most High
shall abide under the shadow of the Almighty.
2 I will say of the Lord,
'He is my refuge and my fortress:
my God; in him will I trust.'
3 Surely he shall deliver thee from the snare
of the fowler,
and from the noisome pestilence.

4 He shall cover thee with his feathers,
and under his wings shalt thou trust:
his truth shall be thy shield and buckler.
5 Thou shalt not be afraid for the terror by night;
nor for the arrow that flieth by day;
6 nor for the pestilence that walketh in darkness;
nor for the destruction that wasteth at noonday.
7 A thousand shall fall at thy side,
and ten thousand at thy right hand;
but it shall not come nigh thee.
8 Only with thine eyes shalt thou behold
and see the reward of the wicked.
9 Because thou hast made the Lord,
which is my refuge,
even the most High, thy habitation;
10 there shall no evil befall thee,
neither shall any plague come nigh thy dwelling.
11 For he shall give his angels charge over thee,
to keep thee in all thy ways.
12 They shall bear thee up in their hands,
lest thou dash thy foot against a stone.
13 Thou shalt tread upon the lion and adder:
the young lion and the dragon
shalt thou trample under feet.
14 Because he hath set his love upon me,
therefore will I deliver him:
I will set him on high,
because he hath known my name.

15 He shall call upon me,
and I will answer him;
I will be with him in trouble;
I will deliver him, and honour him.
16 With long life will I satisfy him,
and shew him my salvation.

92

A psalm or song for the sabbath day.

It is a good thing to give thanks unto the Lord,
and to sing praises unto thy name,
O most High,
2 to shew forth thy lovingkindness in the morning,
and thy faithfulness every night,
3 upon an instrument of ten strings,
and upon the psaltery;
upon the harp with a solemn sound.
4 For thou, Lord, hast made me glad
through thy work:
I will triumph in the works of thy hands.
5 O Lord, how great are thy works!
And thy thoughts are very deep.
6 A brutish man knoweth not;
neither doth a fool understand this.
7 When the wicked spring as the grass,
and when all the workers of iniquity do flourish;
it is that they shall be destroyed for ever;
8 but thou, Lord, art most high for evermore.

9 For, lo, thine enemies, O Lord,
for, lo, thine enemies shall perish;
all the workers of iniquity shall be scattered.
10 But my horn shalt thou exalt like the horn
of an unicorn:
I shall be anointed with fresh oil.
11 Mine eye also shall see my desire on mine enemies,
and mine ears shall hear my desire
of the wicked that rise up against me.
12 The righteous shall flourish like the palm tree:
he shall grow like a cedar in Lebanon.
13 Those that be planted in the house of the Lord
shall flourish in the courts of our God.
14 They shall still bring forth fruit in old age;
they shall be fat and flourishing;
15 to shew that the Lord is upright: he is my rock,
and there is no unrighteousness in him.

93

The Lord reigneth, he is clothed with majesty;
the Lord is clothed with strength,
wherewith he hath girded himself:
the world also is stablished,
that it cannot be moved.
2 Thy throne is established of old:
thou art from everlasting.
3 The floods have lifted up, O Lord,
the floods have lifted up their voice;

the floods lift up their waves.
4 The Lord on high is mightier than the noise
of many waters,
yea, than the mighty waves of the sea.
5 Thy testimonies are very sure:
holiness becometh thine house, O Lord, for ever.

95

O come, let us sing unto the Lord:
let us make a joyful noise to the rock
of our salvation.
2 Let us come before his presence with thanksgiving,
and make a joyful noise unto him with psalms.
3 For the Lord is a great God,
and a great King above all gods.
4 In his hand are the deep places of the earth:
the strength of the hills is his also.
5 The sea is his, and he made it;
and his hands formed the dry land.
6 O come, let us worship and bow down:
let us kneel before the Lord our maker.
7 For he is our God;
and we are the people of his pasture,
and the sheep of his hand.
To day if ye will hear his voice,
8 harden not your heart, as in the provocation,
and as in the day of temptation in the wilderness;
9 when your fathers tempted me,

proved me, and saw my work.
10 Forty years long was I grieved with this generation,
and said, 'It is a people that do err in their heart,
and they have not known my ways,'
11 unto whom I sware in my wrath that they should
not enter into my rest.

96

O sing unto the Lord a new song:
sing unto the Lord, all the earth.
2 Sing unto the Lord, bless his name;
shew forth his salvation from day to day.
3 Declare his glory among the heathen,
his wonders among all people.
4 For the Lord is great, and greatly to be praised:
he is to be feared above all gods.
5 For all the gods of the nations are idols;
but the Lord made the heavens.
6 Honour and majesty are before him:
strength and beauty are in his sanctuary.
7 Give unto the Lord, O ye kindreds of the people,
give unto the Lord glory and strength.
8 Give unto the Lord the glory due unto his name:
bring an offering, and come into his courts.
9 O worship the Lord in the beauty of holiness:
fear before him, all the earth.
10 Say among the heathen that the Lord reigneth:
the world also shall be established

that it shall not be moved:
he shall judge the people righteously.
11 Let the heavens rejoice, and let the earth be glad;
let the sea roar, and the fulness thereof.
12 Let the field be joyful, and all that is therein;
then shall all the trees of the wood rejoice
13 before the Lord; for he cometh,
for he cometh to judge the earth:
he shall judge the world with righteousness,
and the people with his truth.

97

The Lord reigneth; let the earth rejoice;
let the multitude of isles be glad thereof.
2 Clouds and darkness are round about him:
righteousness and judgment are the habitation
of his throne.
3 A fire goeth before him,
and burneth up his enemies round about.
4 His lightnings enlightened the world:
the earth saw, and trembled.
5 The hills melted like wax at the presence
of the Lord,
at the presence of the Lord of the whole earth.
6 The heavens declare his righteousness,
and all the people see his glory.
7 Confounded be all they that serve graven images,
that boast themselves of idols:

worship him, all ye gods.
8 Zion heard, and was glad;
and the daughters of Judah rejoiced
because of thy judgments, O Lord.
9 For thou, Lord, art high above all the earth:
thou art exalted far above all gods.
10 Ye that love the Lord, hate evil;
he preserveth the souls of his saints;
he delivereth them out of the hand
of the wicked.
11 Light is sown for the righteous,
and gladness for the upright in heart.
12 Rejoice in the Lord, ye righteous;
and give thanks at the remembrance
of his holiness.

98

A psalm.

O sing unto the Lord a new song;
for he hath done marvellous things:
his right hand, and his holy arm,
hath gotten him the victory.
2 The Lord hath made known his salvation:
his righteousness hath he openly shewed
in the sight of the heathen.
3 He hath remembered his mercy and his truth
toward the house of Israel:
all the ends of the earth have seen

the salvation of our God.
4 Make a joyful noise unto the Lord,
all the earth: make a loud noise,
and rejoice, and sing praise.
5 Sing unto the Lord with the harp;
with the harp, and the voice of a psalm.
6 With trumpets and sound of cornet
make a joyful noise before the Lord, the King.
7 Let the sea roar, and the fulness thereof;
the world, and they that dwell therein.
8 Let the floods clap their hands;
let the hills be joyful together
9 Before the Lord; for he cometh to judge the earth;
with righteousness shall he judge the world,
and the people with equity.

100

A Psalm of praise.

Make a joyful noise unto the Lord, all ye lands.
2 Serve the Lord with gladness:
come before his presence with singing.
3 Know ye that the Lord he is God;
it is he that hath made us, and not we ourselves;
we are his people,
and the sheep of his pasture.
4 Enter into his gates with thanksgiving,
and into his courts with praise:
be thankful unto him, and bless his name.

5 For the Lord is good; his mercy is everlasting;
and his truth endureth to all generations.

102

A prayer of the afflicted, when he is overwhelmed, and poureth out his complaint before the Lord.

Hear my prayer, O Lord,
and let my cry come unto thee.
2 Hide not thy face from me in the day
when I am in trouble; incline thine ear unto me:
in the day when I call answer me speedily.
3 For my days are consumed like smoke,
and my bones are burned as an hearth.
4 My heart is smitten, and withered like grass;
so that I forget to eat my bread.
5 By reason of the voice of my groaning my bones
cleave to my skin.
6 I am like a pelican of the wilderness:
I am like an owl of the desert.
7 I watch, and am as a sparrow
alone upon the house top.
8 Mine enemies reproach me all the day;
and they that are mad against me are sworn
against me.
9 For I have eaten ashes like bread,
and mingled my drink with weeping,
10 because of thine indignation and thy wrath;

for thou hast lifted me up, and cast me down.
11 My days are like a shadow that declineth;
and I am withered like grass.
12 But thou, O Lord, shalt endure for ever;
and thy remembrance unto all generations.
13 Thou shalt arise, and have mercy upon Zion;
for the time to favour her, yea,
the set time, is come.
14 For thy servants take pleasure in her stones,
and favour the dust thereof.
15 So the heathen shall fear the name of the Lord,
and all the kings of the earth thy glory.
16 When the Lord shall build up Zion,
he shall appear in his glory.
17 He will regard the prayer of the destitute,
and not despise their prayer.
18 This shall be written for the generation to come;
and the people which shall be created
shall praise the Lord.
19 For he hath looked down from the height
of his sanctuary;
from heaven did the Lord behold the earth;
20 to hear the groaning of the prisoner;
to loose those that are appointed to death;
21 to declare the name of the Lord in Zion,
and his praise in Jerusalem;
22 when the people are gathered together,
and the kingdoms, to serve the Lord.

23 He weakened my strength in the way;
he shortened my days.
24 I said, 'O my God, take me not away
in the midst of my days;
thy years are throughout all generations.'
25 Of old hast thou laid the foundation of the earth;
and the heavens are the work of thy hands.
26 They shall perish, but thou shalt endure:
yea, all of them shall wax old like a garment;
as a vesture shalt thou change them,
and they shall be changed;
27 but thou art the same,
and thy years shall have no end.
28 The children of thy servants shall continue,
and their seed shall be established before thee.

103

A psalm of David.

Bless the Lord, O my soul;
and all that is within me, bless his holy name.
2 Bless the Lord, O my soul,
and forget not all his benefits;
3 who forgiveth all thine iniquities;
who healeth all thy diseases;
4 who redeemeth thy life from destruction;
who crowneth thee with lovingkindness
and tender mercies;
5 who satisfieth thy mouth with good things;

so that thy youth is renewed like the eagle's.
6 The Lord executeth righteousness
and judgment for all that are oppressed.
7 He made known his ways unto Moses,
his acts unto the children of Israel.
8 The Lord is merciful and gracious,
slow to anger, and plenteous in mercy.
9 He will not always chide;
neither will he keep his anger for ever.
10 He hath not dealt with us after our sins;
nor rewarded us according to our iniquities.
11 For as the heaven is high above the earth,
so great is his mercy toward them that fear him.
12 As far as the east is from the west,
so far hath he removed our transgressions
from us.
13 Like as a father pitieth his children,
so the Lord pitieth them that fear him.
14 For he knoweth our frame;
he remembereth that we are dust.
15 As for man, his days are as grass:
as a flower of the field, so he flourisheth.
16 For the wind passeth over it, and it is gone;
and the place thereof shall know it no more.
17 But the mercy of the Lord is from everlasting
to everlasting upon them that fear him,
and his righteousness unto children's children;
18 to such as keep his covenant,

and to those that remember his commandments
to do them.
19 The Lord hath prepared his throne in the heavens;
and his kingdom ruleth over all.
20 Bless the Lord, ye his angels, that excel in strength,
that do his commandments,
hearkening unto the voice of his word.
21 Bless ye the Lord, all ye his hosts;
ye ministers of his, that do his pleasure.
22 Bless the Lord, all his works in all places
of his dominion: bless the Lord, O my soul.

104 Bless the Lord, O my soul.
O Lord my God, thou art very great;
thou art clothed with honour and majesty.
2 Who coverest thyself with light as with a garment;
who stretchest out the heavens like a curtain;
3 who layeth the beams of his chambers
in the waters;
who maketh the clouds his chariot;
who walketh upon the wings of the wind;
4 who maketh his angels spirits;
his ministers a flaming fire;
5 who laid the foundations of the earth,
that it should not be removed for ever.
6 Thou coveredst it with the deep as with a garment:
the waters stood above the mountains.

7 At thy rebuke they fled;
at the voice of thy thunder they hasted away.
8 They go up by the mountains;
they go down by the valleys unto the place
which thou hast founded for them.
9 Thou hast set a bound that they may not pass over;
that they turn not again to cover the earth.
10 He sendeth the springs into the valleys,
which run among the hills.
11 They give drink to every beast of the field:
the wild asses quench their thirst.
12 By them shall the fowls of the heaven
have their habitation,
which sing among the branches.
13 He watereth the hills from his chambers:
the earth is satisfied with the fruit of thy works.
14 He causeth the grass to grow for the cattle,
and herb for the service of man,
that he may bring forth food out of the earth;
15 and wine that maketh glad the heart of man,
and oil to make his face to shine,
and bread which strengtheneth man's heart.
16 The trees of the Lord are full of sap;
the cedars of Lebanon, which he hath planted;
17 where the birds make their nests:
as for the stork, the fir trees are her house.
18 The high hills are a refuge for the wild goats;
and the rocks for the conies.

19 He appointed the moon for seasons;
the sun knoweth his going down.
20 Thou makest darkness, and it is night;
wherein all the beasts of the forest do creep forth.
21 The young lions roar after their prey,
and seek their meat from God.
22 The sun ariseth, they gather themselves together,
and lay them down in their dens.
23 Man goeth forth unto his work and to his labour
until the evening.
24 O Lord, how manifold are thy works!
In wisdom hast thou made them all;
the earth is full of thy riches.
25 So is this great and wide sea,
wherein are things creeping innumerable,
both small and great beasts.
26 There go the ships;
there is that leviathan,
whom thou hast made to play therein.
27 These wait all upon thee,
that thou mayest give them their meat
in due season.
28 That thou givest them they gather:
thou openest thine hand,
they are filled with good.
29 Thou hidest thy face, they are troubled:
thou takest away their breath,
they die, and return to their dust.

30 Thou sendest forth thy spirit, they are created:
and thou renewest the face of the earth.
31 The glory of the Lord shall endure for ever:
the Lord shall rejoice in his works.
32 He looketh on the earth, and it trembleth:
he toucheth the hills, and they smoke.
33 I will sing unto the Lord as long as I live:
I will sing praise to my God
while I have my being.
34 My meditation of him shall be sweet:
I will be glad in the Lord.
35 Let the sinners be consumed out of the earth,
and let the wicked be no more.
Bless thou the Lord, O my soul.
Praise ye the Lord.

105

O give thanks unto the Lord;
call upon his name;
make known his deeds among the people.
2 Sing unto him, sing psalms unto him;
talk ye of all his wondrous works.
3 Glory ye in his holy name;
let the heart of them rejoice that seek the Lord.
4 Seek the Lord, and his strength;
seek his face evermore.
5 Remember his marvellous works that he hath done;
his wonders, and the judgments of his mouth;

6 O ye seed of Abraham his servant,
ye children of Jacob his chosen.
7 He is the Lord our God;
his judgments are in all the earth.
8 He hath remembered his covenant for ever,
the word which he commanded
to a thousand generations.
9 Which covenant he made with Abraham,
and his oath unto Isaac;
10 and confirmed the same unto Jacob for a law,
and to Israel for an everlasting covenant,
11 saying, 'Unto thee will I give the land of Canaan,
the lot of your inheritance,'
12 when they were but a few men in number;
yea, very few, and strangers in it.
13 When they went from one nation to another,
from one kingdom to another people;
14 he suffered no man to do them wrong:
yea, he reproved kings for their sakes,
15 saying, 'Touch not mine anointed,
and do my prophets no harm.'
16 Moreover he called for a famine upon the land:
he brake the whole staff of bread.
17 He sent a man before them,
even Joseph, who was sold for a servant,
18 whose feet they hurt with fetters:
he was laid in iron:
19 until the time that his word came:

the word of the Lord tried him.
20 The king sent and loosed him;
even the ruler of the people, and let him go free.
21 He made him lord of his house,
and ruler of all his substance:
22 to bind his princes at his pleasure;
and teach his senators wisdom.
23 Israel also came into Egypt;
and Jacob sojourned in the land of Ham.
24 And he increased his people greatly;
and made them stronger than their enemies.
25 He turned their heart to hate his people,
to deal subtilly with his servants.
26 He sent Moses his servant;
and Aaron whom he had chosen.
27 They shewed his signs among them,
and wonders in the land of Ham.
28 He sent darkness, and made it dark;
and they rebelled not against his word.
29 He turned their waters into blood,
and slew their fish.
30 Their land brought forth frogs in abundance,
in the chambers of their kings.
31 He spake, and there came divers sorts of flies,
and lice in all their coasts.
32 He gave them hail for rain,
and flaming fire in their land.
33 He smote their vines also and their fig trees;

and brake the trees of their coasts.
34 He spake, and the locusts came,
and caterpillers, and that without number,
35 and did eat up all the herbs in their land,
and devoured the fruit of their ground.
36 He smote also all the firstborn in their land,
the chief of all their strength.
37 He brought them forth also with silver and gold;
and there was not one feeble person
among their tribes.
38 Egypt was glad when they departed,
for the fear of them fell upon them.
39 He spread a cloud for a covering;
and fire to give light in the night.
40 The people asked, and he brought quails,
and satisfied them with the bread of heaven.
41 He opened the rock, and the waters gushed out;
they ran in the dry places like a river.
42 For he remembered his holy promise,
and Abraham his servant.
43 And he brought forth his people with joy,
and his chosen with gladness;
44 and gave them the lands of the heathen;
and they inherited the labour of the people;
45 that they might observe his statutes,
and keep his laws. Praise ye the Lord.

107

O Give thanks unto the Lord,
for he is good, for his mercy endureth for ever.
2 Let the redeemed of the Lord say so,
whom he hath redeemed from the hand
of the enemy;
3 and gathered them out of the lands,
from the east, and from the west,
from the north, and from the south.
4 They wandered in the wilderness in a solitary way;
they found no city to dwell in.
5 Hungry and thirsty,
their soul fainted in them.
6 Then they cried unto the Lord in their trouble,
and he delivered them out of their distresses.
7 And he led them forth by the right way,
that they might go to a city of habitation.
8 Oh that men would praise the Lord
for his goodness,
and for his wonderful works
to the children of men!
9 For he satisfieth the longing soul,
and filleth the hungry soul with goodness.
10 Such as sit in darkness and in the shadow of death,
being bound in affliction and iron,
11 because they rebelled against the words of God,
and contemned the counsel of the most High;
12 therefore he brought down their heart with labour;
they fell down, and there was none to help.

13 Then they cried unto the Lord in their trouble,
and he saved them out of their distresses.
14 He brought them out of darkness
and the shadow of death,
and brake their bands in sunder.
15 Oh that men would praise the Lord
for his goodness, and for his wonderful works
to the children of men!
16 For he hath broken the gates of brass,
and cut the bars of iron in sunder.
17 Fools because of their transgression,
and because of their iniquities, are afflicted.
18 Their soul abhorreth all manner of meat;
and they draw near unto the gates of death.
19 Then they cry unto the Lord in their trouble,
and he saveth them out of their distresses.
20 He sent his word, and healed them,
and delivered them from their destructions.
21 Oh that men would praise the Lord
for his goodness, and for his wonderful works
to the children of men!
22 And let them sacrifice the sacrifices
of thanksgiving,
and declare his works with rejoicing.
23 They that go down to the sea in ships,
that do business in great waters;
24 these see the works of the Lord,
and his wonders in the deep.

25 For he commandeth, and raiseth the stormy wind,
which lifteth up the waves thereof.
26 They mount up to the heaven,
they go down again to the depths:
their soul is melted because of trouble.
27 They reel to and fro, and stagger
like a drunken man, and are at their wits' end.
28 Then they cry unto the Lord in their trouble,
and he bringeth them out of their distresses.
29 He maketh the storm a calm,
so that the waves thereof are still.
30 Then are they glad because they be quiet;
so he bringeth them unto their desired haven.
31 Oh that men would praise the Lord
for his goodness, and for his wonderful works
to the children of men!
32 Let them exalt him also in the congregation
of the people, and praise him
in the assembly of the elders.
33 He turneth rivers into a wilderness,
and the watersprings into dry ground,
34 a fruitful land into barrenness,
for the wickedness of them that dwell therein.
35 He turneth the wilderness into a standing water,
and dry ground into watersprings.
36 And there he maketh the hungry to dwell,
that they may prepare a city for habitation,
37 and sow the fields, and plant vineyards,

which may yield fruits of increase.
38 He blesseth them also,
so that they are multiplied greatly;
and suffereth not their cattle to decrease.
39 Again, they are minished and brought low
through oppression, affliction, and sorrow.
40 He poureth contempt upon princes,
and causeth them to wander in the wilderness,
where there is no way.
41 Yet setteth he the poor on high from affliction,
and maketh him families like a flock.
42 The righteous shall see it, and rejoice;
and all inquity shall stop her mouth.
43 Whoso is wise, and will observe these things,
even they shall understand the lovingkindness
of the Lord.

111

Praise ye the Lord.
I will praise the Lord with my whole heart,
in the assembly of the upright,
and in the congregation.
2 The works of the Lord are great, sought out
of all them that have pleasure therein.
3 His work is honourable and glorious;
and his righteousness endureth for ever.
4 He hath made his wonderful works
to be remembered:

the Lord is gracious and full of compassion.
5 He hath given meat unto them that fear him:
he will ever be mindful of his covenant.
6 He hath shewed his people the power of his works,
that he may give them the heritage
of the heathen.
7 The works of his hands are verity and judgment;
all his commandments are sure.
8 They stand fast for ever and ever,
and are done in truth and uprightness.
9 He sent redemption unto his people:
he hath commanded his covenant for ever:
holy and reverend is his name.
10 The fear of the Lord is the beginning of wisdom:
a good understanding have all they
that do his commandments:
his praise endureth for ever.

113

Praise ye the Lord.
Praise, O ye servants of the Lord,
praise the name of the Lord.
2 Blessed be the name of the Lord
from this time forth and for evermore.
3 From the rising of the sun unto the going down
of the same the Lord's name is to be praised.
4 The Lord is high above all nations,
and his glory above the heavens.

5 Who is like unto the Lord our God,
who dwelleth on high,
6 who humbleth himself to behold the things
that are in heaven, and in the earth!
7 He raiseth up the poor out of the dust,
and lifteth the needy out of the dunghill,
8 that he may set him with princes,
even with the princes of his people.
9 He maketh the barren woman to keep house,
and to be a joyful mother of children.
Praise ye the Lord.

115

Not unto us, O Lord, not unto us,
but unto thy name give glory, for thy mercy,
and for thy truth's sake.
2 Wherefore should the heathen say,
'Where is now their God?'
3 But our God is in the heavens:
he hath done whatsoever he hath pleased.
4 Their idols are silver and gold,
the work of men's hands.
5 They have mouths, but they speak not:
eyes have they, but they see not:
6 they have ears, but they hear not:
noses have they, but they smell not:
7 they have hands, but they handle not:
feet have they, but they walk not:

neither speak they through their throat.
8 They that make them are like unto them;
so is every one that trusteth in them.
9 O Israel, trust thou in the Lord:
he is their help and their shield.
10 O house of Aaron, trust in the Lord:
he is their help and their shield.
11 Ye that fear the Lord; trust in the Lord:
he is their help and their shield.
12 The Lord hath been mindful of us:
he will bless us;
he will bless the house of Israel;
he will bless the house of Aaron.
13 He will bless them that fear the Lord,
both small and great.
14 The Lord shall increase you more and more,
you and your children.
15 Ye are blessed of the Lord
which made heaven and earth.
16 The heaven, even the heavens, are the Lord's:
but the earth hath he given to the children
of men.
17 The dead praise not the Lord,
neither any that go down into silence.
18 But we will bless the Lord from this time forth
and for evermore. Praise the Lord.

116 I love the Lord, because he hath heard
my voice and my supplications.
2 Because he hath inclined his ear unto me,
therefore will I call upon him as long as I live.
3 The sorrows of death compassed me,
and the pains of hell gat hold upon me:
I found trouble and sorrow.
4 Then called I upon the name of the Lord:
'O Lord, I beseech thee, deliver my soul.'
5 Gracious is the Lord, and righteous;
yea, our God is merciful.
6 The Lord preserveth the simple:
I was brought low, and he helped me.
7 Return unto thy rest, O my soul;
for the Lord hath dealt bountifully with thee.
8 For thou hast delivered my soul from death,
mine eyes from tears, and my feet from falling.
9 I will walk before the Lord
in the land of the living.
10 I believed, therefore have I spoken:
I was greatly afflicted:
11 I said in my haste, 'All men are liars.'
12 What shall I render unto the Lord
for all his benefits toward me?
13 I will take the cup of salvation,
and call upon the name of the Lord.
14 I will pay my vows unto the Lord
now in the presence of all his people.

15 Precious in the sight of the Lord
is the death of his saints.
16 O Lord, truly I am thy servant;
I am thy servant, and the son of thine handmaid:
thou hast loosed my bonds.
17 I will offer to thee the sacrifice of thanksgiving,
and will call upon the name of the Lord.
18 I will pay my vows unto the Lord,
now in the presence of all his people,
19 in the courts of the Lord's house,
in the midst of thee, O Jerusalem.
Praise ye the Lord.

117 O praise the Lord, all ye nations:
praise him, all ye people.
2 For his merciful kindness is great toward us:
and the truth of the Lord endureth for ever.
Praise ye the Lord.

118 O give thanks unto the Lord; for he is good,
because his mercy endureth for ever.
2 Let Israel now say
that his mercy endureth for ever.
3 Let the house of Aaron now say
that his mercy endureth for ever.
4 Let them now that fear the Lord say
that his mercy endureth for ever.

5 I called upon the Lord in distress:
the Lord answered me,
and set me in a large place.
6 The Lord is on my side;
I will not fear: what can man do unto me?
7 The Lord taketh my part with them that help me;
therefore shall I see my desire
upon them that hate me.
8 It is better to trust in the Lord
than to put confidence in man.
9 It is better to trust in the Lord
than to put confidence in princes.
10 All nations compassed me about;
but in the name of the Lord will I destroy them.
11 They compassed me about;
yea, they compassed me about;
but in the name of the Lord I will destroy
them.
12 They compassed me about like bees;
they are quenched as the fire of thorns,
for in the name of the Lord
I will destroy them.
13 Thou hast thrust sore at me that I might fall;
but the Lord helped me.
14 The Lord is my strength and song,
and is become my salvation.
15 The voice of rejoicing and salvation is in the
tabernacles of the righteous:

the right hand of the Lord doeth valiantly.
16 The right hand of the Lord is exalted:
the right hand of the Lord doeth valiantly.
17 I shall not die, but live,
and declare the works of the Lord.
18 The Lord hath chastened me sore;
but he hath not given me over unto death.
19 Open to me the gates of righteousness:
I will go into them, and I will praise the Lord:
20 this gate of the Lord, into which
the righteous shall enter.
21 I will praise thee; for thou hast heard me,
and art become my salvation.
22 The stone which the builders refused
is become the head stone of the corner.
23 This is the Lord's doing;
it is marvellous in our eyes.
24 This is the day which the Lord hath made;
we will rejoice and be glad in it.
25 Save now, I beseech thee, O Lord:
O Lord, I beseech thee, send now prosperity.
26 Blessed be he that cometh in the name of the Lord:
we have blessed you out of the house of the Lord.
27 God is the Lord, which hath shewed us light:
bind the sacrifice with cords, even unto the horns
of the altar.
28 Thou art my God, and I will praise thee:
thou art my God, I will exalt thee.

29 O give thanks unto the Lord; for he is good;
for his mercy endureth for ever.

119

ALEPH

Blessed are the undefiled in the way,
who walk in the law of the Lord.
2 Blessed are they that keep his testimonies,
and that seek him with the whole heart.
3 They also do no iniquity: they walk in his ways.
4 Thou hast commanded us to keep
thy precepts diligently.
5 O that my ways were directed to keep thy statutes!
6 Then shall I not be ashamed,
when I have respect unto all thy commandments.
7 I will praise thee with uprightness of heart,
when I shall have learned
thy righteous judgments.
8 I will keep thy statutes;
O forsake me not utterly.

BETH

9 Wherewithal shall a young man cleanse his way?
By taking heed thereto according to thy word.
10 With my whole heart have I sought thee;
O let me not wander from thy commandments.
11 Thy word have I hid in mine heart,
that I might not sin against thee.

[12] Blessed art thou, O Lord: teach me thy statutes.
[13] With my lips have I declared
all the judgments of thy mouth.
[14] I have rejoiced in the way of thy testimonies,
as much as in all riches.
[15] I will meditate in thy precepts,
and have respect unto thy ways.
[16] I will delight myself in thy statutes;
I will not forget thy word.

GIMEL

[17] Deal bountifully with thy servant,
that I may live, and keep thy word.
[18] Open thou mine eyes, that I may behold
wondrous things out of thy law.
[19] I am a stranger in the earth:
hide not thy commandments from me.
[20] My soul breaketh for the longing that it hath unto
thy judgments at all times.
[21] Thou hast rebuked the proud that are cursed,
which do err from thy commandments.
[22] Remove from me reproach and contempt,
for I have kept thy testimonies.
[23] Princes also did sit and speak against me;
but thy servant did meditate in thy statutes.
[24] Thy testimonies also are my delight
and my counsellors.

DALETH

25 My soul cleaveth unto the dust;
quicken thou me according to thy word.
26 I have declared my ways, and thou heardest me:
teach me thy statutes.
27 Make me to understand the way of thy precepts;
so shall I talk of thy wondrous works.
28 My soul melteth for heaviness:
strengthen thou me according unto thy word.
29 Remove from me the way of lying;
and grant me thy law graciously.
30 I have chosen the way of truth:
thy judgments have I laid before me.
31 I have stuck unto thy testimonies:
O Lord, put me not to shame.
32 I will run the way of thy commandments,
when thou shalt enlarge my heart.

HE

33 Teach me, O Lord, the way of thy statutes;
and I shall keep it unto the end.
34 Give me understanding, and I shall keep thy law;
yea, I shall observe it with my whole heart.
35 Make me to go in the path of thy commandments;
for therein do I delight.
36 Incline my heart unto thy testimonies,
and not to covetousness.

37 Turn away mine eyes from beholding vanity;
and quicken thou me in thy way.
38 Stablish thy word unto thy servant,
who is devoted to thy fear.
39 Turn away my reproach which I fear;
for thy judgments are good.
40 Behold, I have longed after thy precepts:
quicken me in thy righteousness.

VAU

41 Let thy mercies come also unto me, O Lord,
even thy salvation, according to thy word.
42 So shall I have wherewith to answer him
that reproacheth me; for I trust in thy word.
43 And take not the word of truth utterly
out of my mouth;
for I have hoped in thy judgments.
44 So shall I keep thy law continually
for ever and ever.
45 And I will walk at liberty; for I seek thy precepts.
46 I will speak of thy testimonies also before kings,
and will not be ashamed.
47 And I will delight myself in thy commandments,
which I have loved.
48 My hands also will I lift up
unto thy commandments, which I have loved;
and I will meditate in thy statutes.

ZAIN

49 Remember the word unto thy servant,
upon which thou hast caused me to hope.
50 This is my comfort in my affliction;
for thy word hath quickened me.
51 The proud have had me greatly in derision;
yet have I not declined from thy law.
52 I remembered thy judgments of old, O Lord;
and have comforted myself.
53 Horror hath taken hold upon me
because of the wicked that forsake thy law.
54 Thy statutes have been my songs
in the house of my pilgrimage.
55 I have remembered thy name, O Lord,
in the night, and have kept thy law.
56 This I had, because I kept thy precepts.

CHETH

57 Thou art my portion, O Lord:
I have said that I would keep thy words.
58 I intreated thy favour with my whole heart:
be merciful unto me according to thy word.
59 I thought on my ways,
and turned my feet unto thy testimonies.
60 I made haste,
and delayed not to keep thy commandments.
61 The bands of the wicked have robbed me;
but I have not forgotten thy law.

62 At midnight I will rise to give thanks unto thee
because of thy righteous judgments.
63 I am a companion of all them that fear thee,
and of them that keep thy precepts.
64 The earth, O Lord, is full of thy mercy:
teach me thy statutes.

TETH

65 Thou hast dealt well with thy servant, O Lord,
according unto thy word.
66 Teach me good judgment and knowledge;
for I have believed thy commandments.
67 Before I was afflicted I went astray;
but now have I kept thy word.
68 Thou art good, and doest good;
teach me thy statutes.
69 The proud have forged a lie against me;
but I will keep thy precepts with my whole heart.
70 Their heart is as fat as grease;
but I delight in thy law.
71 It is good for me that I have been afflicted;
that I might learn thy statutes.
72 The law of thy mouth is better unto me
than thousands of gold and silver.

JOD

73 Thy hands have made me and fashioned me:
give me understanding,
that I may learn thy commandments.

74 They that fear thee will be glad when they see me;
because I have hoped in thy word.
75 I know, O Lord, that thy judgments are right,
and that thou in faithfulness hast afflicted me.
76 Let, I pray thee, thy merciful kindness
be for my comfort,
according to thy word unto thy servant.
77 Let thy tender mercies come unto me,
that I may live; for thy law is my delight.
78 Let the proud be ashamed;
for they dealt perversely with me
without a cause;
but I will meditate in thy precepts.
79 Let those that fear thee turn unto me,
and those that have known thy testimonies.
80 Let my heart be sound in thy statutes;
that I be not ashamed.

CAPH

81 My soul fainteth for thy salvation;
but I hope in thy word.
82 Mine eyes fail for thy word, saying,
'When wilt thou comfort me?'
83 For I am become like a bottle in the smoke;
yet do I not forget thy statutes.
84 How many are the days of thy servant?
When wilt thou execute judgment on them
that persecute me?

85 The proud have digged pits for me,
which are not after thy law.
86 All thy commandments are faithful;
they persecute me wrongfully;
help thou me.
87 They had almost consumed me upon earth;
but I forsook not thy precepts.
88 Quicken me after thy lovingkindness;
so shall I keep the testimony of thy mouth.

LAMED

89 For ever, O Lord, thy word is settled in heaven.
90 Thy faithfulness is unto all generations:
thou hast established the earth, and it abideth.
91 They continue this day according to
thine ordinances; for all are thy servants.
92 Unless thy law had been my delights,
I should then have perished in mine affliction.
93 I will never forget thy precepts;
for with them thou hast quickened me.
94 I am thine, save me;
for I have sought thy precepts.
95 The wicked have waited for me to destroy me;
but I will consider thy testimonies.
96 I have seen an end of all perfection;
but thy commandment is exceeding broad.

MEM

97 O how love I thy law!
It is my meditation all the day.
98 Thou through thy commandments hast made
me wiser than mine enemies;
for they are ever with me.
99 I have more understanding than all my teachers;
for thy testimonies are my meditation.
100 I understand more than the ancients,
because I keep thy precepts.
101 I have refrained my feet from every evil way,
that I might keep thy word.
102 I have not departed from thy judgments;
for thou hast taught me.
103 How sweet are thy words unto my taste!
Yea, sweeter than honey to my mouth!
104 Through thy precepts I get understanding;
therefore I hate every false way.

NUN

105 Thy word is a lamp unto my feet,
and a light unto my path.
106 I have sworn, and I will perform it,
that I will keep thy righteous judgments.
107 I am afflicted very much: quicken me, O Lord,
according unto thy word.
108 Accept, I beseech thee,

the freewill offerings of my mouth, O Lord,
and teach me thy judgments.
109 My soul is continually in my hand;
yet do I not forget thy law.
110 The wicked have laid a snare for me;
yet I erred not from thy precepts.
111 Thy testimonies have I taken as an heritage for ever;
for they are the rejoicing of my heart.
112 I have inclined mine heart to perform thy statutes
alway, even unto the end.

SAMECH

113 I hate vain thoughts; but thy law do I love.
114 Thou art my hiding place and my shield:
I hope in thy word.
115 Depart from me, ye evildoers;
for I will keep the commandments of my God.
116 Uphold me according unto thy word,
that I may live;
and let me not be ashamed of my hope.
117 Hold thou me up, and I shall be safe;
and I will have respect unto thy statutes continually.
118 Thou hast trodden down all them that err
from thy statutes; for their deceit is falsehood.
119 Thou puttest away all the wicked of the earth
like dross; therefore I love thy testimonies.
120 My flesh trembleth for fear of thee;

and I am afraid of thy judgments.

AIN

121 I have done judgment and justice:
leave me not to mine oppressors.
122 Be surety for thy servant for good:
let not the proud oppress me.
123 Mine eyes fail for thy salvation,
and for the word of thy righteousness.
124 Deal with thy servant according unto thy mercy,
and teach me thy statutes.
125 I am thy servant; give me understanding,
that I may know thy testimonies.
126 It is time for thee, Lord, to work;
for they have made void thy law.
127 Therefore I love thy commandments above gold;
yea, above fine gold.
128 Therefore I esteem all thy precepts concerning
all things to be right;
and I hate every false way.

PE

129 Thy testimonies are wonderful;
therefore doth my soul keep them.
130 The entrance of thy words giveth light;
it giveth understanding unto the simple.
131 I opened my mouth, and panted;
for I longed for thy commandments.

132 Look thou upon me, and be merciful unto me,
as thou usest to do unto those that love thy name.
133 Order my steps in thy word;
and let not any iniquity have dominion over me.
134 Deliver me from the oppression of man:
so will I keep thy precepts.
135 Make thy face to shine upon thy servant;
and teach me thy statutes.
136 Rivers of waters run down mine eyes,
because they keep not thy law.

TZADDI

137 Righteous art thou, O Lord,
and upright are thy judgments.
138 Thy testimonies that thou hast commanded
are righteous and very faithful.
139 My zeal hath consumed me,
because mine enemies have forgotten thy words.
140 Thy word is very pure;
therefore thy servant loveth it.
141 I am small and despised;
yet do not I forget thy precepts.
142 Thy righteousness is an everlasting righteousness,
and thy law is the truth.
143 Trouble and anguish have taken hold on me;
yet thy commandments are my delights.

144 The righteousness of thy testimonies is everlasting:
give me understanding, and I shall live.

KOPH

145 I cried with my whole heart;
hear me, O Lord: I will keep thy statutes.
146 I cried unto thee;
save me, and I shall keep thy testimonies.
147 I prevented the dawning of the morning,
and cried: 'I hoped in thy word.'
148 Mine eyes prevent the night watches,
that I might meditate in thy word.
149 Hear my voice according unto thy lovingkindness:
'O Lord, quicken me according to thy judgment.'
150 They draw nigh that follow after mischief:
they are far from thy law.
151 Thou art near, O Lord;
and all thy commandments are truth.
152 Concerning thy testimonies,
I have known of old that thou hast founded
them for ever.

RESH

153 Consider mine affliction, and deliver me;
for I do not forget thy law.
154 Plead my cause, and deliver me:
quicken me according to thy word.
155 Salvation is far from the wicked;

for they seek not thy statutes.
156 Great are thy tender mercies, O Lord:
quicken me according to thy judgments.
157 Many are my persecutors and mine enemies;
yet do I not decline from thy testimonies.
158 I beheld the transgressors, and was grieved;
because they kept not thy word.
159 Consider how I love thy precepts:
quicken me, O Lord, according to thy
lovingkindness.
160 Thy word is true from the beginning;
and every one of thy righteous judgments
endureth for ever.

SCHIN

161 Princes have persecuted me without a cause;
but my heart standeth in awe of thy word.
162 I rejoice at thy word,
as one that findeth great spoil.
163 I hate and abhor lying;
but thy law do I love.
164 Seven times a day do I praise thee
because of thy righteous judgments.
165 Great peace have they which love thy law;
and nothing shall offend them.
166 Lord, I have hoped for thy salvation,
and done thy commandments.
167 My soul hath kept thy testimonies;

and I love them exceedingly.
168 I have kept thy precepts and thy testimonies;
for all my ways are before thee.

TAU

169 Let my cry come near before thee, O Lord:
give me understanding according to thy word.
170 Let my supplication come before thee:
deliver me according to thy word.
171 My lips shall utter praise,
when thou hast taught me thy statutes.
172 My tongue shall speak of thy word;
for all thy commandments are righteousness.
173 Let thine hand help me;
for I have chosen thy precepts.
174 I have longed for thy salvation, O Lord;
and thy law is my delight.
175 Let my soul live, and it shall praise thee;
and let thy judgments help me.
176 I have gone astray like a lost sheep;
seek thy servant;
for I do not forget thy commandments.

121

A song of degrees.

I will lift up mine eyes unto the hills,
from whence cometh my help.
2 My help cometh from the Lord,

which made heaven and earth.
3 He will not suffer thy foot to be moved:
he that keepeth thee will not slumber.
4 Behold, he that keepeth Israel shall neither
slumber nor sleep.
5 The Lord is thy keeper:
the Lord is thy shade upon thy right hand.
6 The sun shall not smite thee by day,
nor the moon by night.
7 The Lord shall preserve thee from all evil:
he shall preserve thy soul.
8 The Lord shall preserve thy going out
and thy coming in from this time forth,
and even for evermore.

122

A song of degrees of David.

I was glad when they said unto me,
'Let us go into the house of the Lord.'
2 Our feet shall stand within thy gates,
O Jerusalem.
3 Jerusalem is builded as a city
that is compact together.
4 Whither the tribes go up, the tribes of the Lord,
unto the testimony of Israel,
to give thanks unto the name of the Lord.
5 For there are set thrones of judgment,
the thrones of the house of David.

6 Pray for the peace of Jerusalem:
they shall prosper that love thee.
7 Peace be within thy walls,
and prosperity within thy palaces.
8 For my brethren and companions' sakes,
I will now say, 'Peace be within thee.'
9 Because of the house of the Lord our God
I will seek thy good.

124

A song of degrees of David.

If it had not been the Lord who was on our side,
now may Israel say;
2 if it had not been the Lord who was on our side,
when men rose up against us,
3 then they had swallowed us up quick,
when their wrath was kindled against us;
4 then the waters had overwhelmed us,
the stream had gone over our soul;
5 then the proud waters had gone over our soul.
6 Blessed be the Lord,
who hath not given us as a prey to their teeth.
7 Our soul is escaped as a bird out of the snare
of the fowlers:
the snare is broken, and we are escaped.
8 Our help is in the name of the Lord,
who made heaven and earth.

126

A song of degrees.

When the Lord turned again the captivity of Zion,
we were like them that dream.
2 Then was our mouth filled with laughter,
and our tongue with singing;
then said they among the heathen,
'The Lord hath done great things for them.'
3 The Lord hath done great things for us;
whereof we are glad.
4 Turn again our captivity, O Lord,
as the streams in the south.
5 They that sow in tears shall reap in joy.
6 He that goeth forth and weepeth,
bearing precious seed,
shall doubtless come again with rejoicing,
bringing his sheaves with him.

127

A song of degrees for Solomon.

Except the Lord build the house,
they labour in vain that build it;
except the Lord keep the city,
the watchman waketh but in vain.
2 It is vain for you to rise up early,
to sit up late, to eat the bread of sorrows;
for so he giveth his beloved sleep.
3 Lo, children are an heritage of the Lord;
and the fruit of the womb is his reward.

4 As arrows are in the hand of a mighty man;
so are children of the youth.
5 Happy is the man that hath his quiver full of them:
they shall not be ashamed,
but they shall speak with the enemies
in the gate.

128

A song of degrees.

Blessed is every one that feareth the Lord;
that walketh in his ways.
2 For thou shalt eat the labour of thine hands:
happy shalt thou be,
and it shall be well with thee.
3 Thy wife shall be as a fruitful vine by the sides
of thine house: thy children like olive plants
round about thy table.
4 Behold, that thus shall the man be blessed
that feareth the Lord.
5 The Lord shall bless thee out of Zion;
and thou shalt see the good of Jerusalem
all the days of thy life.
6 Yea, thou shalt see thy children's children,
and peace upon Israel.

130

A song of degrees.

Out of the depths have I cried unto thee, O Lord.

²Lord, hear my voice: let thine ears be attentive
to the voice of my supplications.
³If thou, Lord, shouldest mark inquities,
O Lord, who shall stand?
⁴But there is forgiveness with thee,
that thou mayest be feared.
⁵I wait for the Lord, my soul doth wait,
and in his word do I hope.
⁶My soul waiteth for the Lord more than they that
watch for the morning:
I say, more than they that watch
for the morning.
⁷Let Israel hope in the Lord;
for with the Lord there is mercy,
and with him is plenteous redemption.
⁸And he shall redeem Israel from all his iniquities.

133

A song of degrees of David.

Behold, how good and how pleasant it is
for brethren to dwell together in unity!
²It is like the precious ointment upon the head,
that ran down upon the beard,
even Aaron's beard;
that went down to the skirts of his garments;
³as the dew of Hermon,
and as the dew that descended upon
the mountains of Zion;

for there the Lord commanded the blessing,
even life for evermore.

134

A song of degrees.

Behold, bless ye the Lord,
all ye servants of the Lord,
which by night stand in the house of the Lord.
2 Lift up your hands in the sanctuary,
and bless the Lord.
3 The Lord that made heaven and earth
bless thee out of Zion.

136

O Give thanks unto the Lord; for he is good;
for his mercy endureth for ever.
2 O give thanks unto the God of gods;
for his mercy endureth for ever.
3 O give thanks to the Lord of lords;
for his mercy endureth for ever.
4 To him who alone doeth great wonders;
for his mercy endureth for ever.
5 To him that by wisdom made the heavens;
for his mercy endureth for ever.
6 To him that stretched out the earth
above the waters;
for his mercy endureth for ever.
7 To him that made great lights;

for his mercy endureth for ever:
8 the sun to rule by day;
for his mercy endureth for ever:
9 the moon and stars to rule by night;
for his mercy endureth for ever.
10 To him that smote Egypt in their firstborn;
for his mercy endureth for ever;
11 and brought out Israel from among them;
for his mercy endureth for ever;
12 with a strong hand, and with a stretched out arm;
for his mercy endureth for ever.
13 To him which divided the Red sea into parts;
for his mercy endureth for ever;
14 and made Israel to pass through the midst of it;
for his mercy endureth for ever;
15 but overthrew Pharaoh and his host in the Red sea;
for his mercy endureth for ever.
16 To him which led his people
through the wilderness;
for his mercy endureth for ever.
17 To him which smote great kings;
for his mercy endureth for ever;
18 and slew famous kings;
for his mercy endureth for ever;
19 Sihon king of the Amorites;
for his mercy endureth for ever;
20 and Og the king of Bashan;
for his mercy endureth for ever;
21 and gave their land for an heritage;

for his mercy endureth for ever;
22 even an heritage unto Israel his servant;
for his mercy endureth for ever.
23 Who remembered us in our low estate;
for his mercy endureth for ever;
24 and hath redeemed us from our enemies;
for his mercy endureth for ever.
25 Who giveth food to all flesh;
for his mercy endureth for ever.
26 O give thanks unto the God of heaven;
for his mercy endureth for ever.

137

By the rivers of Babylon, there we sat down,
yea, we wept, when we remembered Zion.
2 We hanged our harps upon the willows
in the midst thereof.
3 For there they that carried us away captive
required of us a song;
and they that wasted us required of us mirth,
saying, 'Sing us one of the songs of Zion.'
4 How shall we sing the Lord's song
in a strange land?
5 If I forget thee, O Jerusalem,
let my right hand forget her cunning.
6 If I do not remember thee,
let my tongue cleave to the roof of my mouth;
if I prefer not Jerusalem above my chief joy.

7 Remember, O Lord,
the children of Edom in the day of Jerusalem;
who said, 'Rase it, rase it,
even to the foundation thereof.'
8 O daughter of Babylon, who art to be destroyed;
happy shall he be, that rewardeth thee
as thou hast served us.
9 Happy shall he be,
that taketh and dasheth thy little ones
against the stones.

138

A psalm of David.

I will praise thee with my whole heart:
before the gods will I sing praise unto thee.
2 I will worship toward thy holy temple,
and praise thy name for thy loving-kindness
and for thy truth;
for thou hast magnified thy word above
all thy name.
3 In the day when I cried thou answeredst me,
and strengthenedst me with strength
in my soul.
4 All the kings of the earth shall praise thee, O Lord,
when they hear the words of thy mouth.
5 Yea, they shall sing in the ways of the Lord;
for great is the glory of the Lord.
6 Though the Lord be high,

yet hath he respect unto the lowly;
but the proud he knoweth afar off.
7 Though I walk in the midst of trouble,
thou wilt revive me;
thou shalt stretch forth thine hand
against the wrath of mine enemies,
and thy right hand shall save me.
8 The Lord will perfect that which concerneth me:
thy mercy, O Lord, endureth for ever:
forsake not the works of thine own hands.

139

To the chief musician, a psalm of David.

O Lord, thou hast searched me, and known me.
2 Thou knowest my downsitting and mine uprising,
thou understandest my thought afar off.
3 Thou compassest my path and my lying down,
and art acquainted with all my ways.
4 For there is not a word in my tongue,
but, lo, O Lord, thou knowest it altogether.
5 Thou hast beset me behind and before,
and laid thine hand upon me.
6 Such knowledge is too wonderful for me;
it is high, I cannot attain unto it.
7 Whither shall I go from thy spirit?
Or whither shall I flee from thy presence?
8 If I ascend up into heaven, thou art there:
if I make my bed in hell, behold, thou art there.

9 If I take the wings of the morning,
and dwell in the uttermost parts of the sea;
10 even there shall thy hand lead me,
and thy right hand shall hold me.
11 If I say, 'Surely the darkness shall cover me;
even the night shall be light about me.'
12 Yea, the darkness hideth not from thee;
but the night shineth as the day;
the darkness and the light are both
alike to thee.
13 For thou hast possessed my reins:
thou hast covered me in my mother's womb.
14 I will praise thee;
for I am fearfully and wonderfully made;
marvellous are thy works;
and that my soul knoweth right well.
15 My substance was not hid from thee,
when I was made in secret,
and curiously wrought in the lowest parts
of the earth.
16 Thine eyes did see my substance,
yet being unperfect; and in thy book
all my members were written,
which in continuance were fashioned when
as yet there was none of them.
17 How precious also are thy thoughts unto me,
O God! How great is the sum of them!
18 If I should count them, they are more in number

than the sand:
when I awake, I am still with thee.
19 Surely thou wilt slay the wicked, O God:
depart from me therefore, ye bloody men.
20 For they speak against thee wickedly,
and thine enemies take thy name in vain.
21 Do not I hate them, O Lord, that hate thee?
And am not I grieved with those that rise up
against thee?
22 I hate them with perfect hatred:
I count them mine enemies.
23 Search me, O God, and know my heart:
try me, and know my thoughts:
24 and see if there be any wicked way in me,
and lead me in the way everlasting.

141

A psalm of David.

Lord, I cry unto thee: make haste unto me;
give ear unto my voice, when I cry unto thee.
2 Let my prayer be set forth before thee as incense;
and the lifting up of my hands
as the evening sacrifice.
3 Set a watch, O Lord, before my mouth;
keep the door of my lips.
4 Incline not my heart to any evil thing,
to practise wicked works with men
that work iniquity;

and let me not eat of their dainties.
5 Let the righteous smite me;
it shall be a kindness; and let him reprove me;
it shall be an excellent oil,
which shall not break my head;
for yet my prayer also shall be in their calamities.
6 When their judges are overthrown in stony places,
they shall hear my words; for they are sweet.
7 Our bones are scattered at the grave's mouth,
as when one cutteth and cleaveth wood
upon the earth.
8 But mine eyes are unto thee, O God the Lord:
in thee is my trust; leave not my soul destitute.
9 Keep me from the snares
which they have laid for me,
and the gins of the workers of iniquity.
10 Let the wicked fall into their own nets,
whilst that I withal escape.

142

Maschil of David; a prayer when he was in the cave.

I cried unto the Lord with my voice;
with my voice unto the Lord
did I make my supplication.
2 I poured out my complaint before him;
I shewed before him my trouble.

3 When my spirit was overwhelmed within me,
then thou knewest my path.
In the way wherein I walked
have they privily laid a snare for me.
4 I looked on my right hand, and beheld,
but there was no man that would know me;
refuge failed me;
no man cared for my soul.
5 I cried unto thee, O Lord; I said,
'Thou art my refuge and my portion
in the land of the living.'
6 Attend unto my cry; for I am brought very low;
deliver me from my persecutors;
for they are stronger than I.
7 Bring my soul out of prison, that I may praise
thy name;
the righteous shall compass me about;
for thou shalt deal bountifully with me.

143

A psalm of David.

Hear my prayer, O Lord,
give ear to my supplications:
in thy faithfulness answer me,
and in thy righteousness.
2 And enter not into judgment with thy servant;
for in thy sight shall no man living
be justified.

3 For the enemy hath persecuted my soul;
he hath smitten my life down to the ground;
he hath made me to dwell in darkness,
as those that have been long dead.
4 Therefore is my spirit overwhelmed within me;
my heart within me is desolate.
5 I remember the days of old;
I meditate on all thy works;
I muse on the work of thy hands.
6 I stretch forth my hands unto thee:
my soul thirsteth after thee,
as a thirsty land. Selah.
7 Hear me speedily, O Lord: my spirit faileth:
hide not thy face from me, lest I be like unto
them that go down into the pit.
8 Cause me to hear thy lovingkindness in
the morning; for in thee do I trust:
cause me to know the way wherein
I should walk; for I lift up my soul unto thee.
9 Deliver me, O Lord, from mine enemies:
I flee unto thee to hide me.
10 Teach me to do thy will;
for thou art my God: thy spirit is good;
lead me into the land of uprightness.
11 Quicken me, O Lord, for thy name's sake;
for thy righteousness' sake bring my soul
out of trouble.
12 And of thy mercy cut off mine enemies,

and destroy all them that afflict my soul;
for I am thy servant.

145

David's psalm of praise.

I will extol thee, my God, O king;
and I will bless thy name for ever and ever.
2 Every day will I bless thee;
and I will praise thy name for ever and ever.
3 Great is the Lord, and greatly to be praised;
and his greatness is unsearchable.
4 One generation shall praise thy works to another,
and shall declare thy mighty acts.
5 I will speak of the glorious honour of thy majesty,
and of thy wondrous works.
6 And men shall speak of the might
of thy terrible acts;
and I will declare thy greatness.
7 They shall abundantly utter the memory
of thy great goodness,
and shall sing of thy righteousness.
8 The Lord is gracious, and full of compassion;
slow to anger, and of great mercy.
9 The Lord is good to all;
and his tender mercies are over all his works.
10 All thy works shall praise thee, O Lord;
and thy saints shall bless thee.
11 They shall speak of the glory of thy kingdom,

and talk of thy power;
12 to make known to the sons of men his mighty acts,
and the glorious majesty of his kingdom.
13 Thy kingdom is an everlasting kingdom,
and thy dominion endureth throughout
all generations.
14 The Lord upholdeth all that fall,
and raiseth up all those that be bowed down.
15 The eyes of all wait upon thee;
and thou givest them their meat in due season.
16 Thou openest thine hand,
and satisfiest the desire of every living thing.
17 The Lord is righteous in all his ways,
and holy in all his works.
18 The Lord is nigh unto all them that call upon him,
to all that call upon him in truth.
19 He will fulfil the desire of them that fear him;
he also will hear their cry, and will save them.
20 The Lord preserveth all them that love him;
but all the wicked will he destroy.
21 My mouth shall speak the praise of the Lord;
and let all flesh bless his holy name
for ever and ever.

146

Praise ye the Lord. Praise the Lord, O my soul.
2 While I live will I praise the Lord:
I will sing praises unto my God while I have

any being.
3 Put not your trust in princes, nor in
the son of man, in whom there is no help.
4 His breath goeth forth, he returneth to his earth;
in that very day his thoughts perish.
5 Happy is he that hath the God of Jacob for his help,
whose hope is in the Lord his God,
6 which made heaven, and earth, the sea,
and all that therein is;
which keepeth truth for ever;
7 which executeth judgment for the oppressed;
which giveth food to the hungry.
The Lord looseth the prisoners.
8 The Lord openeth the eyes of the blind;
the Lord raiseth them that are bowed down;
the Lord loveth the righteous;
9 the Lord preserveth the strangers;
he relieveth the fatherless and widow;
but the way of the wicked
he turneth upside down.
10 The Lord shall reign for ever,
even thy God, O Zion, unto all generations.
Praise ye the Lord.

147

Praise ye the Lord;
for it is good to sing praises unto our God;
for it is pleasant; and praise is comely.

2 The Lord doth build up Jerusalem:
he gathereth together the outcasts of Israel.
3 He healeth the broken in heart,
and bindeth up their wounds.
4 He telleth the number of the stars;
he calleth them all by their names.
5 Great is our Lord, and of great power:
his understanding is infinite.
6 The Lord lifteth up the meek:
he casteth the wicked down to the ground.
7 Sing unto the Lord with thanksgiving;
sing praise upon the harp unto our God,
8 who covereth the heaven with clouds,
who prepareth rain for the earth,
who maketh grass to grow upon
the mountains.
9 He giveth to the beast his food,
and to the young ravens which cry.
10 He delighteth not in the strength of the horse:
he taketh not pleasure in the legs of a man.
11 The Lord taketh pleasure in them that fear him,
in those that hope in his mercy.
12 Praise the Lord, O Jerusalem;
praise thy God, O Zion.
13 For he hath strengthened the bars of thy gates;
he hath blessed thy children within thee.
14 He maketh peace in thy borders,
and filleth thee with the finest of the wheat.

15 He sendeth forth his commandment upon earth:
his word runneth very swiftly.
16 He giveth snow like wool:
he scattereth the hoarfrost like ashes.
17 He casteth forth his ice like morsels.
Who can stand before his cold?
18 He sendeth out his word, and melteth them:
he causeth his wind to blow, and the waters flow.
19 He sheweth his word unto Jacob,
his statutes and his judgments unto
Israel.
20 He hath not dealt so with any nation;
and as for his judgments,
they have not known them.
Praise ye the Lord.

148

Praise ye the Lord.
Praise ye the Lord from the heavens:
praise him in the heights.
2 Praise ye him, all his angels:
praise ye him, all his hosts.
3 Praise ye him, sun and moon:
praise him, all ye stars of light.
4 Praise him, ye heavens of heavens,
and ye waters that be above the heavens.
5 Let them praise the name of the Lord;
for he commanded, and they were created.

6 He hath also stablished them for ever and ever:
he hath made a decree which shall not pass.
7 Praise the Lord from the earth,
ye dragons, and all deeps;
8 fire, and hail; snow, and vapour;
stormy wind fulfilling his word.
9 Mountains, and all hills;
fruitful trees, and all cedars;
10 beasts, and all cattle;
creeping things, and flying fowl.
11 Kings of the earth, and all people;
princes, and all judges of the earth;
12 both young men, and maidens;
old men, and children.
13 Let them praise the name of the Lord;
for his name alone is excellent;
his glory is above the earth and heaven.
14 He also exalteth the horn of his people,
the praise of all his saints;
even of the children of Israel,
a people near unto him. Praise ye the Lord.

149

Praise ye the Lord.
Sing unto the Lord a new song,
and his praise in the congregation of saints.
2 Let Israel rejoice in him that made him:
let the children of Zion be joyful in their King.

3 Let them praise his name in the dance:
let them sing praises unto him
with the timbrel and harp.
4 For the Lord taketh pleasure in his people:
he will beautify the meek with salvation.
5 Let the saints be joyful in glory:
let them sing aloud upon their beds.
6 Let the high praises of God be in their mouth,
and a twoedged sword in their hand;
7 to execute vengeance upon the heathen,
and punishments upon the people;
8 to bind their kings with chains,
and their nobles with fetters of iron;
9 to execute upon them the judgment written:
this honour have all his saints.
Praise ye the Lord.

150 Praise ye the Lord.
Praise God in his sanctuary:
praise him in the firmament of his power.
2 Praise him for his mighty acts:
praise him according to his excellent greatness.
3 Praise him with the sound of the trumpet:
praise him with the psaltery and harp.
4 Praise him with the timbrel and dance:
praise him with stringed instruments and organs.
5 Praise him upon the loud cymbals:

praise him upon the high sounding cymbals.
6 Let every thing that hath breath praise the Lord.
Praise ye the Lord.

proverbs

proverbs

authorized king james version

grove press
new york

with an introduction by | charles johnson

The Pocket Canons were originally published in the U.K. in 1998 by Canongate Books, Ltd.
Published simultaneously in Canada
Printed in the United States of America

FIRST AMERICAN EDITION

Copyright information is on file with the Library of Congress
ISBN 0-8021-3613-3

Design by Paddy Cramsie

Grove Press
841 Broadway
New York, NY 10003

99 00 01 02 10 9 8 7 6 5 4 3 2 1

a note about pocket canons

The Authorized King James Version of the Bible, translated between 1603 and 1611, coincided with an extraordinary flowering of English literature. This version, more than any other, and possibly more than any other work in history, has had an influence in shaping the language we speak and write today. Presenting individual books from the Bible as separate volumes, as they were originally conceived, encourages the reader to approach them as literary works in their own right.

The first twelve books in this series encompass categories as diverse as history, fiction, philosophy, love poetry, and law. Each Pocket Canon also has its own introduction, specially commissioned from an impressive range of writers, which provides a personal interpretation of the text and explores its contemporary relevance.

Charles Johnson won the National Book Award in the USA *in 1990 for his novel* Middle Passage. *A widely published literary critic, philosopher, cartoonist, screenwriter, essayist and lecturer, he is one of twelve African-American authors honoured in an international series of stamps celebrating great writers of the twentieth century. He is currently the Pollock Professor of English at the University of Washington. His new novel,* Dreamer, *was published to great acclaim in October 1998.*

introduction by charles johnson

Where there is no vision, the people perish.

Of all the practical observations in that most pragmatic of texts in the Old Testament, *The Book of Proverbs,* this one sentence linking vision and life comes singing off the page as the most profound. Meditate, please, on the possibility that in life there is a *goal,* an end that makes all our worldly efforts intelligible. Carefully think it through: without a *vision,* either personal or political, the individual (or society) is 'like a city that is broken down, and without walls'. This is not simply a question for the schools, for without a comprehensive and capacious philosophy life fails. The unsentimental implication here – the basic, philosophical and secular premise – is that life can be a perilous journey. Perhaps a social minefield. (Just read today's newspaper if you need proof that the world is and has always been a dangerous place.) And any young person hesitantly starting out on this odyssey, now or in the days of King Solomon, soon discovers that his (or her) chances for survival, prosperity and happiness are enhanced a hundred-fold if – and only if – they have a good map.

Put simply, *Proverbs* is that richly detailed, many-splendored map. A timeless wake-up call. More importantly, along with its companion books, the poetic 'wisdom' literature of the Old Testament (*Job, Ecclesiastes, The Song of Solomon,* and *Psalms*), it is a two-millennium-old blue-print for the staggering challenge of living a truly *civilized* life. Culture, we realize after reading *Proverbs*, is an on-going project. We are not born with culture. Or wisdom. And both are but *one* generation deep. Achieving either is a daily task requiring as much work for the individual as an artist puts into a perfectly balanced painting, or a musician into a flawless performance. (Thus one wonders if the great bulk of human-kind can be truthfully called either cultured or civilized.) Here, in this repository of moral instruction, in its 31 chapters, 915 verses, approximately 900 proverbs, and 15,043 words, the journey that we call a life is presented as a canvas upon which the individual paints skillfully a civilized self-portrait – an offering – that will please himself and the Lord. In chapter 3, we are told, 'Happy is the man that findeth wisdom.' The Hebrew word for 'wisdom' is *chokmah*. It occurs no less than thirty-seven times in *Proverbs*. *Chokmah* also means skillfulness in dealing with the job that is before us – life itself – and I believe it is comparable to the Greek word *techne*, the rational application of principles aimed at making or doing something well. The reader who takes *Proverbs* to heart, who believes like the Greeks that 'the unexamined life is not worth living', is by nature a lover of wisdom: a philosopher. For that is precisely what the word 'philosophy' means (*philein*, to love – *sophia*, wisdom).

I'm aware those words – 'wisdom', 'civilized' and 'philosophy' – may sound musty and antique to modern (or post-modern) ears. As so many have said, ours is an Era of

Relativism, or situational ethics, perhaps even of nihilism, an historical period in which *Proverbs* will for some readers seem right-wing and patriarchal, oppressive and harsh, dogmatic and illiberal. Many will regard its contents as obsolete for the conditions we face at the eleventh hour of the twentieth century because, above all else, we moderns value individual freedom. Unfortunately, our passion for liberty is often misunderstood as license or, more accurately, as licentiousness. Personally, as a Buddhist, I was at first wary of writing about this book, though I was raised on its vision in a midwestern, African Methodist Episcopal church. But after going over *Proverbs* a half dozen times, after opening myself to its spiritual core, which complements nicely the world's other great religious traditions, I re-discovered the gems it has offered western humanity for centuries. I saw in its gnostic truths the reason why Professor C E M Joad once defined decadence as 'the loss of an object in life'. In fact, I realized that *Proverbs* not only speaks powerfully to our morally adrift era, but describes rather well my own often benighted, rebellious-on-principle generation (the Baby Boomers) when it says, 'There is a generation that curseth their father, and doth not bless their mother. There is a generation that are pure in their own eyes, and yet is not washed from their filthiness' (30:11-12).

Chilling.

Like all rich, multi-layered digests, *Proverbs* was not the work of a day. Nor is it the product of a single author, though King Solomon, that Ur-figure among ancient wise men, is credited with having contributed two of its oldest sections

(1:1 and 1:10). Several centuries after the death of Israel's king, the men of Hezekiah (700 BCE) added chapters 25 through 29 from Solomonic material. In short, the book was built layer upon layer, one tissue at a time, borrowing its synthesized instructions from many ancient sources, and did not achieve its finished form until the fourth or fifth century BCE. It favors, one might say, an old, old coin that has traversed continents, picking up something from each one as it was passed down through centuries – advice on social etiquette, philanthropy, how to choose a wife, and why children may need an occasional dose of Dr Spanker's tonic (the 'rod') – and bears the sweat and palm-oil of millions who have handled it. Bible scholar Kenneth T Aitken persuasively argues in his commentary *Proverbs* that the third section of the text (chapter 22) takes a few pages from the *Instructions of Amenemopet*.* That work, dating back to between 1000 and 600 BCE, was strictly a manual of professional training aimed at helping Egyptian civil servants achieve successful careers as they served the state. The sages of Israel, says Aitken, reworked some of the precepts from *Instructions* and at the same time re-contextualized them in a book far broader in its teachings for a triumphant life.

And these were, of course, originally *oral* teachings. They were delivered by a sage to pupils he addressed as a father would his children. His young charges were expected to memorize the proverbs until they were hard-wired into their

* Kenneth T Aitken, *Proverbs* (The Westminster Press: Philadelphia, 1968), p. 3.

hearts. Thus, this book was written for the ear. It relies heavily on repetition, a mnemonic device (which might weary modern eyes), and in its compositional strategies employs couplets linked by parallelisms. In his exegesis of *Proverbs,* J Vernon McGee identifies three forms of parallelisms that occur in the text: (1) *Synonymous Parallelism,* where the second clause restates the content of the first ('Judgments are prepared for scorners, and stripes for the back of the fool', 19:29). (2) *Antithetic (Contrast) Parallelism* that states a truth in the first clause, then contrasts it with an opposite truth in the second ('The light of the righteous rejoiceth, but the lamp of the wicked shall be put out', 13:9). And (3) *Synthetic Parallelism* in which the second clause develops the truth of the first ('The terror of a king is as the roaring of a lion; whoso provoketh him to anger sinneth against his own life', 20:2).*

Yet, for all the sophisticated architectonics in *Proverbs,* and for all the complexity of its literary pedigree, this is a book that sketches out a compelling, classic story: a pilgrim's progress. Imagine a young man (or woman) about to embark on life's journey. Call him – well, Pilgrim. Then, as now, the world teemed with a kaleidoscope of temptations, stramash and confusion. In the bustling cities where colorful bazaars, beggers, thieves, perfumed harlots, con-men, murderers, insouciant idlers and false teachers eager to entice a young person toward wrong-doing and sin (one hoary meaning of which is 'to miss the mark'), all can be found in great

---

* J Vernon McGee, *Proverbs* (Thomas Nelson Publishers: Nashville, 1991), p. x.

abundance. Indeed, these players, some as beautiful as Satan and who say, 'Let us lay wait for blood, let us lurk privily for the innocent', have from time immemorial taken advantage of callow youths (as well as given writers as diverse as Voltaire, De Sade, Dickens, Fielding and Maugham inexhaustible material for the *Bildungsroman*). Given a strictly materialistic viewpoint, it follows that the world of matter, mere *stuff*, will be dominated everywhere and in any era by those who treat objects and others as *things* to be used for their own pleasure and profit, and view everything through the lens of their own limited consciousness. Surveying this social field, we can imagine the authors of *Proverbs* agreeing with Thomas à Kempis who, in *The Imitation of Christ*, wearily quotes the Stoic philosopher Seneca, 'A wise man once said, "As often as I have been among men, I have returned home a lesser man"... No man can live in the public eye without risk to his soul ...'*

As we have seen, if our young Pilgrim is not to lose his (or her) soul on this planet where everything is provisional, if he is not to end bellied up and bottomed out, he needs a damned good map. Ethically, he should not have to reinvent the wheel each time he is confronted by a new moral dilemma. That, I believe, would be like a physicist claiming he can learn nothing from Galileo, Newton, Copernicus or Einstein because the conditions of their time differed so much from his own. But young people are notorious for for-

* Thomas à Kempis, *The Imitation of Christ*, trans. by Leo Sherley-Price (Penguin Books Ltd: Middlesex, 1953), p. 50.

getting instructions (ask any teacher about that), especially the 900 lessons on living delivered in *Proverbs*. What Pilgrim needs is the teaching condensed into *one* simple, bare-knuckled mantra that encapsulates the pith of all the other proverbs. Anticipating just this problem, the *Proverbs* authors provide that axiom in the very first chapter: 'The fear of the Lord is the beginning of knowledge: but fools despise wisdom and instruction.' From this one antithetic parallelism, this stern and admonishing couplet – moment by moment mindfulness of the Most High – all else in *Proverbs* follows with Mandarin exactitude and the necessity of a logical proof. Pilgrim is counseled to 'Commit thy works unto the Lord, and thy thoughts shall be established' (16:3), for the authors of this text understood the irrefragable fact that all we are is the result of what we have thought. From intellection comes desire. From desire, will. From will, our deeds. And from deeds, our destiny. Self-control, therefore, is so essential for the spiritual life and a practical life well led that it is even favorably compared to martial conquest: 'He that is slow to anger is better than the mighty; and he that ruleth his spirit than he that taketh a city' (16:32) in a line strikingly similar to one equally famous that we find in the first-century BCE Buddhist *Dhammapada* ('Path of Virtue') – 'If one man conquer in battle a thousand times a thousand men, and if another conquers himself, he is the greatest of conquerors.'* In the world's religious traditions, eastern and

* *The Dhammapada*, trans. by Irving Babbitt (New Directions: New York, 1965), p. 18.

western, the Way of understanding and wisdom begins by sumptuously feeding the spirit and starving the illusory sense of the ego into extinction ('Trust in the Lord with all thine heart; and lean not unto thine own understanding. In all thy ways acknowledge him, and he shall direct thy paths. Be not wise in thine own eyes:' (3:5-7)), and is realized through a worldly practice that gives priority to the experience of our elders (our global inheritance) over ephemerae in a life that embodies humility, service, and a culture's loftiest ideals, which in Pilgrim's case would be the Ten Commandments.

Wisdom in *Proverbs*, we might say, is thought winging its way home.

Naturally, many couplets in *Proverbs* inveigh against people who are *not* mindful, those who 'eat the bread of wickedness and drink the wine of violence', and break the Commandments. This book does not suffer fools gladly. At first glance, Pilgrim might see the less demanding, hedonistic path and its players as alluring and sweet – and fun! But the seeds of *Proverbs* (practical wisdom) cannot grow in that polluted soil (the 'froward'). Pilgrim is advised not to envy or even 'fret' over the fallen state of these caitiffs and poltroons, for the Lord shall 'render to every man according to his works'. In other words, just as there is inexorable causation in the physical realm, so too is there cause-and-effect in the moral universe. The kingdom of God, at bottom, is a meritocracy; its logic is that of *karma* ('as you sow so shall you reap'). The unmindful cause their own downfall – they 'eat of the fruit of their own way'. Time and again,

Proverbs drives this point home, and nowhere more vividly than in its parable-like description of the industrious ant, or when the book cautions against lapses of vigilance in language so lovely the words almost pirouette and leap on the page: 'Yet a little sleep, a little slumber, a little folding of the hands to sleep: so shall thy poverty come as one that traveleth; and thy want as an armed man' (25:33-4).

However, it would be wrong to say that *Proverbs* is simply a map for avoiding life's pitfalls in order to bow one's knees to Baal. Throughout its chapters, Pilgrim is urged, 'Labor not to be rich' and he is reminded how 'riches certainly make themselves wings; they fly away as an eagle toward heaven', and 'Better is the poor that walketh in his uprightness, than he that is perverse in his ways, though he be rich'. Does this advice contradict the practicality that infuses *Proverbs*? Does it ask us to be poor? No, for a crucial distinction is drawn: 'Wealth gotten by vanity shall be diminished: but he that gathereth by labor shall increase'. The book points our Pilgrim toward industry, not that he might be 'greedy of gain', but rather that he or she might become the sort of provider who 'leaveth an inheritance to his children's children', honors his mother and father (and, one might add, his teachers), and 'stretcheth out her hand to the poor'. In effect, Pilgrim's labor is for others. Always life's true wealth in *Proverbs* is found in God, in wisdom and love; and love is realized through work and indefatigable service to the things loved.

In *Proverbs*, the portrait – the character sketch – that emerges of a successful pilgrim is that of a man or woman who is a quiet embodiment of culture. Not perfect by any means because he knows all too well his flaws. But in his life of building, serving, creating, he mightily strives to be righteous. He is soft-spoken and hates lying. In him there is the continuity of generations, one of the requisites for civilization itself. He is the joy of his mother and father and his children as well, for by honoring the wisdom of his predecessors and transmitting that (along with the fruit of his industry) to his posterity, his past (parents) meets his present (children) and vouchsafes their future. His good name the pilgrim values highly, and he is not garrulous, knowing how to hold his tongue and keep his own counsel. He never acts rashly or 'answereth a matter before he heareth it'. Concerning the needy, he is socially conscious and never 'stoppeth his ears at the cry of the poor'. Though he experiences failure and 'falleth seven times', the just man struggles to his feet again to do the Lord's work, ignoring his weariness. According to *Proverbs*, at night his sleep is 'sweet'. Such a person always heeds the helpful criticism of friends, but never wearies them with his presence or overstays his welcome. And, despite his hard-won victories and integrity, he never boasts, allowing instead 'another man [to] praise thee, and not thine own mouth'. Finally, the man of mindfulness is the very foundation of society – 'bold as a lion', the sort of citizen who, if he assumes a position of authority in the state, makes the 'people rejoice'.

Clearly, the path mapped out in *Proverbs* is exacting. Straight and narrow, 'like the edge of a sword', as Mahatma Gandhi once described the spiritual life. It is fitting, then, that *Proverbs* ends by letting our pilgrim know that he need not – indeed *can*not – travel to his goal alone. The righteous man needs a companion, a spouse equally mindful and just who will 'do him good and not evil all the days of her life'. A life-partner of such luminous morality that his heart 'doth safely trust in her, so that he shall have no need of spoil'. And so, in its remarkable finale – just before the curtain falls – this Old Testament book extolling wisdom and virtue closes by incarnating its heady idealism in an astonishing homage to the *concrete* beauty and goodness of God-fearing women (one surely influential for Chaucer's Wife of Bath), a breathtaking, unforgettable praise-song to this 'good thing', this 'favor of the Lord', this ravishing 'wife of thy youth':

> Strength and honor are her clothing;
> and she shall rejoice in time to come.
> She openeth her mouth with wisdom;
> and in her tongue is the law of kindness.
> She looketh well to the ways of her household,
> and eateth not the bread of idleness.
> Her children arise up and call her blessed;
> her husband also, and he praiseth her.

May we all be blessed with such radiant partners. And, as we travel through this life, may we recognize that *Proverbs*, in its fierce, uncompromising purity, is a work worthy of our trust.

the proverbs

The proverbs of Solomon the son of David, king of Israel:

2 to know wisdom and instruction;
to perceive the words of understanding;
3 to receive the instruction of wisdom, justice,
and judgment, and equity;
4 to give subtilty to the simple,
to the young man knowledge and discretion.
5 A wise man will hear, and will increase learning;
and a man of understanding
shall attain unto wise counsels:
6 to understand a proverb, and the interpretation;
the words of the wise, and their dark sayings.

7 The fear of the Lord is the beginning of knowledge:
but fools despise wisdom and instruction.
8 My son, hear the instruction of thy father,
and forsake not the law of thy mother,
9 for they shall be an ornament of grace unto thy head,
and chains about thy neck.

10 My son, if sinners entice thee, consent thou not.

11 If they say, 'Come with us, let us lay wait for blood,
let us lurk privily for the innocent without cause':
12 Let us swallow them up alive as the grave;
and whole, as those that go down into the pit:
13 We shall find all precious substance,
we shall fill our houses with spoil.
14 Cast in thy lot among us;
let us all have one purse:
15 My son, walk not thou in the way with them;
refrain thy foot from their path:
16 For their feet run to evil,
and make haste to shed blood.
17 Surely in vain the net is spread
in the sight of any bird.
18 And they lay wait for their own blood;
they lurk privily for their own lives.
19 So are the ways of every one that is greedy of gain,
which taketh away the life of the owners thereof.

20 Wisdom crieth without;
she uttereth her voice in the streets.
21 She crieth in the chief place of concourse,
in the openings of the gates:
in the city she uttereth her words, saying,
22 'How long, ye simple ones, will ye love simplicity?'
And the scorners delight in their scorning,
and fools hate knowledge?

23 Turn you at my reproof;
behold, I will pour out my spirit unto you,
I will make known my words unto you.

24 'Because I have called, and ye refused;
I have stretched out my hand,
and no man regarded;
25 but ye have set at nought all my counsel,
and would none of my reproof.
26 I also will laugh at your calamity;
I will mock when your fear cometh;
27 when your fear cometh as desolation,
and your destruction cometh as a whirlwind;
when distress and anguish cometh upon you.
28 Then shall they call upon me, but I will not answer;
they shall seek me early,
but they shall not find me:
29 for that they hated knowledge,
and did not choose the fear of the Lord.
30 They would none of my counsel;
they despised all my reproof.
31 Therefore shall they eat of the fruit of their own way,
and be filled with their own devices.
32 For the turning away of the simple shall slay them,
and the prosperity of fools shall destroy them.
33 But whoso hearkeneth unto me shall dwell safely,
and shall be quiet from fear of evil.

2 My son, if thou wilt receive my words,
and hide my commandments with thee;
2 so that thou incline thine ear unto wisdom,
and apply thine heart to understanding;
3 yea, if thou criest after knowledge,
and liftest up thy voice for understanding,
4 if thou seekest her as silver,
and searchest for her as for hid treasures:
5 then shalt thou understand the fear of the Lord,
and find the knowledge of God.
6 For the Lord giveth wisdom:
out of his mouth cometh knowledge
and understanding.
7 He layeth up sound wisdom for the righteous;
he is a buckler to them that walk uprightly.
8 He keepeth the paths of judgment,
and preserveth the way of his saints.
9 Then shalt thou understand righteousness,
and judgment, and equity;
yea, every good path.

10 When wisdom entereth into thine heart,
and knowledge is pleasant unto thy soul;
11 discretion shall preserve thee,
understanding shall keep thee:
12 To deliver thee from the way of the evil man,
from the man that speaketh froward things;

13 who leave the paths of uprightness,
to walk in the ways of darkness;
14 who rejoice to do evil,
and delight in the frowardness of the wicked;
15 whose ways are crooked,
and they froward in their paths:
16 to deliver thee from the strange woman,
even from the stranger
which flattereth with her words;
17 which forsaketh the guide of her youth,
and forgetteth the covenant of her God.
18 For her house inclineth unto death,
and her paths unto the dead.
19 None that go unto her return again,
neither take they hold of the paths of life.
20 That thou mayest walk in the way of good men,
and keep the paths of the righteous.
21 For the upright shall dwell in the land,
and the perfect shall remain in it.
22 But the wicked shall be cut off from the earth,
and the transgressors shall be rooted out of it.

3 My son, forget not my law;
but let thine heart keep my commandments:
2 For length of days, and long life,
and peace, shall they add to thee.

3 Let not mercy and truth forsake thee:
bind them about thy neck;
write them upon the table of thine heart:
4 so shalt thou find favour and good understanding
in the sight of God and man.

5 Trust in the Lord with all thine heart;
and lean not unto thine own understanding.
6 In all thy ways acknowledge him,
and he shall direct thy paths.

7 Be not wise in thine own eyes:
fear the Lord, and depart from evil.
8 It shall be health to thy navel,
and marrow to thy bones.
9 Honour the Lord with thy substance,
and with the first-fruits of all thine increase:
10 so shall thy barns be filled with plenty,
and thy presses shall burst out with new wine.

11 My son, despise not the chastening of the Lord;
neither be weary of his correction:
12 for whom the Lord loveth he correcteth;
even as a father the son in whom he delighteth.

13 Happy is the man that findeth wisdom,
and the man that getteth understanding.

14 For the merchandise of it is better
than the merchandise of silver,
and the gain thereof than fine gold.
15 She is more precious than rubies:
and all the things thou canst desire
are not to be compared unto her.
16 Length of days is in her right hand;
and in her left hand riches and honour.
17 Her ways are ways of pleasantness,
and all her paths are peace.
18 She is a tree of life to them that lay hold upon her:
and happy is every one that retaineth her.
19 The Lord by wisdom hath founded the earth;
by understanding hath he established the heavens.
20 By his knowledge the depths are broken up,
and the clouds drop down the dew.
21 My son, let not them depart from thine eyes:
keep sound wisdom and discretion:
22 so shall they be life unto thy soul,
and grace to thy neck.
23 Then shalt thou walk in thy way safely,
and thy foot shall not stumble.
24 When thou liest down, thou shalt not be afraid:
yea, thou shalt lie down,
and thy sleep shall be sweet.

25 Be not afraid of sudden fear,
neither of the desolation of the wicked,
when it cometh.
26 For the Lord shall be thy confidence,
and shall keep thy foot from being taken.

27 Withhold not good from them to whom it is due,
when it is in the power of thine hand to do it.
28 Say not unto thy neighbour,
'Go, and come again, and tomorrow I will give,'
when thou hast it by thee.
29 Devise not evil against thy neighbour,
seeing he dwelleth securely by thee.

30 Strive not with a man without cause,
if he have done thee no harm.

31 Envy thou not the oppressor,
and choose none of his ways.
32 For the froward is abomination to the Lord:
but his secret is with the righteous.

33 The curse of the Lord is in the house of the wicked:
but he blesseth the habitation of the just.
34 Surely he scorneth the scorners:
but he giveth grace unto the lowly.
35 The wise shall inherit glory:
but shame shall be the promotion of fools.

4

Hear, ye children, the instruction of a father,
and attend to know understanding.
2 For I give you good doctrine,
forsake ye not my law.
3 For I was my father's son,
tender and only beloved in the sight of my mother.
4 He taught me also, and said unto me,
'Let thine heart retain my words:
keep my commandments, and live.
5 Get wisdom, get understanding:
forget it not;
neither decline from the words of my mouth.
6 Forsake her not, and she shall preserve thee:
love her, and she shall keep thee.
7 Wisdom is the principal thing;
therefore get wisdom:
and with all thy getting get understanding.
8 Exalt her, and she shall promote thee:
she shall bring thee to honour,
when thou dost embrace her.
9 She shall give to thine head an ornament of grace:
a crown of glory shall she deliver to thee.'
10 Hear, O my son, and receive my sayings;
and the years of thy life shall be many.
11 I have taught thee in the way of wisdom;
I have led thee in right paths.

12 When thou goest, thy steps shall not be straitened;
and when thou runnest, thou shalt not stumble.
13 Take fast hold of instruction;
let her not go: keep her; for she is thy life.

14 Enter not into the path of the wicked,
and go not in the way of evil men.
15 Avoid it, pass not by it,
turn from it, and pass away.
16 For they sleep not, except they have done mischief;
and their sleep is taken away,
unless they cause some to fall.
17 For they eat the bread of wickedness,
and drink the wine of violence.
18 But the path of the just is as the shining light,
that shineth more and more unto the perfect day.
19 The way of the wicked is as darkness:
they know not at what they stumble.

20 My son, attend to my words;
incline thine ear unto my sayings.
21 Let them not depart from thine eyes;
keep them in the midst of thine heart.
22 For they are life unto those that find them,
and health to all their flesh.

23 Keep thy heart with all diligence;
for out of it are the issues of life.

24 Put away from thee a froward mouth,
and perverse lips put far from thee.
25 Let thine eyes look right on,
and let thine eyelids
look straight before thee.
26 Ponder the path of thy feet,
and let all thy ways be established.
27 Turn not to the right hand nor to the left:
remove thy foot from evil.

5 My son, attend unto my wisdom,
and bow thine ear to my understanding:
2 that thou mayest regard discretion,
and that thy lips may keep knowledge.

3 For the lips of a strange woman
drop as an honeycomb,
and her mouth is smoother than oil:
4 But her end is bitter as wormwood,
sharp as a two-edged sword.
5 Her feet go down to death;
her steps take hold on hell.
6 Lest thou shouldest ponder the path of life,
her ways are moveable,
that thou canst not know them.
7 Hear me now therefore, O ye children,
and depart not from the words of my mouth.

8 Remove thy way far from her,
and come not nigh the door of her house:
9 Lest thou give thine honour unto others,
and thy years unto the cruel:
10 lest strangers be filled with thy wealth;
and thy labours be in the house of a stranger;
11 and thou mourn at the last,
when thy flesh and thy body are consumed,
12 and say, 'How have I hated instruction,
and my heart despised reproof;
13 and have not obeyed the voice of my teachers,
nor inclined mine ear
to them that instructed me!'
14 I was almost in all evil
in the midst of the congregation and assembly.

15 Drink waters out of thine own cistern,
and running waters out of thine own well.
16 Let thy fountains be dispersed abroad,
and rivers of waters in the streets.
17 Let them be only thine own,
and not strangers with thee.
18 Let thy fountain be blessed:
and rejoice with the wife of thy youth.
19 Let her be as the loving hind and pleasant roe;
let her breasts satisfy thee at all times;
and be thou ravished
always with her love.

20 And why wilt thou, my son,
be ravished with a strange woman,
and embrace the bosom of a stranger?
21 For the ways of man are before the eyes of the Lord,
and he pondereth all his goings.
22 His own iniquities shall take the wicked himself,
and he shall be holden with the cords of his sins.
23 He shall die without instruction;
and in the greatness of his folly
he shall go astray.

6 My son, if thou be surety for thy friend,
if thou hast stricken thy hand with a stranger,
2 thou art snared with the words of thy mouth,
thou art taken with the words of thy mouth.
3 Do this now, my son, and deliver thyself,
when thou art come into the hand of thy friend;
go, humble thyself, and make sure thy friend.
4 Give not sleep to thine eyes,
nor slumber to thine eyelids.
5 Deliver thyself as a roe from the hand of the hunter,
and as a bird from the hand of the fowler.

6 Go to the ant, thou sluggard;
consider her ways, and be wise:
7 which having no guide, overseer, or ruler,
8 provideth her meat in the summer,
and gathereth her food in the harvest.

9 How long wilt thou sleep, O sluggard?
When wilt thou arise out of thy sleep?
10 Yet a little sleep, a little slumber,
a little folding of the hands to sleep:
11 so shall thy poverty come as one that travaileth,
and thy want as an armed man.

12 A naughty person, a wicked man,
walketh with a froward mouth.
13 He winketh with his eyes,
he speaketh with his feet,
he teacheth with his fingers;
14 frowardness is in his heart,
he deviseth mischief continually;
he soweth discord.
15 Therefore shall his calamity come suddenly;
suddenly shall he be broken without remedy.

16 These six things doth the Lord hate;
yea, seven are an abomination unto him:
17 a proud look, a lying tongue,
and hands that shed innocent blood,
18 an heart that deviseth wicked imaginations,
feet that be swift in running to mischief,
19 a false witness that speaketh lies,
and he that soweth discord among brethren.

20 My son, keep thy father's commandment,
and forsake not the law of thy mother:

21 bind them continually upon thine heart,
and tie them about thy neck.
22 When thou goest, it shall lead thee;
when thou sleepest, it shall keep thee;
and when thou awakest,
it shall talk with thee.
23 For the commandment is a lamp;
and the law is light;
and reproofs of instruction are the way of life:
24 To keep thee from the evil woman,
from the flattery
of the tongue of a strange woman.
25 Lust not after her beauty in thine heart;
neither let her take thee with her eyelids.
26 For by means of a whorish woman
a man is brought to a piece of bread:
and the adulteress will hunt for
the precious life.
27 Can a man take fire in his bosom,
and his clothes not be burned?
28 Can one go upon hot coals,
and his feet not be burned?
29 So he that goeth in to his neighbour's wife;
whosoever toucheth her shall not be innocent.
30 Men do not despise a thief,
if he steal to satisfy his soul when he is hungry;
31 but if he be found, he shall restore sevenfold;
he shall give all the substance of his house.

32 But whoso committeth adultery with a woman
lacketh understanding:
he that doeth it destroyeth his own soul.
33 A wound and dishonour shall he get;
and his reproach shall not be wiped away.
34 For jealousy is the rage of a man:
therefore he will not spare
in the day of vengeance.
35 He will not regard any ransom;
neither will he rest content,
though thou givest many gifts.

7 My son, keep my words,
and lay up my commandments with thee.
2 Keep my commandments, and live;
and my law as the apple of thine eye.
3 Bind them upon thy fingers,
write them upon the table of thine heart.
4 Say unto wisdom, 'Thou art my sister,'
and call understanding thy kinswoman:
5 that they may keep thee
from the strange woman,
from the stranger
which flattereth
with her words.
6 For at the window of my house
I looked through my casement,

7 and beheld among the simple ones,
I discerned among the youths,
a young man void of understanding,
8 passing through the street near her corner;
and he went the way to her house,
9 in the twilight, in the evening,
in the black and dark night:
10 And, behold, there met him a woman
with the attire of an harlot, and subtil of heart.
11 (She is loud and stubborn;
her feet abide not in her house:
12 now is she without, now in the streets,
and lieth in wait at every corner.)
13 So she caught him, and kissed him,
and with an impudent face said unto him,
14 'I have peace offerings with me;
this day have I payed my vows.
15 Therefore came I forth to meet thee,
diligently to seek thy face, and I have found thee.
16 I have decked my bed with coverings of tapestry,
with carved works, with fine linen of Egypt.
17 I have perfumed my bed with myrrh,
aloes, and cinnamon.
18 Come, let us take our fill of love until the morning;
let us solace ourselves with loves.
19 For the goodman is not at home,
he is gone a long journey:

[20] he hath taken a bag of money with him,
and will come home at the day appointed.'
[21] With her much fair speech she caused him to yield,
with the flattering of her lips she forced him.
[22] He goeth after her straightway,
as an ox goeth to the slaughter,
or as a fool to the correction of the stocks;
[23] till a dart strike through his liver;
as a bird hasteth to the snare,
and knoweth not that it is for his life.

[24] Hearken unto me now therefore, O ye children,
and attend to the words of my mouth.
[25] Let not thine heart decline to her ways,
go not astray in her paths.
[26] For she hath cast down many wounded;
yea, many strong men have been slain by her.
[27] Her house is the way to hell,
going down to the chambers of death.

8 Doth not wisdom cry?
And understanding put forth her voice?
[2] She standeth in the top of high places,
by the way in the places of the paths.
[3] She crieth at the gates, at the entry of the city,
at the coming in at the doors,
[4] 'Unto you, O men, I call;

and my voice is to the sons of man.
5 O ye simple, understand wisdom, and, ye fools,
be ye of an understanding heart.
6 Hear; for I will speak of excellent things;
and the opening of my lips shall be right things.
7 For my mouth shall speak truth;
and wickedness is an abomination to my lips.
8 All the words of my mouth are in righteousness;
there is nothing froward or perverse in them.
9 They are all plain to him that understandeth,
and right to them that find knowledge.
10 Receive my instruction, and not silver;
and knowledge rather than choice gold.
11 For wisdom is better than rubies;
and all the things that may be desired
are not to be compared to it.

12 I wisdom dwell with prudence,
and find out knowledge of witty inventions.
13 The fear of the Lord is to hate evil;
pride, and arrogancy, and the evil way,
and the froward mouth, do I hate.
14 Counsel is mine, and sound wisdom.
I am understanding; I have strength.
15 By me kings reign, and princes decree justice.
16 By me princes rule, and nobles,
even all the judges of the earth.

17 I love them that love me;
    and those that seek me early shall find me.
18 Riches and honour are with me;
    yea, durable riches and righteousness.
19 My fruit is better than gold, yea, than fine gold;
    and my revenue than choice silver.
20 I lead in the way of righteousness,
    in the midst of the paths of judgment:
21 that I may cause those that love me
    to inherit substance;
        and I will fill their treasures.

22 The Lord possessed me in the beginning of his way,
    before his works of old.
23 I was set up from everlasting,
    from the beginning, or ever the earth was.
24 When there were no depths, I was brought forth;
    when there were no fountains
        abounding with water.
25 Before the mountains were settled,
    before the hills was I brought forth:
26 while as yet he had not made the earth, nor the fields,
    nor the highest part of the dust of the world.
27 When he prepared the heavens, I was there:
    when he set a compass upon the face of the depth:
28 when he established the clouds above:
    when he strengthened the fountains of the deep:

29 when he gave to the sea his decree,
that the waters should not
pass his commandment:
when he appointed the foundations of the earth:
30 then I was by him, as one brought up with him:
and I was daily his delight,
rejoicing always before him;
31 rejoicing in the habitable part of his earth;
and my delights were with the sons of men.

32 Now therefore hearken unto me, O ye children:
for blessed are they that keep my ways.
33 Hear instruction, and be wise, and refuse it not.
34 Blessed is the man that heareth me,
watching daily at my gates,
waiting at the posts of my doors.
35 For whoso findeth me findeth life,
and shall obtain favour of the Lord.
36 But he that sinneth against me
wrongeth his own soul:
all they that hate me love death.'

9 Wisdom hath builded her house,
she hath hewn out her seven pillars.
2 She hath killed her beasts;
she hath mingled her wine;
she hath also furnished her table.

3 She hath sent forth her maidens:
she crieth upon the highest places of the city,
4 'Whoso is simple, let him turn in hither.'
As for him that wanteth understanding,
she saith to him,
5 'Come, eat of my bread, and drink of the wine
which I have mingled.
6 Forsake the foolish, and live;
and go in the way of understanding.'
7 He that reproveth a scorner getteth to himself shame:
and he that rebuketh a wicked man
getteth himself a blot.
8 Reprove not a scorner, lest he hate thee:
rebuke a wise man, and he will love thee.
9 Give instruction to a wise man,
and he will be yet wiser:
teach a just man,
and he will increase in learning.

10 The fear of the Lord is the beginning of wisdom:
and the knowledge of the holy is understanding.
11 For by me thy days shall be multiplied,
and the years of thy life shall be increased.
12 If thou be wise, thou shalt be wise for thyself:
but if thou scornest, thou alone shalt bear it.

13 A foolish woman is clamorous:
she is simple, and knoweth nothing.

14 For she sitteth at the door of her house,
on a seat in the high places of the city,
15 to call passengers who go right on their ways:
16 'Whoso is simple, let him turn in hither,'
and as for him that wanteth understanding,
she saith to him,
17 'Stolen waters are sweet,
and bread eaten in secret is pleasant.'
18 But he knoweth not that the dead are there;
and that her guests are in the depths of hell.

10

The proverbs of Solomon.

A wise son maketh a glad father:
but a foolish son is the heaviness of his mother.

2 Treasures of wickedness profit nothing:
but righteousness delivereth from death.

3 The Lord will not suffer
the soul of the righteous to famish:
but he casteth away
the substance of the wicked.

4 He becometh poor that dealeth with a slack hand:
but the hand of the diligent maketh rich.

5 He that gathereth in summer is a wise son:
but he that sleepeth in harvest
is a son that causeth shame.

[6] Blessings are upon the head of the just:
but violence covereth the mouth of the wicked.

[7] The memory of the just is blessed:
but the name of the wicked shall rot.

[8] The wise in heart will receive commandments:
but a prating fool shall fall.

[9] He that walketh uprightly walketh surely:
but he that perverteth his ways shall be known.

[10] He that winketh with the eye causeth sorrow:
but a prating fool shall fall.

[11] The mouth of a righteous man is a well of life:
but violence covereth the mouth of the wicked.

[12] Hatred stirreth up strifes:
but love covereth all sins.

[13] In the lips of him that hath understanding
wisdom is found:
but a rod is for the back of him
that is void of understanding.

[14] Wise men lay up knowledge:
but the mouth of the foolish
is near destruction.

[15] The rich man's wealth is his strong city:
the destruction of the poor is their poverty.

16 The labour of the righteous tendeth to life:
the fruit of the wicked to sin.

17 He is in the way of life that keepeth instruction:
but he that refuseth reproof erreth.

18 He that hideth hatred with lying lips,
and he that uttereth a slander, is a fool.

19 In the multitude of words there wanteth not sin:
but he that refraineth his lips is wise.

20 The tongue of the just is as choice silver:
the heart of the wicked is little worth.

21 The lips of the righteous feed many:
but fools die for want of wisdom.

22 The blessing of the Lord, it maketh rich,
and he addeth no sorrow with it.

23 It is as sport to a fool to do mischief:
but a man of understanding hath wisdom:

24 The fear of the wicked, it shall come upon him:
but the desire of the righteous shall be granted.

25 As the whirlwind passeth, so is the wicked no more:
but the righteous is an everlasting foundation.

26 As vinegar to the teeth, and as smoke to the eyes,
so is the sluggard to them that send him.

27 The fear of the Lord prolongeth days:
but the years of the wicked shall be shortened.

28 The hope of the righteous shall be gladness:
but the expectation of the wicked shall perish.

29 The way of the Lord is strength to the upright:
but destruction shall be to the workers of iniquity.

30 The righteous shall never be removed:
but the wicked shall not inhabit the earth.

31 The mouth of the just bringeth forth wisdom:
but the froward tongue shall be cut out.

32 The lips of the righteous know what is acceptable:
but the mouth of the wicked speaketh frowardness.

11 A false balance is abomination to the Lord:
but a just weight is his delight.

2 When pride cometh, then cometh shame:
but with the lowly is wisdom.

3 The integrity of the upright shall guide them:
but the perverseness of transgressors
shall destroy them.

4 Riches profit not in the day of wrath:
but righteousness delivereth from death.

5 The righteousness of the perfect
shall direct his way:
but the wicked
shall fall by his own wickedness.

6 The righteousness of the upright shall deliver them:
but transgressors shall be taken
in their own naughtiness.

7 When a wicked man dieth,
his expectation shall perish:
and the hope of unjust men perisheth.

8 The righteous is delivered out of trouble,
and the wicked cometh in his stead.

9 An hypocrite with his mouth
destroyeth his neighbour:
but through knowledge
shall the just be delivered.

10 When it goeth well with the righteous,
the city rejoiceth:
and when the wicked perish, there is shouting.

11 By the blessing of the upright the city is exalted:
but it is overthrown by the mouth of the wicked.

12 He that is void of wisdom despiseth his neighbour:
but a man of understanding holdeth his peace.

13 A talebearer revealeth secrets:
but he that is of a faithful spirit
concealeth the matter.

14 Where no counsel is, the people fall:
but in the multitude of counsellors there is safety.

15 He that is surety for a stranger shall smart for it:
and he that hateth suretiship is sure.

16 A gracious woman retaineth honour:
and strong men retain riches.

17 The merciful man doeth good to his own soul:
but he that is cruel troubleth his own flesh.

18 The wicked worketh a deceitful work:
but to him that soweth righteousness
shall be a sure reward.

19 As righteousness tendeth to life:
so he that pursueth evil pursueth it
to his own death.

20 They that are of a froward heart
are abomination to the Lord:
but such as are upright in their way
are his delight.

21 Though hand join in hand,
the wicked shall not be unpunished:
but the seed of the righteous shall be delivere

22 As a jewel of gold in a swine's snout,
so is a fair woman which is without discretion.

23 The desire of the righteous is only good:
but the expectation of the wicked is wrath.

24 There is that scattereth, and yet increaseth;
and there is that withholdeth more than is meet,
but it tendeth to poverty.

25 The liberal soul shall be made fat:
and he that watereth shall be watered also himself.

26 He that withholdeth corn, the people shall curse him:
but blessing shall be upon the head of him
that selleth it.

27 He that diligently seeketh good procureth favour,
but he that seeketh mischief,
it shall come unto him.

28 He that trusteth in his riches shall fall,
but the righteous shall flourish as a branch.

29 He that troubleth his own house
shall inherit the wind:
and the fool shall be servant
to the wise of heart.

30 The fruit of the righteous is a tree of life;
and he that winneth souls is wise.

[31]Behold, the righteous shall be recompensed
in the earth:
much more the wicked and the sinner.

12 Whoso loveth instruction loveth knowledge:
but he that hateth reproof is brutish.

[2]A good man obtaineth favour of the Lord:
but a man of wicked devices will he condemn.

[3]A man shall not be established by wickedness:
but the root of the righteous shall not be moved.

[4]A virtuous woman is a crown to her husband:
but she that maketh ashamed
is as rottenness in his bones.

[5]The thoughts of the righteous are right:
but the counsels of the wicked are deceit.

[6]The words of the wicked
are to lie in wait for blood:
but the mouth of the upright
shall deliver them.

[7]The wicked are overthrown, and are not:
but the house of the righteous shall stand.

[8]A man shall be commended according to his wisdo
but he that is of a perverse heart shall be despise

9 He that is despised, and hath a servant,
is better than he that honoureth himself,
and lacketh bread.

10 A righteous man regardeth the life of his beast,
but the tender mercies of the wicked are cruel.

11 He that tilleth his land shall be satisfied with bread:
but he that followeth vain persons
is void of understanding.

12 The wicked desireth the net of evil men:
but the root of the righteous yieldeth fruit.

13 The wicked is snared by the transgression of his lips:
but the just shall come out of trouble.

14 A man shall be satisfied with good
by the fruit of his mouth,
and the recompence of a man's hands
shall be rendered unto him.

15 The way of a fool is right in his own eyes:
but he that hearkeneth unto counsel is wise.

16 A fool's wrath is presently known:
but a prudent man covereth shame.

17 He that speaketh truth sheweth forth righteousness:
but a false witness deceit.

[18] There is that speaketh like the piercings of a sword:
but the tongue of the wise is health.

[19] The lip of truth shall be established for ever:
but a lying tongue is but for a moment.

[20] Deceit is in the heart of them that imagine evil:
but to the counsellors of peace is joy.

[21] There shall no evil happen to the just:
but the wicked shall be filled with mischief.

[22] Lying lips are abomination to the Lord:
but they that deal truly are his delight.

[23] A prudent man concealeth knowledge:
but the heart of fools proclaimeth foolishness.

[24] The hand of the diligent shall bear rule:
but the slothful shall be under tribute.

[25] Heaviness in the heart of man maketh it stoop:
but a good word maketh it glad.

[26] The righteous is more excellent than his neighbour:
but the way of the wicked seduceth them.

[27] The slothful man roasteth
not that which he took in hunting:
but the substance of a diligent man is precious.

[28] In the way of righteousness is life;
and in the pathway thereof there is no death.

13 A wise son heareth his father's instruction:
but a scorner heareth not rebuke.

2 A man shall eat good by the fruit of his mouth:
but the soul of the transgressors
shall eat violence.

3 He that keepeth his mouth keepeth his life:
but he that openeth wide his lips
shall have destruction.

4 The soul of the sluggard desireth, and hath nothing:
but the soul of the diligent shall be made fat.

5 A righteous man hateth lying:
but a wicked man is loathsome,
and cometh to shame.

6 Righteousness keepeth him
that is upright in the way:
but wickedness overthroweth the sinner.

7 There is that maketh himself rich,
yet hath nothing:
there is that maketh himself poor,
yet hath great riches.

8 The ransom of a man's life are his riches:
but the poor heareth not rebuke.

9 The light of the righteous rejoiceth:
but the lamp of the wicked shall be put out.

10 Only by pride cometh contention:
but with the well advised is wisdom.

11 Wealth gotten by vanity shall be diminished:
but he that gathereth by labour shall increase.

12 Hope deferred maketh the heart sick:
but when the desire cometh, it is a tree of life.

13 Whoso despiseth the word shall be destroyed:
but he that feareth the commandment
shall be rewarded.

14 The law of the wise is a fountain of life,
to depart from the snares of death.

15 Good understanding giveth favour:
but the way of transgressors is hard.

16 Every prudent man dealeth with knowledge:
but a fool layeth open his folly.

17 A wicked messenger falleth into mischief:
but a faithful ambassador is health.

18 Poverty and shame shall be
to him that refuseth instruction:
but he that regardeth reproof
shall be honoured.

19 The desire accomplished is sweet to the soul:
but it is abomination to fools to depart from evil.

20 He that walketh with wise men shall be wise:
but a companion of fools shall be destroyed.

21 Evil pursueth sinners:
but to the righteous good shall be repayed.

22 A good man leaveth an inheritance
to his children's children:
and the wealth of the sinner
is laid up for the just.

23 Much food is in the tillage of the poor:
but there is that is destroyed
for want of judgment.

24 He that spareth his rod hateth his son:
but he that loveth him chasteneth him betimes.

25 The righteous eateth to the satisfying of his soul:
but the belly of the wicked shall want.

14 Every wise woman buildeth her house:
but the foolish plucketh it down with her hands.

2 He that walketh in his uprightness
feareth the Lord:
but he that is perverse in his ways
despiseth him.

3 In the mouth of the foolish is a rod of pride:
but the lips of the wise shall preserve them.

4 Where no oxen are, the crib is clean:
but much increase is by the strength of the ox.

5 A faithful witness will not lie:
but a false witness will utter lies.

6 A scorner seeketh wisdom, and findeth it not:
but knowledge is easy unto him
that understandeth.

7 Go from the presence of a foolish man,
when thou perceivest not in him
the lips of knowledge.

8 The wisdom of the prudent
is to understand his way:
but the folly of fools is deceit.

9 Fools make a mock at sin:
but among the righteous there is favour.

10 The heart knoweth his own bitterness;
and a stranger doth not intermeddle with his joy.

11 The house of the wicked shall be overthrown:
but the tabernacle of the upright shall flourish.

12 There is a way which seemeth right unto a man,
but the end thereof are the ways of death.

13 Even in laughter the heart is sorrowful;
and the end of that mirth is heaviness.

14 The backslider in heart shall be filled
with his own ways:
and a good man shall be satisfied
from himself.

15 The simple believeth every word:
but the prudent man looketh well to his going.

16 A wise man feareth, and departeth from evil:
but the fool rageth, and is confident.

17 He that is soon angry dealeth foolishly:
and a man of wicked devices is hated.

18 The simple inherit folly:
but the prudent are crowned with knowledge.

19 The evil bow before the good;
and the wicked at the gates of the righteous.

20 The poor is hated even of his own neighbour:
but the rich hath many friends.

21 He that despiseth his neighbour sinneth:
but he that hath mercy on the poor, happy is he.

22 Do they not err that devise evil?
But mercy and truth shall be to them
that devise good.

23 In all labour there is profit:
but the talk of the lips tendeth only to penury.

24 The crown of the wise is their riches:
but the foolishness of fools is folly.

25 A true witness delivereth souls:
but a deceitful witness
speaketh lies.

26 In the fear of the Lord is strong confidence:
and his children shall have a place of refuge.

27 The fear of the Lord is a fountain of life,
to depart from the snares of death.

28 In the multitude of people is the king's honour:
but in the want of people
is the destruction of the prince.

29 He that is slow to wrath
is of great understanding:
but he that is hasty of spirit
exalteth folly.

30 A sound heart is the life of the flesh:
but envy the rottenness of the bones.

31 He that oppresseth the poor
reproacheth his Maker:
but he that honoureth him
hath mercy on the poor.

32 The wicked is driven away in his wickedness:
but the righteous hath hope in his death.

33 Wisdom resteth in the heart of him
that hath understanding:
but that which is in the midst of fools
is made known.

34 Righteousness exalteth a nation:
but sin is a reproach to any people.

35 The king's favour is toward a wise servant:
but his wrath is against him that causeth shame.

15 A soft answer turneth away wrath:
but grievous words stir up anger.

2 The tongue of the wise useth knowledge aright:
but the mouth of fools poureth out foolishness.

3 The eyes of the Lord are in every place,
beholding the evil and the good.

4 A wholesome tongue is a tree of life:
but perverseness therein is a breach in the spirit.

5 A fool despiseth his father's instruction:
but he that regardeth reproof is prudent.

6 In the house of the righteous is much treasure:
but in the revenues of the wicked is trouble.

7 The lips of the wise disperse knowledge:
but the heart of the foolish doeth not so.

8 The sacrifice of the wicked
is an abomination to the Lord:
but the prayer of the upright is his delight.

9 The way of the wicked
is an abomination unto the Lord:
but he loveth him
that followeth after righteousness.

10 Correction is grievous unto him
that forsaketh the way:
and he that hateth reproof shall die.

11 Hell and destruction are before the Lord:
how much more then
the hearts of the children of men?

12 A scorner loveth not one that reproveth him:
neither will he go unto the wise.

13 A merry heart maketh a cheerful countenance:
but by sorrow of the heart the spirit is broken.

14 The heart of him that hath understanding
seeketh knowledge:
but the mouth of fools feedeth on foolishness.

15 All the days of the afflicted are evil:
but he that is of a merry heart
hath a continual feast.

[16] Better is little with the fear of the Lord
than great treasure and trouble therewith.

[17] Better is a dinner of herbs where love is,
than a stalled ox and hatred therewith.

[18] A wrathful man stirreth up strife:
but he that is slow to anger appeaseth strife.

[19] The way of the slothful man
is as an hedge of thorns:
but the way of the righteous is made plain.

[20] A wise son maketh a glad father:
but a foolish man despiseth his mother.

[21] Folly is joy to him that is destitute of wisdom:
but a man of understanding walketh uprightly.

[22] Without counsel purposes are disappointed:
but in the multitude of counsellors
they are established.

[23] A man hath joy by the answer of his mouth:
and a word spoken in due season, how good is it!

[24] The way of life is above to the wise,
that he may depart from hell beneath.

[25] The Lord will destroy the house of the proud:
but he will establish the border of the widow.

26 The thoughts of the wicked
are an abomination to the Lord:
but the words of the pure
are pleasant words.

27 He that is greedy of gain troubleth his own house:
but he that hateth gifts shall live.

28 The heart of the righteous studieth to answer:
but the mouth of the wicked
poureth out evil things.

29 The Lord is far from the wicked:
but he heareth the prayer of the righteous.

30 The light of the eyes rejoiceth the heart:
and a good report maketh the bones fat.

31 The ear that heareth the reproof of life
abideth among the wise.

32 He that refuseth instruction
despiseth his own soul:
but he that heareth reproof
getteth understanding.

33 The fear of the Lord is the instruction of wisdom;
and before honour is humility.

16 The preparations of the heart in man,
and the answer of the tongue, is from the Lord.

2 All the ways of a man are clean in his own eyes;
but the Lord weigheth the spirits.

3 Commit thy works unto the Lord,
and thy thoughts shall be established.

4 The Lord hath made all things for himself:
yea, even the wicked for the day of evil.

5 Every one that is proud in heart
is an abomination to the Lord:
though hand join in hand,
he shall not be unpunished.

6 By mercy and truth iniquity is purged:
and by the fear of the Lord men depart from evil.

7 When a man's ways please the Lord,
he maketh even his enemies
to be at peace with him.

8 Better is a little with righteousness
than great revenues without right.

9 A man's heart deviseth his way:
but the Lord directeth his steps.

10 A divine sentence is in the lips of the king:
his mouth transgresseth not in judgment.

11 A just weight and balance are the Lord's:
all the weights of the bag are his work.

12 It is an abomination to kings to commit wickedness:
for the throne is established by righteousness.

13 Righteous lips are the delight of kings;
and they love him that speaketh right.

14 The wrath of a king is as messengers of death:
but a wise man will pacify it.

15 In the light of the king's countenance is life;
and his favour is as a cloud of the latter rain.

16 How much better is it to get wisdom than gold!
And to get understanding
rather to be chosen than silver!

17 The highway of the upright is to depart from evil:
he that keepeth his way preserveth his soul.

18 Pride goeth before destruction,
and an haughty spirit before a fall.

19 Better it is to be of an humble spirit with the lowly,
than to divide the spoil with the proud.

20 He that handleth a matter wisely shall find good:
and whoso trusteth in the Lord, happy is he.

21 The wise in heart shall be called prudent:
and the sweetness of the lips increaseth learning.

22 Understanding is a wellspring of life
unto him that hath it:
but the instruction of fools is folly.

23 The heart of the wise teacheth his mouth,
and addeth learning to his lips.

24 Pleasant words are as an honeycomb,
sweet to the soul, and health to the bones.

25 There is a way that seemeth right unto a man,
but the end thereof are the ways of death.

26 He that laboureth laboureth for himself:
for his mouth craveth it of him.

27 An ungodly man diggeth up evil:
and in his lips there is as a burning fire.

28 A froward man soweth strife,
and a whisperer separateth chief friends.

29 A violent man enticeth his neighbour,
and leadeth him into the way that is not good.

30 He shutteth his eyes to devise froward things:
moving his lips he bringeth evil to pass.

31 The hoary head is a crown of glory,
if it be found in the way of righteousness.

32 He that is slow to anger is better than the mighty;
and he that ruleth his spirit
than he that taketh a city.

33 The lot is cast into the lap;
but the whole disposing thereof is of the Lord.

17

Better is a dry morsel, and quietness therewith,
than an house full of sacrifices with strife.

2 A wise servant shall have rule over a son
that causeth shame,
and shall have part of the inheritance
among the brethren.

3 The fining pot is for silver, and the furnace for gold:
but the Lord trieth the hearts.

4 A wicked doer giveth heed to false lips;
and a liar giveth ear to a naughty tongue.

5 Whoso mocketh the poor reproacheth his Maker:
and he that is glad at calamities
shall not be unpunished.

6 Children's children are the crown of old men;
and the glory of children are their fathers.

7 Excellent speech becometh not a fool:
much less do lying lips a prince.

8 A gift is as a precious stone
in the eyes of him that hath it:
whithersoever it turneth, it prospereth.

9 He that covereth a transgression
seeketh love;
but he that repeateth a matter
separateth very friends.

10 A reproof entereth more into a wise man
than an hundred stripes into a fool.

11 An evil man seeketh only rebellion:
therefore a cruel messenger
shall be sent against him.

12 Let a bear robbed of her whelps meet a man,
rather than a fool in his folly.

13 Whoso rewardeth evil for good,
evil shall not depart from his house.

14 The beginning of strife
is as when one letteth out water:
therefore leave off contention,
before it be meddled with.

15 He that justifieth the wicked,
and he that condemneth the just,
even they both are
abomination to the Lord.

16 Wherefore is there a price
in the hand of a fool to get wisdom,
seeing he hath no heart to it?

17 A friend loveth at all times,
and a brother is born for adversity.

18 A man void of understanding striketh hands,
and becometh surety
in the presence of his friend.

19 He loveth transgression that loveth strife:
and he that exalteth his gate seeketh destruction.

20 He that hat a froward heart findeth no good:
and he that hath a perverse tongue
falleth into mischief.

21 He that begetteth a fool doeth it to his sorrow:
and the father of a fool hath no joy.

22 A merry heart doeth good like a medicine:
but a broken spirit drieth the bones.

23 A wicked man taketh a gift out of the bosom
to pervert the ways of judgment.

24 Wisdom is before him that hath understanding;
but the eyes of a fool are in the ends of the earth.

25 A foolish son is a grief to his father,
and bitterness to her that bare him.

26 Also to punish the just is not good,
nor to strike princes for equity.

27 He that hath knowledge
spareth his words:
and a man of understanding
is of an excellent spirit.

28 Even a fool, when he holdeth his peace,
is counted wise:
and he that shutteth his lips
is esteemed a man of understanding.

18 Through desire a man, having separated himself,
seeketh and intermeddleth with all wisdom.

2 A fool hath no delight in understanding,
but that his heart may discover itself.

3 When the wicked cometh,
then cometh also contempt,
and with ignominy reproach.

4 The words of a man's mouth are as deep waters,
and the wellspring of wisdom as a flowing brook.

5 It is not good to accept the person of the wicked,
to overthrow the righteous in judgment.

6 A fool's lips enter into contention,
and his mouth calleth for strokes.

7 A fool's mouth is his destruction,
and his lips are the snare of his soul.

8 The words of a tale-bearer are as wounds,
and they go down into
the innermost parts of the belly.

9 He also that is slothful in his work
is brother to him that is a great waster.

10 The name of the Lord is a strong tower:
the righteous runneth into it, and is safe.

11 The rich man's wealth is his strong city,
and as an high wall in his own conceit.

12 Before destruction the heart of man is haughty,
and before honour is humility.

13 He that answereth a matter before he heareth it,
it is folly and shame unto him.

14 The spirit of a man will sustain his infirmity;
but a wounded spirit who can bear?

15 The heart of the prudent getteth knowledge;
and the ear of the wise seeketh knowledge.

16 A man's gift maketh room for him,
and bringeth him before great men.

17 He that is first in his own cause seemeth just;
but his neighbour cometh and searcheth him.

18 The lot causeth contentions to cease,
and parteth between the mighty.

19 A brother offended is harder to be won
than a strong city:
and their contentions are like
the bars of a castle.

20 A man's belly shall be satisfied
with the fruit of his mouth;
and with the increase of his lips
shall he be filled.

21 Death and life are in the power of the tongue:
and they that love it
shall eat the fruit thereof.

22 Whoso findeth a wife findeth a good thing,
and obtaineth favour of the Lord.

23 The poor useth intreaties;
but the rich answereth roughly.

24 A man that hath friends
must shew himself friendly:
and there is a friend
that sticketh closer than a brother.

19 Better is the poor that walketh in his integrity,
than he that is perverse in his lips, and is a fool.

2 Also, that the soul be without knowledge,
it is not good;
and he that hasteth with his feet sinneth.

3 The foolishness of man perverteth his way:
and his heart fretteth against the Lord.

4 Wealth maketh many friends;
but the poor is separated from his neighbour.

5 A false witness shall not be unpunished,
and he that speaketh lies shall not escape.

6 Many will intreat the favour of the prince:
and every man is a friend
to him that giveth gifts.

7 All the brethren of the poor do hate him:
how much more do his friends go far from him?
He pursueth them with words,
yet they are wanting to him.

8 He that getteth wisdom loveth his own soul;
he that keepeth understanding shall find good.

9 A false witness shall not be unpunished,
and he that speaketh lies shall perish.

10 Delight is not seemly for a fool;
much less for a servant to have rule over princes.

11 The discretion of a man deferreth his anger;
and it is his glory to pass over a transgression.

12 The king's wrath is as the roaring of a lion;
but his favour is as dew upon the grass.

13 A foolish son is the calamity of his father:
and the contentions of a wife
are a continual dropping.

14 House and riches are the inheritance of fathers:
and a prudent wife is from the Lord.

15 Slothfulness casteth into a deep sleep;
and an idle soul shall suffer hunger.

16 He that keepeth the commandment
keepeth his own soul;
but he that despiseth his ways shall die.

17 He that hath pity upon the poor
lendeth unto the Lord;
and that which he hath given
will he pay him again.

18 Chasten thy son while there is hope,
and let not thy soul spare for his crying.

19 A man of great wrath shall suffer punishment:
for if thou deliver him, yet thou must do it again.

20 Hear counsel, and receive instruction,
that thou mayest be wise in thy latter end.

21 There are many devices in a man's heart;
nevertheless the counsel of the Lord,
that shall stand.

22 The desire of a man is his kindness:
and a poor man is better than a liar.

23 The fear of the Lord tendeth to life:
and he that hath it shall abide satisfied;
he shall not be visited with evil.

24 A slothful man hideth his hand in his bosom,
and will not so much as
bring it to his mouth again.

25 Smite a scorner, and the simple will beware:
and reprove one that hath understanding,
and he will understand knowledge.

26 He that wasteth his father,
and chaseth away his mother,
is a son that causeth shame,
and bringeth reproach.

27 Cease, my son, to hear the instruction
that causeth to err from the words of knowledge.

28 An ungodly witness scorneth judgment:
and the mouth of the wicked devoureth iniquity.

29 Judgments are prepared for scorners,
and stripes for the back of fools.

20 Wine is a mocker, strong drink is raging:
and whosoever is deceived thereby
is not wise.

2 The fear of a king is as the roaring of a lion:
whoso provoketh him to anger
sinneth against his own soul.

3 It is an honour for a man to cease from strife:
but every fool will be meddling.

4 The sluggard will not plow by reason of the cold:
therefore shall he beg in harvest,
and have nothing.

5 Counsel in the heart of man is like deep water;
but a man of understanding will draw it out.

6 Most men will proclaim every one
his own goodness,
but a faithful man who can find?

7 The just man walketh in his integrity:
his children are blessed after him.

8 A king that sitteth in the throne of judgment
scattereth away all evil with his eyes.

9 Who can say, 'I have made my heart clean,
I am pure from my sin'?

10 Divers weights, and divers measures:
both of them are alike abomination to the Lord.

11 Even a child is known by his doings,
whether his work be pure,
and whether it be right.

12 The hearing ear, and the seeing eye,
the Lord hath made even both of them.

13 Love not sleep, lest thou come to poverty;
open thine eyes,
and thou shalt be satisfied with bread.

14 'It is naught, it is naught,' saith the buyer,
but when he is gone his way, then he boasteth.

15 There is gold, and a multitude of rubies:
but the lips of knowledge are a precious jewel.

16 Take his garment that is surety for a stranger:
and take a pledge of him for a strange woman.

17 Bread of deceit is sweet to a man;
but afterwards his mouth shall be filled
with gravel.

18 Every purpose is established by counsel:
and with good advice make war.

19 He that goeth about as a tale-bearer
revealeth secrets:
therefore meddle not with him
that flattereth with his lips.

20 Whoso curseth his father or his mother,
his lamp shall be put out in obscure darkness.

21 An inheritance may be gotten hastily
at the beginning;
but the end thereof shall not be blessed.

22 Say not thou, 'I will recompense evil';
but wait on the Lord, and he shall save thee.

23 Divers weights are an abomination unto the Lord;
and a false balance is not good.

24 Man's goings are of the Lord;
how can a man then understand his own way?

25 It is a snare to the man who devoureth
that which is holy,
and after vows to make enquiry.

26 A wise king scattereth the wicked,
and bringeth the wheel over them.

27 The spirit of man is the candle of the Lord,
searching all the inward parts of the belly.

28 Mercy and truth preserve the king:
and his throne is upholden by mercy.

29 The glory of young men is their strength:
and the beauty of old men is the gray head.

30 The blueness of a wound cleanseth away evil:
so do stripes the inward parts of the belly.

21 The king's heart is in the hand of the Lord,
as the rivers of water:
he turneth it whithersoever he will.

2 Every way of a man is right in his own eyes:
but the Lord pondereth the hearts.

3 To do justice and judgment
is more acceptable to the Lord than sacrifice.

4 An high look, and a proud heart,
and the plowing of the wicked, is sin.

5 The thoughts of the diligent
tend only to plenteousness;
but of every one that is hasty only to want.

6 The getting of treasures
by a lying tongue is a vanity
tossed to and fro of them that seek death.

7 The robbery of the wicked shall destroy them;
because they refuse to do judgment.

8 The way of man is froward and strange:
but as for the pure, his work is right.

9 It is better to dwell in a corner of the housetop
than with a brawling woman in a wide house.

10 The soul of the wicked desireth evil:
his neighbour findeth no favour in his eyes.

11 When the scorner is punished,
the simple is made wise:
and when the wise is instructed,
he receiveth knowledge.

12 The righteous man wisely considereth
the house of the wicked:
but God overthroweth the wicked
for their wickedness.

13 Whoso stoppeth his ears at the cry of the poor,
he also shall cry himself, but shall not be heard.

14 A gift in secret pacifieth anger:
and a reward in the bosom strong wrath.

15 It is joy to the just to do judgment:
but destruction shall be
to the workers of iniquity.

16 The man that wandereth
out of the way of understanding
shall remain in the congregation of the dead.

17 He that loveth pleasure shall be a poor man:
he that loveth wine and oil shall not be rich.

18 The wicked shall be a ransom for the righteous,
and the transgressor for the upright.

19 It is better to dwell in the wilderness,
than with a contentious and an angry woman.

20 There is treasure to be desired
and oil in the dwelling of the wise;
but a foolish man spendeth it up.

21 He that followeth after righteousness and mercy
findeth life, righteousness, and honour.

22 A wise man scaleth the city of the mighty,
and casteth down the strength
of the confidence thereof.

23 Whoso keepeth his mouth and his tongue
keepeth his soul from troubles.

24 Proud and haughty scorner is his name,
who dealeth in proud wrath.

25 The desire of the slothful killeth him,
for his hands refuse to labour.
26 He coveteth greedily all the day long,
but the righteous giveth and spareth not.

27 The sacrifice of the wicked is abomination:
how much more,
when he bringeth it with a wicked mind?

28 A false witness shall perish:
but the man that heareth speaketh constantly.

29 A wicked man hardeneth his face:
but as for the upright, he directeth his way.

30 There is no wisdom nor understanding
nor counsel against the Lord.

31 The horse is prepared against the day of battle:
but safety is of the Lord.

22 A good name is rather to be chosen
than great riches,
and loving favour
rather than silver and gold.

2 The rich and poor meet together:
the Lord is the maker of them all.

3 A prudent man foreseeth the evil,
and hideth himself:
but the simple pass on,
and are punished.

4 By humility and the fear of the Lord are riches,
and honour, and life.

5 Thorns and snares are in the way of the froward:
he that doth keep his soul shall be far from them.

6 Train up a child in the way he should go:
and when he is old, he will not depart from it.

7 The rich ruleth over the poor,
and the borrower is servant to the lender.

8 He that soweth iniquity shall reap vanity:
and the rod of his anger shall fail.

9 He that hath a bountiful eye shall be blessed;
for he giveth of his bread to the poor.

10 Cast out the scorner, and contention shall go out;
yea, strife and reproach shall cease.

11 He that loveth pureness of heart,
for the grace of his lips
the king shall be his friend.

12 The eyes of the Lord preserve knowledge,
and he overthroweth the words
of the transgressor.

13 The slothful man saith,
'There is a lion without,
I shall be slain in the streets.'

14 The mouth of strange women is a deep pit:
he that is abhorred of the Lord shall fall therein.

15 Foolishness is bound in the heart of a child;
but the rod of correction
shall drive it far from him.

16 He that oppresseth the poor to increase his riches,
and he that giveth to the rich,
shall surely come to want.

17 Bow down thine ear, and hear the words of the wise,
and apply thine heart unto my knowledge.
18 For it is a pleasant thing
if thou keep them within thee;
they shall withal be fitted in thy lips.
19 That thy trust may be in the Lord,
I have made known to thee this day, even to thee.

20 Have not I written to thee excellent things
in counsels and knowledge,
21 that I might make thee know the certainty
of the words of truth;
that thou mightest answer the words of truth
to them that send unto thee?

22 Rob not the poor, because he is poor:
neither oppress the afflicted in the gate:
23 for the Lord will plead their cause,
and spoil the soul of those that spoiled them.

24 Make no friendship with an angry man;
and with a furious man thou shalt not go:
25 lest thou learn his ways,
and get a snare to thy soul.

26 Be not thou one of them that strike hands,
or of them that are sureties for debts.
27 If thou hast nothing to pay,
why should he take away thy bed
from under thee?

28 Remove not the ancient landmark,
which thy fathers have set.

29 Seest thou a man diligent in his business?
He shall stand before kings;
he shall not stand before mean men.

23 When thou sittest to eat with a ruler,
consider diligently what is before thee:
2 and put a knife to thy throat,
if thou be a man given to appetite.
3 Be not desirous of his dainties:
for they are deceitful meat.

4 Labour not to be rich:
cease from thine own wisdom.
5 Wilt thou set thine eyes upon that which is not?
For riches certainly make themselves wings;
they fly away as an eagle toward heaven.

6 Eat thou not the bread of him that hath an evil eye,
neither desire thou his dainty meats:

7 for as he thinketh in his heart, so is he.
'Eat and drink,' saith he to thee;
but his heart is not with thee.
8 The morsel which thou hast eaten
shalt thou vomit up,
and lose thy sweet words.

9 Speak not in the ears of a fool:
for he will despise
the wisdom of thy words.

10 Remove not the old landmark;
and enter not into the fields of the fatherless:
11 for their redeemer is mighty;
he shall plead their cause with thee.

12 Apply thine heart unto instruction,
and thine ears to the words of knowledge.

13 Withhold not correction from the child:
for if thou beatest him with the rod,
he shall not die.
14 Thou shalt beat him with the rod,
and shalt deliver his soul from hell.

15 My son, if thine heart be wise,
my heart shall rejoice, even mine.
16 Yea, my reins shall rejoice,
when thy lips speak right things.

17 Let not thine heart envy sinners:
but be thou in the fear of the Lord
all the day long.
18 For surely there is an end;
and thine expectation shall not be cut off.

19 Hear thou, my son, and be wise,
and guide thine heart in the way.
20 Be not among winebibbers;
among riotous eaters of flesh:
21 for the drunkard and the glutton
shall come to poverty:
and drowsiness shall clothe a man with rags.

22 Hearken unto thy father that begat thee,
and despise not thy mother when she is old.
23 Buy the truth, and sell it not; also wisdom,
and instruction, and understanding.
24 The father of the righteous shall greatly rejoice:
and he that begetteth a wise child
shall have joy of him.
25 Thy father and thy mother shall be glad,
and she that bare thee shall rejoice.

26 My son, give me thine heart,
and let thine eyes observe my ways.
27 For a whore is a deep ditch;
and a strange woman is a narrow pit.

28 She also lieth in wait as for a prey,
and increaseth the transgressors among men.

29 Who hath woe? Who hath sorrow?
Who hath contentions? Who hath babbling?
Who hath wounds without cause?
Who hath redness of eyes?
30 They that tarry long at the wine,
they that go to seek mixed wine.
31 Look not thou upon the wine when it is red,
when it giveth his colour in the cup,
when it moveth itself aright.
32 At the last it biteth like a serpent,
and stingeth like an adder.
33 Thine eyes shall behold strange women,
and thine heart shall utter perverse things.
34 Yea, thou shalt be as he that lieth down
in the midst of the sea,
or as he that lieth upon the top of a mast.
35 'They have stricken me,' shalt thou say,
'and I was not sick;
they have beaten me, and I felt it not.
When shall I awake? I will seek it yet again.'

24 Be not thou envious against evil men,
neither desire to be with them.
2 For their heart studieth destruction,
and their lips talk of mischief.

3 Through wisdom is an house builded;
and by understanding it is established:
4 and by knowledge shall the chambers be filled
with all precious and pleasant riches.

5 A wise man is strong;
yea, a man of knowledge increaseth strength.
6 For by wise counsel thou shalt make thy war:
and in multitude of counsellors
there is safety.

7 Wisdom is too high for a fool:
he openeth not his mouth in the gate.

8 He that deviseth to do evil
shall be called a mischievous person.
9 The thought of foolishness is sin:
and the scorner is an abomination to men.

10 If thou faint in the day of adversity,
thy strength is small.
11 If thou forbear to deliver
them that are drawn unto death,
and those that are ready to be slain;

12 if thou sayest, 'Behold, we knew it not,'
doth not he that pondereth the heart consider it?
And he that keepeth thy soul,
doth not he know it?
And shall not he render to every man
according to his works?

13 My son, eat thou honey, because it is good;
and the honeycomb, which is sweet to thy taste:
14 so shall the knowledge of wisdom be unto thy soul:
when thou hast found it,
then there shall be a reward,
and thy expectation shall not be cut off.

15 Lay not wait, O wicked man,
against the dwelling of the righteous;
spoil not his resting place:
16 for a just man falleth seven times,
and riseth up again:
but the wicked shall fall into mischief.

17 Rejoice not when thine enemy falleth,
and let not thine heart be glad
when he stumbleth:
18 lest the Lord see it, and it displease him,
and he turn away his wrath from him.

19 Fret not thyself because of evil men,
neither be thou envious at the wicked;

20 for there shall be no reward to the evil man;
the candle of the wicked shall be put out.

21 My son, fear thou the Lord and the king,
and meddle not with them
that are given to change:
22 for their calamity shall rise suddenly;
and who knoweth the ruin of them both?

23 These things also belong to the wise.

It is not good to have respect of persons in judgment.
24 He that saith unto the wicked,
'Thou art righteous,' him shall the people curse,
nations shall abhor him:
25 but to them that rebuke him shall be delight,
and a good blessing shall come upon them.
26 Every man shall kiss his lips
that giveth a right answer.

27 Prepare thy work without,
and make it fit for thyself in the field;
and afterwards build thine house.

28 Be not a witness against thy neighbour
without cause;
and deceive not with thy lips.
29 Say not, 'I will do so to him as he hath done to me:
I will render to the man according to his work.'

30 I went by the field of the slothful,
and by the vineyard of the man
void of understanding;
31 and, lo, it was all grown over with thorns,
and nettles had covered the face thereof,
and the stone wall thereof was broken down.
32 Then I saw, and considered it well:
I looked upon it,
and received instruction.
33 Yet a little sleep, a little slumber,
a little folding of the hands to sleep:
34 so shall thy poverty come as one that travelleth;
and thy want as an armed man.

25 These are also proverbs of Solomon, which the men of
Hezekiah king of Judah copied out.

2 It is the glory of God to conceal a thing:
but the honour of kings is to search out a matter.
3 The heaven for height, and the earth for depth,
and the heart of kings is unsearchable.

4 Take away the dross from the silver,
and there shall come forth a vessel for the finer.
5 Take away the wicked from before the king,
and his throne shall be established
in righteousness.

6 Put not forth thyself in the presence of the king,
and stand not in the place of great men:
7 for better it is that it be said unto thee,
'Come up hither,' than that thou shouldest be put
lower in the presence of the prince
whom thine eyes have seen.

8 Go not forth hastily to strive,
lest thou know not what to do in the end thereof,
when thy neighbour hath put thee to shame.

9 Debate thy cause with thy neighbour himself;
and discover not a secret to another:
10 lest he that heareth it put thee to shame,
and thine infamy turn not away.

11 A word fitly spoken is like apples of gold
in pictures of silver.
12 As an earring of gold, and an ornament of fine gold,
so is a wise reprover upon an obedient ear.

13 As the cold of snow in the time of harvest,
so is a faithful messenger to them that send him:
for he refresheth the soul of his masters.

14 Whoso boasteth himself of a false gift
is like clouds and wind without rain.

15 By long forbearing is a prince persuaded,
and a soft tongue breaketh the bone.

16 Hast thou found honey?
Eat so much as is sufficient for thee,
lest thou be filled therewith, and vomit it.

17 Withdraw thy foot from thy neighbour's house;
lest he be weary of thee, and so hate thee.

18 A man that beareth false witness
against his neighbour
is a maul, and a sword, and a sharp arrow.

19 Confidence in an unfaithful man in time of trouble
is like a broken tooth, and a foot out of joint.

20 As he that taketh away a garment in cold weather,
and as vinegar upon nitre,
so is he that singeth songs to an heavy heart.

21 If thine enemy be hungry, give him bread to eat;
and if he be thirsty, give him water to drink:
22 for thou shalt heap coals of fire upon his head,
and the Lord shall reward thee.

23 The north wind driveth away rain:
so doth an angry countenance
a backbiting tongue.

24 It is better to dwell in the corner of the housetop,
than with a brawling woman
and in a wide house.

25 As cold waters to a thirsty soul,
so is good news from a far country.

26 A righteous man falling down before the wicked
is as a troubled fountain, and a corrupt spring.

27 It is not good to eat much honey:
so for men to search their own glory is not glory.

28 He that hath no rule over his own spirit
is like a city that is broken down,
and without walls.

26 As snow in summer, and as rain in harvest,
so honour is not seemly for a fool.

2 As the bird by wandering, as the swallow by flying,
so the curse causeless shall not come.

3 A whip for the horse, a bridle for the ass,
and a rod for the fool's back.

4 Answer not a fool according to his folly,
lest thou also be like unto him.

5 Answer a fool according to his folly,
lest he be wise in his own conceit.

6 He that sendeth a message by the hand of a fool
cutteth off the feet, and drinketh damage.

7 The legs of the lame are not equal:
so is a parable in the mouth of fools.

8 As he that bindeth a stone in a sling,
so is he that giveth honour to a fool.

9 As a thorn goeth up into the hand of a drunkard,
so is a parable in the mouth of fools.

10 The great God that formed all things
both rewardeth the fool,
and rewardeth transgressors.

11 As a dog returneth to his vomit,
so a fool returneth to his folly.

12 Seest thou a man wise in his own conceit?
There is more hope of a fool than of him.

13 The slothful man saith,
'There is a lion in the way;
a lion is in the streets.'

14 As the door turneth upon his hinges,
so doth the slothful upon his bed.

15 The slothful hideth his hand in his bosom;
it grieveth him to bring it again to his mouth.

16 The sluggard is wiser in his own conceit
than seven men that can render a reason.

17 He that passeth by, and meddleth with strife
belonging not to him,
is like one that taketh a dog by the ears.

18 As a mad man who casteth firebrands,
arrows, and death,
19 so is the man that deceiveth his neighbour,
and saith, 'Am not I in sport?'

20 Where no wood is, there the fire goeth out:
so where there is no talebearer,
the strife ceaseth.

21 As coals are to burning coals, and wood to fire;
so is a contentious man to kindle strife.

22 The words of a talebearer are as wounds,
and they go down
into the innermost parts of the belly.
23 Burning lips and a wicked heart
are like a potsherd covered with silver dross.

24 He that hateth dissembleth with his lips,
and layeth up deceit within him;
25 when he speaketh fair, believe him not:
for there are seven abominations in his heart.
26 Whose hatred is covered by deceit,
his wickedness shall be shewed
before the whole congregation.

27 Whoso diggeth a pit shall fall therein:
and he that rolleth a stone,
it will return upon him.

28 A lying tongue hateth those that are afflicted by it;
and a flattering mouth worketh ruin.

27 Boast not thyself of tomorrow;
for thou knowest not what a day may bring forth.

2 Let another man praise thee,
and not thine own mouth;
a stranger, and not thine own lips.

3 A stone is heavy, and the sand weighty;
but a fool's wrath is heavier than them both.

4 Wrath is cruel, and anger is outrageous;
but who is able to stand before envy?

5 Open rebuke is better than secret love.

6 Faithful are the wounds of a friend;
but the kisses of an enemy are deceitful.

7 The full soul loatheth an honeycomb;
but to the hungry soul every bitter thing is sweet.

8 As a bird that wandereth from her nest,
so is a man that wandereth from his place.

[9] Ointment and perfume rejoice the heart:
so doth the sweetness of a man's friend
by hearty counsel.

[10] Thine own friend, and thy father's friend,
forsake not;
neither go into thy brother's house
in the day of thy calamity:
for better is a neighbour
that is near than a brother far off.

[11] My son, be wise, and make my heart glad,
that I may answer him that reproacheth me.

[12] A prudent man foreseeth the evil, and hideth himself;
but the simple pass on, and are punished.

[13] Take his garment that is surety for a stranger,
and take a pledge of him for a strange woman.

[14] He that blesseth his friend with a loud voice,
rising early in the morning,
it shall be counted a curse to him.

[15] A continual dropping in a very rainy day
and a contentious woman are alike.
[16] Whosoever hideth her hideth the wind,
and the ointment of his right hand,
which bewrayeth itself.

17 Iron sharpeneth iron; so a man sharpeneth
the countenance of his friend.

18 Whoso keepeth the fig tree shall eat the fruit thereof:
so he that waiteth on his master shall be honoured.

19 As in water face answereth to face,
so the heart of man to man.

20 Hell and destruction are never full;
so the eyes of man are never satisfied.

21 As the fining pot for silver,
and the furnace for gold;
so is a man to his praise.

22 Though thou shouldest bray a fool in a mortar
among wheat with a pestle,
yet will not his foolishness depart from him.

23 Be thou diligent to know the state of thy flocks,
and look well to thy herds.
24 For riches are not for ever:
and doth the crown endure to every generation?
25 The hay appeareth,
and the tender grass sheweth itself,
and herbs of the mountains are gathered.
26 The lambs are for thy clothing,
and the goats are the price of the field.

27 And thou shalt have goats' milk enough
for thy food, for the food of thy household,
and for the maintenance for thy maidens.

28

The wicked flee when no man pursueth:
but the righteous are bold as a lion.

2 For the transgression of a land
many are the princes thereof,
but by a man of understanding and knowledge
the state thereof shall be prolonged.

3 A poor man that oppresseth the poor
is like a sweeping rain which leaveth no food.

4 They that forsake the law praise the wicked:
but such as keep the law contend with them.

5 Evil men understand not judgment:
but they that seek the
Lord understand all things.

6 Better is the poor that walketh in his uprightness,
than he that is perverse in his ways,
though he be rich.

7 Whoso keepeth the law is a wise son:
but he that is a companion of riotous men
shameth his father.

8 He that by usury and unjust gain
increaseth his substance,
he shall gather it for him
that will pity the poor.

9 He that turneth away his ear from hearing the law,
even his prayer shall be abomination.

10 Whoso causeth the righteous to go astray
in an evil way,
he shall fall himself into his own pit:
but the upright shall have good things
in possession.

11 The rich man is wise in his own conceit;
but the poor that hath understanding
searcheth him out.

12 When righteous men do rejoice,
there is great glory:
but when the wicked rise, a man is hidden.

13 He that covereth his sins shall not prosper:
but whoso confesseth and forsaketh them
shall have mercy.

14 Happy is the man that feareth alway:
but he that hardeneth his heart
shall fall into mischief.

15 As a roaring lion, and a ranging bear;
so is a wicked ruler over the poor people.

16 The prince that wanteth understanding
is also a great oppressor:
but he that hateth covetousness
shall prolong his days.

17 A man that doeth violence
to the blood of any person
shall flee to the pit;
let no man stay him.

18 Whoso walketh uprightly shall be saved,
but he that is perverse in his ways
shall fall at once.

19 He that tilleth his land
shall have plenty of bread:
but he that followeth after vain persons
shall have poverty enough.

20 A faithful man shall abound with blessings:
but he that maketh haste to be rich
shall not be innocent.

21 To have respect of persons is not good,
for for a piece of bread that man will transgress.

22 He that hasteth to be rich hath an evil eye,
and considereth not
that poverty shall come upon him.

23 He that rebuketh a man
afterwards shall find more favour
than he that flattereth with the tongue.

24 Whoso robbeth his father or his mother, and saith,
'It is no transgression,'
the same is the companion of a destroyer.

25 He that is of a proud heart stirreth up strife:
but he that putteth his trust in the Lord
shall be made fat.

26 He that trusteth in his own heart is a fool:
but whoso walketh wisely, he shall be delivered.

27 He that giveth unto the poor shall not lack:
but he that hideth his eyes
shall have many a curse.

28 When the wicked rise, men hide themselves:
but when they perish, the righteous increase.

29 He, that being often reproved, hardeneth his neck,
shall suddenly be destroyed,
and that without remedy.

2 When the righteous are in authority,
the people rejoice:
but when the wicked beareth rule,
the people mourn.

3 Whoso loveth wisdom rejoiceth his father:
but he that keepeth company with harlots
spendeth his substance.

4 The king by judgment establisheth the land:
but he that receiveth gifts overthroweth it.

5 A man that flattereth his neighbour
spreadeth a net for his feet.

6 In the transgression of an evil man there is a snare:
but the righteous doth sing and rejoice.

7 The righteous considereth the cause of the poor:
but the wicked regardeth not to know it.

8 Scornful men bring a city into a snare:
but wise men turn away wrath.

9 If a wise man contendeth with a foolish man,
whether he rage or laugh, there is no rest.

10 The bloodthirsty hate the upright:
but the just seek his soul.

11 A fool uttereth all his mind:
but a wise man keepeth it in till afterwards.

12 If a ruler hearken to lies,
all his servants are wicked.

13 The poor and the deceitful man meet together:
the Lord lighteneth both their eyes.

14 The king that faithfully judgeth the poor,
his throne shall be established for ever.

15 The rod and reproof give wisdom:
but a child left to himself
bringeth his mother to shame.

16 When the wicked are multiplied,
transgression increaseth:
but the righteous shall see their fall.

17 Correct thy son, and he shall give thee rest;
yea, he shall give delight unto thy soul.

18 Where there is no vision, the people perish:
but he that keepeth the law, happy is he.

19 A servant will not be corrected by words:
for though he understand he will not answer.

20 Seest thou a man that is hasty in his words?
There is more hope of a fool than of him.

21 He that delicately bringeth up
his servant from a child
shall have him become his son at the length.

22 An angry man stirreth up strife,
and a furious man aboundeth in transgression.

23 A man's pride shall bring him low:
but honour shall uphold the humble in spirit.

[24] Whoso is partner with a thief hateth his own soul:
he heareth cursing, and bewrayeth it not.

[25] The fear of man bringeth a snare:
but whoso putteth his trust in the Lord
shall be safe.

[26] Many seek the ruler's favour;
but every man's judgment
cometh from the Lord.

[27] An unjust man is an abomination to the just:
and he that is upright in the way
is abomination to the wicked.

30 The words of Agur the son of Jakeh, even the prophecy:
the man spake unto Ithiel, even unto Ithiel and Ucal,

[2] 'Surely I am more brutish than any man,
and have not the understanding of a man.
[3] I neither learned wisdom,
nor have the knowledge of the holy.
[4] Who hath ascended up into heaven, or descended?
Who hath gathered the wind in his fists?
Who hath bound the waters in a garment?
Who hath established all the ends of the earth?
What is his name, and what is his son's name,
if thou canst tell?

5 'Every word of God is pure;
he is a shield unto them
that put their trust in him.
6 Add thou not unto his words,
lest he reprove thee, and thou be found a liar.

7 'Two things have I required of thee;
deny me them not before I die:
8 remove far from me vanity and lies:
give me neither poverty nor riches;
feed me with food convenient for me:
9 lest I be full, and deny thee, and say,
"Who is the Lord?" or lest I be poor, and steal,
and take the name of my God in vain.

10 'Accuse not a servant unto his master,
lest he curse thee, and thou be found guilty.

11 'There is a generation that curseth their father,
and doth not bless their mother.
12 There is a generation that are pure in their own eyes,
and yet is not washed from their filthiness.
13 There is a generation, O how lofty are their eyes!
And their eyelids are lifted up.
14 There is a generation, whose teeth are as swords,
and their jaw teeth as knives,
to devour the poor from off the earth,
and the needy from among men.

15 'The horseleach hath two daughters, crying,
"Give, give."

There are three things that are never satisfied,
yea, four things say not, "It is enough."
16 The grave; and the barren womb;
the earth that is not filled with water;
and the fire that saith not, "It is enough."

17 'The eye that mocketh at his father,
and despiseth to obey his mother,
the ravens of the valley shall pick it out,
and the young eagles shall eat it.

18 There be three things which are too wonderful for me
yea, four which I know not:
19 the way of an eagle in the air;
the way of a serpent upon a rock;
the way of a ship in the midst of the sea;
and the way of a man with a maid.

20 'Such is the way of an adulterous woman;
she eateth, and wipeth her mouth, and saith,
"I have done no wickedness."

21 'For three things the earth is disquieted,
and for four which it cannot bear:
22 for a servant when he reigneth;
and a fool when he is filled with meat;

23 for an odious woman when she is married;
and an handmaid that is heir to her mistress.

24 'There be four things
which are little upon the earth,
but they are exceeding wise:
25 the ants are a people not strong,
yet they prepare their meat in the summer;
26 the conies are but a feeble folk,
yet make they their houses in the rocks;
27 the locusts have no king,
yet go they forth all of them by bands;
28 the spider taketh hold with her hands,
and is in kings' palaces.

29 There be three things which go well,
yea, four are comely in going:
30 a lion which is strongest among beasts,
and turneth not away for any;
31 a greyhound; an he-goat also;
and a king, against whom there is no rising up.

32 If thou hast done foolishly in lifting up thyself,
or if thou hast thought evil,
lay thine hand upon thy mouth.
33 Surely the churning of milk bringeth forth butter,
and the wringing of the nose bringeth forth blood:
so the forcing of wrath bringeth forth strife.'

31 The words of king Lemuel, the prophecy that his mother taught him.

[2] What, my son? And what, the son of my womb?
And what, the son of my vows?
[3] Give not thy strength unto women,
nor thy ways to that which destroyeth kings.

[4] It is not for kings, O Lemuel,
it is not for kings to drink wine;
nor for princes strong drink:
[5] lest they drink, and forget the law,
and pervert the judgment of any of the afflicted.
[6] Give strong drink unto him that is ready to perish,
and wine unto those that be of heavy hearts.
[7] Let him drink, and forget his poverty,
and remember his misery no more.

[8] Open thy mouth for the dumb
in the cause of all
such as are appointed to destruction.
[9] Open thy mouth, judge righteously,
and plead the cause of the poor and needy.

[10] Who can find a virtuous woman?
For her price is far above rubies.
[11] The heart of her husband
doth safely trust in her,
so that he shall have no need of spoil.

12 She will do him good and not evil
all the days of her life.
13 She seeketh wool, and flax,
and worketh willingly with her hands.
14 She is like the merchants' ships;
she bringeth her food from afar.
15 She riseth also while it is yet night,
and giveth meat to her household,
and a portion to her maidens.
16 She considereth a field, and buyeth it:
with the fruit of her hands
she planteth a vineyard.
17 She girdeth her loins with strength,
and strengtheneth her arms.
18 She perceiveth that her merchandise is good:
her candle goeth not out by night.
19 She layeth her hands to the spindle,
and her hands hold the distaff.
20 She stretcheth out her hand to the poor;
yea, she reacheth forth her hands to the needy.
21 She is not afraid of the snow for her household:
for all her household are clothed with scarlet.
22 She maketh herself coverings of tapestry;
her clothing is silk and purple.
23 Her husband is known in the gates,
when he sitteth among the elders of the land.
24 She maketh fine linen, and selleth it;

and delivereth girdles unto the merchant.
25 Strength and honour are her clothing;
and she shall rejoice in time to come.
26 She openeth her mouth with wisdom;
and in her tongue is the law of kindness.
27 She looketh well to the ways of her household,
and eateth not the bread of idleness.
28 Her children arise up, and call her blessed;
her husband also, and he praiseth her.
29 Many daughters have done virtuously,
but thou excellest them all.
30 Favour is deceitful, and beauty is vain:
but a woman that feareth the Lord,
she shall be praised.
31 Give her of the fruit of her hands;
and let her own works praise her in the gates.

titles in the series

genesis – *introduced by e. l. doctorow*
exodus – *introduced by david grossman*
job – *introduced by charles frazier*
selections from the book of psalms – *introduced by bono*
proverbs – *introduced by charles johnson*
ecclesiastes – *introduced by doris lessing*
matthew – *introduced by francisco goldman*
mark – *introduced by barry hannah*
luke – *introduced by thomas cahill*
john – *introduced by darcey steinke*
corinthians – *introduced by fay weldon*
revelation – *introduced by kathleen norris*

ecclesiastes

ecclesiastes

or, the preacher

authorized king james version

grove press
new york

with an introduction by | doris lessing

The Pocket Canons were originally published in the U.K. in 1998 by Canongate Books, Ltd.
Published simultaneously in Canada
Printed in the United States of America

FIRST AMERICAN EDITION

Copyright information is on file with the Library of Congress
ISBN 0-8021-3614-1

Design by Paddy Cramsie

Grove Press
841 Broadway
New York, NY 10003

99 00 01 02 10 9 8 7 6 5 4 3 2 1

a note about pocket canons

The Authorized King James Version of the Bible, translated between 1603 and 1611, coincided with an extraordinary flowering of English literature. This version, more than any other, and possibly more than any other work in history, has had an influence in shaping the language we speak and write today. Presenting individual books from the Bible as separate volumes, as they were originally conceived, encourages the reader to approach them as literary works in their own right.

The first twelve books in this series encompass categories as diverse as history, fiction, philosophy, love poetry, and law. Each Pocket Canon also has its own introduction, specially commissioned from an impressive range of writers, which provides a personal interpretation of the text and explores its contemporary relevance.

Doris Lessing was born of British parents in Persia in 1919 and was taken to Southern Rhodesia when she was five. She arrived in England in 1949 with her first novel, The Grass is Singing, *which was published in 1950. Since then her international reputation, not only as a novelist but also as a non-fiction and short story writer, has flourished. She has won countless prizes and awards and some of her most celebrated novels include* The Golden Notebook, The Summer Before Dark, Memoirs of a Survivor *and the* Martha Quest *series. Her most recent works include* African Laughter *and two volumes of her autobiography,* Under My Skin *and* Walking in the Shade.

introduction by doris lessing

It is something of an undertaking, to write even a few words about a text that has inspired mountains of exegetics, commentaries, analyses, over so many centuries, and in so many languages: and you have not read one word. Immodesty, it could be called, and when I allow myself to think about my audacity, I do feel a little breeze of elation which, considered, turns out to be a mild attack of panic. But most readers will be in the same innocent condition, if they have read *Ecclesiastes* at all. Once, and not so long ago, everybody in Britain and for that matter everyone in the Christian world, was subjected to that obligation, going to church, where every Sunday was heard the thundering magnificence of this prose, and so, ever after, they would have been able to identify the origin of phrases and sayings which are as much a part of our language as Shakespeare. These days, if someone hears, 'There is a time to be born and a time to die ...' they probably do think it is Shakespeare, since the Bible these days is the experience of so few. Ecclesiastes? Who's he! But an innocent, even an ignorant, reader may discover a good deal by using simple observation.

The book begins with a description, 'The words of the

Preacher, the son of David, king in Jerusalem.' That is to say, the words have been collected from notes, or memories, of the Preacher, by disciples or pupils or friends, and made into a whole: probably after he was dead. He did not himself make this book, and it is tempting to remember that he said, 'Of the making of books there is no end, and much study is a weariness of the flesh.' Other great teachers, such as Socrates, Jesus, Confucius, many others, refrained from making books and testaments, leaving this task to other people. Why did they not see the necessity to preserve their 'image' or to edit a testament to make sure that posterity would see them as they saw themselves? Was the reason that they knew their influence – what they said, how they lived – had impressed their pupils and their contemporaries so strongly in their lifetimes that written records were superfluous? I think it is worthwhile to at least consider this possibility.

It is not until the twelfth verse that we hear his own words, with 'I, the Preacher, was king over Israel, in Jerusalem.' He tells us he devoted himself to the acquisition of wisdom, which is the task given to the sons of men by God, but there was pain in it. 'For in much wisdom there is much grief; and he that increaseth knowledge increaseth sorrow.' So then he decided to experience pleasure and the satisfactions of worldly accomplishment. He built houses and planted gardens and vineyards and orchards; he made pools and streams; he acquired male and female servants and all kinds of possessions, and silver and gold, and male and female singers. Whatever he had a fancy to have – so he tells us – he got; he was like the people now who decide that they are going to have a good time and not care about serious things. But then, having done all that, he had a good long look at his life and his property and his riches and knew it was all vanity and vexation of spirit (vanity in the sense of futility, illusion) and that happiness is not to be found in pleasure and that wisdom is better – making a full circle, one might say, if it were not that even a casual reading reveals that verse by verse this is contradictory stuff, a confusing message – if he ever intended what he said to be considered as a message. What we have here is sayings from different occasions, and different contexts, and with different people. There is a deep and terrible need in us all to systematise and make order, and perhaps it is helpful to imagine this material in a pre-book stage, when it was scribbled notes made when listening to the Preacher; or what happened when pupils met after he was dead: 'What do you remember of him? And you? And you?'

What unites the book, is precisely that this is some of the most wonderful English prose ever written. My father, young at a time when not to accept church religion was to invite persecution and social ostracism, said that Sundays, when he had to go to church three times, and also to Sunday school, was like a great black hole every week, but later said that it was listening to the prose of the Bible and the prayer book that taught him to love language and good literature. Generations of writers have been influenced by the rhythms of the Bible, which may be observed in the prose of the best of them – as well as the worst – and we are very much the poorer because the Bible is no longer a book to be found in every home, and heard every week.

We should remember that this prose was written to be heard as much as to be read. The difference between now and then is emphasised by the fact that people used to say, not, 'Let us go and see a play', but 'Let us hear a play'. Shakespeare was not long dead. Surely the translators of this Bible had that sea of sound in their ears, or had been influenced by it. Ears expected to be royally fed.

It was Latin that had been heard in churches. That means that for centuries the common people who did not know Latin did not understand what was going on up there between the priests and God. It is safe to assume they weren't listening much. And now, suddenly, with the translations into English, there was this feast of sound.

From the very first verse of *Ecclesiastes* you are carried along on a running tide of sound, incantatory, almost hypnotic, and it is easy to imagine yourself sitting among this man's pupils, listening to – for instance, 'Remember now thy creator in the days of thy youth, while the evil days come not, nor the years draw nigh when thou shalt say, I have no pleasure in them.' Your ears are entranced, but at the same time you are very much alert. You have to be old to understand that verse, to see your whole life, from early heedlessness to present regret for heedlessness; you find yourself drifting off into speculation. Was this particular admonition addressed to young people, to remind them that old age will come for them too? Or reserved for grey heads who would hear it with the ears of experience? Or flung out in an assembly, to be caught by anyone who could – who had the ears to hear, as Jesus put it.

Towards the end, verse 9 of chapter 12, suddenly it is not his voice, not 'I' speaking, and we are back to description; '... because the preacher was wise, he still taught the people knowledge; yea, he gave good heed, and sought out, and set in order many proverbs.' That is how one contributor to the book saw what Ecclesiastes was doing. And, yet again, we are reading a document that to us is ancient, but it records people who saw themselves as successors in a long line, stretching back into their antiquity.

Between the man, Ecclesiastes, and ourselves, are many veils. One is translation. Over the exact meaning of a word or phrase scholars have laboured and many sermons have been delivered in churches. That word 'Preacher' for instance. In what other ways could the original have been translated? 'Preacher' is so much a concept from organised Christianity, which spawned preachers by the thousand men (and now women) standing in pulpits to expound their views of life to a congregation, and their quite amazing intimacy with God's thinking. Should that 'Preacher' have been 'Teacher'? – a very different thing.

Spiritual teachers were and are part of the Eastern traditions, and that they are not part of ours is precisely because the concept of 'Preacher' was imposed instead – not the aspiration towards the experiential Path to God (or Jehovah, or Allah, or Buddha) but a passive congregation being lectured by God's Spokesman. Or Spokeswoman. *Do what you are told* – by priests, by mullahs.

Another barrier is the nature of the people who recorded the words, or who remembered them. We all know that what we say to a friend will be filtered through the character and experience of that person, and it is safe to assume that Ecclesiastes' pupils were not on the same level as he was, any more that Jesus's disciples were on his level, and that they, like us, had to strain to understand a nobility of mind that was beyond their ordinary selves. There is a little cry of despair in this text, the tale of a small city, besieged by a great king; a poor wise man saved the city, and yet no one remembered the poor man. 'Wisdom is better than strength' is the conclusion, 'nevertheless, the poor man's wisdom is despised and his words not heard.'

There is an interesting deduction or two to be made. This man was the son of David, that is to say, of the Royal House of David, at a time when kings were considered to be God-chosen and God-inspired. The word 'ecclesiastic' now means a clergyman, or describes a clergyman, or what appertains to churches. There is a little encapsulated history here: this 'Preacher' was no churchman, and nowhere does he mention a church: thus do the living springs of knowledge, of wisdom, become captured by institutions, and by churches of various kinds.

ecclesiastes or, the preacher

The words of the Preacher, the son of David, king in Jerusalem.

2 'Vanity of vanities,' saith the Preacher,
'Vanity of vanities; all is vanity.
3 What profit hath a man of all his labour
which he taketh under the sun?
4 One generation passeth away,
and another generation cometh,
but the earth abideth for ever.
5 The sun also ariseth, and the sun goeth down,
and hasteth to his place where he arose.
6 The wind goeth toward the south,
and turneth about unto the north;
it whirleth about continually,
and the wind returneth again
according to his circuits.
7 All the rivers run into the sea; yet the sea is not full;
unto the place from whence the rivers come,
thither they return again.
8 All things are full of labour; man cannot utter it.
The eye is not satisfied with seeing,
nor the ear filled with hearing.
9 The thing that hath been, it is that which shall be;
and that which is done is that which shall be done;

and there is no new thing under the sun.
10 Is there any thing whereof it may be said,
"See, this is new"?
It hath been already of old time,
which was before us.
11 There is no remembrance of former things;
neither shall there be any remembrance
of things that are to come
with those that shall come after.
12 I the Preacher was king over Israel in Jerusalem.
13 And I gave my heart to seek and search out
by wisdom concerning all things
that are done under heaven;
this sore travail hath God given
to the sons of man to be exercised therewith.
14 I have seen all the works that are done under the sun;
and, behold, all is vanity and vexation of spirit.
15 That which is crooked cannot be made straight,
and that which is wanting cannot be numbered.
16 I communed with mine own heart, saying,
"Lo, I am come to great estate,
and have gotten more wisdom than all they
that have been before me in Jerusalem;
yea, my heart had great experience
of wisdom and knowledge."
17 And I gave my heart to know wisdom,
and to know madness and folly.
I perceived that this also is vexation of spirit.
18 For in much wisdom is much grief;
and he that increaseth knowledge increaseth sorrow.

2

1 I said in mine heart,
"Go to now, I will prove thee with mirth,
therefore enjoy pleasure,"
and, behold, this also is vanity.
2 I said of laughter, "It is mad"
and of mirth, "What doeth it?"
3 I sought in mine heart to give myself unto wine,
yet acquainting mine heart with wisdom;
and to lay hold on folly,
till I might see what was that good
for the sons of men,
which they should do under the heaven
all the days of their life.
4 I made me great works; I builded me houses;
I planted me vineyards:
5 I made me gardens and orchards,
and I planted trees in them of all kind of fruits.
6 I made me pools of water, to water therewith
the wood that bringeth forth trees.
7 I got me servants and maidens,
and had servants born in my house;
also I had great possessions
of great and small cattle
above all that were in Jerusalem before me.
8 I gathered me also silver and gold, and
the peculiar treasure of kings and of the provinces.
I gat me men singers and women singers,
and the delights of the sons of men,
as musical instruments, and that of all sorts.
9 So I was great, and increased more

than all that were before me in Jerusalem;
also my wisdom remained with me.
10 And whatsoever mine eyes desired
I kept not from them,
I withheld not my heart from any joy,
for my heart rejoiced in all my labour,
and this was my portion of all my labour.
11 Then I looked on all the works
that my hands had wrought,
and on the labour that I had laboured to do,
and, behold, all was vanity and vexation of spirit,
and there was no profit under the sun.
12 And I turned myself to behold wisdom,
and madness, and folly:
for what can the man do
that cometh after the king?
Even that which hath been already done.
13 Then I saw that wisdom excelleth folly,
as far as light excelleth darkness.
14 The wise man's eyes are in his head;
but the fool walketh in darkness:
and I myself perceived also
that one event happeneth to them all.
15 Then said I in my heart,
"As it happeneth to the fool,
so it happeneth even to me;
and why was I then more wise?"
Then I said in my heart, that this also is vanity.
16 For there is no remembrance of the wise
more than of the fool for ever;

seeing that which now is in the days to come
shall all be forgotten.
And how dieth the wise man?
As the fool.
17 Therefore I hated life;
because the work that is wrought under the sun
is grievous unto me,
for all is vanity and vexation of spirit.
18 Yea, I hated all my labour
which I had taken under the sun,
because I should leave it unto the man
that shall be after me.
19 And who knoweth whether he shall be
a wise man or a fool?
Yet shall he have rule over all my labour
wherein I have laboured,
and wherein I have shewed myself
wise under the sun. This is also vanity.
20 Therefore I went about to cause my heart to despair
of all the labour which I took under the sun.
21 For there is a man whose labour is in wisdom,
and in knowledge, and in equity;
yet to a man that hath not laboured therein
shall he leave it for his portion.
This also is vanity and a great evil.
22 For what hath man of all his labour,
and of the vexation of his heart,
wherein he hath laboured under the sun?
23 For all his days are sorrows, and his travail grief;
yea, his heart taketh not rest in the night.

This is also vanity.
24 There is nothing better for a man,
than that he should eat and drink,
and that he should make his soul
enjoy good in his labour.
This also I saw,
that it was from the hand of God.
25 For who can eat,
or who else can hasten hereunto, more than I?
26 For God giveth to a man that is good in his sight
wisdom, and knowledge, and joy,
but to the sinner he giveth travail,
to gather and to heap up,
that he may give to him
that is good before God.
This also is vanity and vexation of spirit.

3 [1]To every thing there is a season,
and a time to every purpose under the heaven:
2 a time to be born, and a time to die;
a time to plant, and a time to pluck up
that which is planted;
3 a time to kill, and a time to heal;
a time to break down, and a time to build up;
4 a time to weep, and a time to laugh;
a time to mourn, and a time to dance;
5 a time to cast away stones,
and a time to gather stones together;
a time to embrace,
and a time to refrain from embracing;

6 a time to get, and a time to lose;
a time to keep, and a time to cast away;
7 a time to rend, and a time to sew;
a time to keep silence, and a time to speak;
8 a time to love, and a time to hate;
a time of war, and a time of peace.
9 What profit hath he
that worketh in that wherein he laboureth?
10 I have seen the travail,
which God hath given to the sons of men
to be exercised in it.
11 He hath made every thing beautiful in his time;
also he hath set the world in their heart,
so that no man can find out the work
that God maketh from the beginning to the end.
12 I know that there is no good in them,
but for a man to rejoice,
and to do good in his life.
13 And also that every man should eat and drink,
and enjoy the good of all his labour,
it is the gift of God.
14 I know that, whatsoever God doeth,
it shall be for ever; nothing can be put to it,
nor any thing taken from it;
and God doeth it,
that men should fear before him.
15 That which hath been is now;
and that which is to be hath already been;
and God requireth that which is past.
16 And moreover I saw under the sun

the place of judgment,
that wickedness was there;
and the place of righteousness,
that iniquity was there.
17 I said in mine heart,
"God shall judge the righteous and the wicked,
for there is a time there
for every purpose and for every work."
18 I said in mine heart
concerning the estate of the sons of men,
that God might manifest them,
and that they might see
that they themselves are beasts.
19 For that which befalleth the sons of men
befalleth beasts;
even one thing befalleth them.
As the one dieth, so dieth the other;
yea, they have all one breath;
so that a man hath no preeminence above a beast,
for all is vanity.
20 All go unto one place; all are of the dust,
and all turn to dust again.
21 Who knoweth the spirit of man that goeth upward,
and the spirit of the beast
that goeth downward to the earth?
22 Wherefore I perceive that there is nothing better,
than that a man should rejoice in his own works,
for that is his portion,
for who shall bring him to see
what shall be after him?

4 ‘So I returned, and considered all the oppressions
that are done under the sun;
and behold the tears of such as were oppressed,
and they had no comforter;
and on the side of their oppressors
there was power;
but they had no comforter.
2 Wherefore I praised the dead which are already dead
more than the living which are yet alive.
3 Yea, better is he than both they,
which hath not yet been,
who hath not seen the evil work
that is done under the sun.
4 Again, I considered all travail, and every right work,
that for this a man is envied of his neighbour.
This is also vanity and vexation of spirit.
5 The fool foldeth his hands together,
and eateth his own flesh.
6 Better is an handful with quietness,
than both the hands full
with travail and vexation of spirit.
7 Then I returned, and I saw vanity under the sun.
8 There is one alone, and there is not a second;
yea, he hath neither child nor brother;
yet is there no end of all his labour;
neither is his eye satisfied with riches;
neither saith he, “For whom do I labour,
and bereave my soul of good?”
This is also vanity, yea, it is a sore travail.
9 Two are better than one,

because they have a good reward for their labour.
10 For if they fall, the one will lift up his fellow,
but woe to him that is alone when he falleth;
for he hath not another to help him up.
11 Again, if two lie together, then they have heat,
but how can one be warm alone?
12 And if one prevail against him,
two shall withstand him;
and a threefold cord is not quickly broken.
13 Better is a poor and a wise child
than an old and foolish king,
who will no more be admonished.
14 For out of prison he cometh to reign;
whereas also he that is born in his kingdom
becometh poor.
15 I considered all the living which walk under the sun,
with the second child
that shall stand up in his stead.
16 There is no end of all the people,
even of all that have been before them;
they also that come after shall not rejoice in him.
Surely this also is vanity and vexation of spirit.

5 1 Keep thy foot when thou goest to the house of God,
and be more ready to hear,
than to give the sacrifice of fools,
for they consider not that they do evil.
2 Be not rash with thy mouth,
and let not thine heart be hasty
to utter any thing before God,

for God is in heaven, and thou upon earth;
therefore let thy words be few.
3 For a dream cometh
through the multitude of business;
and a fool's voice
is known by multitude of words.
4 When thou vowest a vow unto God,
defer not to pay it;
for he hath no pleasure in fools.
Pay that which thou hast vowed.
5 Better is it that thou shouldest not vow,
than that thou shouldest vow and not pay.
6 Suffer not thy mouth to cause thy flesh to sin;
neither say thou before the angel,
that it was an error.
Wherefore should God be angry at thy voice,
and destroy the work of thine hands?
7 For in the multitude of dreams and many words
there are also divers vanities, but fear thou God.
8 If thou seest the oppression of the poor,
and violent perverting of judgment
and justice in a province,
marvel not at the matter,
for he that is higher than the highest regardeth;
and there be higher than they.
9 Moreover the profit of the earth is for all;
the king himself is served by the field.
10 He that loveth silver shall not be satisfied with silver;
nor he that loveth abundance with increase;
this is also vanity.

11 When goods increase,
they are increased that eat them,
and what good is there to the owners thereof,
saving the beholding of them with their eyes?
12 The sleep of a labouring man is sweet,
whether he eat little or much,
but the abundance of the rich
will not suffer him to sleep.
13 There is a sore evil which I have seen
under the sun, namely,
riches kept for the owners thereof to their hurt.
14 But those riches perish by evil travail,
and he begetteth a son,
and there is nothing in his hand.
15 As he came forth of his mother's womb,
naked shall he return to go as he came,
and shall take nothing of his labour,
which he may carry away in his hand.
16 And this also is a sore evil,
that in all points as he came, so shall he go,
and what profit hath he
that hath laboured for the wind?
17 All his days also he eateth in darkness,
and he hath much sorrow and wrath
with his sickness.
18 Behold that which I have seen;
it is good and comely for one to eat and to drink,
and to enjoy the good of all his labour
that he taketh under the sun
all the days of his life, which God giveth him,

for it is his portion.
19 Every man also to whom God hath given
riches and wealth,
and hath given him power to eat thereof,
and to take his portion, and to rejoice in his labour;
this is the gift of God.
20 For he shall not much remember the days of his life;
because God answereth him in the joy of his heart.

6

1 There is an evil which I have seen under the sun,
and it is common among men:
2 A man to whom God hath given riches,
wealth, and honour,
so that he wanteth nothing for his soul
of all that he desireth,
yet God giveth him not power to eat thereof,
but a stranger eateth it;
this is vanity, and it is an evil disease.
3 If a man beget an hundred children,
and live many years,
so that the days of his years be many,
and his soul be not filled with good,
and also that he have no burial,
I say, that an untimely birth is better than he.
4 For he cometh in with vanity,
and departeth in darkness,
and his name shall be covered with darkness.
5 Moreover he hath not seen the sun,
nor known any thing;
this hath more rest than the other.

6 Yea, though he live a thousand years twice told,
yet hath he seen no good:
do not all go to one place?
7 All the labour of man is for his mouth,
and yet the appetite is not filled.
8 For what hath the wise more than the fool?
What hath the poor,
that knoweth to walk before the living?
9 Better is the sight of the eyes
than the wandering of the desire;
this is also vanity and vexation of spirit.
10 That which hath been is named already,
and it is known that it is man;
neither may he contend with him
that is mightier than he.
11 Seeing there be many things that increase vanity,
what is man the better?
12 For who knoweth what is good for man in this life,
all the days of his vain life
which he spendeth as a shadow?
For who can tell a man
what shall be after him under the sun?

7

1 A good name is better than precious ointment;
and the day of death than the day of one's birth.
2 It is better to go to the house of mourning,
than to go to the house of feasting,
for that is the end of all men;
and the living will lay it to his heart.
3 Sorrow is better than laughter,

for by the sadness of the countenance
the heart is made better.
4 The heart of the wise is in the house of mourning;
but the heart of fools is in the house of mirth.
5 It is better to hear the rebuke of the wise,
than for a man to hear the song of fools.
6 For as the crackling of thorns under a pot,
so is the laughter of the fool; this also is vanity.
7 Surely oppression maketh a wise man mad;
and a gift destroyeth the heart.
8 Better is the end of a thing than the beginning thereof:
and the patient in spirit
is better than the proud in spirit.
9 Be not hasty in thy spirit to be angry,
for anger resteth in the bosom of fools.
10 Say not thou, "What is the cause
that the former days were better than these?"
for thou dost not enquire wisely concerning this.
11 Wisdom is good with an inheritance,
and by it there is profit to them that see the sun.
12 For wisdom is a defence, and money is a defence,
but the excellency of knowledge is,
that wisdom giveth life to them that have it.
13 Consider the work of God,
for who can make that straight,
which he hath made crooked?
14 In the day of prosperity be joyful,
but in the day of adversity consider:
God also hath set the one over against the other,
to the end that man should find nothing after him.

15 All things have I seen in the days of my vanity:
there is a just man that perisheth
in his righteousness,
and there is a wicked man
that prolongeth his life in his wickedness.
16 Be not righteous over much;
neither make thyself over wise;
why shouldest thou destroy thyself?
17 Be not over much wicked, neither be thou foolish;
why shouldest thou die before thy time?
18 It is good that thou shouldest take hold of this;
yea, also from this withdraw not thine hand,
for he that feareth God
shall come forth of them all.
19 Wisdom strengtheneth the wise
more than ten mighty men which are in the city.
20 For there is not a just man upon earth,
that doeth good, and sinneth not.
21 Also take no heed unto all words that are spoken,
lest thou hear thy servant curse thee:
22 For oftentimes also thine own heart knoweth
that thou thyself likewise hast cursed others.
23 All this have I proved by wisdom;
I said, "I will be wise," but it was far from me.
24 That which is far off, and exceeding deep,
who can find it out?
25 I applied mine heart to know, and to search,
and to seek out wisdom, and the reason of things,
and to know the wickedness of folly,
even of foolishness and madness.

26 And I find more bitter than death the woman,
whose heart is snares and nets,
and her hands as bands;
whoso pleaseth God shall escape from her;
but the sinner shall be taken by her.'
27 'Behold, this have I found,' saith the Preacher,
'counting one by one, to find out the account,
28 which yet my soul seeketh, but I find not.
One man among a thousand have I found;
but a woman among all those have I not found.
29 Lo, this only have I found,
that God hath made man upright;
but they have sought out many inventions.

8 'Who is as the wise man?
And who knoweth the interpretation of a thing?
A man's wisdom maketh his face to shine,
and the boldness of his face shall be changed.
2 I counsel thee to keep the king's commandment,
and that in regard of the oath of God.
3 Be not hasty to go out of his sight:
stand not in an evil thing;
for he doeth whatsoever pleaseth him.
4 Where the word of a king is, there is power,
and who may say unto him, "What doest thou?"
5 Whoso keepeth the commandment
shall feel no evil thing and a wise man's heart
discerneth both time and judgment.
6 Because to every purpose there is time and judgment,
therefore the misery of man is great upon him.

26 And I find more bitter than death the woman,
whose heart is snares and nets,
and her hands as bands:
whoso pleaseth God shall escape from her;
but the sinner shall be taken by her.
27 Behold, this have I found, saith the Preacher,
counting one by one, to find out the account:
28 which yet my soul seeketh, but I find not:
one man among a thousand have I found;
but a woman among all those have I not found.
29 Lo, this only have I found,
that God hath made man upright;
but they have sought out many inventions.

8

Who is as the wise man?
and who knoweth the interpretation of a thing?
A man's wisdom maketh his face to shine,
and the boldness of his face shall be changed.
2 I counsel thee to keep the king's commandment,
and that in regard of the oath of God.
3 Be not hasty to go out of his sight:
stand not in an evil thing;
for he doeth whatsoever pleaseth him.
4 Where the word of a king is, there is power:
and who may say unto him, What doest thou?
5 Whoso keepeth the commandment shall feel no evil thing:
and a wise man's heart discerneth both time and judgment.
6 Because to every purpose there is time and judgment,
therefore the misery of man is great upon him.

7 For he knoweth not that which shall be;
for who can tell him when it shall be?
8 There is no man that hath power over the spirit
to retain the spirit;
neither hath he power in the day of death,
and there is no discharge in that war;
neither shall wickedness deliver those
that are given to it.
9 All this have I seen, and applied my heart
unto every work that is done under the sun.
There is a time wherein
one man ruleth over another to his own hurt.
10 And so I saw the wicked buried,
who had come and gone from the place of the holy,
and they were forgotten in the city
where they had so done; this is also vanity.
11 Because sentence against an evil work
is not executed speedily,
therefore the heart of the sons of men
is fully set in them to do evil.
12 Though a sinner do evil an hundred times,
and his days be prolonged,
yet surely I know that it shall be well
with them that fear God, which fear before him.
13 But it shall not be well with the wicked,
neither shall he prolong his days,
which are as a shadow;
because he feareth not before God.
14 There is a vanity which is done upon the earth;
that there be just men unto whom it happeneth

according to the work of the wicked;
again, there be wicked men, to whom it happeneth
according to the work of the righteous;
I said that this also is vanity.
15 Then I commended mirth,
because a man hath no better thing under the sun,
than to eat, and to drink, and to be merry:
for that shall abide with him
of his labour the days of his life,
which God giveth him under the sun.
16 When I applied mine heart to know wisdom,
and to see the business that is done upon the earth
(for also there is that neither day
nor night seeth sleep with his eyes),
17 then I beheld all the work of God,
that a man cannot find out the work
that is done under the sun:
because though a man labour to seek it out,
yet he shall not find it;
yea further; though a wise man think to know it,
yet shall he not be able to find it.

9 1 For all this I considered in my heart
even to declare all this, that the righteous,
and the wise, and their works,
are in the hand of God;
no man knoweth either love or hatred
by all that is before them.
2 All things come alike to all;
there is one event to the righteous,

and to the wicked;
to the good and to the clean, and to the unclean;
to him that sacrificeth,
and to him that sacrificeth not:
as is the good, so is the sinner;
and he that sweareth, as he that feareth an oath.
3 This is an evil among all things
that are done under the sun,
that there is one event unto all;
yea, also the heart of the sons of men is full of evil,
and madness is in their heart while they live,
and after that they go to the dead.
4 For to him that is joined to all the living there is hope,
for a living dog is better than a dead lion.
5 For the living know that they shall die,
but the dead know not any thing,
neither have they any more a reward;
for the memory of them is forgotten.
6 Also their love, and their hatred, and their envy,
is now perished;
neither have they any more a portion
for ever in any thing that is done under the sun.
7 Go thy way, eat thy bread with joy,
and drink thy wine with a merry heart;
for God now accepteth thy works.
8 Let thy garments be always white;
and let thy head lack no ointment.
9 Live joyfully with the wife whom thou lovest
all the days of the life of thy vanity,
which he hath given thee under the sun,

all the days of thy vanity,
for that is thy portion in this life,
and in thy labour which thou takest under the sun.
10 Whatsoever thy hand findeth to do,
do it with thy might;
for there is no work, nor device,
nor knowledge, nor wisdom, in the grave,
whither thou goest.
11 I returned, and saw under the sun,
that the race is not to the swift,
nor the battle to the strong,
neither yet bread to the wise,
nor yet riches to men of understanding,
nor yet favour to men of skill;
but time and chance happeneth to them all.
12 For man also knoweth not his time,
as the fishes that are taken in an evil net,
and as the birds that are caught in the snare;
so are the sons of men snared in an evil time,
when it falleth suddenly upon them.
13 This wisdom have I seen also under the sun,
and it seemed great unto me.
14 There was a little city, and few men within it;
and there came a great king against it,
and besieged it,
and built great bulwarks against it.
15 Now there was found in it a poor wise man,
and he by his wisdom delivered the city;
yet no man remembered that same poor man.
16 Then said I, "Wisdom is better than strength:

nevertheless the poor man's wisdom is despised,
and his words are not heard."
17 The words of wise men are heard in quiet more
than the cry of him that ruleth among fools.
18 Wisdom is better than weapons of war;
but one sinner destroyeth much good.

10

1 Dead flies cause the ointment of the apothecary
to send forth a stinking savour;
so doth a little folly him
that is in reputation for wisdom and honour.
2 A wise man's heart is at his right hand;
but a fool's heart at his left.
3 Yea also, when he that is a fool walketh by the way,
his wisdom faileth him,
and he saith to every one that he is a fool.
4 If the spirit of the ruler rise up against thee,
leave not thy place,
for yielding pacifieth great offences.
5 There is an evil which I have seen under the sun,
as an error which proceedeth from the ruler:
6 folly is set in great dignity,
and the rich sit in low place.
7 I have seen servants upon horses,
and princes walking as servants upon the earth.
8 He that diggeth a pit shall fall into it;
and whoso breaketh an hedge,
a serpent shall bite him.
9 Whoso removeth stones shall be hurt therewith;
and he that cleaveth wood

shall be endangered thereby.
10 If the iron be blunt, and he do not whet the edge,
then must he put to more strength,
but wisdom is profitable to direct.
11 Surely the serpent will bite without enchantment;
and a babbler is no better.
12 The words of a wise man's mouth are gracious;
but the lips of a fool will swallow up himself.
13 The beginning of the words of his mouth
is foolishness,
and the end of his talk is mischievous madness.
14 A fool also is full of words.
A man cannot tell what shall be;
and what shall be after him, who can tell him?
15 The labour of the foolish wearieth every one of them,
because he knoweth not how to go to the city.
16 Woe to thee, O land, when thy king is a child,
and thy princes eat in the morning!
17 Blessed art thou, O land,
when thy king is the son of nobles,
and thy princes eat in due season,
for strength, and not for drunkenness!
18 By much slothfulness the building decayeth;
and through idleness of the hands
the house droppeth through.
19 A feast is made for laughter,
and wine maketh merry,
but money answereth all things.
20 Curse not the king, no not in thy thought;
and curse not the rich in thy bedchamber,

for a bird of the air shall carry the voice,
and that which hath wings shall tell the matter.

11 [1]Cast thy bread upon the waters,
for thou shalt find it after many days.
[2]Give a portion to seven, and also to eight;
for thou knowest not what evil
shall be upon the earth.
[3]If the clouds be full of rain,
they empty themselves upon the earth,
and if the tree fall toward the south,
or toward the north,
in the place where the tree falleth, there it shall be.
[4]He that observeth the wind shall not sow;
and he that regardeth the clouds shall not reap.
[5]As thou knowest not what is the way of the spirit,
nor how the bones do grow
in the womb of her that is with child,
even so thou knowest not
the works of God who maketh all.
[6]In the morning sow thy seed,
and in the evening withhold not thine hand,
for thou knowest not whether shall prosper,
either this or that,
or whether they both shall be alike good.
[7]Truly the light is sweet, and a pleasant thing it is
for the eyes to behold the sun.
[8]But if a man live many years, and rejoice in them all,
yet let him remember the days of darkness,
for they shall be many.

All that cometh is vanity.
9 Rejoice, O young man, in thy youth;
and let thy heart cheer thee in the days of thy youth,
and walk in the ways of thine heart,
and in the sight of thine eyes:
but know thou, that for all these things
God will bring thee into judgment.
10 Therefore remove sorrow from thy heart,
and put away evil from thy flesh,
for childhood and youth are vanity.

12 1 Remember now thy Creator in the days of thy youth,
while the evil days come not,
nor the years draw nigh, when thou shalt say,
"I have no pleasure in them,"
2 while the sun, or the light, or the moon,
or the stars, be not darkened,
nor the clouds return after the rain;
3 in the day when the keepers of the house shall tremble,
and the strong men shall bow themselves,
and the grinders cease because they are few,
and those that look out of the windows
be darkened,
4 and the doors shall be shut in the streets,
when the sound of the grinding is low,
and he shall rise up at the voice of the bird,
and all the daughters of musick shall be brought low;
5 also when they shall be afraid of that which is high,
and fears shall be in the way,
and the almond tree shall flourish,

and the grasshopper shall be a burden,
and desire shall fail,
because man goeth to his long home,
and the mourners go about the streets;
6 or ever the silver cord be loosed,
or the golden bowl be broken,
or the pitcher be broken at the fountain,
or the wheel broken at the cistern.
7 Then shall the dust return to the earth as it was,
and the spirit shall return unto God who gave it.
8 Vanity of vanities,' saith the preacher. 'All is vanity.'
9 And moreover, because the preacher was wise,
he still taught the people knowledge;
yea, he gave good heed, and sought out,
and set in order many proverbs.
10 The preacher sought to find out acceptable words,
and that which was written was upright,
even words of truth.
11 The words of the wise are as goads,
and as nails fastened by the masters of assemblies,
which are given from one shepherd.
12 And further, by these, my son, be admonished;
of making many books there is no end;
and much study is a weariness of the flesh.
13 Let us hear the conclusion of the whole matter:
Fear God, and keep his commandments,
for this is the whole duty of man.
14 For God shall bring every work into judgment,
with every secret thing,
whether it be good, or whether it be evil.

titles in the series

genesis – *introduced by e. l. doctorow*
exodus – *introduced by david grossman*
job – *introduced by charles frazier*
selections from the book of psalms – *introduced by bono*
proverbs – *introduced by charles johnson*
ecclesiastes – *introduced by doris lessing*
matthew – *introduced by francisco goldman*
mark – *introduced by barry hannah*
luke – *introduced by thomas cahill*
john – *introduced by darcey steinke*
corinthians – *introduced by fay weldon*
revelation – *introduced by kathleen norris*

matthew

the gospel according to

matthew

authorized king james version

grove press
new york

with an introduction by | francisco goldman

The Pocket Canons were originally published in the U.K. in 1998 by Canongate Books, Ltd.
Published simultaneously in Canada
Printed in the United States of America

FIRST AMERICAN EDITION

Copyright information is on file with the Library of Congress
ISBN 0-8021-3616-8

Design by Paddy Cramsie

Grove Press
841 Broadway
New York, NY 10003

99 00 01 02 10 9 8 7 6 5 4 3 2 1

a note about pocket canons

The Authorized King James Version of the Bible, translated between 1603 and 1611, coincided with an extraordinary flowering of English literature. This version, more than any other, and possibly more than any other work in history, has had an influence in shaping the language we speak and write today. Presenting individual books from the Bible as separate volumes, as they were originally conceived, encourages the reader to approach them as literary works in their own right.

The first twelve books in this series encompass categories as diverse as history, fiction, philosophy, love poetry, and law. Each Pocket Canon also has its own introduction, specially commissioned from an impressive range of writers, which provides a personal interpretation of the text and explores its contemporary relevance.

Francisco Goldman is the author of the novels The Long Night of White Chickens, *which won the Sue Kaufman Prize for First Fiction from the American Academy of Arts & Letters, and* The Ordinary Seaman, *which was a finalist for the IMPAC Dublin International Literary Prize. Both novels were short-listed for the PEN/Faulkner Award. He has also been awarded a Guggenheim Fellowship. He divides his time between Brooklyn and Mexico City*

introduction by francisco goldman

> *Spina proposed various goals. One was to form gatherings for reading the Bible. Another—which must have seemed quite strange—was to practice Christianity.*
>
> —*Jorge Luis Borges,*
> *"German Literature in the Age of Bach"*

In Gabriel García Márquez's *Love in the Time of Cholera,* Dr. Juvenal Urbino teaches his insolent parrot "selected passages from the Gospel according to Saint Matthew." Climbing into the upper branches of a mango tree to rescue the parrot, the elderly doctor plunges to his death. So the parrot is a harbinger of chaos and death, but the doctor's demise also sets in motion the novel's extraordinary love story. The metaphorical choice of putting the Gospel of Saint Matthew in the mouth of a Caribbean parrot is apt in more ways than one.

Without a doubt, the greatest event of the millennium now ending was the discovery and conquest of the New World. The Spanish historian Francisco López de Gomara called it "the most major thing since the creation of the world, only excepting the incarnation and death of He who created it." The story of the Bible among us in the Americas—and I speak as an American, the son of immigrants to the United States, a Russian-Jewish father and a Guatemalan-Catholic mother—is of course completely different from its story in the Old World. The Old and New Testaments evolved over millennia there alongside the civilizations that wrote them and formed themselves according to their teachings, but in the Americas, the Bible arrived all at once, a completed text, undoubtedly spreading chaos and death, but also beauty and love and mystery.

The classic narrative of the first prolonged encounter between Europeans and *los naturales*, the Indians, is *The True History of the Conquest of New Spain*, written by Bernal Díaz del Castillo, who marched with Hernán Cortés through Mexico. As the relatively small army of conquistadores marched from village to village on their fateful way to the bloody denouement in the capital of the Aztec Empire, they encountered a civilization clearly in the grip of Satan, one that worshiped horrific "dragon-like" stone idols through bloody human sacrifice and practiced cannibalism—practiced it with gluttonous enthusiasm. The native priests were smeared in blood and reeked of human carrion, wore their hair down to their waists, and liked to sodomize each other in their sacred pyramid sanctums, while Indian caciques offered their aristocratic virgin young daughters up to Cortés and his captains in submissive (and sometimes treacherous) gestures of brotherhood. In village after village, when violence could be avoided, Cortés responded in the same way: speaking through Doña Marina, "La Malintzín," his Indian translator and lover, he introduced the Indians to Christianity. Indeed, strikingly in the manner of the Jesus of the Gospel according to Saint Matthew, Cortés wandered in the wilderness and from village to village, teaching, "Stop your sacrifices and do not eat the meat of your fellow man, nor commit sodomy, nor the other ugly things you tend to do, because that is the command of Our Lord God, who we adore and believe, and gives us life and death, and leads us to heaven." And Cortés would tell the caciques that not until their virgin daughters had been baptized would the Spanish consent to receive and "know them as women." The Spanish friars accompanying Cortés would attempt to teach about the Virgin Mary, who conceived without sin, and the Divine Infant, who was the Son of God, and the meaning of the crucifixion. Sometimes, if they found themselves in a position of uncontested strength, the Spaniards would smash the Indian idols; usually, they built an altar and attempted to conduct a mass and, before marching on, raise a cross, and sometimes cleaned up one of the Indian priests, dressed him in white robes, and instructed him in how to keep the altar neat. Once one of the friars protested that it was too early to be leaving a cross "in the power of such a pueblo, because they are shameless and without fear," and this might well have been when one of the most well known of the many instantly recognizable proverbs from Matthew was first spoken in the New World: "Give not that which is holy unto the dogs, neither cast ye your pearls before swine, lest they trample them under their feet, and turn again and rend you."

It probably would have been this book, Matthew, that the Spanish friars would have preached and read from. Jorge Luis Borges called Jesus Christ "the greatest of oral teachers" and reminded us that, except for a few words drawn on the ground, Jesus left no writings. It fell to his disciples and followers to write up his life and teachings. Out of the many Gospels subsequently written, only four were canonized in the New Testament, and the rest were eventually designated as "apocryphal." Matthew's Gospel is the most fundamental, the one that is perhaps most like a manifesto of the new religion. (The apocryphal Gospels include one attributed to the "pseudo Matthew" and another, attributed to Thomas, which amusingly describes the growing pains and antics of an impudent child Jesus.) Composed sometime toward the end of the first century after Jesus' death, Matthew's Gospel displays a sense of limited continuity with Judaism while enunciating the manifold terms of a sharp split. A. N. Wilson has described Matthew as "by paradox an intensely Jewish, and an intensely anti-Jewish work—it is indeed the great Ur-text of anti-Semitism." In Matthew, which is constructed as "a miniature Torah," Jesus, like Moses, "goes up to a mountain and delivers a New Law to his followers." And that law is like a step-by-step primer, delivered mainly in parables, on how to live one's life in preparation for the Final Judgment. Matthew defines and explains the will of God, and where to look for God, and what the comportment of a Christian should be. Eternal salvation is set forth as the fruit of a life of discipline and faith and work, rather than as the result of a long-awaited messianic apocalypse.

Of course, there are many ways of reading, hearing, experiencing Matthew—for example, through the heavenly music of Bach's *Saint Matthew's Passion*. Or through the fire-and-brimstone castigations of a fundamentalist pastor, locked into Matthew's graphic images of the eternal suffering awaiting all sinners, which, if this implacably exacting book is the only authority (this is the Gospel that announces that not only adultery but merely looking with lust in your heart is a sin) condemns nearly every last one of us. A contemporary reader might peruse the Gospel with no other object than to deduce which passages Dr. Urbino might have chosen to teach his parrot. But I am not a partisan of simply literary readings of the Bible. I admire the attitude of the Catholic Flannery O'Connor, who, when Mary McCarthy said that she thought of the Host as a symbol, responded, "Well, if it's a symbol, to hell with it." I do not practice a religion, but I try to read the Bible with respect for its intentions, as the Holy Book to which all of us who live in the West are, one way or another, inextricably bound. It was to worship this book as they pleased that the Protestant English and Dutch settled North America, the heathen-devils they found already living there be damned—or exterminated. In Spanish America, this book was imposed as essential to the faith of the Catholic empire, in whose dominion everyone had to either profess belief or be enslaved and killed, often slowly and horribly.

That newly washed and shorn Indian priest, in his new white linen smock. Did he keep the altar clean? Did he spread the new teachings? Did he compose an apocryphal Aztec Gospel of his own that has since been lost to time? What most impressed him in the teachings of the Spanish fathers?

Was he impressed when they read from the Gospel according to Saint Matthew, "The Kingdom of heaven is at hand." and "Heal the sick, cleanse the lepers, raise the dead, cast out devils: freely have ye received, freely give. Provide neither gold, nor silver, nor brass in your purses." How did this sound, coming from the gold-obsessed, smallpox-plague-spreading Spanish conquistadores and their friars?

Or: "Behold, I send you forth as sheep in the midst of wolves: be ye therefore as wise as serpents, and harmless as doves. But beware of men: for they will deliver you up to the councils, and they will scourge you in their synagogues." This certainly must have sounded like good advice: the enemy warning against himself.

Did he respond to the thrillingly strange images, the poetry of angels, the bewitching mysteries of parable and metaphor: "and, behold, the whole herd of swine ran violently down a steep place into the sea, and perished in the waters"; "But the very hairs of your head are all numbered." And: "The son of man shall send forth his angels, and they shall gather out of his kingdom all things that offend, and them which do iniquity, and shall cast them into a furnace of fire: there shall be wailing and gnashing of teeth."

Did he weep during the eternally moving scene of the crucifixion, with pity for the Jesus who cries, "My God, my God, why hast thou forsaken me?" and with offended pity for the Jews, an entire people condemned unto eternity in this Gospel as those responsible for the revilement, suffering, and death of Jesus? (Perhaps, as we enter a new millennium, it is time for a Third Testament, one that will preserve the beautiful and give us many new and as yet unimagined teachings, and not set religion against religion—to be dictated and written by both Jesus and "J" the redactor, returned to earth.)

In Matthew, Jesus defines the greatest commandant as "Thou shalt love the Lord thy God with all thy heart, and with all thy soul, and with all thy mind." The second greatest, he says, "is like unto it, Thou shalt love thy neighbor as thyself."

For all of its beautiful teachings, indeed because of them, it is impossible, in our American, in our worldly, context not to read and regard the Gospel According to Saint Matthew as its own negation as well—as inevitably evocative of all the horrors, injustice, and racist and hypocritical acts committed in its name. Thus the exemplary response of Hatuy, the cacique of the Indians being exterminated in Cuba, who said that if Heaven was where the Spaniards went, then he wanted to go to Hell.

Then why is Latin America so devoutly and often inspiringly and movingly Christian? At least one answer (I don't deny that there are many) is to be found at the heart of the teachings in the Gospel According to Saint Matthew. A Catholic priest in Guatemala once told me that this teaching was, for him, the heart of Catholicism, that you could throw out all the rest and, keeping just that one parable, justify faith.

Guatemala certainly feels biblical. Sheep, swine, donkeys, serpents—these are everywhere, as are centurions, all manner of wandering false prophets, pharisees, lepers, and whores. The poor, rural, mainly Mayan landscape has an aura of the miraculous; as a setting it is the perfect backdrop for religious parables about fields both barren and fertile, fruits and harvests, hunger and plenty.

For thirty-six years a civil war spread death over the country as if in a biblical plague. An evangelical Protestant pastor who became military dictator of the country directed one of the most horrifying campaigns of violence, invoking the name of God to justify waging a campaign of genocide (as the United Nations has defined it) against the rural Mayan population. It is a country so astoundingly gripped by greed and corruption that a mere 2 percent of the population owns some 98 percent of the wealth. Children routinely die of diseases that were probably curable even in the time of Jesus. I have a relative in Guatemala who once tried to establish a barefoot doctor program so that rudimentarily trained people could at least give out such basics as dysentery medicine; his first seventeen barefoot doctors were almost immediately murdered or chased into exile; he was derided as a "communist" and, in grief and guilt, suffered a massive stroke. I remember how, only a few years ago, sitting in his upscale clinic's office, I asked him what he thought Guatemala most needed and he said, "For Jesus Christ to come back to earth and teach people how to act better." That wasn't a very scientific answer; the doctor smiled back at what must have been my openly skeptical expression. "Isn't this the devil's reign?" he asked. "Is that any more unbelievable?"

During those years, I began to realize that it was religious faith—whether essentially Catholic or Protestant or Catholic-Mayan or even Jewish (I am thinking of certain fellow Jews in that country's human-rights community, of the Jewish sense of justice and the twentieth-century commitment to fight Nazism in all its strains)—that sustained so many, with dignity and even courage, through so much harrowing and unrelenting hardship. And only the Catholic Church, for all its internal contradictions, stood up with any effectiveness and consistency on behalf of the poor. Of course, because of this many priests and nuns and religious activists were murdered. I'll never forget the defiance on display on the walls of the ancient church in Santiago Atitlán, where in 1979 Father Stan Rother had been murdered by soldiers in the rectory, a martyr to the same violence still engulfing the town a decade and a half later. With little pastel pieces of paper, each piece of paper bearing someone's hand-printed name, two large paper crosses had been put up on the wall, one commemorating all those from the town known to have been murdered in the violence, and the other all those who had been "disappeared." Those paper crosses seemed the work of angels, the naming of unnameable names.

"Whoever shall lose his life for my sake shall find it," says Jesus in the Gospel According to Saint Matthew, and from Father Rother to the great human rights activist Bishop Juan Gerardi, murdered in Guatemala City a year ago, Guatemalan clergy have shown their readiness to live by that word. But what did Jesus mean, by "for my sake"?

Of course, one of the most controversial teachings of Jesus in Matthew is the remarkably strong stance taken against the rich, and on behalf of the poor. This is the Gospel wherein it is said, "It is easier for a camel to go through the eye of a needle, than for a rich man to enter the kingdom of God." (And even the disciples, as if exasperated, respond, "Who then can be saved?") But is Jesus' hostility to the rich, and his insistence on the superiority of the poor, enough to inspire martyrs, or enough even to solely comfort the poor?

The great metaphor at the heart of the Gospel According to Saint Matthew is that those who suffer and those who show love for those who suffer are joined through suffering and grace to Jesus Christ. That is the lesson of the great parable the priest told me was enough to justify his faith. Jesus announces, "Come, ye blessed of my Father, inherit the kingdom prepared for you from the foundation of the world: For I was an hungered, and ye gave me meat: I was thirsty, and ye gave me drink: I was a stranger, and ye took me in . . . I was in prison, and ye came unto me." And the righteous people Jesus is addressing answer, "Lord, when saw we thee an hungered, and fed thee?" They don't recall helping or feeding Jesus, or finding him in prison, because they saw only poor, hungry, imprisoned people. And Jesus answers, "Verily I say unto you, Inasmuch as ye have done it unto one of the least of these my brethren, ye have done it unto me."

the gospel according to st matthew

The book of the generation of Jesus Christ, the son of David,
the son of Abraham.

[2]Abraham begat Isaac; and Isaac begat Jacob; and Jacob
begat Judas and his brethren. [3]And Judas begat Phares and
Zara of Thamar; and Phares begat Esrom; and Esrom begat
Aram. [4]And Aram begat Aminadab; and Aminadab begat Naasson; and Naasson begat Salmon. [5]And Salmon begat Booz
of Rachab; and Booz begat Obed of Ruth; and Obed begat
Jesse. [6]And Jesse begat David the king; and David the king
begat Solomon of her that had been the wife of Urias. [7]And
Solomon begat Roboam; and Roboam begat Abia; and Abia
begat Asa. [8]And Asa begat Josaphat; and Josaphat begat Joram;
and Joram begat Ozias. [9]And Ozias begat Joatham; and Joatham begat Achaz; and Achaz begat Ezekias. [10]And Ezekias
begat Manasses; and Manasses begat Amon; and Amon begat
Josias. [11]And Josias begat Jechonias and his brethren, about
the time they were carried away to Babylon. [12]And after they
were brought to Babylon, Jechonias begat Salathiel; and
Salathiel begat Zorobabel. [13]And Zorobabel begat Abiud;
and Abiud begat Eliakim; and Eliakim begat Azor. [14]And
Azor begat Sadoc; and Sadoc begat Achim; and Achim begat
Eliud. [15]And Eliud begat Eleazar; and Eleazar begat Matthan; and Matthan begat Jacob. [16]And Jacob begat Joseph the

husband of Mary, of whom was born Jesus, who is called
Christ. 17 So all the generations from Abraham to David are fourteen generations; and from David until the carrying away
into Babylon are fourteen generations; and from the carrying away into Babylon unto Christ are fourteen generations.
18 Now the birth of Jesus Christ was on this wise. When as
his mother Mary was espoused to Joseph, before they came
together, she was found with child of the Holy Ghost. 19 Then
Joseph her husband, being a just man, and not willing to make
her a publick example, was minded to put her away privily.
20 But while he thought on these things, behold, the angel of
the Lord appeared unto him in a dream, saying, 'Joseph, thou
son of David, fear not to take unto thee Mary thy wife, for
that which is conceived in her is of the Holy Ghost. 21 And she
shall bring forth a son, and thou shalt call his name "Jesus":
for he shall save his people from their sins.' 22 Now all this
was done, that it might be fulfilled which was spoken of the
Lord by the prophet, saying, 23 'Behold, a virgin shall be with
child, and shall bring forth a son, and they shall call his
name "Emmanuel", which being interpreted is, "God with
us". 24 Then Joseph being raised from sleep did as the angel
of the Lord had bidden him, and took unto him his wife;
25 and knew her not till she had brought forth her firstborn
son, and he called his name 'Jesus'.

2 Now when Jesus was born in Bethlehem of Judæa in the
days of Herod the king, behold, there came wise men
from the east to Jerusalem, 2 saying, 'Where is he that is born
King of the Jews? For we have seen his star in the east, and

are come to worship him.' 3 When Herod the king had heard
these things, he was troubled, and all Jerusalem with him.
4 And when he had gathered all the chief priests and scribes
of the people together, he demanded of them where Christ
should be born. 5 And they said unto him, 'In Bethlehem of
Judæa, for thus it is written by the prophet, 6 "And thou
Bethlehem, in the land of Juda, art not the least among the
princes of Juda, for out of thee shall come a Governor, that
shall rule my people Israel."' 7 Then Herod, when he had
privily called the wise men, enquired of them diligently
what time the star appeared. 8 And he sent them to Bethlehem, and said, 'Go and search diligently for the young
child; and when ye have found him, bring me word again,
that I may come and worship him also.' 9 When they had
heard the king, they departed; and, lo, the star, which they
saw in the east, went before them, till it came and stood over
where the young child was. 10 When they saw the star, they
rejoiced with exceeding great joy.

11 And when they were come into the house, they saw the
young child with Mary his mother, and fell down, and worshipped him, and when they had opened their treasures, they
presented unto him gifts: gold, and frankincense, and myrrh.
12 And being warned of God in a dream that they should not
return to Herod, they departed into their own country another
way. 13 And when they were departed, behold, the angel of
the Lord appeareth to Joseph in a dream, saying, 'Arise, and
take the young child and his mother, and flee into Egypt,
and be thou there until I bring thee word, for Herod will
seek the young child to destroy him.' 14 When he arose, he

took the young child and his mother by night, and departed
into Egypt, 15 and was there until the death of Herod, that it
might be fulfilled which was spoken of the Lord by the
prophet, saying, 'Out of Egypt have I called my son.'
16 Then Herod, when he saw that he was mocked of the
wise men, was exceeding wroth, and sent forth, and slew all
the children that were in Bethlehem, and in all the coasts
thereof, from two years old and under, according to the time
which he had diligently enquired of the wise men. 17 Then was
fulfilled that which was spoken by Jeremy the prophet, saying,
18 'In Rama was there a voice heard, lamentation, and weeping, and great mourning, Rachel weeping for her children,
and would not be comforted, because they are not.'
19 But when Herod was dead, behold, an angel of the Lord
appeareth in a dream to Joseph in Egypt, 20 saying, 'Arise,
and take the young child and his mother, and go into the
land of Israel, for they are dead which sought the young
child's life.' 21 And he arose, and took the young child and his
mother, and came into the land of Israel. 22 But when he
heard that Archelaus did reign in Judæa in the room of his
father Herod, he was afraid to go thither; notwithstanding,
being warned of God in a dream, he turned aside into the
parts of Galilee. 23 And he came and dwelt in a city called
Nazareth, that it might be fulfilled which was spoken by the
prophets, 'He shall be called a Nazarene.'

3 In those days came John the Baptist, preaching in the
wilderness of Judæa, 2 and saying, 'Repent ye, for the
kingdom of heaven is at hand.' 3 For this is he that was spoken

of by the prophet Esaias, saying, 'The voice of one crying in
the wilderness, "Prepare ye the way of the Lord, make his
paths straight."' 4 And the same John had his raiment of
camel's hair, and a leathern girdle about his loins; and his meat
was locusts and wild honey. 5 Then went out to him Jerusalem, and all Judæa, and all the region round about Jordan,
6 and were baptized of him in Jordan, confessing their sins.

7 But when he saw many of the Pharisees and Sadducees
come to his baptism, he said unto them, 'O generation of
vipers, who hath warned you to flee from the wrath to come?
8 Bring forth therefore fruits meet for repentance, 9 and think
not to say within yourselves, "We have Abraham to our father,"
for I say unto you that God is able of these stones to raise up
children unto Abraham. 10 And now also the axe is laid unto
the root of the trees: therefore every tree which bringeth not
forth good fruit is hewn down, and cast into the fire. 11 I
indeed baptize you with water unto repentance, but he that
cometh after me is mightier than I, whose shoes I am not
worthy to bear. He shall baptize you with the Holy Ghost, and
with fire, 12 whose fan is in his hand, and he will throughly
purge his floor, and gather his wheat into the garner; but he
will burn up the chaff with unquenchable fire.'

13 Then cometh Jesus from Galilee to Jordan unto John, to
be baptized of him. 14 But John forbad him, saying, 'I have need
to be baptized of thee, and comest thou to me?' 15 And Jesus
answering said unto him, 'Suffer it to be so now, for thus it
becometh us to fulfil all righteousness.' Then he suffered
him. 16 And Jesus, when he was baptized, went up straightway out of the water, and, lo, the heavens were opened unto

him, and he saw the Spirit of God descending like a dove,
and lighting upon him: 17and lo a voice from heaven, saying,
'This is my beloved Son, in whom I am well pleased.'

4 Then was Jesus led up of the Spirit into the wilderness
to be tempted of the devil. 2And when he had fasted
forty days and forty nights, he was afterward an hungred.
3And when the tempter came to him, he said, 'If thou be the
Son of God, command that these stones be made bread.'
4But he answered and said, 'It is written, "Man shall not live
by bread alone, but by every word that proceedeth out of the
mouth of God."' 5Then the devil taketh him up into the holy
city, and setteth him on a pinnacle of the temple, 6and saith
unto him, 'If thou be the Son of God, cast thyself down, for it
is written, "He shall give his angels charge concerning thee,
and in their hands they shall bear thee up, lest at any time
thou dash thy foot against a stone."' 7Jesus said unto him, 'It
is written again, "Thou shalt not tempt the Lord thy God."'
8Again, the devil taketh him up into an exceeding high
mountain, and sheweth him all the kingdoms of the world,
and the glory of them; 9and saith unto him, 'All these things
will I give thee, if thou wilt fall down and worship me.'
10Then saith Jesus unto him, 'Get thee hence, Satan: for it is
written, "Thou shalt worship the Lord thy God, and him
only shalt thou serve."' 11Then the devil leaveth him, and,
behold, angels came and ministered unto him.

12Now when Jesus had heard that John was cast into
prison, he departed into Galilee; 13and leaving Nazareth, he
came and dwelt in Capernaum, which is upon the sea coast,

in the borders of Zabulon and Nephthalim, 14 that it might be
fulfilled which was spoken by Esaias the prophet, saying,
15 'The land of Zabulon, and the land of Nephthalim, by the
way of the sea, beyond Jordan, Galilee of the Gentiles; 16 the people which sat in darkness saw great light; and to them which
sat in the region and shadow of death light is sprung up.'

17 From that time Jesus began to preach, and to say, 'Repent,
for the kingdom of heaven is at hand.'

18 And Jesus, walking by the sea of Galilee, saw two brethren, Simon called Peter, and Andrew his brother, casting a net
into the sea, for they were fishers. 19 And he saith unto them,
'Follow me, and I will make you fishers of men.' 20 And they
straightway left their nets, and followed him. 21 And going on
from thence, he saw other two brethren, James the son of
Zebedee, and John his brother, in a ship with Zebedee their
father, mending their nets; and he called them. 22 And they
immediately left the ship and their father, and followed him.

23 And Jesus went about all Galilee, teaching in their synagogues, and preaching the gospel of the kingdom, and healing all manner of sickness and all manner of disease among
the people. 24 And his fame went throughout all Syria, and
they brought unto him all sick people that were taken with
divers diseases and torments, and those which were possessed with devils, and those which were lunatick, and those
that had the palsy; and he healed them. 25 And there followed
him great multitudes of people from Galilee, and from Decapolis, and from Jerusalem, and from Judæa, and from
beyond Jordan.

5 And seeing the multitudes, he went up into a mountain, and when he was set, his disciples came unto him, 2 and he opened his mouth, and taught them, saying,

3 Blessed are the poor in spirit,
for theirs is the kingdom of heaven.
4 Blessed are they that mourn,
for they shall be comforted.
5 Blessed are the meek,
for they shall inherit the earth.
6 Blessed are they which do hunger
and thirst after righteousness,
for they shall be filled.
7 Blessed are the merciful,
for they shall obtain mercy.
8 Blessed are the pure in heart,
for they shall see God.
9 Blessed are the peacemakers,
for they shall be called the children of God.
10 Blessed are they which are persecuted
for righteousness' sake,
for theirs is the kingdom of heaven.
11 Blessed are ye, when men shall revile you,
and persecute you, and shall say all manner
of evil against you falsely, for my sake.

12 'Rejoice, and be exceeding glad, for great is your reward in heaven, for so persecuted they the prophets which were before you.

13 'Ye are the salt of the earth: but if the salt have lost his

savour, wherewith shall it be salted? It is thenceforth good
for nothing, but to be cast out, and to be trodden under foot
of men. [14] Ye are the light of the world. A city that is set on an
hill cannot be hid. [15] Neither do men light a candle, and put it
under a bushel, but on a candlestick; and it giveth light unto
all that are in the house. [16] Let your light so shine before men,
that they may see your good works, and glorify your Father
which is in heaven.

[17] 'Think not that I am come to destroy the law, or the
prophets; I am not come to destroy, but to fulfil. [18] For verily I
say unto you, till heaven and earth pass, one jot or one tittle
shall in no wise pass from the law, till all be fulfilled. [19] Whosoever therefore shall break one of these least commandments, and shall teach men so, he shall be called the least in
the kingdom of heaven: but whosoever shall do and teach
them, the same shall be called great in the kingdom of
heaven. [20] For I say unto you that, except your righteousness
shall exceed the righteousness of the scribes and Pharisees,
ye shall in no case enter into the kingdom of heaven.

[21] 'Ye have heard that it was said by them of old time,
"Thou shalt not kill", and whosoever shall kill shall be in
danger of the judgment: [22] but I say unto you that whosoever
is angry with his brother without a cause shall be in danger
of the judgment, and whosoever shall say to his brother,
"Raca," shall be in danger of the council, but whosoever
shall say, "Thou fool," shall be in danger of hell fire. [23] Therefore if thou bring thy gift to the altar, and there rememberest
that thy brother hath ought against thee, [24] leave there thy
gift before the altar, and go thy way; first be reconciled to

thy brother, and then come and offer thy gift. 25 Agree with
thine adversary quickly, whiles thou art in the way with
him; lest at any time the adversary deliver thee to the judge,
and the judge deliver thee to the officer, and thou be cast
into prison. 26 Verily I say unto thee, thou shalt by no means
come out thence, till thou hast paid the uttermost farthing.
27 'Ye have heard that it was said by them of old time,
"Thou shalt not commit adultery," 28 but I say unto you that
whosoever looketh on a woman to lust after her hath committed adultery with her already in his heart. 29 And if thy
right eye offend thee, pluck it out, and cast it from thee: for it
is profitable for thee that one of thy members should perish,
and not that thy whole body should be cast into hell. 30 And if
thy right hand offend thee, cut it off, and cast it from thee:
for it is profitable for thee that one of thy members should
perish, and not that thy whole body should be cast into hell.
31 It hath been said, "Whosoever shall put away his wife, let
him give her a writing of divorcement." 32 But I say unto you
that whosoever shall put away his wife, saving for the cause
of fornication, causeth her to commit adultery, and whosoever shall marry her that is divorced committeth adultery.
33 'Again, ye have heard that it hath been said by them of
old time, "Thou shalt not forswear thyself, but shalt perform
unto the Lord thine oaths." 34 But I say unto you, "Swear not
at all; neither by heaven, for it is God's throne, 35 nor by the
earth, for it is his footstool, neither by Jerusalem, for it is the
city of the great King." 36 Neither shalt thou swear by thy
head, because thou canst not make one hair white or black.
37 But let your communication be "Yea, yea", "Nay, nay", for

whatsoever is more than these cometh of evil.
38 'Ye have heard that it hath been said, "An eye for an
eye, and a tooth for a tooth": 39 but I say unto you that ye
resist not evil, but whosoever shall smite thee on thy right
cheek, turn to him the other also. 40 And if any man will sue
thee at the law, and take away thy coat, let him have thy
cloke also. 41 And whosoever shall compel thee to go a mile,
go with him twain. 42 Give to him that asketh thee, and from
him that would borrow of thee turn not thou away.
43 'Ye have heard that it hath been said, "Thou shalt love
thy neighbour, and hate thine enemy." 44 But I say unto you,
"Love your enemies, bless them that curse you, do good to
them that hate you, and pray for them which despitefully
use you, and persecute you"; 45 that ye may be the children of
your Father which is in heaven, for he maketh his sun to rise
on the evil and on the good, and sendeth rain on the just and
on the unjust. 46 For if ye love them which love you, what
reward have ye? Do not even the publicans the same? 47 And
if ye salute your brethren only, what do ye more than others?
Do not even the publicans so? 48 Be ye therefore perfect, even
as your Father which is in heaven is perfect.

6 'Take heed that ye do not your alms before men, to be
seen of them; otherwise ye have no reward of your Father
which is in heaven. 2 Therefore when thou doest thine alms,
do not sound a trumpet before thee, as the hypocrites do in
the synagogues and in the streets, that they may have glory
of men. Verily I say unto you, "They have their reward." 3 But
when thou doest alms, let not thy left hand know what thy

right hand doeth, [4]that thine alms may be in secret, and thy
Father which seeth in secret himself shall reward thee openly.
[5]'And when thou prayest, thou shalt not be as the hypocrites are, for they love to pray standing in the synagogues
and in the corners of the streets, that they may be seen of
men. Verily I say unto you, "They have their reward." [6]But
thou, when thou prayest, enter into thy closet, and when thou
hast shut thy door, pray to thy Father which is in secret; and
thy Father which seeth in secret shall reward thee openly.
[7]But when ye pray, use not vain repetitions, as the heathen
do, for they think that they shall be heard for their much
speaking. [8]Be not ye therefore like unto them, for your
Father knoweth what things ye have need of, before ye ask
him. [9]After this manner therefore pray ye:

Our Father which art in heaven,
    Hallowed be thy name.
[10]Thy kingdom come.
    Thy will be done in earth, as it is in heaven.
[11]Give us this day our daily bread.
[12]And forgive us our debts,
    as we forgive our debtors.
[13]And lead us not into temptation,
    but deliver us from evil:
        for thine is the kingdom,
    and the power, and the glory,
        for ever. Amen.

[14]'For if ye forgive men their trespasses, your heavenly Father
will also forgive you, [15]but if ye forgive not men their

trespasses, neither will your Father forgive your trespasses.
16 'Moreover when ye fast, be not, as the hypocrites, of a
sad countenance: for they disfigure their faces, that they may
appear unto men to fast. Verily I say unto you, "They have
their reward." 17 But thou, when thou fastest, anoint thine
head, and wash thy face, 18 that thou appear not unto men to
fast, but unto thy Father which is in secret: and thy Father,
which seeth in secret, shall reward thee openly.
19 'Lay not up for yourselves treasures upon earth, where
moth and rust doth corrupt, and where thieves break through
and steal, 20 but lay up for yourselves treasures in heaven,
where neither moth nor rust doth corrupt, and where thieves
do not break through nor steal: 21 for where your treasure is,
there will your heart be also. 22 The light of the body is the
eye: if therefore thine eye be single, thy whole body shall be
full of light. 23 But if thine eye be evil, thy whole body shall
be full of darkness. If therefore the light that is in thee be
darkness, how great is that darkness!
24 'No man can serve two masters: for either he will hate
the one, and love the other; or else he will hold to the one,
and despise the other. Ye cannot serve God and mammon.
25 Therefore I say unto you, take no thought for your life,
what ye shall eat, or what ye shall drink; nor yet for your
body, what ye shall put on. Is not the life more than meat,
and the body than raiment? 26 Behold the fowls of the air, for
they sow not, neither do they reap, nor gather into barns; yet
your heavenly Father feedeth them. Are ye not much better
than they? 27 Which of you by taking thought can add one
cubit unto his stature? 28 And why take ye thought for

raiment? Consider the lilies of the field, how they grow; they
toil not, neither do they spin, 29 and yet I say unto you that
even Solomon in all his glory was not arrayed like one of
these. 30 Wherefore, if God so clothe the grass of the field,
which today is, and tomorrow is cast into the oven, shall he
not much more clothe you, O ye of little faith? 31 Therefore
take no thought, saying, "What shall we eat?" or, "What shall
we drink?" or, "Wherewithal shall we be clothed?" 32 (For
after all these things do the Gentiles seek) for your heavenly
Father knoweth that ye have need of all these things. 33 But
seek ye first the kingdom of God, and his righteousness; and
all these things shall be added unto you. 34 Take therefore no
thought for the morrow, for the morrow shall take thought
for the things of itself. Sufficient unto the day is the evil thereof.

7 1 'Judge not, that ye be not judged. 2 For with what judgment ye judge, ye shall be judged, and with what measure ye mete, it shall be measured to you again. 3 And why
beholdest thou the mote that is in thy brother's eye, but con-
siderest not the beam that is in thine own eye? 4 Or how wilt
thou say to thy brother, "Let me pull out the mote out of
thine eye," and, behold, a beam is in thine own eye? 5 Thou
hypocrite, first cast out the beam out of thine own eye; and
then shalt thou see clearly to cast out the mote out of thy
brother's eye.

6 'Give not that which is holy unto the dogs, neither cast
ye your pearls before swine, lest they trample them under
their feet, and turn again and rend you.

7 'Ask, and it shall be given you; seek, and ye shall find;

knock, and it shall be opened unto you: 8 for every one that
asketh receiveth; and he that seeketh findeth; and to him
that knocketh it shall be opened. 9 Or what man is there of
you, whom if his son ask bread, will he give him a stone?
10 Or if he ask a fish, will he give him a serpent? 11 If ye then,
being evil, know how to give good gifts unto your children,
how much more shall your Father which is in heaven give
good things to them that ask him? 12 Therefore all things
whatsoever ye would that men should do to you, do ye even
so to them: for this is the law and the prophets.

13 'Enter ye in at the strait gate, for wide is the gate, and
broad is the way, that leadeth to destruction, and many there
be which go in thereat. 14 Because strait is the gate, and narrow is the way, which leadeth unto life, and few there be
that find it.

15 'Beware of false prophets, which come to you in sheep's
clothing, but inwardly they are ravening wolves. 16 Ye shall
know them by their fruits. Do men gather grapes of thorns,
or figs of thistles? 17 Even so every good tree bringeth forth
good fruit; but a corrupt tree bringeth forth evil fruit. 18 A
good tree cannot bring forth evil fruit, neither can a corrupt
tree bring forth good fruit. 19 Every tree that bringeth not forth
good fruit is hewn down, and cast into the fire. 20 Wherefore
by their fruits ye shall know them.

21 'Not every one that saith unto me, "Lord, Lord," shall
enter into the kingdom of heaven; but he that doeth the will
of my Father which is in heaven. 22 Many will say to me in
that day, "Lord, Lord, have we not prophesied in thy name?
And in thy name have cast out devils? And in thy name done

many wonderful works?" 23And then will I profess unto them,
"I never knew you: depart from me, ye that work iniquity."
24'Therefore whosoever heareth these sayings of mine,
and doeth them, I will liken him unto a wise man, which
built his house upon a rock: 25and the rain descended, and
the floods came, and the winds blew, and beat upon that
house; and it fell not: for it was founded upon a rock. 26And
every one that heareth these sayings of mine, and doeth
them not, shall be likened unto a foolish man, which built
his house upon the sand, 27and the rain descended, and the
floods came, and the winds blew, and beat upon that house;
and it fell, and great was the fall of it.' 28And it came to pass,
when Jesus had ended these sayings, the people were astonished at his doctrine: 29for he taught them as one having
authority, and not as the scribes.

8 When he was come down from the mountain, great
multitudes followed him. 2And, behold, there came a
leper and worshipped him, saying, 'Lord, if thou wilt, thou
canst make me clean.' 3And Jesus put forth his hand, and
touched him, saying, 'I will; be thou clean.' And immediately
his leprosy was cleansed. 4And Jesus saith unto him, 'See
thou tell no man; but go thy way, shew thyself to the priest,
and offer the gift that Moses commanded, for a testimony
unto them.'

5And when Jesus was entered into Capernaum, there
came unto him a centurion, beseeching him, 6and saying,
'Lord, my servant lieth at home sick of the palsy, grievously
tormented.' 7And Jesus saith unto him, 'I will come and heal

him.' [8]The centurion answered and said, 'Lord, I am not
worthy that thou shouldest come under my roof: but speak
the word only, and my servant shall be healed. [9]For I am a
man under authority, having soldiers under me, and I say to
this man, "Go," and he goeth; and to another, "Come," and
he cometh; and to my servant, "Do this," and he doeth it.'
[10]When Jesus heard it, he marvelled, and said to them that
followed, 'Verily I say unto you, I have not found so great
faith, no, not in Israel. [11]And I say unto you that many shall
come from the east and west, and shall sit down with Abraham, and Isaac, and Jacob, in the kingdom of heaven. [12]But
the children of the kingdom shall be cast out into outer darkness: there shall be weeping and gnashing of teeth.' [13]And
Jesus said unto the centurion, 'Go thy way; and as thou hast
believed, so be it done unto thee.' And his servant was healed
in the selfsame hour.

[14]And when Jesus was come into Peter's house, he saw
his wife's mother laid, and sick of a fever. [15]And he touched
her hand, and the fever left her, and she arose, and ministered unto them.

[16]When the even was come, they brought unto him many
that were possessed with devils, and he cast out the spirits
with his word, and healed all that were sick, [17]that it might
be fulfilled which was spoken by Esaias the prophet, saying,
'Himself took our infirmities, and bare our sicknesses.'

[18]Now when Jesus saw great multitudes about him, he
gave commandment to depart unto the other side. [19]And a
certain scribe came, and said unto him, 'Master, I will follow
thee whithersoever thou goest.' [20]And Jesus saith unto him,

'The foxes have holes, and the birds of the air have nests; but
the Son of man hath not where to lay his head.' 21And another
of his disciples said unto him, 'Lord, suffer me first to go and
bury my father.' 22 But Jesus said unto him, 'Follow me; and
let the dead bury their dead.'

23And when he was entered into a ship, his disciples followed him. 24And, behold, there arose a great tempest in the
sea, insomuch that the ship was covered with the waves; but
he was asleep. 25And his disciples came to him, and awoke
him, saying, 'Lord, save us. We perish.' 26And he saith unto
them, 'Why are ye fearful, O ye of little faith?' Then he arose,
and rebuked the winds and the sea; and there was a great
calm. 27 But the men marvelled, saying, 'What manner of
man is this, that even the winds and the sea obey him!'

28And when he was come to the other side into the country of the Gergesenes, there met him two possessed with
devils, coming out of the tombs, exceeding fierce, so that no
man might pass by that way. 29And, behold, they cried out,
saying, 'What have we to do with thee, Jesus, thou Son of
God? Art thou come hither to torment us before the time?'
30And there was a good way off from them an herd of many
swine feeding. 31 So the devils besought him, saying, 'If thou
cast us out, suffer us to go away into the herd of swine.'
32And he said unto them, 'Go.' And when they were come
out, they went into the herd of swine, and, behold, the whole
herd of swine ran violently down a steep place into the sea,
and perished in the waters. 33And they that kept them fled,
and went their ways into the city, and told every thing, and
what was befallen to the possessed of the devils. 34And,

behold, the whole city came out to meet Jesus, and when
they saw him, they besought him that he would depart out
of their coasts.

9 And he entered into a ship, and passed over, and came
into his own city. 2 And, behold, they brought to him a
man sick of the palsy, lying on a bed: and Jesus seeing their
faith said unto the sick of the palsy, 'Son, be of good cheer;
thy sins be forgiven thee.' 3 And, behold, certain of the scribes
said within themselves, 'This man blasphemeth.' 4 And Jesus
knowing their thoughts said, 'Wherefore think ye evil in
your hearts? 5 For whether is easier, to say, "Thy sins be forgiven thee," or to say, "Arise, and walk"? 6 But that ye may
know that the Son of man hath power on earth to forgive
sins,' then saith he to the sick of the palsy, 'Arise, take up thy
bed, and go unto thine house.' 7 And he arose, and departed to
his house. 8 But when the multitudes saw it, they marvelled,
and glorified God, which had given such power unto men.

9 And as Jesus passed forth from thence, he saw a man,
named Matthew, sitting at the receipt of custom, and he saith
unto him, 'Follow me.' And he arose, and followed him.

10 And it came to pass, as Jesus sat at meat in the house,
behold, many publicans and sinners came and sat down
with him and his disciples. 11 And when the Pharisees saw it,
they said unto his disciples, 'Why eateth your Master with
publicans and sinners?' 12 But when Jesus heard that, he said
unto them, 'They that be whole need not a physician, but
they that are sick. 13 But go ye and learn what that meaneth,
"I will have mercy, and not sacrifice," for I am not come to

call the righteous, but sinners to repentance.'

14 Then came to him the disciples of John, saying, 'Why
do we and the Pharisees fast oft, but thy disciples fast not?'
15 And Jesus said unto them, 'Can the children of the bridechamber mourn, as long as the bridegroom is with them?
But the days will come, when the bridegroom shall be taken
from them, and then shall they fast. 16 No man putteth a piece
of new cloth unto an old garment, for that which is put in to fill
it up taketh from the garment, and the rent is made worse.
17 Neither do men put new wine into old bottles: else the bottles break, and the wine runneth out, and the bottles perish; but
they put new wine into new bottles, and both are preserved.'

18 While he spake these things unto them, behold, there
came a certain ruler, and worshipped him, saying, 'My daughter is even now dead, but come and lay thy hand upon her,
and she shall live.' 19 And Jesus arose, and followed him, and
so did his disciples.

20 And, behold, a woman, which was diseased with an issue
of blood twelve years, came behind him, and touched the
hem of his garment, 21 for she said within herself, 'If I may
but touch his garment, I shall be whole.' 22 But Jesus turned
him about, and when he saw her, he said, 'Daughter, be of
good comfort; thy faith hath made thee whole.' And the
woman was made whole from that hour. 23 And when Jesus
came into the ruler's house, and saw the minstrels and the
people making a noise, 24 he said unto them, 'Give place, for
the maid is not dead, but sleepeth.' And they laughed him to
scorn. 25 But when the people were put forth, he went in, and
took her by the hand, and the maid arose. 26 And the fame

hereof went abroad into all that land.
[27]And when Jesus departed thence, two blind men followed him, crying, and saying, 'Thou Son of David, have
mercy on us.' [28]And when he was come into the house, the
blind men came to him, and Jesus saith unto them, 'Believe
ye that I am able to do this?' They said unto him, 'Yea, Lord.'
[29]Then touched he their eyes, saying, 'According to your
faith be it unto you.' [30]And their eyes were opened; and Jesus
straitly charged them, saying, 'See that no man know it.'
[31]But they, when they were departed, spread abroad his fame
in all that country.
[32]As they went out, behold, they brought to him a dumb
man possessed with a devil. [33]And when the devil was cast
out, the dumb spake, and the multitudes marvelled, saying,
'It was never so seen in Israel.' [34]But the Pharisees said, 'He
casteth out devils through the prince of the devils.' [35]And
Jesus went about all the cities and villages, teaching in their
synagogues, and preaching the gospel of the kingdom, and
healing every sickness and every disease among the people.
[36]But when he saw the multitudes, he was moved with
compassion on them, because they fainted, and were scattered abroad, as sheep having no shepherd. [37]Then saith he
unto his disciples, 'The harvest truly is plenteous, but the
labourers are few; [38]pray ye therefore the Lord of the harvest, that he will send forth labourers into his harvest.'

10 And when he had called unto him his twelve disciples,
he gave them power against unclean spirits, to cast
them out, and to heal all manner of sickness and all manner

of disease. [2] Now the names of the twelve apostles are these:
the first, Simon, who is called Peter, and Andrew his brother;
James the son of Zebedee, and John his brother; [3] Philip, and
Bartholomew; Thomas, and Matthew the publican; James
the son of Alphæus, and Lebbæus, whose surname was
Thaddæus; [4] Simon the Canaanite, and Judas Iscariot, who
also betrayed him. [5] These twelve Jesus sent forth, and commanded them, saying, 'Go not into the way of the Gentiles,
and into any city of the Samaritans enter ye not: [6] but go
rather to the lost sheep of the house of Israel. [7] And as ye go,
preach, saying, "The kingdom of heaven is at hand." [8] Heal
the sick, cleanse the lepers, raise the dead, cast out devils:
freely ye have received, freely give. [9] Provide neither gold,
nor silver, nor brass in your purses, [10] nor scrip for your journey, neither two coats, neither shoes, nor yet staves, for the
workman is worthy of his meat. [11] And into whatsoever city
or town ye shall enter, enquire who in it is worthy; and there
abide till ye go thence. [12] And when ye come into an house,
salute it. [13] And if the house be worthy, let your peace come
upon it: but if it be not worthy, let your peace return to you.
[14] And whosoever shall not receive you, nor hear your words,
when ye depart out of that house or city, shake off the dust
of your feet. [15] Verily I say unto you, it shall be more tolerable
for the land of Sodom and Gomorrha in the day of judgment,
than for that city.

[16] 'Behold, I send you forth as sheep in the midst of wolves:
be ye therefore wise as serpents, and harmless as doves. [17] But
beware of men, for they will deliver you up to the councils,
and they will scourge you in their synagogues; [18] and ye shall

be brought before governors and kings for my sake, for a
testimony against them and the Gentiles. [19]But when they
deliver you up, take no thought how or what ye shall speak,
for it shall be given you in that same hour what ye shall speak.
[20]For it is not ye that speak, but the Spirit of your Father
which speaketh in you. [21]And the brother shall deliver up the
brother to death, and the father the child, and the children
shall rise up against their parents, and cause them to be put
to death. [22]And ye shall be hated of all men for my name's
sake: but he that endureth to the end shall be saved. [23]But
when they persecute you in this city, flee ye into another, for
verily I say unto you, ye shall not have gone over the cities
of Israel, till the Son of man be come. [24]The disciple is not
above his master, nor the servant above his lord. [25]It is enough
for the disciple that he be as his master, and the servant as
his lord. If they have called the master of the house Beelzebub, how much more shall they call them of his household?
[26]Fear them not therefore, for there is nothing covered, that
shall not be revealed; and hid, that shall not be known. [27]What
I tell you in darkness, that speak ye in light: and what ye
hear in the ear, that preach ye upon the housetops. [28]And
fear not them which kill the body, but are not able to kill the
soul, but rather fear him which is able to destroy both soul
and body in hell. [29]Are not two sparrows sold for a farthing?
And one of them shall not fall on the ground without your
Father. [30]But the very hairs of your head are all numbered.
[31]Fear ye not therefore, ye are of more value than many sparrows. [32]Whosoever therefore shall confess me before men,
him will I confess also before my Father which is in heaven.

33 But whosoever shall deny me before men, him will I also
deny before my Father which is in heaven. 34 Think not that I
am come to send peace on earth; I came not to send peace,
but a sword. 35 For I am come to set a man at variance against
his father, and the daughter against her mother, and the
daughter-in-law against her mother-in-law. 36 And a man's
foes shall be they of his own household. 37 He that loveth
father or mother more than me is not worthy of me: and he
that loveth son or daughter more than me is not worthy of
me. 38 And he that taketh not his cross, and followeth after
me, is not worthy of me. 39 He that findeth his life shall lose
it: and he that loseth his life for my sake shall find it.

40 'He that receiveth you receiveth me, and he that receiveth me receiveth him that sent me. 41 He that receiveth a
prophet in the name of a prophet shall receive a prophet's
reward; and he that receiveth a righteous man in the name
of a righteous man shall receive a righteous man's reward.
42 And whosoever shall give to drink unto one of these little
ones a cup of cold water only in the name of a disciple, verily I say unto you, he shall in no wise lose his reward.'

11 And it came to pass, when Jesus had made an end of
commanding his twelve disciples, he departed thence
to teach and to preach in their cities. 2 Now when John had
heard in the prison the works of Christ, he sent two of his
disciples, 3 and said unto him, 'Art thou he that should come,
or do we look for another?' 4 Jesus answered and said unto
them, 'Go and shew John again those things which ye do
hear and see: 5 the blind receive their sight, and the lame

walk, the lepers are cleansed, and the deaf hear, the dead are
raised up, and the poor have the gospel preached to them.
6And blessed is he, whosoever shall not be offended in me.'
7And as they departed, Jesus began to say unto the multitudes concerning John, 'What went ye out into the wilderness to see? A reed shaken with the wind? 8 But what went
ye out for to see? A man clothed in soft raiment? Behold,
they that wear soft clothing are in kings' houses. 9 But what
went ye out for to see? A prophet? Yea, I say unto you, and
more than a prophet. 10 For this is he, of whom it is written,
"Behold, I send my messenger before thy face, which shall
prepare thy way before thee." 11 Verily I say unto you, among
them that are born of women there hath not risen a greater
than John the Baptist; notwithstanding he that is least in the
kingdom of heaven is greater than he. 12 And from the days of
John the Baptist until now the kingdom of heaven suffereth
violence, and the violent take it by force. 13 For all the prophets
and the law prophesied until John. 14 And if ye will receive it,
this is Elias, which was for to come. 15 He that hath ears to
hear, let him hear.
16 'But whereunto shall I liken this generation? It is like
unto children sitting in the markets, and calling unto their
fellows, 17 and saying, "We have piped unto you, and ye have
not danced; we have mourned unto you, and ye have not
lamented." 18 For John came neither eating nor drinking, and
they say, "He hath a devil." 19 The Son of man came eating
and drinking, and they say, "Behold a man gluttonous, and a
winebibber, a friend of publicans and sinners." But wisdom
is justified of her children.'

20 Then began he to upbraid the cities wherein most of his
mighty works were done, because they repented not. 21 'Woe
unto thee, Chorazin! Woe unto thee, Bethsaida! For if the
mighty works, which were done in you, had been done in Tyre
and Sidon, they would have repented long ago in sackcloth
and ashes. 22 But I say unto you, it shall be more tolerable for
Tyre and Sidon at the day of judgment, than for you. 23 And
thou, Capernaum, which art exalted unto heaven, shalt be
brought down to hell: for if the mighty works, which have
been done in thee, had been done in Sodom, it would have
remained until this day. 24 But I say unto you, that it shall be
more tolerable for the land of Sodom in the day of judgment,
than for thee.'

25 At that time Jesus answered and said, 'I thank thee, O
Father, Lord of heaven and earth, because thou hast hid these
things from the wise and prudent, and hast revealed them
unto babes. 26 Even so, Father, for so it seemed good in thy
sight. 27 All things are delivered unto me of my Father, and
no man knoweth the Son, but the Father; neither knoweth
any man the Father, save the Son, and he to whomsoever the
Son will reveal him.

28 'Come unto me, all ye that labour and are heavy laden,
and I will give you rest. 29 Take my yoke upon you, and learn of
me; for I am meek and lowly in heart: and ye shall find rest
unto your souls. 30 For my yoke is easy, and my burden is light.'

12 At that time Jesus went on the sabbath day through
the corn; and his disciples were an hungred, and began
to pluck the ears of corn, and to eat. 2 But when the Pharisees

saw it, they said unto him, 'Behold, thy disciples do that
which is not lawful to do upon the sabbath day.' [3] But he said
unto them, 'Have ye not read what David did, when he was
an hungred, and they that were with him; [4] how he entered
into the house of God, and did eat the shewbread, which
was not lawful for him to eat, neither for them which were
with him, but only for the priests? [5] Or have ye not read in
the law, how that on the sabbath days the priests in the temple profane the sabbath, and are blameless? [6] But I say unto
you that in this place is one greater than the temple. [7] But if
ye had known what this meaneth, I will have mercy, and not
sacrifice, ye would not have condemned the guiltless. [8] For
the Son of man is Lord even of the sabbath day.' [9] And when
he was departed thence, he went into their synagogue.

[10] And, behold, there was a man which had his hand withered. And they asked him, saying, 'Is it lawful to heal on the
sabbath days?' that they might accuse him. [11] And he said
unto them, 'What man shall there be among you, that shall
have one sheep, and if it fall into a pit on the sabbath day,
will he not lay hold on it, and lift it out? [12] How much then is
a man better than a sheep? Wherefore it is lawful to do well
on the sabbath days.' [13] Then saith he to the man, 'Stretch
forth thine hand.' And he stretched it forth; and it was restored
whole, like as the other.

[14] Then the Pharisees went out, and held a council against
him, how they might destroy him. [15] But when Jesus knew it,
he withdrew himself from thence, and great multitudes followed him, and he healed them all; [16] and charged them that
they should not make him known, [17] that it might be fulfilled

which was spoken by Esaias the prophet, saying, [18]'Behold
my servant, whom I have chosen; my beloved, in whom my
soul is well pleased: I will put my spirit upon him, and he
shall shew judgment to the Gentiles. [19]He shall not strive, nor
cry; neither shall any man hear his voice in the streets. [20]A
bruised reed shall he not break, and smoking flax shall he
not quench, till he send forth judgment unto victory. [21]And
in his name shall the Gentiles trust.'

[22]Then was brought unto him one possessed with a devil,
blind, and dumb: and he healed him, insomuch that the blind
and dumb both spake and saw. [23]And all the people were
amazed, and said, 'Is not this the son of David?' [24]But when
the Pharisees heard it, they said, 'This fellow doth not cast
out devils, but by Beelzebub the prince of the devils.' [25]And
Jesus knew their thoughts, and said unto them, 'Every kingdom divided against itself is brought to desolation; and every
city or house divided against itself shall not stand. [26]And if
Satan cast out Satan, he is divided against himself; how shall
then his kingdom stand? [27]And if I by Beelzebub cast out
devils, by whom do your children cast them out? Therefore
they shall be your judges. [28]But if I cast out devils by the
Spirit of God, then the kingdom of God is come unto you.
[29]Or else how can one enter into a strong man's house, and
spoil his goods, except he first bind the strong man? And
then he will spoil his house. [30]He that is not with me is against
me; and he that gathereth not with me scattereth abroad.

[31]'Wherefore I say unto you, all manner of sin and blasphemy shall be forgiven unto men: but the blasphemy against
the Holy Ghost shall not be forgiven unto men. [32]And who-

soever speaketh a word against the Son of man, it shall be
forgiven him: but whosoever speaketh against the Holy Ghost,
it shall not be forgiven him, neither in this world, neither in
the world to come. 33 Either make the tree good, and his fruit
good, or else make the tree corrupt, and his fruit corrupt: for
the tree is known by his fruit. 34 O generation of vipers, how
can ye, being evil, speak good things? For out of the abundance of the heart the mouth speaketh. 35 A good man out of
the good treasure of the heart bringeth forth good things:
and an evil man out of the evil treasure bringeth forth evil
things. 36 But I say unto you that every idle word that men
shall speak, they shall give account thereof in the day of
judgment. 37 For by thy words thou shalt be justified, and by
thy words thou shalt be condemned.'

38 Then certain of the scribes and of the Pharisees answered,
saying, 'Master, we would see a sign from thee.' 39 But he
answered and said unto them, 'An evil and adulterous generation seeketh after a sign; and there shall no sign be given
to it, but the sign of the prophet Jonas: 40 for as Jonas was
three days and three nights in the whale's belly; so shall the
Son of man be three days and three nights in the heart of the
earth. 41 The men of Nineveh shall rise in judgment with this
generation, and shall condemn it: because they repented at
the preaching of Jonas; and, behold, a greater than Jonas is
here. 42 The queen of the south shall rise up in the judgment
with this generation, and shall condemn it: for she came from
the uttermost parts of the earth to hear the wisdom of Solomon; and, behold, a greater than Solomon is here. 43 When
the unclean spirit is gone out of a man, he walketh through

dry places, seeking rest, and findeth none. 44 Then he saith, "I
will return into my house from whence I came out"; and when
he is come, he findeth it empty, swept, and garnished. 45 Then
goeth he, and taketh with himself seven other spirits more
wicked than himself, and they enter in and dwell there, and
the last state of that man is worse than the first. Even so shall
it be also unto this wicked generation.'

46 While he yet talked to the people, behold, his mother
and his brethren stood without, desiring to speak with
him. 47 Then one said unto him, 'Behold, thy mother and thy
brethren stand without, desiring to speak with thee.' 48 But
he answered and said unto him that told him, 'Who is my
mother? And who are my brethren?' 49 And he stretched
forth his hand toward his disciples, and said, 'Behold my
mother and my brethren! 50 For whosoever shall do the will
of my Father which is in heaven, the same is my brother, and
sister, and mother.'

13 The same day went Jesus out of the house, and sat by
the sea side. 2 And great multitudes were gathered
together unto him, so that he went into a ship, and sat; and
the whole multitude stood on the shore. 3 And he spake
many things unto them in parables, saying, 'Behold, a sower
went forth to sow; 4 and when he sowed, some seeds fell by
the way side, and the fowls came and devoured them up.
5 Some fell upon stony places, where they had not much
earth: and forthwith they sprung up, because they had no
deepness of earth. 6 And when the sun was up, they were
scorched; and because they had no root, they withered away.

7 And some fell among thorns; and the thorns sprung up, and
choked them. 8 But other fell into good ground, and brought
forth fruit, some an hundredfold, some sixtyfold, some thirtyfold. 9 Who hath ears to hear, let him hear.' 10 And the disciples came, and said unto him, 'Why speakest thou unto them
in parables?' 11 He answered and said unto them, 'Because it
is given unto you to know the mysteries of the kingdom of
heaven, but to them it is not given. 12 For whosoever hath, to
him shall be given, and he shall have more abundance: but
whosoever hath not, from him shall be taken away even that
he hath. 13 Therefore speak I to them in parables: because they
seeing see not; and hearing they hear not, neither do they
understand. 14 And in them is fulfilled the prophecy of Esaias,
which saith, "By hearing ye shall hear, and shall not understand; and seeing ye shall see, and shall not perceive: 15 for
this people's heart is waxed gross, and their ears are dull of
hearing, and their eyes they have closed, lest at any time
they should see with their eyes, and hear with their ears, and
should understand with their heart, and should be converted, and I should heal them." 16 But blessed are your eyes,
for they see, and your ears, for they hear. 17 For verily I say unto
you that many prophets and righteous men have desired to
see those things which ye see, and have not seen them; and
to hear those things which ye hear, and have not heard them.

18 'Hear ye therefore the parable of the sower. 19 When any
one heareth the word of the kingdom, and understandeth it
not, then cometh the wicked one, and catcheth away that
which was sown in his heart. This is he which received seed
by the way side. 20 But he that received the seed into stony

places, the same is he that heareth the word, and anon with joy
receiveth it; 21 yet hath he not root in himself, but dureth for a
while: for when tribulation or persecution ariseth because of
the word, by and by he is offended. 22 He also that received
seed among the thorns is he that heareth the word; and the
care of this world, and the deceitfulness of riches, choke the
word, and he becometh unfruitful. 23 But he that received
seed into the good ground is he that heareth the word, and
understandeth it; which also beareth fruit, and bringeth forth,
some an hundredfold, some sixty, some thirty.'

24 Another parable put he forth unto them, saying, 'The
kingdom of heaven is likened unto a man which sowed good
seed in his field: 25 but while men slept, his enemy came and
sowed tares among the wheat, and went his way. 26 But when
the blade was sprung up, and brought forth fruit, then
appeared the tares also. 27 So the servants of the householder
came and said unto him, "Sir, didst not thou sow good seed
in thy field? From whence then hath it tares?" 28 He said
unto them, "An enemy hath done this." The servants said
unto him, "Wilt thou then that we go and gather them up?"
29 But he said, "Nay, lest while ye gather up the tares, ye root
up also the wheat with them. 30 Let both grow together until
the harvest: and in the time of harvest I will say to the reapers,
'Gather ye together first the tares, and bind them in bundles
to burn them, but gather the wheat into my barn.'"'

31 Another parable put he forth unto them, saying, 'The
kingdom of heaven is like to a grain of mustard seed, which
a man took, and sowed in his field, 32 which indeed is the least
of all seeds: but when it is grown, it is the greatest among

herbs, and becometh a tree, so that the birds of the air come
and lodge in the branches thereof.'

33 Another parable spake he unto them. 'The kingdom of
heaven is like unto leaven, which a woman took, and hid in
three measures of meal, till the whole was leavened.' 34 All
these things spake Jesus unto the multitude in parables; and
without a parable spake he not unto them, 35 that it might be
fulfilled which was spoken by the prophet, saying, 'I will
open my mouth in parables; I will utter things which have
been kept secret from the foundation of the world.' 36 Then
Jesus sent the multitude away, and went into the house, and
his disciples came unto him, saying, 'Declare unto us the parable of the tares of the field.' 37 He answered and said unto
them, 'He that soweth the good seed is the Son of man; 38 the
field is the world; the good seed are the children of the kingdom; but the tares are the children of the wicked one; 39 the
enemy that sowed them is the devil; the harvest is the end of
the world; and the reapers are the angels. 40 As therefore the
tares are gathered and burned in the fire, so shall it be in the
end of this world. 41 The Son of man shall send forth his angels,
and they shall gather out of his kingdom all things that offend,
and them which do iniquity, 42 and shall cast them into a furnace of fire: there shall be wailing and gnashing of teeth.
43 Then shall the righteous shine forth as the sun in the kingdom of their Father. Who hath ears to hear, let him hear.

44 'Again, the kingdom of heaven is like unto treasure hid
in a field; the which when a man hath found, he hideth, and
for joy thereof goeth and selleth all that he hath, and buyeth
that field.

[45] 'Again, the kingdom of heaven is like unto a merchant
man, seeking goodly pearls, [46] who, when he had found one
pearl of great price, went and sold all that he had, and
bought it.

[47] 'Again, the kingdom of heaven is like unto a net, that
was cast into the sea, and gathered of every kind: [48] which,
when it was full, they drew to shore, and sat down, and
gathered the good into vessels, but cast the bad away. [49] So
shall it be at the end of the world. The angels shall come
forth, and sever the wicked from among the just, [50] and shall
cast them into the furnace of fire: there shall be wailing and
gnashing of teeth.' [51] Jesus saith unto them, 'Have ye understood all these things?' They say unto him, 'Yea, Lord.' [52] Then
said he unto them, 'Therefore every scribe which is instructed
unto the kingdom of heaven is like unto a man that is an
householder, which bringeth forth out of his treasure things
new and old.'

[53] And it came to pass, that when Jesus had finished these
parables, he departed thence. [54] And when he was come into
his own country, he taught them in their synagogue, insomuch that they were astonished, and said, 'Whence hath this
man this wisdom, and these mighty works? [55] Is not this the
carpenter's son? Is not his mother called Mary? And his
brethren, James, and Joses, and Simon, and Judas? [56] And his
sisters, are they not all with us? Whence then hath this man
all these things?' [57] And they were offended in him. But Jesus
said unto them, 'A prophet is not without honour, save in his
own country, and in his own house.' [58] And he did not many
mighty works there because of their unbelief.

14 At that time Herod the tetrarch heard of the fame of
Jesus, 2 and said unto his servants, 'This is John the Baptist; he is risen from the dead; and therefore mighty works
do shew forth themselves in him.'

3 For Herod had laid hold on John, and bound him, and
put him in prison for Herodias' sake, his brother Philip's wife.
4 For John said unto him, 'It is not lawful for thee to have
her.' 5 And when he would have put him to death, he feared
the multitude, because they counted him as a prophet. 6 But
when Herod's birthday was kept, the daughter of Herodias
danced before them, and pleased Herod. 7 Whereupon he
promised with an oath to give her whatsoever she would
ask. 8 And she, being before instructed of her mother, said,
'Give me here John Baptist's head in a charger.' 9 And the
king was sorry; nevertheless for the oath's sake, and them
which sat with him at meat, he commanded it to be given
her. 10 And he sent, and beheaded John in the prison. 11 And
his head was brought in a charger, and given to the damsel,
and she brought it to her mother. 12 And his disciples came,
and took up the body, and buried it, and went and told Jesus.

13 When Jesus heard of it, he departed thence by ship into
a desert place apart, and when the people had heard thereof,
they followed him on foot out of the cities. 14 And Jesus went
forth, and saw a great multitude, and was moved with compassion toward them, and he healed their sick.

15 And when it was evening, his disciples came to him,
saying, 'This is a desert place, and the time is now past; send
the multitude away, that they may go into the villages, and
buy themselves victuals.' 16 But Jesus said unto them, 'They

need not depart; give ye them to eat.' 17 And they say unto
him, 'We have here but five loaves, and two fishes.' 18 He said,
'Bring them hither to me.' 19 And he commanded the multitude to sit down on the grass, and took the five loaves, and
the two fishes, and looking up to heaven, he blessed, and
brake, and gave the loaves to his disciples, and the disciples
to the multitude. 20 And they did all eat, and were filled: and
they took up of the fragments that remained twelve baskets
full. 21 And they that had eaten were about five thousand
men, beside women and children.

22 And straightway Jesus constrained his disciples to get
into a ship, and to go before him unto the other side, while
he sent the multitudes away. 23 And when he had sent the
multitudes away, he went up into a mountain apart to pray:
and when the evening was come, he was there alone. 24 But
the ship was now in the midst of the sea, tossed with waves:
for the wind was contrary. 25 And in the fourth watch of the
night Jesus went unto them, walking on the sea. 26 And when
the disciples saw him walking on the sea, they were troubled, saying, 'It is a spirit' and they cried out for fear. 27 But
straightway Jesus spake unto them, saying, 'Be of good cheer;
it is I; be not afraid.' 28 And Peter answered him and said, 'Lord,
if it be thou, bid me come unto thee on the water.' 29 And he
said, 'Come.' And when Peter was come down out of the ship,
he walked on the water, to go to Jesus. 30 But when he saw the
wind boisterous, he was afraid; and beginning to sink, he
cried, saying, 'Lord, save me.' 31 And immediately Jesus stretched forth his hand, and caught him, and said unto him, 'O
thou of little faith, wherefore didst thou doubt?' 32 And when

they were come into the ship, the wind ceased. 33 Then they
that were in the ship came and worshipped him, saying, 'Of
a truth thou art the Son of God.'

34 And when they were gone over, they came into the land
of Gennesaret. 35 And when the men of that place had knowledge of him, they sent out into all that country round about,
and brought unto him all that were diseased; 36 and besought
him that they might only touch the hem of his garment: and
as many as touched were made perfectly whole.

15 Then came to Jesus scribes and Pharisees, which were
of Jerusalem, saying, 2 'Why do thy disciples transgress
the tradition of the elders? For they wash not their hands
when they eat bread.' 3 But he answered and said unto them,
'Why do ye also transgress the commandment of God by
your tradition? 4 For God commanded, saying, "Honour thy
father and mother," and, "He that curseth father or mother,
let him die the death." 5 But ye say, "Whosoever shall say to
his father or his mother, 'It is a gift, by whatsoever thou mightest be profited by me' 6 and honour not his father or his mother,
he shall be free." Thus have ye made the commandment of
God of none effect by your tradition. 7 Ye hypocrites, well did
Esaias prophesy of you, saying, 8 "This people draweth nigh
unto me with their mouth, and honoureth me with their lips;
but their heart is far from me. 9 But in vain they do worship
me, teaching for doctrines the commandments of men."'

10 And he called the multitude, and said unto them, 'Hear,
and understand: 11 not that which goeth into the mouth
defileth a man; but that which cometh out of the mouth, this

defileth a man.' 12 Then came his disciples, and said unto him,
'Knowest thou that the Pharisees were offended, after they
heard this saying?' 13 But he answered and said, 'Every plant,
which my heavenly Father hath not planted, shall be rooted
up. 14 Let them alone: they be blind leaders of the blind. And
if the blind lead the blind, both shall fall into the ditch.'
15 Then answered Peter and said unto him, 'Declare unto us
this parable.' 16 And Jesus said, 'Are ye also yet without understanding? 17 Do not ye yet understand, that whatsoever
entereth in at the mouth goeth into the belly, and is cast out
into the draught? 18 But those things which proceed out of
the mouth come forth from the heart; and they defile the
man. 19 For out of the heart proceed evil thoughts, murders,
adulteries, fornications, thefts, false witness, blasphemies.
20 These are the things which defile a man: but to eat with
unwashen hands defileth not a man.'

21 Then Jesus went thence, and departed into the coasts of
Tyre and Sidon. 22 And, behold, a woman of Canaan came out
of the same coasts, and cried unto him, saying, 'Have mercy
on me, O Lord, thou Son of David; my daughter is grievously vexed with a devil.' 23 But he answered her not a word.
And his disciples came and besought him, saying, 'Send her
away; for she crieth after us.' 24 But he answered and said, 'I
am not sent but unto the lost sheep of the house of Israel.'
25 Then came she and worshipped him, saying, 'Lord, help
me.' 26 But he answered and said, 'It is not meet to take the
children's bread, and to cast it to dogs.' 27 And she said,
'Truth, Lord, yet the dogs eat of the crumbs which fall from
their masters' table.' 28 Then Jesus answered and said unto

her, 'O woman, great is thy faith. Be it unto thee even as thou
wilt.' And her daughter was made whole from that very
hour. 29 And Jesus departed from thence, and came nigh unto
the sea of Galilee; and went up into a mountain, and sat down
there. 30 And great multitudes came unto him, having with
them those that were lame, blind, dumb, maimed, and many
others, and cast them down at Jesus' feet; and he healed them,
31 insomuch that the multitude wondered, when they saw the
dumb to speak, the maimed to be whole, the lame to walk,
and the blind to see, and they glorified the God of Israel.

32 Then Jesus called his disciples unto him, and said, 'I have
compassion on the multitude, because they continue with
me now three days, and have nothing to eat, and I will not
send them away fasting, lest they faint in the way.' 33 And his
disciples say unto him, 'Whence should we have so much
bread in the wilderness, as to fill so great a multitude?' 34 And
Jesus saith unto them, 'How many loaves have ye?' And they
said, 'Seven, and a few little fishes.' 35 And he commanded
the multitude to sit down on the ground. 36 And he took the
seven loaves and the fishes, and gave thanks, and brake them,
and gave to his disciples, and the disciples to the multitude.
37 And they did all eat, and were filled, and they took up of
the broken meat that was left seven baskets full. 38 And they
that did eat were four thousand men, beside women and
children. 39 And he sent away the multitude, and took ship,
and came into the coasts of Magdala.

16 The Pharisees also with the Sadducees came, and tempting desired him that he would shew them a sign from

heaven. 2 He answered and said unto them, 'When it is evening, ye say, "It will be fair weather, for the sky is red." 3 And
in the morning, "It will be foul weather today, for the sky is
red and lowring." O ye hypocrites, ye can discern the face of
the sky; but can ye not discern the signs of the times? 4 A
wicked and adulterous generation seeketh after a sign; and
there shall no sign be given unto it, but the sign of the
prophet Jonas.' And he left them, and departed. 5 And when
his disciples were come to the other side, they had forgotten
to take bread.

6 Then Jesus said unto them, 'Take heed and beware of
the leaven of the Pharisees and of the Sadducees.' 7 And they
reasoned among themselves, saying, 'It is because we have
taken no bread,' 8 which when Jesus perceived, he said unto
them, 'O ye of little faith, why reason ye among yourselves,
because ye have brought no bread? 9 Do ye not yet understand, neither remember the five loaves of the five thousand,
and how many baskets ye took up? 10 Neither the seven loaves
of the four thousand, and how many baskets ye took up?
11 How is it that ye do not understand that I spake it not to
you concerning bread, that ye should beware of the leaven
of the Pharisees and of the Sadducees?' 12 Then understood
they how that he bade them not beware of the leaven of bread,
but of the doctrine of the Pharisees and of the Sadducees.

13 When Jesus came into the coasts of Cæsarea Philippi,
he asked his disciples, saying, 'Whom do men say that I the
Son of man am?' 14 And they said, 'Some say that thou art
John the Baptist: some, Elias; and others, Jeremias, or one of
the prophets.' 15 He saith unto them, 'But whom say ye that I

am?' 16And Simon Peter answered and said, 'Thou art the
Christ, the Son of the living God.' 17And Jesus answered and
said unto him, 'Blessed art thou, Simon Bar-jona, for flesh
and blood hath not revealed it unto thee, but my Father
which is in heaven. 18And I say also unto thee that thou art
Peter, and upon this rock I will build my church; and the
gates of hell shall not prevail against it. 19And I will give unto
thee the keys of the kingdom of heaven, and whatsoever
thou shalt bind on earth shall be bound in heaven, and whatsoever thou shalt loose on earth shall be loosed in heaven.'
20Then charged he his disciples that they should tell no man
that he was Jesus the Christ.

21From that time forth began Jesus to shew unto his
disciples, how that he must go unto Jerusalem, and suffer
many things of the elders and chief priests and scribes, and
be killed, and be raised again the third day. 22Then Peter
took him, and began to rebuke him, saying, 'Be it far from
thee, Lord: this shall not be unto thee.' 23But he turned, and
said unto Peter, 'Get thee behind me, Satan. Thou art an
offence unto me, for thou savourest not the things that be of
God, but those that be of men.'

24Then said Jesus unto his disciples, 'If any man will come
after me, let him deny himself, and take up his cross, and
follow me. 25For whosoever will save his life shall lose it,
and whosoever will lose his life for my sake shall find it.
26For what is a man profited, if he shall gain the whole world,
and lose his own soul? Or what shall a man give in exchange
for his soul? 27For the Son of man shall come in the glory of
his Father with his angels; and then he shall reward every

man according to his works. 28 Verily I say unto you, there be
some standing here, which shall not taste of death, till they
see the Son of man coming in his kingdom.'

17 And after six days Jesus taketh Peter, James, and John
his brother, and bringeth them up into an high mountain apart, 2 and was transfigured before them, and his face
did shine as the sun, and his raiment was white as the light.
3 And, behold, there appeared unto them Moses and Elias
talking with him. 4 Then answered Peter, and said unto Jesus,
'Lord, it is good for us to be here: if thou wilt, let us make
here three tabernacles; one for thee, and one for Moses, and
one for Elias.' 5 While he yet spake, behold, a bright cloud
overshadowed them, and behold a voice out of the cloud,
which said, 'This is my beloved Son, in whom I am well
pleased; hear ye him.' 6 And when the disciples heard it, they
fell on their face, and were sore afraid. 7 And Jesus came and
touched them, and said, 'Arise, and be not afraid.' 8 And when
they had lifted up their eyes, they saw no man, save Jesus
only. 9 And as they came down from the mountain, Jesus
charged them, saying, 'Tell the vision to no man, until the
Son of man be risen again from the dead.' 10 And his disciples
asked him, saying, 'Why then say the scribes that Elias must
first come?' 11 And Jesus answered and said unto them, 'Elias
truly shall first come, and restore all things. 12 But I say unto
you that Elias is come already, and they knew him not, but
have done unto him whatsoever they listed. Likewise shall
also the Son of man suffer of them.' 13 Then the disciples
understood that he spake unto them of John the Baptist.

14And when they were come to the multitude, there came
to him a certain man, kneeling down to him, and saying,
15'Lord, have mercy on my son, for he is lunatick, and sore
vexed, for ofttimes he falleth into the fire, and oft into the
water. 16And I brought him to thy disciples, and they could
not cure him.' 17Then Jesus answered and said, 'O faithless
and perverse generation, how long shall I be with you? How
long shall I suffer you? Bring him hither to me.' 18And Jesus
rebuked the devil; and he departed out of him, and the child
was cured from that very hour. 19Then came the disciples to
Jesus apart, and said, 'Why could not we cast him out?' 20And
Jesus said unto them, 'Because of your unbelief: for verily I
say unto you, if ye have faith as a grain of mustard seed, ye
shall say unto this mountain, "Remove hence to yonder
place," and it shall remove; and nothing shall be impossible
unto you. 21Howbeit this kind goeth not out but by prayer
and fasting.'

22And while they abode in Galilee, Jesus said unto them,
'The Son of man shall be betrayed into the hands of men:
23and they shall kill him, and the third day he shall be raised
again.' And they were exceeding sorry.

24And when they were come to Capernaum, they that
received tribute money came to Peter, and said, 'Doth not
your master pay tribute?' 25He saith, 'Yes.' And when he
was come into the house, Jesus prevented him, saying, 'What
thinkest thou, Simon? Of whom do the kings of the earth take
custom or tribute? Of their own children, or of strangers?'
26Peter saith unto him, 'Of strangers.' Jesus saith unto him,
'Then are the children free. 27Notwithstanding, lest we should

offend them, go thou to the sea, and cast an hook, and take up the fish that first cometh up; and when thou hast opened his mouth, thou shalt find a piece of money; that take, and give unto them for me and thee.'

18 At the same time came the disciples unto Jesus, saying, 'Who is the greatest in the kingdom of heaven?' 2And Jesus called a little child unto him, and set him in the midst of them, 3and said, 'Verily I say unto you, except ye be converted, and become as little children, ye shall not enter into the kingdom of heaven. 4Whosoever therefore shall humble himself as this little child, the same is greatest in the kingdom of heaven. 5And whoso shall receive one such little child in my name receiveth me. 6But whoso shall offend one of these little ones which believe in me, it were better for him that a millstone were hanged about his neck, and that he were drowned in the depth of the sea.

7'Woe unto the world because of offences! For it must needs be that offences come; but woe to that man by whom the offence cometh! 8Wherefore if thy hand or thy foot offend thee, cut them off, and cast them from thee: it is better for thee to enter into life halt or maimed, rather than having two hands or two feet to be cast into everlasting fire. 9And if thine eye offend thee, pluck it out, and cast it from thee: it is better for thee to enter into life with one eye, rather than having two eyes to be cast into hell fire. 10Take heed that ye despise not one of these little ones; for I say unto you, that in heaven their angels do always behold the face of my Father which is in heaven. 11For the Son of man is come to save that

which was lost. 12 How think ye? If a man have an hundred
sheep, and one of them be gone astray, doth he not leave the
ninety and nine, and goeth into the mountains, and seeketh
that which is gone astray? 13 And if so be that he find it, verily
I say unto you, he rejoiceth more of that sheep, than of the
ninety and nine which went not astray. 14 Even so it is not the
will of your Father which is in heaven, that one of these little
ones should perish.

15 'Moreover if thy brother shall trespass against thee, go
and tell him his fault between thee and him alone: if he shall
hear thee, thou hast gained thy brother. 16 But if he will not
hear thee, then take with thee one or two more, that in the
mouth of two or three witnesses every word may be established. 17 And if he shall neglect to hear them, tell it unto the
church: but if he neglect to hear the church, let him be unto
thee as an heathen man and a publican. 18 Verily I say unto
you, whatsoever ye shall bind on earth shall be bound in
heaven, and whatsoever ye shall loose on earth shall be loosed
in heaven. 19 Again I say unto you that if two of you shall
agree on earth as touching any thing that they shall ask, it
shall be done for them of my Father which is in heaven.
20 For where two or three are gathered together in my name,
there am I in the midst of them.'

21 Then came Peter to him, and said, 'Lord, how oft shall
my brother sin against me, and I forgive him? Till seven
times?' 22 Jesus saith unto him, 'I say not unto thee, "Until seven
times," but, "Until seventy times seven."

23 'Therefore is the kingdom of heaven likened unto a certain king, which would take account of his servants. 24 And

when he had begun to reckon, one was brought unto him,
which owed him ten thousand talents. [25] But forasmuch as he
had not to pay, his lord commanded him to be sold, and his
wife, and children, and all that he had, and payment to be
made. [26] The servant therefore fell down, and worshipped
him, saying, "Lord, have patience with me, and I will pay thee
all." [27] Then the lord of that servant was moved with compassion, and loosed him, and forgave him the debt. [28] But the
same servant went out, and found one of his fellowservants,
which owed him an hundred pence, and he laid hands on
him, and took him by the throat, saying, "Pay me that thou
owest." [29] And his fellowservant fell down at his feet, and
besought him, saying, "Have patience with me, and I will
pay thee all." [30] And he would not, but went and cast him
into prison, till he should pay the debt. [31] So when his fellowservants saw what was done, they were very sorry, and
came and told unto their lord all that was done. [32] Then his
lord, after that he had called him, said unto him, "O thou
wicked servant, I forgave thee all that debt, because thou
desiredst me. [33] Shouldest not thou also have had compassion on thy fellowservant, even as I had pity on thee?" [34] And
his lord was wroth, and delivered him to the tormentors, till
he should pay all that was due unto him. [35] So likewise shall
my heavenly Father do also unto you, if ye from your hearts
forgive not every one his brother their trespasses.'

19 And it came to pass, that when Jesus had finished
these sayings, he departed from Galilee, and came into
the coasts of Judæa beyond Jordan; [2] and great multitudes

followed him; and he healed them there.
3 The Pharisees also came unto him, tempting him, and
saying unto him, 'Is it lawful for a man to put away his wife
for every cause?' 4 And he answered and said unto them,
'Have ye not read, that he which made them at the beginning made them male and female, 5 and said, "For this cause
shall a man leave father and mother, and shall cleave to his
wife, and they twain shall be one flesh"? 6 Wherefore they
are no more twain, but one flesh. What therefore God hath
joined together, let not man put asunder.' 7 They say unto him,
'Why did Moses then command to give a writing of divorcement, and to put her away?' 8 He saith unto them, 'Moses,
because of the hardness of your hearts suffered you to put
away your wives: but from the beginning it was not so. 9 And
I say unto you, whosoever shall put away his wife, except it
be for fornication, and shall marry another, committeth
adultery: and whoso marrieth her which is put away doth
commit adultery.'

10 His disciples say unto him, 'If the case of the man be so
with his wife, it is not good to marry.' 11 But he said unto them,
'All men cannot receive this saying, save they to whom it is
given. 12 For there are some eunuchs, which were so born from
their mother's womb, and there are some eunuchs, which were
made eunuchs of men, and there be eunuchs, which have
made themselves eunuchs for the kingdom of heaven's sake.
He that is able to receive it, let him receive it.'

13 Then were there brought unto him little children, that
he should put his hands on them, and pray, and the disciples
rebuked them. 14 But Jesus said, 'Suffer little children, and

forbid them not, to come unto me, for of such is the kingdom
of heaven.' 15 And he laid his hands on them, and departed thence.
16 And, behold, one came and said unto him, 'Good Master, what good thing shall I do, that I may have eternal life?'
17 And he said unto him, 'Why callest thou me good? There is
none good but one, that is, God: but if thou wilt enter into
life, keep the commandments.' 18 He saith unto him, 'Which?'
Jesus said, 'Thou shalt do no murder, thou shalt not commit
adultery, thou shalt not steal, thou shalt not bear false witness, 19 honour thy father and thy mother, and thou shalt
love thy neighbour as thyself.' 20 The young man saith unto
him, 'All these things have I kept from my youth up; what
lack I yet?' 21 Jesus said unto him, 'If thou wilt be perfect, go
and sell that thou hast, and give to the poor, and thou shalt
have treasure in heaven, and come and follow me.' 22 But
when the young man heard that saying, he went away sorrowful, for he had great possessions.

23 Then said Jesus unto his disciples, 'Verily I say unto
you, that a rich man shall hardly enter into the kingdom of
heaven. 24 And again I say unto you, it is easier for a camel to
go through the eye of a needle, than for a rich man to enter
into the kingdom of God.' 25 When his disciples heard it, they
were exceedingly amazed, saying, 'Who then can be saved?'
26 But Jesus beheld them, and said unto them, 'With men this
is impossible; but with God all things are possible.'

27 Then answered Peter and said unto him, 'Behold, we
have forsaken all, and followed thee; what shall we have
therefore?' 28 And Jesus said unto them, 'Verily I say unto
you that ye which have followed me, in the regeneration

when the Son of man shall sit in the throne of his glory, ye also shall sit upon twelve thrones, judging the twelve tribes of Israel. 29 And every one that hath forsaken houses, or brethren, or sisters, or father, or mother, or wife, or children, or lands, for my name's sake, shall receive an hundredfold, and shall inherit everlasting life. 30 But many that are first shall be last; and the last shall be first.

20 1 For the kingdom of heaven is like unto a man that is an householder, which went out early in the morning to hire labourers into his vineyard. 2 And when he had agreed with the labourers for a penny a day, he sent them into his vineyard. 3 And he went out about the third hour, and saw others standing idle in the marketplace, 4 and said unto them, "Go ye also into the vineyard, and whatsoever is right I will give you." And they went their way. 5 Again he went out about the sixth and ninth hour, and did likewise. 6 And about the eleventh hour he went out, and found others standing idle, and saith unto them, "Why stand ye here all the day idle?" 7 They say unto him, "Because no man hath hired us." He saith unto them, "Go ye also into the vineyard; and whatsoever is right, that shall ye receive." 8 So when even was come, the lord of the vineyard saith unto his steward, "Call the labourers, and give them their hire, beginning from the last unto the first." 9 And when they came that were hired about the eleventh hour, they received every man a penny. 10 But when the first came, they supposed that they should have received more; and they likewise received every man a penny. 11 And when they had received it, they

murmured against the goodman of the house, [12]saying,
"These last have wrought but one hour, and thou hast made
them equal unto us, which have borne the burden and heat
of the day." [13]But he answered one of them, and said,
"Friend, I do thee no wrong; didst not thou agree with me
for a penny? [14]Take that thine is, and go thy way: I will give
unto this last, even as unto thee. [15]Is it not lawful for me to
do what I will with mine own? Is thine eye evil, because I
am good?" [16]So the last shall be first, and the first last: for
many be called, but few chosen.'

[17]And Jesus going up to Jerusalem took the twelve disciples
apart in the way, and said unto them, [18]'Behold, we go up to
Jerusalem; and the Son of man shall be betrayed unto the
chief priests and unto the scribes, and they shall condemn
him to death, [19]and shall deliver him to the Gentiles to mock,
and to scourge, and to crucify him, and the third day he
shall rise again.'

[20]Then came to him the mother of Zebedee's children
with her sons, worshipping him, and desiring a certain thing
of him. [21]And he said unto her, 'What wilt thou?' She saith
unto him, 'Grant that these my two sons may sit, the one on
thy right hand, and the other on the left, in thy kingdom.'
[22]But Jesus answered and said, 'Ye know not what ye ask.
Are ye able to drink of the cup that I shall drink of, and to be
baptized with the baptism that I am baptized with?' They
say unto him, 'We are able.' [23]And he saith unto them, 'Ye
shall drink indeed of my cup, and be baptized with the baptism that I am baptized with: but to sit on my right hand,
and on my left, is not mine to give, but it shall be given to

them for whom it is prepared of my Father.' 24 And when the
ten heard it, they were moved with indignation against the
two brethren. 25 But Jesus called them unto him, and said, 'Ye
know that the princes of the Gentiles exercise dominion over
them, and they that are great exercise authority upon them.
26 But it shall not be so among you: but whosoever will be
great among you, let him be your minister; 27 and whosoever
will be chief among you, let him be your servant. 28 Even as
the Son of man came not to be ministered unto, but to minister, and to give his life a ransom for many. 29 And as they
departed from Jericho, a great multitude followed him.

30 And, behold, two blind men sitting by the way side,
when they heard that Jesus passed by, cried out, saying, 'Have
mercy on us, O Lord, thou Son of David.' 31 And the multitude rebuked them, because they should hold their peace:
but they cried the more, saying, 'Have mercy on us, O Lord,
thou Son of David.' 32 And Jesus stood still, and called them,
and said, 'What will ye that I shall do unto you?' 33 They say
unto him, 'Lord, that our eyes may be opened.' 34 So Jesus had
compassion on them, and touched their eyes, and immediately their eyes received sight, and they followed him.

21 And when they drew nigh unto Jerusalem, and were
come to Bethphage, unto the mount of Olives, then
sent Jesus two disciples, 2 saying unto them, 'Go into the village over against you, and straightway ye shall find an ass
tied, and a colt with her; loose them, and bring them unto
me. 3 And if any man say ought unto you, ye shall say, "The
Lord hath need of them," and straightway he will send them.'

4All this was done, that it might be fulfilled which was spoken by the prophet, saying, 5'Tell ye the daughter of Sion,
"Behold, thy King cometh unto thee, meek, and sitting upon
an ass, and a colt the foal of an ass."' 6And the disciples went,
and did as Jesus commanded them, 7and brought the ass,
and the colt, and put on them their clothes, and they set him
thereon. 8And a very great multitude spread their garments
in the way; others cut down branches from the trees, and
strawed them in the way. 9And the multitudes that went
before, and that followed, cried, saying, 'Hosanna to the Son
of David. Blessed is he that cometh in the name of the Lord.
Hosanna in the highest.' 10And when he was come into Jerusalem, all the city was moved, saying, 'Who is this?' 11And the
multitude said, 'This is Jesus the prophet of Nazareth of Galilee.'

12And Jesus went into the temple of God, and cast out all
them that sold and bought in the temple, and overthrew the
tables of the moneychangers, and the seats of them that sold
doves, 13and said unto them, 'It is written, "My house shall
be called the house of prayer," but ye have made it a den of
thieves.' 14And the blind and the lame came to him in the
temple; and he healed them. 15And when the chief priests
and scribes saw the wonderful things that he did, and the
children crying in the temple, and saying, 'Hosanna to the
Son of David,' they were sore displeased, 16and said unto
him, 'Hearest thou what these say?' And Jesus saith unto
them, 'Yea; have ye never read, "Out of the mouth of babes
and sucklings thou hast perfected praise"?'

17And he left them, and went out of the city into Bethany;
and he lodged there. 18Now in the morning as he returned

into the city, he hungered. 19And when he saw a fig tree in
the way, he came to it, and found nothing thereon, but leaves
only, and said unto it, 'Let no fruit grow on thee hencefor-
ward for ever.' And presently the fig tree withered away.
20And when the disciples saw it, they marvelled, saying,
'How soon is the fig tree withered away!' 21Jesus answered
and said unto them, 'Verily I say unto you, if ye have faith,
and doubt not, ye shall not only do this which is done to the
fig tree, but also if ye shall say unto this mountain, "Be thou
removed, and be thou cast into the sea," it shall be done.
22And all things, whatsoever ye shall ask in prayer, believing, ye shall receive.'

23And when he was come into the temple, the chief priests
and the elders of the people came unto him as he was teaching, and said, 'By what authority doest thou these things?
And who gave thee this authority?' 24And Jesus answered
and said unto them, 'I also will ask you one thing, which if
ye tell me, I in like wise will tell you by what authority I do
these things. 25The baptism of John, whence was it? From
heaven, or of men?' And they reasoned with themselves,
saying, 'If we shall say, "From heaven," he will say unto us,
"Why did ye not then believe him?" 26But if we shall say,
"Of men," we fear the people, for all hold John as a prophet.'
27And they answered Jesus, and said, 'We cannot tell.' And
he said unto them, 'Neither tell I you by what authority I do
these things.

28'But what think ye? A certain man had two sons; and
he came to the first, and said, "Son, go work to day in my vineyard." 29He answered and said, "I will not," but afterward he

repented, and went. 30 And he came to the second, and said
likewise. And he answered and said, "I go, sir," and went
not. 31 Whether of them twain did the will of his father?'
They say unto him, 'The first.' Jesus saith unto them, 'Verily I
say unto you that the publicans and the harlots go into the
kingdom of God before you. 32 For John came unto you in the
way of righteousness, and ye believed him not: but the publicans and the harlots believed him, and ye, when ye had
seen it, repented not afterward, that ye might believe him.

33 'Hear another parable. There was a certain householder,
which planted a vineyard, and hedged it round about, and
digged a winepress in it, and built a tower, and let it out to
husbandmen, and went into a far country. 34 And when the
time of the fruit drew near, he sent his servants to the husbandmen, that they might receive the fruits of it. 35 And the
husbandmen took his servants, and beat one, and killed
another, and stoned another. 36 Again, he sent other servants
more than the first, and they did unto them likewise. 37 But
last of all he sent unto them his son, saying, "They will reverence my son." 38 But when the husbandmen saw the son,
they said among themselves, "This is the heir; come, let us
kill him, and let us seize on his inheritance." 39 And they caught
him, and cast him out of the vineyard, and slew him. 40 When
the lord therefore of the vineyard cometh, what will he do
unto those husbandmen?' 41 They say unto him, 'He will mis-
erably destroy those wicked men, and will let out his vineyard unto other husbandmen, which shall render him the
fruits in their seasons.' 42 Jesus saith unto them, 'Did ye never
read in the scriptures, "The stone which the builders rejected,

the same is become the head of the corner: this is the Lord's
doing, and it is marvellous in our eyes"? 43 Therefore say I
unto you, the kingdom of God shall be taken from you, and
given to a nation bringing forth the fruits thereof. 44 And
whosoever shall fall on this stone shall be broken, but on
whomsoever it shall fall, it will grind him to powder.' 45 And
when the chief priests and Pharisees had heard his parables,
they perceived that he spake of them. 46 But when they sought
to lay hands on him, they feared the multitude, because they
took him for a prophet.

22 And Jesus answered and spake unto them again by
parables, and said, 2 'The kingdom of heaven is like
unto a certain king, which made a marriage for his son, 3 and
sent forth his servants to call them that were bidden to the
wedding, and they would not come. 4 Again, he sent forth
other servants, saying, "Tell them which are bidden, 'Behold,
I have prepared my dinner: my oxen and my fatlings are
killed, and all things are ready; come unto the marriage.'" 5 But
they made light of it, and went their ways, one to his farm,
another to his merchandise, 6 and the remnant took his servants, and entreated them spitefully, and slew them. 7 But when
the king heard thereof, he was wroth, and he sent forth his
armies, and destroyed those murderers, and burned up their
city. 8 Then saith he to his servants, "The wedding is ready,
but they which were bidden were not worthy. 9 Go ye therefore into the highways, and as many as ye shall find, bid to
the marriage." 10 So those servants went out into the highways, and gathered together all as many as they found, both

bad and good, and the wedding was furnished with guests.
[11]'And when the king came in to see the guests, he saw
there a man which had not on a wedding garment, [12] and he
saith unto him, "Friend, how camest thou in hither not having a wedding garment?" And he was speechless. [13] Then
said the king to the servants, "Bind him hand and foot, and
take him away, and cast him into outer darkness: there shall
be weeping and gnashing of teeth." [14] For many are called,
but few are chosen.'
[15] Then went the Pharisees, and took counsel how they
might entangle him in his talk. [16] And they sent out unto him
their disciples with the Herodians, saying, 'Master, we know
that thou art true, and teachest the way of God in truth, neither carest thou for any man, for thou regardest not the person
of men. [17] Tell us therefore, what thinkest thou? Is it lawful to
give tribute unto Caesar, or not?' [18] But Jesus perceived their
wickedness, and said, 'Why tempt ye me, ye hypocrites?
[19] Shew me the tribute money.' And they brought unto him a
penny. [20] And he saith unto them, 'Whose is this image and
superscription?' [21] They say unto him, 'Caesar's.' Then saith
he unto them, 'Render therefore unto Caesar the things which
are Caesar's; and unto God the things that are God's.' [22] When
they had heard these words, they marvelled, and left him,
and went their way.
[23] The same day came to him the Sadducees, which say
that there is no resurrection, and asked him, [24] saying, 'Master, Moses said, "If a man die, having no children, his brother
shall marry his wife, and raise up seed unto his brother."
[25] Now there were with us seven brethren, and the first,

when he had married a wife, deceased, and, having no issue,
left his wife unto his brother: 26 likewise the second also, and
the third, unto the seventh. 27 And last of all the woman died
also. 28 Therefore in the resurrection whose wife shall she be
of the seven? For they all had her.' 29 Jesus answered and
said unto them, 'Ye do err, not knowing the scriptures, nor
the power of God. 30 For in the resurrection they neither marry,
nor are given in marriage, but are as the angels of God in
heaven. 31 But as touching the resurrection of the dead, have
ye not read that which was spoken unto you by God, saying,
32 "I am the God of Abraham, and the God of Isaac, and the
God of Jacob?" God is not the God of the dead, but of the
living.' 33 And when the multitude heard this, they were
astonished at his doctrine.

34 But when the Pharisees had heard that he had put the
Sadducees to silence, they were gathered together. 35 Then one
of them, which was a lawyer, asked him a question, tempting him, and saying, 36 'Master, which is the great commandment in the law?' 37 Jesus said unto him, '"Thou shalt love
the Lord thy God with all thy heart, and with all thy soul, and
with all thy mind." 38 This is the first and great commandment. 39 And the second is like unto it, "Thou shalt love thy
neighbour as thyself." 40 On these two commandments hang
all the law and the prophets.'

41 While the Pharisees were gathered together, Jesus asked
them, 42 saying, 'What think ye of Christ? Whose son is he?'
They say unto him, 'The Son of David.' 43 He saith unto them,
'How then doth David in spirit call him "Lord", saying,
44 "The Lord said unto my Lord, 'Sit thou on my right hand,

till I make thine enemies thy footstool'?" 45 If David then call him "Lord", how is he his son?' 46 And no man was able to answer him a word, neither durst any man from that day forth ask him any more questions.

23 Then spake Jesus to the multitude, and to his disciples, 2 saying, 'The scribes and the Pharisees sit in Moses' seat; 3 all therefore whatsoever they bid you observe, that observe and do; but do not ye after their works, for they say, and do not. 4 For they bind heavy burdens and grievous to be borne, and lay them on men's shoulders; but they themselves will not move them with one of their fingers. 5 But all their works they do for to be seen of men; they make broad their phylacteries, and enlarge the borders of their garments, 6 and love the uppermost rooms at feasts, and the chief seats in the synagogues, 7 and greetings in the markets, and to be called of men, "Rabbi, Rabbi". 8 But be not ye called Rabbi: for one is your Master, even Christ; and all ye are brethren. 9 And call no man your father upon the earth: for one is your Father, which is in heaven. 10 Neither be ye called masters: for one is your Master, even Christ. 11 But he that is greatest among you shall be your servant. 12 And whosoever shall exalt himself shall be abased; and he that shall humble himself shall be exalted.

13 'But woe unto you, scribes and Pharisees, hypocrites! For ye shut up the kingdom of heaven against men, for ye neither go in yourselves, neither suffer ye them that are entering to go in. 14 Woe unto you, scribes and Pharisees, hypocrites! For ye devour widows' houses, and for a pretence

make long prayer: therefore ye shall receive the greater
damnation. 15 Woe unto you, scribes and Pharisees, hypocrites!
For ye compass sea and land to make one proselyte, and
when he is made, ye make him twofold more the child of
hell than yourselves. 16 Woe unto you, ye blind guides, which
say, "Whosoever shall swear by the temple, it is nothing; but
whosoever shall swear by the gold of the temple, he is a
debtor!" 17 Ye fools and blind: for whether is greater, the gold,
or the temple that sanctifieth the gold? 18 And, "Whosoever
shall swear by the altar, it is nothing; but whosoever sweareth by the gift that is upon it, he is guilty." 19 Ye fools and
blind: for whether is greater, the gift, or the altar that sanctifieth the gift? 20 Whoso therefore shall swear by the altar,
sweareth by it, and by all things thereon. 21 And whoso shall
swear by the temple, sweareth by it, and by him that dwelleth therein. 22 And he that shall swear by heaven, sweareth
by the throne of God, and by him that sitteth thereon. 23 Woe
unto you, scribes and Pharisees, hypocrites! For ye pay tithe
of mint and anise and cummin, and have omitted the weight-
ier matters of the law, judgment, mercy, and faith. These
ought ye to have done, and not to leave the other undone.
24 Ye blind guides, which strain at a gnat, and swallow a camel.
25 Woe unto you, scribes and Pharisees, hypocrites! For ye
make clean the outside of the cup and of the platter, but within
they are full of extortion and excess. 26 Thou blind Pharisee,
cleanse first that which is within the cup and platter, that the
outside of them may be clean also. 27 Woe unto you, scribes
and Pharisees, hypocrites! For ye are like unto whited sepulchres, which indeed appear beautiful outward, but are within

full of dead men's bones, and of all uncleanness. 28 Even so ye
also outwardly appear righteous unto men, but within ye are
full of hypocrisy and iniquity. 29 Woe unto you, scribes and
Pharisees, hypocrites! Because ye build the tombs of the
prophets, and garnish the sepulchres of the righteous, 30 and
say, "If we had been in the days of our fathers, we would not
have been partakers with them in the blood of the prophets."
31 Wherefore ye be witnesses unto yourselves, that ye are the
children of them which killed the prophets. 32 Fill ye up then
the measure of your fathers. 33 Ye serpents, ye generation of
vipers, how can ye escape the damnation of hell?

34 'Wherefore, behold, I send unto you prophets, and wise
men, and scribes: and some of them ye shall kill and crucify;
and some of them shall ye scourge in your synagogues, and
persecute them from city to city: 35 that upon you may come
all the righteous blood shed upon the earth, from the blood
of righteous Abel unto the blood of Zacharias son of Bara-
chias, whom ye slew between the temple and the altar. 36 Verily
I say unto you, all these things shall come upon this generation. 37 O Jerusalem, Jerusalem, thou that killest the prophets, and stonest them which are sent unto thee, how often
would I have gathered thy children together, even as a hen
gathereth her chickens under her wings, and ye would not!
38 Behold, your house is left unto you desolate. 39 For I say
unto you, ye shall not see me henceforth, till ye shall say,
"Blessed is he that cometh in the name of the Lord."'

24 And Jesus went out, and departed from the temple,
and his disciples came to him for to shew him the

buildings of the temple. 2And Jesus said unto them, 'See ye not
all these things? Verily I say unto you, there shall not be left
here one stone upon another, that shall not be thrown down.'

3And as he sat upon the mount of Olives, the disciples
came unto him privately, saying, 'Tell us, when shall these
things be? And what shall be the sign of thy coming, and of
the end of the world?' 4And Jesus answered and said unto
them, 'Take heed that no man deceive you. 5For many shall
come in my name, saying, "I am Christ," and shall deceive
many. 6And ye shall hear of wars and rumours of wars; see
that ye be not troubled, for all these things must come to pass,
but the end is not yet. 7For nation shall rise against nation,
and kingdom against kingdom, and there shall be famines,
and pestilences, and earthquakes, in diverse places. 8All these
are the beginning of sorrows. 9Then shall they deliver you
up to be afflicted, and shall kill you, and ye shall be hated of
all nations for my name's sake. 10And then shall many be
offended, and shall betray one another, and shall hate one
another. 11And many false prophets shall rise, and shall
deceive many. 12And because iniquity shall abound, the love
of many shall wax cold. 13But he that shall endure unto the
end, the same shall be saved. 14And this gospel of the kingdom shall be preached in all the world for a witness unto all
nations; and then shall the end come. 15When ye therefore
shall see the abomination of desolation, spoken of by Daniel
the prophet, stand in the holy place (whoso readeth, let him
understand), 16then let them which be in Judæa flee into the
mountains; 17let him which is on the housetop not come
down to take any thing out of his house: 18neither let him

which is in the field return back to take his clothes. 19 And
woe unto them that are with child, and to them that give
suck in those days! 20 But pray ye that your flight be not in
the winter, neither on the sabbath day. 21 For then shall be
great tribulation, such as was not since the beginning of the
world to this time, no, nor ever shall be. 22 And except those
days should be shortened, there should no flesh be saved,
but for the elect's sake those days shall be shortened. 23 Then
if any man shall say unto you, "Lo, here is Christ," or "There,"
believe it not. 24 For there shall arise false Christs, and false
prophets, and shall shew great signs and wonders; insomuch
that, if it were possible, they shall deceive the very elect.
25 Behold, I have told you before. 26 Wherefore if they shall say
unto you, "Behold, he is in the desert," go not forth; "Behold,
he is in the secret chambers," believe it not. 27 For as the lightning cometh out of the east, and shineth even unto the west;
so shall also the coming of the Son of man be. 28 For wheresoever the carcase is, there will the eagles be gathered together.

29 'Immediately after the tribulation of those days shall
the sun be darkened, and the moon shall not give her light,
and the stars shall fall from heaven, and the powers of the
heavens shall be shaken. 30 And then shall appear the sign of
the Son of man in heaven, and then shall all the tribes of the
earth mourn, and they shall see the Son of man coming in
the clouds of heaven with power and great glory. 31 And he
shall send his angels with a great sound of a trumpet, and
they shall gather together his elect from the four winds,
from one end of heaven to the other. 32 Now learn a parable
of the fig tree. When his branch is yet tender, and putteth

forth leaves, ye know that summer is nigh: 33 so likewise ye,
when ye shall see all these things, know that it is near, even
at the doors. 34 Verily I say unto you, this generation shall not
pass, till all these things be fulfilled. 35 Heaven and earth shall
pass away, but my words shall not pass away.

36 'But of that day and hour knoweth no man, no, not the
angels of heaven, but my Father only. 37 But as the days of
Noe were, so shall also the coming of the Son of man be. 38 For
as in the days that were before the flood they were eating
and drinking, marrying and giving in marriage, until the day
that Noe entered into the ark, 39 and knew not until the flood
came, and took them all away; so shall also the coming of the
Son of man be. 40 Then shall two be in the field; the one shall
be taken, and the other left. 41 Two women shall be grinding at
the mill; the one shall be taken, and the other left.

42 'Watch therefore: for ye know not what hour your Lord
doth come. 43 But know this, that if the goodman of the house
had known in what watch the thief would come, he would
have watched, and would not have suffered his house to be
broken up. 44 Therefore be ye also ready: for in such an hour
as ye think not the Son of man cometh. 45 Who then is a faithful and wise servant, whom his lord hath made ruler over
his household, to give them meat in due season? 46 Blessed is
that servant, whom his lord when he cometh shall find so
doing. 47 Verily I say unto you that he shall make him ruler
over all his goods. 48 But and if that evil servant shall say in
his heart, "My lord delayeth his coming," 49 and shall begin
to smite his fellow-servants, and to eat and drink with the
drunken; 50 the lord of that servant shall come in a day when

he looketh not for him, and in an hour that he is not aware of,
51and shall cut him asunder, and appoint him his portion with
the hypocrites: there shall be weeping and gnashing of teeth.

25 'Then shall the kingdom of heaven be likened unto
ten virgins, which took their lamps, and went forth
to meet the bridegroom. 2And five of them were wise, and
five were foolish. 3They that were foolish took their lamps,
and took no oil with them, 4but the wise took oil in their vessels with their lamps. 5While the bridegroom tarried, they
all slumbered and slept. 6And at midnight there was a cry
made, "Behold, the bridegroom cometh; go ye out to meet
him." 7Then all those virgins arose, and trimmed their lamps.
8And the foolish said unto the wise, "Give us of your oil; for
our lamps are gone out." 9But the wise answered, saying,
"Not so, lest there be not enough for us and you, but go ye
rather to them that sell, and buy for yourselves." 10And while
they went to buy, the bridegroom came; and they that were
ready went in with him to the marriage; and the door was
shut. 11Afterward came also the other virgins, saying, "Lord,
Lord, open to us." 12But he answered and said, "Verily I say
unto you, I know you not." 13Watch therefore, for ye know
neither the day nor the hour wherein the Son of man cometh.
14'For the kingdom of heaven is as a man travelling into a
far country, who called his own servants, and delivered unto
them his goods, 15and unto one he gave five talents, to another
two, and to another one; to every man according to his several ability; and straightway took his journey. 16Then he that
had received the five talents went and traded with the same,

and made them other five talents. 17 And likewise he that had
received two, he also gained other two. 18 But he that had
received one went and digged in the earth, and hid his lord's
money. 19 After a long time the lord of those servants cometh,
and reckoneth with them. 20 And so he that had received five
talents came and brought other five talents, saying, "Lord,
thou deliveredst unto me five talents; behold, I have gained
beside them five talents more." 21 His lord said unto him,
"Well done, thou good and faithful servant: thou hast been
faithful over a few things; I will make thee ruler over many
things; enter thou into the joy of thy lord." 22 He also that had
received two talents came and said, "Lord, thou deliveredst
unto me two talents; behold, I have gained two other talents
beside them." 23 His lord said unto him, "Well done, good
and faithful servant; thou hast been faithful over a few
things, I will make thee ruler over many things; enter thou
into the joy of thy lord." 24 Then he which had received the
one talent came and said, "Lord, I knew thee that thou art an
hard man, reaping where thou hast not sown, and gathering
where thou hast not strawed, 25 and I was afraid, and went
and hid thy talent in the earth: lo, there thou hast that is
thine." 26 His lord answered and said unto him, "Thou wicked
and slothful servant, thou knewest that I reap where I sowed
not, and gather where I have not strawed. 27 Thou oughtest
therefore to have put my money to the exchangers, and then
at my coming I should have received mine own with usury.
28 Take therefore the talent from him, and give it unto him
which hath ten talents. 29 For unto every one that hath shall
be given, and he shall have abundance: but from him that

hath not shall be taken away even that which he hath. 30 And
cast ye the unprofitable servant into outer darkness: there
shall be weeping and gnashing of teeth."
31 'When the Son of man shall come in his glory, and all
the holy angels with him, then shall he sit upon the throne of
his glory, 32 and before him shall be gathered all nations, and
he shall separate them one from another, as a shepherd divideth his sheep from the goats, 33 and he shall set the sheep
on his right hand, but the goats on the left. 34 Then shall the
King say unto them on his right hand, "Come, ye blessed of
my Father, inherit the kingdom prepared for you from the
foundation of the world; 35 for I was an hungred, and ye gave
me meat; I was thirsty, and ye gave me drink; I was a stranger, and ye took me in; 36 naked, and ye clothed me; I was
sick, and ye visited me; I was in prison, and ye came unto
me." 37 Then shall the righteous answer him, saying, "Lord,
when saw we thee an hungred, and fed thee? Or thirsty, and
gave thee drink? 38 When saw we thee a stranger, and took
thee in? Or naked, and clothed thee? 39 Or when saw we thee
sick, or in prison, and came unto thee?" 40 And the King shall
answer and say unto them, "Verily I say unto you, inasmuch
as ye have done it unto one of the least of these my brethren,
ye have done it unto me." 41 Then shall he say also unto them
on the left hand, "Depart from me, ye cursed, into everlasting fire, prepared for the devil and his angels: 42 for I was an
hungred, and ye gave me no meat; I was thirsty, and ye gave
me no drink; 43 I was a stranger, and ye took me not in; naked,
and ye clothed me not; sick, and in prison, and ye visited me
not." 44 Then shall they also answer him, saying, "Lord, when

saw we thee an hungred, or athirst, or a stranger, or naked,
or sick, or in prison, and did not minister unto thee?" 45 Then
shall he answer them, saying, "Verily I say unto you, inasmuch as ye did it not to one of the least of these, ye did it not
to me." 46 And these shall go away into everlasting punishment, but the righteous into life eternal.'

26 And it came to pass, when Jesus had finished all
these sayings, he said unto his disciples, 2 'Ye know
that after two days is the feast of the passover, and the
Son of man is betrayed to be crucified.' 3 Then assembled
together the chief priests, and the scribes, and the elders of
the people, unto the palace of the high priest, who was
called Caiaphas, 4 and consulted that they might take Jesus
by subtilty, and kill him. 5 But they said, 'Not on the feast
day, lest there be an uproar among the people.'

6 Now when Jesus was in Bethany, in the house of Simon
the leper, 7 there came unto him a woman having an alabaster
box of very precious ointment, and poured it on his head, as
he sat at meat. 8 But when his disciples saw it, they had
indignation, saying, 'To what purpose is this waste? 9 For
this ointment might have been sold for much, and given to
the poor.' 10 When Jesus understood it, he said unto them,
'Why trouble ye the woman? For she hath wrought a good
work upon me. 11 For ye have the poor always with you; but
me ye have not always. 12 For in that she hath poured this
ointment on my body, she did it for my burial. 13 Verily I say
unto you, wheresoever this gospel shall be preached in the
whole world, there shall also this, that this woman hath

done, be told for a memorial of her.'
14 Then one of the twelve, called Judas Iscariot, went unto
the chief priests, 15 and said unto them, 'What will ye give
me, and I will deliver him unto you?' And they covenanted
with him for thirty pieces of silver. 16 And from that time he
sought opportunity to betray him.

17 Now the first day of the feast of unleavened bread the
disciples came to Jesus, saying unto him, 'Where wilt thou
that we prepare for thee to eat the passover?' 18 And he said,
'Go into the city to such a man, and say unto him, "The Master saith, 'My time is at hand; I will keep the passover at thy
house with my disciples.'"' 19 And the disciples did as Jesus
had appointed them; and they made ready the passover.
20 Now when the even was come, he sat down with the twelve.
21 And as they did eat, he said, 'Verily I say unto you that one
of you shall betray me.' 22 And they were exceeding sorrowful, and began every one of them to say unto him, 'Lord, is it
I?' 23 And he answered and said, 'He that dippeth his hand
with me in the dish, the same shall betray me. 24 The Son of
man goeth as it is written of him, but woe unto that man by
whom the Son of man is betrayed! It had been good for that
man if he had not been born.' 25 Then Judas, which betrayed
him, answered and said, 'Master, is it I?' He said unto him,
'Thou hast said.'

26 And as they were eating, Jesus took bread, and blessed
it, and brake it, and gave it to the disciples, and said, 'Take,
eat; this is my body.' 27 And he took the cup, and gave thanks,
and gave it to them, saying, 'Drink ye all of it, 28 for this is my
blood of the new testament, which is shed for many for the

remission of sins. [29] But I say unto you, I will not drink henceforth of this fruit of the vine, until that day when I drink it
new with you in my Father's kingdom.' [30] And when they
had sung an hymn, they went out into the mount of Olives.
[31] Then saith Jesus unto them, 'All ye shall be offended because
of me this night, for it is written, "I will smite the shepherd,
and the sheep of the flock shall be scattered abroad." [32] But
after I am risen again, I will go before you into Galilee.' [33] Peter
answered and said unto him, 'Though all men shall be
offended because of thee, yet will I never be offended.' [34] Jesus
said unto him, 'Verily I say unto thee that this night, before
the cock crow, thou shalt deny me thrice.' [35] Peter said unto
him, 'Though I should die with thee, yet will I not deny
thee.' Likewise also said all the disciples.

[36] Then cometh Jesus with them unto a place called Gethsemane, and saith unto the disciples, 'Sit ye here, while I go
and pray yonder.' [37] And he took with him Peter and the two
sons of Zebedee, and began to be sorrowful and very heavy.
[38] Then saith he unto them, 'My soul is exceeding sorrowful,
even unto death; tarry ye here, and watch with me.' [39] And he
went a little farther, and fell on his face, and prayed, saying,
'O my Father, if it be possible, let this cup pass from me:
nevertheless not as I will, but as thou wilt.' [40] And he cometh
unto the disciples, and findeth them asleep, and saith unto
Peter, 'What, could ye not watch with me one hour? [41] Watch
and pray, that ye enter not into temptation: the spirit indeed
is willing, but the flesh is weak.' [42] He went away again the
second time, and prayed, saying, 'O my Father, if this cup
may not pass away from me, except I drink it, thy will be

done.’ 43 And he came and found them asleep again: for their
eyes were heavy. 44 And he left them, and went away again,
and prayed the third time, saying the same words. 45 Then
cometh he to his disciples, and saith unto them, ‘Sleep on
now, and take your rest: behold, the hour is at hand, and the
Son of man is betrayed into the hands of sinners. 46 Rise, let
us be going: behold, he is at hand that doth betray me.’

47 And while he yet spake, lo, Judas, one of the twelve,
came, and with him a great multitude with swords and staves,
from the chief priests and elders of the people. 48 Now he
that betrayed him gave them a sign, saying, ‘Whomsoever I
shall kiss, that same is he; hold him fast.’ 49 And forthwith he
came to Jesus, and said, ‘Hail, master,’ and kissed him. 50 And
Jesus said unto him, ‘Friend, wherefore art thou come?’ Then
came they, and laid hands on Jesus, and took him. 51 And,
behold, one of them which were with Jesus stretched out his
hand, and drew his sword, and struck a servant of the high
priest’s, and smote off his ear. 52 Then said Jesus unto him,
‘Put up again thy sword into his place: for all they that take
the sword shall perish with the sword. 53 Thinkest thou that I
cannot now pray to my Father, and he shall presently give
me more than twelve legions of angels? 54 But how then shall
the scriptures be fulfilled, that thus it must be?’ 55 In that
same hour said Jesus to the multitudes, ‘Are ye come out as
against a thief with swords and staves for to take me? I sat
daily with you teaching in the temple, and ye laid no hold
on me. 56 But all this was done, that the scriptures of the
prophets might be fulfilled.’ Then all the disciples forsook
him, and fled.

57 And they that had laid hold on Jesus led him away to Caiaphas the high priest, where the scribes and the elders were assembled. 58 But Peter followed him afar off unto the high priest's palace, and went in, and sat with the servants, to see the end. 59 Now the chief priests, and elders, and all the council, sought false witness against Jesus, to put him to death, 60 but found none; yea, though many false witnesses came, yet found they none. At the last came two false witnesses, 61 and said, 'This fellow said, "I am able to destroy the temple of God, and to build it in three days."' 62 And the high priest arose, and said unto him, 'Answerest thou nothing? What is it which these witness against thee?' 63 But Jesus held his peace. And the high priest answered and said unto him, 'I adjure thee by the living God, that thou tell us whether thou be the Christ, the Son of God.' 64 Jesus saith unto him, 'Thou hast said: nevertheless I say unto you, hereafter shall ye see the Son of man sitting on the right hand of power, and coming in the clouds of heaven.' 65 Then the high priest rent his clothes, saying, 'He hath spoken blasphemy; what further need have we of witnesses? Behold, now ye have heard his blasphemy. 66 What think ye?' They answered and said, 'He is guilty of death.' 67 Then did they spit in his face, and buffeted him; and others smote him with the palms of their hands, 68 saying, 'Prophesy unto us, thou Christ. Who is he that smote thee?'

69 Now Peter sat without in the palace, and a damsel came unto him, saying, 'Thou also wast with Jesus of Galilee.' 70 But he denied before them all, saying, 'I know not what thou sayest.' 71 And when he was gone out into the porch,

another maid saw him, and said unto them that were there,
'This fellow was also with Jesus of Nazareth.' 72 And again he
denied with an oath: 'I do not know the man.' 73 And after a
while came unto him they that stood by, and said to Peter,
'Surely thou also art one of them; for thy speech bewrayeth
thee.' 74 Then began he to curse and to swear, saying, 'I know
not the man.' And immediately the cock crew. 75 And Peter
remembered the word of Jesus, which said unto him, 'Before
the cock crow, thou shalt deny me thrice.' And he went out,
and wept bitterly.

27 When the morning was come, all the chief priests
and elders of the people took counsel against Jesus to
put him to death: 2 and when they had bound him, they led
him away, and delivered him to Pontius Pilate the governor.
3 Then Judas, which had betrayed him, when he saw that
he was condemned, repented himself, and brought again the
thirty pieces of silver to the chief priests and elders, 4 saying,
'I have sinned in that I have betrayed the innocent blood.'
And they said, 'What is that to us? See thou to that.' 5 And he
cast down the pieces of silver in the temple, and departed,
and went and hanged himself. 6 And the chief priests took
the silver pieces, and said, 'It is not lawful for to put them
into the treasury, because it is the price of blood.' 7 And they
took counsel, and bought with them the potter's field, to
bury strangers in. 8 Wherefore that field was called 'the field
of blood' unto this day. 9 Then was fulfilled that which was
spoken by Jeremy the prophet, saying, 'And they took the
thirty pieces of silver, the price of him that was valued,

whom they of the children of Israel did value, [10]and gave
them for the potter's field, as the Lord appointed me.' [11]And
Jesus stood before the governor, and the governor asked
him, saying, 'Art thou the King of the Jews?' And Jesus said
unto him, 'Thou sayest.' [12]And when he was accused of the
chief priests and elders, he answered nothing. [13]Then said
Pilate unto him, 'Hearest thou not how many things they witness against thee?' [14]And he answered him to never a word;
insomuch that the governor marvelled greatly. [15]Now at that
feast the governor was wont to release unto the people a
prisoner, whom they would. [16]And they had then a notable
prisoner, called Barabbas. [17]Therefore when they were gathered together, Pilate said unto them, 'Whom will ye that I
release unto you? Barabbas, or Jesus which is called Christ?'
[18]For he knew that for envy they had delivered him.

[19]When he was set down on the judgment seat, his wife
sent unto him, saying, 'Have thou nothing to do with that
just man: for I have suffered many things this day in a dream
because of him.' [20]But the chief priests and elders persuaded
the multitude that they should ask Barabbas, and destroy
Jesus. [21]The governor answered and said unto them, 'Whether
of the twain will ye that I release unto you?' They said,
'Barabbas.' [22]Pilate saith unto them, 'What shall I do then
with Jesus which is called Christ?' They all say unto him,
'Let him be crucified.' [23]And the governor said, 'Why, what
evil hath he done?' But they cried out the more, saying, 'Let
him be crucified.'

[24]When Pilate saw that he could prevail nothing, but that
rather a tumult was made, he took water, and washed his

hands before the multitude, saying, 'I am innocent of the
blood of this just person: see ye to it.' 25 Then answered all
the people, and said, 'His blood be on us, and on our children.'
26 Then released he Barabbas unto them, and when he
had scourged Jesus, he delivered him to be crucified. 27 Then
the soldiers of the governor took Jesus into the common hall,
and gathered unto him the whole band of soldiers. 28 And
they stripped him, and put on him a scarlet robe.
29 And when they had platted a crown of thorns, they put
it upon his head, and a reed in his right hand, and they
bowed the knee before him, and mocked him, saying, 'Hail,
King of the Jews!' 30 And they spit upon him, and took the
reed, and smote him on the head. 31 And after that they had
mocked him, they took the robe off from him, and put his
own raiment on him, and led him away to crucify him. 32 And
as they came out, they found a man of Cyrene, Simon by
name: him they compelled to bear his cross. 33 And when
they were come unto a place called Golgotha, that is to say, a
place of a skull, 34 they gave him vinegar to drink mingled
with gall, and when he had tasted thereof, he would not
drink. 35 And they crucified him, and parted his garments,
casting lots: that it might be fulfilled which was spoken by
the prophet, 'They parted my garments among them, and
upon my vesture did they cast lots.' 36 And sitting down they
watched him there; 37 and set up over his head his accusation
written, 'This is Jesus the King of the Jews.' 38 Then were there
two thieves crucified with him, one on the right hand, and
another on the left.
39 And they that passed by reviled him, wagging their

heads, 40 and saying, 'Thou that destroyest the temple, and
buildest it in three days, save thyself. If thou be the Son of
God, come down from the cross.' 41 Likewise also the chief
priests, mocking him, with the scribes and elders, said, 42 'He
saved others; himself he cannot save. If he be the King of
Israel, let him now come down from the cross, and we will
believe him. 43 He trusted in God; let him deliver him now, if
he will have him: for he said, "I am the Son of God."' 44 The
thieves also, which were crucified with him, cast the same in
his teeth. 45 Now from the sixth hour there was darkness over
all the land unto the ninth hour. 46 And about the ninth hour
Jesus cried with a loud voice, saying, 'Eli, Eli, lama sabachthani?' that is to say, 'My God, my God, why hast thou forsaken me?' 47 Some of them that stood there, when they heard
that, said, 'This man calleth for Elias.' 48 And straightway one
of them ran, and took a spunge, and filled it with vinegar,
and put it on a reed, and gave him to drink. 49 The rest said,
'Let be, let us see whether Elias will come to save him.'

50 Jesus, when he had cried again with a loud voice, yielded
up the ghost. 51 And, behold, the veil of the temple was rent
in twain from the top to the bottom; and the earth did quake,
and the rocks rent; 52 and the graves were opened; and many
bodies of the saints which slept arose, 53 and came out of the
graves after his resurrection, and went into the holy city, and
appeared unto many. 54 Now when the centurion, and they
that were with him, watching Jesus, saw the earthquake, and
those things that were done, they feared greatly, saying,
'Truly this was the Son of God.' 55 And many women were
there beholding afar off, which followed Jesus from Galilee,

ministering unto him, 56 among which was Mary Magdalene, and Mary the mother of James and Joses, and the mother of Zebedee's children. 57 When the even was come, there came a rich man of Arimathæa, named Joseph, who also himself was Jesus' disciple. 58 He went to Pilate, and begged the body of Jesus. Then Pilate commanded the body to be delivered. 59 And when Joseph had taken the body, he wrapped it in a clean linen cloth, 60 and laid it in his own new tomb, which he had hewn out in the rock, and he rolled a great stone to the door of the sepulchre, and departed. 61 And there was Mary Magdalene, and the other Mary, sitting over against the sepulchre.

62 Now the next day, that followed the day of the preparation, the chief priests and Pharisees came together unto Pilate, 63 saying, 'Sir, we remember that that deceiver said, while he was yet alive, "After three days I will rise again." 64 Command therefore that the sepulchre be made sure until the third day, lest his disciples come by night, and steal him away, and say unto the people, "He is risen from the dead," so the last error shall be worse than the first.' 65 Pilate said unto them, 'Ye have a watch: go your way, make it as sure as ye can.' 66 So they went, and made the sepulchre sure, sealing the stone, and setting a watch.

28 In the end of the sabbath, as it began to dawn toward the first day of the week, came Mary Magdalene and the other Mary to see the sepulchre. 2 And, behold, there was a great earthquake: for the angel of the Lord descended from heaven, and came and rolled back the stone from the door,

and sat upon it. 3 His countenance was like lightning, and his
raiment white as snow, 4 and for fear of him the keepers did
shake, and became as dead men. 5 And the angel answered
and said unto the women, 'Fear not ye, for I know that ye
seek Jesus, which was crucified. 6 He is not here: for he is risen,
as he said. Come, see the place where the Lord lay. 7 And go
quickly, and tell his disciples that he is risen from the dead;
and, behold, he goeth before you into Galilee; there shall ye
see him: lo, I have told you.' 8 And they departed quickly
from the sepulchre with fear and great joy; and did run to
bring his disciples word.

9 And as they went to tell his disciples, behold, Jesus met
them, saying, 'All hail.' And they came and held him by the
feet, and worshipped him. 10 Then said Jesus unto them, 'Be
not afraid: go tell my brethren that they go into Galilee, and
there shall they see me.'

11 Now when they were going, behold, some of the watch
came into the city, and shewed unto the chief priests all the
things that were done. 12 And when they were assembled with
the elders, and had taken counsel, they gave large money unto
the soldiers, 13 saying, 'Say ye, "His disciples came by night,
and stole him away while we slept." 14 And if this come to the
governor's ears, we will persuade him, and secure you.' 15 So
they took the money, and did as they were taught, and this
saying is commonly reported among the Jews until this day.

16 Then the eleven disciples went away into Galilee, into a
mountain where Jesus had appointed them. 17 And when
they saw him, they worshipped him, but some doubted.
18 And Jesus came and spake unto them, saying, 'All power is

given unto me in heaven and in earth.
[19] 'Go ye therefore, and teach all nations, baptizing them
in the name of the Father, and of the Son, and of the Holy
Ghost, [20] teaching them to observe all things whatsoever I
have commanded you, and, lo, I am with you alway, even
unto the end of the world. Amen.'

titles in the series

genesis – *introduced by e. l. doctorow*
exodus – *introduced by david grossman*
job – *introduced by charles frazier*
selections from the book of psalms – *introduced by bono*
proverbs – *introduced by charles johnson*
ecclesiastes – *introduced by doris lessing*
matthew – *introduced by francisco goldman*
mark – *introduced by barry hannah*
luke – *introduced by thomas cahill*
john – *introduced by darcey steinke*
corinthians – *introduced by fay weldon*
revelation – *introduced by kathleen norris*

mark

the gospel according to

mark

authorized king james version

grove press
new york

---

with an introduction by | barry hannah

The Pocket Canons were originally published in the U.K. in 1998 by Canongate Books, Ltd.
Published simultaneously in Canada
Printed in the United States of America

FIRST AMERICAN EDITION

Copyright information is on file with the Library of Congress
ISBN 0-8021-3617-6

Design by Paddy Cramsie

Grove Press
841 Broadway
New York, NY 10003

99 00 01 02 10 9 8 7 6 5 4 3 2 1

a note about pocket canons

The Authorized King James Version of the Bible, translated between 1603 and 1611, coincided with an extraordinary flowering of English literature. This version, more than any other, and possibly more than any other work in history, has had an influence in shaping the language we speak and write today. Presenting individual books from the Bible as separate volumes, as they were originally conceived, encourages the reader to approach them as literary works in their own right.

The first twelve books in this series encompass categories as diverse as history, fiction, philosophy, love poetry, and law. Each Pocket Canon also has its own introduction, specially commissioned from an impressive range of writers, which provides a personal interpretation of the text and explores its contemporary relevance.

Barry Hannah is the author of eleven novels and collections of short stories. His books include the novels Geronimo Rex *(winner of the William Faulkner Prize and a National Book Award finalist) and* Ray *(an American Book Award nominee), and the collection of stories* Airships, *which is regarded as a contemporary classic. His awards include recognition from the American Academy of Arts & Letters for achievement in fiction and the Robert Penn Warren Award from the Fellowship of Southern Writers. He lives in Oxford, Mississippi.*

introduction by barry hannah

Mark, leanest of the Gospels, composed around 70 A.D., when the Jewish War saw the destruction of the temple by the army of Titus, was written in a climate of misery and apocalypse. Mark invented the form of the gospel, which means "good news." Yet much of his work countenances despair, doubt, treachery, and death.

These are the same conditions that attend the Turkish earthquake as I write now in the final months of the millennium. Whole cities have collapsed, forty-five thousand body bags have been requested by the government, the rebuilding cost surpasses the state resources, and signs of hope seem far away, even alien.

Mark may have addressed persecuted and refugee Christians of a community in the Roman province of Syria. They looked for an imminent Parousia (second coming) upon the destruction of the temple, and were disappointed when the end had not come, as the scholar Wilfrid Harrington explains.*

This gospel is neglected, and the least quoted. Thomas Jefferson hardly includes material from Mark at all in the Jefferson Bible, wherein he intended to concretize, from the Gospels, "the most sublime and benevolent code of morals which has ever been offered to man." Mark may have seemed

* In *Mark*, Collegeville, Minn.: Liturgical Press, 1991.

obscure or elliptical to him. Harrington accounts for the neglect of Mark: "The gospel is uncompromisingly uncomfortable . . . suffering Messiahship and suffering discipleship . . . between the times of resurrection and consummation."

Scholars seem to agree that the most reliable manuscripts of Mark's gospel end at 16:8, not at 16:20, as supplied by many versions. It is helpful to look at the final verses for a tone of the whole gospel:

> And when the sabbath was past, Mary Magdalene, and Mary the mother of James, and Salome, had brought sweet spices, that they might come and anoint him. And very early in the morning the first day of the week, they came into the sepulchre at the rising of the sun. And they said among themselves, "Who shall roll us away the stone at the door of the sepulchre?" And when they looked, they saw the stone was rolled away; for it was very great. And entering the sepulchre, they saw a young man sitting on the right side, clothed in a long white garment; and they were affrighted. And he saith unto them, "Be not affrighted; ye seek Jesus of Nazareth, which was crucified. He is risen; he is not here; behold the place where they laid him. But go your way, tell his disciples and Peter that he goeth before you into Galilee: there shall ye see him, as he said unto you." And they went out quickly, and fled from the sepulchre; for they trembled and were amazed; neither said they any thing to any man; for they were afraid.

There is plainly more fear than hope here, even from the women who have remained faithful throughout the crucifixion while the disciples fled for reasons of personal safety—the very men who dropped their nets to follow Jesus, who saw the healing and the miracles and the walk on water; four of whom heard God speak to Christ from a bright cloud, and one of whom, Peter, the famous denier of Christ three times before the cock crew twice, would be the rock on which Christianity was built. These men could not honor the last hours of Christ by staying awake while he pled with his Father to commute his sentence of death on the cross.

Fear and fatigue, the atheism of evident biology, wherein no man returns from death—these beset the *best* men Christ was able to assemble and appoint as apostles, that is, missionaries of the good news. Judas Iscariot, the crassest and most cowardly of all, has already betrayed Christ to the officials for thirty pieces of silver and then hanged himself in a late attack of conscience. We should remember, however, that Judas *was* a disciple. He was no stranger.

Mark is a book of utter realism, very uncomfortable. It is the vase, basic, without the amplified blooms given to it by the later gospellers Matthew, Luke, and John. The vase, in its abiding economy, has great beauty and holds promise of eternal life, but its theme is heavy on bafflement, misunderstanding, and grief. Even Jesus seems to misunderstand the capabilities of his chosen twelve. He constantly upbraids them and is surprised by their obtuseness. Simply, he has found the men too human—skeptical, cowardly, unimaginative, power seeking, weak. They have quit their professions to follow him, but they never intended to follow him into the precincts of death.

They behave like the deists who had much to do with founding America. God has created the world but then forgotten it. They behave like present bad Christians, like many of us, in fact. The disciples may even be worse than modern believers. They have had hard evidence to believe—visual, aural, physical. We have manuscripts two thousand years old and the testimonies, quite often, of those we dislike and distrust, many who seem a plague of new Pharisees, the screaming Law.

Here is a curious example of the complaint of a modern man against apostles of Christ: Englishman H. E. Arnhold, leading businessman and former chairman of the Shanghai Municipal Council, protests the behavior of a large number of up-country American missionaries in a Japanese internment camp at Chapei (China) during World War II. The missionaries would not comply with camp rules, neglected cleanliness in the lavatories, occupied more floor space than they were entitled to, interfered with the distribution of eggs, and, most annoying of all, propagated the species.

> Considering the overcrowded and undernourished condition of the camp one would have thought that self-restraint would have been exercised, so that the camp would not have been deprived of most necessary food (eggs and milk) to provide for this increase in population, apart from the indecency of sexual intercourse in over-crowded dormitories and the embarrassment, annoyance, and disturbance caused to other inmates. . . . One person went through the nightly per-

formance of quoting the Bible to an unwilling spouse until she submitted to his importunities.*

I have never heard Christians accused of being too sexy in public.

Such reportings of the worldly have trailed Christians ever since I have been alive, and there is hardly need to list the more lethal depredations of the Crusades, the Inquisition, the Conquistadors, the Witch Trials, and the collusion of the Vatican with anticommunist fascists, even Hitler; or the late squalor and greed of Jim and Tammy Bakker and Jimmy Swaggart, or other hypocrites and wolves unto the sheep, in order to fill the cyclorama of misdeeds that we are invited to by secular humanists, liberal atheists, and common gleeful wags. We breathe the very air of disbelief and doubt and are currently led by an ostentatious Baptist Bible-toter who delighted in fellatio in the Oval Office just minutes after the funeral of his supposed pal Ron Brown. We did not need to know this, but apparently we adored it when we did. Because we are assured that nobody is better than we are, and this gives comfort to our nasty republican hearts.

But remember that the disciples, constantly upbraided, cowardly, treacherous, obtuse, much weaker than their women, became the apostles of light and went on to their own heroic sufferings, persecutions, jails, and crucifixions.

They were good enough.

* Bernard Wasserstein, *Secret War in Shanghai*, Boston: Houghton Mifflin, 1998, pp. 139-140.

Christ appeared living to them in Galilee and sent them out. They were not only forgiven but adored. They were promised constant friendship and direction by the Savior. This at a time when by all outer appearances the day was doomed, men were confused and abandoned, women huddled in slavish existences, their Savior mocked and destroyed in the humiliating scandal of the cross.

The message of Mark is heartening to bad Christians such as myself, who doubt daily, in our comfort, and even doubt the earthly thing that has brought them the most joy—the writing of stories, in my case. But what serious writer has not doubted the efficacy of words themselves, or their relative courage and truth? We might all be set aside under the leisure section, in the club of idlers and dabblers, of the Great Newspaper in the Sky. Sunday newspaper hell. Such doubts have led to total renunciation of earlier works by born-again converts like Tolstoy, or just rational despair, as with Beckett, who, when bragged upon by some last visitor to his deathbed, said, "But it's just words. Only words. Nothing."

Every day, honest men and women awake to misery, restlessness, doubt, even torture, *if* they awake, and we forget that things were always so, and much worse. We are not in Turkey, dead, or bereft of loved ones overnight. We are in the great nation founded on Christian inclusiveness and forgiveness and tolerance, are we not? That it is an inconceivably wasteful ant colony of Darwinian fascism, the crassest, most materialistic monster the world has ever witnessed, does not occur to us that often, as it does to foreigners, many of whom clamor to enter and drain their brains therein. An exponential amplitude of old Rome, inflicting itself internationally almost with the perfection of flood water.

But it is hopeful to know that not only forgiveness but the power of the Savior's friendship remain available to each unworthy one. And that through the layers of comfort we can reach a decision that will make us happier and the world much better, although Christ has warned that this is the most unlikely decision of all, more difficult than the decision of the early disciples. They were merely fishermen and had only to drop their nets.

Now I offer a poem inspired by Mark's gospel, a brutal and exquisite work, in paravoice of the Savior as I have perceived it.

> Do not think so much.
> Surrender. Believe.
> Unprepared, move out to the world and testify.
> The words will come. Serve.
> From now on service is kingly.
> There are no more kings.
> Serve. Help. Love. Others as thyself.
> This is impossible but do it.
> You have seen enough. You have seen it all,
> The miracles, the walk on water, Father speaking
> from a bright cloud.
> You were not there but the centurion was,
> Through the last hour.
> The women, faithful, down the hill, waiting and
> watching.
> "Truly this was the Son of God," told the centurion.

To all near the cross. Not you, craven.
The temple did not fall but its veil was rent
Top to bottom. Enough. You do not need the whole
  catastrophe,
For it has already taken place.
God is not in the temple anymore.
You cowards, keep running, but now you are mine,
My brothers and sisters.
Tell them. Help. Love. Service.
My good cowards, weaklings, doubters,
How I love you,
Whom I serve, and will see in Galilee.

I am not aroused to poetry very often but Mark has done it, with his mysterious compact power. I hope the poem will be forgiven its deficiencies, as I do not those of my students, in the spirit of Mark and a recent movie by Robert Duvall, *The Apostle*. The movie is exceptional in modern circumstances because of its favorable testimony to a Christian apostle (a murderer) and the power of his tiny church.

The apostle invited everyone to bring their instruments to the first service. An old black man has brought a trumpet and blurts on it horribly in praise of the Lord. The apostle chuckles—one of Duvall's best faces ever—and exclaims something like "Beautiful!" It put me in mind of Christ himself, in His love for our spirits despite all outward proof.

the gospel according to st mark

The beginning of the gospel of Jesus Christ, the Son of God;
2 as it is written in the prophets, 'Behold, I send my messenger before thy face, which shall prepare thy way before thee.
3 The voice of one crying in the wilderness, "Prepare ye the
way of the Lord, make his paths straight."' 4 John did baptize
in the wilderness, and preach the baptism of repentance for
the remission of sins. 5 And there went out unto him all the
land of Judæa, and they of Jerusalem, and were all baptized
of him in the river of Jordan, confessing their sins.

6 And John was clothed with camel's hair, and with a girdle of a skin about his loins; and he did eat locusts and wild
honey; 7 and preached, saying, 'There cometh one mightier
than I after me, the latchet of whose shoes I am not worthy
to stoop down and unloose. 8 I indeed have baptized you
with water; but he shall baptize you with the Holy Ghost.'

9 And it came to pass in those days, that Jesus came from
Nazareth of Galilee, and was baptized of John in Jordan.
10 And straightway coming up out of the water, he saw the
heavens opened, and the Spirit like a dove descending upon
him. 11 And there came a voice from heaven, saying, 'Thou art
my beloved Son, in whom I am well pleased.'

12 And immediately the Spirit driveth him into the wilderness. 13 And he was there in the wilderness forty days, tempted

of Satan; and was with the wild beasts; and the angels ministered unto him.
[14] Now after that John was put in prison, Jesus came into
Galilee, preaching the gospel of the kingdom of God, [15] and
saying, 'The time is fulfilled, and the kingdom of God is at
hand; repent ye, and believe the gospel.'
[16] Now as he walked by the sea of Galilee, he saw Simon
and Andrew his brother casting a net into the sea, for they
were fishers. [17] And Jesus said unto them, 'Come ye after me,
and I will make you to become fishers of men.' [18] And straightway they forsook their nets, and followed him.
[19] And when he had gone a little further thence, he saw
James the son of Zebedee, and John his brother, who also
were in the ship mending their nets. [20] And straightway he
called them: and they left their father Zebedee in the ship
with the hired servants, and went after him.
[21] And they went into Capernaum; and straightway on
the sabbath day he entered into the synagogue, and taught.
[22] And they were astonished at his doctrine: for he taught
them as one that had authority, and not as the scribes. [23] And
there was in their synagogue a man with an unclean spirit;
and he cried out, [24] saying, 'Let us alone; what have we to do
with thee, thou Jesus of Nazareth? Art thou come to destroy
us? I know thee who thou art, the Holy One of God.' [25] And
Jesus rebuked him, saying, 'Hold thy peace, and come out of
him.' [26] And when the unclean spirit had torn him, and cried
with a loud voice, he came out of him. [27] And they were all
amazed, insomuch that they questioned among themselves,
saying, 'What thing is this? What new doctrine is this? For

with authority commandeth he even the unclean spirits, and
they do obey him.' 28 And immediately his fame spread abroad
throughout all the region round about Galilee.

29 And forthwith, when they were come out of the synagogue, they entered into the house of Simon and Andrew,
with James and John. 30 But Simon's wife's mother lay sick of
a fever, and anon they tell him of her. 31 And he came and
took her by the hand, and lifted her up; and immediately the
fever left her, and she ministered unto them.

32 And at even, when the sun did set, they brought unto
him all that were diseased, and them that were possessed
with devils. 33 And all the city was gathered together at the
door. 34 And he healed many that were sick of divers diseases,
and cast out many devils; and suffered not the devils to
speak, because they knew him.

35 And in the morning, rising up a great while before day,
he went out, and departed into a solitary place, and there
prayed. 36 And Simon and they that were with him followed
after him. 37 And when they had found him, they said unto
him, 'All men seek for thee.' 38 And he said unto them, 'Let us
go into the next towns, that I may preach there also; for therefore came I forth.' 39 And he preached in their synagogues
throughout all Galilee, and cast out devils.

40 And there came a leper to him, beseeching him, and
kneeling down to him, and saying unto him, 'If thou wilt, thou
canst make me clean.' 41 And Jesus, moved with compassion,
put forth his hand, and touched him, and saith unto him, 'I
will; be thou clean.' 42 And as soon as he had spoken, immediately the leprosy departed from him, and he was cleansed.

43 And he straitly charged him, and forthwith sent him away;
44 and saith unto him, 'See thou say nothing to any man; but
go thy way, shew thyself to the priest, and offer for thy clean-
sing those things which Moses commanded, for a testimony
unto them.' 45 But he went out, and began to publish it much,
and to blaze abroad the matter, insomuch that Jesus could
no more openly enter into the city, but was without in desert
places; and they came to him from every quarter.

2 And again he entered into Capernaum after some days;
and it was noised that he was in the house. 2 And straightway many were gathered together, insomuch that there was
no room to receive them, no, not so much as about the door;
and he preached the word unto them. 3 And they come unto
him, bringing one sick of the palsy, which was borne of four.
4 And when they could not come nigh unto him for the press,
they uncovered the roof where he was; and when they had
broken it up, they let down the bed wherein the sick of the
palsy lay. 5 When Jesus saw their faith, he said unto the sick
of the palsy, 'Son, thy sins be forgiven thee.'

6 But there were certain of the scribes sitting there, and
reasoning in their hearts, 7 'Why doth this man thus speak
blasphemies? Who can forgive sins but God only?' 8 And
immediately when Jesus perceived in his spirit that they so
reasoned within themselves, he said unto them, 'Why reason
ye these things in your hearts? 9 Whether is it easier to say to
the sick of the palsy, "Thy sins be forgiven thee," or to say,
"Arise, and take up thy bed, and walk"? 10 But that ye may
know that the Son of man hath power on earth to forgive

sins,' he saith to the sick of the palsy, 11 'I say unto thee, Arise,
and take up thy bed, and go thy way into thine house.' 12 And
immediately he arose, took up the bed, and went forth before
them all; insomuch that they were all amazed, and glorified
God, saying, 'We never saw it on this fashion.'

13 And he went forth again by the sea side; and all the multitude resorted unto him, and he taught them. 14 And as he
passed by, he saw Levi the son of Alphæus sitting at the
receipt of custom, and said unto him, 'Follow me.' And Levi
arose and followed him.

15 And it came to pass, that, as Jesus sat at meat in his
house, many publicans and sinners sat also together with
Jesus and his disciples; for there were many, and they followed him. 16 And when the scribes and Pharisees saw him
eat with publicans and sinners, they said unto his disciples,
'How is it that he eateth and drinketh with publicans and
sinners?' 17 When Jesus heard it, he saith unto them, 'They that
are whole have no need of the physician, but they that are sick;
I came not to call the righteous, but sinners to repentance.'

18 And the disciples of John and of the Pharisees used to
fast; and they come and say unto him, 'Why do the disciples
of John and of the Pharisees fast, but thy disciples fast not?'
19 And Jesus said unto them, 'Can the children of the bridechamber fast, while the bridegroom is with them? As long as
they have the bridegroom with them, they cannot fast. 20 But
the days will come, when the bridegroom shall be taken
away from them, and then shall they fast in those days.

21 'No man also seweth a piece of new cloth on an old garment; else the new piece that filled it up taketh away from

the old, and the rent is made worse. [22]And no man putteth
new wine into old bottles; else the new wine doth burst the
bottles, and the wine is spilled, and the bottles will be marred;
but new wine must be put into new bottles.' [23]And it came to
pass that he went through the corn fields on the sabbath
day; and his disciples began, as they went, to pluck the ears
of corn. [24]And the Pharisees said unto him, 'Behold, why do
they on the sabbath day that which is not lawful?' [25]And he
said unto them, 'Have ye never read what David did, when
he had need, and was an hungred, he, and they that were
with him? [26]How he went into the house of God in the days
of Abiathar the high priest, and did eat the shewbread, which
is not lawful to eat but for the priests, and gave also to them
which were with him?'

[27]And he said unto them, 'The sabbath was made for man,
and not man for the sabbath; [28]therefore the Son of man is
Lord also of the sabbath.'

3 And he entered again into the synagogue; and there
was a man there which had a withered hand. [2]And they
watched him, whether he would heal him on the sabbath
day; that they might accuse him.

[3]And he saith unto the man which had the withered
hand, 'Stand forth.' [4]And he saith unto them, 'Is it lawful to
do good on the sabbath days, or to do evil? To save life, or to
kill?' But they held their peace. [5]And when he had looked
round about on them with anger, being grieved for the hardness of their hearts, he saith unto the man, 'Stretch forth thine
hand.' And he stretched it out; and his hand was restored

whole as the other. 6 And the Pharisees went forth, and straightway took counsel with the Herodians against him, how they
might destroy him.

7 But Jesus withdrew himself with his disciples to the sea;
and a great multitude from Galilee followed him, and from
Judæa, 8 and from Jerusalem, and from Idumæa, and from
beyond Jordan; and they about Tyre and Sidon, a great multitude, when they had heard what great things he did, came
unto him. 9 And he spake to his disciples, that a small ship
should wait on him because of the multitude, lest they should
throng him. 10 For he had healed many; insomuch that they
pressed upon him for to touch him, as many as had plagues.
11 And unclean spirits, when they saw him, fell down before
him, and cried, saying, 'Thou art the Son of God.' 12 And he
straitly charged them that they should not make him known.

13 And he goeth up into a mountain, and calleth unto him
whom he would: and they came unto him. 14 And he ordained
twelve, that they should be with him, and that he might send
them forth to preach, 15 and to have power to heal sicknesses,
and to cast out devils: 16 and Simon he surnamed Peter; 17 and
James the son of Zebedee, and John the brother of James; and
he surnamed them Boanerges, which is, The sons of thunder;
18 and Andrew, and Philip, and Bartholomew, and Matthew,
and Thomas, and James the son of Alphæus, and Thaddæus,
and Simon the Canaanite; 19 and Judas Iscariot, which also
betrayed him. And they went into an house. 20 And the multitude cometh together again, so that they could not so much
as eat bread. 21 And when his friends heard of it, they went
out to lay hold on him; for they said, 'He is beside himself.'

22 And the scribes which came down from Jerusalem said,
'He hath Beelzebub, and by the prince of the devils casteth
he out devils.' 23 And he called them unto him, and said unto
them in parables, 'How can Satan cast out Satan? 24 And if a
kingdom be divided against itself, that kingdom cannot stand.
25 And if a house be divided against itself, that house cannot
stand. 26 And if Satan rise up against himself, and be divided,
he cannot stand, but hath an end.

27 'No man can enter into a strong man's house, and spoil
his goods, except he will first bind the strong man; and then
he will spoil his house.

28 'Verily I say unto you, all sins shall be forgiven unto the
sons of men, and blasphemies wherewith soever they shall
blaspheme; 29 but he that shall blaspheme against the Holy
Ghost hath never forgiveness, but is in danger of eternal damnation, 30 because they said, "He hath an unclean spirit."'

31 There came then his brethren and his mother, and, standing without, sent unto him, calling him. 32 And the multitude
sat about him, and they said unto him, 'Behold, thy mother
and thy brethren without seek for thee.' 33 And he answered
them, saying, 'Who is my mother, or my brethren?' 34 And he
looked round about on them which sat about him, and said,
'Behold my mother and my brethren! 35 For whosoever shall
do the will of God, the same is my brother, and my sister,
and mother.'

4 And he began again to teach by the sea side; and there
was gathered unto him a great multitude, so that he entered into a ship, and sat in the sea; and the whole multitude

was by the sea on the land. [2]And he taught them many things
by parables, and said unto them in his doctrine, [3]'Hearken;
behold, there went out a sower to sow. [4]And it came to pass,
as he sowed, some fell by the way side, and the fowls of the
air came and devoured it up. [5]And some fell on stony ground,
where it had not much earth; and immediately it sprang up,
because it had no depth of earth. [6]But when the sun was up,
it was scorched; and because it had no root, it withered
away. [7]And some fell among thorns, and the thorns grew up,
and choked it, and it yielded no fruit. [8]And other fell on
good ground, and did yield fruit that sprang up and
increased; and brought forth, some thirty, and some sixty,
and some an hundred.' [9]And he said unto them, 'He that
hath ears to hear, let him hear.'

[10]And when he was alone, they that were about him with
the twelve asked of him the parable. [11]And he said unto them,
'Unto you it is given to know the mystery of the kingdom of
God; but unto them that are without, all these things are
done in parables; [12]that seeing they may see, and not perceive; and hearing they may hear, and not understand; lest
at any time they should be converted, and their sins should
be forgiven them.'

[13]And he said unto them, 'Know ye not this parable? And
how then will ye know all parables?

[14]'The sower soweth the word. [15]And these are they by
the way side, where the word is sown; but when they have
heard, Satan cometh immediately, and taketh away the word
that was sown in their hearts. [16]And these are they likewise
which are sown on stony ground; who, when they have

heard the word, immediately receive it with gladness; [17]and have no root in themselves, and so endure but for a time; afterward, when affliction or persecution ariseth for the word's sake, immediately they are offended. [18]And these are they which are sown among thorns; such as hear the word, [19]and the cares of this world, and the deceitfulness of riches, and the lusts of other things entering in, choke the word, and it becometh unfruitful. [20]And these are they which are sown on good ground; such as hear the word, and receive it, and bring forth fruit, some thirtyfold, some sixty, and some an hundred.'

[21]And he said unto them, 'Is a candle brought to be put under a bushel, or under a bed? And not to be set on a candlestick? [22]For there is nothing hid, which shall not be manifested; neither was any thing kept secret, but that it should come abroad. [23]If any man have ears to hear, let him hear.' [24]And he said unto them, 'Take heed what ye hear: with what measure ye mete, it shall be measured to you; and unto you that hear shall more be given. [25]For he that hath, to him shall be given; and he that hath not, from him shall be taken even that which he hath.'

[26]And he said, 'So is the kingdom of God, as if a man should cast seed into the ground; [27]and should sleep, and rise night and day, and the seed should spring and grow up, he knoweth not how. [28]For the earth bringeth forth fruit of herself; first the blade, then the ear, after that the full corn in the ear. [29]But when the fruit is brought forth, immediately he putteth in the sickle, because the harvest is come.'

[30]And he said, 'Whereunto shall we liken the kingdom of

God? Or with what comparison shall we compare it? 31 It is
like a grain of mustard seed, which, when it is sown in the
earth, is less than all the seeds that be in the earth; 32 but when
it is sown, it groweth up, and becometh greater than all
herbs, and shooteth out great branches; so that the fowls of
the air may lodge under the shadow of it.'

33 And with many such parables spake he the word unto
them, as they were able to hear it. 34 But without a parable
spake he not unto them; and when they were alone, he expounded all things to his disciples.

35 And the same day, when the even was come, he saith
unto them, 'Let us pass over unto the other side.' 36 And when
they had sent away the multitude, they took him even as he
was in the ship. And there were also with him other little
ships. 37 And there arose a great storm of wind, and the waves
beat into the ship, so that it was now full. 38 And he was in
the hinder part of the ship, asleep on a pillow; and they
awake him, and say unto him, 'Master, carest thou not that
we perish?' 39 And he arose, and rebuked the wind, and said
unto the sea, 'Peace, be still.' And the wind ceased, and there
was a great calm. 40 And he said unto them, 'Why are ye so
fearful? How is it that ye have no faith?' 41 And they feared
exceedingly, and said one to another, 'What manner of man
is this, that even the wind and the sea obey him?'

5 And they came over unto the other side of the sea, into
the country of the Gadarenes. 2 And when he was come
out of the ship, immediately there met him out of the tombs
a man with an unclean spirit, 3 who had his dwelling among

the tombs; and no man could bind him, no, not with chains;
[4]because that he had been often bound with fetters and
chains, and the chains had been plucked asunder by him, and
the fetters broken in pieces; neither could any man tame him.

[5]And always, night and day, he was in the mountains,
and in the tombs, crying, and cutting himself with stones.
[6]But when he saw Jesus afar off, he ran and worshipped
him, [7]and cried with a loud voice, and said, 'What have I to
do with thee, Jesus, thou Son of the most high God? I adjure
thee by God, that thou torment me not.' [8]For Jesus said unto
him, 'Come out of the man, thou unclean spirit.' [9]And he
asked him, 'What is thy name?' And the man answered, saying, 'My name is Legion: for we are many.' [10]And he besought him much that he would not send them away out of
the country.

[11]Now there was there nigh unto the mountains a great
herd of swine feeding. [12]And all the devils besought him,
saying, 'Send us into the swine, that we may enter into them.'
[13]And forthwith Jesus gave them leave. And the unclean
spirits went out, and entered into the swine; and the herd
ran violently down a steep place into the sea (they were
about two thousand) and were choked in the sea.

[14]And they that fed the swine fled, and told it in the city,
and in the country. And they went out to see what it was
that was done. [15]And they come to Jesus, and see him that
was possessed with the devil, and had the legion, sitting, and
clothed, and in his right mind; and they were afraid. [16]And
they that saw it told them how it befell to him that was possessed with the devil, and also concerning the swine. [17]And

they began to pray him to depart out of their coasts. 18 And
when he was come into the ship, he that had been possessed
with the devil prayed him that he might be with him.
19 Howbeit Jesus suffered him not, but saith unto him, 'Go
home to thy friends, and tell them how great things the Lord
hath done for thee, and hath had compassion on thee.' 20 And
he departed, and began to publish in Decapolis how great
things Jesus had done for him; and all men did marvel.

21 And when Jesus was passed over again by ship unto
the other side, much people gathered unto him: and he was
nigh unto the sea. 22 And, behold, there cometh one of the
rulers of the synagogue, Jairus by name; and when he saw
him, he fell at his feet, 23 and besought him greatly, saying,
'My little daughter lieth at the point of death; I pray thee,
come and lay thy hands on her, that she may be healed; and
she shall live.' 24 And Jesus went with him; and much people
followed him, and thronged him.

25 And a certain woman, which had an issue of blood twelve
years, 26 and had suffered many things of many physicians,
and had spent all that she had, and was nothing bettered, but
rather grew worse, 27 when she had heard of Jesus, came in the
press behind, and touched his garment. 28 For she said, 'If I
may touch but his clothes, I shall be whole.' 29 And straightway
the fountain of her blood was dried up; and she felt in her
body that she was healed of that plague. 30 And Jesus, immediately knowing in himself that virtue had gone out of him,
turned him about in the press, and said, 'Who touched my
clothes?' 31 And his disciples said unto him, 'Thou seest the multitude thronging thee, and sayest thou, "Who touched me?"'

[32]And he looked round about to see her that had done this
thing. [33]But the woman fearing and trembling, knowing what
was done in her, came and fell down before him, and told him
all the truth. [34]And he said unto her, 'Daughter, thy faith hath
made thee whole; go in peace, and be whole of thy plague.'

[35]While he yet spake, there came from the ruler of the
synagogue's house certain which said, 'Thy daughter is dead;
why troublest thou the Master any further?' [36]As soon as
Jesus heard the word that was spoken, he saith unto the
ruler of the synagogue, 'Be not afraid, only believe.' [37]And he
suffered no man to follow him, save Peter, and James, and
John the brother of James. [38]And he cometh to the house of
the ruler of the synagogue, and seeth the tumult, and them
that wept and wailed greatly. [39]And when he was come in,
he saith unto them, 'Why make ye this ado, and weep? The
damsel is not dead, but sleepeth.' [40]And they laughed him to
scorn. But when he had put them all out, he taketh the father
and the mother of the damsel, and them that were with him,
and entereth in where the damsel was lying. [41]And he took
the damsel by the hand, and said unto her, 'Talitha cumi,'
which is, being interpreted, 'Damsel, I say unto thee, arise.'
[42]And straightway the damsel arose, and walked; for she
was of the age of twelve years. And they were astonished
with a great astonishment. [43]And he charged them straitly
that no man should know it; and commanded that something should be given her to eat.

6 And he went out from thence, and came into his own
country; and his disciples follow him. [2]And when the

sabbath day was come, he began to teach in the synagogue;
and many hearing him were astonished, saying, 'From
whence hath this man these things? And what wisdom is
this which is given unto him, that even such mighty works
are wrought by his hands? 3 Is not this the carpenter, the son
of Mary, the brother of James, and Joses, and of Juda, and
Simon? And are not his sisters here with us?' And they were
offended at him. 4 But Jesus said unto them, 'A prophet is not
without honour, but in his own country, and among his own
kin, and in his own house.' 5 And he could there do no mighty
work, save that he laid his hands upon a few sick folk, and
healed them. 6 And he marvelled because of their unbelief.
And he went round about the villages, teaching.

7 And he called unto him the twelve, and began to send
them forth by two and two; and gave them power over unclean
spirits; 8 and commanded them that they should take nothing for their journey, save a staff only; no scrip, no bread, no
money in their purse; 9 but be shod with sandals; and not put
on two coats. 10 And he said unto them, 'In what place soever
ye enter into an house, there abide till ye depart from that
place. 11 And whosoever shall not receive you, nor hear you,
when ye depart thence, shake off the dust under your feet
for a testimony against them. Verily I say unto you, It shall be
more tolerable for Sodom and Gomorrha in the day of judgment, than for that city.' 12 And they went out, and preached
that men should repent. 13 And they cast out many devils,
and anointed with oil many that were sick, and healed them.

14 And king Herod heard of him (for his name was spread
abroad) and he said, 'That John the Baptist was risen from

the dead, and therefore mighty works do shew forth themselves in him.' 15 Others said, 'That it is Elias.' And others said, 'That it is a prophet, or as one of the prophets.' 16 But when Herod heard thereof, he said, 'It is John, whom I beheaded; he is risen from the dead.'

17 For Herod himself had sent forth and laid hold upon John, and bound him in prison for Herodias' sake, his brother Philip's wife; for he had married her. 18 For John had said unto Herod, 'It is not lawful for thee to have thy brother's wife.' 19 Therefore Herodias had a quarrel against him, and would have killed him; but she could not; 20 for Herod feared John, knowing that he was a just man and an holy, and observed him; and when he heard him, he did many things, and heard him gladly.

21 And when a convenient day was come, that Herod on his birthday made a supper to his lords, high captains, and chief estates of Galilee; 22 and when the daughter of the said Herodias came in, and danced, and pleased Herod and them that sat with him, the king said unto the damsel, 'Ask of me whatsoever thou wilt, and I will give it thee.' 23 And he sware unto her, 'Whatsoever thou shalt ask of me, I will give it thee, unto the half of my kingdom.' 24 And she went forth, and said unto her mother, 'What shall I ask?' And she said, 'The head of John the Baptist.' 25 And she came in straightway with haste unto the king, and asked, saying, 'I will that thou give me by and by in a charger the head of John the Baptist.' 26 And the king was exceeding sorry; yet for his oath's sake, and for their sakes which sat with him, he would not reject her. 27 And immediately the king sent an executioner,

and commanded his head to be brought; and he went and
beheaded him in the prison, 28 and brought his head in a
charger, and gave it to the damsel; and the damsel gave it to
her mother.

29 And when his disciples heard of it, they came and took
up his corpse, and laid it in a tomb.

30 And the apostles gathered themselves together unto
Jesus, and told him all things, both what they had done, and
what they had taught. 31 And he said unto them, 'Come ye
yourselves apart into a desert place, and rest a while,' for
there were many coming and going, and they had no leisure
so much as to eat. 32 And they departed into a desert place by
ship privately. 33 And the people saw them departing, and
many knew him, and ran afoot thither out of all cities, and
outwent them, and came together unto him. 34 And Jesus,
when he came out, saw much people, and was moved with
compassion toward them, because they were as sheep not
having a shepherd; and he began to teach them many things.
35 And when the day was now far spent, his disciples came
unto him, and said, 'This is a desert place, and now the time
is far passed; 36 send them away, that they may go into the
country round about, and into the villages, and buy themselves bread; for they have nothing to eat.' 37 He answered
and said unto them, 'Give ye them to eat.' And they say unto
him, 'Shall we go and buy two hundred pennyworth of bread,
and give them to eat?' 38 He saith unto them, 'How many
loaves have ye? Go and see.' And when they knew, they say,
'Five, and two fishes.' 39 And he commanded them to make
all sit down by companies upon the green grass. 40 And they

sat down in ranks, by hundreds, and by fifties. 41 And when
he had taken the five loaves and the two fishes, he looked up
to heaven, and blessed, and brake the loaves, and gave them to
his disciples to set before them; and the two fishes divided
he among them all. 42 And they did all eat, and were filled.
43 And they took up twelve baskets full of the fragments, and
of the fishes. 44 And they that did eat of the loaves were about
five thousand men.

45 And straightway he constrained his disciples to get into
the ship, and to go to the other side before unto Bethsaida,
while he sent away the people. 46 And when he had sent them
away, he departed into a mountain to pray. 47 And when even
was come, the ship was in the midst of the sea, and he alone
on the land. 48 And he saw them toiling in rowing; for the
wind was contrary unto them; and about the fourth watch of
the night he cometh unto them, walking upon the sea, and
would have passed by them. 49 But when they saw him walking upon the sea, they supposed it had been a spirit, and cried
out; 50 for they all saw him, and were troubled. And immediately he talked with them, and saith unto them, 'Be of
good cheer: it is I; be not afraid.' 51 And he went up unto them
into the ship; and the wind ceased; and they were sore
amazed in themselves beyond measure, and wondered. 52 For
they considered not the miracle of the loaves; for their heart
was hardened.

53 And when they had passed over, they came into the
land of Gennesaret, and drew to the shore. 54 And when they
were come out of the ship, straightway they knew him, 55 and
ran through that whole region round about, and began to

carry about in beds those that were sick, where they heard
he was. 56 And whithersoever he entered, into villages, or cities,
or country, they laid the sick in the streets, and besought him
that they might touch if it were but the border of his garment: and as many as touched him were made whole.

7 Then came together unto him the Pharisees, and certain
of the scribes, which came from Jerusalem. 2 And when
they saw some of his disciples eat bread with defiled, that is
to say, with unwashen, hands, they found fault. 3 For the
Pharisees, and all the Jews, except they wash their hands oft,
eat not, holding the tradition of the elders. 4 And when they
come from the market, except they wash, they eat not. And
many other things there be, which they have received to
hold, as the washing of cups, and pots, brasen vessels, and of
tables. 5 Then the Pharisees and scribes asked him, 'Why walk
not thy disciples according to the tradition of the elders, but
eat bread with unwashen hands?' 6 He answered and said
unto them, 'Well hath Esaias prophesied of you hypocrites,
as it is written, "This people honoureth me with their lips,
but their heart is far from me. 7 Howbeit in vain do they worship me, teaching for doctrines the commandments of men."
8 For laying aside the commandment of God, ye hold the tradition of men, as the washing of pots and cups; and many
other such like things ye do.'

9 And he said unto them, 'Full well ye reject the commandment of God, that ye may keep your own tradition. 10 For
Moses said, "Honour thy father and thy mother," and, "Whoso curseth father or mother, let him die the death." 11 But ye

say, "If a man shall say to his father or mother, 'It is Corban,'
that is to say, a gift, by whatsoever thou mightest be profited
by me; he shall be free." 12And ye suffer him no more to do
ought for his father or his mother; 13 making the word of God
of none effect through your tradition, which ye have delivered: and many such like things do ye.'

14And when he had called all the people unto him, he said
unto them, 'Hearken unto me every one of you, and understand: 15 there is nothing from without a man, that entering
into him can defile him; but the things which come out of
him, those are they that defile the man. 16 If any man have
ears to hear, let him hear.'

17And when he was entered into the house from the people, his disciples asked him concerning the parable. 18And he
saith unto them, 'Are ye so without understanding also? Do
ye not perceive, that whatsoever thing from without entereth into the man, it cannot defile him; 19 because it entereth
not into his heart, but into the belly, and goeth out into the
draught, purging all meats?' 20And he said, 'That which
cometh out of the man, that defileth the man. 21 For from
within, out of the heart of men, proceed evil thoughts, adulteries, fornications, murders, 22 thefts, covetousness, wickedness, deceit, lasciviousness, an evil eye, blasphemy, pride,
foolishness: 23 all these evil things come from within, and
defile the man.'

24And from thence he arose, and went into the borders of
Tyre and Sidon, and entered into an house, and would have
no man know it; but he could not be hid. 25 For a certain
woman, whose young daughter had an unclean spirit, heard

of him, and came and fell at his feet. 26 The woman was a
Greek, a Syrophenician by nation; and she besought him that
he would cast forth the devil out of her daughter. 27 But Jesus
said unto her, 'Let the children first be filled: for it is not
meet to take the children's bread, and to cast it unto the dogs.'
28 And she answered and said unto him, 'Yes, Lord: yet the
dogs under the table eat of the children's crumbs.' 29 And he
said unto her, 'For this saying go thy way; the devil is gone
out of thy daughter.' 30 And when she was come to her house,
she found the devil gone out, and her daughter laid upon
the bed.

31 And again, departing from the coasts of Tyre and Sidon,
he came unto the sea of Galilee, through the midst of the
coasts of Decapolis. 32 And they bring unto him one that was
deaf, and had an impediment in his speech; and they beseech
him to put his hand upon him. 33 And he took him aside from
the multitude, and put his fingers into his ears, and he spit,
and touched his tongue; 34 and looking up to heaven, he
sighed, and saith unto him, 'Ephphatha,' that is, 'Be opened.'
35 And straightway his ears were opened, and the string of
his tongue was loosed, and he spake plain. 36 And he charged
them that they should tell no man; but the more he charged
them, so much the more a great deal they published it; 37 and
were beyond measure astonished, saying, 'He hath done all
things well: he maketh both the deaf to hear, and the dumb
to speak.'

8 In those days the multitude being very great, and having nothing to eat, Jesus called his disciples unto him,

and saith unto them, 2 'I have compassion on the multitude,
because they have now been with me three days, and have
nothing to eat; 3 and if I send them away fasting to their own
houses, they will faint by the way; for divers of them came
from far.' 4 And his disciples answered him, 'From whence
can a man satisfy these men with bread here in the wilderness?' 5 And he asked them, 'How many loaves have ye?'
And they said, 'Seven.' 6 And he commanded the people to
sit down on the ground: and he took the seven loaves, and
gave thanks, and brake, and gave to his disciples to set before
them; and they did set them before the people. 7 And they
had a few small fishes; and he blessed, and commanded to
set them also before them. 8 So they did eat, and were filled;
and they took up of the broken meat that was left seven baskets. 9 And they that had eaten were about four thousand;
and he sent them away.

10 And straightway he entered into a ship with his disciples, and came into the parts of Dalmanutha. 11 And the Pharisees came forth, and began to question with him, seeking of
him a sign from heaven, tempting him. 12 And he sighed
deeply in his spirit, and saith, 'Why doth this generation seek
after a sign? Verily I say unto you, There shall no sign be
given unto this generation.' 13 And he left them, and entering
into the ship again departed to the other side.

14 Now the disciples had forgotten to take bread, neither
had they in the ship with them more than one loaf. 15 And he
charged them, saying, 'Take heed, beware of the leaven of
the Pharisees, and of the leaven of Herod.' 16 And they reasoned among themselves, saying, 'It is because we have no

bread.' 17And when Jesus knew it, he saith unto them, 'Why
reason ye, because ye have no bread? Perceive ye not yet,
neither understand? Have ye your heart yet hardened?
18Having eyes, see ye not? And having ears, hear ye not?
And do ye not remember? 19When I brake the five loaves
among five thousand, how many baskets full of fragments
took ye up?' They say unto him, 'Twelve.' 20'And when the
seven among four thousand, how many baskets full of fragments took ye up?' And they said, 'Seven.' 21And he said
unto them, 'How is it that ye do not understand?'

22And he cometh to Bethsaida; and they bring a blind
man unto him, and besought him to touch him. 23And he
took the blind man by the hand, and led him out of the
town; and when he had spit on his eyes, and put his hands
upon him, he asked him if he saw ought. 24And he looked
up, and said, 'I see men as trees, walking.' 25After that he put
his hands again upon his eyes, and made him look up: and
he was restored, and saw every man clearly. 26And Jesus sent
him away to his house, saying, 'Neither go into the town,
nor tell it to any in the town.'

27And Jesus went out, and his disciples, into the towns of
Cæsarea Philippi: and by the way he asked his disciples, saying unto them, 'Whom do men say that I am?' 28And they
answered, 'John the Baptist: but some say, Elias; and others,
one of the prophets.' 29And he saith unto them, 'But whom
say ye that I am?' And Peter answereth and saith unto him,
'Thou art the Christ.' 30And he charged them that they should
tell no man of him. 31And he began to teach them, that the
Son of man must suffer many things, and be rejected of the

elders, and of the chief priests, and scribes, and be killed,
and after three days rise again. 32 And he spake that saying
openly. And Peter took him, and began to rebuke him. 33 But
when he had turned about and looked on his disciples, he
rebuked Peter, saying, 'Get thee behind me, Satan: for thou
savourest not the things that be of God, but the things that
be of men.'

34 And when he had called the people unto him with his
disciples also, he said unto them, 'Whosoever will come after
me, let him deny himself, and take up his cross, and follow
me. 35 For whosoever will save his life shall lose it; but whosoever shall lose his life for my sake and the gospel's, the
same shall save it. 36 For what shall it profit a man, if he shall
gain the whole world, and lose his own soul? 37 Or what shall
a man give in exchange for his soul? 38 Whosoever therefore
shall be ashamed of me and of my words in this adulterous
and sinful generation; of him also shall the Son of man be
ashamed, when he cometh in the glory of his Father with the
holy angels.'

9 And he said unto them, 'Verily I say unto you, that
there be some of them that stand here, which shall not
taste of death, till they have seen the kingdom of God come
with power.'

2 And after six days Jesus taketh with him Peter, and James,
and John, and leadeth them up into an high mountain apart
by themselves; and he was transfigured before them. 3 And
his raiment became shining, exceeding white as snow; so as
no fuller on earth can white them. 4 And there appeared unto

them Elias with Moses; and they were talking with Jesus.
5And Peter answered and said to Jesus, 'Master, it is good for
us to be here; and let us make three tabernacles: one for thee,
and one for Moses, and one for Elias.' 6 For he wist not what
to say; for they were sore afraid. 7And there was a cloud that
overshadowed them; and a voice came out of the cloud, saying, 'This is my beloved Son: hear him.' 8And suddenly, when
they had looked round about, they saw no man any more,
save Jesus only with themselves. 9And as they came down
from the mountain, he charged them that they should tell no
man what things they had seen, till the Son of man were
risen from the dead. 10And they kept that saying with themselves, questioning one with another what the rising from
the dead should mean.

11And they asked him, saying, 'Why say the scribes that
Elias must first come?' 12And he answered and told them,
'Elias verily cometh first, and restoreth all things; and how it
is written of the Son of man, that he must suffer many things,
and be set at nought. 13 But I say unto you, that Elias is indeed
come, and they have done unto him whatsoever they listed,
as it is written of him.'

14And when he came to his disciples, he saw a great multitude about them, and the scribes questioning with them.
15And straightway all the people, when they beheld him,
were greatly amazed, and running to him saluted him. 16And
he asked the scribes, 'What question ye with them?' 17And
one of the multitude answered and said, 'Master, I have
brought unto thee my son, which hath a dumb spirit; 18 and
wheresoever he taketh him, he teareth him: and he foameth,

and gnasheth with his teeth, and pineth away; and I spake to
thy disciples that they should cast him out; and they could
not.' [19] He answereth him, and saith, 'O faithless generation,
how long shall I be with you? How long shall I suffer you?
Bring him unto me.' [20] And they brought him unto him: and
when he saw him, straightway the spirit tare him; and he fell
on the ground, and wallowed foaming. [21] And he asked his
father, 'How long is it ago since this came unto him?' And he
said, 'Of a child. [22] And ofttimes it hath cast him into the fire,
and into the waters, to destroy him; but if thou canst do any
thing, have compassion on us, and help us.' [23] Jesus said unto
him, 'If thou canst believe, all things are possible to him that
believeth.' [24] And straightway the father of the child cried out,
and said with tears, 'Lord, I believe; help thou mine unbelief.'
[25] When Jesus saw that the people came running together, he
rebuked the foul spirit, saying unto him, 'Thou dumb and
deaf spirit, I charge thee, come out of him, and enter no more
into him.' [26] And the spirit cried, and rent him sore, and came
out of him: and he was as one dead; insomuch that many
said, 'He is dead.' [27] But Jesus took him by the hand, and
lifted him up; and he arose. [28] And when he was come into
the house, his disciples asked him privately, 'Why could not
we cast him out?' [29] And he said unto them, 'This kind can
come forth by nothing, but by prayer and fasting.'

[30] And they departed thence, and passed through Galilee;
and he would not that any man should know it. [31] For he
taught his disciples, and said unto them, 'The Son of man is
delivered into the hands of men, and they shall kill him; and
after that he is killed, he shall rise the third day.' [32] But they

understood not that saying, and were afraid to ask him.

33 And he came to Capernaum: and being in the house he
asked them, 'What was it that ye disputed among yourselves
by the way?' 34 But they held their peace: for by the way they
had disputed among themselves, who should be the greatest. 35 And he sat down, and called the twelve, and saith unto
them, 'If any man desire to be first, the same shall be last of
all, and servant of all.' 36 And he took a child, and set him in
the midst of them; and when he had taken him in his arms,
he said unto them, 37 'Whosoever shall receive one of such
children in my name, receiveth me; and whosoever shall
receive me, receiveth not me, but him that sent me.'

38 And John answered him, saying, 'Master, we saw one
casting out devils in thy name, and he followeth not us; and
we forbad him, because he followeth not us.' 39 But Jesus said,
'Forbid him not; for there is no man which shall do a miracle
in my name, that can lightly speak evil of me. 40 For he that
is not against us is on our part. 41 For whosoever shall give
you a cup of water to drink in my name, because ye belong
to Christ, verily I say unto you, he shall not lose his reward.

42 'And whosoever shall offend one of these little ones
that believe in me, it is better for him that a millstone were
hanged about his neck, and he were cast into the sea. 43 And
if thy hand offend thee, cut it off; it is better for thee to enter
into life maimed, than having two hands to go into hell, into
the fire that never shall be quenched, 44 where their worm
dieth not, and the fire is not quenched. 45 And if thy foot
offend thee, cut it off: it is better for thee to enter halt into
life, than having two feet to be cast into hell, into the fire that

never shall be quenched, 46 where their worm dieth not, and
the fire is not quenched. 47 And if thine eye offend thee, pluck
it out; it is better for thee to enter into the kingdom of God
with one eye, than having two eyes to be cast into hell fire,
48 where their worm dieth not, and the fire is not quenched.
49 For every one shall be salted with fire, and every sacrifice
shall be salted with salt. 50 Salt is good; but if the salt have
lost his saltness, wherewith will ye season it? Have salt in
yourselves, and have peace one with another.'

10 And he arose from thence, and cometh into the coasts of
Judæa by the farther side of Jordan; and the people resort
unto him again; and, as he was wont, he taught them again.
2 And the Pharisees came to him, and asked him, 'Is it lawful for a man to put away his wife?' tempting him. 3 And he
answered and said unto them, 'What did Moses command
you?' 4 And they said, 'Moses suffered to write a bill of divorcement, and to put her away.' 5 And Jesus answered and said
unto them, 'For the hardness of your heart he wrote you this
precept. 6 But from the beginning of the creation God made
them male and female. 7 For this cause shall a man leave his
father and mother, and cleave to his wife; 8 and they twain
shall be one flesh; so then they are no more twain, but one
flesh. 9 What therefore God hath joined together, let not man
put asunder.' 10 And in the house his disciples asked him again
of the same matter. 11 And he saith unto them, 'Whosoever
shall put away his wife, and marry another, committeth adultery against her. 12 And if a woman shall put away her husband, and be married to another, she committeth adultery.'

13And they brought young children to him, that he should
touch them; and his disciples rebuked those that brought
them. 14But when Jesus saw it, he was much displeased, and
said unto them, 'Suffer the little children to come unto me,
and forbid them not; for of such is the kingdom of God.
15Verily I say unto you, whosoever shall not receive the kingdom of God as a little child, he shall not enter therein.' 16And
he took them up in his arms, put his hands upon them, and
blessed them.

17And when he was gone forth into the way, there came
one running, and kneeled to him, and asked him, 'Good
Master, what shall I do that I may inherit eternal life?' 18And
Jesus said unto him, 'Why callest thou me good? There is
none good but one, that is, God. 19Thou knowest the commandments, "Do not commit adultery, Do not kill, Do not
steal, Do not bear false witness, Defraud not, Honour thy
father and mother."' 20And he answered and said unto him,
'Master, all these have I observed from my youth.' 21Then
Jesus beholding him loved him, and said unto him, 'One thing
thou lackest: go thy way, sell whatsoever thou hast, and give
to the poor, and thou shalt have treasure in heaven; and come,
take up the cross, and follow me.' 22And he was sad at that
saying, and went away grieved; for he had great possessions.

23And Jesus looked round about, and saith unto his disciples, 'How hardly shall they that have riches enter into the
kingdom of God!' 24And the disciples were astonished at his
words. But Jesus answereth again, and saith unto them,
'Children, how hard is it for them that trust in riches to enter
into the kingdom of God! 25It is easier for a camel to go

through the eye of a needle, than for a rich man to enter into
the kingdom of God.' 26And they were astonished out of
measure, saying among themselves, 'Who then can be saved?'
27And Jesus looking upon them saith, 'With men it is impossible, but not with God; for with God all things are possible.'

28Then Peter began to say unto him, 'Lo, we have left all,
and have followed thee.' 29And Jesus answered and said, 'Verily I say unto you, there is no man that hath left house, or
brethren, or sisters, or father, or mother, or wife, or children,
or lands, for my sake, and the gospel's, 30but he shall receive
an hundredfold now in this time, houses, and brethren, and
sisters, and mothers, and children, and lands, with persecutions; and in the world to come eternal life. 31But many that
are first shall be last; and the last first.'

32And they were in the way going up to Jerusalem; and
Jesus went before them; and they were amazed; and as they
followed, they were afraid. And he took again the twelve,
and began to tell them what things should happen unto him,
33saying, 'Behold, we go up to Jerusalem; and the Son of man
shall be delivered unto the chief priests, and unto the scribes;
and they shall condemn him to death, and shall deliver him
to the Gentiles; 34and they shall mock him, and shall scourge
him, and shall spit upon him, and shall kill him: and the
third day he shall rise again.'

35And James and John, the sons of Zebedee, come unto
him, saying, 'Master, we would that thou shouldest do for
us whatsoever we shall desire.' 36And he said unto them,
'What would ye that I should do for you?' 37They said unto
him, 'Grant unto us that we may sit, one on thy right hand,

and the other on thy left hand, in thy glory.' [38] But Jesus said
unto them, 'Ye know not what ye ask: can ye drink of the
cup that I drink of? And be baptized with the baptism that I
am baptized with?' [39] And they said unto him, 'We can.' And
Jesus said unto them, 'Ye shall indeed drink of the cup that I
drink of; and with the baptism that I am baptized withal
shall ye be baptized; [40] but to sit on my right hand and on my
left hand is not mine to give; but it shall be given to them for
whom it is prepared.' [41] And when the ten heard it, they began
to be much displeased with James and John. [42] But Jesus
called them to him, and saith unto them, 'Ye know that they
which are accounted to rule over the Gentiles exercise lordship over them; and their great ones exercise authority upon
them. [43] But so shall it not be among you; but whosoever will
be great among you, shall be your minister; [44] and whosoever of you will be the chiefest, shall be servant of all. [45] For
even the Son of man came not to be ministered unto, but to
minister, and to give his life a ransom for many.'

[46] And they came to Jericho; and as he went out of Jericho
with his disciples and a great number of people, blind Bar-
timæus, the son of Timæus, sat by the highway side begging.
[47] And when he heard that it was Jesus of Nazareth, he began
to cry out, and say, 'Jesus, thou Son of David, have mercy on
me.' [48] And many charged him that he should hold his peace;
but he cried the more a great deal, 'Thou Son of David, have
mercy on me.' [49] And Jesus stood still, and commanded him
to be called. And they call the blind man, saying unto him,
'Be of good comfort, rise; he calleth thee.' [50] And he, casting
away his garment, rose, and came to Jesus. [51] And Jesus

answered and said unto him, 'What wilt thou that I should
do unto thee?' The blind man said unto him, 'Lord, that I
might receive my sight.' 52And Jesus said unto him, 'Go thy
way; thy faith hath made thee whole.' And immediately he
received his sight, and followed Jesus in the way.

11 And when they came nigh to Jerusalem, unto Bethphage and Bethany, at the mount of Olives, he sendeth
forth two of his disciples, 2and saith unto them, 'Go your way
into the village over against you; and as soon as ye be entered into it, ye shall find a colt tied, whereon never man sat;
loose him, and bring him. 3And if any man say unto you,
"Why do ye this?" say ye that the Lord hath need of him; and
straightway he will send him hither.' 4And they went their
way, and found the colt tied by the door without in a place
where two ways met; and they loose him. 5And certain of them
that stood there said unto them, 'What do ye, loosing the colt?'
6And they said unto them even as Jesus had commanded;
and they let them go. 7And they brought the colt to Jesus,
and cast their garments on him; and he sat upon him. 8And
many spread their garments in the way; and others cut down
branches off the trees, and strawed them in the way. 9And
they that went before, and they that followed, cried, saying,
'Hosanna; blessed is he that cometh in the name of the Lord;
10blessed be the kingdom of our father David, that cometh in
the name of the Lord; hosanna in the highest.' 11And Jesus
entered into Jerusalem, and into the temple; and when he
had looked round about upon all things, and now the eventide was come, he went out unto Bethany with the twelve.

[12]And on the morrow, when they were come from Bethany, he was hungry; [13]and seeing a fig tree afar off having
leaves, he came, if haply he might find any thing thereon; and
when he came to it, he found nothing but leaves; for the time
of figs was not yet. [14]And Jesus answered and said unto it,
'No man eat fruit of thee hereafter for ever.' And his disciples heard it.

[15]And they come to Jerusalem; and Jesus went into the
temple, and began to cast out them that sold and bought in
the temple, and overthrew the tables of the moneychangers,
and the seats of them that sold doves; [16]and would not suffer
that any man should carry any vessel through the temple.
[17]And he taught, saying unto them, 'Is it not written, "My
house shall be called of all nations the house of prayer"? But
ye have made it a den of thieves.' [18]And the scribes and chief
priests heard it, and sought how they might destroy him; for
they feared him, because all the people was astonished at his
doctrine. [19]And when even was come, he went out of the city.

[20]And in the morning, as they passed by, they saw the fig
tree dried up from the roots. [21]And Peter calling to remembrance saith unto him, 'Master, behold, the fig tree which
thou cursedst is withered away.' [22]And Jesus answering saith
unto them, 'Have faith in God. [23]For verily I say unto you, that
whosoever shall say unto this mountain, "Be thou removed,
and be thou cast into the sea"; and shall not doubt in his
heart, but shall believe that those things which he saith shall
come to pass; he shall have whatsoever he saith. [24]Therefore
I say unto you, what things soever ye desire, when ye pray,
believe that ye receive them, and ye shall have them. [25]And

when ye stand praying, forgive, if ye have ought against
any: that your Father also which is in heaven may forgive
you your trespasses. 26 But if ye do not forgive, neither will
your Father which is in heaven forgive your trespasses.'

27 And they come again to Jerusalem; and as he was walking in the temple, there come to him the chief priests, and
the scribes, and the elders, 28 and say unto him, 'By what
authority doest thou these things? And who gave thee this
authority to do these things?' 29 And Jesus answered and said
unto them, 'I will also ask of you one question, and answer
me, and I will tell you by what authority I do these things.
30 The baptism of John, was it from heaven, or of men? Answer
me.' 31 And they reasoned with themselves, saying, 'If we
shall say, "From heaven," he will say, "Why then did ye not
believe him?" 32 But if we shall say, "Of men,"' they feared
the people; for all men counted John, that he was a prophet
indeed.' 33 And they answered and said unto Jesus, 'We cannot tell.' And Jesus answering saith unto them, 'Neither do I
tell you by what authority I do these things.'

12 And he began to speak unto them by parables. 'A certain man planted a vineyard, and set an hedge about
it, and digged a place for the winefat, and built a tower, and
let it out to husbandmen, and went into a far country. 2 And
at the season he sent to the husbandmen a servant, that he
might receive from the husbandmen of the fruit of the vineyard. 3 And they caught him, and beat him, and sent him
away empty. 4 And again he sent unto them another servant;
and at him they cast stones, and wounded him in the head,

and sent him away shamefully handled. [5]And again he sent
another; and him they killed, and many others; beating
some, and killing some. [6]Having yet therefore one son, his
wellbeloved, he sent him also last unto them, saying, "They
will reverence my son." [7]But those husbandmen said among
themselves, "This is the heir; come, let us kill him, and the
inheritance shall be ours." [8]And they took him, and killed
him, and cast him out of the vineyard. [9]What shall therefore
the lord of the vineyard do? He will come and destroy the
husbandmen, and will give the vineyard unto others. [10]And
have ye not read this scripture: "The stone which the builders
rejected is become the head of the corner. [11]This was the
Lord's doing, and it is marvellous in our eyes"?' [12]And they
sought to lay hold on him, but feared the people; for
they knew that he had spoken the parable against them:
and they left him, and went their way.

[13]And they send unto him certain of the Pharisees and of
the Herodians, to catch him in his words. [14]And when they
were come, they say unto him, 'Master, we know that thou
art true, and carest for no man; for thou regardest not the
person of men, but teachest the way of God in truth. Is it
lawful to give tribute to Caesar, or not? [15]Shall we give, or
shall we not give?' But he, knowing their hypocrisy, said
unto them, 'Why tempt ye me? Bring me a penny, that I may
see it.' [16]And they brought it. And he saith unto them, 'Whose
is this image and superscription?' And they said unto him,
'Caesar's.' [17]And Jesus answering said unto them, 'Render to
Caesar the things that are Caesar's, and to God the things
that are God's.' And they marvelled at him.

18 Then come unto him the Sadducees, which say there is
no resurrection; and they asked him, saying, 19 'Master, Moses
wrote unto us, "If a man's brother die, and leave his wife
behind him, and leave no children, that his brother should
take his wife, and raise up seed unto his brother." 20 Now there
were seven brethren; and the first took a wife, and dying left
no seed. 21 And the second took her, and died, neither left he
any seed; and the third likewise. 22 And the seven had her,
and left no seed; last of all the woman died also. 23 In the resurrection therefore, when they shall rise, whose wife shall
she be of them? For the seven had her to wife.' 24 And Jesus
answering said unto them, 'Do ye not therefore err, because
ye know not the scriptures, neither the power of God? 25 For
when they shall rise from the dead, they neither marry, nor
are given in marriage; but are as the angels which are in
heaven. 26 And as touching the dead, that they rise; have ye
not read in the book of Moses, how in the bush God spake
unto him, saying, "I am the God of Abraham, and the God of
Isaac, and the God of Jacob?" 27 He is not the God of the dead,
but the God of the living; ye therefore do greatly err.'

28 And one of the scribes came, and having heard them reasoning together, and perceiving that he had answered them
well, asked him, 'Which is the first commandment of all?'
29 And Jesus answered him, 'The first of all the commandments is, "Hear, O Israel; the Lord our God is one Lord: 30 and
thou shalt love the Lord thy God with all thy heart, and with
all thy soul, and with all thy mind, and with all thy strength":
this is the first commandment. 31 And the second is like,
namely this, "Thou shalt love thy neighbour as thyself." There

is none other commandment greater than these.' [32]And the
scribe said unto him, 'Well, Master, thou hast said the truth:
for there is one God; and there is none other but he; [33] and to
love him with all the heart, and with all the understanding,
and with all the soul, and with all the strength, and to love his
neighbour as himself, is more than all whole burnt offerings
and sacrifices.' [34]And when Jesus saw that he answered dis-
creetly, he said unto him, 'Thou art not far from the kingdom
of God.' And no man after that durst ask him any question.

[35]And Jesus answered and said, while he taught in the
temple, 'How say the scribes that Christ is the Son of David?
[36] For David himself said by the Holy Ghost, "The Lord said
to my Lord, 'Sit thou on my right hand, till I make thine enemies thy footstool.'" [37] David therefore himself calleth him
"Lord"; and whence is he then his son?' And the common
people heard him gladly.

[38]And he said unto them in his doctrine, 'Beware of the
scribes, which love to go in long clothing, and love saluta-
tions in the marketplaces, [39] and the chief seats in the synagogues, and the uppermost rooms at feasts, [40] which devour
widows' houses, and for a pretence make long prayers:
these shall receive greater damnation.'

[41]And Jesus sat over against the treasury, and beheld how
the people cast money into the treasury; and many that were
rich cast in much. [42]And there came a certain poor widow,
and she threw in two mites, which make a farthing. [43]And he
called unto him his disciples, and saith unto them, 'Verily I
say unto you, that this poor widow hath cast more in, than
all they which have cast into the treasury: [44] for all they did

cast in of their abundance; but she of her want did cast in all
that she had, even all her living.'

13 And as he went out of the temple, one of his disciples
saith unto him, 'Master, see what manner of stones and
what buildings are here!' 2And Jesus answering said unto
him, 'Seest thou these great buildings? There shall not be left
one stone upon another, that shall not be thrown down.'
3And as he sat upon the mount of Olives over against the
temple, Peter and James and John and Andrew asked him
privately, 4'Tell us, when shall these things be? And what
shall be the sign when all these things shall be fulfilled?'
5And Jesus answering them began to say, 'Take heed lest any
man deceive you; 6for many shall come in my name, saying,
"I am Christ," and shall deceive many. 7And when ye shall
hear of wars and rumours of wars, be ye not troubled; for
such things must needs be; but the end shall not be yet. 8For
nation shall rise against nation, and kingdom against kingdom; and there shall be earthquakes in divers places, and
there shall be famines and troubles: these are the beginnings
of sorrows.

9'But take heed to yourselves: for they shall deliver you
up to councils; and in the synagogues ye shall be beaten;
and ye shall be brought before rulers and kings for my sake,
for a testimony against them. 10And the gospel must first be
published among all nations. 11But when they shall lead you,
and deliver you up, take no thought beforehand what ye
shall speak, neither do ye premeditate; but whatsoever shall
be given you in that hour, that speak ye: for it is not ye that

speak, but the Holy Ghost. [12] Now the brother shall betray the
brother to death, and the father the son; and children shall rise
up against their parents, and shall cause them to be put to
death. [13] And ye shall be hated of all men for my name's sake:
but he that shall endure unto the end, the same shall be saved.

[14] 'But when ye shall see the abomination of desolation,
spoken of by Daniel the prophet, standing where it ought
not (let him that readeth understand) then let them that be in
Judæa flee to the mountains; [15] and let him that is on the
house-top not go down into the house, neither enter therein,
to take any thing out of his house; [16] and let him that is in the
field not turn back again for to take up his garment. [17] But
woe to them that are with child, and to them that give suck
in those days! [18] And pray ye that your flight be not in the
winter. [19] For in those days shall be affliction, such as was not
from the beginning of the creation which God created unto
this time, neither shall be. [20] And except that the Lord had
shortened those days, no flesh should be saved; but for the
elect's sake, whom he hath chosen, he hath shortened the days.
[21] And then if any man shall say to you, "Lo, here is Christ,"
or, "lo, he is there," believe him not; [22] for false Christs and
false prophets shall rise, and shall shew signs and wonders,
to seduce, if it were possible, even the elect. [23] But take ye
heed: behold, I have foretold you all things.

[24] 'But in those days, after that tribulation, the sun shall
be darkened, and the moon shall not give her light, [25] and the
stars of heaven shall fall, and the powers that are in heaven
shall be shaken. [26] And then shall they see the Son of man
coming in the clouds with great power and glory. [27] And then

shall he send his angels, and shall gather together his elect
from the four winds, from the uttermost part of the earth to
the uttermost part of heaven. 28 Now learn a parable of the
fig tree: when her branch is yet tender, and putteth forth
leaves, ye know that summer is near; 29 so ye in like manner,
when ye shall see these things come to pass, know that it is
nigh, even at the doors. 30 Verily I say unto you, that this generation shall not pass, till all these things be done. 31 Heaven
and earth shall pass away: but my words shall not pass away.

32 'But of that day and that hour knoweth no man, no, not
the angels which are in heaven, neither the Son, but the Father.
33 Take ye heed, watch and pray: for ye know not when the
time is. 34 For the Son of man is as a man taking a far journey,
who left his house, and gave authority to his servants, and to
every man his work, and commanded the porter to watch.
35 Watch ye therefore: for ye know not when the master of
the house cometh, at even, or at midnight, or at the cockcrow-
ing, or in the morning, 36 lest coming suddenly he find you
sleeping. 37 And what I say unto you I say unto all, Watch.'

14 After two days was the feast of the passover, and of
unleavened bread; and the chief priests and the scribes
sought how they might take him by craft, and put him to
death. 2 But they said, 'Not on the feast day, lest there be an
uproar of the people.'

3 And being in Bethany in the house of Simon the leper,
as he sat at meat, there came a woman having an alabaster
box of ointment of spikenard very precious; and she brake
the box, and poured it on his head. 4 And there were some

that had indignation within themselves, and said, 'Why was
this waste of the ointment made?' 5 For it might have been
sold for more than three hundred pence, and have been given
to the poor.' And they murmured against her. 6 And Jesus
said, 'Let her alone; why trouble ye her? She hath wrought a
good work on me. 7 For ye have the poor with you always,
and whensoever ye will ye may do them good; but me ye
have not always. 8 She hath done what she could: she is come
aforehand to anoint my body to the burying. 9 Verily I say
unto you, wheresoever this gospel shall be preached throughout the whole world, this also that she hath done shall be
spoken of for a memorial of her.'

10 And Judas Iscariot, one of the twelve, went unto the
chief priests, to betray him unto them. 11 And when they heard
it, they were glad, and promised to give him money. And he
sought how he might conveniently betray him.

12 And the first day of unleavened bread, when they killed
the passover, his disciples said unto him, 'Where wilt thou
that we go and prepare that thou mayest eat the passover?'
13 And he sendeth forth two of his disciples, and saith unto
them, 'Go ye into the city, and there shall meet you a man
bearing a pitcher of water; follow him. 14 And wheresoever
he shall go in, say ye to the goodman of the house, "The Master saith, 'Where is the guestchamber, where I shall eat the
passover with my disciples?'" 15 And he will shew you a
large upper room furnished and prepared; there make ready
for us.' 16 And his disciples went forth, and came into the city,
and found as he had said unto them; and they made ready
the passover. 17 And in the evening he cometh with the twelve.

18 And as they sat and did eat, Jesus said, 'Verily I say unto
you, one of you which eateth with me shall betray me.' 19 And
they began to be sorrowful, and to say unto him one by one,
'Is it I?' and another said, 'Is it I?' 20 And he answered and said
unto them, 'It is one of the twelve, that dippeth with me in
the dish. 21 The Son of man indeed goeth, as it is written of him;
but woe to that man by whom the Son of man is betrayed!
Good were it for that man if he had never been born.'

22 And as they did eat, Jesus took bread, and blessed, and
brake it, and gave to them, and said, 'Take, eat: this is my
body.' 23 And he took the cup, and when he had given thanks,
he gave it to them; and they all drank of it. 24 And he said
unto them, 'This is my blood of the new testament, which is
shed for many. 25 Verily I say unto you, I will drink no more
of the fruit of the vine, until that day that I drink it new in
the kingdom of God.'

26 And when they had sung an hymn, they went out into
the mount of Olives. 27 And Jesus saith unto them, 'All ye
shall be offended because of me this night; for it is written, I
will smite the shepherd, and the sheep shall be scattered.
28 But after that I am risen, I will go before you into Galilee.'
29 But Peter said unto him, 'Although all shall be offended,
yet will not I.' 30 And Jesus saith unto him, 'Verily I say unto
thee, that this day, even in this night, before the cock crow
twice, thou shalt deny me thrice.' 31 But he spake the more
vehemently, 'If I should die with thee, I will not deny thee in
any wise.' Likewise also said they all. 32 And they came to a
place which was named Gethsemane; and he saith to his disciples, 'Sit ye here, while I shall pray.' 33 And he taketh with

him Peter and James and John, and began to be sore amazed,
and to be very heavy; 34 and saith unto them, 'My soul is
exceeding sorrowful unto death; tarry ye here, and watch.'
35 And he went forward a little, and fell on the ground, and
prayed that, if it were possible, the hour might pass from
him. 36 And he said, 'Abba, Father, all things are possible unto
thee; take away this cup from me; nevertheless not what I
will, but what thou wilt.' 37 And he cometh, and findeth them
sleeping, and saith unto Peter, 'Simon, sleepest thou? Could-
est not thou watch one hour? 38 Watch ye and pray, lest ye
enter into temptation. The spirit truly is ready, but the flesh
is weak.' 39 And again he went away, and prayed, and spake
the same words. 40 And when he returned, he found them
asleep again (for their eyes were heavy), neither wist they
what to answer him. 41 And he cometh the third time, and
saith unto them, 'Sleep on now, and take your rest: it is
enough, the hour is come; behold, the Son of man is betrayed
into the hands of sinners. 42 Rise up, let us go; lo, he that
betrayeth me is at hand.'

43 And immediately, while he yet spake, cometh Judas,
one of the twelve, and with him a great multitude with swords
and staves, from the chief priests and the scribes and the elders. 44 And he that betrayed him had given them a token, saying, 'Whomsoever I shall kiss, that same is he; take him, and
lead him away safely.' 45 And as soon as he was come, he
goeth straightway to him, and saith, 'Master, master,' and
kissed him.

46 And they laid their hands on him, and took him. 47 And
one of them that stood by drew a sword, and smote a servant

of the high priest, and cut off his ear. 48And Jesus answered
and said unto them, 'Are ye come out, as against a thief, with
swords and with staves to take me? 49I was daily with you in
the temple teaching, and ye took me not: but the scriptures
must be fulfilled.' 50And they all forsook him, and fled. 51And
there followed him a certain young man, having a linen cloth
cast about his naked body; and the young men laid hold on
him; 52and he left the linen cloth, and fled from them naked.

53And they led Jesus away to the high priest; and with
him were assembled all the chief priests and the elders and
the scribes. 54And Peter followed him afar off, even into the
palace of the high priest: and he sat with the servants, and
warmed himself at the fire. 55And the chief priests and all the
council sought for witness against Jesus to put him to death;
and found none. 56For many bare false witness against him,
but their witness agreed not together. 57And there arose certain, and bare false witness against him, saying, 58'We heard
him say, "I will destroy this temple that is made with hands,
and within three days I will build another made without
hands."' 59But neither so did their witness agree together.
60And the high priest stood up in the midst, and asked Jesus,
saying, 'Answerest thou nothing? What is it which these witness against thee?' 61But he held his peace, and answered
nothing. Again the high priest asked him, and said unto him,
'Art thou the Christ, the Son of the Blessed?' 62And Jesus said,
'I am; and ye shall see the Son of man sitting on the right
hand of power, and coming in the clouds of heaven.' 63Then
the high priest rent his clothes, and saith, 'What need we any
further witnesses? 64Ye have heard the blasphemy: what think

ye?' And they all condemned him to be guilty of death. 65And
some began to spit on him, and to cover his face, and to buffet him, and to say unto him, 'Prophesy,' and the servants
did strike him with the palms of their hands.

66And as Peter was beneath in the palace, there cometh
one of the maids of the high priest; 67and when she saw Peter
warming himself, she looked upon him, and said, 'And thou
also wast with Jesus of Nazareth.' 68But he denied, saying, 'I
know not, neither understand I what thou sayest.' And he
went out into the porch; and the cock crew. 69And a maid
saw him again, and began to say to them that stood by, 'This
is one of them.' 70And he denied it again. And a little after,
they that stood by said again to Peter, 'Surely thou art one of
them; for thou art a Galilæan, and thy speech agreeth thereto.'
71But he began to curse and to swear, saying, 'I know not this
man of whom ye speak.' 72And the second time the cock crew.
And Peter called to mind the word that Jesus said unto him,
'Before the cock crow twice, thou shalt deny me thrice.' And
when he thought thereon, he wept.

15 And straightway in the morning the chief priests held
a consultation with the elders and scribes and the whole
council, and bound Jesus, and carried him away, and delivered him to Pilate. 2And Pilate asked him, 'Art thou the King
of the Jews?' And he answering said unto him, 'Thou sayest
it.' 3And the chief priests accused him of many things: but he
answered nothing. 4And Pilate asked him again, saying,
'Answerest thou nothing? Behold how many things they witness against thee.' 5But Jesus yet answered nothing; so that

Pilate marvelled. [6]Now at that feast he released unto them
one prisoner, whomsoever they desired. [7]And there was one
named Barabbas, which lay bound with them that had made
insurrection with him, who had committed murder in the
insurrection. [8]And the multitude crying aloud began to
desire him to do as he had ever done unto them. [9]But Pilate
answered them, saying, 'Will ye that I release unto you the
King of the Jews?' [10]For he knew that the chief priests had
delivered him for envy. [11]But the chief priests moved the
people, that he should rather release Barabbas unto them.
[12]And Pilate answered and said again unto them, 'What will
ye then that I shall do unto him whom ye call the King of the
Jews?' [13]And they cried out again, 'Crucify him.' [14]Then Pilate
said unto them, 'Why, what evil hath he done?' And they
cried out the more exceedingly, 'Crucify him.'

[15]And so Pilate, willing to content the people, released
Barabbas unto them, and delivered Jesus, when he had
scourged him, to be crucified. [16]And the soldiers led him
away into the hall, called Prætorium; and they call together
the whole band. [17]And they clothed him with purple, and
platted a crown of thorns, and put it about his head, [18]and
began to salute him, 'Hail, King of the Jews!' [19]And they smote
him on the head with a reed, and did spit upon him, and
bowing their knees worshipped him. [20]And when they had
mocked him, they took off the purple from him, and put his
own clothes on him, and led him out to crucify him. [21]And
they compel one Simon a Cyrenian, who passed by, coming
out of the country, the father of Alexander and Rufus, to
bear his cross. [22]And they bring him unto the place Golgotha,

which is, being interpreted, 'The place of a skull.' 23And they
gave him to drink wine mingled with myrrh: but he received
it not. 24And when they had crucified him, they parted his
garments, casting lots upon them, what every man should
take. 25And it was the third hour, and they crucified him.
26And the superscription of his accusation was written over,
'The king of the Jews'. 27And with him they crucify two
thieves; the one on his right hand, and the other on his left.
28And the scripture was fulfilled, which saith, 'And he was
numbered with the transgressors.' 29And they that passed by
railed on him, wagging their heads, and saying, 'Ah, thou
that destroyest the temple, and buildest it in three days,
30 save thyself, and come down from the cross.' 31 Likewise
also the chief priests mocking said among themselves with
the scribes, 'He saved others; himself he cannot save. 32 Let
Christ the King of Israel descend now from the cross, that
we may see and believe.' And they that were crucified with
him reviled him. 33And when the sixth hour was come, there
was darkness over the whole land until the ninth hour. 34And
at the ninth hour Jesus cried with a loud voice, saying, 'Eloi,
Eloi, lama sabachthani?' which is, being interpreted, 'My
God, my God, why hast thou forsaken me?' 35And some of
them that stood by, when they heard it, said, 'Behold, he calleth Elias.' 36And one ran and filled a spunge full of vinegar,
and put it on a reed, and gave him to drink, saying, 'Let alone;
let us see whether Elias will come to take him down.' 37And
Jesus cried with a loud voice, and gave up the ghost. 38And the
veil of the temple was rent in twain from the top to the bottom.

39And when the centurion, which stood over against him,

saw that he so cried out, and gave up the ghost, he said, 'Truly
this man was the Son of God.' 40There were also women looking on afar off; among whom was Mary Magdalene, and
Mary the mother of James the less and of Joses, and Salome
41(who also, when he was in Galilee, followed him, and ministered unto him), and many other women which came up
with him unto Jerusalem.

42And now when the even was come, because it was the
preparation, that is, the day before the sabbath, 43Joseph of
Arimathæa, an honourable counsellor, which also waited for
the kingdom of God, came, and went in boldly unto Pilate,
and craved the body of Jesus. 44And Pilate marvelled if he
were already dead; and calling unto him the centurion, he
asked him whether he had been any while dead. 45And when
he knew it of the centurion, he gave the body to Joseph.
46And he bought fine linen, and took him down, and wrapped
him in the linen, and laid him in a sepulchre which was
hewn out of a rock, and rolled a stone unto the door of the
sepulchre. 47And Mary Magdalene and Mary the mother of
Joses beheld where he was laid.

16 And when the sabbath was past, Mary Magdalene, and
Mary the mother of James, and Salome, had bought
sweet spices, that they might come and anoint him. 2And
very early in the morning the first day of the week, they
came unto the sepulchre at the rising of the sun. 3And they
said among themselves, 'Who shall roll us away the stone
from the door of the sepulchre?' 4And when they looked,
they saw that the stone was rolled away; for it was very great.

5And entering into the sepulchre, they saw a young man sitting on the right side, clothed in a long white garment; and
they were affrighted. 6And he saith unto them, 'Be not affrighted: ye seek Jesus of Nazareth, which was crucified. He
is risen; he is not here; behold the place where they laid him.
7But go your way, tell his disciples and Peter that he goeth
before you into Galilee: there shall ye see him, as he said unto
you.' 8And they went out quickly, and fled from the sepulchre; for they trembled and were amazed; neither said they
any thing to any man; for they were afraid.

* 9Now when Jesus was risen early the first day of the
week, he appeared first to Mary Magdalene, out of whom he
had cast seven devils. 10And she went and told them that had
been with him, as they mourned and wept. 11And they, when
they had heard that he was alive, and had been seen of her,
believed not.

12After that he appeared in another form unto two of
them, as they walked, and went into the country. 13And they
went and told it unto the residue; neither believed they them.

14Afterward he appeared unto the eleven as they sat at
meat, and upbraided them with their unbelief and hardness
of heart, because they believed not them which had seen
him after he was risen. 15And he said unto them, 'Go ye into
all the world, and preach the gospel to every creature. 16He
that believeth and is baptised shall be saved; but he that
believeth not shall be damned. 17And these signs shall follow
them that believe: in my name shall they cast out devils;
they shall speak with new tongues; 18they shall take up serpents; and if they drink any deadly thing, it shall not hurt

them; they shall lay hands on the sick, and they shall recover.'
19 So then after the Lord had spoken unto them, he was
received up into heaven, and sat on the right hand of God.
20 And they went forth, and preached every where, the Lord
working with them, and confirming the word with signs following. Amen.

* *In the most reliable manuscripts Mark's gospel ends at ch. 16:8.*

the gospel according to

luke

authorized king james version

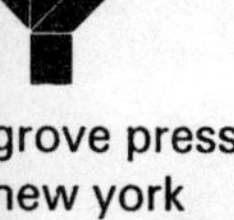

grove press
new york

with an introduction by | thomas cahill

The Pocket Canons were originally published in the U.K. in 1998 by Canongate Books, Ltd.
Published simultaneously in Canada
Printed in the United States of America

FIRST AMERICAN EDITION

Copyright information is on file with the Library of Congress
ISBN 0-8021-3618-4

Design by Paddy Cramsie

Grove Press
841 Broadway
New York, NY 10003

99 00 01 02 10 9 8 7 6 5 4 3 2 1

a note about pocket canons

The Authorized King James Version of the Bible, translated between 1603 and 1611, coincided with an extraordinary flowering of English literature. This version, more than any other, and possibly more than any other work in history, has had an influence in shaping the language we speak and write today. Presenting individual books from the Bible as separate volumes, as they were originally conceived, encourages the reader to approach them as literary works in their own right.

The first twelve books in this series encompass categories as diverse as history, fiction, philosophy, love poetry, and law. Each Pocket Canon also has its own introduction, specially commissioned from an impressive range of writers, which provides a personal interpretation of the text and explores its contemporary relevance.

Thomas Cahill is the author of the bestselling Hinges of History series, which includes How the Irish Saved Civilization, The Gifts of the Jews, *and* Desire of the Everlasting Hills. *He has studied with some of America's most distinguished literary and biblical scholars at New York's Union Theological Seminary, Columbia University, Fordham University, and the Jewish Theological Seminary of America. The former director of religious publishing at Doubleday, he divides his time between New York City and Rome.*

introduction by thomas cahill

Within the covers of the New Testament we find four Gospels (or accounts of the life and teachings of Jesus), written in Greek by four evangelists (or Gospel writers) whose names ancient tradition has given us as Matthew, Mark, Luke, and John. Though three of these men were what publishers today would call "one-book authors," one of them, Luke, wrote a second book, the Acts of the Apostles. This second book continues the story of Jesus into the period *after* his earthly life in order to show us how Jesus remained present to his followers even when he was no longer with them physically. The four Gospels, together with the Acts of the Apostles, make up the first five books of the New Testament, and correspond in position and importance to the Five Books of Moses, which the Jews placed at the head of their Sacred Scriptures, usually called by Christians the Old Testament.

Among the four evangelists, Luke stands out for several reasons, especially because he is the best writer of the bunch. As far as we can tell, he was not a Jew (probably the only non-Jew to author a book of the Bible) but a Greek-speaking Syrian of the first century who knew Paul (Paul described him as "the beloved physician") and other figures prominent in the early Christian Church but who did not know the earthly Jesus—because he had come to the Christian "Way" only after Jesus' departure. His Gospel shares many things with the other Gospels, particularly those of Matthew and Mark, but whereas the other evangelists write like Aramaic-speaking, Hebrew-reading Jews who had picked up Greek somewhere along the line, Luke writes with the high style of someone who absorbed Greek with his mother's milk and understands how to use it with elegant balance and refinement. He is a beautiful writer. His Gospel, indeed, was called by Ernest Renan *"le plus beau livre qu'il y ait,"* the most beautiful book ever written. (Its sequel, the Acts of the Apostles, bids fair to be considered the most beautiful sequel ever written.)

I hope someday to write a passage-by-passage appreciation of Luke's writing. Mine will not be the appreciation of a theologian or Scripture scholar but of a writer who can only admire Luke's magisterial construct. I shall, as needed, take into account Luke's influence on theology and Christian history and shall tap the best resources of Scripture scholarship to keep me on track, but the goal of the hunt will be to catch not Luke the theologian or Luke the ecclesiastical controversialist or Luke the linguist but Luke the writer. It is the essence of his art that I would hope to bag. Here I can sound only the first notes of such an appreciation—by offering an analysis of Luke's first twenty-seven verses.

Luke 1:1–4

Luke's very first sentence alerts us to his facility. A long, perfectly sustained periodic sentence, it exhibits all the modest indirection of true classical writing while at the same time reassuring the reader that Luke has done his job diligently: he has consulted eyewitnesses and other accounts, and he will deal with all this material with completeness, accuracy, and thoroughness—and, perhaps most important to a Greek reader, the account will be systematic, that is, presented according to the classical rules of Order, the great virtue of Greco-Roman civilization.

Even in his first sentence, Luke strikes the first notes of a theme that will be repeated throughout his account: "the events that have come to fulfillment among us" (a more accurate translation than the King James's "those things which are most surely believed among us"). So this will be a story, not a thesis, packed with "events" that are not just happenings but *fruitions*: the effects will be intended, not haphazard. Intended by whom? Luke does not say as yet, but we must already suspect that he is not talking about the effects a writer can produce by his craft. No, Luke means to bring on the stage a force much more powerful than himself. So the ultimate assurance that the reader has is not Luke's diligence or intelligence but the assurance of someone quite other and much larger than the author. In the Greek, the last word of the sentence, *asphaleia*, "assurance" ("certainty" in the King James Version), creates an effect that is virtually impossible to render in English. For the last word of a Greek periodic sentence must bear all the accumulated weight of the sentence's meaning. So the promise Luke is making to Theophilus is a bold one, indeed; he is promising a great deal.

We have no idea who Theophilus was or why he is addressed as "Your Excellency," but the name means Lover of God, so we may assume that Luke is addressing a person of some importance whose name suggests that he has already taken his first steps in exploring the new "Way" of the Christians. Given this, there is no reason to doubt that Luke also meant to address each one of us, you and me. For, in Luke's view, the events have come to fulfillment *among us*—and he means to include even us. To know that this ancient writer, who wrote in a language few of us can understand, really intended to address even *us* across all the centuries alerts us to the fact that what we are about to read is, at the least, an unusual story.

Luke 1:5–25

By invoking the name of King Herod, Luke anchors his narrative in a historical time familiar to his initial readers and no more distant from them than, say, Woodrow Wilson is from us—in other words, in a time their parents or grandparents could remember. But Greek (not unlike Hebrew before it) had two words for time: *chronos*, meaning the measure of time, as in "What time is it now?" and *kairos*, meaning the *right* time, as in "Now is the time!" Luke repeatedly uses *kairos* when he means the right time, the time of fulfillment, God's time. "God's time" is not the easiest idea to get hold of, for we human beings have no way of measuring it. Only God knows when is the right time for something to happen. But more than this, Luke sees the whole of human history—the whole human story—as God's time, in which he brings to fruition those things that he has ordained, according to his own promises to human beings whom he has chosen for his own utterly mysterious reasons. Right now, in the wicked reign of Herod, God has decided: this is the right time for his promised fulfillment to begin to come to fruition.

The passage about Zechariah's encounter with Gabriel is full of notes of fulfillment, words that speak to us subliminally or forthrightly of fruition: *descendant, children, barren, bear you a son, he will be great, the children of Israel, parents turning to their children, old, well on in years, the day these things will take place, my words which will find fulfillment in their own time, sometime later, Elizabeth became pregnant, how the Lord has dealt with me at the time he saw fit*! These are a great many chords of fulfillment for a few short paragraphs—so much so that we can say that it is as if Luke wants us to think of the cosmos itself as pregnant with God's meaning, of the whole of the created universe as groaning in labor, heavy with the fruit it is about to drop.

The purpose of human history itself is about to be revealed, and Luke's text invokes, for a reader who knows the Old Testament, some of the greatest figures of Jewish history: Abraham and Sarah, whose old age also brought forth a son, despite their initial skepticism, so like Zechariah's; the spirit and power of the prophet Elijah, who left such an impression on Jewish imagination, because he never died but was taken up into the heavens in a chariot of fire; the prophet Malachi, who first spoke the ringing phrase that promised an age in which "the hearts of parents" would be turned "to their children." All these figures Luke, as it were, summons as witnesses to a momentous revelation.

And what will this revelation, this fulfillment, be exactly? Whatever it will be it will involve reconciliation, love, and justice—"to make ready a people fit for the Lord." For the other set of notes that these paragraphs contain are the great qualities repeatedly emphasized throughout the Jewish Scriptures, the qualities by which man becomes like God: *blameless* and *upright*, the qualities that bring *joy* and *delight*. This passage, then, is a kind of fugue in which two themes are intertwined and finally fused together, as the upright Zechariah and the blameless Elizabeth, both ancient representatives of those who understand, the upright of Israel, conceive out of their ancientness a child of joy and delight, a boy of greatness, filled from his birth with a holy Spirit.

Even in this early passage we may take note that the mysterious fulfillment to come, though obviously communal—that is, meant for the whole nation—is also to be individual, for it involves these two very human characters, Zechariah, the understandably skeptical old priest, and Elizabeth, who ground her teeth over "the disgrace that [she] endured among people." It involves too the child to come, the mysteriously great John; and soon it will involve an even larger cast of quite distinct personalities.

Is Zechariah made mute as a punishment for his skepticism, which is no greater than Abraham's or Sarah's, nor greater than (as we shall soon see) Mary's? To me, at least, this muteness is simply an instance of the great truth that God treats individuals individually. Apparently, Abraham, Sarah, and Mary, though all quite as skeptical as Zechariah, were able to grasp the revelation they had received without God having to resort to making them mute. Zechariah—we don't know why—was not. His personality, for reasons we are not told directly, required this remedy. He was, after all, a priest, someone used to being listened to, in all likelihood not someone used to listening. But in the coming nine months of enforced silence, God will succeed in getting through to him in a spectacular manner—which will blossom forth in his thrilling song (Luke 1:68–79).

Most of us are somewhat like Zechariah, unable to believe that God has chosen us for his purpose. We too need a time of quiet in which we obey not our own interminable voice but the voice of the Other, who has been trying to speak to us for so long. We need to pray the insightful prayer of Cardinal Newman:

> God has created me to do him some definite service: he has committed some work to me which he has not committed to another. I have my mission—I never may know it in this life, but I shall be told in the next. Somehow I am necessary for His purposes. . . . I have a part in this great work; I am a link in a chain, a bond of connection between persons. He has not created me for nought.

Like Zechariah, most of us need a time of withdrawal, of retreat from our ordinary tasks and daily busyness, of mute silence, if God is ever to get through to us and impress on us what it is that he means us to do. It is unlikely that what God has in mind for us involves great matters of state—that we are meant to advise prime ministers or presidents or popes. But whatever it is, God surely expects of us that we will do our part to "make ready a people fit for" him, that we will play our role, however humble, to enable the coming of *kairos,* the acceptable time.

Luke 1:26–27

When Elizabeth is six months pregnant, Gabriel, the busy angelic messenger, appears in Galilee to a virgin whose name is Mary. Much ink has been spilled over this virgin, most recently in an attempt to prove that she was no virgin—just another pregnant teenager in need of a cover story. But there is no reason to think that Luke has any doubts on this score or that he doesn't really mean "virgin," only "young girl." Matthew, in his account of Mary's pregnancy, makes direct reference to Isaiah's prophecy "A virgin shall conceive . . ." and while it is true that Matthew is quoting the traditional Greek translation of this prophecy, which uses *parthenos*, the Greek word for "virgin," it is also true that the original Hebrew uses a word that means "young girl." So while it is possible (though pretty unlikely) that Matthew thinks that Mary was no virgin, there can scarcely be any doubt about Luke's meaning: "But how can this be," Mary will ask skeptically in verse 34, "since I have no relations with a man?" Luke's meaning is clear as crystal: Mary, betrothed, probably in childhood (after the tradition of Palestinian Jews), long before actual congress with her husband, has not yet come to live with him.

What we see here is a great instance of parallelism, the chief device ancient Hebrew writers used to achieve emphasis. Parallelism courses through the Psalms, to such an extent that it may be found in couplets and triplets everywhere. It is the simple but extremely effective device of repeating an idea in new words:

> Sweeter than honey,
> than honey dripping from the honeycomb.
>
> For you will not abandon me to Hell,
> Nor can you allow your faithful servant to see the Abyss.

In Luke's account the parallelism is on a grander scale and occurs between the events leading up to (and including) the birth of John the Baptist and the events leading up to (and including) the birth of Jesus. One set of events is a repetition in different words of the other—but with a difference: the birth of Jesus is accorded more importance and requires even greater intervention on God's part. This is called step parallelism.

Mary's name (Miryam, in all likelihood, in her original Aramaic, though the name Maria was not unknown among Palestinian Jews) means something like summit, pinnacle, apogee: she is, therefore, the culmination of all this fruitfulness. And, once again, Luke's writing is full of fruit and offspring, wombs and promises of miraculous births. We are about to experience a cosmic explosion of fecundity. Fulfillment is at hand, so reality itself is pregnant.

Luke's allusions remind me of a Flemish painting of the Annunciation (as this scene is called) that hangs among the paintings of the northern Renaissance in the Metropolitan Museum of Art in New York. It depicts a modest, almost tentative Mary, her eyes downcast in the presence of the angelic apparition who is very nearly her mirror image—but slightly more ruddy and vigorous, coming as he does from Heaven. The artist (the painting has most recently been attributed to Memling, but who knows?) has surrounded the scene with symbolic reminders of fertility: an upended vase, a blooming lily, a riotous summer garden beyond the open window, pillows and bedroom draperies arranged to mimic the protrusion of pregnancy, even (I think) the "buzz" between the two principals.

And, as in the scene with Zechariah, the long procession of Old Testament figures is once again invoked. Elizabeth is the descendant of Aaron, the brother of Moses. Mary's husband is a descendant of David, the great king, and his name calls up our memory of the Joseph of Genesis, the son of Jacob, who was also called Israel. All the many passages of the Old Testament in which one generation begat another is now come to its culmination. All that vigorous begetting is about to have its final issue.

We have considered only the first twenty-seven verses of Luke's Gospel, one-fifth of his prologue (which is his first two chapters). Now—in Mary's encounter with the angel—the story commences in earnest. As you read on, allow Luke to continue to speak to you in his exquisitely thoughtful way. Take time to appreciate Luke's unique material, the stories only he tells us. One wonders how Christianity would have managed without the episodes found only in his Gospel. Besides this prologue of pregnancies and births, there are Luke's other unique stories: the Good Samaritan (Luke 10:29–37), Martha and Mary (10:38–42), the Rich Fool (12:16–21), the Prodigal Son (15:11–32), Dives and Lazarus (16:19–31), the Pharisee and the Publican (18:10–14), Zaccheus (19:1–10), the Lament over Jerusalem (19:41–44), and the Good Thief (23:39–43), as well as Luke's delicious coda of the Disciples on the Road to Emmaus (24:13–35). Do not fail to note Luke's juxtapositions, which are always full of significance. (Consider, for instance, the unified trilogy of anecdotes that stretches from 10:29 to 11:4, in which Jesus teaches us that kindness to others is primary but only possible if we are willing to take time out from our daily preoccupations and pray to the Father.) From the Good Samaritan to the Good Thief, Luke, whose zephyr-like prose caresses his readers, is telling us always of the mercy of God. This mercy is Luke's profoundest theme, the one to which all his other themes are subservient. With good reason Dante called him "*il scriba della gentilezza di Cristo*," the scribe of the kindness of Christ.

the gospel according to st luke

Forasmuch as many have taken in hand to set forth in order
a declaration of those things which are most surely believed
among us, 2 even as they delivered them unto us, which from
the beginning were eye-witnesses, and ministers of the word;
3 it seemed good to me also, having had perfect understanding of all things from the very first, to write unto thee in
order, most excellent Theophilus, 4 that thou mightest know
the certainty of those things, wherein thou hast been instructed.

5 There was in the days of Herod, the king of Judæa, a
certain priest named Zacharias, of the course of Abia; and
his wife was of the daughters of Aaron, and her name was
Elisabeth. 6 And they were both righteous before God, walking in all the commandments and ordinances of the Lord
blameless. 7 And they had no child, because that Elisabeth
was barren, and they both were now well stricken in years.

8 And it came to pass, that while he executed the priest's
office before God in the order of his course, 9 according to the
custom of the priest's office, his lot was to burn incense
when he went into the temple of the Lord. 10 And the whole
multitude of the people were praying without at the time of
incense. 11 And there appeared unto him an angel of the Lord
standing on the right side of the altar of incense. 12 And when
Zacharias saw him, he was troubled, and fear fell upon him.
13 But the angel said unto him, 'Fear not, Zacharias, for thy

prayer is heard; and thy wife Elisabeth shall bear thee a son,
and thou shalt call his name John. [14]And thou shalt have joy
and gladness; and many shall rejoice at his birth. [15]For he
shall be great in the sight of the Lord, and shall drink neither
wine nor strong drink; and he shall be filled with the Holy
Ghost, even from his mother's womb. [16]And many of the
children of Israel shall he turn to the Lord their God. [17]And
he shall go before him in the spirit and power of Elias, to
turn the hearts of the fathers to the children, and the disobe-
dient to the wisdom of the just; to make ready a people prepared for the Lord.' [18]And Zacharias said unto the angel,
'Whereby shall I know this? For I am an old man, and my
wife well stricken in years.' [19]And the angel answering said
unto him, 'I am Gabriel, that stand in the presence of God;
and am sent to speak unto thee, and to shew thee these glad
tidings. [20]And, behold, thou shalt be dumb, and not able to
speak, until the day that these things shall be performed,
because thou believest not my words, which shall be fulfilled in their season.'

[21]And the people waited for Zacharias, and marvelled
that he tarried so long in the temple. [22]And when he came
out, he could not speak unto them; and they perceived that
he had seen a vision in the temple, for he beckoned unto
them, and remained speechless. [23]And it came to pass, that,
as soon as the days of his ministration were accomplished,
he departed to his own house.

[24]And after those days his wife Elisabeth conceived, and
hid herself five months, saying, [25]'Thus hath the Lord dealt
with me in the days wherein he looked on me, to take away
my reproach among men.'

26 And in the sixth month the angel Gabriel was sent from
God unto a city of Galilee, named Nazareth, 27 to a virgin
espoused to a man whose name was Joseph, of the house of
David; and the virgin's name was Mary. 28 And the angel came
in unto her, and said, 'Hail, thou that art highly favoured,
the Lord is with thee: blessed art thou among women.' 29 And
when she saw him, she was troubled at his saying, and cast
in her mind what manner of salutation this should be. 30 And
the angel said unto her, 'Fear not, Mary, for thou hast found
favour with God. 31 And, behold, thou shalt conceive in thy
womb, and bring forth a son, and shalt call his name JESUS.
32 He shall be great, and shall be called the Son of the Highest; and the Lord God shall give unto him the throne of his
father David. 33 And he shall reign over the house of Jacob for
ever; and of his kingdom there shall be no end.' 34 Then said
Mary unto the angel, 'How shall this be, seeing I know not a
man?' 35 And the angel answered and said unto her, 'The Holy
Ghost shall come upon thee, and the power of the Highest
shall overshadow thee; therefore also that holy thing which
shall be born of thee shall be called the Son of God. 36 And,
behold, thy cousin Elisabeth, she hath also conceived a son
in her old age; and this is the sixth month with her, who was
called barren. 37 For with God nothing shall be impossible.'
38 And Mary said, 'Behold the handmaid of the Lord; be it unto
me according to thy word.' And the angel departed from her.

39 And Mary arose in those days, and went into the hill
country with haste, into a city of Juda; 40 and entered into the
house of Zacharias, and saluted Elisabeth. 41 And it came to
pass, that, when Elisabeth heard the salutation of Mary, the
babe leaped in her womb; and Elisabeth was filled with the

Holy Ghost. 42 And she spake out with a loud voice, and said,
'Blessed art thou among women, and blessed is the fruit of
thy womb. 43 And whence is this to me, that the mother of my
Lord should come to me? 44 For, lo, as soon as the voice of
thy salutation sounded in mine ears, the babe leaped in my
womb for joy. 45 And blessed is she that believed: for there
shall be a performance of those things which were told her
from the Lord.' 46 And Mary said,

'My soul doth magnify the Lord,
47 and my spirit hath rejoiced in God my Saviour.
48 For he hath regarded the low estate
of his handmaiden;
for, behold, from henceforth
all generations shall call me blessed.
49 For he that is mighty hath done to me great things;
and holy is his name.
50 And his mercy is on them that fear him
from generation to generation.
51 He hath shewed strength with his arm;
he hath scattered the proud
in the imagination of their hearts.
52 He hath put down the mighty from their seats,
and exalted them of low degree.
53 He hath filled the hungry with good things;
and the rich he hath sent empty away.
54 He hath holpen his servant Israel,
in remembrance of his mercy;
55 as he spake to our fathers, to Abraham,
and to his seed for ever.'

56 And Mary abode with her about three months, and
returned to her own house.

57 Now Elisabeth's full time came that she should be delivered; and she brought forth a son. 58 And her neighbours and
her cousins heard how the Lord had shewed great mercy
upon her; and they rejoiced with her.

59 And it came to pass, that on the eighth day they came to
circumcise the child; and they called him Zacharias, after the
name of his father. 60 And his mother answered and said,
'Not so; but he shall be called John.' 61 And they said unto
her, 'There is none of thy kindred that is called by this name.'
62 And they made signs to his father, how he would have him
called. 63 And he asked for a writing table, and wrote, saying,
'His name is John.' And they marvelled all. 64 And his mouth
was opened immediately, and his tongue loosed, and he
spake, and praised God. 65 And fear came on all that dwelt
round about them: and all these sayings were noised abroad
throughout all the hill country of Judæa. 66 And all they that
heard them laid them up in their hearts, saying, 'What manner
of child shall this be!' And the hand of the Lord was with him.

67 And his father Zacharias was filled with the Holy
Ghost, and prophesied, saying, 68 'Blessed be the Lord God
of Israel; for he hath visited and redeemed his people, 69 and
hath raised up an horn of salvation for us in the house of his
servant David, 70 as he spake by the mouth of his holy prophets, which have been since the world began, 71 that we should
be saved from our enemies, and from the hand of all that
hate us, 72 to perform the mercy promised to our fathers, and
to remember his holy covenant, 73 the oath which he sware to
our father Abraham, 74 that he would grant unto us, that we

being delivered out of the hand of our enemies might serve
him without fear, 75 in holiness and righteousness before him,
all the days of our life. 76 And thou, child, shalt be called the
prophet of the Highest; for thou shalt go before the face of the
Lord to prepare his ways, 77 to give knowledge of salvation
unto his people by the remission of their sins, 78 through the
tender mercy of our God; whereby the dayspring from on
high hath visited us, 79 to give light to them that sit in darkness and in the shadow of death, to guide our feet into the
way of peace.' 80 And the child grew, and waxed strong in spirit,
and was in the deserts till the day of his shewing unto Israel.

2 And it came to pass in those days, that there went out a
decree from Caesar Augustus, that all the world should
be taxed. 2 (And this taxing was first made when Cyrenius
was governor of Syria.) 3 And all went to be taxed, every one
into his own city. 4 And Joseph also went up from Galilee, out
of the city of Nazareth, into Judæa, unto the city of David,
which is called Bethlehem (because he was of the house and
lineage of David), 5 to be taxed with Mary his espoused wife,
being great with child. 6 And so it was, that, while they were
there, the days were accomplished that she should be delivered. 7 And she brought forth her firstborn son, and wrapped
him in swaddling clothes, and laid him in a manger; because
there was no room for them in the inn. 8 And there were in
the same country shepherds abiding in the field, keeping
watch over their flock by night. 9 And, lo, the angel of the Lord
came upon them, and the glory of the Lord shone round
about them; and they were sore afraid. 10 And the angel said
unto them, 'Fear not: for, behold, I bring you good tidings of

great joy, which shall be to all people. [11]For unto you is born
this day in the city of David a Saviour, which is Christ the
Lord. [12]And this shall be a sign unto you: ye shall find the
babe wrapped in swaddling clothes, lying in a manger.'
[13]And suddenly there was with the angel a multitude of the
heavenly host praising God, and saying, [14]'Glory to God in
the highest, and on earth peace, good will toward men.'

[15]And it came to pass, as the angels were gone away from
them into heaven, the shepherds said one to another, 'Let us
now go even unto Bethlehem, and see this thing which is
come to pass, which the Lord hath made known unto us.'
[16]And they came with haste, and found Mary, and Joseph,
and the babe lying in a manger. [17]And when they had seen it,
they made known abroad the saying which was told them
concerning this child. [18]And all they that heard it wondered
at those things which were told them by the shepherds. [19]But
Mary kept all these things, and pondered them in her heart.
[20]And the shepherds returned, glorifying and praising God
for all the things that they had heard and seen, as it was told
unto them.

[21]And when eight days were accomplished for the circum-
cising of the child, his name was called JESUS, which was so
named of the angel before he was conceived in the womb.

[22]And when the days of her purification according to the
law of Moses were accomplished, they brought him to Jerusalem, to present him to the Lord [23](as it is written in the law
of the Lord, 'Every male that openeth the womb shall be
called holy to the Lord'), [24]and to offer a sacrifice according
to that which is said in the law of the Lord, 'a pair of turtle-
doves, or two young pigeons.' [25]And, behold, there was a man

in Jerusalem, whose name was Simeon; and the same man
was just and devout, waiting for the consolation of Israel,
and the Holy Ghost was upon him. [26]And it was revealed
unto him by the Holy Ghost that he should not see death
before he had seen the Lord's Christ. [27]And he came by the
Spirit into the temple; and when the parents brought in the
child Jesus, to do for him after the custom of the law, [28] then
took he him up in his arms, and blessed God, and said,
[29] 'Lord, now lettest thou thy servant depart in peace, according to thy word: [30] 'For mine eyes have seen thy salvation,
[31] which thou hast prepared before the face of all people, [32] a
light to lighten the Gentiles, and the glory of thy people Israel.'

[33]And Joseph and his mother marvelled at those things
which were spoken of him. [34]And Simeon blessed them, and
said unto Mary his mother, 'Behold, this child is set for the
fall and rising again of many in Israel; and for a sign which
shall be spoken against [35] (yea, a sword shall pierce through
thy own soul also), that the thoughts of many hearts may be
revealed.'

[36]And there was one Anna, a prophetess, the daughter of
Phanuel, of the tribe of Aser. She was of a great age, and had
lived with an husband seven years from her virginity; [37]and
she was a widow of about fourscore and four years, which
departed not from the temple, but served God with fastings
and prayers night and day. [38]And she coming in that instant
gave thanks likewise unto the Lord, and spake of him to all
them that looked for redemption in Jerusalem.

[39]And when they had performed all things according to the
law of the Lord, they returned into Galilee, to their own city
Nazareth. [40]And the child grew, and waxed strong in spirit,

filled with wisdom; and the grace of God was upon him.
41 Now his parents went to Jerusalem every year at the
feast of the passover. 42 And when he was twelve years old,
they went up to Jerusalem after the custom of the feast.
43 And when they had fulfilled the days, as they returned, the
child Jesus tarried behind in Jerusalem; and Joseph and his
mother knew not of it. 44 But they, supposing him to have
been in the company, went a day's journey; and they sought
him among their kinsfolk and acquaintance. 45 And when
they found him not, they turned back again to Jerusalem,
seeking him. 46 And it came to pass, that after three days they
found him in the temple, sitting in the midst of the doctors,
both hearing them, and asking them questions. 47 And all that
heard him were astonished at his understanding and answers.
48 And when they saw him, they were amazed; and his
mother said unto him, 'Son, why hast thou thus dealt with
us? Behold, thy father and I have sought thee sorrowing.'

49 And he said unto them, 'How is it that ye sought me?
Wist ye not that I must be about my Father's business?' 50 And
they understood not the saying which he spake unto them.
51 And he went down with them, and came to Nazareth, and
was subject unto them; but his mother kept all these sayings
in her heart.

52 And Jesus increased in wisdom and stature, and in
favour with God and man.

3 Now in the fifteenth year of the reign of Tiberius Cæsar,
Pontius Pilate being governor of Judæa, and Herod being
tetrarch of Galilee, and his brother Philip tetrarch of Ituræa
and of the region of Trachonitis, and Lysanias the tetrarch of

Abilene, [2]Annas and Caiaphas being the high priests, the word of God came unto John the son of Zacharias in the wilderness. [3]And he came into all the country about Jordan, preaching the baptism of repentance for the remission of sins; [4]as it is written in the book of the words of Esaias the prophet, saying, 'The voice of one crying in the wilderness, "Prepare ye the way of the Lord, make his paths straight. [5]Every valley shall be filled, and every mountain and hill shall be brought low; and the crooked shall be made straight, and the rough ways shall be made smooth; [6]and all flesh shall see the salvation of God."' [7]Then said he to the multitude that came forth to be baptized of him, 'O generation of vipers, who hath warned you to flee from the wrath to come? [8]Bring forth therefore fruits worthy of repentance, and begin not to say within yourselves, "We have Abraham to our father," for I say unto you that God is able of these stones to raise up children unto Abraham. [9]And now also the axe is laid unto the root of the trees; every tree therefore which bringeth not forth good fruit is hewn down, and cast into the fire.'

[10]And the people asked him, saying, 'What shall we do then?' [11]He answereth and saith unto them, 'He that hath two coats, let him impart to him that hath none; and he that hath meat, let him do likewise.' [12]Then came also publicans to be baptized, and said unto him, 'Master, what shall we do?' [13]And he said unto them, 'Exact no more than that which is appointed you.' [14]And the soldiers likewise demanded of him, saying, 'And what shall we do?' And he said unto them, 'Do violence to no man, neither accuse any falsely; and be content with your wages.'

[15]And as the people were in expectation, and all men

mused in their hearts of John, whether he were the Christ, or
not, 16 John answered, saying unto them all, 'I indeed baptize
you with water; but one mightier than I cometh, the latchet
of whose shoes I am not worthy to unloose; he shall baptize
you with the Holy Ghost and with fire, 17 whose fan is in his
hand, and he will throughly purge his floor, and will gather
the wheat into his garner; but the chaff he will burn with fire
unquenchable.'

18 And many other things in his exhortation preached he
unto the people. 19 But Herod the tetrarch, being reproved by
him for Herodias his brother Philip's wife, and for all the
evils which Herod had done, 20 added yet this above all, that
he shut up John in prison.

21 Now when all the people were baptized, it came to pass,
that Jesus also being baptized, and praying, the heaven was
opened, 22 and the Holy Ghost descended in a bodily shape
like a dove upon him, and a voice came from heaven, which
said, 'Thou art my beloved Son; in thee I am well pleased.'

23 And Jesus himself began to be about thirty years of age,
being (as was supposed) the son of Joseph, which was the son
of Heli, 24 which was the son of Matthat, which was the son of
Levi, which was the son of Melchi, which was the son of Janna,
which was the son of Joseph, 25 which was the son of Mat-
tathias, which was the son of Amos, which was the son of
Naum, which was the son of Esli, which was the son of Nagge,
26 which was the son of Maath, which was the son of Mat-
tathias, which was the son of Semei, which was the son of Joseph, which was the son of Juda, 27 which was the son of Joanna,
which was the son of Rhesa, which was the son of Zorobabel, which was the son of Salathiel, which was the son of Neri,

28 which was the son of Melchi, which was the son of Addi,
which was the son of Cosam, which was the son of Elmo-
dam, which was the son of Er, 29 which was the son of Jose,
which was the son of Eliezer, which was the son of Jorim,
which was the son of Matthat, which was the son of Levi,
30 which was the son of Simeon, which was the son of Juda,
which was the son of Joseph, which was the son of Jonan,
which was the son of Eliakim, 31 which was the son of Melea,
which was the son of Menan, which was the son of Mattatha,
which was the son of Nathan, which was the son of David,
32 which was the son of Jesse, which was the son of Obed,
which was the son of Booz, which was the son of Salmon,
which was the son of Naasson, 33 which was the son of Aminadab, which was the son of Aram, which was the son of Esrom,
which was the son of Phares, which was the son of Juda,
34 which was the son of Jacob, which was the son of Isaac,
which was the son of Abraham, which was the son of Thara,
which was the son of Nachor, 35 which was the son of Saruch,
which was the son of Ragau, which was the son of Phalec,
which was the son of Heber, which was the son of Sala,
36 which was the son of Cainan, which was the son of Arphaxad, which was the son of Sem, which was the son of Noe,
which was the son of Lamech, 37 which was the son of Math-
usala, which was the son of Enoch, which was the son of Jared,
which was the son of Maleleel, which was the son of Cainan,
38 which was the son of Enos, which was the son of Seth,
which was the son of Adam, which was the son of God.

4 And Jesus being full of the Holy Ghost returned from
Jordan, and was led by the Spirit into the wilderness,

2 being forty days tempted of the devil. And in those days he
did eat nothing: and when they were ended, he afterward
hungered. 3 And the devil said unto him, 'If thou be the Son
of God, command this stone that it be made bread.' 4 And
Jesus answered him, saying, 'It is written, "That man shall
not live by bread alone, but by every word of God."'

5 And the devil, taking him up into an high mountain,
shewed unto him all the kingdoms of the world in a moment
of time. 6 And the devil said unto him, 'All this power will I
give thee, and the glory of them; for that is delivered unto
me, and to whomsoever I will I give it. 7 If thou therefore wilt
worship me, all shall be thine.' 8 And Jesus answered and
said unto him, 'Get thee behind me, Satan; for it is written,
"Thou shalt worship the Lord thy God, and him only shalt
thou serve."'

9 And he brought him to Jerusalem, and set him on a
pinnacle of the temple, and said unto him, 'If thou be the Son
of God, cast thyself down from hence. 10 For it is written, "He
shall give his angels charge over thee, to keep thee: 11 and in
their hands they shall bear thee up, lest at any time thou
dash thy foot against a stone."' 12 And Jesus answering said
unto him, 'It is said, "Thou shalt not tempt the Lord thy
God."' 13 And when the devil had ended all the temptation,
he departed from him for a season.

14 And Jesus returned in the power of the Spirit into
Galilee: and there went out a fame of him through all the
region round about. 15 And he taught in their synagogues,
being glorified of all.

16 And he came to Nazareth, where he had been brought
up: and, as his custom was, he went into the synagogue on

the sabbath day, and stood up for to read. [17]And there was
delivered unto him the book of the prophet Esaias. And
when he had opened the book, he found the place where it
was written, [18]'The Spirit of the Lord is upon me, because he
hath anointed me to preach the gospel to the poor; he hath
sent me to heal the brokenhearted, to preach deliverance to
the captives, and recovering of sight to the blind, to set at liberty them that are bruised, [19]to preach the acceptable year of
the Lord.' [20]And he closed the book, and he gave it again to
the minister, and sat down. And the eyes of all them that
were in the synagogue were fastened on him. [21]And he
began to say unto them, 'This day is this scripture fulfilled in
your ears.' [22]And all bare him witness, and wondered at the
gracious words which proceeded out of his mouth. And they
said, 'Is not this Joseph's son?' [23]And he said unto them, 'Ye
will surely say unto me this proverb, "Physician, heal thyself: whatsoever we have heard done in Capernaum, do also
here in thy country."' [24]And he said, 'Verily I say unto you,
no prophet is accepted in his own country. [25]But I tell you of
a truth, many widows were in Israel in the days of Elias,
when the heaven was shut up three years and six months,
when great famine was throughout all the land; [26]but unto
none of them was Elias sent, save unto Sarepta, a city of
Sidon, unto a woman that was a widow. [27]And many lepers
were in Israel in the time of Eliseus the prophet; and none of
them was cleansed, saving Naaman the Syrian.' [28]And all
they in the synagogue, when they heard these things, were
filled with wrath, [29]and rose up, and thrust him out of the
city, and led him unto the brow of the hill whereon their city
was built, that they might cast him down headlong. [30]But he

passing through the midst of them went his way, [31] and came
down to Capernaum, a city of Galilee, and taught them on
the sabbath days. [32] And they were astonished at his doctrine: for his word was with power.

[33] And in the synagogue there was a man, which had a
spirit of an unclean devil, and cried out with a loud voice,
[34] saying, 'Let us alone; what have we to do with thee, thou
Jesus of Nazareth? Art thou come to destroy us? I know thee
who thou art; the Holy One of God.' [35] And Jesus rebuked
him, saying, 'Hold thy peace, and come out of him.' And when
the devil had thrown him in the midst, he came out of him,
and hurt him not. [36] And they were all amazed, and spake
among themselves, saying, 'What a word is this! For with
authority and power he commandeth the unclean spirits,
and they come out.' [37] And the fame of him went out into
every place of the country round about.

[38] And he arose out of the synagogue, and entered into
Simon's house. And Simon's wife's mother was taken with a
great fever; and they besought him for her. [39] And he stood
over her, and rebuked the fever, and it left her; and immediately she arose and ministered unto them.

[40] Now when the sun was setting, all they that had any
sick with divers diseases brought them unto him; and he
laid his hands on every one of them, and healed them. [41] And
devils also came out of many, crying out, and saying, 'Thou
art Christ the Son of God.' And he rebuking them suffered
them not to speak; for they knew that he was Christ. [42] And
when it was day, he departed and went into a desert place;
and the people sought him, and came unto him, and stayed
him, that he should not depart from them. [43] And he said

unto them, 'I must preach the kingdom of God to other cities
also: for therefore am I sent.' 44And he preached in the synagogues of Galilee.

5 And it came to pass, that, as the people pressed upon
him to hear the word of God, he stood by the lake of
Gennesaret, 2and saw two ships standing by the lake; but
the fishermen were gone out of them, and were washing
their nets. 3And he entered into one of the ships, which was
Simon's, and prayed him that he would thrust out a little
from the land. And he sat down, and taught the people out
of the ship. 4Now when he had left speaking, he said unto
Simon, 'Launch out into the deep, and let down your nets for
a draught.' 5And Simon answering said unto him, 'Master,
we have toiled all the night, and have taken nothing; nevertheless at thy word I will let down the net.' 6And when they
had this done, they inclosed a great multitude of fishes; and
their net brake. 7And they beckoned unto their partners, which
were in the other ship, that they should come and help them.
And they came, and filled both the ships, so that they began
to sink. 8When Simon Peter saw it, he fell down at Jesus' knees,
saying, 'Depart from me; for I am a sinful man, O Lord.' 9For
he was astonished, and all that were with him, at the draught
of the fishes which they had taken. 10And so was also James,
and John, the sons of Zebedee, which were partners with
Simon. And Jesus said unto Simon, 'Fear not; from henceforth thou shalt catch men.' 11And when they had brought
their ships to land, they forsook all, and followed him.

12And it came to pass, when he was in a certain city, behold
a man full of leprosy, who seeing Jesus fell on his face, and

besought him, saying, 'Lord, if thou wilt, thou canst make
me clean.' [13]And he put forth his hand, and touched him,
saying, 'I will: be thou clean.' And immediately the leprosy
departed from him. [14]And he charged him to tell no man, 'But
go, and shew thyself to the priest, and offer for thy cleans-
ing, according as Moses commanded, for a testimony unto
them.' [15]But so much the more went there a fame abroad of
him; and great multitudes came together to hear, and to be
healed by him of their infirmities.

[16]And he withdrew himself into the wilderness, and
prayed. [17]And it came to pass on a certain day, as he was
teaching, that there were Pharisees and doctors of the law
sitting by, which were come out of every town of Galilee,
and Judæa, and Jerusalem; and the power of the Lord was
present to heal them.

[18]And, behold, men brought in a bed a man which was
taken with a palsy: and they sought means to bring him in,
and to lay him before him. [19]And when they could not find
by what way they might bring him in because of the multitude, they went upon the housetop, and let him down through
the tiling with his couch into the midst before Jesus. [20]And
when he saw their faith, he said unto him, 'Man, thy sins are
forgiven thee.' [21]And the scribes and the Pharisees began to
reason, saying, 'Who is this which speaketh blasphemies?
Who can forgive sins, but God alone?' [22]But when Jesus perceived their thoughts, he answering said unto them, 'What
reason ye in your hearts? [23]Whether is easier, to say, "Thy
sins be forgiven thee," or to say, "Rise up and walk"? [24]But
that ye may know that the Son of man hath power upon
earth to forgive sins (he said unto the sick of the palsy), I say

unto thee, "Arise, and take up thy couch, and go into thine house."' 25And immediately he rose up before them, and took up that whereon he lay, and departed to his own house, glorifying God. 26And they were all amazed, and they glorified God, and were filled with fear, saying, 'We have seen strange things today.'

27And after these things he went forth, and saw a publican, named Levi, sitting at the receipt of custom; and he said unto him, 'Follow me.' 28And he left all, rose up, and followed him. 29And Levi made him a great feast in his own house; and there was a great company of publicans and of others that sat down with them. 30 But their scribes and Pharisees murmured against his disciples, saying, 'Why do ye eat and drink with publicans and sinners?' 31And Jesus answering said unto them, 'They that are whole need not a physician; but they that are sick. 32 I came not to call the righteous, but sinners to repentance.'

33And they said unto him, 'Why do the disciples of John fast often, and make prayers, and likewise the disciples of the Pharisees; but thine eat and drink?' 34And he said unto them, 'Can ye make the children of the bridechamber fast, while the bridegroom is with them? 35 But the days will come, when the bridegroom shall be taken away from them, and then shall they fast in those days.'

36And he spake also a parable unto them: 'No man putteth a piece of a new garment upon an old; if otherwise, then both the new maketh a rent, and the piece that was taken out of the new agreeth not with the old. 37And no man putteth new wine into old bottles; else the new wine will burst the bottles, and be spilled, and the bottles shall perish. 38 But new

wine must be put into new bottles; and both are preserved.
39 No man also having drunk old wine straightway desireth
new: for he saith, "The old is better."'

6 And it came to pass on the second sabbath after the first,
that he went through the corn fields; and his disciples
plucked the ears of corn, and did eat, rubbing them in their
hands. 2 And certain of the Pharisees said unto them, 'Why
do ye that which is not lawful to do on the sabbath days?'
3 And Jesus answering them said, 'Have ye not read so much
as this, what David did, when himself was an hungred, and
they which were with him; 4 how he went into the house of
God, and did take and eat the shewbread, and gave also to
them that were with him; which it is not lawful to eat but for
the priests alone?' 5 And he said unto them that 'The Son of
man is Lord also of the sabbath.'

6 And it came to pass also on another sabbath, that he
entered into the synagogue and taught; and there was a man
whose right hand was withered. 7 And the scribes and Pharisees watched him, whether he would heal on the sabbath
day; that they might find an accusation against him. 8 But he
knew their thoughts, and said to the man which had the withered hand, 'Rise up, and stand forth in the midst.' And he
arose and stood forth. 9 Then said Jesus unto them, 'I will ask
you one thing: Is it lawful on the sabbath days to do good, or
to do evil? To save life, or to destroy it?' 10 And looking
round about upon them all, he said unto the man, 'Stretch
forth thy hand.' And he did so; and his hand was restored
whole as the other. 11 And they were filled with madness; and
communed one with another what they might do to Jesus.

12 And it came to pass in those days, that he went out into
a mountain to pray, and continued all night in prayer to God.
13 And when it was day, he called unto him his disciples: and
of them he chose twelve, whom also he named apostles:
14 Simon (whom he also named Peter) and Andrew his
brother, James and John, Philip and Bartholomew, 15 Matthew
and Thomas, James the son of Alphæus, and Simon called
Zelotes, 16 and Judas the brother of James, and Judas Iscariot,
which also was the traitor.

17 And he came down with them, and stood in the plain,
and the company of his disciples, and a great multitude of
people out of all Judæa and Jerusalem, and from the sea
coast of Tyre and Sidon, which came to hear him, and to be
healed of their diseases; 18 and they that were vexed with
unclean spirits. And they were healed. 19 And the whole multitude sought to touch him; for there went virtue out of him,
and healed them all.

20 And he lifted up his eyes on his disciples, and said, 'Blessed be ye poor; for yours is the kingdom of God. 21 Blessed
are ye that hunger now; for ye shall be filled. Blessed are ye
that weep now; for ye shall laugh. 22 Blessed are ye, when
men shall hate you, and when they shall separate you from
their company, and shall reproach you, and cast out your
name as evil, for the Son of man's sake. 23 Rejoice ye in that
day, and leap for joy; for, behold, your reward is great in
heaven, for in the like manner did their fathers unto the
prophets. 24 But woe unto you that are rich! For ye have
received your consolation. 25 Woe unto you that are full! For
ye shall hunger. Woe unto you that laugh now! For ye shall
mourn and weep. 26 Woe unto you, when all men shall speak

well of you! For so did their fathers to the false prophets.

27 'But I say unto you which hear, Love your enemies, do
good to them which hate you, 28 bless them that curse you,
and pray for them which despitefully use you. 29 And unto
him that smiteth thee on the one cheek offer also the other;
and him that taketh away thy cloke forbid not to take thy
coat also. 30 Give to every man that asketh of thee; and of him
that taketh away thy goods ask them not again. 31 And as ye
would that men should do to you, do ye also to them likewise. 32 For if ye love them which love you, what thank have
ye? For sinners also love those that love them. 33 And if ye do
good to them which do good to you, what thank have ye?
For sinners also do even the same. 34 And if ye lend to them
of whom ye hope to receive, what thank have ye? For sinners also lend to sinners, to receive as much again. 35 But love
ye your enemies, and do good, and lend, hoping for nothing
again; and your reward shall be great, and ye shall be the
children of the Highest: for he is kind unto the unthankful
and to the evil. 36 Be ye therefore merciful, as your Father also
is merciful. 37 Judge not, and ye shall not be judged; condemn
not, and ye shall not be condemned; forgive, and ye shall be
forgiven; 38 give, and it shall be given unto you; good measure, pressed down, and shaken together, and running over,
shall men give into your bosom. For with the same measure
that ye mete withal it shall be measured to you again.'

39 And he spake a parable unto them, 'Can the blind lead
the blind? Shall they not both fall into the ditch? 40 The disciple is not above his master: but every one that is perfect shall
be as his master. 41 And why beholdest thou the mote that is
in thy brother's eye, but perceivest not the beam that is in

thine own eye? [42] Either how canst thou say to thy brother,
"Brother, let me pull out the mote that is in thine eye," when
thou thyself beholdest not the beam that is in thine own eye?
Thou hypocrite, cast out first the beam out of thine own eye,
and then shalt thou see clearly to pull out the mote that is in
thy brother's eye. [43] For a good tree bringeth not forth corrupt
fruit; neither doth a corrupt tree bring forth good fruit. [44] For
every tree is known by his own fruit. For of thorns men do
not gather figs, nor of a bramble bush gather they grapes. [45] A
good man out of the good treasure of his heart bringeth
forth that which is good; and an evil man out of the evil
treasure of his heart bringeth forth that which is evil: for of
the abundance of the heart his mouth speaketh.

[46] 'And why call ye me, "Lord, Lord," and do not the
things which I say? [47] Whosoever cometh to me, and heareth
my sayings, and doeth them, I will shew you to whom he is
like. [48] He is like a man which built an house, and digged
deep, and laid the foundation on a rock: and when the flood
arose, the stream beat vehemently upon that house, and
could not shake it: for it was founded upon a rock. [49] But he
that heareth, and doeth not, is like a man that without a
foundation built an house upon the earth; against which the
stream did beat vehemently, and immediately it fell; and the
ruin of that house was great.'

7 Now when he had ended all his sayings in the audience
of the people, he entered into Capernaum. [2] And a certain centurion's servant, who was dear unto him, was sick,
and ready to die. [3] And when he heard of Jesus, he sent unto
him the elders of the Jews, beseeching him that he would

come and heal his servant. [4]And when they came to Jesus,
they besought him instantly, saying, that 'He was worthy for
whom he should do this, [5]for he loveth our nation, and he
hath built us a synagogue.' [6]Then Jesus went with them.
And when he was now not far from the house, the centurion
sent friends to him, saying unto him, 'Lord, trouble not thyself; for I am not worthy that thou shouldest enter under my
roof. [7]Wherefore neither thought I myself worthy to come
unto thee; but say in a word, and my servant shall be healed.
[8]For I also am a man set under authority, having under me
soldiers, and I say unto one, "Go," and he goeth; and to
another, "Come," and he cometh; and to my servant, "Do
this," and he doeth it.' [9]When Jesus heard these things, he
marvelled at him, and turned him about, and said unto the
people that followed him, 'I say unto you, I have not found
so great faith, no, not in Israel.' [10]And they that were sent,
returning to the house, found the servant whole that had
been sick.

[11]And it came to pass the day after, that he went into a
city called Nain; and many of his disciples went with him,
and much people. [12]Now when he came nigh to the gate of
the city, behold, there was a dead man carried out, the only
son of his mother, and she was a widow; and much people
of the city was with her. [13]And when the Lord saw her, he
had compassion on her, and said unto her, 'Weep not.' [14]And
he came and touched the bier: and they that bare him stood
still. And he said, 'Young man, I say unto thee, Arise.' [15]And
he that was dead sat up, and began to speak. And he delivered him to his mother. [16]And there came a fear on all: and
they glorified God, saying, that 'a great prophet is risen up

among us'; and, that 'God hath visited his people.' 17And this
rumour of him went forth throughout all Judæa, and
throughout all the region round about. 18And the disciples of
John shewed him of all these things.

19And John calling unto him two of his disciples sent them
to Jesus, saying, 'Art thou he that should come? Or look we
for another?' 20When the men were come unto him, they
said, 'John Baptist hath sent us unto thee, saying, "Art thou
he that should come? Or look we for another?"' 21And in that
same hour he cured many of their infirmities and plagues,
and of evil spirits; and unto many that were blind he gave
sight. 22Then Jesus answering said unto them, 'Go your way,
and tell John what things ye have seen and heard; how that
the blind see, the lame walk, the lepers are cleansed, the deaf
hear, the dead are raised, to the poor the gospel is preached.
23And blessed is he, whosoever shall not be offended in me.'

24And when the messengers of John were departed, he
began to speak unto the people concerning John, 'What went
ye out into the wilderness for to see? A reed shaken with the
wind? 25But what went ye out for to see? A man clothed in
soft raiment? Behold, they which are gorgeously apparelled,
and live delicately, are in kings' courts. 26But what went ye out
for to see? A prophet? Yea, I say unto you, and much more
than a prophet. 27This is he, of whom it is written, "Behold, I
send my messenger before thy face, which shall prepare thy
way before thee." 28For I say unto you, Among those that are
born of women there is not a greater prophet than John the
Baptist: but he that is least in the kingdom of God is greater
than he.' 29And all the people that heard him, and the publicans, justified God, being baptized with the baptism of John.

30 But the Pharisees and lawyers rejected the counsel of God
against themselves, being not baptized of him.
31 And the Lord said, 'Whereunto then shall I liken the
men of this generation? And to what are they like? 32 They
are like unto children sitting in the marketplace, and calling
one to another, and saying, "We have piped unto you, and
ye have not danced; we have mourned to you, and ye have
not wept." 33 For John the Baptist came neither eating bread
nor drinking wine; and ye say, "He hath a devil." 34 The Son
of man is come eating and drinking; and ye say, "Behold a
gluttonous man, and a winebibber, a friend of publicans and
sinners!" 35 But wisdom is justified of all her children.'
36 And one of the Pharisees desired him that he would eat
with him. And he went into the Pharisee's house, and sat
down to meat. 37 And, behold, a woman in the city, which
was a sinner, when she knew that Jesus sat at meat in the
Pharisee's house, brought an alabaster box of ointment, 38 and
stood at his feet behind him weeping, and began to wash his
feet with tears, and did wipe them with the hairs of her
head, and kissed his feet, and anointed them with the ointment. 39 Now when the Pharisee which had bidden him saw
it, he spake within himself, saying, 'This man, if he were a
prophet, would have known who and what manner of
woman this is that toucheth him: for she is a sinner.' 40 And
Jesus answering said unto him, 'Simon, I have somewhat to
say unto thee.' And he saith, 'Master, say on.' 41 'There was a
certain creditor which had two debtors: the one owed five
hundred pence, and the other fifty. 42 And when they had
nothing to pay, he frankly forgave them both. Tell me therefore, which of them will love him most?' 43 Simon answered

and said, 'I suppose that he, to whom he forgave most.' And
he said unto him, 'Thou hast rightly judged.' 44 And he turned
to the woman, and said unto Simon, 'Seest thou this woman?
I entered into thine house, thou gavest me no water for my
feet: but she hath washed my feet with tears, and wiped
them with the hairs of her head. 45 Thou gavest me no kiss:
but this woman since the time I came in hath not ceased to
kiss my feet. 46 My head with oil thou didst not anoint: but
this woman hath anointed my feet with ointment. 47 Wherefore I say unto thee, her sins, which are many, are forgiven;
for she loved much; but to whom little is forgiven, the same
loveth little.' 48 And he said unto her, 'Thy sins are forgiven.'
49 And they that sat at meat with him began to say within
themselves, 'Who is this that forgiveth sins also?' 50 And he
said to the woman, 'Thy faith hath saved thee; go in peace.'

8 And it came to pass afterward, that he went throughout
every city and village, preaching and shewing the glad
tidings of the kingdom of God; and the twelve were with
him, 2 and certain women, which had been healed of evil
spirits and infirmities: Mary called Magdalene, out of whom
went seven devils, 3 and Joanna the wife of Chuza Herod's
steward, and Susanna, and many others, which ministered
unto him of their substance.

4 And when much people were gathered together, and
were come to him out of every city, he spake by a parable:
5 'A sower went out to sow his seed; and as he sowed, some
fell by the way side; and it was trodden down, and the fowls
of the air devoured it. 6 And some fell upon a rock; and as
soon as it was sprung up, it withered away, because it lacked

moisture. 7 And some fell among thorns; and the thorns
sprang up with it, and choked it. 8 And other fell on good
ground, and sprang up, and bare fruit an hundred-fold.'
And when he had said these things, he cried, 'He that hath
ears to hear, let him hear.'

9 And his disciples asked him, saying, 'What might this
parable be?' 10 And he said, 'Unto you it is given to know the
mysteries of the kingdom of God; but to others in parables,
that seeing they might not see, and hearing they might not
understand. 11 Now the parable is this: The seed is the word
of God. 12 Those by the way side are they that hear; then
cometh the devil, and taketh away the word out of their
hearts, lest they should believe and be saved. 13 They on the
rock are they, which, when they hear, receive the word with
joy; and these have no root, which for a while believe, and in
time of temptation fall away. 14 And that which fell among
thorns are they, which, when they have heard, go forth, and
are choked with cares and riches and pleasures of this life,
and bring no fruit to perfection. 15 But that on the good
ground are they, which in an honest and good heart, having
heard the word, keep it, and bring forth fruit with patience.

16 'No man, when he hath lighted a candle, covereth it with
a vessel, or putteth it under a bed; but setteth it on a candlestick, that they which enter in may see the light. 17 For nothing is secret, that shall not be made manifest; neither any
thing hid, that shall not be known and come abroad. 18 Take
heed therefore how ye hear; for whosoever hath, to him
shall be given; and whosoever hath not, from him shall be
taken even that which he seemeth to have.'

19 Then came to him his mother and his brethren, and

could not come at him for the press. [20]And it was told him by
certain which said, 'Thy mother and thy brethren stand without, desiring to see thee.' [21]And he answered and said unto
them, 'My mother and my brethren are these which hear the
word of God, and do it.'

[22]Now it came to pass on a certain day, that he went into
a ship with his disciples; and he said unto them, 'Let us go
over unto the other side of the lake.' And they launched
forth. [23]But as they sailed he fell asleep; and there came down
a storm of wind on the lake; and they were filled with water,
and were in jeopardy. [24]And they came to him, and awoke
him, saying, 'Master, master, we perish.' Then he arose, and
rebuked the wind and the raging of the water; and they
ceased, and there was a calm. [25]And he said unto them,
'Where is your faith?' And they being afraid wondered, saying one to another, 'What manner of man is this! For he
commandeth even the winds and water, and they obey him.'

[26]And they arrived at the country of the Gadarenes, which
is over against Galilee. [27]And when he went forth to land,
there met him out of the city a certain man, which had devils
long time, and ware no clothes, neither abode in any house,
but in the tombs. [28]When he saw Jesus, he cried out, and fell
down before him, and with a loud voice said, 'What have I
to do with thee, Jesus, thou Son of God most high? I beseech
thee, torment me not.' [29](For he had commanded the unclean
spirit to come out of the man. For often-times it had caught
him; and he was kept bound with chains and in fetters; and
he brake the bands, and was driven of the devil into the
wilderness.) [30]And Jesus asked him, saying, 'What is thy
name?' And he said, 'Legion', because many devils were

entered into him. [31]And they besought him that he would
not command them to go out into the deep.
[32]And there was there an herd of many swine feeding on
the mountain; and they besought him that he would suffer
them to enter into them. And he suffered them. [33]Then went
the devils out of the man, and entered into the swine; and
the herd ran violently down a steep place into the lake, and
were choked. [34]When they that fed them saw what was
done, they fled, and went and told it in the city and in the
country. [35]Then they went out to see what was done; and
came to Jesus, and found the man, out of whom the devils
were departed, sitting at the feet of Jesus, clothed, and in his
right mind; and they were afraid. [36]They also which saw it
told them by what means he that was possessed of the devils
was healed.

[37]Then the whole multitude of the country of the Gadarenes round about besought him to depart from them; for
they were taken with great fear: and he went up into the
ship, and returned back again. [38]Now the man out of whom
the devils were departed besought him that he might be
with him; but Jesus sent him away, saying, [39]'Return to thine
own house, and shew how great things God hath done unto
thee.' And he went his way, and published throughout the
whole city how great things Jesus had done unto him. [40]And
it came to pass, that, when Jesus was returned, the people
gladly received him; for they were all waiting for him.

[41]And, behold, there came a man named Jairus, and he
was a ruler of the synagogue; and he fell down at Jesus' feet,
and besought him that he would come into his house. [42]For
he had one only daughter, about twelve years of age, and

she lay a dying. But as he went the people thronged him.
[43]And a woman having an issue of blood twelve years,
which had spent all her living upon physicians, neither could
be healed of any, [44]came behind him, and touched the border
of his garment: and immediately her issue of blood stanched.
[45]And Jesus said, 'Who touched me?' When all denied, Peter
and they that were with him said, 'Master, the multitude
throng thee and press thee, and sayest thou, "Who touched
me?"' [46]And Jesus said, 'Somebody hath touched me; for I perceive that virtue is gone out of me.' [47]And when the woman
saw that she was not hid, she came trembling, and falling
down before him, she declared unto him before all the people for what cause she had touched him, and how she was
healed immediately. [48]And he said unto her, 'Daughter, be of
good comfort: thy faith hath made thee whole; go in peace.'
[49]While he yet spake, there cometh one from the ruler of
the synagogue's house, saying to him, 'Thy daughter is dead;
trouble not the Master.' [50]But when Jesus heard it, he
answered him, saying, 'Fear not: believe only, and she shall
be made whole.' [51]And when he came into the house, he suffered no man to go in, save Peter, and James, and John, and
the father and the mother of the maiden. [52]And all wept, and
bewailed her; but he said, 'Weep not; she is not dead, but
sleepeth.' [53]And they laughed him to scorn, knowing that
she was dead. [54]And he put them all out, and took her by the
hand, and called, saying, 'Maid, arise.' [55]And her spirit came
again, and she arose straightway: and he commanded to
give her meat. [56]And her parents were astonished: but he
charged them that they should tell no man what was done.

9 Then he called his twelve disciples together, and gave
them power and authority over all devils, and to cure
diseases. [2]And he sent them to preach the kingdom of God,
and to heal the sick. [3]And he said unto them, 'Take nothing
for your journey, neither staves, nor scrip, neither bread, neither money; neither have two coats apiece. [4]And whatsoever
house ye enter into, there abide, and thence depart. [5]And
whosoever will not receive you, when ye go out of that city,
shake off the very dust from your feet for a testimony against
them.' [6]And they departed, and went through the towns,
preaching the gospel, and healing every where.

[7]Now Herod the tetrarch heard of all that was done by
him: and he was perplexed, because that it was said of some,
that John was risen from the dead; [8]and of some, that Elias
had appeared; and of others, that one of the old prophets
was risen again. [9]And Herod said, 'John have I beheaded:
but who is this, of whom I hear such things?' And he desired
to see him.

[10]And the apostles, when they were returned, told him all
that they had done. And he took them, and went aside privately into a desert place belonging to the city called Bethsaida. [11]And the people, when they knew it, followed him:
and he received them, and spake unto them of the kingdom
of God, and healed them that had need of healing. [12]And
when the day began to wear away, then came the twelve,
and said unto him, 'Send the multitude away, that they may
go into the towns and country round about, and lodge, and
get victuals: for we are here in a desert place.' [13]But he said
unto them, 'Give ye them to eat.' And they said, 'We have no
more but five loaves and two fishes; except we should go

and buy meat for all this people.' [14] For they were about five
thousand men. And he said to his disciples, 'Make them sit
down by fifties in a company.' [15] And they did so, and made
them all sit down. [16] Then he took the five loaves and the two
fishes, and looking up to heaven, he blessed them, and
brake, and gave to the disciples to set before the multitude.
[17] And they did eat, and were all filled: and there was taken
up of fragments that remained to them twelve baskets.

[18] And it came to pass, as he was alone praying, his disciples were with him: and he asked them, saying, 'Whom say
the people that I am?' [19] They answering said, 'John the Baptist; but some say, Elias; and others say, that one of the old
prophets is risen again.' [20] He said unto them, 'But whom say
ye that I am?' Peter answering said, 'The Christ of God.'
[21] And he straitly charged them, and commanded them to tell
no man that thing, [22] saying, 'The Son of man must suffer
many things, and be rejected of the elders and chief priests
and scribes, and be slain, and be raised the third day.'

[23] And he said to them all, 'If any man will come after me,
let him deny himself, and take up his cross daily, and follow
me. [24] For whosoever will save his life shall lose it; but
whosoever will lose his life for my sake, the same shall save
it. [25] For what is a man advantaged, if he gain the whole
world, and lose himself, or be cast away? [26] For whosoever
shall be ashamed of me and of my words, of him shall the
Son of man be ashamed, when he shall come in his own
glory, and in his Father's, and of the holy angels. [27] But I tell
you of a truth, there be some standing here, which shall not
taste of death, till they see the kingdom of God.'

[28] And it came to pass about an eight days after these

sayings, he took Peter and John and James, and went up into
a mountain to pray. [29]And as he prayed, the fashion of his
countenance was altered, and his raiment was white and
glistering. [30]And, behold, there talked with him two men,
which were Moses and Elias, [31]who appeared in glory, and
spake of his decease which he should accomplish at Jerusalem. [32]But Peter and they that were with him were heavy
with sleep; and when they were awake, they saw his glory,
and the two men that stood with him. [33]And it came to pass,
as they departed from him, Peter said unto Jesus, 'Master, it
is good for us to be here: and let us make three tabernacles:
one for thee, and one for Moses, and one for Elias,' not knowing what he said. [34]While he thus spake, there came a cloud,
and overshadowed them; and they feared as they entered
into the cloud. [35]And there came a voice out of the cloud,
saying, 'This is my beloved Son: hear him.' [36]And when the
voice was past, Jesus was found alone. And they kept it
close, and told no man in those days any of those things
which they had seen.

[37]And it came to pass that on the next day, when they
were come down from the hill, much people met him. [38]And,
behold, a man of the company cried out, saying, 'Master, I
beseech thee, look upon my son; for he is mine only child.
[39]And, lo, a spirit taketh him, and he suddenly crieth out; and
it teareth him that he foameth again, and bruising him hardly
departeth from him. [40]And I besought thy disciples to cast
him out; and they could not.' [41]And Jesus answering said, 'O
faithless and perverse generation, how long shall I be with
you, and suffer you? Bring thy son hither.' [42]And as he was
yet a coming, the devil threw him down, and tare him. And

Jesus rebuked the unclean spirit, and healed the child, and
delivered him again to his father.

43 And they were all amazed at the mighty power of God.
But while they wondered every one at all things which Jesus
did, he said unto his disciples, 44 'Let these sayings sink down
into your ears: for the Son of man shall be delivered into the
hands of men.' 45 But they understood not this saying, and it
was hid from them, that they perceived it not: and they
feared to ask him of that saying.

46 Then there arose a reasoning among them, which of
them should be greatest. 47 And Jesus, perceiving the thought
of their heart, took a child, and set him by him, 48 and said
unto them, 'Whosoever shall receive this child in my name
receiveth me: and whosoever shall receive me receiveth him
that sent me; for he that is least among you all, the same
shall be great.'

49 And John answered and said, 'Master, we saw one casting out devils in thy name; and we forbad him, because he
followeth not with us.' 50 And Jesus said unto him, 'Forbid
him not: for he that is not against us is for us.'

51 And it came to pass, when the time was come that he
should be received up, he stedfastly set his face to go to Jerusalem, 52 and sent messengers before his face: and they went,
and entered into a village of the Samaritans, to make ready
for him. 53 And they did not receive him, because his face was
as though he would go to Jerusalem. 54 And when his disciples James and John saw this, they said, 'Lord, wilt thou that
we command fire to come down from heaven, and consume
them, even as Elias did?' 55 But he turned, and rebuked them,
and said, 'Ye know not what manner of spirit ye are of. 56 For

the Son of man is not come to destroy men's lives, but to
save them.' And they went to another village.
57 And it came to pass, that, as they went in the way, a certain man said unto him, 'Lord, I will follow thee whithersoever thou goest.' 58 And Jesus said unto him, 'Foxes have holes,
and birds of the air have nests; but the Son of man hath not
where to lay his head.' 59 And he said unto another, 'Follow
me.' But he said, 'Lord, suffer me first to go and bury my
father.' 60 Jesus said unto him, 'Let the dead bury their dead;
but go thou and preach the kingdom of God.' 61 And another
also said, 'Lord, I will follow thee; but let me first go bid
them farewell, which are at home at my house.' 62 And Jesus
said unto him, 'No man, having put his hand to the plough,
and looking back, is fit for the kingdom of God.'

10 After these things the Lord appointed other seventy
also, and sent them two and two before his face into
every city and place, whither he himself would come.
2 Therefore said he unto them, 'The harvest truly is great, but
the labourers are few; pray ye therefore the Lord of the harvest, that he would send forth labourers into his harvest.
3 Go your ways: behold, I send you forth as lambs among
wolves. 4 Carry neither purse, nor scrip, nor shoes: and salute
no man by the way. 5 And into whatsoever house ye enter,
first say, "Peace be to this house." 6 And if the son of peace be
there, your peace shall rest upon it: if not, it shall turn to you
again. 7 And in the same house remain, eating and drinking
such things as they give: for the labourer is worthy of his
hire. Go not from house to house. 8 And into whatsoever city
ye enter, and they receive you, eat such things as are set

before you. 9And heal the sick that are therein, and say unto
them, "The kingdom of God is come nigh unto you." 10But
into whatsoever city ye enter, and they receive you not, go
your ways out into the streets of the same, and say, 11"Even
the very dust of your city, which cleaveth on us, we do wipe
off against you; notwithstanding be ye sure of this, that the
kingdom of God is come nigh unto you." 12But I say unto
you, that it shall be more tolerable in that day for Sodom,
than for that city. 13Woe unto thee, Chorazin! Woe unto thee,
Bethsaida! For if the mighty works had been done in Tyre
and Sidon, which have been done in you, they had a great
while ago repented, sitting in sackcloth and ashes. 14But it
shall be more tolerable for Tyre and Sidon at the judgment,
than for you. 15And thou, Capernaum, which art exalted to
heaven, shalt be thrust down to hell. 16He that heareth you
heareth me; and he that despiseth you despiseth me; and he
that despiseth me despiseth him that sent me.'

17And the seventy returned again with joy, saying, 'Lord,
even the devils are subject unto us through thy name.' 18And
he said unto them, 'I beheld Satan as lightning fall from
heaven. 19Behold, I give unto you power to tread on serpents
and scorpions, and over all the power of the enemy; and
nothing shall by any means hurt you. 20Notwithstanding in
this rejoice not, that the spirits are subject unto you; but
rather rejoice, because your names are written in heaven.'

21In that hour Jesus rejoiced in spirit, and said, 'I thank
thee, O Father, Lord of heaven and earth, that thou hast hid
these things from the wise and prudent, and hast revealed
them unto babes: even so, Father; for so it seemed good in
thy sight. 22All things are delivered to me of my Father; and

no man knoweth who the Son is, but the Father; and who
the Father is, but the Son, and he to whom the Son will
reveal him.'

23 And he turned him unto his disciples, and said privately,
'Blessed are the eyes which see the things that ye see. 24 For I
tell you that many prophets and kings have desired to see
those things which ye see, and have not seen them; and to
hear those things which ye hear, and have not heard them.'

25 And, behold, a certain lawyer stood up, and tempted
him, saying, 'Master, what shall I do to inherit eternal life?'
26 He said unto him, 'What is written in the law? How read-
est thou?' 27 And he answering said, 'Thou shalt love the Lord
thy God with all thy heart, and with all thy soul, and with all
thy strength, and with all thy mind; and thy neighbour as
thyself.' 28 And he said unto him, 'Thou hast answered right:
this do, and thou shalt live.' 29 But he, willing to justify himself, said unto Jesus, 'And who is my neighbour?' 30 And Jesus
answering said, 'A certain man went down from Jerusalem
to Jericho, and fell among thieves, which stripped him of his
raiment, and wounded him, and departed, leaving him half
dead. 31 And by chance there came down a certain priest that
way: and when he saw him, he passed by on the other side.
32 And likewise a Levite, when he was at the place, came and
looked on him, and passed by on the other side. 33 But a certain Samaritan, as he journeyed, came where he was; and
when he saw him, he had compassion on him, 34 and went to
him, and bound up his wounds, pouring in oil and wine, and
set him on his own beast, and brought him to an inn, and
took care of him. 35 And on the morrow when he departed, he
took out two pence, and gave them to the host, and said

unto him, "Take care of him; and whatsoever thou spendest
more, when I come again, I will repay thee." 36 Which now of
these three, thinkest thou, was neighbour unto him that fell
among the thieves?' 37 And he said, 'He that shewed mercy on
him.' Then said Jesus unto him, 'Go, and do thou likewise.'

38 Now it came to pass, as they went, that he entered into
a certain village: and a certain woman named Martha received him into her house. 39 And she had a sister called Mary,
which also sat at Jesus' feet, and heard his word. 40 But Martha
was cumbered about much serving, and came to him, and
said, 'Lord, dost thou not care that my sister hath left me to
serve alone? Bid her therefore that she help me.' 41 And Jesus
answered and said unto her, 'Martha, Martha, thou art care-
ful and troubled about many things, 42 but one thing is need-
ful; and Mary hath chosen that good part, which shall not be
taken away from her.'

11 And it came to pass, that, as he was praying in a certain
place, when he ceased, one of his disciples said unto
him, 'Lord, teach us to pray, as John also taught his disciples.' 2 And he said unto them, 'When ye pray, say,

Our Father which art in heaven,
Hallowed be thy name.
Thy kingdom come.
Thy will be done, as in heaven, so in earth.
3 Give us day by day our daily bread.
4 And forgive us our sins;
for we also forgive every one
that is indebted to us.

And lead us not into temptation;
but deliver us from evil.'

[5]And he said unto them, 'Which of you shall have a friend,
and shall go unto him at midnight, and say unto him, "Friend,
lend me three loaves; [6]for a friend of mine in his journey is
come to me, and I have nothing to set before him?" [7]And he
from within shall answer and say, "Trouble me not: the door
is now shut, and my children are with me in bed; I cannot
rise and give thee." [8]I say unto you, though he will not rise
and give him, because he is his friend, yet because of his im-
portunity he will rise and give him as many as he needeth.

[9]'And I say unto you, ask, and it shall be given you; seek,
and ye shall find; knock, and it shall be opened unto you.
[10]For every one that asketh receiveth; and he that seeketh
findeth; and to him that knocketh it shall be opened. [11]If a
son shall ask bread of any of you that is a father, will he give
him a stone? Or if he ask a fish, will he for a fish give him a
serpent? [12]Or if he shall ask an egg, will he offer him a scorpion? [13]If ye then, being evil, know how to give good gifts
unto your children, how much more shall your heavenly
Father give the Holy Spirit to them that ask him?'

[14]And he was casting out a devil, and it was dumb. And it
came to pass, when the devil was gone out, the dumb spake;
and the people wondered. [15]But some of them said, 'He casteth out devils through Beelzebub the chief of the devils.'
[16]And others, tempting him, sought of him a sign from heaven.
[17]But he, knowing their thoughts, said unto them, 'Every
kingdom divided against itself is brought to desolation; and
a house divided against a house falleth. [18]If Satan also be

divided against himself, how shall his kingdom stand?
Because ye say that I cast out devils through Beelzebub. 19And
if I by Beelzebub cast out devils, by whom do your sons cast
them out? Therefore shall they be your judges. 20 But if I with
the finger of God cast out devils, no doubt the kingdom of
God is come upon you. 21 When a strong man armed keepeth
his palace, his goods are in peace. 22 But when a stronger
man than he shall come upon him, and overcome him, he
taketh from him all his armour wherein he trusted, and
divideth his spoils. 23 He that is not with me is against me;
and he that gathereth not with me scattereth. 24 When the
unclean spirit is gone out of a man, he walketh through dry
places, seeking rest; and finding none, he saith, "I will return
unto my house whence I came out." 25And when he cometh,
he findeth it swept and garnished. 26 Then goeth he, and
taketh to him seven other spirits more wicked than himself;
and they enter in, and dwell there; and the last state of that
man is worse than the first.'

27And it came to pass, as he spake these things, a certain
woman of the company lifted up her voice, and said unto
him, 'Blessed is the womb that bare thee, and the paps which
thou hast sucked.' 28 But he said, 'Yea rather, blessed are they
that hear the word of God, and keep it.'

29And when the people were gathered thick together, he
began to say, 'This is an evil generation: they seek a sign;
and there shall no sign be given it, but the sign of Jonas the
prophet. 30 For as Jonas was a sign unto the Ninevites, so
shall also the Son of man be to this generation. 31 The queen
of the south shall rise up in the judgment with the men of
this generation, and condemn them; for she came from the

utmost parts of the earth to hear the wisdom of Solomon;
and, behold, a greater than Solomon is here. 32 The men of
Nineve shall rise up in the judgment with this generation,
and shall condemn it; for they repented at the preaching of
Jonas; and, behold, a greater than Jonas is here. 33 No man,
when he hath lighted a candle, putteth it in a secret place,
neither under a bushel, but on a candlestick, that they which
come in may see the light. 34 The light of the body is the eye:
therefore when thine eye is single, thy whole body also is
full of light; but when thine eye is evil, thy body also is full
of darkness. 35 Take heed therefore that the light which is in
thee be not darkness. 36 If thy whole body therefore be full of
light, having no part dark, the whole shall be full of light, as
when the bright shining of a candle doth give thee light.'

37 And as he spake, a certain Pharisee besought him to
dine with him; and he went in, and sat down to meat. 38 And
when the Pharisee saw it, he marvelled that he had not first
washed before dinner. 39 And the Lord said unto him, 'Now
do ye Pharisees make clean the outside of the cup and the
platter; but your inward part is full of ravening and wickedness. 40 Ye fools, did not he that made that which is without
make that which is within also? 41 But rather give alms of
such things as ye have; and, behold, all things are clean unto
you. 42 But woe unto you, Pharisees! For ye tithe mint and
rue and all manner of herbs, and pass over judgment and
the love of God; these ought ye to have done, and not to
leave the other undone. 43 Woe unto you, Pharisees! For ye
love the uppermost seats in the synagogues, and greetings
in the markets. 44 Woe unto you, scribes and Pharisees, hypocrites! For ye are as graves which appear not, and the men

that walk over them are not aware of them.'

45 Then answered one of the lawyers, and said unto him, 'Master, thus saying thou reproachest us also.' 46 And he said, 'Woe unto you also, ye lawyers! For ye lade men with burdens grievous to be borne, and ye yourselves touch not the burdens with one of your fingers. 47 Woe unto you! For ye build the sepulchres of the prophets, and your fathers killed them. 48 Truly ye bear witness that ye allow the deeds of your fathers; for they indeed killed them, and ye build their sepulchres. 49 Therefore also said the wisdom of God, "I will send them prophets and apostles, and some of them they shall slay and persecute," 50 that the blood of all the prophets, which was shed from the foundation of the world, may be required of this generation; 51 from the blood of Abel unto the blood of Zacharias, which perished between the altar and the temple: verily I say unto you, it shall be required of this generation. 52 Woe unto you, lawyers! For ye have taken away the key of knowledge; ye entered not in yourselves, and them that were entering in ye hindered.'

53 And as he said these things unto them, the scribes and the Pharisees began to urge him vehemently, and to provoke him to speak of many things: 54 laying wait for him, and seeking to catch something out of his mouth, that they might accuse him.

12 In the mean time, when there were gathered together an innumerable multitude of people, insomuch that they trode one upon another, he began to say unto his disciples first of all, 'Beware ye of the leaven of the Pharisees, which is hypocrisy. 2 For there is nothing covered, that shall not be revealed; neither hid, that shall not be known. 3 Therefore

whatsoever ye have spoken in darkness shall be heard in the
light; and that which ye have spoken in the ear in closets
shall be proclaimed upon the housetops. [4]And I say unto
you my friends, be not afraid of them that kill the body, and
after that have no more that they can do. [5]But I will fore-
warn you whom ye shall fear: fear him, which after he hath
killed hath power to cast into hell; yea, I say unto you, Fear
him. [6]Are not five sparrows sold for two farthings, and not
one of them is forgotten before God? [7]But even the very
hairs of your head are all numbered. Fear not therefore: ye
are of more value than many sparrows. [8]Also I say unto you,
whosoever shall confess me before men, him shall the Son of
man also confess before the angels of God; [9]but he that deni-
eth me before men shall be denied before the angels of God.
[10]And whosoever shall speak a word against the Son of man,
it shall be forgiven him; but unto him that blasphemeth
against the Holy Ghost it shall not be forgiven. [11]And when
they bring you unto the synagogues, and unto magistrates,
and powers, take ye no thought how or what thing ye shall
answer, or what ye shall say. [12]For the Holy Ghost shall teach
you in the same hour what ye ought to say.'

[13]And one of the company said unto him, 'Master, speak
to my brother, that he divide the inheritance with me.' [14]And
he said unto him, 'Man, who made me a judge or a divider
over you?' [15]And he said unto them, 'Take heed, and beware of
covetousness; for a man's life consisteth not in the abundance
of the things which he possesseth.' [16]And he spake a parable
unto them, saying, 'The ground of a certain rich man brought
forth plentifully, [17]and he thought within himself, saying,
"What shall I do, because I have no room where to bestow

my fruits?" [18]And he said, "This will I do: I will pull down
my barns, and build greater; and there will I bestow all my
fruits and my goods. [19]And I will say to my soul, Soul, thou
hast much goods laid up for many years; take thine ease, eat,
drink, and be merry." [20]But God said unto him, "Thou fool,
this night thy soul shall be required of thee; then whose shall
those things be, which thou hast provided?" [21]So is he that
layeth up treasure for himself, and is not rich toward God.'

[22]And he said unto his disciples, 'Therefore I say unto you,
take no thought for your life, what ye shall eat; neither for
the body, what ye shall put on. [23]The life is more than meat,
and the body is more than raiment. [24]Consider the ravens,
for they neither sow nor reap; which neither have store-
house nor barn; and God feedeth them: how much more are
ye better than the fowls? [25]And which of you with taking
thought can add to his stature one cubit? [26]If ye then be not
able to do that thing which is least, why take ye thought for
the rest? [27]Consider the lilies how they grow: they toil not,
they spin not; and yet I say unto you, that Solomon in all his
glory was not arrayed like one of these. [28]If then God so
clothe the grass, which is today in the field, and tomorrow is
cast into the oven, how much more will he clothe you, O ye of
little faith? [29]And seek not ye what ye shall eat, or what ye
shall drink, neither be ye of doubtful mind. [30]For all these
things do the nations of the world seek after: and your
Father knoweth that ye have need of these things.

[31]'But rather seek ye the kingdom of God; and all these
things shall be added unto you. [32]Fear not, little flock; for it
is your Father's good pleasure to give you the kingdom.
[33]Sell that ye have, and give alms; provide yourselves bags

which wax not old, a treasure in the heavens that faileth not,
where no thief approacheth, neither moth corrupteth. [34] For
where your treasure is, there will your heart be also. [35] Let
your loins be girded about, and your lights burning; [36] and
ye yourselves like unto men that wait for their lord, when he
will return from the wedding; that when he cometh and
knocketh, they may open unto him immediately. [37] Blessed
are those servants whom the lord when he cometh shall find
watching: verily I say unto you that he shall gird himself, and
make them to sit down to meat, and will come forth and
serve them. [38] And if he shall come in the second watch, or
come in the third watch, and find them so, blessed are those
servants. [39] And this know, that if the goodman of the house
had known what hour the thief would come, he would have
watched, and not have suffered his house to be broken
through. [40] Be ye therefore ready also: for the Son of man
cometh at an hour when ye think not.'

[41] Then Peter said unto him, 'Lord, speakest thou this parable unto us, or even to all?' [42] And the Lord said, 'Who then is
that faithful and wise steward, whom his lord shall make ruler
over his household, to give them their portion of meat in due
season? [43] Blessed is that servant, whom his lord when he cometh shall find so doing. [44] Of a truth I say unto you that he will
make him ruler over all that he hath. [45] But and if that servant say in his heart, "My lord delayeth his coming," and shall
begin to beat the menservants and maidens, and to eat and
drink, and to be drunken, [46] the lord of that servant will come
in a day when he looketh not for him, and at an hour when he
is not aware, and will cut him in sunder, and will appoint him
his portion with the unbelievers. [47] And that servant, which

knew his lord's will, and prepared not himself, neither did
according to his will, shall be beaten with many stripes. 48 But
he that knew not, and did commit things worthy of stripes,
shall be beaten with few stripes. For unto whomsoever
much is given, of him shall be much required: and to whom
men have committed much, of him they will ask the more.

49 'I am come to send fire on the earth; and what will I, if
it be already kindled? 50 But I have a baptism to be baptized
with; and how am I straitened till it be accomplished! 51 Suppose ye that I am come to give peace on earth? I tell you,
nay; but rather division. 52 For from henceforth there shall be
five in one house divided, three against two, and two against
three. 53 The father shall be divided against the son, and the
son against the father; the mother against the daughter, and
the daughter against the mother; the mother in law against
her daughter in law, and the daughter in law against her
mother in law.'

54 And he said also to the people, 'When ye see a cloud rise
out of the west, straightway ye say, "There cometh a shower,"
and so it is. 55 And when ye see the south wind blow, ye say,
"There will be heat," and it cometh to pass. 56 Ye hypocrites,
ye can discern the face of the sky and of the earth; but how is
it that ye do not discern this time? 57 Yea, and why even of
yourselves judge ye not what is right?

58 'When thou goest with thine adversary to the magis-
trate, as thou art in the way, give diligence that thou mayest
be delivered from him; lest he hale thee to the judge, and the
judge deliver thee to the officer, and the officer cast thee into
prison. 59 I tell thee, thou shalt not depart thence, till thou
hast paid the very last mite.'

13 There were present at that season some that told him of the Galilæans, whose blood Pilate had mingled with their sacrifices. 2 And Jesus answering said unto them, 'Suppose ye that these Galilæans were sinners above all the Galilæans, because they suffered such things? 3 I tell you, nay: but, except ye repent, ye shall all likewise perish. 4 Or those eighteen, upon whom the tower in Siloam fell, and slew them, think ye that they were sinners above all men that dwelt in Jerusalem? 5 I tell you, nay: but, except ye repent, ye shall all likewise perish.'

6 He spake also this parable: 'A certain man had a fig tree planted in his vineyard; and he came and sought fruit thereon, and found none. 7 Then said he unto the dresser of his vineyard, "Behold, these three years I come seeking fruit on this fig tree, and find none; cut it down; why cumbereth it the ground?" 8 And he answering said unto him, "Lord, let it alone this year also, till I shall dig about it, and dung it; 9 and if it bear fruit, well; and if not, then after that thou shalt cut it down."'

10 And he was teaching in one of the synagogues on the sabbath. 11 And, behold, there was a woman which had a spirit of infirmity eighteen years, and was bowed together, and could in no wise lift up herself. 12 And when Jesus saw her, he called her to him, and said unto her, 'Woman, thou art loosed from thine infirmity.' 13 And he laid his hands on her: and immediately she was made straight, and glorified God. 14 And the ruler of the synagogue answered with indignation, because that Jesus had healed on the sabbath day, and said unto the people, 'There are six days in which men ought to work; in them therefore come and be healed, and

not on the sabbath day.' [15] The Lord then answered him, and
said, 'Thou hypocrite, doth not each one of you on the sabbath loose his ox or his ass from the stall, and lead him away
to watering? [16] And ought not this woman, being a daughter
of Abraham, whom Satan hath bound, lo, these eighteen
years, be loosed from this bond on the sabbath day?' [17] And
when he had said these things, all his adversaries were ashamed: and all the people rejoiced for all the glorious things
that were done by him.

[18] Then said he, 'Unto what is the kingdom of God like?
And whereunto shall I resemble it? [19] It is like a grain of mustard seed, which a man took, and cast into his garden; and it
grew, and waxed a great tree; and the fowls of the air lodged
in the branches of it.' [20] And again he said, 'Whereunto shall
I liken the kingdom of God?' [21] It is like leaven, which a
woman took and hid in three measures of meal, till the
whole was leavened.'

[22] And he went through the cities and villages, teaching,
and journeying toward Jerusalem. [23] Then said one unto him,
'Lord, are there few that be saved?' And he said unto them,
[24] 'Strive to enter in at the strait gate; for many, I say unto
you, will seek to enter in, and shall not be able. [25] When once
the master of the house is risen up, and hath shut to the
door, and ye begin to stand without, and to knock at the
door, saying, "Lord, Lord, open unto us"; and he shall answer
and say unto you, "I know you not whence ye are," [26] then
shall ye begin to say, "We have eaten and drunk in thy presence, and thou hast taught in our streets." [27] But he shall say,
"I tell you, I know you not whence ye are; depart from me,
all ye workers of iniquity." [28] There shall be weeping and

gnashing of teeth, when ye shall see Abraham, and Isaac,
and Jacob, and all the prophets, in the kingdom of God, and
you yourselves thrust out. 29 And they shall come from the
east, and from the west, and from the north, and from the
south, and shall sit down in the kingdom of God. 30 And,
behold, there are last which shall be first, and there are first
which shall be last.'

31 The same day there came certain of the Pharisees, saying unto him, 'Get thee out, and depart hence; for Herod will
kill thee.' 32 And he said unto them, 'Go ye, and tell that fox,
"Behold, I cast out devils, and I do cures today and tomorrow, and the third day I shall be perfected. 33 Nevertheless I
must walk today, and tomorrow, and the day following; for
it cannot be that a prophet perish out of Jerusalem." 34 O
Jerusalem, Jerusalem, which killest the prophets, and stonest
them that are sent unto thee; how often would I have gathered thy children together, as a hen doth gather her brood
under her wings, and ye would not! 35 Behold, your house is
left unto you desolate: and verily I say unto you, ye shall not
see me, until the time come when ye shall say, "Blessed is he
that cometh in the name of the Lord."'

14 And it came to pass, as he went into the house of one
of the chief Pharisees to eat bread on the sabbath day,
that they watched him. 2 And, behold, there was a certain
man before him which had the dropsy. 3 And Jesus answering spake unto the lawyers and Pharisees, saying, 'Is it lawful to heal on the sabbath day?' 4 And they held their peace.
And he took him, and healed him, and let him go; 5 and
answered them, saying, 'Which of you shall have an ass or

an ox fallen into a pit, and will not straightway pull him out
on the sabbath day?' 6And they could not answer him again
to these things.
7And he put forth a parable to those which were bidden,
when he marked how they chose out the chief rooms; saying
unto them, 8'When thou art bidden of any man to a wedding,
sit not down in the highest room, lest a more honourable
man than thou be bidden of him; 9and he that bade thee and
him come and say to thee, "Give this man place"; and thou
begin with shame to take the lowest room. 10But when thou
art bidden, go and sit down in the lowest room; that when
he that bade thee cometh, he may say unto thee, "Friend, go
up higher," then shalt thou have worship in the presence of
them that sit at meat with thee. 11For whosoever exalteth
himself shall be abased; and he that humbleth himself shall
be exalted.'
12Then said he also to him that bade him, 'When thou
makest a dinner or a supper, call not thy friends, nor thy
brethren, neither thy kinsmen, nor thy rich neighbours, lest
they also bid thee again, and a recompence be made thee.
13But when thou makest a feast, call the poor, the maimed,
the lame, the blind; 14and thou shalt be blessed; for they cannot recompense thee; for thou shalt be recompensed at the
resurrection of the just.'
15And when one of them that sat at meat with him heard
these things, he said untc him, 'Blessed is he that shall eat
bread in the kingdom of God.' 16Then said he unto him, 'A
certain man made a great supper, and bade many, 17and sent
his servant at supper time to say to them that were bidden,
"Come; for all things are now ready." 18And they all with

one consent began to make excuse. The first said unto him,
"I have bought a piece of ground, and I must needs go and
see it: I pray thee have me excused." [19]And another said, "I
have bought five yoke of oxen, and I go to prove them: I
pray thee have me excused." [20]And another said, "I have
married a wife, and therefore I cannot come." [21]So that servant came, and shewed his lord these things. Then the master of the house being angry said to his servant, "Go out
quickly into the streets and lanes of the city, and bring in
hither the poor, and the maimed, and the halt, and the blind."
[22]And the servant said, "Lord, it is done as thou hast commanded, and yet there is room." [23]And the lord said unto the
servant, "Go out into the highways and hedges, and compel
them to come in, that my house may be filled. [24]For I say
unto you that none of those men which were bidden shall
taste of my supper."'

[25]And there went great multitudes with him; and he turned, and said unto them, [26]'If any man come to me, and hate
not his father, and mother, and wife, and children, and brethren, and sisters, yea, and his own life also, he cannot be my
disciple. [27]And whosoever doth not bear his cross, and come
after me, cannot be my disciple. [28]For which of you, intend-
ing to build a tower, sitteth not down first, and counteth the
cost, whether he have sufficient to finish it? [29]Lest haply,
after he hath laid the foundation, and is not able to finish it,
all that behold it begin to mock him, [30]saying, "This man
began to build, and was not able to finish." [31]Or what king,
going to make war against another king, sitteth not down
first, and consulteth whether he be able with ten thousand to
meet him that cometh against him with twenty thousand?

32 Or else, while the other is yet a great way off, he sendeth
an ambassage, and desireth conditions of peace. 33 So likewise, whosoever he be of you that forsaketh not all that he
hath, he cannot be my disciple.

34 'Salt is good: but if the salt have lost his savour, wherewith shall it be seasoned? 35 It is neither fit for the land, nor
yet for the dunghill; but men cast it out. He that hath ears to
hear, let him hear.'

15 Then drew near unto him all the publicans and sinners for to hear him. 2 And the Pharisees and scribes
murmured, saying, 'This man receiveth sinners, and eateth
with them.'

3 And he spake this parable unto them, saying, 4 'What
man of you, having an hundred sheep, if he lose one of them,
doth not leave the ninety and nine in the wilderness, and go
after that which is lost, until he find it? 5 And when he hath
found it, he layeth it on his shoulders, rejoicing. 6 And when
he cometh home, he calleth together his friends and neighbours, saying unto them, "Rejoice with me; for I have found
my sheep which was lost." 7 I say unto you, that likewise joy
shall be in heaven over one sinner that repenteth, more than
over ninety and nine just persons, which need no repentance.

8 'Either what woman having ten pieces of silver, if she
lose one piece, doth not light a candle, and sweep the house,
and seek diligently till she find it? 9 And when she hath
found it, she calleth her friends and her neighbours together,
saying, "Rejoice with me; for I have found the piece which I
had lost." 10 Likewise, I say unto you, there is joy in the presence of the angels of God over one sinner that repenteth.'

[11]And he said, 'A certain man had two sons: [12]and the
younger of them said to his father, "Father, give me the portion of goods that falleth to me." And he divided unto them
his living. [13]And not many days after the younger son gathered all together, and took his journey into a far country, and
there wasted his substance with riotous living. [14]And when
he had spent all, there arose a mighty famine in that land;
and he began to be in want. [15]And he went and joined himself to a citizen of that country; and he sent him into his
fields to feed swine. [16]And he would fain have filled his belly
with the husks that the swine did eat; and no man gave unto
him. [17]And when he came to himself, he said, "How many
hired servants of my father's have bread enough and to spare,
and I perish with hunger! [18]I will arise and go to my father,
and will say unto him, Father, I have sinned against heaven,
and before thee, [19]and am no more worthy to be called thy
son; make me as one of thy hired servants." [20]And he arose,
and came to his father. But when he was yet a great way off,
his father saw him, and had compassion, and ran, and fell on
his neck, and kissed him. [21]And the son said unto him, "Father,
I have sinned against heaven, and in thy sight, and am no
more worthy to be called thy son." [22]But the father said to
his servants, "Bring forth the best robe, and put it on him;
and put a ring on his hand, and shoes on his feet: [23]and bring
hither the fatted calf, and kill it; and let us eat, and be merry.
[24]For this my son was dead, and is alive again; he was lost,
and is found." And they began to be merry. [25]Now his elder
son was in the field; and as he came and drew nigh to the
house, he heard musick and dancing. [26]And he called one of
the servants, and asked what these things meant. [27]And he

said unto him, "Thy brother is come; and thy father hath killed the fatted calf, because he hath received him safe and sound." 28 And he was angry, and would not go in; therefore came his father out, and intreated him. 29 And he answering said to his father, "Lo, these many years do I serve thee, neither transgressed I at any time thy commandment: and yet thou never gavest me a kid, that I might make merry with my friends. 30 But as soon as this thy son was come, which hath devoured thy living with harlots, thou hast killed for him the fatted calf." 31 And he said unto him, "Son, thou art ever with me, and all that I have is thine. 32 It was meet that we should make merry, and be glad; for this thy brother was dead, and is alive again; and was lost, and is found."'

16 And he said also unto his disciples, 'There was a certain rich man, which had a steward; and the same was accused unto him that he had wasted his goods. 2 And he called him, and said unto him, "How is it that I hear this of thee? Give an account of thy stewardship; for thou mayest be no longer steward." 3 Then the steward said within himself, "What shall I do? For my lord taketh away from me the stewardship. I cannot dig; to beg I am ashamed. 4 I am resolved what to do, that, when I am put out of the stewardship, they may receive me into their houses." 5 So he called every one of his lord's debtors unto him, and said unto the first, "How much owest thou unto my lord?" 6 And he said, "An hundred measures of oil." And he said unto him, "Take thy bill, and sit down quickly, and write fifty." 7 Then said he to another, "And how much owest thou?" And he said, "An hundred measures of wheat." And he said unto him, "Take

thy bill, and write fourscore." 8And the lord commended the
unjust steward, because he had done wisely: for the children
of this world are in their generation wiser than the children
of light. 9And I say unto you, make to yourselves friends of
the mammon of unrighteousness; that, when ye fail, they
may receive you into everlasting habitations.

10'He that is faithful in that which is least is faithful also
in much: and he that is unjust in the least is unjust also in
much. 11If therefore ye have not been faithful in the unrighteous mammon, who will commit to your trust the true
riches? 12And if ye have not been faithful in that which is
another man's, who shall give you that which is your own?

13'No servant can serve two masters: for either he will hate
the one, and love the other; or else he will hold to the one,
and despise the other. Ye cannot serve God and mammon.'

14And the Pharisees also, who were covetous, heard all
these things: and they derided him. 15And he said unto them,
'Ye are they which justify yourselves before men, but God
knoweth your hearts, for that which is highly esteemed
among men is abomination in the sight of God. 16The law
and the prophets were until John; since that time the kingdom of God is preached, and every man presseth into it. 17And
it is easier for heaven and earth to pass, than one tittle of the
law to fail. 18Whosoever putteth away his wife, and marrieth
another, committeth adultery; and whosoever marrieth her
that is put away from her husband committeth adultery.

19'There was a certain rich man, which was clothed in
purple and fine linen, and fared sumptuously every day;
20and there was a certain beggar named Lazarus, which was
laid at his gate, full of sores, 21and desiring to be fed with the

crumbs which fell from the rich man's table; moreover the
dogs came and licked his sores. 22 And it came to pass that
the beggar died, and was carried by the angels into Abraham's bosom; the rich man also died, and was buried; 23 and
in hell he lift up his eyes, being in torments, and seeth Abraham afar off, and Lazarus in his bosom. 24 And he cried and
said, "Father Abraham, have mercy on me, and send Lazarus
that he may dip the tip of his finger in water, and cool my
tongue; for I am tormented in this flame." 25 But Abraham
said, "Son, remember that thou in thy lifetime receivedst thy
good things, and likewise Lazarus evil things; but now he is
comforted, and thou art tormented. 26 And beside all this,
between us and you there is a great gulf fixed: so that they
which would pass from hence to you cannot; neither can
they pass to us, that would come from thence." 27 Then he
said, "I pray thee therefore, father, that thou wouldest send
him to my father's house, 28 for I have five brethren; that he
may testify unto them, lest they also come into this place of
torment." 29 Abraham saith unto him, "They have Moses and
the prophets; let them hear them." 30 And he said, "Nay,
father Abraham: but if one went unto them from the dead,
they will repent." 31 And he said unto him, "If they hear not
Moses and the prophets, neither will they be persuaded,
though one rose from the dead."'

17 Then said he unto the disciples, 'It is impossible but
that offences will come: but woe unto him, through
whom they come! 2 It were better for him that a millstone
were hanged about his neck, and he cast into the sea, than
that he should offend one of these little ones.

3 'Take heed to yourselves: if thy brother trespass against
thee, rebuke him; and if he repent, forgive him. 4 And if he
trespass against thee seven times in a day, and seven times
in a day turn again to thee, saying, "I repent," thou shalt forgive him.'
5 And the apostles said unto the Lord, 'Increase our faith.'
6 And the Lord said, 'If ye had faith as a grain of mustard seed,
ye might say unto this sycamine tree, "Be thou plucked up
by the root, and be thou planted in the sea"; and it should obey
you. 7 But which of you, having a servant plowing or feeding
cattle, will say unto him by and by, when he is come from
the field, "Go and sit down to meat"? 8 And will not rather
say unto him, "Make ready wherewith I may sup, and gird
thyself, and serve me, till I have eaten and drunken; and afterward thou shalt eat and drink"? 9 Doth he thank that servant
because he did the things that were commanded him? I trow
not. 10 So likewise ye, when ye shall have done all those things
which are commanded you, say, "We are unprofitable servants: we have done that which was our duty to do."'
11 And it came to pass, as he went to Jerusalem, that he
passed through the midst of Samaria and Galilee. 12 And as
he entered into a certain village, there met him ten men that
were lepers, which stood afar off. 13 And they lifted up their
voices, and said, 'Jesus, Master, have mercy on us.' 14 And
when he saw them, he said unto them, 'Go shew yourselves
unto the priests.' And it came to pass, that, as they went,
they were cleansed. 15 And one of them, when he saw that he
was healed, turned back, and with a loud voice glorified
God, 16 and fell down on his face at his feet, giving him
thanks; and he was a Samaritan. 17 And Jesus answering said,

'Were there not ten cleansed? But where are the nine?
[18] There are not found that returned to give glory to God,
save this stranger.' [19] And he said unto him, 'Arise, go thy
way; thy faith hath made thee whole.'
[20] And when he was demanded of the Pharisees, when
the kingdom of God should come, he answered them and
said, 'The kingdom of God cometh not with observation.
[21] Neither shall they say, "Lo here!" or, "Lo there!" For, behold,
the kingdom of God is within you.' [22] And he said unto the
disciples, 'The days will come, when ye shall desire to see
one of the days of the Son of man, and ye shall not see it.
[23] And they shall say to you, "See here," or, "See there": go not
after them, nor follow them. [24] For as the lightning, that lighteneth out of the one part under heaven, shineth unto the
other part under heaven; so shall also the Son of man be in
his day. [25] But first must he suffer many things, and be rejected
of this generation. [26] And as it was in the days of Noe, so shall
it be also in the days of the Son of man. [27] They did eat, they
drank, they married wives, they were given in marriage,
until the day that Noe entered into the ark, and the flood
came, and destroyed them all. [28] Likewise also as it was in
the days of Lot; they did eat, they drank, they bought, they
sold, they planted, they builded; [29] but the same day that Lot
went out of Sodom it rained fire and brimstone from heaven,
and destroyed them all. [30] Even thus shall it be in the day
when the Son of man is revealed. [31] In that day, he which
shall be upon the housetop, and his stuff in the house, let
him not come down to take it away; and he that is in the
field, let him likewise not return back. [32] Remember Lot's
wife. [33] Whosoever shall seek to save his life shall lose it; and

whosoever shall lose his life shall preserve it. 34 I tell you, in
that night there shall be two men in one bed; the one shall be
taken, and the other shall be left. 35 Two women shall be
grinding together; the one shall be taken, and the other left.
36 Two men shall be in the field; the one shall be taken, and
the other left.' 37 And they answered and said unto him,
'Where, Lord?' And he said unto them, 'Wheresoever the
body is, thither will the eagles be gathered together.'

18 And he spake a parable unto them to this end, that
men ought always to pray, and not to faint; 2 saying,
'There was in a city a judge, which feared not God, neither
regarded man; 3 and there was a widow in that city; and she
came unto him, saying, "Avenge me of mine adversary."
4 And he would not for a while; but afterward he said within
himself, "Though I fear not God, nor regard man; 5 yet because
this widow troubleth me, I will avenge her, lest by her continual coming she weary me."' 6 And the Lord said, 'Hear
what the unjust judge saith. 7 And shall not God avenge his
own elect, which cry day and night unto him, though he
bear long with them? 8 I tell you that he will avenge them
speedily. Nevertheless when the Son of man cometh, shall
he find faith on the earth?'

9 And he spake this parable unto certain which trusted in
themselves that they were righteous, and despised others.
10 'Two men went up into the temple to pray: the one a Pharisee,
and the other a publican. 11 The Pharisee stood and prayed thus
with himself, "God, I thank thee, that I am not as other men
are, extortioners, unjust, adulterers, or even as this publican.
12 I fast twice in the week, I give tithes of all that I possess."

13And the publican, standing afar off, would not lift up so
much as his eyes unto heaven, but smote upon his breast,
saying, "God be merciful to me a sinner." 14I tell you, this
man went down to his house justified rather than the other:
for every one that exalteth himself shall be abased; and he
that humbleth himself shall be exalted.'

15And they brought unto him also infants, that he would
touch them; but when his disciples saw it, they rebuked
them. 16But Jesus called them unto him, and said, 'Suffer little children to come unto me, and forbid them not; for of
such is the kingdom of God. 17Verily I say unto you, whosoever shall not receive the kingdom of God as a little child
shall in no wise enter therein.'

18And a certain ruler asked him, saying, 'Good Master,
what shall I do to inherit eternal life?' 19And Jesus said unto
him, 'Why callest thou me good? None is good, save one,
that is, God. 20Thou knowest the commandments: Do not commit adultery, Do not kill, Do not steal, Do not bear false witness, Honour thy father and thy mother.' 21And he said, 'All
these have I kept from my youth up.' 22Now when Jesus heard
these things, he said unto him, 'Yet lackest thou one thing:
sell all that thou hast, and distribute unto the poor, and thou
shalt have treasure in heaven; and come, follow me.' 23And
when he heard this, he was very sorrowful; for he was very
rich. 24And when Jesus saw that he was very sorrowful, he
said, 'How hardly shall they that have riches enter into the
kingdom of God! 25For it is easier for a camel to go through a
needle's eye, than for a rich man to enter into the kingdom of
God.' 26And they that heard it said, 'Who then can be saved?'
27And he said, 'The things which are impossible with men

are possible with God.' 28 Then Peter said, 'Lo, we have left all,
and followed thee.' 29 And he said unto them, 'Verily I say unto
you, there is no man that hath left house, or parents, or
brethren, or wife, or children, for the kingdom of God's sake,
30 who shall not receive manifold more in this present time,
and in the world to come life everlasting.'

31 Then he took unto him the twelve, and said unto them,
'Behold, we go up to Jerusalem, and all things that are written by the prophets concerning the Son of man shall be
accomplished. 32 For he shall be delivered unto the Gentiles,
and shall be mocked, and spitefully entreated, and spitted
on. 33 And they shall scourge him, and put him to death; and
the third day he shall rise again.' 34 And they understood
none of these things; and this saying was hid from them,
neither knew they the things which were spoken.

35 And it came to pass that, as he was come nigh unto Jericho, a certain blind man sat by the way side begging, 36 and
hearing the multitude pass by, he asked what it meant. 37 And
they told him that Jesus of Nazareth passeth by. 38 And he
cried, saying, 'Jesus, thou Son of David, have mercy on me.'
39 And they which went before rebuked him, that he should
hold his peace: but he cried so much the more, 'Thou Son of
David, have mercy on me.' 40 And Jesus stood, and commanded him to be brought unto him; and when he was come
near, he asked him, 41 saying, 'What wilt thou that I shall do
unto thee?' And he said, 'Lord, that I may receive my sight.'
42 And Jesus said unto him, 'Receive thy sight; thy faith hath
saved thee.' 43 And immediately he received his sight, and
followed him, glorifying God: and all the people, when they
saw it, gave praise unto God.

19 And Jesus entered and passed through Jericho. [2]And,
behold, there was a man named Zacchæus, which was
the chief among the publicans, and he was rich. [3]And he
sought to see Jesus who he was; and could not for the press,
because he was little of stature. [4]And he ran before, and
climbed up into a sycomore tree to see him; for he was to
pass that way. [5]And when Jesus came to the place, he looked
up, and saw him, and said unto him, 'Zacchæus, make haste,
and come down; for today I must abide at thy house.' [6]And
he made haste, and came down, and received him joyfully.
[7]And when they saw it, they all murmured, saying that he
was gone to be guest with a man that is a sinner. [8]And Zacchæus stood, and said unto the Lord, 'Behold, Lord, the half
of my goods I give to the poor; and if I have taken any thing
from any man by false accusation, I restore him fourfold.'
[9]And Jesus said unto him, 'This day is salvation come to this
house, forsomuch as he also is a son of Abraham. [10]For the
Son of man is come to seek and to save that which was lost.'

[11]And as they heard these things, he added and spake a
parable, because he was nigh to Jerusalem, and because they
thought that the kingdom of God should immediately
appear. [12]He said therefore, 'A certain nobleman went into a
far country to receive for himself a kingdom, and to return.
[13]And he called his ten servants, and delivered them ten
pounds, and said unto them, "Occupy till I come." [14]But his
citizens hated him, and sent a message after him, saying,
"We will not have this man to reign over us." [15]And it came
to pass that, when he was returned, having received the kingdom, then he commanded these servants to be called unto
him, to whom he had given the money, that he might know

how much every man had gained by trading. 16 Then came
the first, saying, "Lord, thy pound hath gained ten pounds."
17 And he said unto him, "Well, thou good servant, because
thou hast been faithful in a very little, have thou authority
over ten cities." 18 And the second came, saying, "Lord, thy
pound hath gained five pounds." 19 And he said likewise to
him, "Be thou also over five cities." 20 And another came, saying, "Lord, behold, here is thy pound, which I have kept laid
up in a napkin; 21 for I feared thee, because thou art an austere man: thou takest up that thou layedst not down, and
reapest that thou didst not sow." 22 And he saith unto him,
"Out of thine own mouth will I judge thee, thou wicked servant. Thou knewest that I was an austere man, taking up that
I laid not down, and reaping that I did not sow. 23 Wherefore
then gavest not thou my money into the bank, that at my
coming I might have required mine own with usury?" 24 And
he said unto them that stood by, "Take from him the pound,
and give it to him that hath ten pounds." 25 (And they said
unto him, "Lord, he hath ten pounds.") 26 For I say unto you
that unto every one which hath shall be given; and from him
that hath not, even that he hath shall be taken away from
him. 27 But those mine enemies, which would not that I should
reign over them, bring hither, and slay them before me.'

28 And when he had thus spoken, he went before, ascending up to Jerusalem. 29 And it came to pass, when he was
come nigh to Bethphage and Bethany, at the mount called
the mount of Olives, he sent two of his disciples, 30 saying,
'Go ye into the village over against you, in the which at your
entering ye shall find a colt tied, whereon yet never man sat:
loose him, and bring him hither. 31 And if any man ask you,

"Why do ye loose him?" Thus shall ye say unto him, "Because
the Lord hath need of him."' 32And they that were sent went
their way, and found even as he had said unto them. 33And
as they were loosing the colt, the owners thereof said unto
them, 'Why loose ye the colt?' 34And they said, 'The Lord
hath need of him.' 35And they brought him to Jesus: and they
cast their garments upon the colt, and they set Jesus thereon.
36And as he went, they spread their clothes in the way. 37And
when he was come nigh, even now at the descent of the
mount of Olives, the whole multitude of the disciples began
to rejoice and praise God with a loud voice for all the mighty
works that they had seen, 38 saying, 'Blessed be the King that
cometh in the name of the Lord; peace in heaven, and glory
in the highest.' 39And some of the Pharisees from among the
multitude said unto him, 'Master, rebuke thy disciples.'
40And he answered and said unto them, 'I tell you that, if
these should hold their peace, the stones would immediately
cry out.'

41And when he was come near, he beheld the city, and
wept over it, 42 saying, 'If thou hadst known, even thou, at
least in this thy day, the things which belong unto thy peace!
But now they are hid from thine eyes. 43 For the days shall
come upon thee, that thine enemies shall cast a trench about
thee, and compass thee round, and keep thee in on every side,
44 and shall lay thee even with the ground, and thy children
within thee; and they shall not leave in thee one stone upon
another; because thou knewest not the time of thy visitation.'
45And he went into the temple, and began to cast out them
that sold therein, and them that bought, 46 saying unto them,
'It is written, "My house is the house of prayer," but ye have

made it a den of thieves.' [47]And he taught daily in the temple. But the chief priests and the scribes and the chief of the
people sought to destroy him, [48]and could not find what they
might do; for all the people were very attentive to hear him.

20 And it came to pass that on one of those days, as he
taught the people in the temple, and preached the
gospel, the chief priests and the scribes came upon him with
the elders, [2]and spake unto him, saying, 'Tell us, by what
authority doest thou these things? Or who is he that gave
thee this authority?' [3]And he answered and said unto them,
'I will also ask you one thing; and answer me: [4]the baptism
of John, was it from heaven, or of men?' [5]And they reasoned
with themselves, saying, 'If we shall say, "From heaven," he
will say, "Why then believed ye him not?"; [6]but and if we
say, "Of men; all the people will stone us; for they be persuaded that John was a prophet.' [7]And they answered that
they could not tell whence it was. [8]And Jesus said unto
them, 'Neither tell I you by what authority I do these things.'

[9]Then began he to speak to the people this parable: 'A
certain man planted a vineyard, and let it forth to husbandmen, and went into a far country for a long time. [10]And at the
season he sent a servant to the husbandmen, that they should
give him of the fruit of the vineyard; but the husbandmen
beat him, and sent him away empty. [11]And again he sent
another servant: and they beat him also, and entreated him
shamefully, and sent him away empty. [12]And again he sent a
third; and they wounded him also, and cast him out. [13]Then
said the lord of the vineyard, "What shall I do? I will send
my beloved son; it may be they will reverence him when

they see him." [14]But when the husbandmen saw him, they
reasoned among themselves, saying, "This is the heir: come,
let us kill him, that the inheritance may be ours." [15]So they
cast him out of the vineyard, and killed him. What therefore
shall the lord of the vineyard do unto them? [16]He shall come
and destroy these husbandmen, and shall give the vineyard
to others.' And when they heard it, they said, 'God forbid.'
[17]And he beheld them, and said, 'What is this then that is
written, "The stone which the builders rejected, the same is
become the head of the corner"? [18]Whosoever shall fall upon
that stone shall be broken; but on whomsoever it shall fall, it
will grind him to powder.'

[19]And the chief priests and the scribes the same hour
sought to lay hands on him; and they feared the people; for
they perceived that he had spoken this parable against them.
[20]And they watched him, and sent forth spies, which should
feign themselves just men, that they might take hold of his
words, that so they might deliver him unto the power and
authority of the governor. [21]And they asked him, saying, 'Master, we know that thou sayest and teachest rightly, neither
acceptest thou the person of any, but teachest the way of God
truly. [22]Is it lawful for us to give tribute unto Cæsar, or no?'
[23]But he perceived their craftiness, and said unto them, 'Why
tempt ye me? [24]Shew me a penny. Whose image and superscription hath it?' They answered and said, 'Cæsar's.' [25]And
he said unto them, 'Render therefore unto Cæsar the things
which be Cæsar's, and unto God the things which be God's.'
[26]And they could not take hold of his words before the people: and they marvelled at his answer, and held their peace.

[27]Then came to him certain of the Sadducees, which deny

that there is any resurrection; and they asked him, 28 saying,
'Master, Moses wrote unto us, if any man's brother die, having
a wife, and he die without children, that his brother should
take his wife, and raise up seed unto his brother. 29 There were
therefore seven brethren; and the first took a wife, and died
without children. 30 And the second took her to wife, and he
died childless. 31 And the third took her; and in like manner
the seven also: and they left no children, and died. 32 Last of
all the woman died also. 33 Therefore in the resurrection whose
wife of them is she? For seven had her to wife.' 34 And Jesus
answering said unto them, 'The children of this world marry,
and are given in marriage, 35 but they which shall be accounted
worthy to obtain that world, and the resurrection from the
dead, neither marry, nor are given in marriage; 36 neither can
they die any more: for they are equal unto the angels; and
are the children of God, being the children of the resurrection. 37 Now that the dead are raised, even Moses shewed at
the bush, when he calleth the Lord the God of Abraham, and
the God of Isaac, and the God of Jacob. 38 For he is not a God
of the dead, but of the living: for all live unto him.'

39 Then certain of the scribes answering said, 'Master,
thou hast well said.' 40 And after that they durst not ask him
any question at all. 41 And he said unto them, 'How say they
that Christ is David's son? 42 And David himself saith in the
book of Psalms, "The Lord said unto my Lord, 'Sit thou on
my right hand, 43 till I make thine enemies thy footstool."
44 David therefore calleth him Lord, how is he then his son?'

45 Then in the audience of all the people he said unto
his disciples, 46 'Beware of the scribes, which desire to walk
in long robes, and love greetings in the markets, and the

highest seats in the synagogues, and the chief rooms at feasts; [47] which devour widows' houses, and for a shew make long prayers: the same shall receive greater damnation.'

21 And he looked up, and saw the rich men casting their gifts into the treasury. [2]And he saw also a certain poor widow casting in thither two mites. [3]And he said, 'Of a truth I say unto you that this poor widow hath cast in more than they all. [4]For all these have of their abundance cast in unto the offerings of God, but she of her penury hath cast in all the living that she had.'

[5]And as some spake of the temple, how it was adorned with goodly stones and gifts, he said, [6]'As for these things which ye behold, the days will come, in the which there shall not be left one stone upon another, that shall not be thrown down.' [7]And they asked him, saying, 'Master, but when shall these things be? And what sign will there be when these things shall come to pass?' [8]And he said, 'Take heed that ye be not deceived; for many shall come in my name, saying, "I am Christ," and the time draweth near: go ye not therefore after them.

[9]'But when ye shall hear of wars and commotions, be not terrified; for these things must first come to pass, but the end is not by and by.' [10]Then said he unto them, 'Nation shall rise against nation, and kingdom against kingdom. [11]And great earthquakes shall be in divers places, and famines, and pestilences; and fearful sights and great signs shall there be from heaven.

[12]'But before all these, they shall lay their hands on you, and persecute you, delivering you up to the synagogues, and

into prisons, being brought before kings and rulers for my
name's sake. 13 And it shall turn to you for a testimony. 14 Settle it therefore in your hearts, not to meditate before what ye
shall answer, 15 for I will give you a mouth and wisdom, which
all your adversaries shall not be able to gainsay nor resist.
16 And ye shall be betrayed both by parents, and brethren,
and kinsfolks, and friends; and some of you shall they cause
to be put to death. 17 And ye shall be hated of all men for my
name's sake. 18 But there shall not an hair of your head perish. 19 In your patience possess ye your souls. 20 And when ye
shall see Jerusalem compassed with armies, then know that
the desolation thereof is nigh. 21 Then let them which are in
Judæa flee to the mountains; and let them which are in the
midst of it depart out; and let not them that are in the countries enter thereinto. 22 For these be the days of vengeance,
that all things which are written may be fulfilled. 23 But woe
unto them that are with child, and to them that give suck, in
those days! For there shall be great distress in the land, and
wrath upon this people. 24 And they shall fall by the edge of
the sword, and shall be led away captive into all nations:
and Jerusalem shall be trodden down of the Gentiles, until
the times of the Gentiles be fulfilled.

25 'And there shall be signs in the sun, and in the moon,
and in the stars; and upon the earth distress of nations, with
perplexity; the sea and the waves roaring; 26 men's hearts
failing them for fear, and for looking after those things which
are coming on the earth: for the powers of heaven shall be
shaken. 27 And then shall they see the Son of man coming in a
cloud with power and great glory. 28 And when these things
begin to come to pass, then look up, and lift up your heads;

for your redemption draweth nigh.' 29 And he spake to them
a parable: 'Behold the fig tree, and all the trees; 30 when they
now shoot forth, ye see and know of your own selves that
summer is now nigh at hand. 31 So likewise ye, when ye see
these things come to pass, know ye that the kingdom of God
is nigh at hand. 32 Verily I say unto you, this generation shall
not pass away, till all be fulfilled. 33 Heaven and earth shall
pass away, but my words shall not pass away.

34 And take heed to yourselves, lest at any time your hearts
be overcharged with surfeiting, and drunkenness, and cares
of this life, and so that day come upon you unawares. 35 For
as a snare shall it come on all them that dwell on the face of
the whole earth. 36 Watch ye therefore, and pray always, that
ye may be accounted worthy to escape all these things that
shall come to pass, and to stand before the Son of man.'
37 And in the day time he was teaching in the temple; and at
night he went out, and abode in the mount that is called the
mount of Olives. 38 And all the people came early in the
morning to him in the temple, for to hear him.

22 Now the feast of unleavened bread drew nigh,
which is called the Passover. 2 And the chief priests
and scribes sought how they might kill him; for they feared
the people.

3 Then entered Satan into Judas surnamed Iscariot, being
of the number of the twelve. 4 And he went his way, and
communed with the chief priests and captains, how he might
betray him unto them. 5 And they were glad, and covenanted
to give him money. 6 And he promised, and sought opportunity to betray him unto them in the absence of the multitude.

[7]Then came the day of unleavened bread, when the
passover must be killed. [8]And he sent Peter and John, saying, 'Go and prepare us the passover, that we may eat.' [9]And
they said unto him, 'Where wilt thou that we prepare?'
[10]And he said unto them, 'Behold, when ye are entered into
the city, there shall a man meet you, bearing a pitcher of
water; follow him into the house where he entereth in. [11]And
ye shall say unto the goodman of the house, "The Master
saith unto thee, 'Where is the guestchamber, where I shall
eat the passover with my disciples?' " [12]And he shall shew
you a large upper room furnished; there make ready.' [13]And
they went, and found as he had said unto them: and they
made ready the passover.

[14]And when the hour was come, he sat down, and the
twelve apostles with him. [15]And he said unto them, 'With
desire I have desired to eat this passover with you before I
suffer. [16]For I say unto you, I will not any more eat thereof,
until it be fulfilled in the kingdom of God.' [17]And he took the
cup, and gave thanks, and said, 'Take this, and divide it
among yourselves. [18]For I say unto you, I will not drink of
the fruit of the vine, until the kingdom of God shall come.'

[19]And he took bread, and gave thanks, and brake it, and
gave unto them, saying, 'This is my body which is given for
you: this do in remembrance of me.' [20]Likewise also the cup
after supper, saying, 'This cup is the new testament in my
blood, which is shed for you. [21]But, behold, the hand of him
that betrayeth me is with me on the table. [22]And truly the Son
of man goeth, as it was determined: but woe unto that man
by whom he is betrayed!' [23]And they began to enquire among
themselves, which of them it was that should do this thing.

24 And there was also a strife among them, which of them
should be accounted the greatest. 25 And he said unto them,
'The kings of the Gentiles exercise lordship over them; and
they that exercise authority upon them are called benefac-
tors. 26 But ye shall not be so: but he that is greatest among
you, let him be as the younger; and he that is chief, as he that
doth serve. 27 For whether is greater, he that sitteth at meat,
or he that serveth? Is not he that sitteth at meat? But I am
among you as he that serveth. 28 Ye are they which have continued with me in my temptations. 29 And I appoint unto you
a kingdom, as my Father hath appointed unto me; 30 that ye
may eat and drink at my table in my kingdom, and sit on
thrones judging the twelve tribes of Israel.'

31 And the Lord said, 'Simon, Simon, behold, Satan hath
desired to have you, that he may sift you as wheat; 32 but I
have prayed for thee, that thy faith fail not; and when thou
art converted, strengthen thy brethren.' 33 And he said unto
him, 'Lord, I am ready to go with thee, both into prison, and
to death.' 34 And he said, 'I tell thee, Peter, the cock shall not
crow this day, before that thou shalt thrice deny that thou
knowest me.' 35 And he said unto them, 'When I sent you
without purse, and scrip, and shoes, lacked ye any thing?'
And they said, 'Nothing.' 36 Then said he unto them, 'But
now, he that hath a purse, let him take it, and likewise his
scrip: and he that hath no sword, let him sell his garment,
and buy one. 37 For I say unto you that this that is written
must yet be accomplished in me, and he was reckoned among
the transgressors: for the things concerning me have an end.'
38 And they said, 'Lord, behold, here are two swords.' And he
said unto them, 'It is enough.'

39And he came out, and went, as he was wont, to the
mount of Olives; and his disciples also followed him. 40And
when he was at the place, he said unto them, 'Pray that ye
enter not into temptation.' 41And he was withdrawn from
them about a stone's cast, and kneeled down, and prayed,
42 saying, 'Father, if thou be willing, remove this cup from
me; nevertheless not my will, but thine, be done.' 43And
there appeared an angel unto him from heaven, strengthen-
ing him. 44And being in an agony he prayed more earnestly;
and his sweat was as it were great drops of blood falling
down to the ground. 45And when he rose up from prayer,
and was come to his disciples, he found them sleeping for
sorrow, 46 and said unto them, 'Why sleep ye? Rise and pray,
lest ye enter into temptation.'

47And while he yet spake, behold a multitude, and he that
was called Judas, one of the twelve, went before them, and
drew near unto Jesus to kiss him. 48 But Jesus said unto him,
'Judas, betrayest thou the Son of man with a kiss?' 49 When
they which were about him saw what would follow, they
said unto him, 'Lord, shall we smite with the sword?'

50And one of them smote the servant of the high priest,
and cut off his right ear. 51And Jesus answered and said, 'Suffer ye thus far.' And he touched his ear, and healed him.
52 Then Jesus said unto the chief priests, and captains of the
temple, and the elders, which were come to him, 'Be ye come
out, as against a thief, with swords and staves? 53 When I was
daily with you in the temple, ye stretched forth no hands
against me: but this is your hour, and the power of darkness.'

54 Then took they him, and led him, and brought him into
the high priest's house. And Peter followed afar off. 55And

when they had kindled a fire in the midst of the hall, and
were set down together, Peter sat down among them. [56] But a
certain maid beheld him as he sat by the fire, and earnestly
looked upon him, and said, 'This man was also with him.'
[57]And he denied him, saying, 'Woman, I know him not.' [58]And
after a little while another saw him, and said, 'Thou art also
of them.' And Peter said, 'Man, I am not.' [59]And about the
space of one hour after another confidently affirmed, saying,
'Of a truth this fellow also was with him; for he is a Galilæan.' [60]And Peter said, 'Man, I know not what thou sayest.'
And immediately, while he yet spake, the cock crew. [61]And
the Lord turned, and looked upon Peter. And Peter remembered the word of the Lord, how he had said unto him,
'Before the cock crow, thou shalt deny me thrice.' [62]And Peter
went out, and wept bitterly.

[63]And the men that held Jesus mocked him, and smote
him. [64]And when they had blindfolded him, they struck him
on the face, and asked him, saying, 'Prophesy, who is it that
smote thee?' [65]And many other things blasphemously spake
they against him.

[66]And as soon as it was day, the elders of the people and
the chief priests and the scribes came together, and led him
into their council, saying, [67]'Art thou the Christ? Tell us.'
And he said unto them, 'If I tell you, ye will not believe.
[68]And if I also ask you, ye will not answer me, nor let me go.
[69]Hereafter shall the Son of man sit on the right hand of the
power of God.' [70]Then said they all, 'Art thou then the Son of
God?' And he said unto them, 'Ye say that I am.' [71]And they
said, 'What need we any further witness? For we ourselves
have heard of his own mouth.'

23 And the whole multitude of them arose, and led him
unto Pilate. 2And they began to accuse him, saying,
'We found this fellow perverting the nation, and forbidding
to give tribute to Cæsar, saying that he himself is Christ a
King.' 3And Pilate asked him, saying, 'Art thou the King of
the Jews?' And he answered him and said, 'Thou sayest it.'
4Then said Pilate to the chief priests and to the people, 'I find
no fault in this man.' 5And they were the more fierce, saying,
'He stirreth up the people, teaching throughout all Jewry,
beginning from Galilee to this place.' 6When Pilate heard of
Galilee, he asked whether the man were a Galilæan. 7And as
soon as he knew that he belonged unto Herod's jurisdiction,
he sent him to Herod, who himself also was at Jerusalem at
that time.

8And when Herod saw Jesus, he was exceeding glad, for
he was desirous to see him of a long season, because he had
heard many things of him; and he hoped to have seen some
miracle done by him. 9Then he questioned with him in
many words; but he answered him nothing. 10And the chief
priests and scribes stood and vehemently accused him.
11And Herod with his men of war set him at nought, and
mocked him, and arrayed him in a gorgeous robe, and sent
him again to Pilate.

12And the same day Pilate and Herod were made friends
together; for before they were at enmity between themselves.

13And Pilate, when he had called together the chief priests
and the rulers and the people, 14said unto them, 'Ye have
brought this man unto me, as one that perverteth the people:
and, behold, I, having examined him before you, have found
no fault in this man touching those things whereof ye accuse

him. 15 No, nor yet Herod: for I sent you to him; and, lo,
nothing worthy of death is done unto him. 16 I will therefore
chastise him, and release him.' 17 (For of necessity he must
release one unto them at the feast.)

18 And they cried out all at once, saying, 'Away with this
man, and release unto us Barabbas' 19 (who for a certain sedition made in the city, and for murder, was cast into prison).
20 Pilate therefore, willing to release Jesus, spake again to them.
21 But they cried, saying, 'Crucify him, crucify him.' 22 And he
said unto them the third time, 'Why, what evil hath he done?
I have found no cause of death in him: I will therefore chastise him, and let him go.' 23 And they were instant with loud
voices, requiring that he might be crucified. And the voices
of them and of the chief priests prevailed. 24 And Pilate gave
sentence that it should be as they required. 25 And he released
unto them him that for sedition and murder was cast into
prison, whom they had desired; but he delivered Jesus to
their will. 26 And as they led him away, they laid hold upon
one Simon, a Cyrenian, coming out of the country, and on
him they laid the cross, that he might bear it after Jesus.

27 And there followed him a great company of people,
and of women, which also bewailed and lamented him.
28 But Jesus turning unto them said, 'Daughters of Jerusalem,
weep not for me, but weep for yourselves, and for your children. 29 For, behold, the days are coming, in the which they
shall say, "Blessed are the barren, and the wombs that never
bore, and the paps which never gave suck." 30 Then shall
they begin to say to the mountains, "Fall on us," and to the
hills, "Cover us." 31 For if they do these things in a green tree,
what shall be done in the dry?' 32 And there were also two

other, malefactors, led with him to be put to death. 33And
when they were come to the place, which is called Calvary,
there they crucified him, and the malefactors, one on the right
hand, and the other on the left.
34Then said Jesus, 'Father, forgive them; for they know
not what they do.' And they parted his raiment, and cast lots.
35And the people stood beholding. And the rulers also with
them derided him, saying, 'He saved others; let him save
himself, if he be Christ, the chosen of God.' 36And the soldiers also mocked him, coming to him, and offering him
vinegar, 37and saying, 'If thou be the king of the Jews, save
thyself.' 38And a superscription also was written over him in
letters of Greek, and Latin, and Hebrew, 'THIS IS THE
KING OF THE JEWS.'
39And one of the malefactors which were hanged railed
on him, saying, 'If thou be Christ, save thyself and us.' 40But
the other answering rebuked him, saying, 'Dost not thou
fear God, seeing thou art in the same condemnation? 41And
we indeed justly; for we receive the due reward of our
deeds: but this man hath done nothing amiss.' 42And he said
unto Jesus, 'Lord, remember me when thou comest into thy
kingdom.' 43And Jesus said unto him, 'Verily I say unto thee,
today shalt thou be with me in paradise.'
44And it was about the sixth hour, and there was a darkness over all the earth until the ninth hour. 45And the sun
was darkened, and the veil of the temple was rent in the midst.
46And when Jesus had cried with a loud voice, he said,
'Father, into thy hands I commend my spirit,' and having
said thus, he gave up the ghost. 47Now when the centurion
saw what was done, he glorified God, saying, 'Certainly this

was a righteous man.' 48 And all the people that came together to that sight, beholding the things which were done, smote their breasts, and returned. 49 And all his acquaintance, and the women that followed him from Galilee, stood afar off, beholding these things.

50 And, behold, there was a man named Joseph, a counsellor; and he was a good man, and a just. 51 (The same had not consented to the counsel and deed of them.) He was of Arimathæa, a city of the Jews, who also himself waited for the kingdom of God. 52 This man went unto Pilate, and begged the body of Jesus. 53 And he took it down, and wrapped it in linen, and laid it in a sepulchre that was hewn in stone, wherein never man before was laid. 54 And that day was the preparation, and the sabbath drew on. 55 And the women also, which came with him from Galilee, followed after, and beheld the sepulchre, and how his body was laid. 56 And they returned, and prepared spices and ointments; and rested the sabbath day according to the commandment.

24 Now upon the first day of the week, very early in the morning, they came unto the sepulchre, bringing the spices which they had prepared, and certain others with them. 2 And they found the stone rolled away from the sepulchre. 3 And they entered in, and found not the body of the Lord Jesus. 4 And it came to pass, as they were much perplexed thereabout, behold, two men stood by them in shining garments. 5 And as they were afraid, and bowed down their faces to the earth, they said unto them, 'Why seek ye the living among the dead? 6 He is not here, but is risen. Remember how he spake unto you when he was yet in Galilee, 7 saying,

"The Son of man must be delivered into the hands of sinful
men, and be crucified, and the third day rise again.'" 8And they
remembered his words, 9and returned from the sepulchre,
and told all these things unto the eleven, and to all the rest.
10It was Mary Magdalene, and Joanna, and Mary the mother
of James, and other women that were with them, which told
these things unto the apostles. 11And their words seemed to
them as idle tales, and they believed them not. 12Then arose
Peter, and ran unto the sepulchre, and stooping down, he
beheld the linen clothes laid by themselves, and departed,
wondering in himself at that which was come to pass.

13And, behold, two of them went that same day to a village called Emmaus, which was from Jerusalem about threescore furlongs. 14And they talked together of all these things
which had happened. 15And it came to pass, that, while they
communed together and reasoned, Jesus himself drew near,
and went with them. 16But their eyes were holden that they
should not know him. 17And he said unto them, 'What manner of communications are these that ye have one to another,
as ye walk, and are sad?' 18And the one of them, whose name
was Cleopas, answering said unto him, 'Art thou only a stranger in Jerusalem, and hast not known the things which are
come to pass there in these days?' 19And he said unto them,
'What things?' And they said unto him, 'Concerning Jesus of
Nazareth, which was a prophet mighty in deed and word
before God and all the people; 20and how the chief priests
and our rulers delivered him to be condemned to death, and
have crucified him. 21But we trusted that it had been he which
should have redeemed Israel; and beside all this, today is the
third day since these things were done. 22Yea, and certain

women also of our company made us astonished, which
were early at the sepulchre; [23]and when they found not his
body, they came, saying that they had also seen a vision of
angels, which said that he was alive. [24]And certain of them
which were with us went to the sepulchre, and found it even
so as the women had said; but him they saw not.' [25]Then he
said unto them, 'O fools, and slow of heart to believe all that
the prophets have spoken. [26]Ought not Christ to have suffered these things, and to enter into his glory?' [27]And beginning at Moses and all the prophets, he expounded unto them
in all the scriptures the things concerning himself. [28]And
they drew nigh unto the village, whither they went; and he
made as though he would have gone further. [29]But they constrained him, saying, 'Abide with us; for it is toward evening,
and the day is far spent.' And he went in to tarry with them.
[30]And it came to pass, as he sat at meat with them, he took
bread, and blessed it, and brake, and gave to them. [31]And
their eyes were opened, and they knew him; and he van-
ished out of their sight. [32]And they said one to another, 'Did
not our heart burn within us, while he talked with us by the
way, and while he opened to us the scriptures?' [33]And they
rose up the same hour, and returned to Jerusalem, and found
the eleven gathered together, and them that were with them,
[34]saying, 'The Lord is risen indeed, and hath appeared to
Simon.' [35]And they told what things were done in the way,
and how he was known of them in breaking of bread.

[36]And as they thus spake, Jesus himself stood in the midst
of them, and saith unto them, 'Peace be unto you.' [37]But they
were terrified and affrighted, and supposed that they had
seen a spirit. [38]And he said unto them, 'Why are ye troubled?

And why do thoughts arise in your hearts? 39 Behold my hands
and my feet, that it is I myself: handle me, and see; for a spirit
hath no flesh and bones, as ye see me have.' 40 And when he
had thus spoken, he shewed them his hands and his feet.
41 And while they yet believed not for joy, and wondered, he
said unto them, 'Have ye here any meat?' 42 And they gave
him a piece of a broiled fish, and of an honeycomb. 43 And he
took it, and did eat before them. 44 And he said unto them,
'These are the words which I spake unto you, while I was
yet with you, that all things must be fulfilled, which were
written in the law of Moses, and in the prophets, and in the
psalms, concerning me.' 45 Then opened he their understanding, that they might understand the scriptures, 46 and said
unto them, 'Thus it is written, and thus it behoved Christ to
suffer, and to rise from the dead the third day; 47 and that
repentance and remission of sins should be preached in his
name among all nations, beginning at Jerusalem. 48 And ye
are witnesses of these things.

49 'And, behold, I send the promise of my Father upon
you; but tarry ye in the city of Jerusalem, until ye be endued
with power from on high.'

50 And he led them out as far as to Bethany, and he lifted
up his hands, and blessed them. 51 And it came to pass, while
he blessed them, he was parted from them, and carried up
into heaven. 52 And they worshipped him, and returned to
Jerusalem with great joy; 53 and were continually in the temple, praising and blessing God. Amen.

titles in the series

genesis – *introduced by e. l. doctorow*
exodus – *introduced by david grossman*
job – *introduced by charles frazier*
selections from the book of psalms – *introduced by bono*
proverbs – *introduced by charles johnson*
ecclesiastes – *introduced by doris lessing*
matthew – *introduced by francisco goldman*
mark – *introduced by barry hannah*
luke – *introduced by thomas cahill*
john – *introduced by darcey steinke*
corinthians – *introduced by fay weldon*
revelation – *introduced by kathleen norris*

john

the gospel according to

john

authorized king james version

grove press
new york

with an introduction by | darcey steinke

The Pocket Canons were originally published in the U.K. in 1998 by Canongate Books, Ltd.
Published simultaneously in Canada
Printed in the United States of America

FIRST AMERICAN EDITION

Copyright information is on file with the Library of Congress
ISBN 0-8021-3619-2

Design by Paddy Cramsie

Grove Press
841 Broadway
New York, NY 10003

99 00 01 02 10 9 8 7 6 5 4 3 2 1

a note about pocket canons

The Authorized King James Version of the Bible, translated between 1603 and 1611, coincided with an extraordinary flowering of English literature. This version, more than any other, and possibly more than any other work in history, has had an influence in shaping the language we speak and write today. Presenting individual books from the Bible as separate volumes, as they were originally conceived, encourages the reader to approach them as literary works in their own right.

The first twelve books in this series encompass categories as diverse as history, fiction, philosophy, love poetry, and law. Each Pocket Canon also has its own introduction, specially commissioned from an impressive range of writers, which provides a personal interpretation of the text and explores its contemporary relevance.

Darcey Steinke is the author of the novels Up Through the Water, Suicide Blonde, *and* Jesus Saves. *She has also edited a collection of essays with Rick Moody entitled* Joyful Noise: The New Testament Revisited. *Her journalism has appeared in* Spin, George, The Guardian (*London*), Artforum, The Village Voice, *and* The Oxford American. *She lives in Brooklyn, New York, with her husband and daughter.*

introduction by darcey steinke

A stranger once showed up at my father's church during a Sunday potluck supper. The parishioners had just filled their plates with lumps of tuna-fish casserole and Jell-O salad when a man with a white beard came to the back door, stood in the foyer, and ceremoniously unfolded a piece of paper. With a heavy German accent he read his birth date, his parents' names, and the name of the town where he'd been born seventy-seven years earlier, just outside Berlin.

My father jumped up from where we sat at the head table. He was about thirty then, blond, and lean in his black clerical suit. I was six years old and had never seen anyone so jittery and upset. Over and over, the old German repeated his birth date and asked if my father had known his mother, the lovely Berta from Frankfurt. He seemed unsure of his own existence and wanted my father to keep the birth certificate as proof that he was alive. The overhead fluorescent lights slickened the white cement-block walls and made the old German look even more exotic in the confines of the church basement. The man refused to stay and eat, though as he left he seemed calmed by the fact my father had taken down the directions to his house and promised to drive out to visit him the following day.

I waited on the front steps of the parsonage for my father to return from visiting the old German. The cement steps were lined with wrought-iron railings, and as I watched my father through the black latticework get out of the station wagon and walk toward me, I could tell he was discombobulated. His black trench coat swung down from his narrow shoulders, and the way he let his arms dangle at his sides suggested that he was slightly unhinged.

"Is the man lonely?" I asked, grasping at his cold fingers and standing up.

"Yes," my father replied, "the man is very lonely."

I could tell my father was withholding information, so I followed him inside the house. But he was preoccupied and headed immediately downstairs to talk to my mother, who was loading clothes into the washing machine. I pretended to walk upstairs to my room, but then tiptoed back and stood with my ear inside the cracked basement door and listened as my father told my mother that the German's house had been filthy and teaming with cats, that he'd referred to magazine clippings of children as his daughters and to the naked department store mannequin sitting at his kitchen table as his wife.

I'd never heard such a thing! The German was like a character in a fairy tale, a wizard setting up his magic trick, or Cinderella's fairy godmother turning a pumpkin into a carriage and white mice into thoroughbreds. I was young enough to believe that miracles were possible and I understood the need for a lot of cats, but what was wrong with pretending your doll was your wife if you were feeling lonely and just wanted a friend? The old German was sort of like Jesus, a loner, an essentially sad character, never satisfied with reality, always trying to break into the spiritual world.

Dark skinned and hairless, Jesus' thin body hung half dead on the cross in our kitchen like a changeling, someone who could take you to a better place. And like the German, Jesus was also freaky and out of control. I could always tell my mother disapproved of Jesus' behavior; she'd stiffen up as my father read about him changing water into wine and helping prostitutes.

I wanted to see where the old man lived and, though he insisted I wait in the car during the visit, my father let me ride along with him the following week. I was hoping for a derelict gingerbread house, a mailbox shaped like a swan, or kittens that could say the alphabet, some sign that the German did indeed have magical powers, so I was disappointed by the tilted front porch and the cat with sick eyes curled up on the broken-down recliner. The glass panes of the front window were splintered, so that the curtains inside showed brown patches of water damage.

My father left the car running, heat blew up from under the dashboard, and I played with the radio dial, hoping to find the latest Beatles single, "I Want to Hold Your Hand." After knocking on the front door, my father motioned to me that he was going to walk around the back of the house. I watched him disappear around the corner of the building, carrying his traveling communion kit, with velvet nooks for the silver goblet and the tin of dove-stamped wafers. I had just learned in grade school that the planets revolved around the sun, and this fact filled me with admiration for God. What a concept! Gigantic brilliantly colored balls flying around a fireball for all eternity! So I sat there for some time, trying to imagine the earth spinning through space. After a while, when I couldn't convince myself any longer that the car was moving like a rocket ship, I thought about how hard it was going to be to find that one person meant just for me, and then I thought about God's son, Jesus; how if God hadn't sent him down to the earth and if Jesus hadn't told his disciples to love one another, I wouldn't even be sitting here in this car with hot air blowing on my knees waiting for a Beatles song to come on the radio.

I was so preoccupied that I hadn't seen my father walking back to the car, and as he yanked opened the door, I pulled my legs from where I had them sprawled out dreamily over his seat. I could tell by his countenance, shoulders raised, his face drained of all color, that he was angry at me.

"What happened, Daddy?" I asked him.

"It's not you, sweetie," he said, "it's Mr. Kleinburg." I could see him ordering his words. "He's dead."

"Maybe Mr. Kleinburg is just sleeping," I suggested.

My father gripped the steering wheel, his knuckles whitened, and he jerked his head forward, opened his mouth, and gagged. This surprised me so much I decided to stay quiet and thought about Mr. Kleinburg reading from his birth certificate, how he'd been right to worry over his own existence.

Once back on the highway, we stopped at a gas station to call the police. My father dropped me off at home, then drove back to Mr. Kleinburg's house. Late that night, when my father finally got home, I stood outside my parents' bedroom and listened to him detail the suicide scene: blood and tissue splattered up over the magazine pictures of his daughters, the chair flung backward, his body curled sideways on the ground, a shotgun between his legs. His chin was gone.

This fact seemed to upset my father the most. His voice thickened up as it did when he read from the passion on Good Friday. I was so stunned I can still remember the texture of the latex paint on the bedroom door and the sound of branches scraping against the side of the house as I listened to my father's story. The elements of Mr. Kleinburg's suicide—the shotgun, the blood-splattered magazine pictures, the tipped chair—were as vivid to me as Jesus' crown of thorns, his fake king's robe, the vinegar-soaked sponge.

The cadence of my father's first-person account—still quaking from a brush with fanaticism and death—reminds me of John's eyewitness Gospel account of Jesus, and listening to my father's story about the German puts me in the same configuration as someone reading John's version of the life of Christ. John is unique among the Gospels because of the narrator's claim that he witnessed Jesus' life and death. This immediacy and intimacy of detail configures Jesus as a charismatic young radical. Teasing his friend Nathanael about being too enthusiastic about his divinity, Jesus says, "Just because I said unto thee I saw you under the fig tree, believist though? Though shall see greater things than these." Jesus' first miracle in chapter 2 is an aesthetic and rather groovy one; he changes water into wine. Later in that same chapter he commits an act of social anarchy worthy of any '60s revolutionary: making a scourge out of small cords, Jesus drives the money changers out of the temple. But unlike Che Guevara, whose demeanor and public agenda seem close to Jesus', the hero of the Gospels has a trump card to play: supernatural power.

This effusion of magic makes the atmosphere of John hallucinatory: it's the Gospel in which Jesus appears most like the brother from another planet. Structured like an *X-Files* episode, Jesus, a magnetic thirty-three-year-old, claims to be from his father's house in the sky. He performs a variety of trippy miracles—raising Lazarus from the dead, making a few loaves of bread and a couple of fish feed five thousand, and reattaching a severed ear—all the while speaking in cryptic parables about the urgency of the spiritual realm. When attacked by dark governmental forces, he gives up his corporeal envelope and makes a last ghostly appearance before ascending up to the mother ship.

Even the language in John can be as bizarre and distended as a channeled message. "On the next day much people that were come to the feast . . ." and " . . . where was a garden, into the which he entered and his disciples." The staccato rhythm and off-key cadence of these lines signify language operating under intense duress. These words pushed to the edge of comprehension remind me of the time my sister-in-law called to tell us about her husband's death. My own husband's eyes widened as he pulled his mouth away from the phone receiver and said, "Steve gunned himself in the head and then died." Reality was punctured and words were wrestled into configurations to bind together the incision. Shocked syntax straining toward understanding is the stylistic signature of John's prose. Above all the other Gospel writers, John values language. In the beginning he claims, *before everything else,* was the Word, and for him the Word and God are synonymous.

As a little girl listening through my parents' door while my father told the story of the German's demise, I craved *words*. All humans do, especially at that high level of narrative intensity. There is a great power in the authenticity of an eyewitness account, and as humans we also need witnesses—the German wanted my father to witness his lonely death. But even as we listen to the concrete details on the nightly news of the Oklahoma City bombing or the atrocities in Bosnia, or more personal stories of a friend's grandmother's final hour, or the birth of our brother's baby son, even as our emotions attach to the participant's pain or joy, nothing is really cleared up. Instead, mystery takes root inside of us.

Mystery in John is evoked on two levels: the fact that Jesus may actually be a messenger sent by the creator and, more mundanely but no less fascinating, the mysteries intrinsic in the intricacies of Jesus' own character. The evocation of the latter is the real strength of John. John's voice is intimate and urgent. He tells us the story of his crazy fanatical friend, but unlike my father's bleak suicide narrative, unlike any of the sacred human narratives that relay details of pain, death, and violence, John's story claims to contain particles of divinity. That's the message which vaults his account over all other biographies; Jesus was a fenestral opening, a direct communiqué from God. John's narrative affects us viscerally because Jesus' effect on him was so devastating and sublime that all these centuries later, through his unshored and hyperbolic prose, we can still get a contact high.

the gospel according to st john

In the beginning was the Word, and the Word was with God,
and the Word was God. 2 The same was in the beginning
with God. 3 All things were made by him; and without him
was not any thing made that was made. 4 In him was life;
and the life was the light of men. 5 And the light shineth in
darkness; and the darkness comprehended it not.

6 There was a man sent from God, whose name was John.
7 The same came for a witness, to bear witness of the Light,
that all men through him might believe. 8 He was not that
Light, but was sent to bear witness of that Light. 9 That was
the true Light, which lighteth every man that cometh into
the world. 10 He was in the world, and the world was made
by him, and the world knew him not. 11 He came unto his own,
and his own received him not. 12 But as many as received
him, to them gave he power to become the sons of God, even
to them that believe on his name, 13 which were born, not of
blood, nor of the will of the flesh, nor of the will of man, but
of God. 14 And the Word was made flesh, and dwelt among
us (and we beheld his glory, the glory as of the only begotten
of the Father), full of grace and truth.

15 John bare witness of him, and cried, saying, 'This was
he of whom I spake, "He that cometh after me is preferred
before me, for he was before me."' 16 And of his fulness have

all we received, and grace for grace. 17 For the law was given
by Moses, but grace and truth came by Jesus Christ. 18 No
man hath seen God at any time; the only begotten Son,
which is in the bosom of the Father, he hath declared him.

19 And this is the record of John, when the Jews sent
priests and Levites from Jerusalem to ask him, 'Who art
thou?' 20 And he confessed, and denied not; but confessed, 'I
am not the Christ.' 21 And they asked him, 'What then? Art
thou Elias?' And he saith, 'I am not.' 'Art thou that prophet?'
And he answered, 'No.' 22 Then said they unto him, 'Who art
thou? That we may give an answer to them that sent us.
What sayest thou of thyself?' 23 He said, 'I am the voice of
one crying in the wilderness, "Make straight the way of the
Lord,"' as said the prophet Esaias. 24 And they which were
sent were of the Pharisees. 25 And they asked him, and said
unto him, 'Why baptizest thou then, if thou be not that
Christ, nor Elias, neither that prophet?' 26 John answered
them, saying, 'I baptize with water, but there standeth one
among you, whom ye know not. 27 He it is, who coming after
me is preferred before me, whose shoe's latchet I am not
worthy to unloose.' 28 These things were done in Bethabara
beyond Jordan, where John was baptizing.

29 The next day John seeth Jesus coming unto him, and
saith, 'Behold the Lamb of God, which taketh away the sin of
the world. 30 This is he of whom I said, "After me cometh a
man which is preferred before me: for he was before me."
31 And I knew him not: but that he should be made manifest
to Israel, therefore am I come baptizing with water.' 32 And
John bare record, saying, 'I saw the Spirit descending from

heaven like a dove, and it abode upon him. 33And I knew
him not: but he that sent me to baptize with water, the same
said unto me, "Upon whom thou shalt see the Spirit descending, and remaining on him, the same is he which baptizeth
with the Holy Ghost." 34And I saw, and bare record that this
is the Son of God.'

35Again the next day after John stood, and two of his disciples; 36 and looking upon Jesus as he walked, he saith, 'Behold
the Lamb of God!' 37And the two disciples heard him speak,
and they followed Jesus. 38 Then Jesus turned, and saw them
following, and saith unto them, 'What seek ye?' They said
unto him, 'Rabbi (which is to say, being interpreted, Master),
where dwellest thou?' 39 He saith unto them, 'Come and see.
They came and saw where he dwelt, and abode with him
that day, for it was about the tenth hour.' 40 One of the two
which heard John speak, and followed him, was Andrew,
Simon Peter's brother. 41 He first findeth his own brother
Simon, and saith unto him, 'We have found the Messias,
which is, being interpreted, the Christ.' 42And he brought
him to Jesus. And when Jesus beheld him, he said, 'Thou art
Simon the son of Jona: thou shalt be called Cephas, which is
by interpretation, a stone.'

43 The day following Jesus would go forth into Galilee, and
findeth Philip, and saith unto him, 'Follow me.' 44 Now Philip
was of Bethsaida, the city of Andrew and Peter. 45 Philip findeth Nathanael, and saith unto him, 'We have found him, of
whom Moses in the law, and the prophets, did write: Jesus
of Nazareth, the son of Joseph.' 46And Nathanael said unto
him, 'Can there any good thing come out of Nazareth?' Philip

saith unto him, 'Come and see.' 47 Jesus saw Nathanael coming to him, and saith of him, 'Behold an Israelite indeed, in
whom is no guile!' 48 Nathanael saith unto him, 'Whence
knowest thou me?' Jesus answered and said unto him, 'Before
that Philip called thee, when thou wast under the fig tree, I
saw thee.' 49 Nathanael answered and saith unto him, 'Rabbi,
thou art the Son of God; thou art the King of Israel.' 50 Jesus
answered and said unto him, 'Because I said unto thee, I saw
thee under the fig tree, believest thou? Thou shalt see greater
things than these.' 51 And he saith unto him, 'Verily, verily, I say
unto you, hereafter ye shall see heaven open, and the angels
of God ascending and descending upon the Son of man.'

2 And the third day there was a marriage in Cana of Galilee; and the mother of Jesus was there, 2 and both Jesus
was called, and his disciples, to the marriage. 3 And when
they wanted wine, the mother of Jesus saith unto him, 'They
have no wine.' 4 Jesus saith unto her, 'Woman, what have I to
do with thee? Mine hour is not yet come.' 5 His mother saith
unto the servants, 'Whatsoever he saith unto you, do it.'
6 And there were set there six waterpots of stone, after the
manner of the purifying of the Jews, containing two or three
firkins apiece. 7 Jesus saith unto them, 'Fill the waterpots
with water.' And they filled them up to the brim. 8 And he
saith unto them, 'Draw out now, and bear unto the governor
of the feast.' And they bare it. 9 When the ruler of the feast
had tasted the water that was made wine, and knew not
whence it was (but the servants which drew the water knew),
the governor of the feast called the bridegroom, 10 and saith

unto him, 'Every man at the beginning doth set forth good
wine; and when men have well drunk, then that which is
worse: but thou hast kept the good wine until now.' [11]This
beginning of miracles did Jesus in Cana of Galilee, and manifested forth his glory; and his disciples believed on him.

[12]After this he went down to Capernaum, he, and his
mother, and his brethren, and his disciples, and they continued there not many days.

[13]And the Jews' passover was at hand, and Jesus went up
to Jerusalem, [14]and found in the temple those that sold oxen
and sheep and doves, and the changers of money sitting:
[15]and when he had made a scourge of small cords, he drove
them all out of the temple, and the sheep, and the oxen; and
poured out the changers' money, and overthrew the tables;
[16]and said unto them that sold doves, 'Take these things
hence; make not my Father's house an house of merchandise.' [17]And his disciples remembered that it was written,
'The zeal of thine house hath eaten me up.'

[18]Then answered the Jews and said unto him, 'What sign
shewest thou unto us, seeing that thou doest these things?'
[19]Jesus answered and said unto them, 'Destroy this temple,
and in three days I will raise it up.' [20]Then said the Jews, 'Forty
and six years was this temple in building, and wilt thou rear
it up in three days?' [21]But he spake of the temple of his body.
[22]When therefore he was risen from the dead, his disciples
remembered that he had said this unto them; and they
believed the scripture, and the word which Jesus had said.

[23]Now when he was in Jerusalem at the passover, in the
feast day, many believed in his name, when they saw the

miracles which he did. 24 But Jesus did not commit himself
unto them, because he knew all men, 25 and needed not that
any should testify of man, for he knew what was in man.

3 There was a man of the Pharisees, named Nicodemus, a
ruler of the Jews. 2 The same came to Jesus by night, and
said unto him, 'Rabbi, we know that thou art a teacher come
from God, for no man can do these miracles that thou doest,
except God be with him.' 3 Jesus answered and said unto
him, 'Verily, verily, I say unto thee, except a man be born
again, he cannot see the kingdom of God.' 4 Nicodemus saith
unto him, 'How can a man be born when he is old? Can he
enter the second time into his mother's womb, and be born?'
5 Jesus answered, 'Verily, verily, I say unto thee, except a man
be born of water and of the Spirit, he cannot enter into the
kingdom of God. 6 That which is born of the flesh is flesh;
and that which is born of the Spirit is spirit. 7 Marvel not that
I said unto thee, ye must be born again.' 8 The wind bloweth
where it listeth, and thou hearest the sound thereof, but canst
not tell whence it cometh, and whither it goeth: so is every
one that is born of the Spirit.' 9 Nicodemus answered and said
unto him, 'How can these things be?' 10 Jesus answered and
said unto him, 'Art thou a master of Israel, and knowest not
these things? 11 Verily, verily, I say unto thee, we speak that we
do know, and testify that we have seen; and ye receive not
our witness. 12 If I have told you earthly things, and ye believe
not, how shall ye believe, if I tell you of heavenly things?
13 And no man hath ascended up to heaven, but he that came
down from heaven, even the Son of man which is in heaven.

14 'And as Moses lifted up the serpent in the wilderness,
even so must the Son of man be lifted up: 15 that whosoever
believeth in him should not perish, but have eternal life.

16 'For God so loved the world, that he gave his only begotten Son, that whosoever believeth in him should not perish,
but have everlasting life. 17 For God sent not his Son into the
world to condemn the world; but that the world through
him might be saved.

18 'He that believeth on him is not condemned: but he
that believeth not is condemned already, because he hath not
believed in the name of the only begotten Son of God. 19 And
this is the condemnation, that light is come into the world,
and men loved darkness rather than light, because their deeds
were evil. 20 For every one that doeth evil hateth the light, neither cometh to the light, lest his deeds should be reproved.
21 But he that doeth truth cometh to the light, that his deeds
may be made manifest, that they are wrought in God.'

22 After these things came Jesus and his disciples into the
land of Judæa; and there he tarried with them, and baptized.

23 And John also was baptizing in Ænon near to Salim,
because there was much water there, and they came, and were
baptized. 24 For John was not yet cast into prison.

25 Then there arose a question between some of John's disciples and the Jews about purifying. 26 And they came unto
John, and said unto him, 'Rabbi, he that was with thee beyond
Jordan, to whom thou barest witness, behold, the same baptizeth, and all men come to him.' 27 John answered and said,
'A man can receive nothing, except it be given him from
heaven. 28 Ye yourselves bear me witness, that I said, "I am

not the Christ," but that I am sent before him. 29 He that hath
the bride is the bridegroom, but the friend of the bridegroom, which standeth and heareth him, rejoiceth greatly
because of the bridegroom's voice: this my joy therefore is
fulfilled. 30 He must increase, but I must decrease. 31 He that
cometh from above is above all; he that is of the earth is
earthly, and speaketh of the earth; he that cometh from heaven
is above all. 32 And what he hath seen and heard, that he testifieth; and no man receiveth his testimony. 33 He that hath
received his testimony hath set to his seal that God is true.
34 For he whom God hath sent speaketh the words of God,
for God giveth not the Spirit by measure unto him. 35 The
Father loveth the Son, and hath given all things into his
hand. 36 He that believeth on the Son hath everlasting life,
and he that believeth not the Son shall not see life; but the
wrath of God abideth on him.'

4 When therefore the Lord knew how the Pharisees had
heard that Jesus made and baptized more disciples than
John 2 (though Jesus himself baptized not, but his disciples),
3 he left Judæa, and departed again into Galilee. 4 And he must
needs go through Samaria. 5 Then cometh he to a city of Samaria, which is called Sychar, near to the parcel of ground that
Jacob gave to his son Joseph. 6 Now Jacob's well was there.
Jesus therefore, being wearied with his journey, sat thus on
the well, and it was about the sixth hour. 7 There cometh a
woman of Samaria to draw water. Jesus saith unto her, 'Give
me to drink.' 8 (For his disciples were gone away unto the city
to buy meat.) 9 Then saith the woman of Samaria unto him,

'How is it that thou, being a Jew, askest drink of me, which
am a woman of Samaria?' For the Jews have no dealings
with the Samaritans. 10 Jesus answered and said unto her, 'If
thou knewest the gift of God, and who it is that saith to thee,
"Give me to drink," thou wouldest have asked of him, and
he would have given thee living water.' 11 The woman saith
unto him, 'Sir, thou hast nothing to draw with, and the well
is deep; from whence then hast thou that living water? 12 Art
thou greater than our father Jacob, which gave us the well,
and drank thereof himself, and his children, and his cattle?'
13 Jesus answered and said unto her, 'Whosoever drinketh of
this water shall thirst again: 14 but whosoever drinketh of the
water that I shall give him shall never thirst; but the water
that I shall give him shall be in him a well of water springing
up into everlasting life.' 15 The woman saith unto him, 'Sir,
give me this water, that I thirst not, neither come hither to
draw.' 16 Jesus saith unto her, 'Go, call thy husband, and come
hither.' 17 The woman answered and said, 'I have no husband.'
Jesus said unto her, 'Thou hast well said, "I have no husband," 18 for thou hast had five husbands; and he whom thou
now hast is not thy husband; in that saidst thou truly.' 19 The
woman saith unto him, 'Sir, I perceive that thou art a prophet.
20 Our fathers worshipped in this mountain; and ye say, that
in Jerusalem is the place where men ought to worship.'
21 Jesus saith unto her, 'Woman, believe me, the hour cometh,
when ye shall neither in this mountain, nor yet at Jerusalem,
worship the Father. 22 Ye worship ye know not what: we
know what we worship, for salvation is of the Jews. 23 But
the hour cometh, and now is, when the true worshippers

shall worship the Father in spirit and in truth, for the Father seeketh such to worship him. 24 God is a Spirit, and they that worship him must worship him in spirit and in truth.' 25 The woman saith unto him, 'I know that Messias cometh, which is called Christ: when he is come, he will tell us all things.' 26 Jesus saith unto her, 'I that speak unto thee am he.'

27 And upon this came his disciples, and marvelled that he talked with the woman; yet no man said, 'What seekest thou?' or 'Why talkest thou with her?' 28 The woman then left her waterpot, and went her way into the city, and saith to the men, 29 'Come, see a man, which told me all things that ever I did: is not this the Christ?' 30 Then they went out of the city, and came unto him.

31 In the mean while his disciples prayed him, saying, 'Master, eat.' 32 But he said unto them, 'I have meat to eat that ye know not of.' 33 Therefore said the disciples one to another, 'Hath any man brought him ought to eat?' 34 Jesus saith unto them, 'My meat is to do the will of him that sent me, and to finish his work. 35 Say not ye, "There are yet four months, and then cometh harvest"? Behold, I say unto you, lift up your eyes, and look on the fields: for they are white already to harvest. 36 And he that reapeth receiveth wages, and gathereth fruit unto life eternal, that both he that soweth and he that reapeth may rejoice together. 37 And herein is that saying true, "One soweth, and another reapeth." 38 I sent you to reap that whereon ye bestowed no labour; other men laboured, and ye are entered into their labours.'

39 And many of the Samaritans of that city believed on him for the saying of the woman, which testified, 'He told

me all that ever I did.' 40 So when the Samaritans were come
unto him, they besought him that he would tarry with them,
and he abode there two days. 41 And many more believed
because of his own word; 42 and said unto the woman, 'Now
we believe, not because of thy saying, for we have heard him
ourselves, and know that this is indeed the Christ, the Saviour of the world.'

43 Now after two days he departed thence, and went into
Galilee. 44 For Jesus himself testified that a prophet hath no
honour in his own country. 45 Then when he was come into
Galilee, the Galilæans received him, having seen all the
things that he did at Jerusalem at the feast, for they also
went unto the feast. 46 So Jesus came again into Cana of
Galilee, where he made the water wine. And there was a certain nobleman, whose son was sick at Capernaum. 47 When
he heard that Jesus was come out of Judæa into Galilee, he
went unto him, and besought him that he would come
down, and heal his son, for he was at the point of death.
48 Then said Jesus unto him, 'Except ye see signs and wonders, ye will not believe.' 49 The nobleman saith unto him,
'Sir, come down ere my child die.' 50 Jesus saith unto him,
'Go thy way; thy son liveth.' And the man believed the word
that Jesus had spoken unto him, and he went his way. 51 And
as he was now going down, his servants met him, and told
him, saying, 'Thy son liveth.' 52 Then enquired he of them the
hour when he began to amend. And they said unto him,
'Yesterday at the seventh hour the fever left him.' 53 So the
father knew that it was at the same hour, in the which Jesus
said unto him, 'Thy son liveth,' and himself believed, and his

whole house. 54 This is again the second miracle that Jesus
did, when he was come out of Judæa into Galilee.

5 After this there was a feast of the Jews; and Jesus went
up to Jerusalem. 2 Now there is at Jerusalem by the sheep
market a pool, which is called in the Hebrew tongue Beth-
esda, having five porches. 3 In these lay a great multitude of
impotent folk, of blind, halt, withered, waiting for the moving of the water. 4 For an angel went down at a certain season into the pool, and troubled the water: whosoever then
first after the troubling of the water stepped in was made
whole of whatsoever disease he had. 5 And a certain man was
there, which had an infirmity thirty and eight years. 6 When
Jesus saw him lie, and knew that he had been now a long time
in that case, he saith unto him, 'Wilt thou be made whole?'
7 The impotent man answered him, 'Sir, I have no man, when
the water is troubled, to put me into the pool: but while I am
coming, another steppeth down before me.' 8 Jesus saith unto
him, 'Rise, take up thy bed, and walk.' 9 And immediately the
man was made whole, and took up his bed, and walked; and
on the same day was the sabbath.

10 The Jews therefore said unto him that was cured, 'It is
the sabbath day: it is not lawful for thee to carry thy bed.'
11 He answered them, 'He that made me whole, the same said
unto me, "Take up thy bed, and walk."' 12 Then asked they
him, 'What man is that which said unto thee, "Take up thy
bed, and walk?"' 13 And he that was healed wist not who it
was, for Jesus had conveyed himself away, a multitude being
in that place. 14 Afterward Jesus findeth him in the temple,

and said unto him, 'Behold, thou art made whole; sin no more, lest a worse thing come unto thee.' 15 The man departed, and told the Jews that it was Jesus, which had made him whole. 16 And therefore did the Jews persecute Jesus, and sought to slay him, because he had done these things on the sabbath day.

17 But Jesus answered them, 'My Father worketh hitherto, and I work.' 18 Therefore the Jews sought the more to kill him, because he not only had broken the sabbath, but said also that God was his Father, making himself equal with God. 19 Then answered Jesus and said unto them, 'Verily, verily, I say unto you, the Son can do nothing of himself, but what he seeth the Father do: for what things soever he doeth, these also doeth the Son likewise. 20 For the Father loveth the Son, and sheweth him all things that himself doeth, and he will shew him greater works than these, that ye may marvel. 21 For as the Father raiseth up the dead, and quickeneth them; even so the Son quickeneth whom he will. 22 For the Father judgeth no man, but hath committed all judgment unto the Son, 23 that all men should honour the Son, even as they honour the Father. He that honoureth not the Son honoureth not the Father which hath sent him. 24 Verily, verily, I say unto you, he that heareth my word, and believeth on him that sent me, hath everlasting life, and shall not come into condemnation; but is passed from death unto life. 25 Verily, verily, I say unto you, the hour is coming, and now is, when the dead shall hear the voice of the Son of God, and they that hear shall live. 26 For as the Father hath life in himself; so hath he given to the Son to have life in himself; 27 and hath

given him authority to execute judgment also, because he is
the Son of man. [28] Marvel not at this, for the hour is coming,
in the which all that are in the graves shall hear his voice,
[29] and shall come forth; they that have done good, unto the
resurrection of life; and they that have done evil, unto the
resurrection of damnation. [30] I can of mine own self do nothing: as I hear, I judge, and my judgment is just; because I
seek not mine own will, but the will of the Father which hath
sent me. [31] If I bear witness of myself, my witness is not true.

[32] 'There is another that beareth witness of me; and I know
that the witness which he witnesseth of me is true. [33] Ye sent
unto John, and he bare witness unto the truth. [34] But I receive
not testimony from man: but these things I say, that ye might
be saved. [35] He was a burning and a shining light, and ye were
willing for a season to rejoice in his light.

[36] 'But I have greater witness than that of John: for the
works which the Father hath given me to finish, the same
works that I do, bear witness of me, that the Father hath sent
me. [37] And the Father himself, which hath sent me, hath borne
witness of me. Ye have neither heard his voice at any time,
nor seen his shape. [38] And ye have not his word abiding in
you: for whom he hath sent, him ye believe not.

[39] 'Search the scriptures, for in them ye think ye have eternal life: and they are they which testify of me. [40] And ye will
not come to me, that ye might have life. [41] I receive not honour from men. [42] But I know you, that ye have not the love of
God in you. [43] I am come in my Father's name, and ye receive
me not; if another shall come in his own name, him ye will
receive. [44] How can ye believe, which receive honour one of

another, and seek not the honour that cometh from God only?
45 Do not think that I will accuse you to the Father: there is
one that accuseth you, even Moses, in whom ye trust. 46 For
had ye believed Moses, ye would have believed me: for he
wrote of me. 47 But if ye believe not his writings, how shall ye
believe my words?'

6 After these things Jesus went over the sea of Galilee,
which is the sea of Tiberias. 2 And a great multitude followed him, because they saw his miracles which he did on
them that were diseased. 3 And Jesus went up into a mountain, and there he sat with his disciples. 4 And the passover, a
feast of the Jews, was nigh.

5 When Jesus then lifted up his eyes, and saw a great company come unto him, he saith unto Philip, 'Whence shall we
buy bread, that these may eat?' 6 And this he said to prove
him, for he himself knew what he would do. 7 Philip answered
him, 'Two hundred pennyworth of bread is not sufficient for
them, that every one of them may take a little.' 8 One of his
disciples, Andrew, Simon Peter's brother, saith unto him,
9 'There is a lad here, which hath five barley loaves, and two
small fishes, but what are they among so many?' 10 And Jesus
said, 'Make the men sit down.' Now there was much grass in
the place. So the men sat down, in number about five thousand. 11 And Jesus took the loaves; and when he had given
thanks, he distributed to the disciples, and the disciples to
them that were set down; and likewise of the fishes as much
as they would. 12 When they were filled, he said unto his disciples, 'Gather up the fragments that remain, that nothing be

lost.' [13]Therefore they gathered them together, and filled
twelve baskets with the fragments of the five barley loaves,
which remained over and above unto them that had eaten.
[14]Then those men, when they had seen the miracle that Jesus
did, said, 'This is of a truth that prophet that should come
into the world.'

[15]When Jesus therefore perceived that they would come
and take him by force, to make him a king, he departed again
into a mountain himself alone. [16]And when even was now
come, his disciples went down unto the sea, [17]and entered
into a ship, and went over the sea toward Capernaum. And
it was now dark, and Jesus was not come to them. [18]And the
sea arose by reason of a great wind that blew. [19]So when they
had rowed about five and twenty or thirty furlongs, they see
Jesus walking on the sea, and drawing nigh unto the ship,
and they were afraid. [20]But he saith unto them, 'It is I; be not
afraid.' [21]Then they willingly received him into the ship, and
immediately the ship was at the land whither they went.

[22]The day following, when the people which stood on
the other side of the sea saw that there was none other boat
there, save that one whereinto his disciples were entered,
and that Jesus went not with his disciples into the boat, but
that his disciples were gone away alone. [23](Howbeit there
came other boats from Tiberias nigh unto the place where
they did eat bread, after that the Lord had given thanks.)
[24]When the people therefore saw that Jesus was not there,
neither his disciples, they also took shipping, and came to
Capernaum, seeking for Jesus. [25]And when they had found
him on the other side of the sea, they said unto him, 'Rabbi,

when camest thou hither?' 26 Jesus answered them and said,
'Verily, verily, I say unto you, ye seek me, not because ye
saw the miracles, but because ye did eat of the loaves, and
were filled. 27 Labour not for the meat which perisheth, but
for that meat which endureth unto everlasting life, which
the Son of man shall give unto you: for him hath God the
Father sealed.' 28 Then said they unto him, 'What shall we do,
that we might work the works of God?' 29 Jesus answered
and said unto them, 'This is the work of God, that ye believe
on him whom he hath sent.' 30 They said therefore unto him,
'What sign shewest thou then, that we may see, and believe
thee? What dost thou work? 31 Our fathers did eat manna in
the desert; as it is written, "He gave them bread from heaven
to eat."' 32 Then Jesus said unto them, 'Verily, verily, I say
unto you, Moses gave you not that bread from heaven; but
my Father giveth you the true bread from heaven. 33 For the
bread of God is he which cometh down from heaven, and
giveth life unto the world.' 34 Then said they unto him, 'Lord,
evermore give us this bread.' 35 And Jesus said unto them, 'I
am the bread of life: he that cometh to me shall never hunger;
and he that believeth on me shall never thirst. 36 But I said
unto you that ye also have seen me, and believe not. 37 All
that the Father giveth me shall come to me; and him that
cometh to me I will in no wise cast out. 38 For I came down
from heaven, not to do mine own will, but the will of him
that sent me. 39 And this is the Father's will which hath sent
me: that of all which he hath given me I should lose nothing,
but should raise it up again at the last day. 40 And this is the
will of him that sent me: that every one which seeth the Son,

and believeth on him, may have everlasting life, and I will
raise him up at the last day.' 41 The Jews then murmured at
him, because he said, 'I am the bread which came down from
heaven.' 42 And they said, 'Is not this Jesus, the son of Joseph,
whose father and mother we know? How is it then that he
saith, "I came down from heaven"?' 43 Jesus therefore answered
and said unto them, 'Murmur not among yourselves. 44 No
man can come to me, except the Father which hath sent me
draw him, and I will raise him up at the last day. 45 It is written in the prophets, "And they shall be all taught of God."
Every man therefore that hath heard, and hath learned of the
Father, cometh unto me. 46 Not that any man hath seen the
Father, save he which is of God, he hath seen the Father.
47 Verily, verily, I say unto you, he that believeth on me hath
everlasting life. 48 I am that bread of life. 49 Your fathers did
eat manna in the wilderness, and are dead. 50 This is the bread
which cometh down from heaven, that a man may eat thereof,
and not die. 51 I am the living bread which came down from
heaven: if any man eat of this bread, he shall live for ever;
and the bread that I will give is my flesh, which I will give
for the life of the world.' 52 The Jews therefore strove among
themselves, saying, 'How can this man give us his flesh to
eat?' 53 Then Jesus said unto them, 'Verily, verily, I say unto
you, except ye eat the flesh of the Son of man, and drink his
blood, ye have no life in you. 54 Whoso eateth my flesh, and
drinketh my blood, hath eternal life; and I will raise him up
at the last day. 55 For my flesh is meat indeed, and my blood
is drink indeed. 56 He that eateth my flesh, and drinketh my
blood, dwelleth in me, and I in him. 57 As the living Father

hath sent me, and I live by the Father, so he that eateth me,
even he shall live by me. 58 This is that bread which came
down from heaven: not as your fathers did eat manna, and
are dead. He that eateth of this bread shall live for ever.'
59 These things said he in the synagogue, as he taught in
Capernaum. 60 Many therefore of his disciples, when they
had heard this, said, 'This is an hard saying; who can hear
it?' 61 When Jesus knew in himself that his disciples murmured at it, he said unto them, 'Doth this offend you? 62 What
and if ye shall see the Son of man ascend up where he was
before? 63 It is the spirit that quickeneth; the flesh profiteth
nothing; the words that I speak unto you, they are spirit, and
they are life. 64 But there are some of you that believe not.'
For Jesus knew from the beginning who they were that believed not, and who should betray him. 65 And he said,
'Therefore said I unto you, that no man can come unto me,
except it were given unto him of my Father.'

66 From that time many of his disciples went back, and
walked no more with him. 67 Then said Jesus unto the twelve,
'Will ye also go away?' 68 Then Simon Peter answered him,
'Lord, to whom shall we go? Thou hast the words of eternal
life. 69 And we believe and are sure that thou art that Christ,
the Son of the living God.' 70 Jesus answered them, 'Have not
I chosen you twelve, and one of you is a devil?' 71 He spake
of Judas Iscariot the son of Simon: for he it was that should
betray him, being one of the twelve.

7 After these things Jesus walked in Galilee: for he would
not walk in Jewry, because the Jews sought to kill him.

2 Now the Jews' feast of tabernacles was at hand. 3 His brethren therefore said unto him, 'Depart hence, and go into
Judæa, that thy disciples also may see the works that thou
doest. 4 For there is no man that doeth any thing in secret,
and he himself seeketh to be known openly. If thou do these
things, shew thyself to the world.' 5 For neither did his brethren believe in him. 6 Then Jesus said unto them, 'My time is
not yet come, but your time is alway ready. 7 The world cannot hate you; but me it hateth, because I testify of it, that the
works thereof are evil. 8 Go ye up unto this feast. I go not up
yet unto this feast; for my time is not yet full come.' 9 When
he had said these words unto them, he abode still in Galilee.

10 But when his brethren were gone up, then went he also
up unto the feast, not openly, but as it were in secret. 11 Then
the Jews sought him at the feast, and said, 'Where is he?'
12 And there was much murmuring among the people concerning him, for some said, 'He is a good man,' others said,
'Nay; but he deceiveth the people.' 13 Howbeit no man spake
openly of him for fear of the Jews.

14 Now about the midst of the feast Jesus went up into the
temple, and taught. 15 And the Jews marvelled, saying, 'How
knoweth this man letters, having never learned?' 16 Jesus
answered them, and said, 'My doctrine is not mine, but his
that sent me. 17 If any man will do his will, he shall know of
the doctrine, whether it be of God, or whether I speak of
myself. 18 He that speaketh of himself seeketh his own glory:
but he that seeketh his glory that sent him, the same is true,
and no unrighteousness is in him. 19 Did not Moses give you
the law, and yet none of you keepeth the law? Why go ye

about to kill me?' 20 The people answered and said, 'Thou
hast a devil. Who goeth about to kill thee?' 21 Jesus answered
and said unto them, 'I have done one work, and ye all marvel.
22 Moses therefore gave unto you circumcision (not because it
is of Moses, but of the fathers), and ye on the sabbath day
circumcise a man. 23 If a man on the sabbath day receive circumcision, that the law of Moses should not be broken; are
ye angry at me, because I have made a man every whit whole
on the sabbath day? 24 Judge not according to the appearance, but judge righteous judgment.' 25 Then said some of
them of Jerusalem, 'Is not this he, whom they seek to kill?
26 But, lo, he speaketh boldly, and they say nothing unto him.
Do the rulers know indeed that this is the very Christ?
27 Howbeit we know this man whence he is, but when Christ
cometh, no man knoweth whence he is.' 28 Then cried Jesus
in the temple as he taught, saying, 'Ye both know me, and ye
know whence I am; and I am not come of myself, but he that
sent me is true, whom ye know not. 29 But I know him, for I
am from him, and he hath sent me.' 30 Then they sought to
take him: but no man laid hands on him, because his hour
was not yet come. 31 And many of the people believed on him,
and said, 'When Christ cometh, will he do more miracles
than these which this man hath done?'

32 The Pharisees heard that the people murmured such
things concerning him; and the Pharisees and the chief priests
sent officers to take him. 33 Then said Jesus unto them, 'Yet a
little while am I with you, and then I go unto him that sent
me. 34 Ye shall seek me, and shall not find me, and where I
am, thither ye cannot come.' 35 Then said the Jews among

themselves, 'Whither will he go, that we shall not find him?
Will he go unto the dispersed among the Gentiles, and teach
the Gentiles? 36 What manner of saying is this that he said,
"Ye shall seek me, and shall not find me, and where I am,
thither ye cannot come"?' 37 In the last day, that great day of
the feast, Jesus stood and cried, saying, 'If any man thirst, let
him come unto me, and drink. 38 He that believeth on me, as
the scripture hath said, out of his belly shall flow rivers of
living water.' 39 (But this spake he of the Spirit, which they
that believe on him should receive: for the Holy Ghost was
not yet given; because that Jesus was not yet glorified.)

40 Many of the people therefore, when they heard this saying, said, 'Of a truth this is the Prophet.' 41 Others said, 'This
is the Christ.' But some said, 'Shall Christ come out of Galilee?
42 Hath not the scripture said that Christ cometh of the seed
of David, and out of the town of Bethlehem, where David
was?' 43 So there was a division among the people because of
him. 44 And some of them would have taken him; but no man
laid hands on him.

45 Then came the officers to the chief priests and Pharisees;
and they said unto them, 'Why have ye not brought him?'
46 The officers answered, 'Never man spake like this man.'
47 Then answered them the Pharisees, 'Are ye also deceived?
48 Have any of the rulers or of the Pharisees believed on him?
49 But this people who knoweth not the law are cursed.'
50 Nicodemus saith unto them (he that came to Jesus by night,
being one of them), 51 'Doth our law judge any man, before it
hear him, and know what he doeth?' 52 They answered and
said unto him, 'Art thou also of Galilee? Search, and look: for

out of Galilee ariseth no prophet.' 53And every man went
unto his own house.

8 Jesus went unto the mount of Olives. 2And early in the
morning he came again into the temple, and all the people
came unto him; and he sat down, and taught them. 3And the
scribes and Pharisees brought unto him a woman taken in
adultery; and when they had set her in the midst, 4 they say
unto him, 'Master, this woman was taken in adultery, in the
very act. 5 Now Moses in the law commanded us, that such
should be stoned, but what sayest thou?' 6 This they said,
tempting him, that they might have to accuse him. But Jesus
stooped down, and with his finger wrote on the ground, as
though he heard them not. 7 So when they continued asking
him, he lifted up himself, and said unto them, 'He that is
without sin among you, let him first cast a stone at her.' 8And
again he stooped down, and wrote on the ground. 9And they
which heard it, being convicted by their own conscience, went
out one by one, beginning at the eldest, even unto the last,
and Jesus was left alone, and the woman standing in the
midst. 10 When Jesus had lifted up himself, and saw none but
the woman, he said unto her, 'Woman, where are those thine
accusers? Hath no man condemned thee?' 11 She said, 'No man,
Lord.' And Jesus said unto her, 'Neither do I condemn thee:
go, and sin no more.'

12 Then spake Jesus again unto them, saying, 'I am the
light of the world: he that followeth me shall not walk in
darkness, but shall have the light of life.' 13 The Pharisees
therefore said unto him, 'Thou bearest record of thyself; thy

record is not true.' 14 Jesus answered and said unto them,
'Though I bear record of myself, yet my record is true, for I
know whence I came, and whither I go; but ye cannot tell
whence I come, and whither I go. 15 Ye judge after the flesh; I
judge no man. 16 And yet if I judge, my judgment is true, for I
am not alone, but I and the Father that sent me. 17 It is also
written in your law, that the testimony of two men is true. 18 I
am one that bear witness of myself, and the Father that sent
me beareth witness of me.' 19 Then said they unto him, 'Where
is thy Father?' Jesus answered, 'Ye neither know me, nor my
Father. If ye had known me, ye should have known my
Father also.' 20 These words spake Jesus in the treasury, as he
taught in the temple, and no man laid hands on him; for his
hour was not yet come. 21 Then said Jesus again unto them, 'I
go my way, and ye shall seek me, and shall die in your sins.
Whither I go, ye cannot come.' 22 Then said the Jews, 'Will he
kill himself?' because he saith, 'Whither I go, ye cannot come.'
23 And he said unto them, 'Ye are from beneath; I am from
above: ye are of this world; I am not of this world. 24 I said
therefore unto you, that ye shall die in your sins: for if ye
believe not that I am he, ye shall die in your sins.' 25 Then
said they unto him, 'Who art thou?' And Jesus saith unto
them, 'Even the same that I said unto you from the beginning. 26 I have many things to say and to judge of you, but he
that sent me is true; and I speak to the world those things
which I have heard of him.' 27 They understood not that he
spake to them of the Father. 28 Then said Jesus unto them,
'When ye have lifted up the Son of man, then shall ye know
that I am he, and that I do nothing of myself; but as my Father

hath taught me, I speak these things. 29 And he that sent me is
with me: the Father hath not left me alone, for I do always
those things that please him.' 30 As he spake these words,
many believed on him. 31 Then said Jesus to those Jews which
believed on him, 'If ye continue in my word, then are ye my
disciples indeed; 32 and ye shall know the truth, and the truth
shall make you free.'

33 They answered him, 'We be Abraham's seed, and were
never in bondage to any man. How sayest thou, "Ye shall be
made free"?' 34 Jesus answered them, 'Verily, verily, I say unto
you, whosoever committeth sin is the servant of sin. 35 And
the servant abideth not in the house for ever, but the Son
abideth ever. 36 If the Son therefore shall make you free, ye
shall be free indeed. 37 I know that ye are Abraham's seed; but
ye seek to kill me, because my word hath no place in you. 38 I
speak that which I have seen with my Father, and ye do that
which ye have seen with your father.' 39 They answered and
said unto him, 'Abraham is our father.' Jesus saith unto them,
'If ye were Abraham's children, ye would do the works of
Abraham. 40 But now ye seek to kill me, a man that hath told
you the truth, which I have heard of God: this did not Abraham. 41 Ye do the deeds of your father.' Then said they to
him, 'We be not born of fornication; we have one Father,
even God.' 42 Jesus said unto them, 'If God were your Father,
ye would love me: for I proceeded forth and came from
God; neither came I of myself, but he sent me. 43 Why do ye
not understand my speech? Even because ye cannot hear my
word. 44 Ye are of your father the devil, and the lusts of your
father ye will do. He was a murderer from the beginning,

and abode not in the truth, because there is no truth in him.
When he speaketh a lie, he speaketh of his own: for he is a
liar, and the father of it. 45 And because I tell you the truth, ye
believe me not. 46 Which of you convinceth me of sin? And if
I say the truth, why do ye not believe me? 47 He that is of
God heareth God's words: ye therefore hear them not,
because ye are not of God.' 48 Then answered the Jews, and
said unto him, 'Say we not well that thou art a Samaritan,
and hast a devil?' 49 Jesus answered, 'I have not a devil; but I
honour my Father, and ye do dishonour me. 50 And I seek not
mine own glory: there is one that seeketh and judgeth. 51 Verily, verily, I say unto you, if a man keep my saying, he shall
never see death.' 52 Then said the Jews unto him, 'Now we
know that thou hast a devil. Abraham is dead, and the
prophets; and thou sayest, "If a man keep my saying, he
shall never taste of death." 53 Art thou greater than our father
Abraham, which is dead? And the prophets are dead.
Whom makest thou thyself?' 54 Jesus answered, 'If I honour
myself, my honour is nothing: it is my Father that honoureth
me; of whom ye say, that he is your God; 55 yet ye have not
known him; but I know him, and if I should say, "I know
him not" I shall be a liar like unto you; but I know him, and
keep his saying. 56 Your father Abraham rejoiced to see my
day, and he saw it, and was glad.' 57 Then said the Jews unto
him, 'Thou art not yet fifty years old, and hast thou seen
Abraham?' 58 Jesus said unto them, 'Verily, verily, I say unto
you, before Abraham was, I am.' 59 Then took they up stones
to cast at him: but Jesus hid himself, and went out of the
temple, going through the midst of them, and so passed by.

9 And as Jesus passed by, he saw a man which was blind
from his birth. 2 And his disciples asked him, saying,
'Master, who did sin, this man, or his parents, that he was
born blind?' 3 Jesus answered, 'Neither hath this man sinned,
nor his parents, but that the works of God should be made
manifest in him. 4 I must work the works of him that sent me,
while it is day; the night cometh, when no man can work.
5 As long as I am in the world, I am the light of the world.'
6 When he had thus spoken, he spat on the ground, and
made clay of the spittle, and he anointed the eyes of the
blind man with the clay, 7 and said unto him, 'Go, wash in the
pool of Siloam' (which is by interpretation, Sent). He went
his way therefore, and washed, and came seeing.

8 The neighbours therefore, and they which before had
seen him that he was blind, said, 'Is not this he that sat and
begged?' 9 Some said, 'This is he,' others said, 'He is like him,'
but he said, 'I am he.' 10 Therefore said they unto him, 'How
were thine eyes opened?' 11 He answered and said, 'A man
that is called Jesus made clay, and anointed mine eyes, and
said unto me, "Go to the pool of Siloam, and wash," and I
went and washed, and I received sight.' 12 Then said they unto
him, 'Where is he?' He said, 'I know not.'

13 They brought to the Pharisees him that aforetime was
blind. 14 And it was the sabbath day when Jesus made the clay,
and opened his eyes. 15 Then again the Pharisees also asked
him how he had received his sight. He said unto them, 'He
put clay upon mine eyes, and I washed, and do see.' 16 Therefore said some of the Pharisees, 'This man is not of God,
because he keepeth not the sabbath day.' Others said, 'How

can a man that is a sinner do such miracles?' And there was
a division among them. 17 They say unto the blind man again,
'What sayest thou of him, that he hath opened thine eyes?'
He said, 'He is a prophet.' 18 But the Jews did not believe concerning him, that he had been blind, and received his sight,
until they called the parents of him that had received his
sight. 19 And they asked them, saying, 'Is this your son, who
ye say was born blind? How then doth he now see?' 20 His
parents answered them and said, 'We know that this is our
son, and that he was born blind 21 but by what means he now
seeth, we know not; or who hath opened his eyes, we know
not. He is of age; ask him: he shall speak for himself.' 22 These
words spake his parents, because they feared the Jews: for
the Jews had agreed already, that if any man did confess that
he was Christ, he should be put out of the synagogue.
23 Therefore said his parents, 'He is of age; ask him.' 24 Then
again called they the man that was blind, and said unto him,
'Give God the praise; we know that this man is a sinner.'
25 He answered and said, 'Whether he be a sinner or no, I
know not; one thing I know, that, whereas I was blind, now I
see.' 26 Then said they to him again, 'What did he to thee?
How opened he thine eyes?' 27 He answered them, 'I have told
you already, and ye did not hear: wherefore would ye hear it
again? Will ye also be his disciples?' 28 Then they reviled
him, and said, 'Thou art his disciple; but we are Moses' disciples. 29 We know that God spake unto Moses; as for this fellow, we know not from whence he is.' 30 The man answered
and said unto them, 'Why herein is a marvellous thing, that
ye know not from whence he is, and yet he hath opened

mine eyes. 31 Now we know that God heareth not sinners,
but if any man be a worshipper of God, and doeth his will,
him he heareth. 32 Since the world began was it not heard
that any man opened the eyes of one that was born blind. 33 If
this man were not of God, he could do nothing.' 34 They
answered and said unto him, 'Thou wast altogether born in
sins, and dost thou teach us?' And they cast him out. 35 Jesus
heard that they had cast him out; and when he had found
him, he said unto him, 'Dost thou believe on the Son of God?'
36 He answered and said, 'Who is he, Lord, that I might
believe on him?' 37 And Jesus said unto him, 'Thou hast both
seen him, and it is he that talketh with thee.' 38 And he said,
'Lord, I believe.' And he worshipped him.

39 And Jesus said, 'For judgment I am come into this world,
that they which see not might see; and that they which see
might be made blind.' 40 And some of the Pharisees which
were with him heard these words, and said unto him, 'Are
we blind also?' 41 Jesus said unto them, 'If ye were blind, ye
should have no sin, but now ye say, "We see"; therefore your
sin remaineth.'

10 'Verily, verily, I say unto you, he that entereth not by the
door into the sheepfold, but climbeth up some other
way, the same is a thief and a robber. 2 But he that entereth in
by the door is the shepherd of the sheep. 3 To him the porter
openeth; and the sheep hear his voice, and he calleth his
own sheep by name, and leadeth them out. 4 And when he
putteth forth his own sheep, he goeth before them, and the
sheep follow him, for they know his voice. 5 And a stranger

will they not follow, but will flee from him, for they know
not the voice of strangers.' 6 This parable spake Jesus unto
them, but they understood not what things they were which
he spake unto them. 7 Then said Jesus unto them again, 'Verily, verily, I say unto you, I am the door of the sheep. 8 All that
ever came before me are thieves and robbers, but the sheep
did not hear them. 9 I am the door: by me if any man enter in,
he shall be saved, and shall go in and out, and find pasture.
10 The thief cometh not, but for to steal, and to kill, and to
destroy: I am come that they might have life, and that they
might have it more abundantly. 11 I am the good shepherd:
the good shepherd giveth his life for the sheep. 12 But he that
is an hireling, and not the shepherd, whose own the sheep
are not, seeth the wolf coming, and leaveth the sheep, and
fleeth, and the wolf catcheth them, and scattereth the sheep.
13 The hireling fleeth, because he is an hireling, and careth not
for the sheep. 14 I am the good shepherd, and know my sheep,
and am known of mine. 15 As the Father knoweth me, even so
know I the Father, and I lay down my life for the sheep. 16 And
other sheep I have, which are not of this fold: them also I
must bring, and they shall hear my voice; and there shall be
one fold: and one shepherd. 17 Therefore doth my Father love
me, because I lay down my life, that I might take it again.
18 No man taketh it from me, but I lay it down of myself. I
have power to lay it down, and I have power to take it again.
This commandment have I received of my Father.'

19 There was a division therefore again among the Jews
for these sayings. 20 And many of them said, 'He hath a devil,
and is mad; why hear ye him?' 21 Others said, 'These are not

the words of him that hath a devil. Can a devil open the eyes
of the blind?'
22 And it was at Jerusalem the feast of the dedication, and
it was winter. 23 And Jesus walked in the temple in Solomon's
porch. 24 Then came the Jews round about him, and said unto
him, 'How long dost thou make us to doubt? If thou be the
Christ, tell us plainly.' 25 Jesus answered them, 'I told you, and
ye believed not: the works that I do in my Father's name,
they bear witness of me. 26 But ye believe not, because ye are
not of my sheep, as I said unto you. 27 My sheep hear my
voice, and I know them, and they follow me, 28 and I give unto
them eternal life; and they shall never perish, neither shall
any man pluck them out of my hand. 29 My Father, which
gave them me, is greater than all; and no man is able to pluck
them out of my Father's hand. 30 I and my Father are one.'
31 Then the Jews took up stones again to stone him. 32 Jesus
answered them, 'Many good works have I shewed you from
my Father; for which of those works do ye stone me?' 33 The
Jews answered him, saying, 'For a good work we stone thee
not; but for blasphemy; and because that thou, being a man,
makest thyself God.' 34 Jesus answered them, 'Is it not written
in your law, "I said, ye are gods"? 35 If he called them gods,
unto whom the word of God came, and the scripture cannot
be broken; 36 say ye of him, whom the Father hath sanctified,
and sent into the world, "Thou blasphemest," because I said,
"I am the Son of God"? 37 If I do not the works of my Father,
believe me not. 38 But if I do, though ye believe not me, believe
the works: that ye may know, and believe, that the Father is
in me, and I in him.' 39 Therefore they sought again to take

him: but he escaped out of their hand, 40 and went away again
beyond Jordan into the place where John at first baptized;
and there he abode. 41 And many resorted unto him, and said,
'John did no miracle, but all things that John spake of this
man were true.' 42 And many believed on him there.

11 Now a certain man was sick, named Lazarus, of Bethany, the town of Mary and her sister Martha. 2 (It was
that Mary which anointed the Lord with ointment, and wiped
his feet with her hair, whose brother Lazarus was sick.)
3 Therefore his sisters sent unto him, saying, 'Lord, behold,
he whom thou lovest is sick.' 4 When Jesus heard that, he
said, 'This sickness is not unto death, but for the glory of
God, that the Son of God might be glorified thereby.' 5 Now
Jesus loved Martha, and her sister, and Lazarus. 6 When he
had heard therefore that he was sick, he abode two days still
in the same place where he was. 7 Then after that saith he to
his disciples, 'Let us go into Judæa again.' 8 His disciples say
unto him, 'Master, the Jews of late sought to stone thee; and
goest thou thither again?' 9 Jesus answered, 'Are there not
twelve hours in the day? If any man walk in the day, he stumbleth not, because he seeth the light of this world. 10 But if a
man walk in the night, he stumbleth, because there is no light
in him.' 11 These things said he, and after that he saith unto
them, 'Our friend Lazarus sleepeth; but I go, that I may awake
him out of sleep.' 12 Then said his disciples, 'Lord, if he sleep,
he shall do well.' 13 Howbeit Jesus spake of his death, but they
thought that he had spoken of taking of rest in sleep. 14 Then
said Jesus unto them plainly, 'Lazarus is dead. 15 And I am

glad for your sakes that I was not there, to the intent ye may
believe; nevertheless let us go unto him.' 16 Then said Thomas,
which is called Didymus, unto his fellowdisciples, 'Let us
also go, that we may die with him.' 17 Then when Jesus came,
he found that he had lain in the grave four days already.
18 Now Bethany was nigh unto Jerusalem, about fifteen furlongs off, 19 and many of the Jews came to Martha and Mary,
to comfort them concerning their brother. 20 Then Martha, as
soon as she heard that Jesus was coming, went and met him,
but Mary sat still in the house. 21 Then said Martha unto Jesus,
'Lord, if thou hadst been here, my brother had not died. 22 But
I know, that even now, whatsoever thou wilt ask of God,
God will give it thee.' 23 Jesus saith unto her, 'Thy brother shall
rise again.' 24 Martha saith unto him, 'I know that he shall rise
again in the resurrection at the last day.' 25 Jesus said unto
her, 'I am the resurrection, and the life: he that believeth in
me, though he were dead, yet shall he live, 26 and whosoever
liveth and believeth in me shall never die. Believest thou
this?' 27 She saith unto him, 'Yea, Lord, I believe that thou art
the Christ, the Son of God, which should come into the world.'
28 And when she had so said, she went her way, and called
Mary her sister secretly, saying, 'The Master is come, and calleth for thee.' 29 As soon as she heard that, she arose quickly,
and came unto him. 30 Now Jesus was not yet come into the
town, but was in that place where Martha met him. 31 The
Jews then which were with her in the house, and comforted
her, when they saw Mary, that she rose up hastily and went
out, followed her, saying, 'She goeth unto the grave to weep
there.' 32 Then when Mary was come where Jesus was, and

saw him, she fell down at his feet, saying unto him, 'Lord, if
thou hadst been here, my brother had not died.' 33 When
Jesus therefore saw her weeping, and the Jews also weeping
which came with her, he groaned in the spirit, and was troubled, 34 and said, 'Where have ye laid him?' They said unto
him, 'Lord, come and see.' 35 Jesus wept. 36 Then said the Jews,
'Behold how he loved him!' 37 And some of them said, 'Could
not this man, which opened the eyes of the blind, have caused
that even this man should not have died?' 38 Jesus therefore
again groaning in himself cometh to the grave. It was a cave,
and a stone lay upon it. 39 Jesus said, 'Take ye away the stone.'
Martha, the sister of him that was dead, saith unto him, 'Lord,
by this time he stinketh, for he hath been dead four days.'
40 Jesus saith unto her, 'Said I not unto thee, that, if thou wouldest believe, thou shouldest see the glory of God?' 41 Then
they took away the stone from the place where the dead was
laid. And Jesus lifted up his eyes, and said, 'Father, I thank
thee that thou hast heard me. 42 And I knew that thou hearest
me always, but because of the people which stand by I said
it, that they may believe that thou hast sent me.' 43 And when
he thus had spoken, he cried with a loud voice, 'Lazarus,
come forth.' 44 And he that was dead came forth, bound hand
and foot with graveclothes, and his face was bound about
with a napkin. Jesus saith unto them, 'Loose him, and let
him go.' 45 Then many of the Jews which came to Mary, and
had seen the things which Jesus did, believed on him. 46 But
some of them went their ways to the Pharisees, and told
them what things Jesus had done.

47 Then gathered the chief priests and the Pharisees a

council, and said, 'What do we? For this man doeth many miracles. 48 If we let him thus alone, all men will believe on him, and the Romans shall come and take away both our place and nation.' 49 And one of them, named Caiaphas, being the high priest that same year, said unto them, 'Ye know nothing at all, 50 nor consider that it is expedient for us, that one man should die for the people, and that the whole nation perish not.' 51 And this spake he not of himself, but being high priest that year, he prophesied that Jesus should die for that nation; 52 and not for that nation only, but that also he should gather together in one the children of God that were scattered abroad. 53 Then from that day forth they took counsel together for to put him to death. 54 Jesus therefore walked no more openly among the Jews; but went thence unto a country near to the wilderness, into a city called Ephraim, and there continued with his disciples.

55 And the Jews' passover was nigh at hand, and many went out of the country up to Jerusalem before the passover, to purify themselves. 56 Then sought they for Jesus, and spake among themselves, as they stood in the temple, 'What think ye, that he will not come to the feast?' 57 Now both the chief priests and the Pharisees had given a commandment, that, if any man knew where he were, he should shew it, that they might take him.

12 Then Jesus six days before the passover came to Bethany, where Lazarus was which had been dead, whom he raised from the dead. 2 There they made him a supper, and Martha served, but Lazarus was one of them that sat at

the table with him. 3 Then took Mary a pound of ointment of
spikenard, very costly, and anointed the feet of Jesus, and
wiped his feet with her hair, and the house was filled with
the odour of the ointment. 4 Then saith one of his disciples,
Judas Iscariot, Simon's son, which should betray him, 5 'Why
was not this ointment sold for three hundred pence, and
given to the poor?' 6 This he said, not that he cared for the
poor; but because he was a thief, and had the bag, and bare
what was put therein. 7 Then said Jesus, 'Let her alone: against
the day of my burying hath she kept this. 8 For the poor always
ye have with you; but me ye have not always.' 9 Much people
of the Jews therefore knew that he was there, and they came
not for Jesus' sake only, but that they might see Lazarus also,
whom he had raised from the dead.

10 But the chief priests consulted that they might put Lazarus also to death; 11 because that by reason of him many of
the Jews went away, and believed on Jesus.

12 On the next day much people that were come to the
feast, when they heard that Jesus was coming to Jerusalem,
13 took branches of palm trees, and went forth to meet him,
and cried, 'Hosanna: blessed is the King of Israel that cometh
in the name of the Lord.' 14 And Jesus, when he had found a
young ass, sat thereon; as it is written, 15 'Fear not, daughter
of Sion: behold, thy King cometh, sitting on an ass's colt.'
16 These things understood not his disciples at the first, but
when Jesus was glorified, then remembered they that these
things were written of him, and that they had done these
things unto him. 17 The people therefore that was with him
when he called Lazarus out of his grave, and raised him from

the dead, bare record. 18 For this cause the people also met
him, for that they heard that he had done this miracle. 19 The
Pharisees therefore said among themselves, 'Perceive ye
how ye prevail nothing? Behold, the world is gone after him.'

20 And there were certain Greeks among them that came
up to worship at the feast. 21 The same came therefore to
Philip, which was of Bethsaida of Galilee, and desired him,
saying, 'Sir, we would see Jesus.' 22 Philip cometh and telleth
Andrew, and again Andrew and Philip tell Jesus.

23 And Jesus answered them, saying, 'The hour is come,
that the Son of man should be glorified. 24 Verily, verily, I say
unto you, except a corn of wheat fall into the ground and
die, it abideth alone, but if it die, it bringeth forth much fruit.
25 He that loveth his life shall lose it; and he that hateth his
life in this world shall keep it unto life eternal. 26 If any man
serve me, let him follow me; and where I am, there shall also
my servant be: if any man serve me, him will my Father
honour. 27 Now is my soul troubled; and what shall I say?
"Father, save me from this hour." But for this cause came I
unto this hour. 28 Father, glorify thy name.' Then came there
a voice from heaven, saying, 'I have both glorified it, and
will glorify it again.' 29 The people therefore, that stood by,
and heard it, said that it thundered; others said, 'An angel
spake to him.' 30 Jesus answered and said, 'This voice came
not because of me, but for your sakes. 31 Now is the judgment
of this world: now shall the prince of this world be cast out.
32 And I, if I be lifted up from the earth, will draw all men unto
me.' 33 This he said, signifying what death he should die. 34 The
people answered him, 'We have heard out of the law that

Christ abideth for ever, and how sayest thou the Son of man
must be lifted up? Who is this Son of man?' 35 Then Jesus said
unto them, 'Yet a little while is the light with you. Walk
while ye have the light, lest darkness come upon you: for he
that walketh in darkness knoweth not whither he goeth.
36 While ye have light, believe in the light, that ye may be the
children of light.' These things spake Jesus, and departed,
and did hide himself from them.

37 But though he had done so many miracles before them,
yet they believed not on him, 38 that the saying of Esaias the
prophet might be fulfilled, which he spake, 'Lord, who hath
believed our report? And to whom hath the arm of the Lord
been revealed?' 39 Therefore they could not believe, because
that Esaias said again, 40 'He hath blinded their eyes, and
hardened their heart; that they should not see with their eyes,
nor understand with their heart, and be converted, and I
should heal them.' 41 These things said Esaias, when he saw
his glory, and spake of him.

42 Nevertheless among the chief rulers also many believed
on him; but because of the Pharisees they did not confess
him, lest they should be put out of the synagogue, 43 for they
loved the praise of men more than the praise of God.

44 Jesus cried and said, 'He that believeth on me, believeth
not on me, but on him that sent me. 45 And he that seeth me
seeth him that sent me. 46 I am come a light into the world,
that whosoever believeth on me should not abide in darkness. 47 And if any man hear my words, and believe not, I
judge him not: for I came not to judge the world, but to save
the world. 48 He that rejecteth me, and receiveth not my

words, hath one that judgeth him: the word that I have spoken, the same shall judge him in the last day. 49 For I have not
spoken of myself; but the Father which sent me, he gave me
a commandment, what I should say, and what I should speak.
50 And I know that his commandment is life everlasting:
whatsoever I speak therefore, even as the Father said unto
me, so I speak.'

13 Now before the feast of the passover, when Jesus knew
that his hour was come that he should depart out of
this world unto the Father, having loved his own which
were in the world, he loved them unto the end. 2 And supper
being ended, the devil having now put into the heart of
Judas Iscariot, Simon's son, to betray him; 3 Jesus knowing
that the Father had given all things into his hands, and that
he was come from God, and went to God; 4 he riseth from
supper, and laid aside his garments; and took a towel, and
girded himself. 5 After that he poureth water into a bason,
and began to wash the disciples' feet, and to wipe them with
the towel wherewith he was girded. 6 Then cometh he to
Simon Peter, and Peter saith unto him, 'Lord, dost thou wash
my feet?' 7 Jesus answered and said unto him, 'What I do thou
knowest not now; but thou shalt know hereafter.' 8 Peter saith
unto him, 'Thou shalt never wash my feet.' Jesus answered
him, 'If I wash thee not, thou hast no part with me.' 9 Simon
Peter saith unto him, 'Lord, not my feet only, but also my
hands and my head.' 10 Jesus saith to him, 'He that is washed
needeth not save to wash his feet, but is clean every whit:
and ye are clean, but not all.' 11 For he knew who should betray

him; therefore said he, 'Ye are not all clean.' 12 So after he had
washed their feet, and had taken his garments, and was set
down again, he said unto them, 'Know ye what I have done
to you? 13 Ye call me "Master" and "Lord", and ye say well;
for so I am. 14 If I then, your Lord and Master, have washed
your feet, ye also ought to wash one another's feet. 15 For I
have given you an example, that ye should do as I have done
to you. 16 Verily, verily, I say unto you, the servant is not greater
than his lord; neither he that is sent greater than he that sent
him. 17 If ye know these things, happy are ye if ye do them.

18 'I speak not of you all; I know whom I have chosen: but
that the scripture may be fulfilled. He that eateth bread with
me hath lifted up his heel against me. 19 Now I tell you before
it come, that, when it is come to pass, ye may believe that
I am he. 20 Verily, verily, I say unto you, he that receiveth
whomsoever I send receiveth me; and he that receiveth me
receiveth him that sent me.' 21 When Jesus had thus said, he
was troubled in spirit, and testified, and said, 'Verily, verily,
I say unto you, that one of you shall betray me.' 22 Then the
disciples looked one on another, doubting of whom he spake.
23 Now there was leaning on Jesus' bosom one of his disciples, whom Jesus loved. 24 Simon Peter therefore beckoned
to him, that he should ask who it should be of whom he
spake. 25 He then lying on Jesus' breast saith unto him, 'Lord,
who is it?' 26 Jesus answered, 'He it is, to whom I shall give a
sop, when I have dipped it.' And when he had dipped the
sop, he gave it to Judas Iscariot, the son of Simon. 27 And after
the sop Satan entered into him. Then said Jesus unto him,
'That thou doest, do quickly.' 28 Now no man at the table

knew for what intent he spake this unto him. 29 For some of
them thought, because Judas had the bag, that Jesus had said
unto him, 'Buy those things that we have need of against the
feast,' or, that he should give something to the poor. 30 He
then having received the sop went immediately out, and it
was night.

31 Therefore, when he was gone out, Jesus said, 'Now is
the Son of man glorified, and God is glorified in him. 32 If God
be glorified in him, God shall also glorify him in himself,
and shall straightway glorify him. 33 Little children, yet a little while I am with you. Ye shall seek me, and as I said unto
the Jews, "Whither I go, ye cannot come"; so now I say to you.
34 A new commandment I give unto you, that ye love one
another; as I have loved you, that ye also love one another.
35 By this shall all men know that ye are my disciples, if ye
have love one to another.'

36 Simon Peter said unto him, 'Lord, whither goest thou?'
Jesus answered him, 'Whither I go, thou canst not follow me
now; but thou shalt follow me afterwards.' 37 Peter said unto
him, 'Lord, why cannot I follow thee now? I will lay down
my life for thy sake.' 38 Jesus answered him, 'Wilt thou lay
down thy life for my sake? Verily, verily, I say unto thee, the
cock shall not crow, till thou hast denied me thrice.

14 'Let not your heart be troubled: ye believe in God,
believe also in me. 2 In my Father's house are many
mansions: if it were not so, I would have told you. I go to
prepare a place for you. 3 And if I go and prepare a place for
you, I will come again, and receive you unto myself; that

where I am, there ye may be also. 4 And whither I go ye know, and the way ye know.' 5 Thomas saith unto him, 'Lord, we know not whither thou goest; and how can we know the way?' 6 Jesus saith unto him, 'I am the way, the truth, and the life: no man cometh unto the Father, but by me. 7 If ye had known me, ye should have known my Father also: and from henceforth ye know him, and have seen him.' 8 Philip saith unto him, 'Lord, shew us the Father, and it sufficeth us.' 9 Jesus saith unto him, 'Have I been so long time with you, and yet hast thou not known me, Philip? He that hath seen me hath seen the Father; and how sayest thou then, "Shew us the Father"? 10 Believest thou not that I am in the Father, and the Father in me? The words that I speak unto you I speak not of myself; but the Father that dwelleth in me, he doeth the works. 11 Believe me that I am in the Father, and the Father in me, or else believe me for the very works' sake. 12 Verily, verily, I say unto you, he that believeth on me, the works that I do shall he do also; and greater works than these shall he do; because I go unto my Father. 13 And whatsoever ye shall ask in my name, that will I do, that the Father may be glorified in the Son. 14 If ye shall ask any thing in my name, I will do it.

15 'If ye love me, keep my commandments. 16 And I will pray the Father, and he shall give you another Comforter, that he may abide with you for ever; 17 even the Spirit of truth; whom the world cannot receive, because it seeth him not, neither knoweth him, but ye know him; for he dwelleth with you, and shall be in you. 18 I will not leave you comfortless; I will come to you. 19 Yet a little while, and the world seeth me no more; but ye see me: because I live, ye shall live

also. [20]At that day ye shall know that I am in my Father, and
ye in me, and I in you. [21]He that hath my commandments,
and keepeth them, he it is that loveth me: and he that loveth
me shall be loved of my Father, and I will love him, and will
manifest myself to him.' [22]Judas saith unto him, not Iscariot,
'Lord, how is it that thou wilt manifest thyself unto us, and
not unto the world?' [23]Jesus answered and said unto him, 'If
a man love me, he will keep my words: and my Father will
love him, and we will come unto him, and make our abode
with him. [24]He that loveth me not keepeth not my sayings,
and the word which ye hear is not mine, but the Father's
which sent me. [25]These things have I spoken unto you, being
yet present with you. [26]But the Comforter, which is the Holy
Ghost, whom the Father will send in my name, he shall teach
you all things, and bring all things to your remembrance,
whatsoever I have said unto you. [27]Peace I leave with you,
my peace I give unto you: not as the world giveth, give I
unto you. Let not your heart be troubled, neither let it be
afraid. [28]Ye have heard how I said unto you, "I go away, and
come again unto you." If ye loved me, ye would rejoice,
because I said I go unto the Father, for my Father is greater
than I. [29]And now I have told you before it come to pass, that,
when it is come to pass, ye might believe. [30]Hereafter I will
not talk much with you, for the prince of this world cometh,
and hath nothing in me. [31]But that the world may know that
I love the Father; and as the Father gave me commandment,
even so I do. Arise, let us go hence.

15 'I am the true vine, and my Father is the husbandman.
2 Every branch in me that beareth not fruit he taketh
away, and every branch that beareth fruit, he purgeth it, that
it may bring forth more fruit. 3 Now ye are clean through the
word which I have spoken unto you. 4 Abide in me, and I in
you. As the branch cannot bear fruit of itself, except it abide
in the vine; no more can ye, except ye abide in me. 5 I am the
vine, ye are the branches. He that abideth in me, and I in
him, the same bringeth forth much fruit, for without me ye
can do nothing. 6 If a man abide not in me, he is cast forth as
a branch, and is withered; and men gather them, and cast
them into the fire, and they are burned. 7 If ye abide in me,
and my words abide in you, ye shall ask what ye will, and it
shall be done unto you. 8 Herein is my Father glorified, that
ye bear much fruit; so shall ye be my disciples. 9 As the Father
hath loved me, so have I loved you; continue ye in my love.
10 If ye keep my commandments, ye shall abide in my love;
even as I have kept my Father's commandments, and abide
in his love. 11 These things have I spoken unto you, that my
joy might remain in you, and that your joy might be full.

12 'This is my commandment: that ye love one another, as
I have loved you. 13 Greater love hath no man than this, that a
man lay down his life for his friends. 14 Ye are my friends, if
ye do whatsoever I command you. 15 Henceforth I call you
not servants; for the servant knoweth not what his lord
doeth; but I have called you friends, for all things that I have
heard of my Father I have made known unto you. 16 Ye have
not chosen me, but I have chosen you, and ordained you, that
ye should go and bring forth fruit, and that your fruit should

remain: that whatsoever ye shall ask of the Father in my
name, he may give it you. 17 These things I command you, that
ye love one another.

18 'If the world hate you, ye know that it hated me before
it hated you. 19 If ye were of the world, the world would love
his own: but because ye are not of the world, but I have
chosen you out of the world, therefore the world hateth you.
20 Remember the word that I said unto you, "The servant is
not greater than his lord." If they have persecuted me, they
will also persecute you; if they have kept my saying, they
will keep yours also. 21 But all these things will they do unto
you for my name's sake, because they know not him that
sent me. 22 If I had not come and spoken unto them, they had
not had sin: but now they have no cloke for their sin. 23 He
that hateth me hateth my Father also. 24 If I had not done
among them the works which none other man did, they had
not had sin: but now have they both seen and hated both me
and my Father. 25 But this cometh to pass, that the word might
be fulfilled that is written in their law: "They hated me without a cause."

26 'But when the Comforter is come, whom I will send unto
you from the Father, even the Spirit of truth, which proceedeth
from the Father, he shall testify of me. 27 And ye also shall bear
witness, because ye have been with me from the beginning.

16 'These things have I spoken unto you, that ye should
not be offended. 2 They shall put you out of the synagogues: yea, the time cometh, that whosoever killeth you will
think that he doeth God service. 3 And these things will they

do unto you, because they have not known the Father, nor
me. 4 But these things have I told you, that when the time shall
come, ye may remember that I told you of them. And these
things I said not unto you at the beginning, because I was
with you. 5 But now I go my way to him that sent me; and
none of you asketh me, "Whither goest thou?" 6 But because I
have said these things unto you, sorrow hath filled your
heart. 7 Nevertheless I tell you the truth. It is expedient for you
that I go away: for if I go not away, the Comforter will not
come unto you; but if I depart, I will send him unto you. 8 And
when he is come, he will reprove the world of sin, and of
righteousness, and of judgment: 9 of sin, because they believe
not on me; 10 of righteousness, because I go to my Father, and
ye see me no more; 11 of judgment, because the prince of this
world is judged. 12 I have yet many things to say unto you, but
ye cannot bear them now. 13 Howbeit when he, the Spirit of
truth, is come, he will guide you into all truth, for he shall not
speak of himself; but whatsoever he shall hear, that shall he
speak, and he will shew you things to come. 14 He shall glorify
me, for he shall receive of mine, and shall shew it unto you.
15 All things that the Father hath are mine: therefore said I, that
he shall take of mine, and shall shew it unto you.

16 'A little while, and ye shall not see me, and again, a little while, and ye shall see me, because I go to the Father.'
17 Then said some of his disciples among themselves, 'What is
this that he saith unto us, "A little while, and ye shall not see
me, and again, a little while, and ye shall see me," and,
"Because I go to the Father"?' 18 They said therefore, 'What is
this that he saith, "A little while?" We cannot tell what he

saith.' 19 Now Jesus knew that they were desirous to ask him,
and said unto them, 'Do ye enquire among yourselves of that
I said, "A little while, and ye shall not see me, and again, a
little while, and ye shall see me"? 20 Verily, verily, I say unto
you that ye shall weep and lament, but the world shall rejoice;
and ye shall be sorrowful, but your sorrow shall be turned
into joy. 21 A woman when she is in travail hath sorrow,
because her hour is come, but as soon as she is delivered of
the child, she remembereth no more the anguish, for joy that
a man is born into the world. 22 And ye now therefore have
sorrow, but I will see you again, and your heart shall rejoice,
and your joy no man taketh from you. 23 And in that day ye
shall ask me nothing. Verily, verily, I say unto you, whatsoever ye shall ask the Father in my name, he will give it you.
24 Hitherto have ye asked nothing in my name: ask, and ye
shall receive, that your joy may be full.

25 'These things have I spoken unto you in proverbs, but
the time cometh, when I shall no more speak unto you in
proverbs, but I shall shew you plainly of the Father. 26 At that
day ye shall ask in my name, and I say not unto you that I will
pray the Father for you, 27 for the Father himself loveth you,
because ye have loved me, and have believed that I came out
from God. 28 I came forth from the Father, and am come into
the world; again, I leave the world, and go to the Father.'

29 His disciples said unto him, 'Lo, now speakest thou
plainly, and speakest no proverb. 30 Now are we sure that thou
knowest all things, and needest not that any man should ask
thee: by this we believe that thou camest forth from God.'
31 Jesus answered them, 'Do ye now believe? 32 Behold, the

hour cometh, yea, is now come, that ye shall be scattered,
every man to his own, and shall leave me alone, and yet I am
not alone; because the Father is with me. 33 These things I
have spoken unto you, that in me ye might have peace. In
the world ye shall have tribulation: but be of good cheer; I
have overcome the world.'

17 These words spake Jesus, and lifted up his eyes to
heaven, and said, 'Father, the hour is come; glorify thy
Son, that thy Son also may glorify thee. 2 As thou hast given
him power over all flesh, that he should give eternal life to
as many as thou hast given him. 3 And this is life eternal, that
they might know thee the only true God, and Jesus Christ,
whom thou hast sent. 4 I have glorified thee on the earth: I
have finished the work which thou gavest me to do. 5 And
now, O Father, glorify thou me with thine own self with the
glory which I had with thee before the world was.

6 'I have manifested thy name unto the men which thou
gavest me out of the world: thine they were, and thou gavest
them me; and they have kept thy word. 7 Now they have
known that all things whatsoever thou hast given me are of
thee. 8 For I have given unto them the words which thou
gavest me; and they have received them, and have known
surely that I came out from thee, and they have believed that
thou didst send me. 9 I pray for them: I pray not for the world,
but for them which thou hast given me; for they are thine.
10 And all mine are thine, and thine are mine; and I am glorified in them. 11 And now I am no more in the world, but these
are in the world, and I come to thee. Holy Father, keep

through thine own name those whom thou hast given me,
that they may be one, as we are. 12 While I was with them in
the world, I kept them in thy name; those that thou gavest
me I have kept, and none of them is lost, but the son of
perdition; that the scripture might be fulfilled. 13 And now
come I to thee; and these things I speak in the world, that
they might have my joy fulfilled in themselves. 14 I have given
them thy word; and the world hath hated them, because they
are not of the world, even as I am not of the world. 15 I pray
not that thou shouldest take them out of the world, but that
thou shouldest keep them from the evil. 16 They are not of the
world, even as I am not of the world. 17 Sanctify them through
thy truth: thy word is truth. 18 As thou hast sent me into the
world, even so have I also sent them into the world. 19 And
for their sakes I sanctify myself, that they also might be sanctified through the truth.

20 'Neither pray I for these alone, but for them also which
shall believe on me through their word; 21 that they all may
be one; as thou, Father, art in me, and I in thee, that they also
may be one in us: that the world may believe that thou hast
sent me. 22 And the glory which thou gavest me I have given
them; that they may be one, even as we are one: 23 I in them,
and thou in me, that they may be made perfect in one; and
that the world may know that thou hast sent me, and hast
loved them, as thou hast loved me. 24 Father, I will that they
also, whom thou hast given me, be with me where I am; that
they may behold my glory, which thou hast given me, for
thou lovedst me before the foundation of the world.

25 'O righteous Father, the world hath not known thee,

but I have known thee, and these have known that thou hast
sent me. 26And I have declared unto them thy name, and will
declare it, that the love wherewith thou hast loved me may
be in them, and I in them.'

18 When Jesus had spoken these words, he went forth
with his disciples over the brook Cedron, where was a
garden, into the which he entered, and his disciples. 2And
Judas also, which betrayed him, knew the place, for Jesus
ofttimes resorted thither with his disciples. 3Judas then, having received a band of men and officers from the chief priests
and Pharisees, cometh thither with lanterns and torches and
weapons. 4Jesus therefore, knowing all things that should
come upon him, went forth, and said unto them, 'Whom
seek ye?' 5They answered him, 'Jesus of Nazareth.' Jesus saith
unto them, 'I am he.' And Judas also, which betrayed him,
stood with them. 6As soon then as he had said unto them, 'I
am he,' they went backward, and fell to the ground. 7Then
asked he them again, 'Whom seek ye?' And they said, 'Jesus
of Nazareth.' 8Jesus answered, 'I have told you that I am he:
if therefore ye seek me, let these go their way,' 9that the saying might be fulfilled, which he spake: 'Of them which thou
gavest me have I lost none.' 10Then Simon Peter having a
sword drew it, and smote the high priest's servant, and cut
off his right ear. The servant's name was Malchus. 11Then
said Jesus unto Peter, 'Put up thy sword into the sheath; the
cup which my Father hath given me, shall I not drink it?'
12Then the band and the captain and officers of the Jews took
Jesus, and bound him, 13and led him away to Annas first; for

he was father-in-law to Caiaphas, which was the high priest that same year. 14 Now Caiaphas was he, which gave counsel to the Jews, that it was expedient that one man should die for the people.

15 And Simon Peter followed Jesus, and so did another disciple; that disciple was known unto the high priest, and went in with Jesus into the palace of the high priest. 16 But Peter stood at the door without. Then went out that other disciple, which was known unto the high priest, and spake unto her that kept the door, and brought in Peter. 17 Then saith the damsel that kept the door unto Peter, 'Art not thou also one of this man's disciples?' He saith, 'I am not.' 18 And the servants and officers stood there, who had made a fire of coals, for it was cold, and they warmed themselves, and Peter stood with them, and warmed himself.

19 The high priest then asked Jesus of his disciples, and of his doctrine. 20 Jesus answered him, 'I spake openly to the world; I ever taught in the synagogue, and in the temple, whither the Jews always resort; and in secret have I said nothing. 21 Why askest thou me? Ask them which heard me, what I have said unto them; behold, they know what I said.' 22 And when he had thus spoken, one of the officers which stood by struck Jesus with the palm of his hand, saying, 'Answerest thou the high priest so?' 23 Jesus answered him, 'If I have spoken evil, bear witness of the evil, but if well, why smitest thou me?' 24 Now Annas had sent him bound unto Caiaphas the high priest. 25 And Simon Peter stood and warmed himself. They said therefore unto him, 'Art not thou also one of his disciples?' He denied it, and said, 'I am not.'

[26] One of the servants of the high priest, being his kinsman
whose ear Peter cut off, saith, 'Did not I see thee in the garden with him?' [27] Peter then denied again, and immediately
the cock crew.

[28] Then led they Jesus from Caiaphas unto the hall of
judgment, and it was early; and they themselves went not
into the judgment hall, lest they should be defiled; but that
they might eat the passover. [29] Pilate then went out unto
them, and said, 'What accusation bring ye against this man?'
[30] They answered and said unto him, 'If he were not a male-
factor, we would not have delivered him up unto thee.' [31] Then
said Pilate unto them, 'Take ye him, and judge him according to your law.' The Jews therefore said unto him, 'It is not
lawful for us to put any man to death,' [32] that the saying of
Jesus might be fulfilled, which he spake, signifying what
death he should die. [33] Then Pilate entered into the judgment
hall again, and called Jesus, and said unto him, 'Art thou the
King of the Jews?' [34] Jesus answered him, 'Sayest thou this
thing of thyself, or did others tell it thee of me?' [35] Pilate answered, 'Am I a Jew? Thine own nation and the chief priests
have delivered thee unto me; what hast thou done?' [36] Jesus
answered, 'My kingdom is not of this world: if my kingdom
were of this world, then would my servants fight, that I
should not be delivered to the Jews, but now is my kingdom
not from hence.' [37] Pilate therefore said unto him, 'Art thou a
king then?' Jesus answered, 'Thou sayest that I am a king. To
this end was I born, and for this cause came I into the world,
that I should bear witness unto the truth. Every one that is of
the truth heareth my voice.' [38] Pilate saith unto him, 'What is

truth?' And when he had said this, he went out again unto
the Jews, and saith unto them, 'I find in him no fault at all.
39 But ye have a custom, that I should release unto you one at
the passover: will ye therefore that I release unto you the
King of the Jews?' 40 Then cried they all again, saying, 'Not
this man, but Barabbas.' Now Barabbas was a robber.

19 Then Pilate therefore took Jesus, and scourged him.
2 And the soldiers platted a crown of thorns, and put it
on his head, and they put on him a purple robe, 3 and said,
'Hail, King of the Jews!' and they smote him with their hands.
4 Pilate therefore went forth again, and saith unto them, 'Behold, I bring him forth to you, that ye may know that I find
no fault in him.' 5 Then came Jesus forth, wearing the crown
of thorns, and the purple robe. And Pilate saith unto them,
'Behold the man!' 6 When the chief priests therefore and officers saw him, they cried out, saying, 'Crucify him, crucify
him.' Pilate saith unto them, 'Take ye him, and crucify him,
for I find no fault in him.' 7 The Jews answered him, 'We have
a law, and by our law he ought to die, because he made himself the Son of God.'

8 When Pilate therefore heard that saying, he was the
more afraid, 9 and went again into the judgment hall, and
saith unto Jesus, 'Whence art thou?' But Jesus gave him no
answer. 10 Then saith Pilate unto him, 'Speakest thou not unto
me? Knowest thou not that I have power to crucify thee, and
have power to release thee?' 11 Jesus answered, 'Thou could-
est have no power at all against me, except it were given
thee from above: therefore he that delivered me unto thee

hath the greater sin.' 12 And from thenceforth Pilate sought to release him, but the Jews cried out, saying, 'If thou let this man go, thou art not Cæsar's friend; whosoever maketh himself a king speaketh against Cæsar.'

13 When Pilate therefore heard that saying, he brought Jesus forth, and sat down in the judgment seat in a place that is called the Pavement, but in the Hebrew, Gabbatha. 14 And it was the preparation of the passover, and about the sixth hour, and he saith unto the Jews, 'Behold your King!' 15 But they cried out, 'Away with him, away with him, crucify him.' Pilate saith unto them, 'Shall I crucify your King?' The chief priests answered, 'We have no king but Cæsar.' 16 Then delivered he him therefore unto them to be crucified. And they took Jesus, and led him away. 17 And he bearing his cross went forth into a place called the place of a skull, which is called in the Hebrew Golgotha, 18 where they crucified him, and two other with him, on either side one, and Jesus in the midst.

19 And Pilate wrote a title, and put it on the cross. And the writing was, 'Jesus of Nazareth the King of the Jews.' 20 This title then read many of the Jews, for the place where Jesus was crucified was nigh to the city, and it was written in Hebrew, and Greek, and Latin. 21 Then said the chief priests of the Jews to Pilate, 'Write not, "The King of the Jews", but that he said, "I am King of the Jews."' 22 Pilate answered, 'What I have written I have written.'

23 Then the soldiers, when they had crucified Jesus, took his garments, and made four parts, to every soldier a part; and also his coat. Now the coat was without seam, woven from the top throughout. 24 They said therefore among themselves,

'Let us not rend it, but cast lots for it, whose it shall be,' that
the scripture might be fulfilled, which saith, 'They parted
my raiment among them, and for my vesture they did cast
lots.' These things therefore the soldiers did.
25 Now there stood by the cross of Jesus his mother, and
his mother's sister, Mary the wife of Cleophas, and Mary Magdalene. 26 When Jesus therefore saw his mother, and the disciple standing by, whom he loved, he saith unto his mother,
'Woman, behold thy son!' 27 Then saith he to the disciple,
'Behold thy mother!' And from that hour that disciple took
her unto his own home.
28 After this, Jesus knowing that all things were now
accomplished, that the scripture might be fulfilled, saith, 'I
thirst.' 29 Now there was set a vessel full of vinegar, and they
filled a spunge with vinegar, and put it upon hyssop, and
put it to his mouth. 30 When Jesus therefore had received the
vinegar, he said, 'It is finished,' and he bowed his head, and
gave up the ghost. 31 The Jews therefore, because it was the
preparation, that the bodies should not remain upon the
cross on the sabbath day (for that sabbath day was an high
day), besought Pilate that their legs might be broken, and
that they might be taken away. 32 Then came the soldiers,
and brake the legs of the first, and of the other which was
crucified with him. 33 But when they came to Jesus, and saw
that he was dead already, they brake not his legs, 34 but one
of the soldiers with a spear pierced his side, and forthwith
came there out blood and water. 35 And he that saw it bare
record, and his record is true, and he knoweth that he saith
true, that ye might believe. 36 For these things were done,

that the scripture should be fulfilled: 'A bone of him shall not
be broken.' 37And again another scripture saith, 'They shall
look on him whom they pierced.'

38And after this Joseph of Arimathæa, being a disciple of
Jesus, but secretly for fear of the Jews, besought Pilate that
he might take away the body of Jesus, and Pilate gave him
leave. He came therefore, and took the body of Jesus. 39And
there came also Nicodemus, which at the first came to Jesus
by night, and brought a mixture of myrrh and aloes, about
an hundred pound weight. 40Then took they the body of
Jesus, and wound it in linen clothes with the spices, as the
manner of the Jews is to bury. 41Now in the place where he
was crucified there was a garden; and in the garden a new
sepulchre, wherein was never man yet laid. 42There laid they
Jesus therefore because of the Jews' preparation day, for the
sepulchre was nigh at hand.

20 The first day of the week cometh Mary Magdalene
early, when it was yet dark, unto the sepulchre, and
seeth the stone taken away from the sepulchre. 2Then she
runneth, and cometh to Simon Peter, and to the other disciple,
whom Jesus loved, and saith unto them, 'They have taken
away the Lord out of the sepulchre, and we know not where
they have laid him.' 3Peter therefore went forth, and that other
disciple, and came to the sepulchre. 4So they ran both together,
and the other disciple did outrun Peter, and came first to the
sepulchre. 5And he stooping down, and looking in, saw the
linen clothes lying; yet went he not in. 6Then cometh Simon
Peter following him, and went into the sepulchre, and seeth

the linen clothes lie, 7 and the napkin, that was about his head,
not lying with the linen clothes, but wrapped together in a
place by itself. 8 Then went in also that other disciple, which
came first to the sepulchre, and he saw, and believed. 9 For as
yet they knew not the scripture, that he must rise again from
the dead. 10 Then the disciples went away again unto their
own home.

11 But Mary stood without at the sepulchre weeping, and
as she wept, she stooped down, and looked into the sepulchre, 12 and seeth two angels in white sitting, the one at the
head, and the other at the feet, where the body of Jesus had
lain. 13 And they say unto her, 'Woman, why weepest thou?'
She saith unto them, 'Because they have taken away my
Lord, and I know not where they have laid him.' 14 And when
she had thus said, she turned herself back, and saw Jesus
standing, and knew not that it was Jesus. 15 Jesus saith unto
her, 'Woman, why weepest thou? Whom seekest thou?' She,
supposing him to be the gardener, saith unto him, 'Sir, if
thou have borne him hence, tell me where thou hast laid
him, and I will take him away.' 16 Jesus saith unto her, 'Mary.'
She turned herself, and saith unto him, 'Rabboni,' which is to
say, 'Master'. 17 Jesus saith unto her, 'Touch me not, for I am
not yet ascended to my Father, but go to my brethren, and
say unto them, "I ascend unto my Father, and your Father;
and to my God, and your God."' 18 Mary Magdalene came
and told the disciples that she had seen the Lord, and that he
had spoken these things unto her.

19 Then the same day at evening, being the first day of the
week, when the doors were shut where the disciples were

assembled for fear of the Jews, came Jesus and stood in the
midst, and saith unto them, 'Peace be unto you.' 20 And when
he had so said, he shewed unto them his hands and his side.
Then were the disciples glad, when they saw the Lord. 21 Then
said Jesus to them again, 'Peace be unto you: as my Father hath
sent me, even so send I you.' 22 And when he had said this, he
breathed on them, and saith unto them, 'Receive ye the Holy
Ghost. 23 Whose soever sins ye remit, they are remitted unto
them; and whose soever sins ye retain, they are retained.'

24 But Thomas, one of the twelve, called Didymus, was
not with them when Jesus came. 25 The other disciples therefore said unto him, 'We have seen the Lord.' But he said unto
them, 'Except I shall see in his hands the print of the nails,
and put my finger into the print of the nails, and thrust my
hand into his side, I will not believe.'

26 And after eight days again his disciples were within,
and Thomas with them; then came Jesus, the doors being
shut, and stood in the midst, and said, 'Peace be unto you.'
27 Then saith he to Thomas, 'Reach hither thy finger, and
behold my hands; and reach hither thy hand, and thrust it
into my side; and be not faithless, but believing.' 28 And
Thomas answered and said unto him, 'My Lord and my
God.' 29 Jesus saith unto him, 'Thomas, because thou hast
seen me, thou hast believed: blessed are they that have not
seen, and yet have believed.'

30 And many other signs truly did Jesus in the presence of
his disciples, which are not written in this book: 31 but these are
written, that ye might believe that Jesus is the Christ, the Son
of God; and that believing ye might have life through his name.

21 After these things Jesus shewed himself again to the
disciples at the sea of Tiberias; and on this wise shewed
he himself. [2] There were together Simon Peter, and Thomas
called Didymus, and Nathanael of Cana in Galilee, and the
sons of Zebedee, and two other of his disciples. [3] Simon Peter
saith unto them, 'I go a fishing.' They say unto him, 'We also
go with thee.' They went forth, and entered into a ship immediately; and that night they caught nothing. [4] But when
the morning was now come, Jesus stood on the shore, but
the disciples knew not that it was Jesus. [5] Then Jesus saith
unto them, 'Children, have ye any meat?' They answered him,
'No.' [6] And he said unto them, 'Cast the net on the right side
of the ship, and ye shall find.' They cast therefore, and now
they were not able to draw it for the multitude of fishes.
[7] Therefore that disciple whom Jesus loved saith unto Peter,
'It is the Lord.' Now when Simon Peter heard that it was the
Lord, he girt his fisher's coat unto him (for he was naked),
and did cast himself into the sea. [8] And the other disciples
came in a little ship (for they were not far from land, but as it
were two hundred cubits), dragging the net with fishes. [9] As
soon then as they were come to land, they saw a fire of coals
there, and fish laid thereon, and bread. [10] Jesus saith unto
them, 'Bring of the fish which ye have now caught.' [11] Simon
Peter went up, and drew the net to land full of great fishes,
an hundred and fifty and three, and for all there were so
many, yet was not the net broken. [12] Jesus saith unto them,
'Come and dine.' And none of the disciples durst ask
him, 'Who art thou?' knowing that it was the Lord. [13] Jesus
then cometh, and taketh bread, and giveth them, and fish

likewise. 14 This is now the third time that Jesus shewed himself to his disciples, after that he was risen from the dead.
15 So when they had dined, Jesus saith to Simon Peter,
'Simon, son of Jonas, lovest thou me more than these?' He
saith unto him, 'Yea, Lord; thou knowest that I love thee.'
He saith unto him, 'Feed my lambs.' 16 He saith to him again
the second time, 'Simon, son of Jonas, lovest thou me?' He
saith unto him, 'Yea, Lord; thou knowest that I love thee.'
He saith unto him, 'Feed my sheep.' 17 He saith unto him the
third time, 'Simon, son of Jonas, lovest thou me?' Peter was
grieved because he said unto him the third time, 'Lovest thou
me?' And he said unto him, 'Lord, thou knowest all things;
thou knowest that I love thee.' Jesus saith unto him, 'Feed
my sheep.' 18 Verily, verily, I say unto thee, 'When thou wast
young, thou girdedst thyself, and walkedst whither thou
wouldest, but when thou shalt be old, thou shalt stretch
forth thy hands, and another shall gird thee, and carry thee
whither thou wouldest not.' 19 This spake he, signifying by
what death he should glorify God. And when he had spoken
this, he saith unto him, 'Follow me.' 20 Then Peter, turning
about, seeth the disciple whom Jesus loved following, which
also leaned on his breast at supper, and said, 'Lord, which is
he that betrayeth thee?' 21 Peter seeing him saith to Jesus,
'Lord, and what shall this man do?' 22 Jesus saith unto him,
'If I will that he tarry till I come, what is that to thee? Follow
thou me.' 23 Then went this saying abroad among the brethren, that that disciple should not die; yet Jesus said not unto
him, 'He shall not die,' but, 'If I will that he tarry till I come,
what is that to thee?' 24 This is the disciple which testifieth of

these things, and wrote these things, and we know that his
testimony is true. [25]And there are also many other things
which Jesus did, the which, if they should be written every
one, I suppose that even the world itself could not contain
the books that should be written. Amen.

titles in the series

genesis – *introduced by e. l. doctorow*
exodus – *introduced by david grossman*
job – *introduced by charles frazier*
selections from the book of psalms – *introduced by bono*
proverbs – *introduced by charles johnson*
ecclesiastes – *introduced by doris lessing*
matthew – *introduced by francisco goldman*
mark – *introduced by barry hannah*
luke – *introduced by thomas cahill*
john – *introduced by darcey steinke*
corinthians – *introduced by fay weldon*
revelation – *introduced by kathleen norris*

corinthians

the epistles of paul the apostle to the

corinthians

authorized king james version

grove press
new york

with an introduction by | fay weldon

The Pocket Canons were originally published in the U.K. in 1998 by Canongate Books, Ltd.
Published simultaneously in Canada
Printed in the United States of America

FIRST AMERICAN EDITION

Copyright information is on file with the Library of Congress
ISBN 0-8021-3620-6

Design by Paddy Cramsie

Grove Press
841 Broadway
New York, NY 10003

99 00 01 02 10 9 8 7 6 5 4 3 2 1

a note about pocket canons

The Authorized King James Version of the Bible, translated between 1603 and 1611, coincided with an extraordinary flowering of English literature. This version, more than any other, and possibly more than any other work in history, has had an influence in shaping the language we speak and write today. Presenting individual books from the Bible as separate volumes, as they were originally conceived, encourages the reader to approach them as literary works in their own right.

The first twelve books in this series encompass categories as diverse as history, fiction, philosophy, love poetry, and law. Each Pocket Canon also has its own introduction, specially commissioned from an impressive range of writers, which provides a personal interpretation of the text and explores its contemporary relevance.

Fay Weldon was born in England and raised in New Zealand. She took degrees in Economics and Psychology at the University of St Andrews in Scotland and then, after a decade of odd jobs and hard times, began writing fiction. She is now well known as novelist, screenwriter and cultural journalist. Her novels include The Life and Loves of a She-Devil *(a major movie starring Meryl Streep and Roseanne Barr),* Puffball, The Cloning of Joanna May, Affliction *and* Worst Fears. *She is the writer of Channel 4's successful series* Big Women, *and has several collections of short stories to her name, in particular* A Hard Time to be a Father. *She has four sons and lives in London.*

introduction by fay weldon

It is hard to *like* Paul the Apostle. One is not out of sympathy when Ananias the Chief Priest of Jerusalem tries to get him thrown out of town for preaching the Christian gospel and remarks to the Roman authorities, 'We have found him a pestilent fellow'. There seems to be so little love flowing from Paul, other than 'in God' which sometimes seems a way of getting out of the need for it in person, and perhaps why so many cruelties get to be perpetrated in God's name. Certainly, all, at the time, were in awe of this slippery, preaching, threatening, cajoling young man, always one step ahead of his enemies: he who BC would have been a prophet but AD must be an apostle, he who has a hot-line to God and God to him (or so he says), but *like* him? No. Many at the time must have suspected that on the road to Damascus this turncoat Paul, once Saul the persecutor of the Christians, did not see God, but rather a path to personal power, twinkling and beckoning in the desert sun. Perhaps Paul the Apostle simply 'crossed the floor' in the political parlance of our own country, our own age. When all of a sudden it seems the other side is singing the best tunes, over you go. Why hang around? Enemy becomes friend, and vice versa.

Prating 'love', this Apostle Paul rants, rails, reproaches and leads others into mortal danger, preaching the forbidden gospel. Letters to the little groups of Christians, digging in here and there – Corinthia, Galatia, Ephesia, Rome itself – model for all revolutionary movements thereafter, confirming them in their dangerous belief. At the time, 'Behold, I see the heavens opened and the Son of Man standing on the right hand of God' was a statement sufficiently bold to get poor Stephen – 'a man full of faith and the Holy Ghost' – brought before Saul and stoned to death. That was our Saul before Damascus, that was, before he changed his name to Paul; our Saul in full scourging flight, 'breathing out threatenings and slaughter against the disciples of the Lord'. Does the leopard change his spots as he changes sides?

And doesn't Paul take up such an annoyingly large chunk of the Bible, after the romance and passion and savagery of the early days are all finished, after that death upon the cross, with his undramatic letters to here and letters to there? A very Mandelson of religious politics, demanding his united front? Listen to Paul in *Corinthians*. 'Now I beseech you, brethren, by the name of our Lord, that ye all speak the same thing, and that there be no divisions amongst you, but that you be perfectly joined together in the same judgement.' Oh, thanks! And it's to be *your* judgement, isn't it, because you have the hot-line to God? Or say you have. Don't smoke, don't own guns, don't be unrighteous, don't spit in church, let's have no dissension here! Don't, don't, don't. Put away our adulthood and submit – be as a little child. 'For now we see as in a glass, darkly, but then face to face.' How quickly the early church, under Paul's tuition, ceases to be visionary and turns respectable. How short are the days of miracle and wonder. Believe, behave! Consult, unite! We're under threat here, and how many divisions did the intellectuals ever have? Ignore them. 'For it is written I will destroy the wisdom of the wise.'

Judgement is nothing, you men and women of Corinthia, clustering together in your ochre landscape, your rough dwellings squatting low upon the burning land. The spirit is all, and the new faith. And what hope this new faith brings. Life is not so short, and brutish and hard as you thought: only believe and you are saved, the Kingdom of God is at hand: oh fortunate generation, with the marvel of the coming of the Son of Man still in living memory.

Though Paul your Apostle never actually met Him face to face he has talked to those who have, and God himself has appeared to Paul once or twice, and sent an Angel to free him from prison (the two gaolers were put to death as a consequence, which always seemed unfair). The Holy Ghost is a familiar visitor too, bringing with him the gift of tongues, the word of God (so long as you can un-garble it), that same gift which charismatic sects still experience today. Though not so terrifying as once it was, the descent of the Holy Spirit is diminished in these cosy days into something seen rather as a relaxing kind of psychotherapy – or else defined as glossolalia, the mere description of a medical condition.

Love is all, writes Paul, so long of course as it's 'in God' and not in the flesh. 'Marry or burn!' (What a master of the sound-bite is this Paul!) Spare us from fornication, for the flesh can only exist at the expense of the spirit, so the flesh must be subdued, a doctrine which has suited many ever since.

'It is good for a man not to touch a woman,' says Paul and can it be that as a result of these eleven words for near on two thousand years women have been seen as temptation, and blamed, and priests have been celibate, and miserable (or gay) and sex a source of so much shame and degradation? Are men and women so easily led? So easily persuaded to forgo pleasure for the sake of principle? It seems so. Better to be as he himself is, says Paul, and celibate, but if you can't help it, then marry and behave. At least Paul has this much mercy: perhaps he saw the impracticality of what he wanted to achieve: a world without sex. 'Let the husband render unto the wife due benevolence: and likewise also the wife unto the husband.' Well, that's okay. That's generous, that's civilised, that's better than many manage or preach today, let alone then. Kindness and good manners get us a long way.

And next to sex there's bad company. 'Adulterers and effeminates: revilers and abusers of themselves with mankind.' Abhor, abjure! 'A fornicator, or covetous, or an idolater, or a railer, or a drunkard, or an extortioner: with such a one, no, not to eat.' Well, that makes sense. My mother, aged ninety, assures me that the breakdown of family life began on the first occasion a person declared guilty in a divorce case was asked to dinner. Forget when they got allowed into the Royal Enclosure at Ascot. Yes, folks, there was a time when moral blame was levelled at those who erred in sexual matters: when the breakdown of a marriage meant one party was guilty and one was innocent and the Court was prepared to say which. Nowadays there's simply no time for any of that. But who is to say we were not happier then?

And yet because we today don't much like Paul, it does not mean God was not speaking to him. The ways of the Creator are very strange. Our contemporary judgement, our political, emotional and spiritual correctnesses are not His. The magic of the language of Corinthians must be our evidence as to the actuality or otherwise of revelation. Did the Paul we know write the words? Or did the angels, as he claimed, write through him? Write, not speak, I say advisedly, for every writer knows the moment when the words on the page seem driven not by the mind but by an understanding that they already exist and which the hand merely serves. Remember that these are actual letters, written on parchment rolls, laboriously. They are not, unlike the rest of the Bible, spoken words of myth, fable and history mixed, flowing through a dusty landscape, gathered together from a thousand doubtful sources and recorded by those who often had their own interest to serve. They come from the hand of the writer, and can of course change in translation but that's about all.

'Though I speak with the tongues of men and of angels,' writes St Paul the poet, 'and have not charity, I am become as sounding brass or a tinkling cymbal. And though I have the gift of prophecy and understand all mysteries and all knowledge: and though I have all faith, so I could remove mountains, and have not charity, I am nothing ... Charity suffereth long and is kind: charity envieth not: charity vaunteth not itself, is not puffed up … Doth not behave itself unseemly, seeketh not her own: is not easily provoked, thinketh no evil …' We all know the passage, and rightly, for it is part of our Christian heritage, even if only to be spoken to us warningly by teachers. (I suspect Kipling based his poem *If* upon 2 *Corinthians* 1:13.)

'Charity' is often translated as 'love', but that word too has become so misused it begins to lose grandeur. The original word derives from the Roman *caritas*, usually translated as 'affection' but that too in context lacks gravitas. Our new 'empathy' is probably nearer to the actual meaning, but who could use such a base and modern word for so magnificent a usage? What is meant, I think, by 'charity' is the unexpected lurch of the heart towards others which can take the soul by surprise. So that 'now abideth faith, hope and charity, but the greatest of these is charity,' and if Paul, apostate and poet, tells us so, we had better believe him. The timeless truths remain. Two millennia are just the twinkling of an eye in the sight of God, and / or the writer.

the first epistle of paul the apostle to the corinthians

Paul, called to be an apostle of Jesus Christ through the will
of God, and Sosthenes our brother, 2 unto the church of God
which is at Corinth, to them that are sanctified in Christ
Jesus, called to be saints, with all that in every place call
upon the name of Jesus Christ our Lord, both theirs and
ours: 3 Grace be unto you, and peace, from God our Father,
and from the Lord Jesus Christ.

4 I thank my God always on your behalf, for the grace of
God which is given you by Jesus Christ: 5 that in every
thing ye are enriched by him, in all utterance, and in all
knowledge, 6 even as the testimony of Christ was confirmed in you, 7 so that ye come behind in no gift; waiting
for the coming of our Lord Jesus Christ, 8 who shall also
confirm you unto the end, that ye may be blameless in the
day of our Lord Jesus Christ. 9 God is faithful, by whom ye
were called unto the fellowship of his Son Jesus Christ our
Lord.

10 Now I beseech you, brethren, by the name of our Lord
Jesus Christ, that ye all speak the same thing, and that there
be no divisions among you, but that ye be perfectly joined
together in the same mind and in the same judgment. 11 For it
hath been declared unto me of you, my brethren, by them
which are of the house of Chloe, that there are contentions

among you. [12] Now this I say, that every one of you saith, 'I
am of Paul,' and 'I of Apollos,' and 'I of Cephas,' and 'I of
Christ.' [13] Is Christ divided? Was Paul crucified for you? Or
were ye baptized in the name of Paul? [14] I thank God that I
baptized none of you, but Crispus and Gaius, [15] lest any
should say that I had baptized in mine own name. [16] And I
baptized also the household of Stephanas; besides, I know
not whether I baptized any other. [17] For Christ sent me not to
baptize, but to preach the gospel: not with wisdom of words,
lest the cross of Christ should be made of none effect.

[18] For the preaching of the cross is to them that perish
foolishness, but unto us which are saved it is the power of
God. [19] For it is written, 'I will destroy the wisdom of the wise,
and will bring to nothing the understanding of the prudent.'
[20] Where is the wise? Where is the scribe? Where is the dis-
puter of this world? Hath not God made foolish the wisdom
of this world? [21] For after that in the wisdom of God the world
by wisdom knew not God, it pleased God by the foolishness
of preaching to save them that believe. [22] For the Jews require
a sign, and the Greeks seek after wisdom, [23] but we preach
Christ crucified, unto the Jews a stumbling-block, and unto
the Greeks foolishness, [24] but unto them which are called,
both Jews and Greeks, Christ the power of God, and the wisdom of God. [25] Because the foolishness of God is wiser than
men; and the weakness of God is stronger than men.

[26] For ye see your calling, brethren, how that not many
wise men after the flesh, not many mighty, not many noble,
are called, [27] but God hath chosen the foolish things of the
world to confound the wise; and God hath chosen the weak

things of the world to confound the things which are mighty;
28 and base things of the world, and things which are despised,
hath God chosen, yea, and things which are not, to bring to
nought things that are, 29 that no flesh should glory in his
presence. 30 But of him are ye in Christ Jesus, who of God is
made unto us wisdom, and righteousness, and sanctifica-
tion, and redemption, 31 that, according as it is written, 'He
that glorieth, let him glory in the Lord.'

2 And I, brethren, when I came to you, came not with
excellency of speech or of wisdom, declaring unto you
the testimony of God. 2 For I determined not to know any
thing among you, save Jesus Christ, and him crucified. 3 And
I was with you in weakness, and in fear, and in much trembling. 4 And my speech and my preaching was not with
enticing words of man's wisdom, but in demonstration of
the Spirit and of power, 5 that your faith should not stand in
the wisdom of men, but in the power of God.

6 Howbeit we speak wisdom among them that are perfect: yet not the wisdom of this world, nor of the princes of
this world, that come to nought; 7 but we speak the wisdom
of God in a mystery, even the hidden wisdom, which God
ordained before the world unto our glory, 8 which none of
the princes of this world knew, for had they known it, they
would not have crucified the Lord of glory. 9 But as it is written, 'Eye hath not seen, nor ear heard, neither have entered
into the heart of man, the things which God hath prepared
for them that love him.' 10 But God hath revealed them unto
us by his Spirit, for the Spirit searcheth all things, yea, the

deep things of God. [11] For what man knoweth the things of a
man, save the spirit of man which is in him? Even so the
things of God knoweth no man, but the Spirit of God. [12] Now
we have received, not the spirit of the world, but the spirit
which is of God, that we might know the things that are freely
given to us of God. [13] Which things also we speak, not in the
words which man's wisdom teacheth, but which the Holy
Ghost teacheth; comparing spiritual things with spiritual.

[14] But the natural man receiveth not the things of the Spirit
of God, for they are foolishness unto him; neither can he
know them, because they are spiritually discerned. [15] But he
that is spiritual judgeth all things, yet he himself is judged of
no man. [16] 'For who hath known the mind of the Lord, that
he may instruct him?' But we have the mind of Christ.

3 And I, brethren, could not speak unto you as unto spiritual, but as unto carnal, even as unto babes in Christ. [2] I
have fed you with milk, and not with meat, for hitherto ye
were not able to bear it, neither yet now are ye able. [3] For ye
are yet carnal, for whereas there is among you envying, and
strife, and divisions, are ye not carnal, and walk as men?
[4] For while one saith, 'I am of Paul,' and another, 'I am of Apollos,' are ye not carnal?

[5] Who then is Paul, and who is Apollos, but ministers by
whom ye believed, even as the Lord gave to every man? [6] I
have planted, Apollos watered; but God gave the increase.
[7] So then neither is he that planteth any thing, neither he that
watereth; but God that giveth the increase. [8] Now he that
planteth and he that watereth are one, and every man shall

receive his own reward according to his own labour. 9 For
we are labourers together with God; ye are God's husbandry,
ye are God's building.

10 According to the grace of God which is given unto me,
as a wise masterbuilder, I have laid the foundation, and
another buildeth thereon. But let every man take heed how
he buildeth thereupon. 11 For other foundation can no man
lay than that is laid, which is Jesus Christ. 12 Now if any man
build upon this foundation gold, silver, precious stones,
wood, hay, stubble, 13 every man's work shall be made manifest, for the day shall declare it, because it shall be revealed
by fire; and the fire shall try every man's work of what sort it
is. 14 If any man's work abide which he hath built thereupon,
he shall receive a reward. 15 If any man's work shall be
burned, he shall suffer loss, but he himself shall be saved;
yet so as by fire.

16 Know ye not that ye are the temple of God, and that the
Spirit of God dwelleth in you? 17 If any man defile the temple
of God, him shall God destroy, for the temple of God is holy,
which temple ye are. 18 Let no man deceive himself. If any
man among you seemeth to be wise in this world, let him
become a fool, that he may be wise. 19 For the wisdom of
this world is foolishness with God. For it is written, 'He
taketh the wise in their own craftiness,' 20 and again, 'The
Lord knoweth the thoughts of the wise, that they are vain.'
21 Therefore let no man glory in men. For all things are yours,
22 whether Paul, or Apollos, or Cephas, or the world, or life,
or death, or things present, or things to come; all are yours;
23 and ye are Christ's; and Christ is God's.

4 Let a man so account of us, as of the ministers of Christ,
and stewards of the mysteries of God. 2 Moreover it is
required in stewards, that a man be found faithful. 3 But with
me it is a very small thing that I should be judged of you, or
of man's judgment; yea, I judge not mine own self. 4 For I
know nothing by myself; yet am I not hereby justified; but
he that judgeth me is the Lord. 5 Therefore judge nothing
before the time, until the Lord come, who both will bring to
light the hidden things of darkness, and will make manifest
the counsels of the hearts, and then shall every man have
praise of God.

6 And these things, brethren, I have in a figure transferred
to myself and to Apollos for your sakes; that ye might learn
in us not to think of men above that which is written, that no
one of you be puffed up for one against another. 7 For who
maketh thee to differ from another? And what hast thou that
thou didst not receive? Now if thou didst receive it, why
dost thou glory, as if thou hadst not received it?

8 Now ye are full, now ye are rich, ye have reigned as
kings without us, and I would to God ye did reign, that we
also might reign with you. 9 For I think that God hath set
forth us the apostles last, as it were appointed to death, for
we are made a spectacle unto the world, and to angels, and
to men. 10 We are fools for Christ's sake, but ye are wise in
Christ; we are weak, but ye are strong; ye are honourable,
but we are despised. 11 Even unto this present hour we both
hunger, and thirst, and are naked, and are buffeted, and have
no certain dwellingplace; 12 and labour, working with our
own hands. Being reviled, we bless; being persecuted, we

suffer it; [13]being defamed, we intreat. We are made as the
filth of the world, and are the offscouring of all things unto
this day.

[14]I write not these things to shame you, but as my beloved sons I warn you. [15]For though ye have ten thousand
instructers in Christ, yet have ye not many fathers, for in
Christ Jesus I have begotten you through the gospel.
[16]Wherefore I beseech you, be ye followers of me. [17]For this
cause have I sent unto you Timotheus, who is my beloved
son, and faithful in the Lord, who shall bring you into remembrance of my ways which be in Christ, as I teach every
where in every church. [18]Now some are puffed up, as though
I would not come to you. [19]But I will come to you shortly, if
the Lord will, and will know, not the speech of them which
are puffed up, but the power. [20]For the kingdom of God is
not in word, but in power. [21]What will ye? Shall I come unto
you with a rod, or in love, and in the spirit of meekness?

5 It is reported commonly that there is fornication among
you, and such fornication as is not so much as named
among the Gentiles, that one should have his father's wife.
[2]And ye are puffed up, and have not rather mourned, that
he that hath done this deed might be taken away from
among you.

[3]For I verily, as absent in body, but present in spirit, have
judged already, as though I were present, concerning him
that hath so done this deed, [4]in the name of our Lord Jesus
Christ, when ye are gathered together, and my spirit, with
the power of our Lord Jesus Christ, [5]to deliver such an one

unto Satan for the destruction of the flesh, that the spirit may
be saved in the day of the Lord Jesus.

6 Your glorying is not good. Know ye not that a little
leaven leaveneth the whole lump? 7 Purge out therefore the
old leaven, that ye may be a new lump, as ye are unleavened.
For even Christ our passover is sacrificed for us; 8 therefore
let us keep the feast, not with old leaven, neither with the
leaven of malice and wickedness, but with the unleavened
bread of sincerity and truth.

9 I wrote unto you in an epistle not to company with fornicators; 10 yet not altogether with the fornicators of this
world, or with the covetous, or extortioners, or with idolaters,
for then must ye needs go out of the world. 11 But now I have
written unto you not to keep company, if any man that is
called a brother be a fornicator, or covetous, or an idolater,
or a railer, or a drunkard, or an extortioner; with such an one
no not to eat. 12 For what have I to do to judge them also that
are without? Do not ye judge them that are within? 13 But
them that are without God judgeth. Therefore put away
from among yourselves that wicked person.

6 Dare any of you, having a matter against another, go to
law before the unjust, and not before the saints? 2 Do ye
not know that the saints shall judge the world? And if the
world shall be judged by you, are ye unworthy to judge the
smallest matters? 3 Know ye not that we shall judge angels?
How much more things that pertain to this life? 4 If then ye
have judgments of things pertaining to this life, set them to
judge who are least esteemed in the church. 5 I speak to your

shame. Is it so, that there is not a wise man among you? No,
not one that shall be able to judge between his brethren?
6 But brother goeth to law with brother, and that before the
unbelievers.

7 Now therefore there is utterly a fault among you, because ye go to law one with another. Why do ye not rather
take wrong? Why do ye not rather suffer yourselves to be
defrauded? 8 Nay, ye do wrong, and defraud, and that your
brethren.

9 Know ye not that the unrighteous shall not inherit the
kingdom of God? Be not deceived: neither fornicators, nor
idolaters, nor adulterers, nor effeminate, nor abusers of themselves with mankind, 10 nor thieves, nor covetous, nor drunk-
ards, nor revilers, nor extortioners, shall inherit the kingdom
of God. 11 And such were some of you: but ye are washed, but
ye are sanctified, but ye are justified in the name of the Lord
Jesus, and by the Spirit of our God.

12 All things are lawful unto me, but all things are not
expedient; all things are lawful for me, but I will not be
brought under the power of any. 13 Meats for the belly, and
the belly for meats, but God shall destroy both it and them.
Now the body is not for fornication, but for the Lord; and
the Lord for the body. 14 And God hath both raised up the
Lord, and will also raise up us by his own power. 15 Know ye
not that your bodies are the members of Christ? Shall I then
take the members of Christ, and make them the members of
an harlot? God forbid. 16 What? Know ye not that he which is
joined to an harlot is one body? For two, saith he, shall be
one flesh. 17 But he that is joined unto the Lord is one spirit.

18 Flee fornication. Every sin that a man doeth is without the
body, but he that committeth fornication sinneth against his
own body. 19 What? Know ye not that your body is the temple of the Holy Ghost which is in you, which ye have of God,
and ye are not your own? 20 For ye are bought with a price;
therefore glorify God in your body, and in your spirit, which
are God's.

7 Now concerning the things whereof ye wrote unto me:
'It is good for a man not to touch a woman.' 2 Nevertheless, to avoid fornication, let every man have his own wife,
and let every woman have her own husband. 3 Let the husband render unto the wife due benevolence, and likewise
also the wife unto the husband. 4 The wife hath not power of
her own body, but the husband, and likewise also the husband hath not power of his own body, but the wife. 5 Defraud
ye not one the other, except it be with consent for a time, that
ye may give yourselves to fasting and prayer; and come
together again, that Satan tempt you not for your incon-
tinency. 6 But I speak this by permission, and not of commandment. 7 For I would that all men were even as I myself.
But every man hath his proper gift of God, one after this
manner, and another after that.

8 I say therefore to the unmarried and widows: it is good
for them if they abide even as I. 9 But if they cannot contain,
let them marry, for it is better to marry than to burn.

10 And unto the married I command, yet not I, but the
Lord, let not the wife depart from her husband; 11 but and if
she depart, let her remain unmarried, or be reconciled to her

husband, and let not the husband put away his wife.

12 But to the rest speak I, not the Lord: if any brother hath
a wife that believeth not, and she be pleased to dwell with
him, let him not put her away. 13 And the woman which hath
an husband that believeth not, and if he be pleased to dwell
with her, let her not leave him. 14 For the unbelieving husband
is sanctified by the wife, and the unbelieving wife is sanctified by the husband: else were your children unclean; but
now are they holy. 15 But if the unbelieving depart, let him
depart. A brother or a sister is not under bondage in such
cases, but God hath called us to peace. 16 For what knowest
thou, O wife, whether thou shalt save thy husband? Or how
knowest thou, O man, whether thou shalt save thy wife?

17 But as God hath distributed to every man, as the Lord
hath called every one, so let him walk. And so ordain I in all
churches. 18 Is any man called being circumcised? Let him
not become uncircumcised. Is any called in uncircumcision?
Let him not be circumcised. 19 Circumcision is nothing, and
uncircumcision is nothing, but the keeping of the commandments of God. 20 Let every man abide in the same calling
wherein he was called.

21 Art thou called being a servant? Care not for it, but if
thou mayest be made free, use it rather. 22 For he that is called
in the Lord, being a servant, is the Lord's freeman; likewise
also he that is called, being free, is Christ's servant. 23 Ye are
bought with a price; be not ye the servants of men. 24 Brethren,
let every man, wherein he is called, therein abide with God.

25 Now concerning virgins I have no commandment of
the Lord; yet I give my judgment, as one that hath obtained

mercy of the Lord to be faithful. 26 I suppose therefore that this is good for the present distress, I say, that it is good for a man so to be. 27 Art thou bound unto a wife? Seek not to be loosed. Art thou loosed from a wife? Seek not a wife. 28 But and if thou marry, thou hast not sinned; and if a virgin marry, she hath not sinned. Nevertheless such shall have trouble in the flesh, but I spare you. 29 But this I say, brethren, the time is short: it remaineth, that both they that have wives be as though they had none; 30 and they that weep, as though they wept not; and they that rejoice, as though they rejoiced not; and they that buy, as though they possessed not; 31 and they that use this world, as not abusing it; for the fashion of this world passeth away.

32 But I would have you without carefulness. He that is unmarried careth for the things that belong to the Lord, how he may please the Lord, 33 but he that is married careth for the things that are of the world, how he may please his wife. 34 There is difference also between a wife and a virgin. The unmarried woman careth for the things of the Lord, that she may be holy both in body and in spirit, but she that is married careth for the things of the world, how she may please her husband. 35 And this I speak for your own profit; not that I may cast a snare upon you, but for that which is comely, and that ye may attend upon the Lord without distraction.

36 But if any man think that he behaveth himself uncomely toward his virgin, if she pass the flower of her age, and need so require, let him do what he will, he sinneth not: let them marry. 37 Nevertheless he that standeth stedfast in his heart, having no necessity, but hath power over his own will, and

hath so decreed in his heart that he will keep his virgin, doeth
well. 38 So then he that giveth her in marriage doeth well; but
he that giveth her not in marriage doeth better.
39 The wife is bound by the law as long as her husband
liveth; but if her husband be dead, she is at liberty to be married to whom she will; only in the Lord. 40 But she is happier
if she so abide, after my judgment, and I think also that I
have the Spirit of God.

8 Now as touching things offered unto idols, we know
that we all have knowledge. Knowledge puffeth up, but
charity edifieth. 2 And if any man think that he knoweth any
thing, he knoweth nothing yet as he ought to know. 3 But if
any man love God, the same is known of him.
4 As concerning therefore the eating of those things that
are offered in sacrifice unto idols, we know that an idol is
nothing in the world, and that there is none other God but
one. 5 For though there be that are called gods, whether in
heaven or in earth (as there be gods many, and lords many),
6 but to us there is but one God, the Father, of whom are all
things, and we in him, and one Lord Jesus Christ, by whom
are all things, and we by him.
7 Howbeit there is not in every man that knowledge, for
some with conscience of the idol unto this hour eat it as a
thing offered unto an idol; and their conscience being weak
is defiled. 8 But meat commendeth us not to God: for neither,
if we eat, are we the better; neither, if we eat not, are we the
worse. 9 But take heed lest by any means this liberty of yours
become a stumbling-block to them that are weak. 10 For if any

man see thee which hast knowledge sit at meat in the idol's
temple, shall not the conscience of him which is weak be
emboldened to eat those things which are offered to idols,
[11] and through thy knowledge shall the weak brother perish,
for whom Christ died? [12] But when ye sin so against the
brethren, and wound their weak conscience, ye sin against
Christ. [13] Wherefore, if meat make my brother to offend, I
will eat no flesh while the world standeth, lest I make my
brother to offend.

9 Am I not an apostle? Am I not free? Have I not seen
Jesus Christ our Lord? Are not ye my work in the Lord?
[2] If I be not an apostle unto others, yet doubtless I am to you,
for the seal of mine apostleship are ye in the Lord.

[3] Mine answer to them that do examine me is this. [4] Have
we not power to eat and to drink? [5] Have we not power to
lead about a sister, a wife, as well as other apostles, and as
the brethren of the Lord, and Cephas? [6] Or I only and Barn-
abas, have not we power to forbear working? [7] Who goeth a
warfare any time at his own charges? Who planteth a vineyard, and eateth not of the fruit thereof? Or who feedeth a
flock, and eateth not of the milk of the flock?

[8] Say I these things as a man? Or saith not the law the
same also? [9] For it is written in the law of Moses, 'Thou shalt
not muzzle the mouth of the ox that treadeth out the corn.'
Doth God take care for oxen? [10] Or saith he it altogether for
our sakes? For our sakes, no doubt, this is written: 'That he
that ploweth should plow in hope, and that he that thresh-
eth in hope should be partaker of his hope.' [11] If we have

sown unto you spiritual things, is it a great thing if we shall
reap your carnal things? 12 If others be partakers of this power
over you, are not we rather? Nevertheless we have not used
this power; but suffer all things, lest we should hinder the
gospel of Christ. 13 Do ye not know that they which minister
about holy things live of the things of the temple? And they
which wait at the altar are partakers with the altar? 14 Even so
hath the Lord ordained that they which preach the gospel
should live of the gospel.

15 But I have used none of these things; neither have I
written these things, that it should be so done unto me, for it
were better for me to die, than that any man should make
my glorying void. 16 For though I preach the gospel, I have
nothing to glory of, for necessity is laid upon me; yea, woe is
unto me, if I preach not the gospel! 17 For if I do this thing
willingly, I have a reward, but if against my will, a dispensa-
tion of the gospel is committed unto me. 18 What is my
reward then? Verily that, when I preach the gospel, I may
make the gospel of Christ without charge, that I abuse not
my power in the gospel.

19 For though I be free from all men, yet have I made
myself servant unto all, that I might gain the more. 20 And
unto the Jews I became as a Jew, that I might gain the Jews;
to them that are under the law, as under the law, that I might
gain them that are under the law; 21 to them that are without
law, as without law (being not without law to God, but under
the law to Christ), that I might gain them that are without
law. 22 To the weak became I as weak, that I might gain the
weak. I am made all things to all men, that I might by all

means save some. 23 And this I do for the gospel's sake, that I
might be partaker thereof with you.

24 Know ye not that they which run in a race run all, but
one receiveth the prize? So run, that ye may obtain. 25 And
every man that striveth for the mastery is temperate in all
things. Now they do it to obtain a corruptible crown, but we
an incorruptible. 26 I therefore so run, not as uncertainly; so
fight I, not as one that beateth the air, 27 but I keep under
my body, and bring it into subjection, lest that by any means,
when I have preached to others, I myself should be a cast-
away.

10 Moreover, brethren, I would not that ye should be
ignorant, how that all our fathers were under the
cloud, and all passed through the sea, 2 and were all baptized
unto Moses in the cloud and in the sea, 3 and did all eat the
same spiritual meat, 4 and did all drink the same spiritual
drink, for they drank of that spiritual Rock that followed
them, and that Rock was Christ. 5 But with many of them
God was not well pleased, for they were overthrown in the
wilderness.

6 Now these things were our examples, to the intent we
should not lust after evil things, as they also lusted. 7 Neither
be ye idolaters, as were some of them; as it is written, 'The
people sat down to eat and drink, and rose up to play.' 8 Neither let us commit fornication, as some of them committed,
and fell in one day three and twenty thousand. 9 Neither let
us tempt Christ, as some of them also tempted, and were
destroyed of serpents. 10 Neither murmur ye, as some of them

also murmured, and were destroyed of the destroyer. [11] Now
all these things happened unto them for ensamples, and
they are written for our admonition, upon whom the ends of
the world are come. [12] Wherefore let him that thinketh he
standeth take heed lest he fall. [13] There hath no temptation
taken you but such as is common to man, but God is faithful,
who will not suffer you to be tempted above that ye are able,
but will with the temptation also make a way to escape, that
ye may be able to bear it.

[14] Wherefore, my dearly beloved, flee from idolatry. [15] I speak
as to wise men; judge ye what I say. [16] The cup of blessing
which we bless, is it not the communion of the blood of Christ?
The bread which we break, is it not the communion of the
body of Christ? [17] For we being many are one bread, and one
body, for we are all partakers of that one bread. [18] Behold
Israel after the flesh: are not they which eat of the sacrifices
partakers of the altar? [19] What say I then? That the idol is any
thing, or that which is offered in sacrifice to idols is any thing?
[20] But I say, that the things which the Gentiles sacrifice, they
sacrifice to devils, and not to God, and I would not that ye
should have fellowship with devils. [21] Ye cannot drink the
cup of the Lord, and the cup of devils; ye cannot be partakers of the Lord's table, and of the table of devils. [22] Do we
provoke the Lord to jealousy? Are we stronger than he?

[23] All things are lawful for me, but all things are not expedient; all things are lawful for me, but all things edify not.
[24] Let no man seek his own, but every man another's wealth.
[25] Whatsoever is sold in the shambles, that eat, asking no
question for conscience sake, [26] for the earth is the Lord's, and

the fulness thereof. 27 If any of them that believe not bid you
to a feast, and ye be disposed to go; whatsoever is set before
you, eat, asking no question for conscience sake. 28 But if any
man say unto you, 'This is offered in sacrifice unto idols,' eat
not for his sake that shewed it, and for conscience sake, for
the earth is the Lord's, and the fulness thereof. 29 Conscience,
I say, not thine own, but of the other: for why is my liberty
judged of another man's conscience? 30 For if I by grace be a
partaker, why am I evil spoken of for that for which I give
thanks?

31 Whether therefore ye eat, or drink, or whatsoever ye
do, do all to the glory of God. 32 Give none offence, neither to
the Jews, nor to the Gentiles, nor to the church of God.
33 Even as I please all men in all things, not seeking mine
own profit, but the profit of many, that they may be saved.

11 Be ye followers of me, even as I also am of Christ.
2 Now I praise you, brethren, that ye remember me in
all things, and keep the ordinances, as I delivered them to
you. 3 But I would have you know that the head of every
man is Christ; and the head of the woman is the man; and
the head of Christ is God. 4 Every man praying or prophesying, having his head covered, dishonoureth his head. 5 But
every woman that prayeth or prophesieth with her head
uncovered dishonoureth her head, for that is even all one as
if she were shaven. 6 For if the woman be not covered, let her
also be shorn, but if it be a shame for a woman to be shorn or
shaven, let her be covered. 7 For a man indeed ought not to
cover his head, forasmuch as he is the image and glory of

God, but the woman is the glory of the man. 8 For the man is
not of the woman, but the woman of the man. 9 Neither was
the man created for the woman, but the woman for the man.
10 For this cause ought the woman to have power on her head
because of the angels. 11 Nevertheless neither is the man
without the woman, neither the woman without the man, in
the Lord. 12 For as the woman is of the man, even so is the
man also by the woman; but all things of God. 13 Judge in
yourselves: is it comely that a woman pray unto God uncovered? 14 Doth not even nature itself teach you, that, if a man
have long hair, it is a shame unto him? 15 But if a woman
have long hair, it is a glory to her, for her hair is given her for
a covering. 16 But if any man seem to be contentious, we have
no such custom, neither the churches of God.

17 Now in this that I declare unto you I praise you not,
that ye come together not for the better, but for the worse.
18 For first of all, when ye come together in the church, I hear
that there be divisions among you; and I partly believe it.
19 For there must be also heresies among you, that they which
are approved may be made manifest among you. 20 When ye
come together therefore into one place, this is not to eat the
Lord's supper. 21 For in eating every one taketh before other
his own supper, and one is hungry, and another is drunken.
22 What? Have ye not houses to eat and to drink in? Or
despise ye the church of God, and shame them that have
not? What shall I say to you? Shall I praise you in this? I
praise you not.

23 For I have received of the Lord that which also I delivered unto you, that the Lord Jesus the same night in which

he was betrayed took bread, 24 and when he had given thanks,
he brake it, and said, 'Take, eat; this is my body, which is
broken for you; this do in remembrance of me.' 25 After the
same manner also he took the cup, when he had supped,
saying, 'This cup is the new testament in my blood; this do
ye, as oft as ye drink it, in remembrance of me.' 26 For as often
as ye eat this bread, and drink this cup, ye do shew the
Lord's death till he come.

27 Wherefore whosoever shall eat this bread, and drink
this cup of the Lord, unworthily, shall be guilty of the body
and blood of the Lord. 28 But let a man examine himself, and
so let him eat of that bread, and drink of that cup. 29 For he
that eateth and drinketh unworthily, eateth and drinketh
damnation to himself, not discerning the Lord's body. 30 For
this cause many are weak and sickly among you, and many
sleep. 31 For if we would judge ourselves, we should not be
judged. 32 But when we are judged, we are chastened of the
Lord, that we should not be condemned with the world.

33 Wherefore, my brethren, when ye come together to eat,
tarry one for another. 34 And if any man hunger, let him eat at
home; that ye come not together unto condemnation. And
the rest will I set in order when I come.

12 Now concerning spiritual gifts, brethren, I would not
have you ignorant. 2 Ye know that ye were Gentiles,
carried away unto these dumb idols, even as ye were led.
3 Wherefore I give you to understand, that no man speaking
by the Spirit of God calleth Jesus accursed, and that no man
can say that Jesus is the Lord, but by the Holy Ghost.

[4]Now there are diversities of gifts, but the same Spirit.
[5]And there are differences of administrations, but the same
Lord. [6]And there are diversities of operations, but it is the
same God which worketh all in all. [7]But the manifestation of
the Spirit is given to every man to profit withal. [8]For to one
is given by the Spirit the word of wisdom; to another the word
of knowledge by the same Spirit; [9]to another faith by the
same Spirit; to another the gifts of healing by the same Spirit;
[10]to another the working of miracles; to another prophecy; to
another discerning of spirits; to another divers kinds of
tongues; to another the interpretation of tongues; [11]but all
these worketh that one and the selfsame Spirit, dividing to
every man severally as he will.

[12]For as the body is one, and hath many members, and all
the members of that one body, being many, are one body; so
also is Christ. [13]For by one Spirit are we all baptized into one
body, whether we be Jews or Gentiles, whether we be bond
or free, and have been all made to drink into one Spirit.

[14]For the body is not one member, but many. [15]If the foot
shall say, 'Because I am not the hand, I am not of the body,' is
it therefore not of the body? [16]And if the ear shall say,
'Because I am not the eye, I am not of the body,' is it therefore not of the body? [17]If the whole body were an eye, where
were the hearing? If the whole were hearing, where were the
smelling? [18]But now hath God set the members every one of
them in the body, as it hath pleased him. [19]And if they were
all one member, where were the body? [20]But now are they
many members, yet but one body. [21]And the eye cannot say
unto the hand, I have no need of thee; nor again the head to

the feet, I have no need of you. 22 Nay, much more those members of the body, which seem to be more feeble, are necessary; 23 and those members of the body, which we think to be
less honourable, upon these we bestow more abundant honour; and our uncomely parts have more abundant comeli-
ness. 24 For our comely parts have no need, but God hath
tempered the body together, having given more abundant
honour to that part which lacked, 25 that there should be no
schism in the body, but that the members should have the
same care one for another. 26 And whether one member suffer, all the members suffer with it; or one member be honoured, all the members rejoice with it.

27 Now ye are the body of Christ, and members in particular. 28 And God hath set some in the church, first apostles,
secondarily prophets, thirdly teachers, after that miracles, then
gifts of healings, helps, governments, diversities of tongues.
29 Are all apostles? Are all prophets? Are all teachers? Are all
workers of miracles? 30 Have all the gifts of healing? Do all
speak with tongues? Do all interpret? 31 But covet earnestly
the best gifts, and yet shew I unto you a more excellent way.

13 Though I speak with the tongues of men and of angels,
and have not charity,
I am become as sounding brass,
or a tinkling cymbal.
2 And though I have the gift of prophecy,
and understand all mysteries, and all knowledge;
and though I have all faith,
so that I could remove mountains,

and have not charity, I am nothing.
3 And though I bestow all my goods to feed the poor,
and though I give my body to be burned,
and have not charity,
it profiteth me nothing.
4 Charity suffereth long, and is kind;
charity envieth not;
charity vaunteth not itself, is not puffed up,
5 doth not behave itself unseemly,
seeketh not her own, is not easily provoked,
thinketh no evil;
6 rejoiceth not in iniquity, but rejoiceth in the truth;
7 beareth all things, believeth all things,
hopeth all things, endureth all things.
8 Charity never faileth,
but whether there be prophecies, they shall fail;
whether there be tongues,
they shall cease;
whether there be knowledge,
it shall vanish away.
9 For we know in part, and we prophesy in part.
10 But when that which is perfect is come,
then that which is in part shall be done away.
11 When I was a child, I spake as a child,
I understood as a child, I thought as a child,
but when I became a man,
I put away childish things.
12 For now we see through a glass, darkly;
but then face to face.

Now I know in part;
but then shall I know even as also I am known.
13 And now abideth faith, hope, charity, these three;
but the greatest of these is charity.

14 Follow after charity, and desire spiritual gifts, but
rather that ye may prophesy. 2 For he that speaketh in
an unknown tongue speaketh not unto men, but unto God:
for no man understandeth him; howbeit in the spirit he
speaketh mysteries. 3 But he that prophesieth speaketh unto
men to edification, and exhortation, and comfort. 4 He that
speaketh in an unknown tongue edifieth himself, but he
that prophesieth edifieth the church. 5 I would that ye all
spake with tongues, but rather that ye prophesied: for
greater is he that prophesieth than he that speaketh with
tongues, except he interpret, that the church may receive
edifying.

6 Now, brethren, if I come unto you speaking with
tongues, what shall I profit you, except I shall speak to you
either by revelation, or by knowledge, or by prophesying, or
by doctrine? 7 And even things without life giving sound,
whether pipe or harp, except they give a distinction in the
sounds, how shall it be known what is piped or harped?
8 For if the trumpet give an uncertain sound, who shall prepare himself to the battle? 9 So likewise ye, except ye utter by
the tongue words easy to be understood, how shall it be
known what is spoken? For ye shall speak into the air.
10 There are, it may be, so many kinds of voices in the world,
and none of them is without signification. 11 Therefore if I

know not the meaning of the voice, I shall be unto him that
speaketh a barbarian, and he that speaketh shall be a barbarian unto me. 12 Even so ye, forasmuch as ye are zealous of
spiritual gifts, seek that ye may excel to the edifying of the
church.

13 Wherefore let him that speaketh in an unknown tongue
pray that he may interpret. 14 For if I pray in an unknown
tongue, my spirit prayeth, but my understanding is unfruitful. 15 What is it then? I will pray with the spirit, and I will
pray with the understanding also; I will sing with the spirit,
and I will sing with the understanding also. 16 Else when
thou shalt bless with the spirit, how shall he that occupieth
the room of the unlearned say 'Amen' at thy giving of thanks,
seeing he understandeth not what thou sayest? 17 For thou
verily givest thanks well, but the other is not edified. 18 I
thank my God, I speak with tongues more than ye all; 19 yet
in the church I had rather speak five words with my understanding, that by my voice I might teach others also, than ten
thousand words in an unknown tongue.

20 Brethren, be not children in understanding: howbeit in
malice be ye children, but in understanding be men. 21 In the
law it is written, 'With men of other tongues and other lips
will I speak unto this people; and yet for all that will they
not hear me,' saith the Lord. 22 Wherefore tongues are for a
sign, not to them that believe, but to them that believe not,
but prophesying serveth not for them that believe not, but
for them which believe. 23 If therefore the whole church be
come together into one place, and all speak with tongues,
and there come in those that are unlearned, or unbelievers,

will they not say that ye are mad? 24 But if all prophesy, and there come in one that believeth not, or one unlearned, he is convinced of all, he is judged of all, 25 and thus are the secrets of his heart made manifest; and so falling down on his face he will worship God, and report that God is in you of a truth.

26 How is it then, brethren? When ye come together, every one of you hath a psalm, hath a doctrine, hath a tongue, hath a revelation, hath an interpretation. Let all things be done unto edifying. 27 If any man speak in an unknown tongue, let it be by two, or at the most by three, and that by course; and let one interpret. 28 But if there be no interpreter, let him keep silence in the church; and let him speak to himself, and to God. 29 Let the prophets speak two or three, and let the other judge. 30 If any thing be revealed to another that sitteth by, let the first hold his peace. 31 For ye may all prophesy one by one, that all may learn, and all may be comforted. 32 And the spirits of the prophets are subject to the prophets. 33 For God is not the author of confusion, but of peace, as in all churches of the saints. 34 Let your women keep silence in the churches, for it is not permitted unto them to speak, but they are commanded to be under obedience, as also saith the law. 35 And if they will learn any thing, let them ask their husbands at home, for it is a shame for women to speak in the church. 36 What? Came the word of God out from you? Or came it unto you only?

37 If any man think himself to be a prophet, or spiritual, let him acknowledge that the things that I write unto you are the commandments of the Lord. 38 But if any man be ignorant, let him be ignorant. 39 Wherefore, brethren, covet to

prophesy, and forbid not to speak with tongues. 40 Let all things be done decently and in order.

15 Moreover, brethren, I declare unto you the gospel which I preached unto you, which also ye have received, and wherein ye stand, 2 by which also ye are saved, if ye keep in memory what I preached unto you, unless ye have believed in vain.

3 For I delivered unto you first of all that which I also received, how that Christ died for our sins according to the scriptures; 4 and that he was buried, and that he rose again the third day according to the scriptures, 5 and that he was seen of Cephas, then of the twelve. 6 After that, he was seen of above five hundred brethren at once; of whom the greater part remain unto this present, but some are fallen asleep. 7 After that, he was seen of James; then of all the apostles. 8 And last of all he was seen of me also, as of one born out of due time. 9 For I am the least of the apostles, that am not meet to be called an apostle, because I persecuted the church of God. 10 But by the grace of God I am what I am: and his grace which was bestowed upon me was not in vain; but I laboured more abundantly than they all; yet not I, but the grace of God which was with me. 11 Therefore whether it were I or they, so we preach, and so ye believed.

12 Now if Christ be preached that he rose from the dead, how say some among you that there is no resurrection of the dead? 13 But if there be no resurrection of the dead, then is Christ not risen. 14 And if Christ be not risen, then is our preaching vain, and your faith is also vain. 15 Yea, and we are found

false witnesses of God, because we have testified of God that
he raised up Christ, whom he raised not up, if so be that the
dead rise not. 16 For if the dead rise not, then is not Christ
raised, 17 and if Christ be not raised, your faith is vain; ye are
yet in your sins. 18 Then they also which are fallen asleep in
Christ are perished. 19 If in this life only we have hope in
Christ, we are of all men most miserable.

20 But now is Christ risen from the dead, and become the
firstfruits of them that slept. 21 For since by man came death,
by man came also the resurrection of the dead. 22 For as in
Adam all die, even so in Christ shall all be made alive. 23 But
every man in his own order: Christ the firstfruits; afterward
they that are Christ's at his coming. 24 Then cometh the end,
when he shall have delivered up the kingdom to God, even
the Father, when he shall have put down all rule and all
authority and power. 25 For he must reign, till he hath put all
enemies under his feet. 26 The last enemy that shall be destroyed is death. 27 For he hath put all things under his feet.
But when he saith all things are put under him, it is manifest
that he is excepted, which did put all things under him.
28 And when all things shall be subdued unto him, then shall
the Son also himself be subject unto him that put all things
under him, that God may be all in all.

29 Else what shall they do which are baptized for the
dead, if the dead rise not at all? Why are they then baptized
for the dead?

30 And why stand we in jeopardy every hour? 31 I protest
by your rejoicing which I have in Christ Jesus our Lord, I die
daily. 32 If after the manner of men I have fought with beasts

at Ephesus, what advantageth it me, if the dead rise not? Let
us eat and drink, for to morrow we die. 33 Be not deceived:
evil communications corrupt good manners. 34 Awake to
righteousness, and sin not; for some have not the knowledge
of God. I speak this to your shame. 35 But some man will say,
'How are the dead raised up? And with what body do they
come?' 36 Thou fool, that which thou sowest is not quickened, except it die. 37 And that which thou sowest, thou sowest not that body that shall be, but bare grain, it may chance
of wheat, or of some other grain, 38 but God giveth it a body
as it hath pleased him, and to every seed his own body. 39 All
flesh is not the same flesh, but there is one kind of flesh of
men, another flesh of beasts, another of fishes, and another
of birds. 40 There are also celestial bodies, and bodies terrestrial, but the glory of the celestial is one, and the glory of the
terrestrial is another. 41 There is one glory of the sun, and
another glory of the moon, and another glory of the stars, for
one star differeth from another star in glory.

42 So also is the resurrection of the dead. It is sown in corruption; it is raised in incorruption. 43 It is sown in dishonour; it is raised in glory. It is sown in weakness; it is raised in
power. 44 It is sown a natural body; it is raised a spiritual
body. There is a natural body, and there is a spiritual body.
45 And so it is written, 'The first man Adam was made a living soul.' The last Adam was made a quickening spirit.
46 Howbeit that was not first which is spiritual, but that
which is natural; and afterward that which is spiritual. 47 The
first man is of the earth, earthy; the second man is the Lord
from heaven. 48 As is the earthy, such are they also that are

earthy, and as is the heavenly, such are they also that are heavenly. 49 And as we have borne the image of the earthy, we shall also bear the image of the heavenly.

50 Now this I say, brethren, that flesh and blood cannot inherit the kingdom of God; neither doth corruption inherit incorruption. 51 Behold, I shew you a mystery. We shall not all sleep, but we shall all be changed, 52 in a moment, in the twinkling of an eye, at the last trump, for the trumpet shall sound, and the dead shall be raised incorruptible, and we shall be changed. 53 For this corruptible must put on incorruption, and this mortal must put on immortality. 54 So when this corruptible shall have put on incorruption, and this mortal shall have put on immortality, then shall be brought to pass the saying that is written, 'Death is swallowed up in victory.' 55 O death, where is thy sting? O grave, where is thy victory? 56 The sting of death is sin, and the strength of sin is the law. 57 But thanks be to God, which giveth us the victory through our Lord Jesus Christ.

58 Therefore, my beloved brethren, be ye stedfast, unmoveable, always abounding in the work of the Lord, forasmuch as ye know that your labour is not in vain in the Lord.

16 Now concerning the collection for the saints, as I have given order to the churches of Galatia, even so do ye. 2 Upon the first day of the week let every one of you lay by him in store, as God hath prospered him, that there be no gatherings when I come. 3 And when I come, whomsoever ye shall approve by your letters, them will I send to bring your liberality unto Jerusalem. 4 And if it be meet that I go also,

they shall go with me.
5 Now I will come unto you, when I shall pass through
Macedonia, for I do pass through Macedonia. 6 And it may
be that I will abide, yea, and winter with you, that ye may
bring me on my journey whithersoever I go. 7 For I will not
see you now by the way, but I trust to tarry a while with you,
if the Lord permit. 8 But I will tarry at Ephesus until Pente-
cost. 9 For a great door and effectual is opened unto me, and
there are many adversaries.

10 Now if Timotheus come, see that he may be with you
without fear, for he worketh the work of the Lord, as I also
do. 11 Let no man therefore despise him, but conduct him
forth in peace, that he may come unto me, for I look for him
with the brethren.

12 As touching our brother Apollos, I greatly desired him
to come unto you with the brethren: but his will was not at
all to come at this time; but he will come when he shall have
convenient time.

13 Watch ye, stand fast in the faith, quit you like men, be
strong. 14 Let all your things be done with charity.

15 I beseech you, brethren (ye know the house of Stephanas, that it is the firstfruits of Achaia, and that they have
addicted themselves to the ministry of the saints), 16 that ye
submit yourselves unto such, and to every one that helpeth
with us, and laboureth. 17 I am glad of the coming of Stephanas and Fortunatus and Achaicus, for that which was lacking on your part they have supplied. 18 For they have
refreshed my spirit and yours: therefore acknowledge ye
them that are such.

[19] The churches of Asia salute you. Aquila and Priscilla
salute you much in the Lord, with the church that is in their
house. [20] All the brethren greet you. Greet ye one another
with an holy kiss.

[21] The salutation of me Paul with mine own hand. [22] If any
man love not the Lord Jesus Christ, let him be Anathema
Maranatha. [23] The grace of our Lord Jesus Christ be with
you. [24] My love be with you all in Christ Jesus. Amen.

the second epistle of paul the apostle to the corinthians

Paul, an apostle of Jesus Christ by the will of God, and Timo-
thy our brother, unto the church of God which is at Corinth,
with all the saints which are in all Achaia:
2 Grace be to you and peace from God our Father, and
from the Lord Jesus Christ.
3 Blessed be God, even the Father of our Lord Jesus Christ,
the Father of mercies, and the God of all comfort, 4 who comforteth us in all our tribulation, that we may be able to comfort them which are in any trouble, by the comfort wherewith
we ourselves are comforted of God. 5 For as the sufferings of
Christ abound in us, so our consolation also aboundeth by
Christ. 6 And whether we be afflicted, it is for your consolation and salvation, which is effectual in the enduring of the
same sufferings which we also suffer; or whether we be comforted, it is for your consolation and salvation. 7 And our hope
of you is stedfast, knowing, that as ye are partakers of the sufferings, so shall ye be also of the consolation. 8 For we would
not, brethren, have you ignorant of our trouble which came to
us in Asia, that we were pressed out of measure, above strength,
insomuch that we despaired even of life: 9 but we had the sentence of death in ourselves, that we should not trust in ourselves, but in God which raiseth the dead, 10 who delivered us
from so great a death, and doth deliver: in whom we trust that
he will yet deliver us. 11 Ye also helping together by prayer

for us, that for the gift bestowed upon us by the means of
many persons thanks may be given by many on our behalf.

12 For our rejoicing is this, the testimony of our conscience,
that in simplicity and godly sincerity, not with fleshly wisdom, but by the grace of God, we have had our conversation
in the world, and more abundantly to you-ward. 13 For we
write none other things unto you, than what ye read or acknowledge, and I trust ye shall acknowledge even to the end,
14 as also ye have acknowledged us in part, that we are your
rejoicing, even as ye also are ours in the day of the Lord Jesus.

15 And in this confidence I was minded to come unto you
before, that ye might have a second benefit, 16 and to pass by
you into Macedonia, and to come again out of Macedonia
unto you, and of you to be brought on my way toward
Judaea. 17 When I therefore was thus minded, did I use light-
ness? Or the things that I purpose, do I purpose according to
the flesh, that with me there should be yea yea, and nay
nay? 18 But as God is true, our word toward you was not yea
and nay. 19 For the Son of God, Jesus Christ, who was preached
among you by us, even by me and Silvanus and Timotheus,
was not yea and nay, but in him was yea. 20 For all the promises of God in him are yea, and in him amen, unto the glory
of God by us. 21 Now he which stablisheth us with you in
Christ, and hath anointed us, is God, 22 who hath also sealed
us, and given the earnest of the Spirit in our hearts.

23 Moreover I call God for a record upon my soul, that to
spare you I came not as yet unto Corinth. 24 Not for that we
have dominion over your faith, but are helpers of your joy,
for by faith ye stand.

2 But I determined this with myself, that I would not
come again to you in heaviness. [2]For if I make you
sorry, who is he then that maketh me glad, but the same
which is made sorry by me? [3]And I wrote this same unto
you, lest, when I came, I should have sorrow from them of
whom I ought to rejoice; having confidence in you all, that
my joy is the joy of you all. [4]For out of much affliction and
anguish of heart I wrote unto you with many tears; not that
ye should be grieved, but that ye might know the love which
I have more abundantly unto you.

[5]But if any have caused grief, he hath not grieved me, but
in part, that I may not overcharge you all. [6]Sufficient to such
a man is this punishment, which was inflicted of many. [7]So
that contrariwise ye ought rather to forgive him, and comfort
him, lest perhaps such a one should be swallowed up with
overmuch sorrow. [8]Wherefore I beseech you that ye would
confirm your love toward him. [9]For to this end also did I write,
that I might know the proof of you, whether ye be obedient
in all things. [10]To whom ye forgive any thing, I forgive also,
for if I forgave any thing, to whom I forgave it, for your sakes
forgave I it in the person of Christ, [11]lest Satan should get an
advantage of us, for we are not ignorant of his devices.

[12]Furthermore, when I came to Troas to preach Christ's
gospel, and a door was opened unto me of the Lord, [13]I had no
rest in my spirit, because I found not Titus my brother, but
taking my leave of them, I went from thence into Macedonia.

[14]Now thanks be unto God, which always causeth us to
triumph in Christ, and maketh manifest the savour of his
knowledge by us in every place. [15]For we are unto God a

sweet savour of Christ, in them that are saved, and in them
that perish; 16 to the one we are the savour of death unto
death; and to the other the savour of life unto life. And who
is sufficient for these things? 17 For we are not as many,
which corrupt the word of God, but as of sincerity, but as of
God, in the sight of God speak we in Christ.

3 Do we begin again to commend ourselves? Or need we,
as some others, epistles of commendation to you, or letters of commendation from you? 2 Ye are our epistle written
in our hearts, known and read of all men; 3 forasmuch as ye
are manifestly declared to be the epistle of Christ ministered
by us, written not with ink, but with the Spirit of the living
God; not in tables of stone, but in fleshy tables of the heart.
4 And such trust have we through Christ to God-ward:
5 not that we are sufficient of ourselves to think any thing as
of ourselves, but our sufficiency is of God, 6 who also hath
made us able ministers of the new testament; not of the letter,
but of the spirit; for the letter killeth, but the spirit giveth life.
7 But if the ministration of death, written and engraven in
stones, was glorious, so that the children of Israel could not
stedfastly behold the face of Moses for the glory of his countenance, which glory was to be done away. 8 How shall not the
ministration of the spirit be rather glorious? 9 For if the ministration of condemnation be glory, much more doth the ministration of righteousness exceed in glory. 10 For even that which
was made glorious had no glory in this respect, by reason of
the glory that excelleth. 11 For if that which is done away was
glorious, much more that which remaineth is glorious.

12 Seeing then that we have such hope, we use great plain-
ness of speech, 13 and not as Moses, which put a vail over his
face, that the children of Israel could not stedfastly look to
the end of that which is abolished, 14 but their minds were
blinded, for until this day remaineth the same vail untaken
away in the reading of the old testament; which vail is done
away in Christ. 15 But even unto this day, when Moses is read,
the vail is upon their heart. 16 Nevertheless when it shall turn
to the Lord, the vail shall be taken away. 17 Now the Lord is
that Spirit, and where the Spirit of the Lord is, there is liberty. 18 But we all, with open face beholding as in a glass the
glory of the Lord, are changed into the same image from
glory to glory, even as by the Spirit of the Lord.

4 Therefore seeing we have this ministry, as we have received mercy, we faint not, 2 but have renounced the
hidden things of dishonesty, not walking in craftiness, nor
handling the word of God deceitfully; but by manifestation
of the truth commending ourselves to every man's conscience in the sight of God. 3 But if our gospel be hid, it is hid
to them that are lost, 4 in whom the god of this world hath
blinded the minds of them which believe not, lest the light of
the glorious gospel of Christ, who is the image of God,
should shine unto them. 5 For we preach not ourselves, but
Christ Jesus the Lord; and ourselves your servants for Jesus'
sake. 6 For God, who commanded the light to shine out of
darkness, hath shined in our hearts, to give the light of the
knowledge of the glory of God in the face of Jesus Christ.

7 But we have this treasure in earthen vessels, that the

excellency of the power may be of God, and not of us. 8 We are
troubled on every side, yet not distressed; we are perplexed,
but not in despair; 9 persecuted, but not forsaken; cast down,
but not destroyed; 10 always bearing about in the body the
dying of the Lord Jesus, that the life also of Jesus might be
made manifest in our body. 11 For we which live are alway
delivered unto death for Jesus' sake, that the life also of Jesus
might be made manifest in our mortal flesh. 12 So then death
worketh in us, but life in you. 13 We having the same spirit of
faith, according as it is written, 'I believed, and therefore
have I spoken'; we also believe, and therefore speak, 14 knowing that he which raised up the Lord Jesus shall raise up us
also by Jesus, and shall present us with you. 15 For all things
are for your sakes, that the abundant grace might through
the thanksgiving of many redound to the glory of God.

16 For which cause we faint not; but though our outward
man perish, yet the inward man is renewed day by day.
17 For our light affliction, which is but for a moment, worketh
for us a far more exceeding and eternal weight of glory;
18 while we look not at the things which are seen, but at the
things which are not seen: for the things which are seen are
temporal, but the things which are not seen are eternal.

5 For we know that if our earthly house of this tabernacle
were dissolved, we have a building of God, an house
not made with hands, eternal in the heavens. 2 For in this we
groan, earnestly desiring to be clothed upon with our house
which is from heaven, 3 if so be that being clothed we shall
not be found naked. 4 For we that are in this tabernacle do

groan, being burdened, not for that we would be unclothed, but clothed upon, that mortality might be swallowed up of life. 5 Now he that hath wrought us for the selfsame thing is God, who also hath given unto us the earnest of the Spirit. 6 Therefore we are always confident, knowing that, whilst we are at home in the body, we are absent from the Lord 7 (for we walk by faith, not by sight). 8 We are confident, I say, and willing rather to be absent from the body, and to be present with the Lord. 9 Wherefore we labour, that, whether present or absent, we may be accepted of him. 10 For we must all appear before the judgment seat of Christ; that every one may receive the things done in his body, according to that he hath done, whether it be good or bad. 11 Knowing therefore the terror of the Lord, we persuade men; but we are made manifest unto God; and I trust also are made manifest in your consciences. 12 For we commend not ourselves again unto you, but give you occasion to glory on our behalf, that ye may have somewhat to answer them which glory in appearance, and not in heart.

13 For whether we be beside ourselves, it is to God, or whether we be sober, it is for your cause. 14 For the love of Christ constraineth us, because we thus judge, that if one died for all, then were all dead, 15 and that he died for all, that they which live should not henceforth live unto themselves, but unto him which died for them, and rose again.

16 Wherefore henceforth know we no man after the flesh: yea, though we have known Christ after the flesh, yet now henceforth know we him no more. 17 Therefore if any man be in Christ, he is a new creature. Old things are passed away;

behold, all things are become new. 18 And all things are of
God, who hath reconciled us to himself by Jesus Christ, and
hath given to us the ministry of reconciliation; 19 to wit, that
God was in Christ, reconciling the world unto himself, not
imputing their trespasses unto them, and hath committed
unto us the word of reconciliation. 20 Now then we are
ambassadors for Christ, as though God did beseech you by
us. We pray you in Christ's stead, be ye reconciled to God.
21 For he hath made him to be sin for us, who knew no sin,
that we might be made the righteousness of God in him.

6 We then, as workers together with him, beseech you also
that ye receive not the grace of God in vain. 2 (For he saith,
I have heard thee in a time accepted, and in the day of salvation have I succoured thee: behold, now is the accepted time;
behold, now is the day of salvation.) 3 Giving no offence in
any thing, that the ministry be not blamed, 4 but in all things
approving ourselves as the ministers of God, in much
patience, in afflictions, in necessities, in distresses, 5 in stripes,
in imprisonments, in tumults, in labours, in watchings, in
fastings; 6 by pureness, by knowledge, by longsuffering, by
kindness, by the Holy Ghost, by love unfeigned, 7 by the
word of truth, by the power of God, by the armour of righteousness on the right hand and on the left, 8 by honour and
dishonour, by evil report and good report; as deceivers, and
yet true; 9 as unknown, and yet well known; as dying, and,
behold, we live; as chastened, and not killed; 10 as sorrowful,
yet alway rejoicing; as poor, yet making many rich; as
having nothing, and yet possessing all things. 11 O ye

Corinthians, our mouth is open unto you, our heart is
enlarged. 12 Ye are not straitened in us, but ye are straitened
in your own bowels. 13 Now for a recompence in the same (I
speak as unto my children), be ye also enlarged.

14 Be ye not unequally yoked together with unbelievers,
for what fellowship hath righteousness with unrighteousness? And what communion hath light with darkness?
15 And what concord hath Christ with Belial? Or what part
hath he that believeth with an infidel? 16 And what agree-
ment hath the temple of God with idols? For ye are the temple of the living God, as God hath said, 'I will dwell in them,
and walk in them; and I will be their God, and they shall be
my people. 17 Wherefore come out from among them, and be
ye separate,' saith the Lord, 'And touch not the unclean thing;
and I will receive you, 18 and will be a Father unto you, and
ye shall be my sons and daughters,' saith the Lord Almighty.

7 Having therefore these promises, dearly beloved, let us
cleanse ourselves from all filthiness of the flesh and
spirit, perfecting holiness in the fear of God.

2 Receive us; we have wronged no man, we have corrupted no man, we have defrauded no man. 3 I speak not this
to condemn you, for I have said before, that ye are in our
hearts to die and live with you. 4 Great is my boldness of
speech toward you, great is my glorying of you. I am filled
with comfort, I am exceeding joyful in all our tribulation.

5 For, when we were come into Macedonia, our flesh had
no rest, but we were troubled on every side; without were
fightings, within were fears. 6 Nevertheless God, that

comforteth those that are cast down, comforted us by the
coming of Titus; [7]and not by his coming only, but by the consolation wherewith he was comforted in you, when he told
us your earnest desire, your mourning, your fervent mind
toward me; so that I rejoiced the more. [8]For though I made
you sorry with a letter, I do not repent, though I did repent,
for I perceive that the same epistle hath made you sorry,
though it were but for a season. [9]Now I rejoice, not that ye
were made sorry, but that ye sorrowed to repentance, for ye
were made sorry after a godly manner, that ye might receive
damage by us in nothing. [10]For godly sorrow worketh
repentance to salvation not to be repented of, but the sorrow
of the world worketh death. [11]For behold this selfsame thing,
that ye sorrowed after a godly sort, what carefulness it
wrought in you, yea, what clearing of yourselves, yea, what
indignation, yea, what fear, yea, what vehement desire, yea,
what zeal, yea, what revenge! In all things ye have approved
yourselves to be clear in this matter. [12]Wherefore, though I
wrote unto you, I did it not for his cause that had done the
wrong, nor for his cause that suffered wrong, but that our
care for you in the sight of God might appear unto you.

[13]Therefore we were comforted in your comfort; yea, and
exceedingly the more joyed we for the joy of Titus, because his
spirit was refreshed by you all. [14]For if I have boasted any thing
to him of you, I am not ashamed, but as we spake all things
to you in truth, even so our boasting, which I made before
Titus, is found a truth. [15]And his inward affection is more
abundant toward you, whilst he remembereth the obedience
of you all, how with fear and trembling ye received him. [16]I

rejoice therefore that I have confidence in you in all things.

8 Moreover, brethren, we do you to wit of the grace of God
bestowed on the churches of Macedonia; 2 how that in a
great trial of affliction the abundance of their joy and their
deep poverty abounded unto the riches of their liberality.
3 For to their power, I bear record, yea, and beyond their
power they were willing of themselves, 4 praying us with
much intreaty that we would receive the gift, and take upon
us the fellowship of the ministering to the saints. 5 And this
they did, not as we hoped, but first gave their own selves to
the Lord, and unto us by the will of God. 6 Insomuch that we
desired Titus, that as he had begun, so he would also finish
in you the same grace also. 7 Therefore, as ye abound in every
thing, in faith, and utterance, and knowledge, and in all diligence, and in your love to us, see that ye abound in this
grace also.

8 I speak not by commandment, but by occasion of the for-
wardness of others, and to prove the sincerity of your love.
9 For ye know the grace of our Lord Jesus Christ, that, though
he was rich, yet for your sakes he became poor, that ye
through his poverty might be rich. 10 And herein I give my
advice, for this is expedient for you, who have begun before,
not only to do, but also to be forward a year ago. 11 Now therefore perform the doing of it; that as there was a readiness to
will, so there may be a performance also out of that which ye
have. 12 For if there be first a willing mind, it is accepted
according to that a man hath, and not according to that he
hath not. 13 For I mean not that other men be eased, and ye

burdened, [14] But by an equality, that now at this time your
abundance may be a supply for their want, that their abundance also may be a supply for your want, that there may be
equality, [15] as it is written, 'He that had gathered much had
nothing over; and he that had gathered little had no lack.'
[16] But thanks be to God, which put the same earnest care into
the heart of Titus for you. [17] For indeed he accepted the exhortation; but being more forward, of his own accord he went
unto you. [18] And we have sent with him the brother, whose
praise is in the gospel throughout all the churches; [19] and not
that only, but who was also chosen of the churches to travel
with us with this grace, which is administered by us to the
glory of the same Lord, and declaration of your ready mind;
[20] avoiding this, that no man should blame us in this abundance which is administered by us; [21] providing for honest
things, not only in the sight of the Lord, but also in the sight
of men. [22] And we have sent with them our brother, whom
we have oftentimes proved diligent in many things, but now
much more diligent, upon the great confidence which I have
in you. [23] Whether any do enquire of Titus, he is my partner
and fellowhelper concerning you; or our brethren be enquired
of, they are the messengers of the churches, and the glory of
Christ. [24] Wherefore shew ye to them, and before the churches,
the proof of your love, and of our boasting on your behalf.

9 For as touching the ministering to the saints, it is superfluous for me to write to you, [2] for I know the forward-
ness of your mind, for which I boast of you to them of
Macedonia, that Achaia was ready a year ago; and your zeal

hath provoked very many. 3 Yet have I sent the brethren, lest
our boasting of you should be in vain in this behalf; that, as I
said, ye may be ready, 4 lest haply if they of Macedonia come
with me, and find you unprepared, we (that we say not, ye)
should be ashamed in this same confident boasting. 5 Therefore I thought it necessary to exhort the brethren, that they
would go before unto you, and make up beforehand your
bounty, whereof ye had notice before, that the same might
be ready, as a matter of bounty, and not as of covetousness.
6 But this I say: he which soweth sparingly shall reap also
sparingly; and he which soweth bountifully shall reap also
bountifully. 7 Every man according as he purposeth in his
heart, so let him give, not grudgingly, or of necessity, for
God loveth a cheerful giver. 8 And God is able to make all
grace abound toward you, that ye, always having all sufficiency in all things, may abound to every good work: 9 (As it
is written, 'He hath dispersed abroad; he hath given to the
poor; his righteousness remaineth for ever.' 10 Now he that
ministereth seed to the sower doth minister bread for your
food, and multiply your seed sown, and increase the fruits
of your righteousness.) 11 Being enriched in every thing to all
bountifulness, which causeth through us thanksgiving to
God. 12 For the administration of this service not only suppli-
eth the want of the saints, but is abundant also by many
thanksgivings unto God; 13 whiles by the experiment of
this ministration they glorify God for your professed subjection unto the gospel of Christ, and for your liberal distribution unto them, and unto all men, 14 and by their prayer
for you, which long after you for the exceeding grace of

God in you. 15 Thanks be unto God for his unspeakable gift.

10 Now I Paul myself beseech you by the meekness and
gentleness of Christ, who in presence am base among
you, but being absent am bold toward you, 2 but I beseech
you, that I may not be bold when I am present with that confidence, wherewith I think to be bold against some, which
think of us as if we walked according to the flesh. 3 For though
we walk in the flesh, we do not war after the flesh 4 (for the
weapons of our warfare are not carnal, but mighty through
God to the pulling down of strong holds), 5 casting down
imaginations, and every high thing that exalteth itself against
the knowledge of God, and bringing into captivity every
thought to the obedience of Christ; 6 and having in a readiness
to revenge all disobedience, when your obedience is fulfilled.

7 Do ye look on things after the outward appearance? If
any man trust to himself that he is Christ's, let him of himself
think this again, that, as he is Christ's, even so are we Christ's.
8 For though I should boast somewhat more of our authority,
which the Lord hath given us for edification, and not for
your destruction, I should not be ashamed, 9 that I may not
seem as if I would terrify you by letters. 10 For 'His letters,'
say they, 'are weighty and powerful; but his bodily presence
is weak, and his speech contemptible.' 11 Let such an one think
this, that, such as we are in word by letters when we are
absent, such will we be also in deed when we are present.

12 For we dare not make ourselves of the number, or compare ourselves with some that commend themselves, but
they measuring themselves by themselves, and comparing

themselves among themselves, are not wise. 13 But we will
not boast of things without our measure, but according to
the measure of the rule which God hath distributed to us, a
measure to reach even unto you. 14 For we stretch not ourselves beyond our measure, as though we reached not unto
you, for we are come as far as to you also in preaching the
gospel of Christ, 15 not boasting of things without our measure, that is, of other men's labours; but having hope, when
your faith is increased, that we shall be enlarged by you
according to our rule abundantly, 16 to preach the gospel in
the regions beyond you, and not to boast in another man's
line of things made ready to our hand. 17 But he that glorieth,
let him glory in the Lord. 18 For not he that commendeth himself is approved, but whom the Lord commendeth.

11 Would to God ye could bear with me a little in my
folly, and indeed bear with me. 2 For I am jealous over
you with godly jealousy, for I have espoused you to one husband, that I may present you as a chaste virgin to Christ.
3 But I fear, lest by any means, as the serpent beguiled Eve
through his subtilty, so your minds should be corrupted
from the simplicity that is in Christ. 4 For if he that cometh
preacheth another Jesus, whom we have not preached, or if
ye receive another spirit, which ye have not received, or
another gospel, which ye have not accepted, ye might well
bear with him. 5 For I suppose I was not a whit behind the
very chiefest apostles. 6 But though I be rude in speech, yet
not in knowledge; but we have been throughly made manifest among you in all things.

7 Have I committed an offence in abasing myself that ye might be exalted, because I have preached to you the gospel of God freely? 8 I robbed other churches, taking wages of them, to do you service. 9 And when I was present with you, and wanted, I was chargeable to no man, for that which was lacking to me the brethren which came from Macedonia supplied, and in all things I have kept myself from being burdensome unto you, and so will I keep myself. 10 As the truth of Christ is in me, no man shall stop me of this boasting in the regions of Achaia. 11 Wherefore? Because I love you not? God knoweth.

12 But what I do, that I will do, that I may cut off occasion from them which desire occasion; that wherein they glory, they may be found even as we. 13 For such are false apostles, deceitful workers, transforming themselves into the apostles of Christ. 14 And no marvel; for Satan himself is transformed into an angel of light. 15 Therefore it is no great thing if his ministers also be transformed as the ministers of righteousness, whose end shall be according to their works.

16 I say again, let no man think me a fool; if otherwise, yet as a fool receive me, that I may boast myself a little. 17 That which I speak, I speak it not after the Lord, but as it were foolishly, in this confidence of boasting. 18 Seeing that many glory after the flesh, I will glory also. 19 For ye suffer fools gladly, seeing ye yourselves are wise. 20 For ye suffer, if a man bring you into bondage, if a man devour you, if a man take of you, if a man exalt himself, if a man smite you on the face. 21 I speak as concerning reproach, as though we had been weak. Howbeit where-

insoever any is bold (I speak foolishly), I am bold also.
22 Are they Hebrews? So am I. Are they Israelites? So am
I. Are they the seed of Abraham? So am I. 23 Are they ministers of Christ? (I speak as a fool.) I am more; in labours more
abundant, in stripes above measure, in prisons more fre-
quent, in deaths oft. 24 Of the Jews five times received I forty
stripes save one. 25 Thrice was I beaten with rods, once was I
stoned, thrice I suffered shipwreck, a night and a day I have
been in the deep; 26 in journeyings often, in perils of waters,
in perils of robbers, in perils by mine own countrymen, in
perils by the heathen, in perils in the city, in perils in the
wilderness, in perils in the sea, in perils among false
brethren; 27 in weariness and painfulness, in watchings often,
in hunger and thirst, in fastings often, in cold and nakedness. 28 Beside those things that are without, that which
cometh upon me daily, the care of all the churches. 29 Who is
weak, and I am not weak? Who is offended, and I burn not?
30 If I must needs glory, I will glory of the things which con-
cern mine infirmities. 31 The God and Father of our Lord
Jesus Christ, which is blessed for evermore, knoweth that I
lie not. 32 In Damascus the governor under Aretas the king
kept the city of the Damascenes with a garrison, desirous to
apprehend me, 33 and through a window in a basket was I let
down by the wall, and escaped his hands.

12 It is not expedient for me doubtless to glory. I will
come to visions and revelations of the Lord. 2 I knew a
man in Christ above fourteen years ago (whether in the
body, I cannot tell; or whether out of the body, I cannot tell;

God knoweth), such an one caught up to the third heaven.
3 And I knew such a man (whether in the body, or out of the
body, I cannot tell; God knoweth); 4 how that he was caught
up into paradise, and heard unspeakable words, which it is
not lawful for a man to utter. 5 Of such an one will I glory;
yet of myself I will not glory, but in mine infirmities. 6 For
though I would desire to glory, I shall not be a fool; for I will
say the truth; but now I forbear, lest any man should think
of me above that which he seeth me to be, or that he heareth
of me. 7 And lest I should be exalted above measure through
the abundance of the revelations, there was given to me a
thorn in the flesh, the messenger of Satan to buffet me, lest I
should be exalted above measure. 8 For this thing I besought
the Lord thrice, that it might depart from me. 9 And he said
unto me, 'My grace is sufficient for thee, for my strength is
made perfect in weakness.' Most gladly therefore will I
rather glory in my infirmities, that the power of Christ may
rest upon me. 10 Therefore I take pleasure in infirmities, in
reproaches, in necessities, in persecutions, in distresses for
Christ's sake, for when I am weak, then am I strong.

11 I am become a fool in glorying; ye have compelled me,
for I ought to have been commended of you, for in nothing
am I behind the very chiefest apostles, though I be nothing.
12 Truly the signs of an apostle were wrought among you in
all patience, in signs, and wonders, and mighty deeds. 13 For
what is it wherein ye were inferior to other churches, except
it be that I myself was not burdensome to you? Forgive me
this wrong.

14 Behold, the third time I am ready to come to you; and I

will not be burdensome to you, for I seek not yours, but you,
for the children ought not to lay up for the parents, but the
parents for the children. 15 And I will very gladly spend and
be spent for you; though the more abundantly I love you,
the less I be loved. 16 But be it so, I did not burden you; nevertheless, being crafty, I caught you with guile. 17 Did I make
a gain of you by any of them whom I sent unto you? 18 I
desired Titus, and with him I sent a brother. Did Titus make
a gain of you? Walked we not in the same spirit? Walked we
not in the same steps?

19 Again, think ye that we excuse ourselves unto you? We
speak before God in Christ, but we do all things, dearly beloved, for your edifying. 20 For I fear, lest, when I come, I shall
not find you such as I would, and that I shall be found unto
you such as ye would not: lest there be debates, envyings,
wraths, strifes, backbitings, whisperings, swellings, tumults;
21 and lest, when I come again, my God will humble me
among you, and that I shall bewail many which have sinned
already, and have not repented of the uncleanness and fornication and lasciviousness which they have committed.

13 This is the third time I am coming to you. In the mouth
of two or three witnesses shall every word be established. 2 I told you before, and foretell you, as if I were present, the second time; and being absent now I write to them
which heretofore have sinned, and to all other, that, if I come
again, I will not spare, 3 since ye seek a proof of Christ speaking in me, which to you-ward is not weak, but is mighty in
you. 4 For though he was crucified through weakness, yet he

liveth by the power of God. For we also are weak in him, but
we shall live with him by the power of God toward you.

5 Examine yourselves, whether ye be in the faith; prove
your own selves. Know ye not your own selves, how that
Jesus Christ is in you, except ye be reprobates? 6 But I trust
that ye shall know that we are not reprobates. 7 Now I pray
to God that ye do no evil; not that we should appear approved,
but that ye should do that which is honest, though we be as
reprobates. 8 For we can do nothing against the truth, but for
the truth. 9 For we are glad, when we are weak, and ye are
strong, and this also we wish, even your perfection. 10 Therefore I write these things being absent, lest being present I
should use sharpness, according to the power which the
Lord hath given me to edification, and not to destruction.

11 Finally, brethren, farewell. Be perfect, be of good comfort, be of one mind, live in peace; and the God of love and
peace shall be with you. 12 Greet one another with an holy
kiss. 13 All the saints salute you. 14 The grace of the Lord Jesus
Christ, and the love of God, and the communion of the Holy
Ghost, be with you all. Amen.

revelation

revelation

authorized king james version

grove press
new york

with an introduction by | kathleen norris

The Pocket Canons were originally published in the U.K. in 1998 by Canongate Books, Ltd.
Published simultaneously in Canada
Printed in the United States of America

FIRST AMERICAN EDITION

Copyright information is on file with the Library of Congress
ISBN 0-8021-3621-4

Design by Paddy Cramsie

Grove Press
841 Broadway
New York, NY 10003

99 00 01 02 10 9 8 7 6 5 4 3 2 1

a note about pocket canons

The Authorized King James Version of the Bible, translated between 1603 and 1611, coincided with an extraordinary flowering of English literature. This version, more than any other, and possibly more than any other work in history, has had an influence in shaping the language we speak and write today. Presenting individual books from the Bible as separate volumes, as they were originally conceived, encourages the reader to approach them as literary works in their own right.

The first twelve books in this series encompass categories as diverse as history, fiction, philosophy, love poetry, and law. Each Pocket Canon also has its own introduction, specially commissioned from an impressive range of writers, which provides a personal interpretation of the text and explores its contemporary relevance.

Kathleen Norris is an award-winning poet and writer and the author of The Cloister Walk, Dakota: A Spiritual Geography, *and* Amazing Grace: A Vocabulary of Faith, *as well as three volumes of poetry. A recipient of grants from the Bush and Guggenheim foundations, she has twice been in residence at the Institute for Ecumenical and Cultural Research at St. John's Abbey in Collegeville, Minnesota, and has been an oblate at a Benedictine Monastery in North Dakota since 1986. She and her husband live in South Dakota.*

introduction by kathleen norris

I love this unlovable book for many reasons. It's a pretty good description of the writing process—crazed angels directing you to write, and not write, and to eat words that taste sweet in the mouth but soon turn to gall. "Make it new," Ezra Pound said; "Did that," answers Jesus, and you write it out as best you can, letting the images and symbols fly, and then the fools interpret it literally, arguing over what everything *means.*

I am attracted to the Revelation also because it was Emily Dickinson's favorite book of the Bible, and because it takes a stand in favor of singing. In fact, it proclaims that when all is said and done, of the considerable noises human beings are capable of, it is singing that will endure. A new song—if you can imagine—and light will be what remains. I find this a cause for hope, and am further buoyed to learn that the latter prediction, at least, is in tune with the conjectures of contemporary astrophysicists, who have yet to weigh in on the question of song.

The Revelation is a casebook of visionary excess: a man appears holding "in his right hand seven stars: and out of his mouth went a sharp two-edged sword: and his countenance was as the sun shineth in his strength" (1:16); a beast rises out of the sea "having seven heads and ten horns, and upon his horns ten crowns, and upon his heads the name of blasphemy" (13:1). Voices sound like thunder or trumpets, a throne sits in a sea of glass, surrounded by cherubim and lightning, four angels stand at the four corners of the earth, four horses—white, red, black, and pale—herald an apocalypse. But for all of this, the book is also an ordinary human vessel, a letter meant to be read aloud. It begins and ends with a blessing upon those who read it to others, and those who hear and heed it.

Emily Dickinson would have heard the Revelation read aloud many times in daily family devotions and at the church she attended until she was in her mid-thirties. Chapter 21, or the "gem chapter," is known to be a favorite, and it is easy to see how its dense mouthfuls of imagery would have appealed to her, the walls of the holy city of Jerusalem vividly described as having twelve foundations, each one made of a different stone: jasper, sapphire, chalcedony, emerald, sardonyx, sardius, chrysolyte, beryl, topaz, chrysoprasus, jacinth, and amethyst.

Typically, Dickinson puts the Revelation to personal use, writing a jaunty letter in the autumn of 1873 to a dear friend, Mrs. Josiah Gilbert Holland : "To live is Endowment. It puts me in mind of that singular Verse in the Revelation—"Every Several Gate was of one Pearl." But in more chilly weather, after the Christmas of 1882, just a month after the death of her mother, she wrote to the same friend:

> The Fiction of "Santa Claus" always reminds me of the reply to my early question of "Who made the Bible"—"Holy Men by the Holy Ghost," and though I have now ceased my investigations, the Solution is insufficient.

Santa Claus, though, *illustrates* Revelation.
But a Book is only the Heart's Portrait—every Page a Pulse.

As usual, Dickinson's whimsy is dead-on serious. Santa does illustrate a simple moral: act good (at least in front of those who matter) and you will get the goodies. John of Patmos is not so simple. Intent on apocalypse, which at its Greek root means "uncovering," he holds up a mirror to the human heart, and doesn't bother to ask if we like what we see there. As he speaks to the churches, we can see ourselves: how the youthful, earnest heart soon forgets its first fervor and grows lukewarm, distracted by the world, compromising faith and justice and love for comfort or gain.

And John's images do seem to pulse, the work of a visionary in prison on a windswept island, who has to struggle to say in words what those incessant winds have revealed to him. This is a poet's book, which is probably the best argument for reclaiming it from fundamentalists. It doesn't tell, it shows, over and over again, its images unfolding, pushing hard against the limits of language and metaphor, engaging the listener in a tale that has the satisfying yet unsettling logic of a dream.

Perhaps the Revelation is best understood as prison literature, but not necessarily escapist, although many Christians use it for easy reassurance that "when the roll is called up yonder" they'll find themselves securely placed on the list, and too bad about you. More than any other book of the Christian Bible, the Revelation has suffered from bad interpretation: solipsistic, short-sighted, cruel. Cruelty is not a distinguishing feature of the book itself; rather, it describes in stark terms the world we have made and boldly asserts that our cruelties and injustices will not have the last word.

Like the Psalms, the Revelation is a compendium of biblical images and themes, and it is clear that John has drunk deep from the prophets, who consistently warn us not to tip the scales of justice too far in our favor, lest God overturn our precious applecarts. The prophets are difficult for us to bear because they remind us that our measure of discomfort at apocalypse is the measure of our comfort with the way things are. Who really wants to hear about a doomed city, formerly great, where the wealthy fed on dainties and clothed themselves in finery, while the children of the poor begged on the streets for bread? If it sounds familiar, it should, for it is how a prophet sees the here and now:

> And the merchants of the earth shall weep and mourn . . . for no man buyeth their merchandise any more: The merchandise of gold, and silver, and precious stones, and of pearls, and fine linen, and purple, and silk, and scarlet . . . and cinnamon, and odours, and ointments . . . and wine, and oil, and fine flour, and wheat, and beasts, and sheep, and horses, and chariots, and slaves, and souls of men.
>
> And the fruits that thy soul lusted after are departed from thee . . . and thou shalt find them no more at all. (18:11–14)

The here-and-now import of the Revelation is so consistently ignored that I was relieved to find the novelist Mary

Gaitskill stating, in a recent essay, that the book no longer reads to her "like a chronicle of arbitrarily inflicted cruelty . . . [but] like a terrible abstract of how we violate ourselves and others and thus bring down endless suffering on earth." (As I write this, Serbs and Albanians are busy taking revenge on one another in Kosovo; by the time you read this the bloodshed will be somewhere else, the justifications for it somewhat different, though just as finely tuned.) There seems no end to it, but the Revelation insists that there is. It is a healing vision, meant to give us hope. God's wrath is stirred by what we have done to the world he made, and that's the good news. God intends to take our mess and make it come out right.

The hope engendered by the Revelation is as bitter and bracing as the hope one finds in an emergency room or ICU or hospice. All that seemed to matter, all competence, all status, all that was formerly of value is revealed as nothing compared to the beat of a pulse, that next breath. The book embraces a great psychological truth, that the crises and apocalypses of our lives are not meant to not beat us into submission so much as to give us room to change and grow. But we usually don't rise to the challenge; we stick with the devil we know, and John is honest about that as well. Our "blaspheming" and "fornications" are not an intellectual game but, as Mary Gaitskill puts it, a blaspheming "of life itself by failing to have the courage to be honest and kind," an addiction to "sex done in a state of psychic disintegration, with no awareness of one's self or one's partner, let alone any sense of honor or even real playfulness."

The Revelation uncovers the world as it is, and reveals to us our true condition. And John insists that, despite ourselves, God wills to restore this world to a beauty we can scarcely imagine. It is a city, not a solitude, an important distinction in the narcissistic din of American culture. It is a city as only God can envision it, without tears, which we are invited to envision as well, and by implication asked to strive for in the present, even if it means forgoing "getting in touch with ourselves" in order to better constitute a community.

And the God who has been stirred to cataclysmic rage by our stubborn selfishness and lack of love surprises us after all. What is evil has been swept away, until only the good remains. And God desires to be with those who have suffered most in a cruel, unjust, and violent world. This God does not act at all like a vengeful dictator infatuated with power but comes to gently "wipe away all tears from their eyes." If, as the pop psychologists insist, imaging is half the battle, John is already there: "and there shall be no more death, neither sorrow, nor crying, neither shall there be any more pain: for the former things are passed away" (21:4).

the revelation of st john the divine

The Revelation of Jesus Christ, which God gave unto him, to shew unto his servants things which must shortly come to pass; and he sent and signified it by his angel unto his servant John, 2 who bare record of the word of God, and of the testimony of Jesus Christ, and of all things that he saw. 3 Blessed is he that readeth, and they that hear the words of this prophecy, and keep those things which are written therein; for the time is at hand.

4 John to the seven churches which are in Asia: Grace be unto you, and peace, from him which is, and which was, and which is to come; and from the seven Spirits which are before his throne; 5 and from Jesus Christ, who is the faithful witness, and the first begotten of the dead, and the prince of the kings of the earth. Unto him that loved us, and washed us from our sins in his own blood, 6 and hath made us kings and priests unto God and his Father; to him be glory and dominion for ever and ever. Amen. 7 Behold, he cometh with clouds; and every eye shall see him, and they also which pierced him; and all kindreds of the earth shall wail because of him. Even so, Amen.

8 'I am Alpha and Omega, the beginning and the ending,' saith the Lord, which is, and which was, and which is to come, the Almighty. 9 I John, who also am your brother, and companion in tribulation, and in the kingdom and patience of

Jesus Christ, was in the isle that is called Patmos, for the word
of God, and for the testimony of Jesus Christ. [10] I was in the
Spirit on the Lord's day, and heard behind me a great voice,
as of a trumpet, [11] saying, 'I am Alpha and Omega, the first and
the last'; and, 'What thou seest, write in a book, and send it
unto the seven churches which are in Asia; unto Ephesus,
and unto Smyrna, and unto Pergamos, and unto Thyatira,
and unto Sardis, and unto Philadelphia, and unto Laodicea.'

[12] And I turned to see the voice that spake with me. And
being turned, I saw seven golden candlesticks; [13] and in the
midst of the seven candlesticks one like unto the Son of man,
clothed with a garment down to the foot, and girt about the
paps with a golden girdle. [14] His head and his hairs were white
like wool, as white as snow; and his eyes were as a flame of
fire; [15] and his feet like unto fine brass, as if they burned in a
furnace; and his voice as the sound of many waters. [16] And he
had in his right hand seven stars; and out of his mouth went
a sharp twoedged sword; and his countenance was as the
sun shineth in his strength.

[17] And when I saw him, I fell at his feet as dead. And he laid
his right hand upon me, saying unto me, 'Fear not; I am the
first and the last: [18] I am he that liveth, and was dead; and,
behold, I am alive for evermore, Amen; and have the keys of
hell and of death. [19] Write the things which thou hast seen,
and the things which are, and the things which shall be hereafter; [20] the mystery of the seven stars which thou sawest in
my right hand, and the seven golden candlesticks. The seven
stars are the angels of the seven churches; and the seven candlesticks which thou sawest are the seven churches.'

2 'Unto the angel of the church of Ephesus write: These
things saith he that holdeth the seven stars in his right
hand, who walketh in the midst of the seven golden candlesticks: 2 I know thy works, and thy labour, and thy patience,
and how thou canst not bear them which are evil; and thou
hast tried them which say they are apostles, and are not, and
hast found them liars; 3 and hast borne, and hast patience,
and for my name's sake hast laboured, and hast not fainted.
4 Nevertheless I have somewhat against thee, because thou
hast left thy first love. 5 Remember therefore from whence
thou art fallen, and repent, and do the first works; or else I
will come unto thee quickly, and will remove thy candlestick
out of his place, except thou repent. 6 But this thou hast, that
thou hatest the deeds of the Nicolaitans, which I also hate.
7 He that hath an ear, let him hear what the Spirit saith unto
the churches; to him that overcometh will I give to eat of the
tree of life, which is in the midst of the paradise of God.

8 'And unto the angel of the church in Smyrna write: These
things saith the first and the last, which was dead, and is
alive: 9 I know thy works, and tribulation, and poverty (but
thou art rich), and I know the blasphemy of them which say
they are Jews, and are not, but are the synagogue of Satan.
10 Fear none of those things which thou shalt suffer. Behold,
the devil shall cast some of you into prison, that ye may be
tried; and ye shall have tribulation ten days; be thou faithful
unto death, and I will give thee a crown of life. 11 He that hath
an ear, let him hear what the Spirit saith unto the churches;
he that overcometh shall not be hurt of the second death.

12 'And to the angel of the church in Pergamos write: These

things saith he which hath the sharp sword with two edges:
13 I know thy works, and where thou dwellest, even where
Satan's seat is; and thou holdest fast my name, and hast not
denied my faith, even in those days wherein Antipas was
my faithful martyr, who was slain among you, where Satan
dwelleth. 14 But I have a few things against thee, because thou
hast there them that hold the doctrine of Balaam, who taught
Balac to cast a stumblingblock before the children of Israel,
to eat things sacrificed unto idols, and to commit fornication.
15 So hast thou also them that hold the doctrine of the Nicolaitans, which thing I hate. 16 Repent; or else I will come unto
thee quickly, and will fight against them with the sword of
my mouth. 17 He that hath an ear, let him hear what the Spirit
saith unto the churches; to him that overcometh will I give
to eat of the hidden manna, and will give him a white stone,
and in the stone a new name written, which no man knoweth saving he that receiveth it.

18 'And unto the angel of the church in Thyatira write: These
things saith the Son of God, who hath his eyes like unto a
flame of fire, and his feet are like fine brass: 19 I know thy
works, and charity, and service, and faith, and thy patience,
and thy works; and the last to be more than the first. 20 Notwithstanding I have a few things against thee, because thou
sufferest that woman Jezebel, which calleth herself a prophetess, to teach and to seduce my servants to commit fornication, and to eat things sacrificed unto idols. 21 And I gave her
space to repent of her fornication; and she repented not.
22 Behold, I will cast her into a bed, and them that commit
adultery with her into great tribulation, except they repent

of their deeds. 23 And I will kill her children with death; and
all the churches shall know that I am he which searcheth the
reins and hearts; and I will give unto every one of you according to your works. 24 But unto you I say, and unto the rest
in Thyatira, as many as have not this doctrine, and which
have not known the depths of Satan, as they speak; I will put
upon you none other burden. 25 But that which ye have already
hold fast till I come. 26 And he that overcometh, and keepeth
my works unto the end, to him will I give power over the
nations; 27 and he shall rule them with a rod of iron; as the
vessels of a potter shall they be broken to shivers; even as I
received of my Father. 28 And I will give him the morning
star. 29 He that hath an ear, let him hear what the Spirit saith
unto the churches.

3 'And unto the angel of the church in Sardis write: These
things saith he that hath the seven Spirits of God, and
the seven stars: I know thy works, that thou hast a name that
thou livest, and art dead. 2 Be watchful, and strengthen the
things which remain, that are ready to die; for I have not
found thy works perfect before God. 3 Remember therefore
how thou hast received and heard, and hold fast, and repent.
If therefore thou shalt not watch, I will come on thee as a
thief, and thou shalt not know what hour I will come upon
thee. 4 Thou hast a few names even in Sardis which have not
defiled their garments; and they shall walk with me in
white; for they are worthy. 5 He that overcometh, the same
shall be clothed in white raiment; and I will not blot out his
name out of the book of life, but I will confess his name
before my Father, and before his angels. 6 He that hath an
ear, let him hear what the Spirit saith unto the churches.

7 'And to the angel of the church in Philadelphia write:
These things saith he that is holy, he that is true, he that hath
the key of David, he that openeth, and no man shutteth; and
shutteth, and no man openeth: 8 I know thy works; behold, I
have set before thee an open door, and no man can shut it;
for thou hast a little strength, and hast kept my word, and
hast not denied my name. 9 Behold, I will make them of the
synagogue of Satan, which say they are Jews, and are not,
but do lie; behold, I will make them to come and worship
before thy feet, and to know that I have loved thee. 10 Because
thou hast kept the word of my patience, I also will keep thee
from the hour of temptation, which shall come upon all the
world, to try them that dwell upon the earth. 11 Behold, I

come quickly; hold that fast which thou hast, that no man
take thy crown. 12 Him that overcometh will I make a pillar in
the temple of my God, and he shall go no more out: and I
will write upon him the name of my God, and the name of
the city of my God, which is new Jerusalem, which cometh
down out of heaven from my God; and I will write upon
him my new name. 13 He that hath an ear, let him hear what
the Spirit saith unto the churches.

14 'And unto the angel of the church of the Laodiceans
write: These things saith the Amen, the faithful and true witness, the beginning of the creation of God: 15 I know thy works,
that thou art neither cold nor hot; I would thou wert cold or
hot. 16 So then because thou art lukewarm, and neither cold
nor hot, I will spue thee out of my mouth. 17 Because thou
sayest, "I am rich, and increased with goods, and have need
of nothing"; and knowest not that thou art wretched, and
miserable, and poor, and blind, and naked. 18 I counsel thee
to buy of me gold tried in the fire, that thou mayest be rich;
and white raiment, that thou mayest be clothed, and that the
shame of thy nakedness do not appear; and anoint thine
eyes with eyesalve, that thou mayest see. 19 As many as I love, I
rebuke and chasten: be zealous therefore, and repent. 20 Behold,
I stand at the door, and knock: if any man hear my voice,
and open the door, I will come in to him, and will sup with
him, and he with me. 21 To him that overcometh will I grant
to sit with me in my throne, even as I also overcame, and am
set down with my Father in his throne. 22 He that hath an ear,
let him hear what the Spirit saith unto the churches.'

4 After this I looked, and, behold, a door was opened in heaven; and the first voice which I heard was as it were of a
trumpet talking with me; which said, 'Come up hither, and I will
shew thee things which must be hereafter.' 2 And immediately
I was in the spirit; and, behold, a throne was set in heaven, and
one sat on the throne. 3 And he that sat was to look upon like a
jasper and a sardine stone; and there was a rainbow round
about the throne, in sight like unto an emerald. 4 And round
about the throne were four and twenty seats; and upon the
seats I saw four and twenty elders sitting, clothed in white raiment; and they had on their heads crowns of gold. 5 And out of
the throne proceeded lightnings and thunderings and voices;
and there were seven lamps of fire burning before the throne,
which are the seven Spirits of God. 6 And before the throne
there was a sea of glass like unto crystal; and in the midst of
the throne, and round about the throne, were four beasts full
of eyes before and behind. 7 And the first beast was like a lion,
and the second beast like a calf, and the third beast had a face
as a man, and the fourth beast was like a flying eagle. 8 And the
four beasts had each of them six wings about him; and they
were full of eyes within; and they rest not day and night, saying, 'Holy, holy, holy, Lord God Almighty, which was, and is,
and is to come.' 9 And when those beasts give glory and honour
and thanks to him that sat on the throne, who liveth for ever and
ever, 10 the four and twenty elders fall down before him that sat
on the throne, and worship him that liveth for ever and ever, and
cast their crowns before the throne, saying, 11 'Thou art worthy,
O Lord, to receive glory and honour and power; for thou hast
created all things, and for thy pleasure they are and were created.'

5 And I saw in the right hand of him that sat on the throne
a book written within and on the backside, sealed with
seven seals. 2 And I saw a strong angel proclaiming with a
loud voice, 'Who is worthy to open the book, and to loose
the seals thereof?' 3 And no man in heaven, nor in earth, neither under the earth, was able to open the book, neither to
look thereon. 4 And I wept much, because no man was found
worthy to open and to read the book, neither to look thereon.
5 And one of the elders saith unto me, 'Weep not; behold, the
Lion of the tribe of Juda, the Root of David, hath prevailed to
open the book, and to loose the seven seals thereof.'

6 And I beheld, and, lo, in the midst of the throne and of
the four beasts, and in the midst of the elders, stood a Lamb
as it had been slain, having seven horns and seven eyes,
which are the seven Spirits of God sent forth into all the
earth. 7 And he came and took the book out of the right hand
of him that sat upon the throne. 8 And when he had taken the
book, the four beasts and four and twenty elders fell down
before the Lamb, having every one of them harps, and golden
vials full of odours, which are the prayers of saints. 9 And
they sung a new song, saying,

Thou art worthy to take the book,
and to open the seals thereof;
for thou wast slain, and hast redeemed us
to God by thy blood out of every kindred,
and tongue, and people, and nation;
10 and hast made us unto our God kings and priests;
and we shall reign on the earth.

11 And I beheld, and I heard the voice of many angels round
about the throne and the beasts and the elders: and the number of them was ten thousand times ten thousand, and thousands of thousands; 12 saying with a loud voice, 'Worthy is
the Lamb that was slain to receive power, and riches, and
wisdom, and strength, and honour, and glory, and blessing.'
13 And every creature which is in heaven, and on the earth,
and under the earth, and such as are in the sea, and all that
are in them, heard I saying, 'Blessing, and honour, and glory,
and power, be unto him that sitteth upon the throne, and
unto the Lamb for ever and ever.' 14 And the four beasts said,
'Amen.' And the four and twenty elders fell down and worshipped him that liveth for ever and ever.

6 And I saw when the Lamb opened one of the seals, and
I heard, as it were the noise of thunder, one of the four
beasts saying, 'Come and see.' 2And I saw, and behold a white
horse; and he that sat on him had a bow; and a crown was
given unto him; and he went forth conquering, and to conquer.
3And when he had opened the second seal, I heard the
second beast say, 'Come and see.' 4And there went out another
horse that was red; and power was given to him that sat
thereon to take peace from the earth, and that they should
kill one another: and there was given unto him a great sword.
5And when he had opened the third seal, I heard the third
beast say, 'Come and see.' And I beheld, and lo a black horse;
and he that sat on him had a pair of balances in his hand.
6And I heard a voice in the midst of the four beasts say, 'A
measure of wheat for a penny, and three measures of barley
for a penny; and see thou hurt not the oil and the wine.'
7And when he had opened the fourth seal, I heard the
voice of the fourth beast say, 'Come and see.' 8And I looked,
and behold a pale horse; and his name that sat on him was
Death, and Hell followed with him. And power was given
unto them over the fourth part of the earth, to kill with
sword, and with hunger, and with death, and with the beasts
of the earth.
9And when he had opened the fifth seal, I saw under the
altar the souls of them that were slain for the word of God,
and for the testimony which they held. 10And they cried with
a loud voice, saying, 'How long, O Lord, holy and true, dost
thou not judge and avenge our blood on them that dwell on
the earth?' 11And white robes were given unto every one of

them; and it was said unto them that they should rest yet for a
little season, until their fellowservants also and their brethren,
that should be killed as they were, should be fulfilled.
[12]And I beheld when he had opened the sixth seal, and,
lo, there was a great earthquake; and the sun became black
as sackcloth of hair, and the moon became as blood; [13]and
the stars of heaven fell unto the earth, even as a fig tree
casteth her untimely figs, when she is shaken of a mighty
wind. [14]And the heaven departed as a scroll when it is rolled
together; and every mountain and island were moved out of
their places. [15]And the kings of the earth, and the great men,
and the rich men, and the chief captains, and the mighty
men, and every bondman, and every free man, hid themselves in the dens and in the rocks of the mountains; [16]and
said to the mountains and rocks, 'Fall on us, and hide us
from the face of him that sitteth on the throne, and from the
wrath of the Lamb; [17]for the great day of his wrath is come,
and who shall be able to stand?'

7 And after these things I saw four angels standing on
the four corners of the earth, holding the four winds of
the earth, that the wind should not blow on the earth, nor on
the sea, nor on any tree. 2 And I saw another angel ascending
from the east, having the seal of the living God; and he cried
with a loud voice to the four angels, to whom it was given to
hurt the earth and the sea, 3 saying, 'Hurt not the earth, neither
the sea, nor the trees, till we have sealed the servants of our
God in their foreheads.'

4 And I heard the number of them which were sealed;
and there were sealed an hundred and forty and four thousand of all the tribes of the children of Israel. 5 Of the tribe of
Juda were sealed twelve thousand. Of the tribe of Reuben
were sealed twelve thousand. Of the tribe of Gad were sealed
twelve thousand. 6 Of the tribe of Aser were sealed twelve
thousand. Of the tribe of Nepthalim were sealed twelve thousand. Of the tribe of Manasses were sealed twelve thousand.
7 Of the tribe of Simeon were sealed twelve thousand. Of the
tribe of Levi were sealed twelve thousand. Of the tribe of
Issachar were sealed twelve thousand. 8 Of the tribe of Zabulon were sealed twelve thousand. Of the tribe of Joseph were
sealed twelve thousand. Of the tribe of Benjamin were sealed
twelve thousand.

9 After this I beheld, and, lo, a great multitude, which no
man could number, of all nations, and kindreds, and people,
and tongues, stood before the throne, and before the Lamb,
clothed with white robes, and palms in their hands; 10 and
cried with a loud voice, saying, 'Salvation to our God which
sitteth upon the throne, and unto the Lamb.'

[11]And all the angels stood round about the throne, and
about the elders and the four beasts, and fell before the throne
on their faces, and worshipped God, [12] saying, 'Amen: Blessing,
and glory, and wisdom, and thanksgiving, and honour, and
power, and might, be unto our God for ever and ever. Amen.'
[13]And one of the elders answered, saying unto me, 'What
are these which are arrayed in white robes? And whence
came they?' [14]And I said unto him, 'Sir, thou knowest.' And
he said to me, 'These are they which came out of great tribulation, and have washed their robes, and made them white
in the blood of the Lamb. [15]Therefore are they before the
throne of God, and serve him day and night in his temple;
and he that sitteth on the throne shall dwell among them.
[16]They shall hunger no more, neither thirst any more; neither shall the sun light on them, nor any heat. [17] For the Lamb
which is in the midst of the throne shall feed them, and shall
lead them unto living fountains of waters; and God shall
wipe away all tears from their eyes.'

8 And when he had opened the seventh seal, there was
silence in heaven about the space of half an hour. 2 And I
saw the seven angels which stood before God; and to them
were given seven trumpets.
3 And another angel came and stood at the altar, having a
golden censer; and there was given unto him much incense,
that he should offer it with the prayers of all saints upon
the golden altar which was before the throne. 4 And the smoke
of the incense, which came with the prayers of the saints,
ascended up before God out of the angel's hand. 5 And the
angel took the censer, and filled it with fire of the altar, and
cast it into the earth; and there were voices, and thunderings, and lightnings, and an earthquake.
6 And the seven angels which had the seven trumpets
prepared themselves to sound.
7 The first angel sounded, and there followed hail and
fire mingled with blood, and they were cast upon the earth;
and the third part of trees was burnt up, and all green grass
was burnt up.
8 And the second angel sounded, and as it were a great
mountain burning with fire was cast into the sea; and the third
part of the sea became blood; 9 and the third part of the crea-
tures which were in the sea, and had life, died; and the third
part of the ships were destroyed.
10 And the third angel sounded, and there fell a great star
from heaven, burning as it were a lamp, and it fell upon the
third part of the rivers, and upon the fountains of waters;
11 and the name of the star is called Wormwood; and the third
part of the waters became wormwood; and many men died

of the waters, because they were made bitter.
[12]And the fourth angel sounded, and the third part of the
sun was smitten, and the third part of the moon, and the
third part of the stars; so as the third part of them was darkened, and the day shone not for a third part of it, and the
night likewise.
[13]And I beheld, and heard an angel flying through the
midst of heaven, saying with a loud voice, 'Woe, woe, woe,
to the inhabiters of the earth by reason of the other voices of
the trumpet of the three angels, which are yet to sound!'

9 And the fifth angel sounded, and I saw a star fall from
heaven unto the earth; and to him was given the key of
the bottomless pit. 2 And he opened the bottomless pit; and
there arose a smoke out of the pit, as the smoke of a great
furnace; and the sun and the air were darkened by reason of
the smoke of the pit. 3 And there came out of the smoke locusts
upon the earth; and unto them was given power, as the scorpions of the earth have power. 4 And it was commanded
them that they should not hurt the grass of the earth, neither
any green thing, neither any tree; but only those men which
have not the seal of God in their foreheads. 5 And to them it
was given that they should not kill them, but that they
should be tormented five months; and their torment was as
the torment of a scorpion, when he striketh a man. 6 And in
those days shall men seek death, and shall not find it; and
shall desire to die, and death shall flee from them.

7 And the shapes of the locusts were like unto horses prepared unto battle; and on their heads were as it were crowns
like gold, and their faces were as the faces of men. 8 And they
had hair as the hair of women, and their teeth were as the
teeth of lions. 9 And they had breastplates, as it were breastplates of iron; and the sound of their wings was as the sound
of chariots of many horses running to battle. 10 And they had
tails like unto scorpions, and there were stings in their tails;
and their power was to hurt men five months. 11 And they
had a king over them, which is the angel of the bottomless
pit, whose name in the Hebrew tongue is Abaddon, but in
the Greek tongue hath his name Apollyon.

12 One woe is past; and, behold, there come two woes

more hereafter. [13]And the sixth angel sounded, and I heard a
voice from the four horns of the golden altar which is before
God, [14]saying to the sixth angel which had the trumpet,
'Loose the four angels which are bound in the great river
Euphrates.' [15]And the four angels were loosed, which were
prepared for an hour, and a day, and a month, and a year,
for to slay the third part of men. [16]And the number of the
army of the horsemen were two hundred thousand thousand: and I heard the number of them. [17]And thus I saw the
horses in the vision, and them that sat on them, having breastplates of fire, and of jacinth, and brimstone; and the heads of
the horses were as the heads of lions; and out of their mouths
issued fire and smoke and brimstone. [18]By these three was
the third part of men killed, by the fire, and by the smoke,
and by the brimstone, which issued out of their mouths.
[19]For their power is in their mouth, and in their tails; for
their tails were like unto serpents, and had heads, and with
them they do hurt.

[20]And the rest of the men which were not killed by these
plagues yet repented not of the works of their hands, that
they should not worship devils, and idols of gold, and silver,
and brass, and stone, and of wood; which neither can see, nor
hear, nor walk; [21]neither repented they of their murders, nor
of their sorceries, nor of their fornication, nor of their thefts.

10 And I saw another mighty angel come down from heaven, clothed with a cloud; and a rainbow was upon his
head, and his face was as it were the sun, and his feet as pillars of fire; 2 and he had in his hand a little book open; and he
set his right foot upon the sea, and his left foot on the earth,
3 and cried with a loud voice, as when a lion roareth; and when
he had cried, seven thunders uttered their voices. 4 And when
the seven thunders had uttered their voices, I was about to
write; and I heard a voice from heaven saying unto me, 'Seal
up those things which the seven thunders uttered, and write
them not.' 5 And the angel which I saw stand upon the sea and
upon the earth lifted up his hand to heaven, 6 and sware by him
that liveth for ever and ever, who created heaven, and the things
that therein are, and the earth, and the things that therein are,
and the sea, and the things which are therein, that there should
be time no longer; 7 but in the days of the voice of the seventh
angel, when he shall begin to sound, the mystery of God should
be finished, as he hath declared to his servants the prophets.

8 And the voice which I heard from heaven spake unto me
again, and said, 'Go and take the little book which is open in
the hand of the angel which standeth upon the sea and upon
the earth.' 9 And I went unto the angel, and said unto him,
'Give me the little book.' And he said unto me, 'Take it, and
eat it up; and it shall make thy belly bitter, but it shall be in
thy mouth sweet as honey.' 10 And I took the little book out of
the angel's hand, and ate it up; and it was in my mouth sweet
as honey; and as soon as I had eaten it, my belly was bitter.

11 And he said unto me, 'Thou must prophesy again before
many peoples, and nations, and tongues, and kings.'

11 And there was given me a reed like unto a rod; and the angel stood, saying, 'Rise, and measure the temple of God, and the altar, and them that worship therein. 2 But the court which is without the temple leave out, and measure it not; for it is given unto the Gentiles; and the holy city shall they tread under foot forty and two months. 3 And I will give power unto my two witnesses, and they shall prophesy a thousand two hundred and threescore days, clothed in sackcloth.'

4 These are the two olive trees, and the two candlesticks standing before the God of the earth. 5 And if any man will hurt them, fire proceedeth out of their mouth, and devoureth their enemies; and if any man will hurt them, he must in this manner be killed. 6 These have power to shut heaven, that it rain not in the days of their prophecy; and have power over waters to turn them to blood, and to smite the earth with all plagues, as often as they will.

7 And when they shall have finished their testimony, the beast that ascendeth out of the bottomless pit shall make war against them, and shall overcome them, and kill them. 8 And their dead bodies shall lie in the street of the great city, which spiritually is called Sodom and Egypt, where also our Lord was crucified. 9 And they of the people and kindreds and tongues and nations shall see their dead bodies three days and an half, and shall not suffer their dead bodies to be put in graves. 10 And they that dwell upon the earth shall rejoice over them, and make merry, and shall send gifts one to another; because these two prophets tormented them that dwelt on the earth.

11 And after three days and an half the Spirit of life from

God entered into them, and they stood upon their feet; and
great fear fell upon them which saw them. 12And they heard
a great voice from heaven saying unto them, 'Come up hither.'
And they ascended up to heaven in a cloud; and their enemies beheld them. 13And the same hour was there a great
earthquake, and the tenth part of the city fell, and in the
earthquake were slain of men seven thousand; and the remnant were affrighted, and gave glory to the God of heaven.

14The second woe is past; and, behold, the third woe
cometh quickly.

15And the seventh angel sounded; and there were great
voices in heaven, saying, 'The kingdoms of this world are
become the kingdoms of our Lord, and of his Christ; and he
shall reign for ever and ever.'

16And the four and twenty elders, which sat before God
on their seats, fell upon their faces, and worshipped God,
17saying, 'We give thee thanks, O Lord God Almighty, which
art, and wast, and art to come; because thou hast taken to
thee thy great power, and hast reigned. 18And the nations
were angry, and thy wrath is come, and the time of the dead,
that they should be judged, and that thou shouldest give
reward unto thy servants the prophets, and to the saints,
and them that fear thy name, small and great; and shouldest
destroy them which destroy the earth.'

19And the temple of God was opened in heaven, and
there was seen in his temple the ark of his testament; and
there were lightnings, and voices, and thunderings, and an
earthquake, and great hail.

12 And there appeared a great wonder in heaven; a
woman clothed with the sun, and the moon under her
feet, and upon her head a crown of twelve stars; 2and she
being with child cried, travailing in birth, and pained to be
delivered. 3And there appeared another wonder in heaven;
and behold a great red dragon, having seven heads and ten
horns, and seven crowns upon his heads. 4And his tail drew
the third part of the stars of heaven, and did cast them to the
earth; and the dragon stood before the woman which was
ready to be delivered, for to devour her child as soon as it
was born. 5And she brought forth a man child, who was to
rule all nations with a rod of iron; and her child was caught
up unto God, and to his throne. 6And the woman fled into
the wilderness, where she hath a place prepared of God, that
they should feed her there a thousand two hundred and
threescore days.

7And there was war in heaven: Michael and his angels
fought against the dragon; and the dragon fought and his
angels, 8and prevailed not; neither was their place found
any more in heaven. 9And the great dragon was cast out,
that old serpent, called the Devil, and Satan, which deceiveth the whole world: he was cast out into the earth, and his
angels were cast out with him.

10And I heard a loud voice saying in heaven, 'Now is
come salvation, and strength, and the kingdom of our God,
and the power of his Christ; for the accuser of our brethren
is cast down, which accused them before our God day and
night. 11And they overcame him by the blood of the Lamb,
and by the word of their testimony; and they loved not their

lives unto the death. 12 Therefore rejoice, ye heavens, and ye that dwell in them. Woe to the inhabiters of the earth and of the sea! For the devil is come down unto you, having great wrath, because he knoweth that he hath but a short time.'

13 And when the dragon saw that he was cast unto the earth, he persecuted the woman which brought forth the man child. 14 And to the woman were given two wings of a great eagle, that she might fly into the wilderness, into her place, where she is nourished for a time, and times, and half a time, from the face of the serpent. 15 And the serpent cast out of his mouth water as a flood after the woman, that he might cause her to be carried away of the flood. 16 And the earth helped the woman, and the earth opened her mouth, and swallowed up the flood which the dragon cast out of his mouth. 17 And the dragon was wroth with the woman, and went to make war with the remnant of her seed, which keep the commandments of God, and have the testimony of Jesus Christ.

13 And I stood upon the sand of the sea, and saw a beast
rise up out of the sea, having seven heads and ten
horns, and upon his horns ten crowns, and upon his heads
the name of blasphemy. 2And the beast which I saw was like
unto a leopard, and his feet were as the feet of a bear, and his
mouth as the mouth of a lion; and the dragon gave him his
power, and his seat, and great authority. 3And I saw one of
his heads as it were wounded to death; and his deadly
wound was healed; and all the world wondered after the
beast. 4And they worshipped the dragon which gave power
unto the beast; and they worshipped the beast, saying, 'Who
is like unto the beast? Who is able to make war with him?'

5And there was given unto him a mouth speaking great
things and blasphemies; and power was given unto him to
continue forty and two months. 6And he opened his mouth
in blasphemy against God, to blaspheme his name, and his
tabernacle, and them that dwell in heaven. 7And it was given
unto him to make war with the saints, and to overcome them;
and power was given him over all kindreds, and tongues,
and nations. 8And all that dwell upon the earth shall worship him, whose names are not written in the book of life of
the Lamb slain from the foundation of the world.

9If any man have an ear, let him hear. 10He that leadeth
into captivity shall go into captivity; he that killeth with the
sword must be killed with the sword. Here is the patience
and the faith of the saints.

11And I beheld another beast coming up out of the earth;
and he had two horns like a lamb, and he spake as a dragon.
12And he exerciseth all the power of the first beast before

him, and causeth the earth and them which dwell therein to
worship the first beast, whose deadly wound was healed.
[13]And he doeth great wonders, so that he maketh fire come
down from heaven on the earth in the sight of men, [14]and
deceiveth them that dwell on the earth by the means of those
miracles which he had power to do in the sight of the beast;
saying to them that dwell on the earth that they should make
an image to the beast, which had the wound by a sword, and
did live. [15]And he had power to give life unto the image of the
beast, that the image of the beast should both speak, and cause
that as many as would not worship the image of the beast
should be killed. [16]And he causeth all, both small and great, rich
and poor, free and bond, to receive a mark in their right hand,
or in their foreheads; [17]and that no man might buy or sell, save
he that had the mark, or the name of the beast, or the number
of his name. [18]Here is wisdom. Let him that hath understanding count the number of the beast; for it is the number
of a man; and his number is six hundred threescore and six.

14 And I looked, and, lo, a Lamb stood on the mount Sion,
and with him an hundred forty and four thousand, having his Father's name written in their foreheads. [2]And I heard
a voice from heaven, as the voice of many waters, and as the voice
of a great thunder; and I heard the voice of harpers harping
with their harps; [3]and they sung as it were a new song before
the throne, and before the four beasts, and the elders; and no
man could learn that song but the hundred and forty and four
thousand, which were redeemed from the earth. [4]These are
they which were not defiled with women; for they are virgins.
These are they which follow the Lamb whithersoever he goeth.
These were redeemed from among men, being the firstfruits
unto God and to the Lamb. [5]And in their mouth was found
no guile; for they are without fault before the throne of God.

[6]And I saw another angel fly in the midst of heaven, having
the everlasting gospel to preach unto them that dwell on the
earth, and to every nation, and kindred, and tongue, and people, [7]saying with a loud voice, 'Fear God, and give glory to him,
for the hour of his judgment is come; and worship him that
made heaven, and earth, and the sea, and the fountains of waters.'

[8]And there followed another angel, saying, 'Babylon is
fallen, is fallen, that great city, because she made all nations
drink of the wine of the wrath of her fornication.'

[9]And the third angel followed them, saying with a loud
voice, 'If any man worship the beast and his image, and
receive his mark in his forehead, or in his hand, [10]the same
shall drink of the wine of the wrath of God, which is poured
out without mixture into the cup of his indignation; and he
shall be tormented with fire and brimstone in the presence

of the holy angels, and in the presence of the Lamb. 11 And the
smoke of their torment ascendeth up for ever and ever; and
they have no rest day nor night, who worship the beast and
his image, and whosoever receiveth the mark of his name.'
12 Here is the patience of the saints: here are they that
keep the commandments of God, and the faith of Jesus.
13 And I heard a voice from heaven saying unto me, 'Write,
Blessed are the dead which die in the Lord from henceforth.'
'Yea,' saith the Spirit, 'that they may rest from their labours;
and their works do follow them.'
14 And I looked, and behold a white cloud, and upon the
cloud one sat like unto the Son of man, having on his head a
golden crown, and in his hand a sharp sickle. 15 And another
angel came out of the temple, crying with a loud voice to
him that sat on the cloud, 'Thrust in thy sickle, and reap; for
the time is come for thee to reap; for the harvest of the earth
is ripe.' 16 And he that sat on the cloud thrust in his sickle on
the earth; and the earth was reaped.
17 And another angel came out of the temple which is in
heaven, he also having a sharp sickle. 18 And another angel
came out from the altar, which had power over fire; and cried
with a loud cry to him that had the sharp sickle, saying,
'Thrust in thy sharp sickle, and gather the clusters of the vine
of the earth; for her grapes are fully ripe.' 19 And the angel
thrust in his sickle into the earth, and gathered the vine of
the earth, and cast it into the great winepress of the wrath of
God. 20 And the winepress was trodden without the city, and
blood came out of the winepress, even unto the horse brid-
les, by the space of a thousand and six hundred furlongs.

15 And I saw another sign in heaven, great and marvellous, seven angels having the seven last plagues; for in
them is filled up the wrath of God.

2 And I saw as it were a sea of glass mingled with fire;
and them that had gotten the victory over the beast, and over
his image, and over his mark, and over the number of his
name, stand on the sea of glass, having the harps of God. 3 And
they sing the song of Moses the servant of God, and the song
of the Lamb, saying,

Great and marvellous are thy works,
Lord God Almighty;
just and true are thy ways,
thou King of saints.
4 Who shall not fear thee, O Lord,
and glorify thy name?
For thou only art holy;
for all nations shall come and worship before thee;
for thy judgments are made manifest.

5 And after that I looked, and, behold, the temple of the tabernacle of the testimony in heaven was opened. 6 And the seven
angels came out of the temple, having the seven plagues,
clothed in pure and white linen, and having their breasts
girded with golden girdles. 7 And one of the four beasts gave
unto the seven angels seven golden vials full of the wrath of
God, who liveth for ever and ever. 8 And the temple was
filled with smoke from the glory of God, and from his power;
and no man was able to enter into the temple, till the seven
plagues of the seven angels were fulfilled.

16 And I heard a great voice out of the temple saying to
the seven angels, 'Go your ways, and pour out the vials
of the wrath of God upon the earth.'

2 And the first went, and poured out his vial upon the
earth; and there fell a noisome and grievous sore upon the
men which had the mark of the beast, and upon them which
worshipped his image.

3 And the second angel poured out his vial upon the sea;
and it became as the blood of a dead man; and every living
soul died in the sea.

4 And the third angel poured out his vial upon the rivers
and fountains of waters; and they became blood. 5 And I
heard the angel of the waters say, 'Thou art righteous, O Lord,
which art, and wast, and shalt be, because thou hast judged
thus. 6 For they have shed the blood of saints and prophets,
and thou hast given them blood to drink; for they are worthy.' 7 And I heard another out of the altar say, 'Even so, Lord
God Almighty, true and righteous are thy judgments.'

8 And the fourth angel poured out his vial upon the sun;
and power was given unto him to scorch men with fire.
9 And men were scorched with great heat, and blasphemed
the name of God, which hath power over these plagues; and
they repented not to give him glory.

10 And the fifth angel poured out his vial upon the seat of
the beast; and his kingdom was full of darkness; and they
gnawed their tongues for pain, 11 and blasphemed the God of
heaven because of their pains and their sores, and repented
not of their deeds.

12 And the sixth angel poured out his vial upon the great

river Euphrates; and the water thereof was dried up, that the
way of the kings of the east might be prepared. [13]And I saw
three unclean spirits like frogs come out of the mouth of the
dragon, and out of the mouth of the beast, and out of the mouth
of the false prophet. [14]For they are the spirits of devils, working miracles, which go forth unto the kings of the earth and
of the whole world, to gather them to the battle of that great
day of God Almighty. [15]'Behold, I come as a thief. Blessed is
he that watcheth, and keepeth his garments, lest he walk naked,
and they see his shame.' [16]And he gathered them together
into a place called in the Hebrew tongue Armageddon.

[17]And the seventh angel poured out his vial into the air;
and there came a great voice out of the temple of heaven,
from the throne, saying, 'It is done.' [18]And there were voices,
and thunders, and lightnings; and there was a great earthquake, such as was not since men were upon the earth, so
mighty an earthquake, and so great. [19]And the great city was
divided into three parts, and the cities of the nations fell; and
great Babylon came in remembrance before God, to give unto
her the cup of the wine of the fierceness of his wrath. [20]And
every island fled away, and the mountains were not found.
[21]And there fell upon men a great hail out of heaven, every
stone about the weight of a talent; and men blasphemed
God because of the plague of the hail; for the plague thereof
was exceeding great.

17 And there came one of the seven angels which had the
seven vials, and talked with me, saying unto me,'Come
hither; I will shew unto thee the judgment of the great
whore that sitteth upon many waters, 2 with whom the kings
of the earth have committed fornication, and the inhabitants
of the earth have been made drunk with the wine of her fornication.' 3 So he carried me away in the spirit into the wilderness; and I saw a woman sit upon a scarlet coloured beast,
full of names of blasphemy, having seven heads and ten
horns. 4 And the woman was arrayed in purple and scarlet
colour, and decked with gold and precious stones and pearls,
having a golden cup in her hand full of abominations and
filthiness of her fornication: 5 and upon her forehead was a
name written, 'MYSTERY, BABYLON THE GREAT, THE
MOTHER OF HARLOTS AND ABOMINATIONS OF THE
EARTH.' 6 And I saw the woman drunken with the blood of
the saints, and with the blood of the martyrs of Jesus; and
when I saw her, I wondered with great admiration.

7 And the angel said unto me, 'Wherefore didst thou marvel? I will tell thee the mystery of the woman, and of the beast
that carrieth her, which hath the seven heads and ten horns.
8 The beast that thou sawest was, and is not; and shall ascend
out of the bottomless pit, and go into perdition; and they
that dwell on the earth shall wonder, whose names were not
written in the book of life from the foundation of the world,
when they behold the beast that was, and is not, and yet is.

9 'And here is the mind which hath wisdom. The seven
heads are seven mountains, on which the woman sitteth.
10 And there are seven kings: five are fallen, and one is, and

the other is not yet come; and when he cometh, he must continue a short space. [11]And the beast that was, and is not, even
he is the eighth, and is of the seven, and goeth into perdition.
[12]And the ten horns which thou sawest are ten kings, which
have received no kingdom as yet; but receive power as kings
one hour with the beast. [13]These have one mind, and shall
give their power and strength unto the beast. [14]These shall
make war with the Lamb, and the Lamb shall overcome
them; for he is Lord of lords, and King of kings; and they
that are with him are called, and chosen, and faithful.'

[15]And he saith unto me, 'The waters which thou sawest,
where the whore sitteth, are peoples, and multitudes, and
nations, and tongues. [16]And the ten horns which thou sawest
upon the beast, these shall hate the whore, and shall make
her desolate and naked, and shall eat her flesh, and burn her
with fire. [17]For God hath put in their hearts to fulfil his will,
and to agree, and give their kingdom unto the beast, until
the words of God shall be fulfilled. [18]And the woman which
thou sawest is that great city, which reigneth over the kings
of the earth.'

18 And after these things I saw another angel come down
from heaven, having great power; and the earth was
lightened with his glory. 2 And he cried mightily with a strong
voice, saying, 'Babylon the great is fallen, is fallen, and is
become the habitation of devils, and the hold of every foul
spirit, and a cage of every unclean and hateful bird. 3 For all
nations have drunk of the wine of the wrath of her fornication, and the kings of the earth have committed fornication
with her, and the merchants of the earth are waxed rich
through the abundance of her delicacies.'

4 And I heard another voice from heaven, saying, 'Come
out of her, my people, that ye be not partakers of her sins,
and that ye receive not of her plagues. 5 For her sins have
reached unto heaven, and God hath remembered her iniquities. 6 Reward her even as she rewarded you, and double
unto her double according to her works; in the cup which
she hath filled fill to her double. 7 How much she hath glorified herself, and lived deliciously, so much torment and sorrow give her; for she saith in her heart, I sit a queen, and am
no widow, and shall see no sorrow. 8 Therefore shall her
plagues come in one day, death, and mourning, and famine;
and she shall be utterly burned with fire; for strong is the
Lord God who judgeth her.'

9 And the kings of the earth, who have committed fornication and lived deliciously with her, shall bewail her, and
lament for her, when they shall see the smoke of her burning, 10 standing afar off for the fear of her torment, saying,
'Alas, alas, that great city Babylon, that mighty city! For in
one hour is thy judgment come.'

11 And the merchants of the earth shall weep and mourn
over her; for no man buyeth their merchandise any more:
12 the merchandise of gold, and silver, and precious stones, and
of pearls, and fine linen, and purple, and silk, and scarlet,
and all thyine wood, and all manner vessels of ivory, and all
manner vessels of most precious wood, and of brass, and
iron, and marble, 13 and cinnamon, and odours, and ointments,
and frankincense, and wine, and oil, and fine flour, and wheat,
and beasts, and sheep, and horses, and chariots, and slaves,
and souls of men.

14 'And the fruits that thy soul lusted after are departed
from thee, and all things which were dainty and goodly are
departed from thee, and thou shalt find them no more at all.'

15 The merchants of these things, which were made rich
by her, shall stand afar off for the fear of her torment, weeping and wailing, 16 and saying, 'Alas, alas, that great city, that
was clothed in fine linen, and purple, and scarlet, and decked
with gold, and precious stones, and pearls! 17 For in one hour
so great riches is come to nought.' And every shipmaster,
and all the company in ships, and sailors, and as many as
trade by sea, stood afar off, 18 and cried when they saw the
smoke of her burning, saying, 'What city is like unto this great
city!' 19 And they cast dust on their heads, and cried, weeping
and wailing, saying, 'Alas, alas, that great city, wherein were
made rich all that had ships in the sea by reason of her costli-
ness! For in one hour is she made desolate.'

20 Rejoice over her, thou heaven, and ye holy apostles and
prophets; for God hath avenged you on her. 21 And a mighty
angel took up a stone like a great millstone, and cast it into

the sea, saying, 'Thus with violence shall that great city Babylon be thrown down, and shall be found no more at all. 22 And
the voice of harpers, and musicians, and of pipers, and trum-
peters, shall be heard no more at all in thee; and no craftsman,
of whatsoever craft he be, shall be found any more in thee;
and the sound of a millstone shall be heard no more at all in
thee; 23 and the light of a candle shall shine no more at all
in thee; and the voice of the bridegroom and of the bride
shall be heard no more at all in thee; for thy merchants were
the great men of the earth; for by thy sorceries were all nations
deceived. 24 And in her was found the blood of prophets, and
of saints, and of all that were slain upon the earth.'

19 And after these things I heard a great voice of much people in heaven, saying, 'Alleluia; Salvation, and glory, and honour, and power, unto the Lord our God; 2 for true and righteous are his judgments; for he hath judged the great whore, which did corrupt the earth with her fornication, and hath avenged the blood of his servants at her hand.'

3 And again they said, 'Alleluia.' And her smoke rose up for ever and ever. 4 And the four and twenty elders and the four beasts fell down and worshipped God that sat on the throne, saying, 'Amen; Alleluia.'

5 And a voice came out of the throne, saying, 'Praise our God, all ye his servants, and ye that fear him, both small and great.' 6 And I heard as it were the voice of a great multitude, and as the voice of many waters, and as the voice of mighty thunderings, saying, 'Alleluia: for the Lord God omnipotent reigneth. 7 Let us be glad and rejoice, and give honour to him; for the marriage of the Lamb is come, and his wife hath made herself ready. 8 And to her was granted that she should be arrayed in fine linen, clean and white; for the fine linen is the righteousness of saints.'

9 And he saith unto me, 'Write, Blessed are they which are called unto the marriage supper of the Lamb.' And he saith unto me, 'These are the true sayings of God.' 10 And I fell at his feet to worship him. And he said unto me, 'See thou do it not: I am thy fellowservant, and of thy brethren that have the testimony of Jesus; worship God, for the testimony of Jesus is the spirit of prophecy.'

11 And I saw heaven opened, and behold a white horse; and he that sat upon him was called Faithful and True, and

in righteousness he doth judge and make war. [12]His eyes
were as a flame of fire, and on his head were many crowns;
and he had a name written, that no man knew, but he himself. [13]And he was clothed with a vesture dipped in blood;
and his name is called The Word of God. [14]And the armies
which were in heaven followed him upon white horses,
clothed in fine linen, white and clean. [15]And out of his mouth
goeth a sharp sword, that with it he should smite the nations;
and he shall rule them with a rod of iron; and he treadeth
the winepress of the fierceness and wrath of Almighty God.
[16]And he hath on his vesture and on his thigh a name written, 'KING OF KINGS, AND LORD OF LORDS.'

[17]And I saw an angel standing in the sun; and he cried
with a loud voice, saying to all the fowls that fly in the midst
of heaven, 'Come and gather yourselves together unto the
supper of the great God; [18] that ye may eat the flesh of kings,
and the flesh of captains, and the flesh of mighty men, and
the flesh of horses, and of them that sit on them, and the
flesh of all men, both free and bond, both small and great.'
[19]And I saw the beast, and the kings of the earth, and their
armies, gathered together to make war against him that sat
on the horse, and against his army. [20]And the beast was
taken, and with him the false prophet that wrought miracles
before him, with which he deceived them that had received
the mark of the beast, and them that worshipped his image.
These both were cast alive into a lake of fire burning with
brimstone. [21]And the remnant were slain with the sword of
him that sat upon the horse, which sword proceeded out of
his mouth; and all the fowls were filled with their flesh.

20 And I saw an angel come down from heaven, having the key of the bottomless pit and a great chain in his hand. 2 And he laid hold on the dragon, that old serpent, which is the Devil, and Satan, and bound him a thousand years, 3 and cast him into the bottomless pit, and shut him up, and set a seal upon him, that he should deceive the nations no more, till the thousand years should be fulfilled; and after that he must be loosed a little season.

4 And I saw thrones, and they sat upon them, and judgment was given unto them; and I saw the souls of them that were beheaded for the witness of Jesus, and for the word of God, and which had not worshipped the beast, neither his image, neither had received his mark upon their foreheads, or in their hands; and they lived and reigned with Christ a thousand years. 5 But the rest of the dead lived not again until the thousand years were finished. This is the first resurrection. 6 Blessed and holy is he that hath part in the first resurrection; on such the second death hath no power, but they shall be priests of God and of Christ, and shall reign with him a thousand years.

7 And when the thousand years are expired, Satan shall be loosed out of his prison, 8 and shall go out to deceive the nations which are in the four quarters of the earth, Gog and Magog, to gather them together to battle; the number of whom is as the sand of the sea. 9 And they went up on the breadth of the earth, and compassed the camp of the saints about, and the beloved city; and fire came down from God out of heaven, and devoured them. 10 And the devil that deceived them was cast into the lake of fire and brimstone,

where the beast and the false prophet are, and shall be tormented day and night for ever and ever.
11And I saw a great white throne, and him that sat on it,
from whose face the earth and the heaven fled away; and
there was found no place for them. 12And I saw the dead, small
and great, stand before God; and the books were opened;
and another book was opened, which is the book of life; and
the dead were judged out of those things which were written in the books, according to their works. 13And the sea gave
up the dead which were in it; and death and hell delivered
up the dead which were in them; and they were judged every
man according to their works. 14And death and hell were cast
into the lake of fire. This is the second death. 15And whosoever was not found written in the book of life was cast into
the lake of fire.

21 And I saw a new heaven and a new earth; for the first
heaven and the first earth were passed away; and
there was no more sea. 2And I John saw the holy city, new
Jerusalem, coming down from God out of heaven, prepared
as a bride adorned for her husband. 3And I heard a great
voice out of heaven saying, 'Behold, the tabernacle of God is
with men, and he will dwell with them, and they shall be his
people, and God himself shall be with them, and be their
God. 4And God shall wipe away all tears from their eyes;
and there shall be no more death, neither sorrow, nor crying,
neither shall there be any more pain; for the former things
are passed away.'

5And he that sat upon the throne said, 'Behold, I make all
things new.' And he said unto me, 'Write: for these words
are true and faithful.' 6And he said unto me, 'It is done. I am
Alpha and Omega, the beginning and the end. I will give
unto him that is athirst of the fountain of the water of life
freely. 7He that overcometh shall inherit all things; and I will
be his God, and he shall be my son. 8But the fearful, and
unbelieving, and the abominable, and murderers, and whoremongers, and sorcerers, and idolaters, and all liars, shall
have their part in the lake which burneth with fire and brimstone; which is the second death.'

9And there came unto me one of the seven angels which
had the seven vials full of the seven last plagues, and talked
with me, saying, 'Come hither, I will shew thee the bride, the
Lamb's wife.' 10And he carried me away in the spirit to a great
and high mountain, and shewed me that great city, the holy
Jerusalem, descending out of heaven from God, 11having the

glory of God; and her light was like unto a stone most precious, even like a jasper stone, clear as crystal; 12 and had a
wall great and high, and had twelve gates, and at the gates
twelve angels, and names written thereon, which are the
names of the twelve tribes of the children of Israel: 13 on the
east three gates; on the north three gates; on the south three
gates; and on the west three gates. 14 And the wall of the city
had twelve foundations, and in them the names of the twelve
apostles of the Lamb.

15 And he that talked with me had a golden reed to measure the city, and the gates thereof, and the wall thereof. 16 And
the city lieth foursquare, and the length is as large as the
breadth; and he measured the city with the reed, twelve thous-
and furlongs. The length and the breadth and the height of it
are equal. 17 And he measured the wall thereof, an hundred
and forty and four cubits, according to the measure of a man,
that is, of the angel. 18 And the building of the wall of it was
of jasper; and the city was pure gold, like unto clear glass.
19 And the foundations of the wall of the city were garnished
with all manner of precious stones. The first foundation was
jasper; the second, sapphire; the third, a chalcedony; the
fourth, an emerald; 20 the fifth, sardonyx; the sixth, sardius;
the seventh, chrysolite; the eighth, beryl; the ninth, a topaz;
the tenth, a chrysoprasus; the eleventh, a jacinth; the twelfth,
an amethyst. 21 And the twelve gates were twelve pearls; every
several gate was of one pearl; and the street of the city was
pure gold, as it were transparent glass.

22 And I saw no temple therein; for the Lord God Almighty
and the Lamb are the temple of it. 23 And the city had no need

of the sun, neither of the moon, to shine in it: for the glory of
God did lighten it, and the Lamb is the light thereof. 24And
the nations of them which are saved shall walk in the light of
it; and the kings of the earth do bring their glory and honour
into it. 25And the gates of it shall not be shut at all by day; for
there shall be no night there. 26And they shall bring the glory
and honour of the nations into it. 27And there shall in no wise
enter into it any thing that defileth, neither whatsoever worketh abomination, or maketh a lie; but they which are written in the Lamb's book of life.

22 And he shewed me a pure river of water of life, clear as crystal, proceeding out of the throne of God and of the Lamb. 2 In the midst of the street of it, and on either side of the river, was there the tree of life, which bare twelve manner of fruits, and yielded her fruit every month; and the leaves of the tree were for the healing of the nations. 3 And there shall be no more curse, but the throne of God and of the Lamb shall be in it; and his servants shall serve him; 4 and they shall see his face; and his name shall be in their foreheads. 5 And there shall be no night there; and they need no candle, neither light of the sun; for the Lord God giveth them light; and they shall reign for ever and ever.

6 And he said unto me, 'These sayings are faithful and true; and the Lord God of the holy prophets sent his angel to shew unto his servants the things which must shortly be done. 7 Behold, I come quickly; blessed is he that keepeth the sayings of the prophecy of this book.'

8 And I John saw these things, and heard them. And when I had heard and seen, I fell down to worship before the feet of the angel which shewed me these things. 9 Then saith he unto me, 'See thou do it not; for I am thy fellowservant, and of thy brethren the prophets, and of them which keep the sayings of this book: worship God.' 10 And he saith unto me, 'Seal not the sayings of the prophecy of this book; for the time is at hand. 11 He that is unjust, let him be unjust still; and he which is filthy, let him be filthy still; and he that is righteous, let him be righteous still; and he that is holy, let him be holy still.

12 'And, behold, I come quickly; and my reward is with

me, to give every man according as his work shall be. [13] I am
Alpha and Omega, the beginning and the end, the first and
the last.'

[14] Blessed are they that do his commandments, that they
may have right to the tree of life, and may enter in through
the gates into the city. [15] For without are dogs, and sorcerers,
and whoremongers, and murderers, and idolaters, and whosoever loveth and maketh a lie.

[16] 'I Jesus have sent mine angel to testify unto you these
things in the churches. I am the root and the offspring of
David, and the bright and morning star.' [17] And the Spirit and
the bride say, 'Come.' And let him that heareth say, 'Come.'
And let him that is athirst come. And whosoever will, let
him take the water of life freely. [18] For I testify unto every
man that heareth the words of the prophecy of this book, if
any man shall add unto these things, God shall add unto
him the plagues that are written in this book. [19] And if any
man shall take away from the words of the book of this
prophecy, God shall take away his part out of the book of
life, and out of the holy city, and from the things which are
written in this book. [20] He which testifieth these things saith,
'Surely I come quickly.' Amen. Even so, come, Lord Jesus.
[21] The grace of our Lord Jesus Christ be with you all. Amen.

titles in the series

genesis – *introduced by e. l. doctorow*
exodus – *introduced by david grossman*
job – *introduced by charles frazier*
selections from the book of psalms – *introduced by bono*
proverbs – *introduced by charles johnson*
ecclesiastes – *introduced by doris lessing*
matthew – *introduced by francisco goldman*
mark – *introduced by barry hannah*
luke – *introduced by thomas cahill*
john – *introduced by darcey steinke*
corinthians – *introduced by fay weldon*
revelation – *introduced by kathleen norris*